GOODNIGHT PUNPUN

4

Story and Art by INIO ASANO

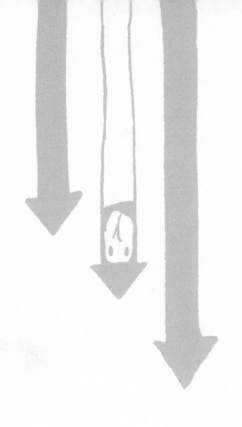

GOODNIGHT PUNPUN
Part Seven

CONTENTS

STORY THUS FAR...

Nothing to speak of.

CAST OF CHARACTERS

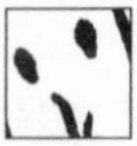

PUNPUN ONODERA
Punpun of the Onoderas.
A senior in high school.

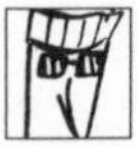

YUICHI ONODERA
Punpun's uncle.

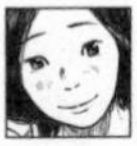

MIDORI ONODERA
Yuichi's wife.

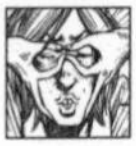

YUKINOSHIN MIMURA
A legendary giant reborn after 300 years.

Chapter 68

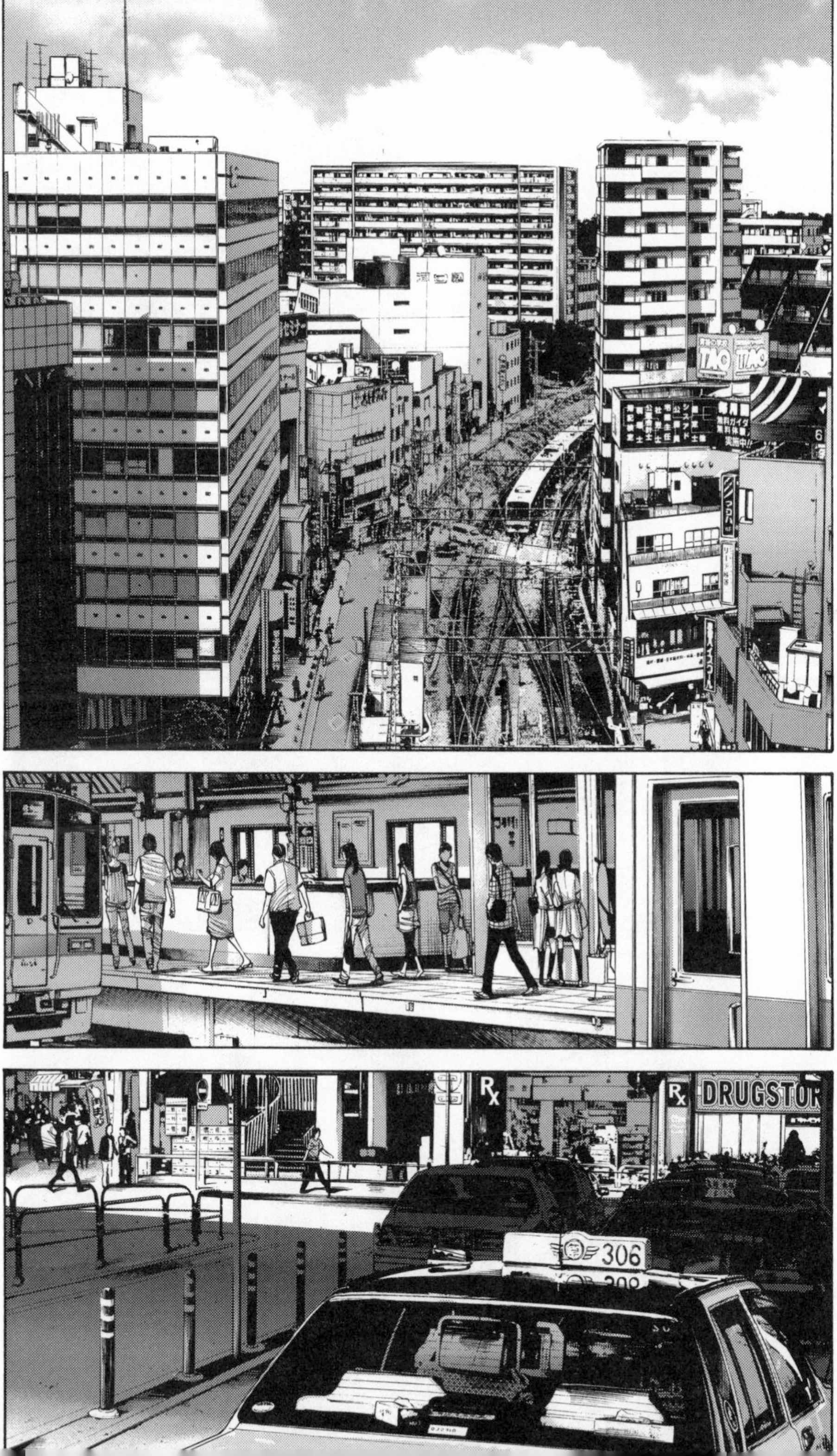
TAC
TAC
DRUGSTOR
306

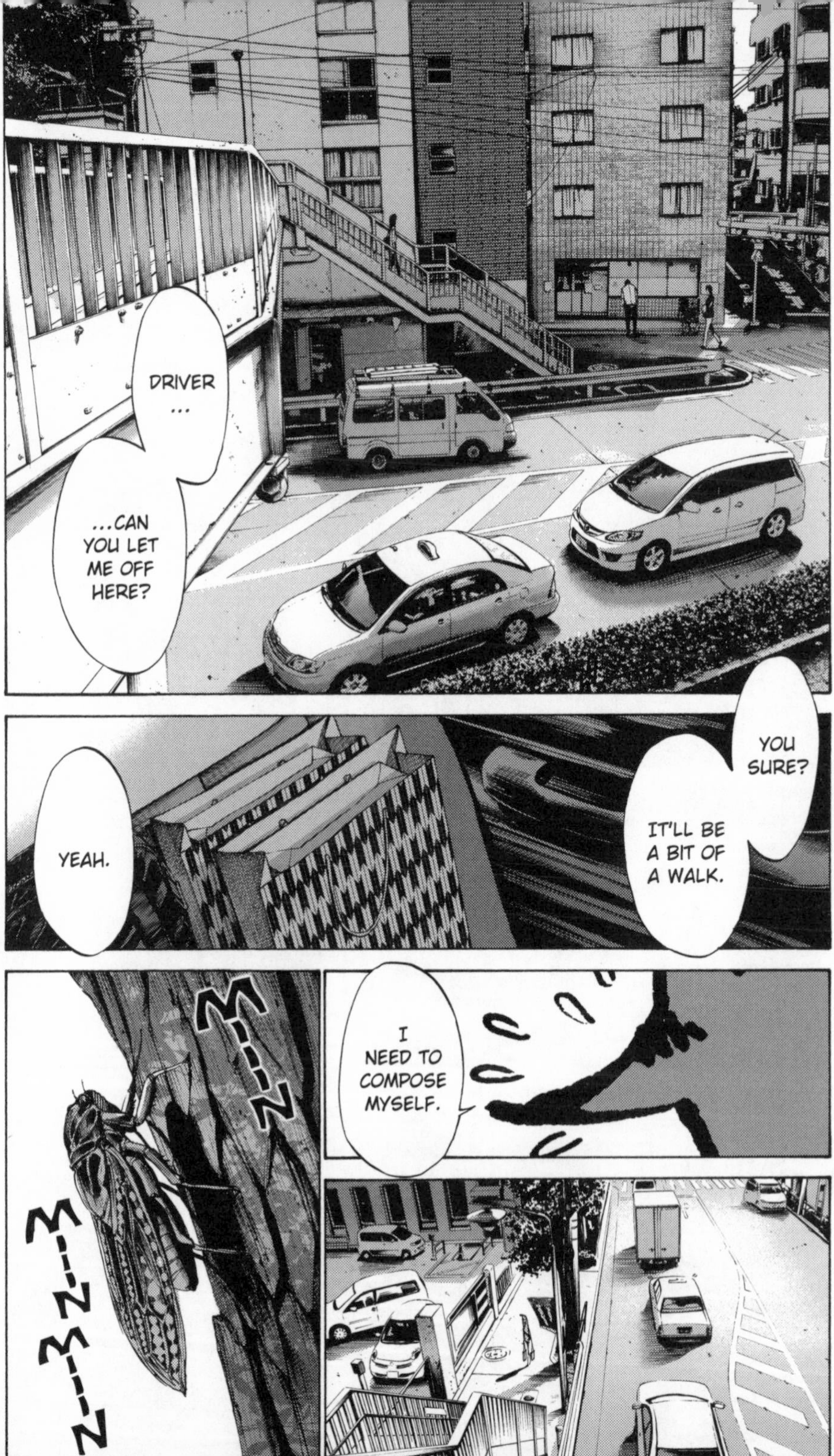
DRIVER ...
...CAN YOU LET ME OFF HERE?
YOU SURE?
IT'LL BE A BIT OF A WALK.
YEAH.
I NEED TO COMPOSE MYSELF.
MIIN
MIIN MIIN

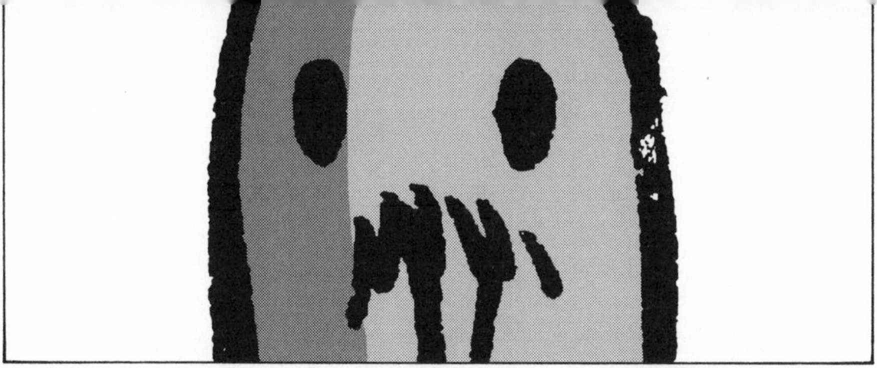

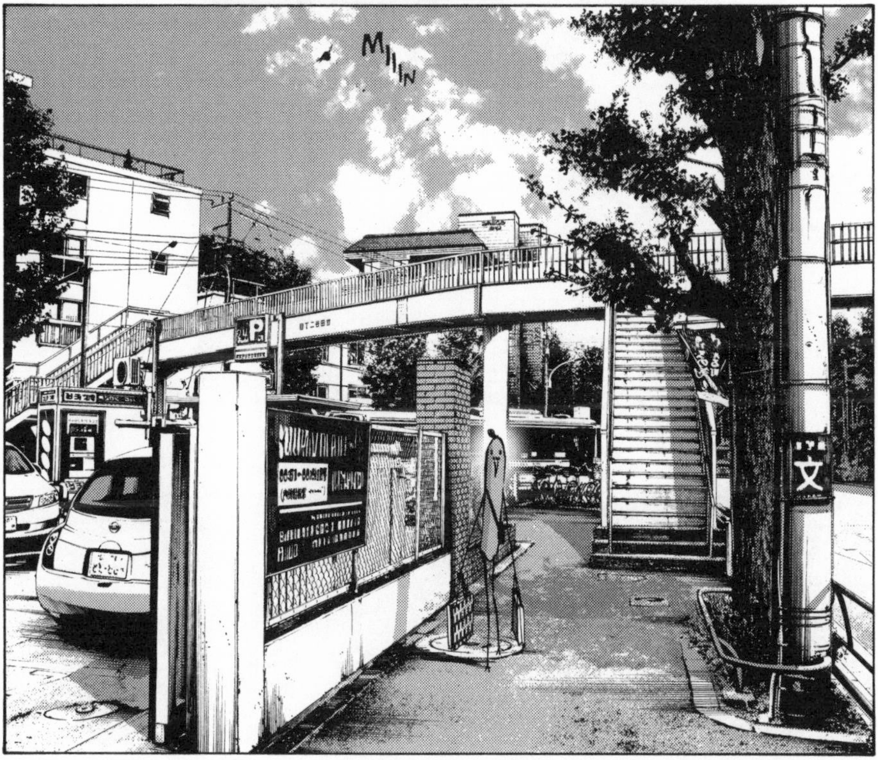
MIIIN

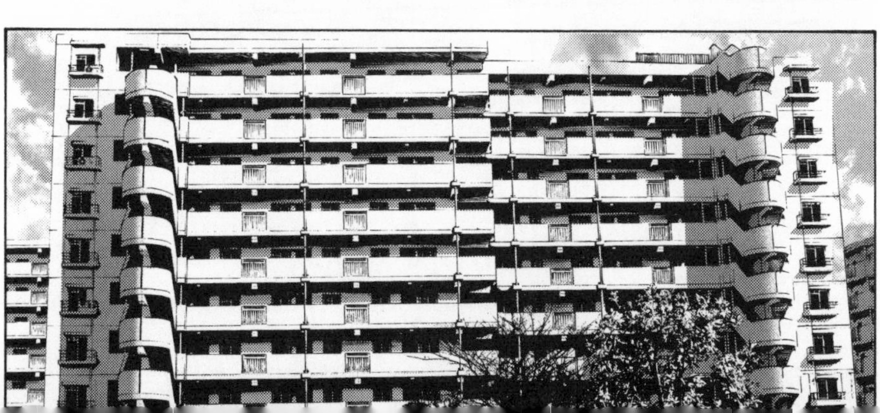

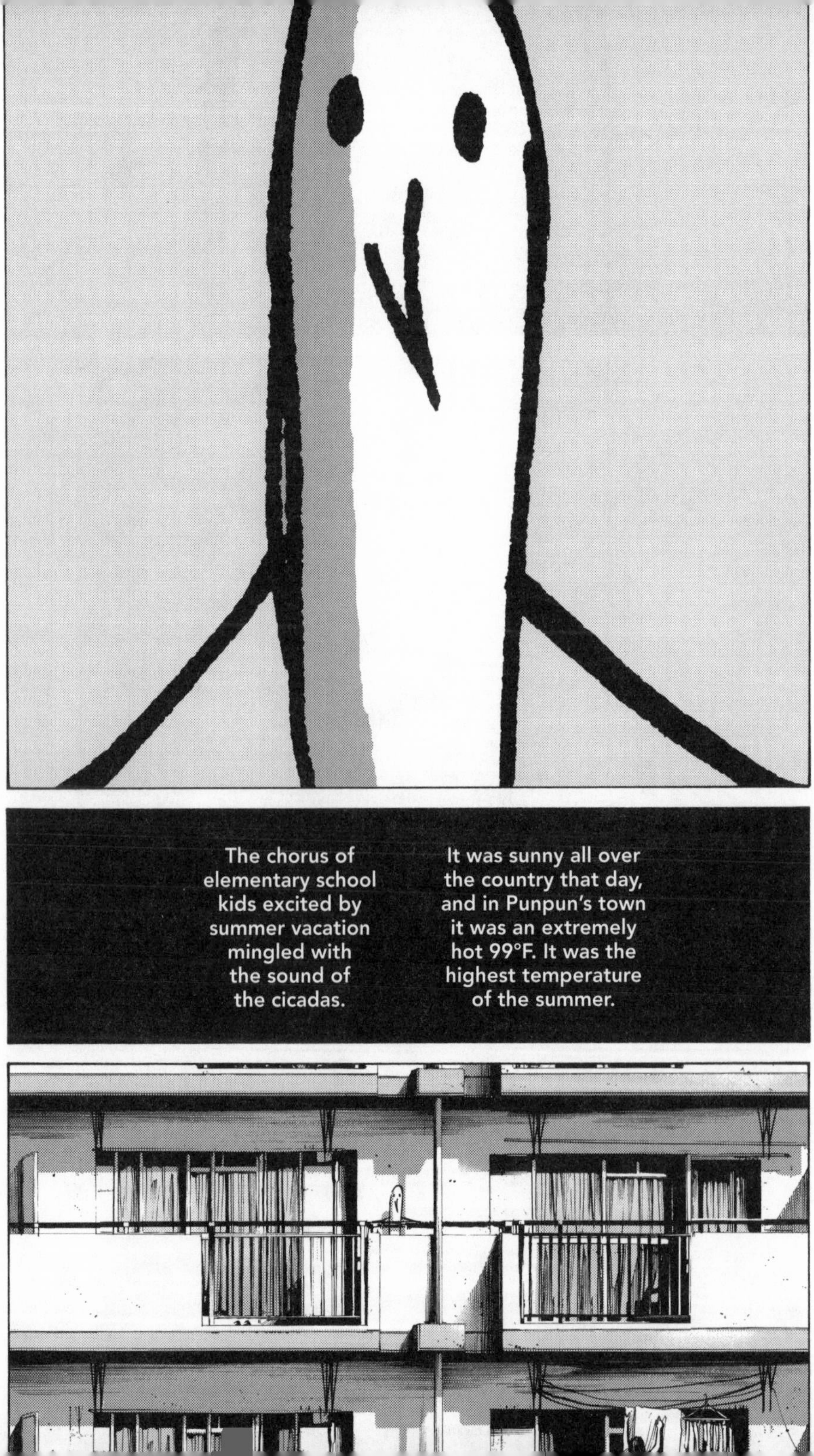
It was sunny all over the country that day, and in Punpun's town it was an extremely hot 99°F. It was the highest temperature of the summer.
The chorus of elementary school kids excited by summer vacation mingled with the sound of the cicadas.

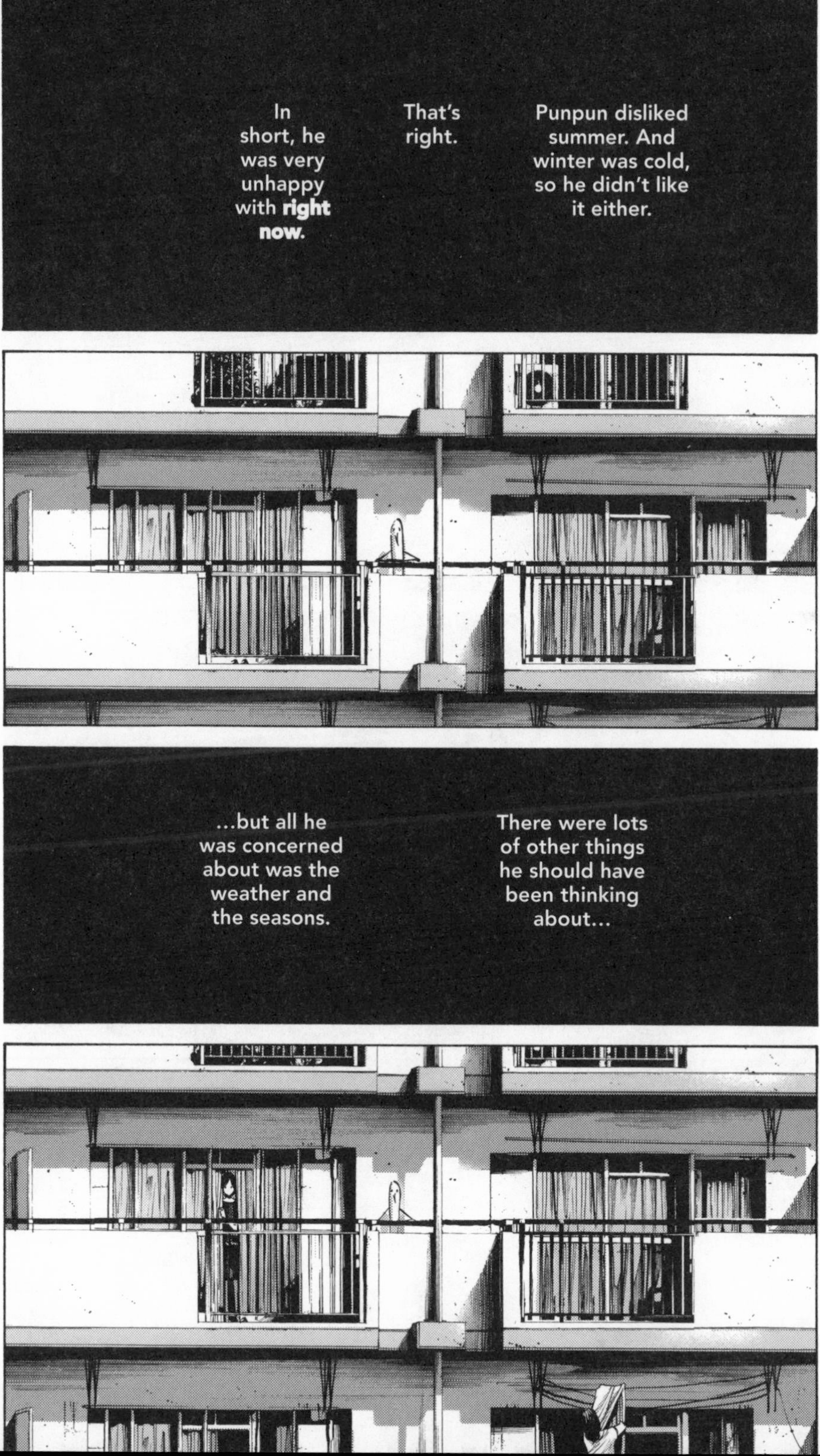
Punpun disliked summer. And winter was cold, so he didn't like it either.
That's right.
In short, he was very unhappy with **right now.**
There were lots of other things he should have been thinking about...
...but all he was concerned about was the weather and the seasons.

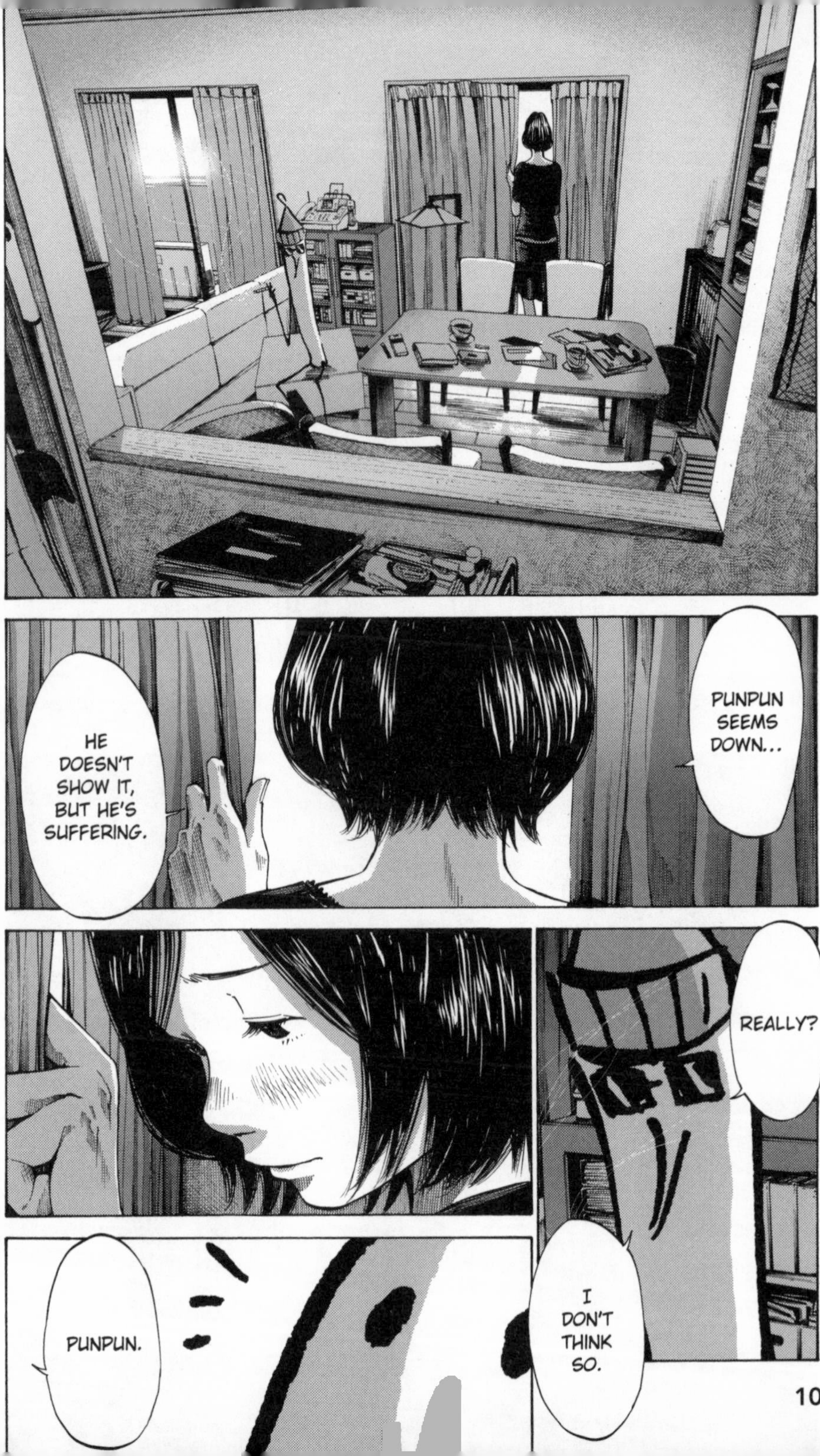
PUNPUN SEEMS DOWN...
HE DOESN'T SHOW IT, BUT HE'S SUFFERING.
REALLY?
I DON'T THINK SO.
PUNPUN.

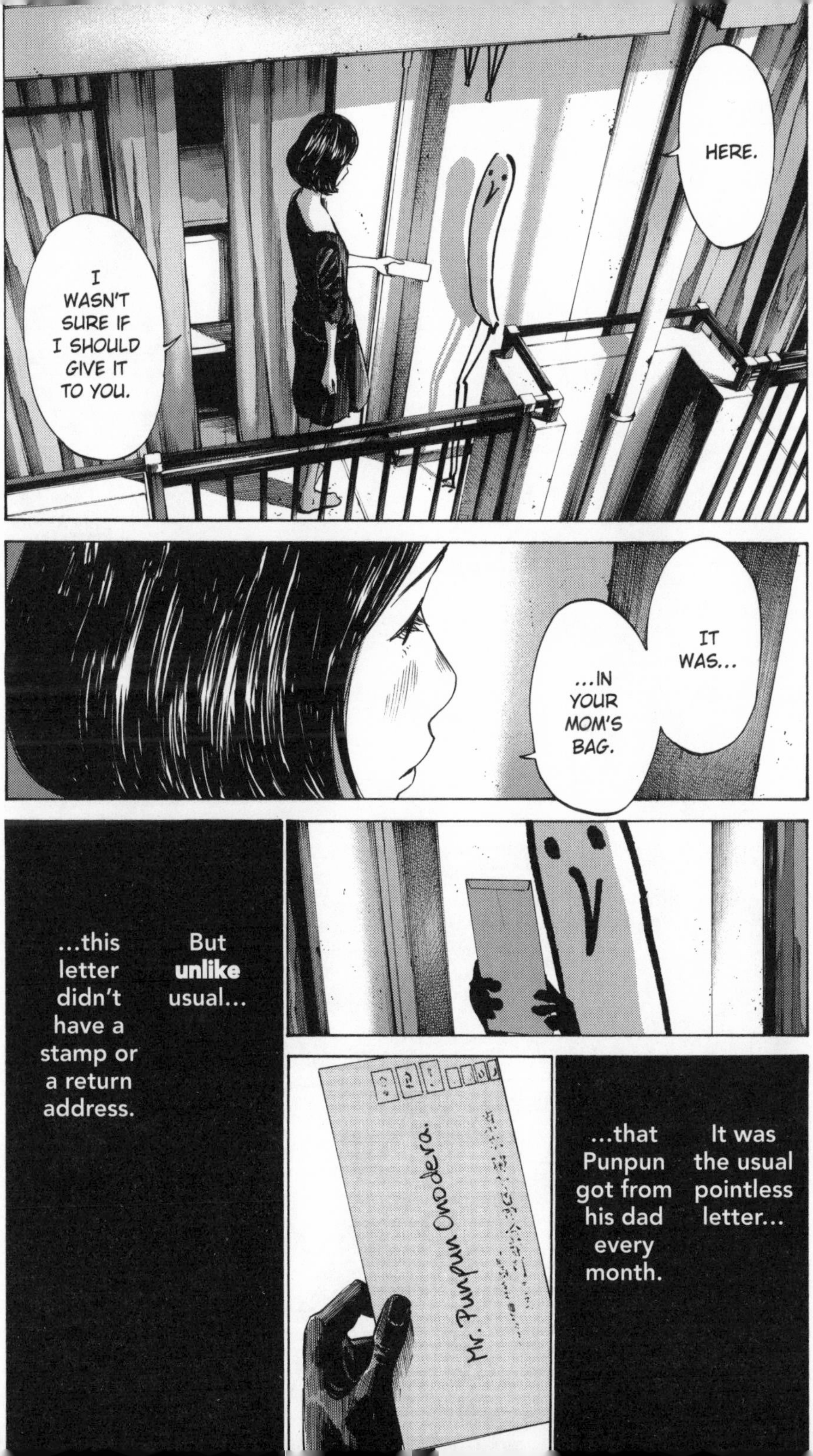
HERE.
I WASN'T SURE IF I SHOULD GIVE IT TO YOU.
IT WAS...
...IN YOUR MOM'S BAG.
It was the usual pointless letter...
...that Punpun got from his dad every month.
Mr. Punpun Onodera.
But **unlike** usual...
...this letter didn't have a stamp or a return address.

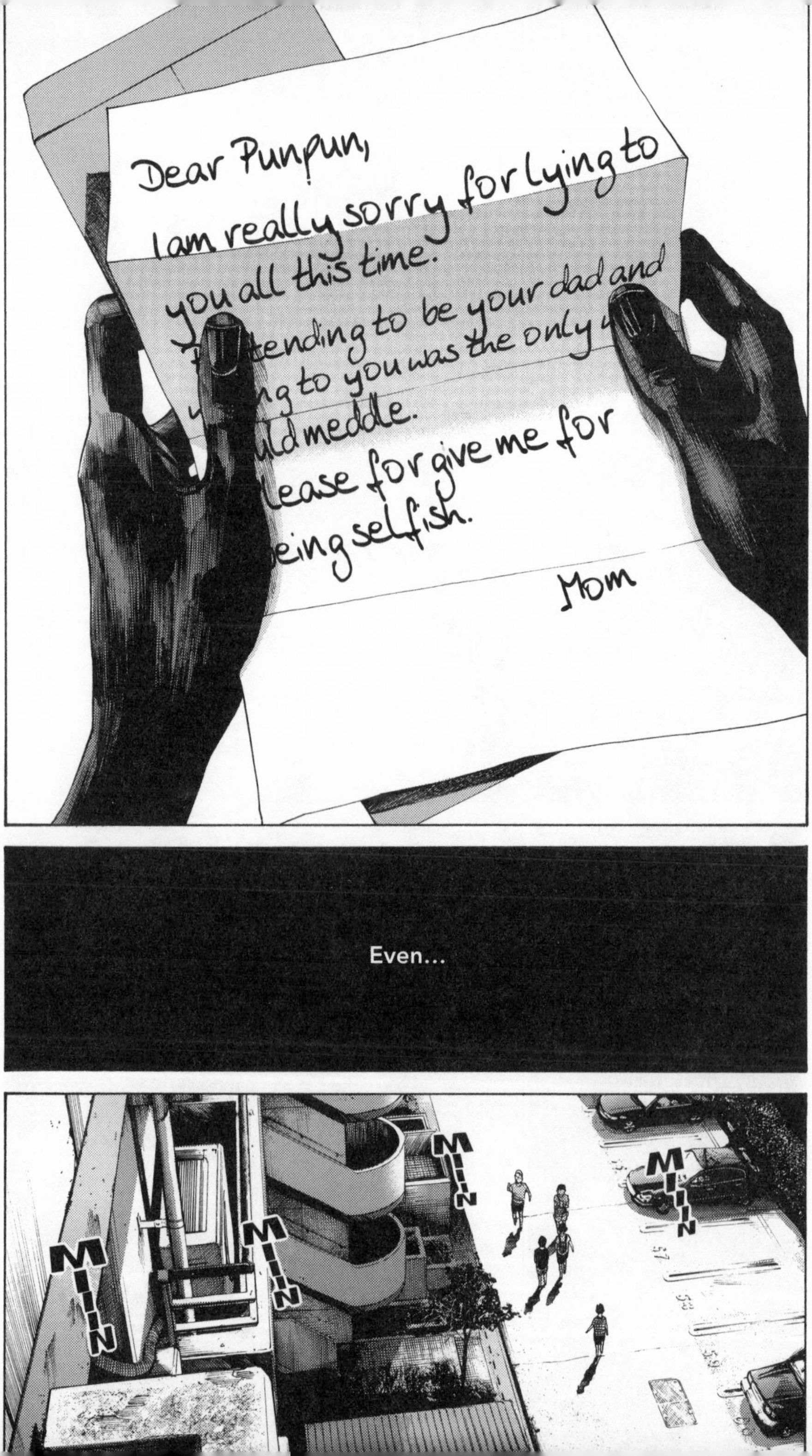
Dear Punpun,
I am really sorry for lying to
you all this time.
tending to be your dad and
g to you was the only
uld meddle.
lease forgive me for
eing selfish.
Mom
Even...
MIIN
MIIN
MIIN
MIIN

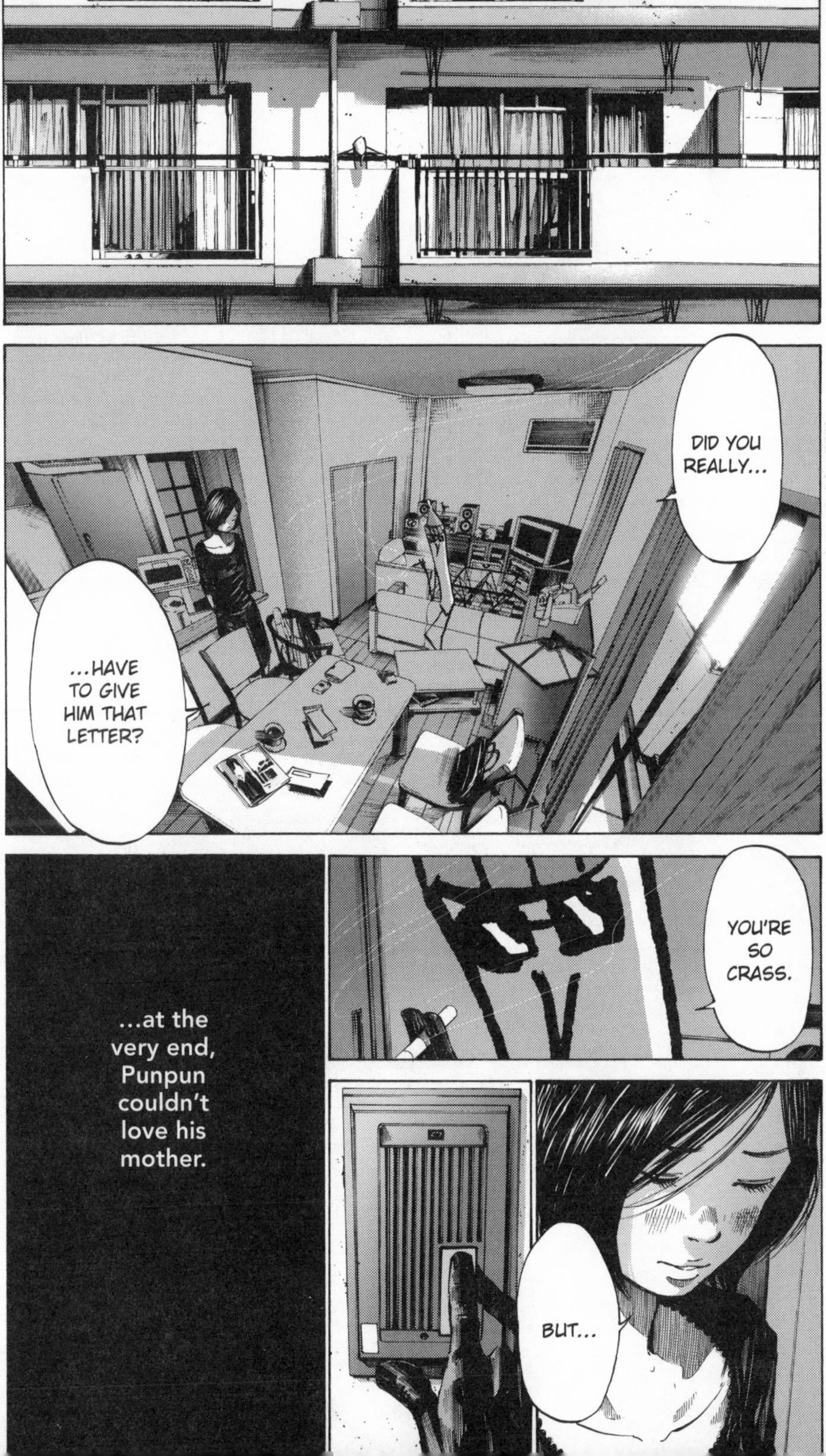
DID YOU REALLY...
...HAVE TO GIVE HIM THAT LETTER?
YOU'RE SO CRASS.
BUT...
...at the very end, Punpun couldn't love his mother.

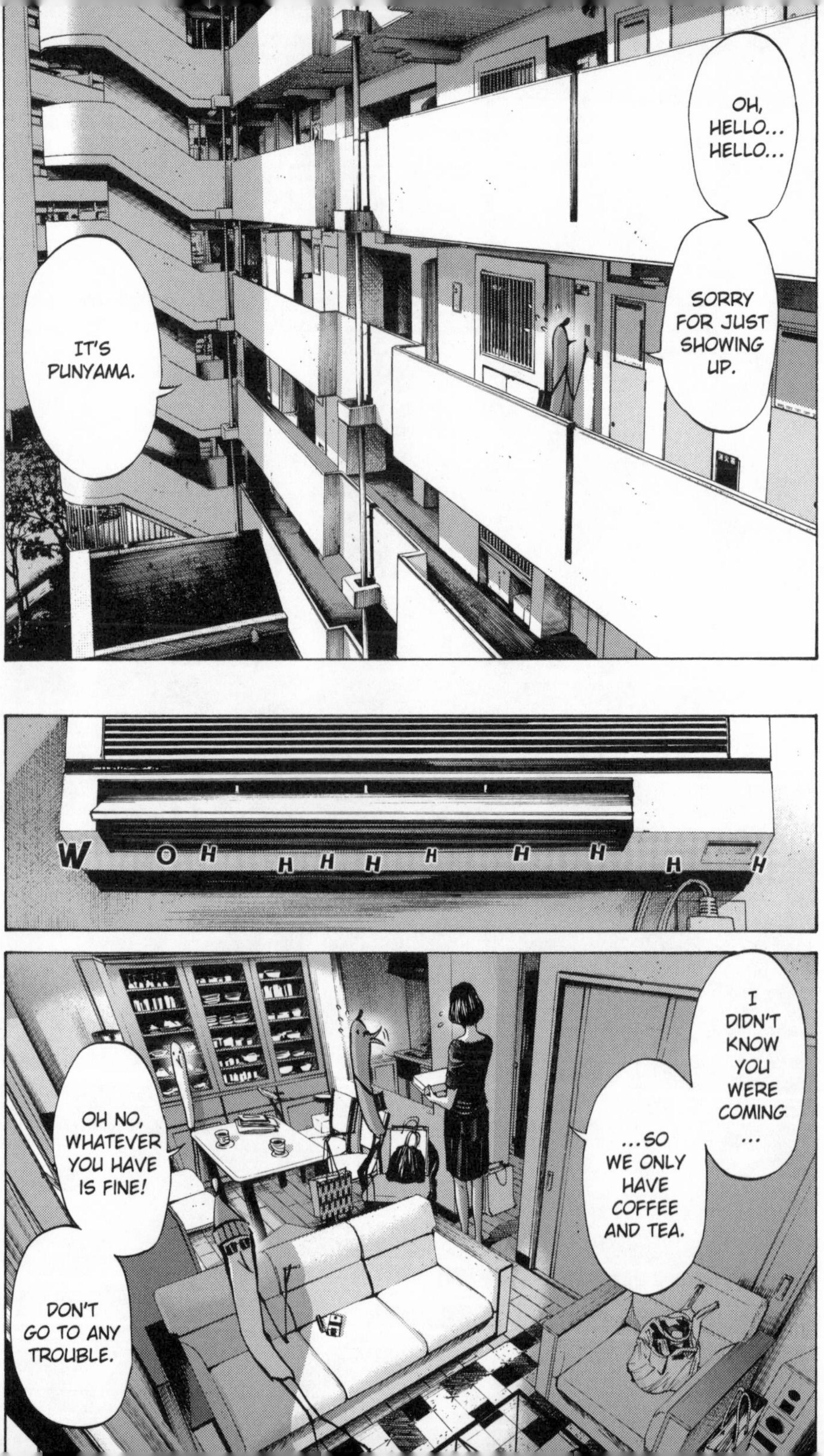
OH, HELLO... HELLO...
SORRY FOR JUST SHOWING UP.
IT'S PUNYAMA.
WOHHHHHHHHH
I DIDN'T KNOW YOU WERE COMING ...
...SO WE ONLY HAVE COFFEE AND TEA.
OH NO, WHATEVER YOU HAVE IS FINE!
DON'T GO TO ANY TROUBLE.

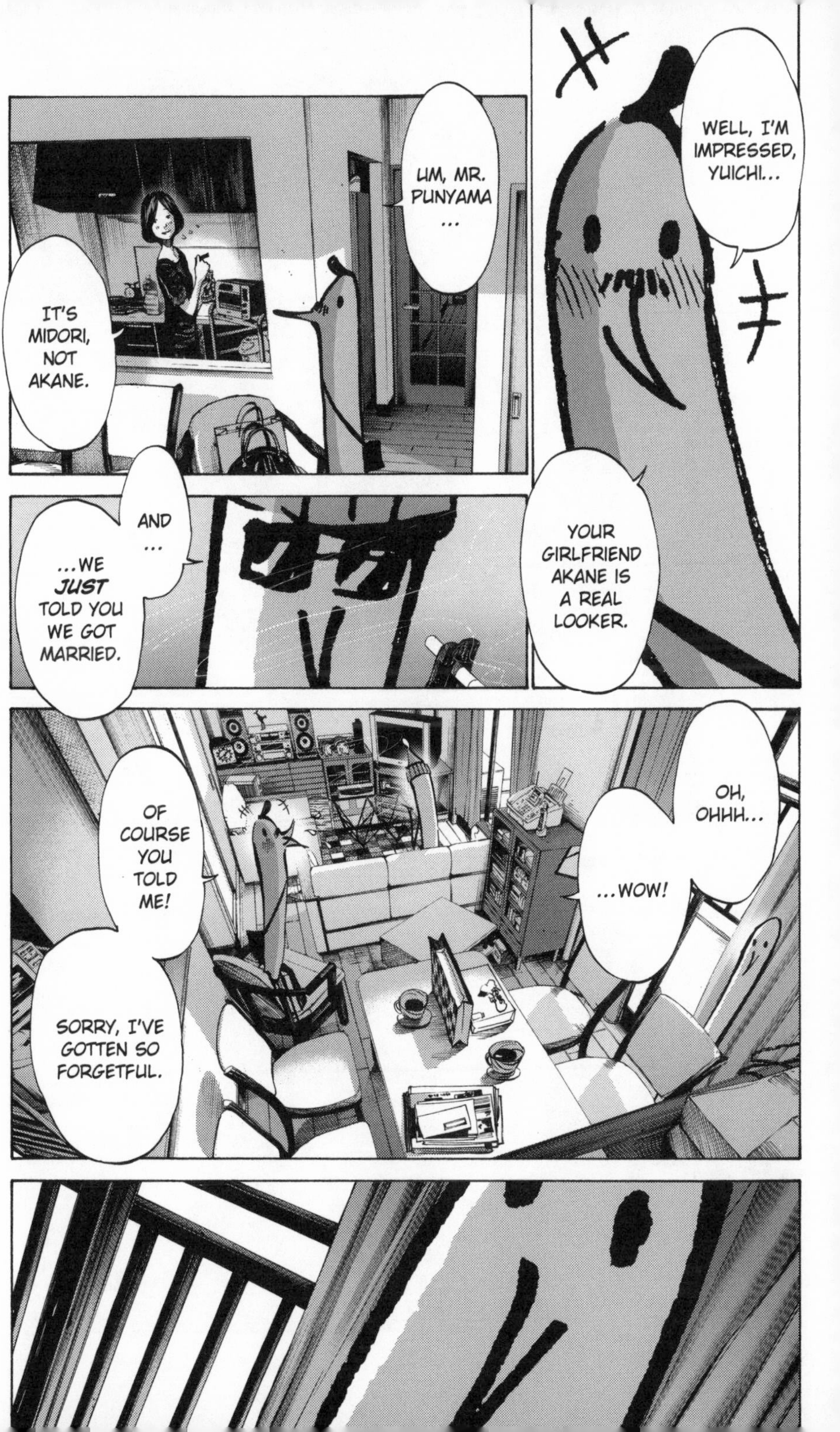
WELL, I'M IMPRESSED, YUICHI...
YOUR GIRLFRIEND AKANE IS A REAL LOOKER.
UM, MR. PUNYAMA ...
IT'S MIDORI, NOT AKANE.
AND ...
...WE **JUST** TOLD YOU WE GOT MARRIED.
OH, OHHH...
...WOW!
OF COURSE YOU TOLD ME!
SORRY, I'VE GOTTEN SO FORGETFUL.

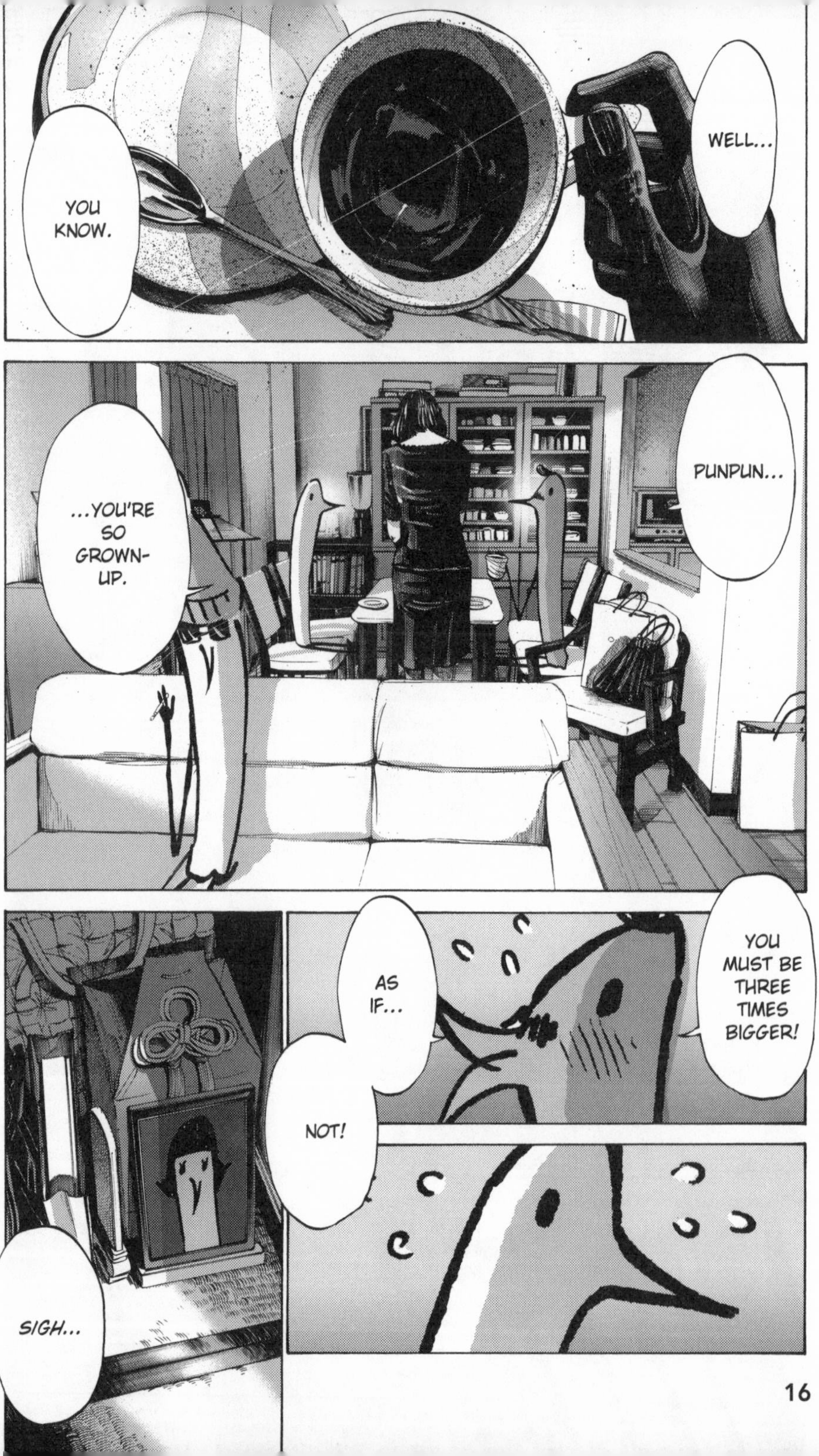

WELL...
YOU KNOW.
PUNPUN...
...YOU'RE SO GROWN-UP.
YOU MUST BE THREE TIMES BIGGER!
AS IF...
NOT!
SIGH...

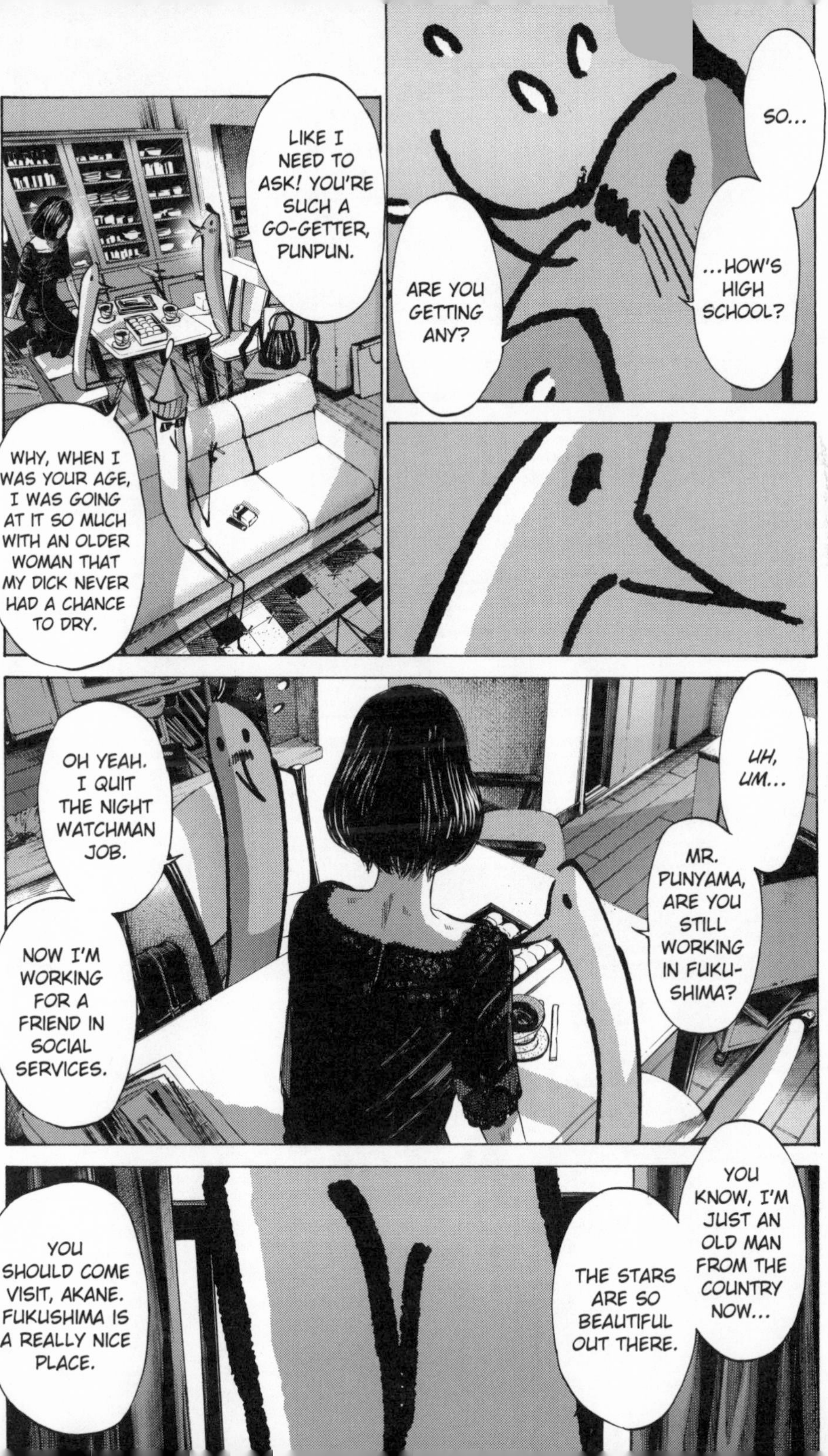
SO...
...HOW'S HIGH SCHOOL?
ARE YOU GETTING ANY?
LIKE I NEED TO ASK! YOU'RE SUCH A GO-GETTER, PUNPUN.
WHY, WHEN I WAS YOUR AGE, I WAS GOING AT IT SO MUCH WITH AN OLDER WOMAN THAT MY DICK NEVER HAD A CHANCE TO DRY.
UH, UM...
MR. PUNYAMA, ARE YOU STILL WORKING IN FUKU-SHIMA?
OH YEAH. I QUIT THE NIGHT WATCHMAN JOB.
NOW I'M WORKING FOR A FRIEND IN SOCIAL SERVICES.
YOU KNOW, I'M JUST AN OLD MAN FROM THE COUNTRY NOW...
THE STARS ARE SO BEAUTIFUL OUT THERE.
YOU SHOULD COME VISIT, AKANE. FUKUSHIMA IS A REALLY NICE PLACE.

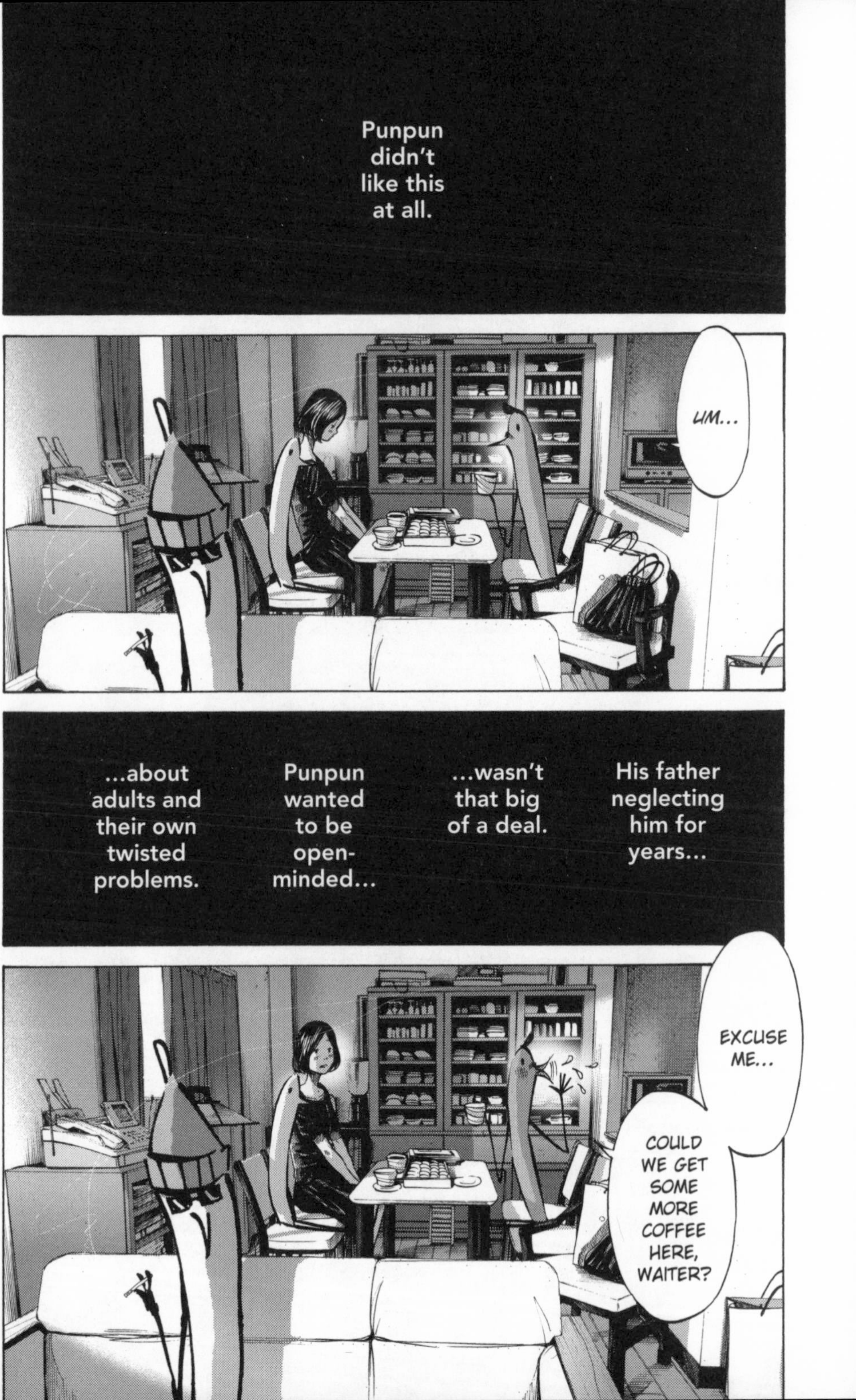
Punpun didn't like this at all.
UM...
His father neglecting him for years...
...wasn't that big of a deal.
Punpun wanted to be open-minded...
...about adults and their own twisted problems.
EXCUSE ME...
COULD WE GET SOME MORE COFFEE HERE, WAITER?

His dad's appearance, his voice, his demeanor...

Nothing had changed much.

He was the same funny, kind dad he'd always been.

But the poisonous sense of wrongness was so painful...

...that Punpun kept observing his dad in the hopes of figuring out **why**.

"I see..."

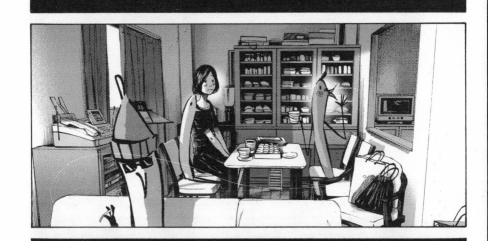

Punpun figured out what had changed the most.

GEEZ, I MISTOOK THIS FOR A COFFEE SHOP...
I'M SORRY, AKANE, COULD I HAVE ANOTHER CUP?
I'LL PUT THE KETTLE ON.
AND BY THE WAY, IT'S MIDORI.

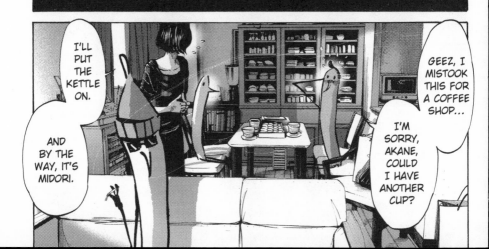

It was
himself.

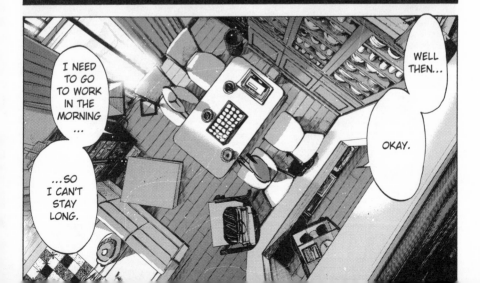

I NEED TO GO TO WORK IN THE MORNING...

...SO I CAN'T STAY LONG.

WELL THEN...

OKAY.

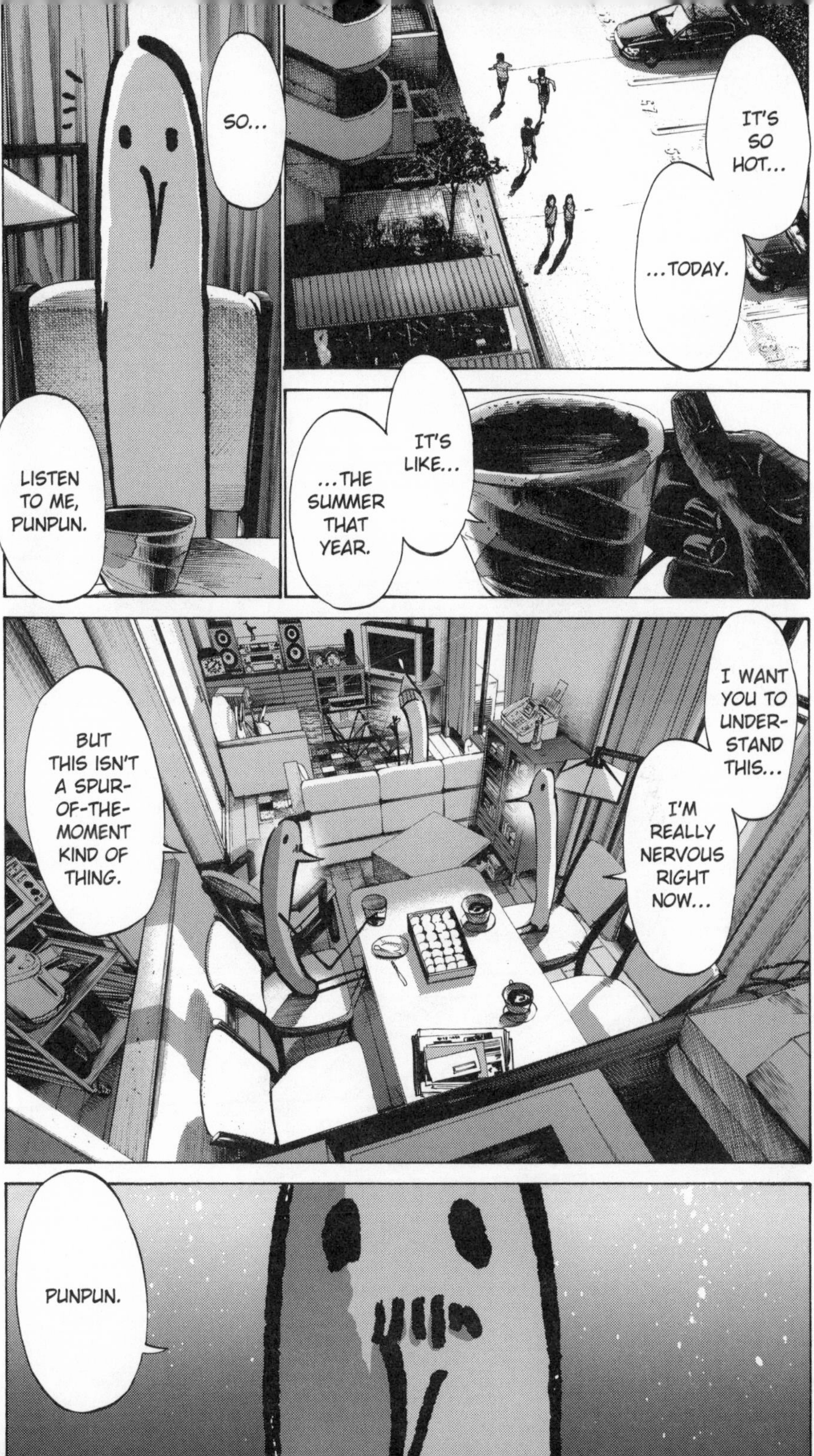
IT'S SO HOT...
...TODAY.
IT'S LIKE...
...THE SUMMER THAT YEAR.
SO...
LISTEN TO ME, PUNPUN.
I WANT YOU TO UNDER-STAND THIS...
I'M REALLY NERVOUS RIGHT NOW...
BUT THIS ISN'T A SPUR-OF-THE-MOMENT KIND OF THING.
PUNPUN.

DO YOU WANT...

...TO COME LIVE WITH ME IN FUKUSHIMA?

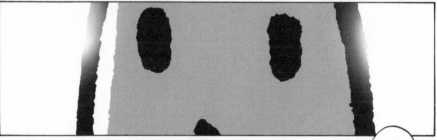

WE CAN HAVE A NEW BEGINNING.

JUST THE TWO OF US.

Chapter 69

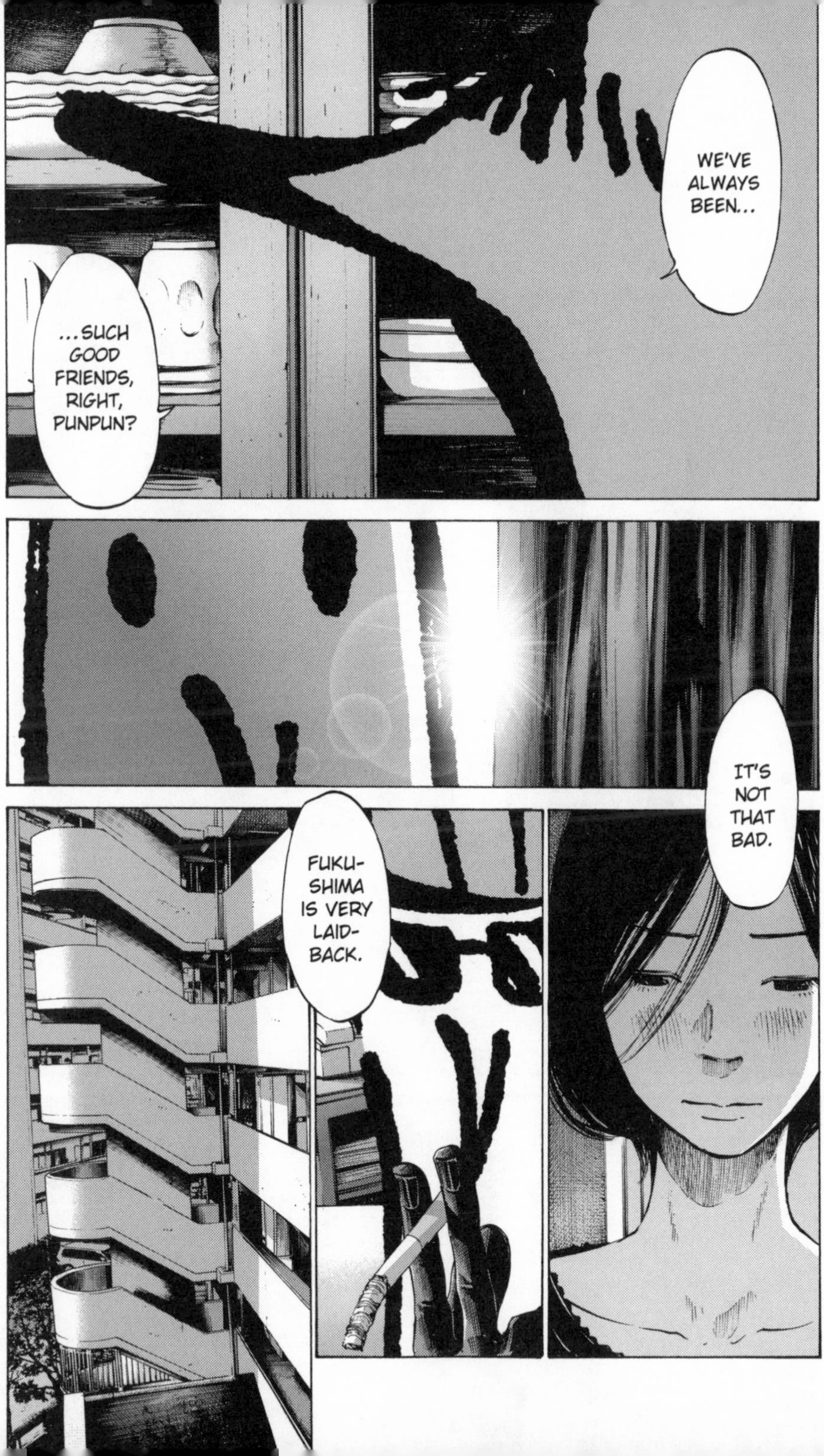
WE'VE ALWAYS BEEN...
...SUCH GOOD FRIENDS, RIGHT, PUNPUN?
IT'S NOT THAT BAD.
FUKU-SHIMA IS VERY LAID-BACK.

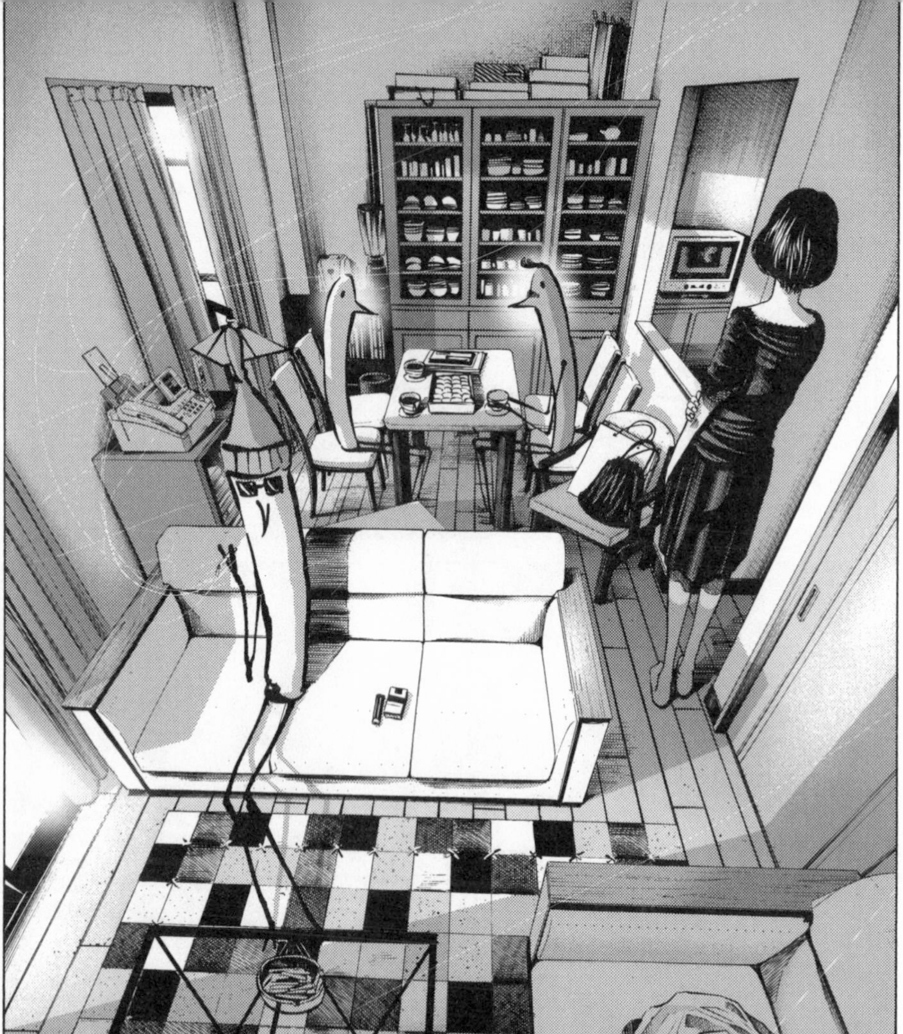

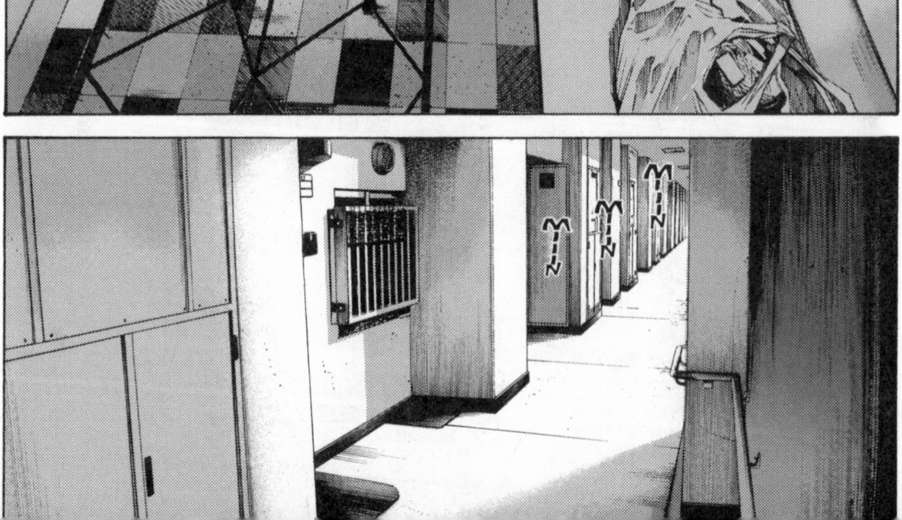
MIIN
MIIN
MIIN

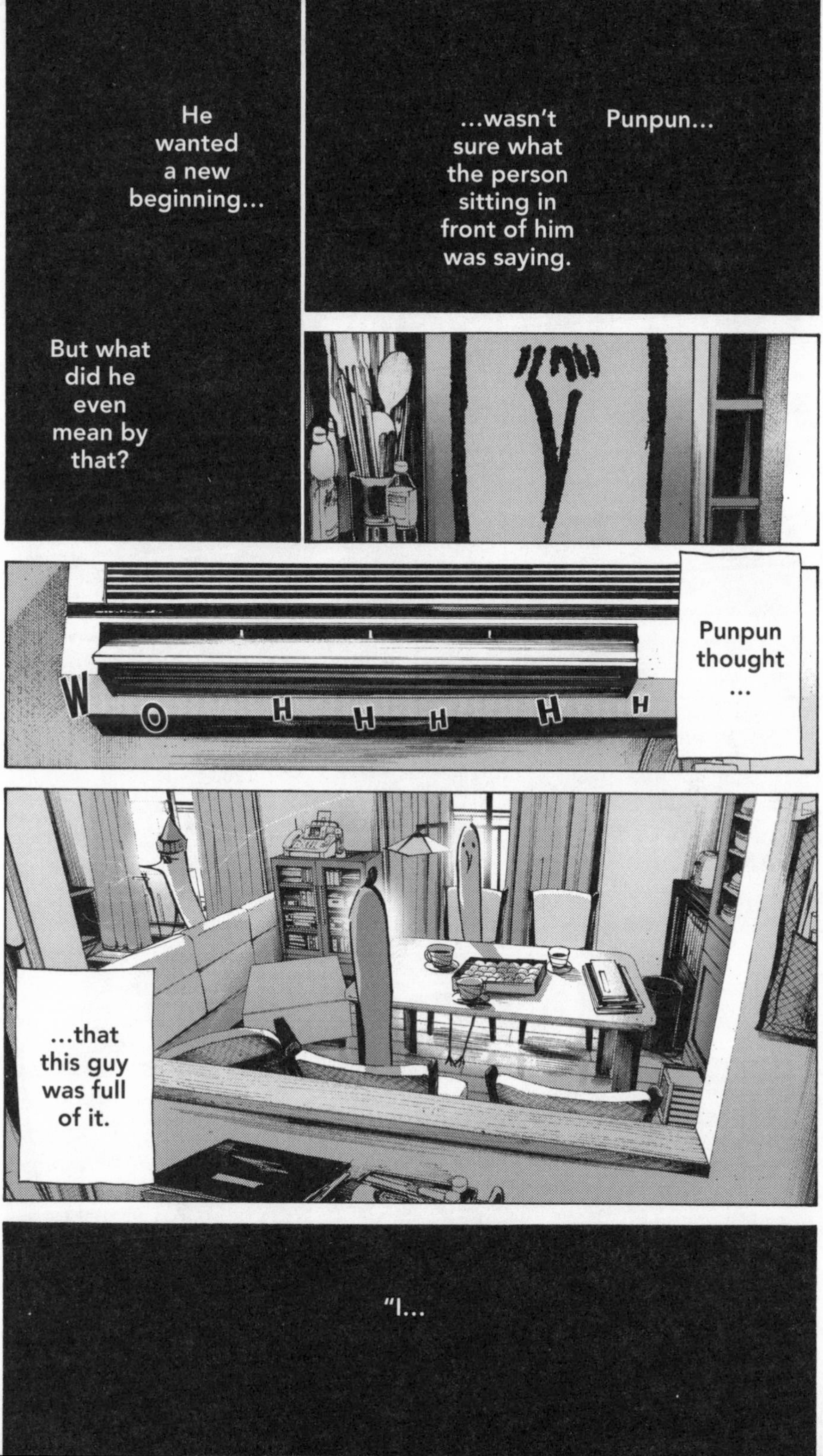
Punpun...
...wasn't sure what the person sitting in front of him was saying.
He wanted a new beginning...
But what did he even mean by that?
Punpun thought ...
WOHHHHH
...that this guy was full of it.
"I...

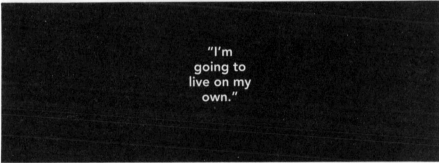

"I'm
going to
live on my
own."

OKAY
...

... RIGHT.

I
UNDER-
STAND.

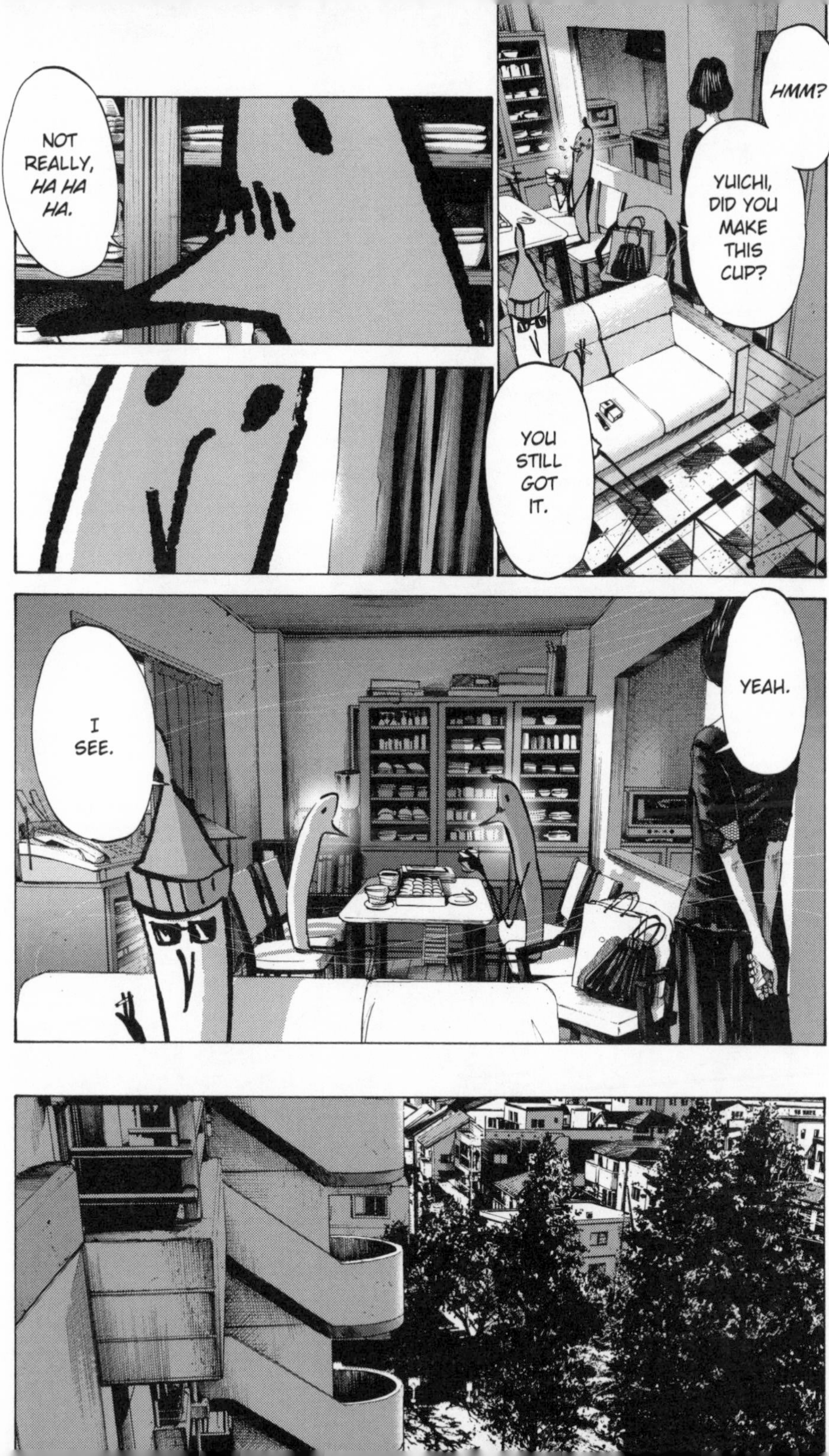
HMM?
YUICHI, DID YOU MAKE THIS CUP?
YOU STILL GOT IT.
NOT REALLY, HA HA HA.
YEAH.
I SEE.

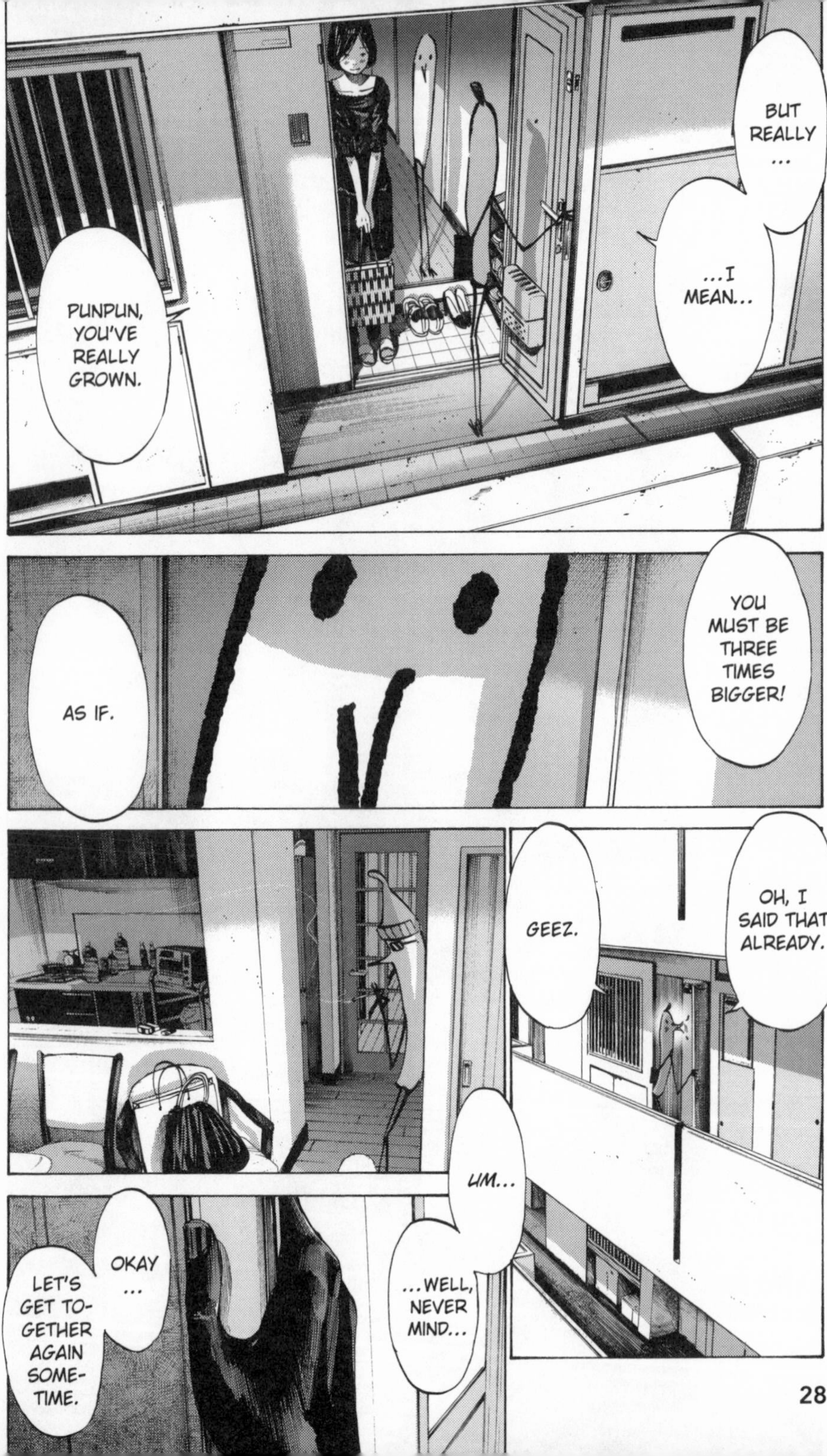
BUT REALLY ...
...I MEAN...
PUNPUN, YOU'VE REALLY GROWN.
YOU MUST BE THREE TIMES BIGGER!
AS IF.
OH, I SAID THAT ALREADY.
GEEZ.
UM...
...WELL, NEVER MIND...
OKAY ...
LET'S GET TO-GETHER AGAIN SOME-TIME.

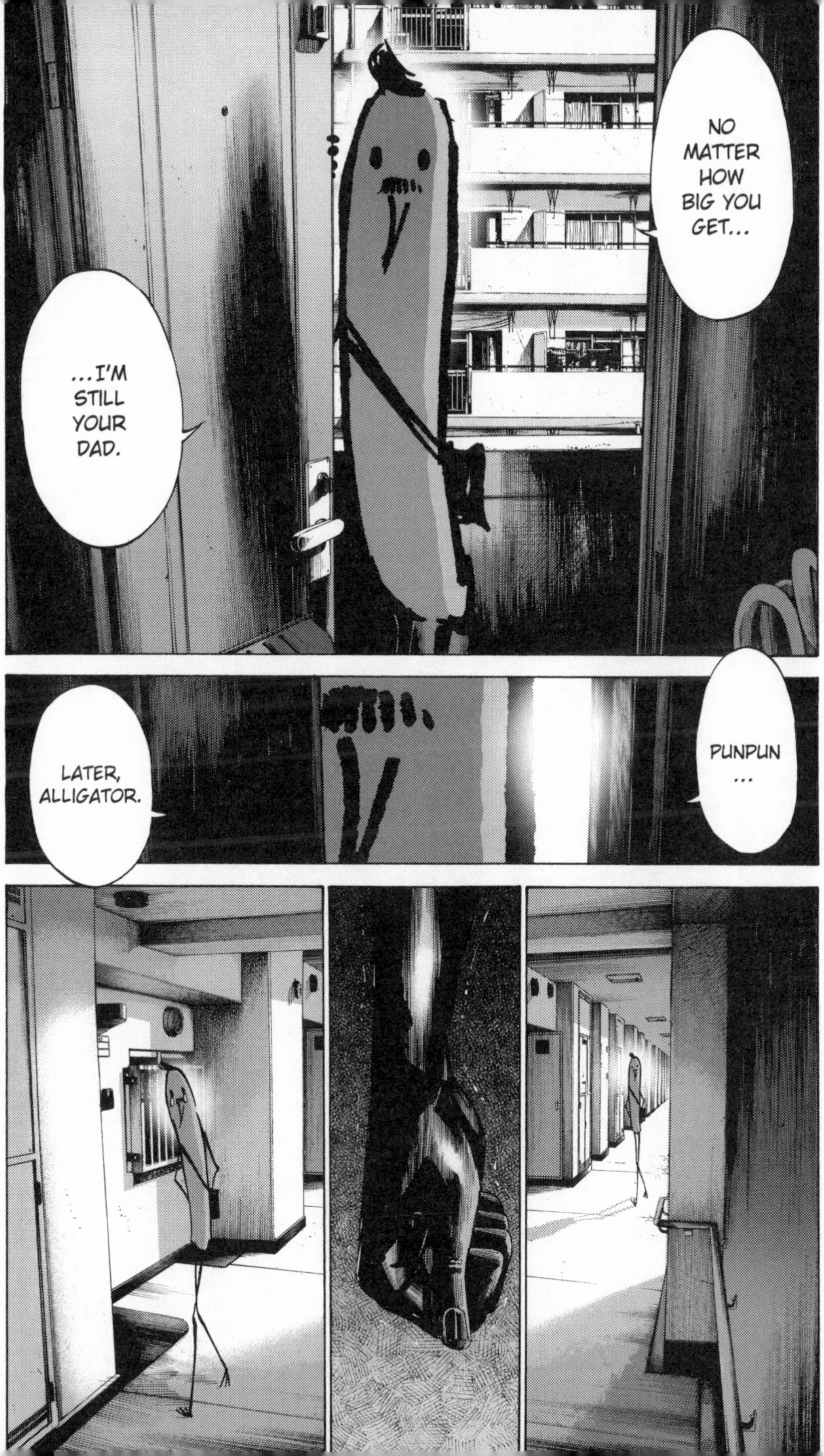
NO MATTER HOW BIG YOU GET...
...I'M STILL YOUR DAD.
PUNPUN ...
LATER, ALLIGATOR.

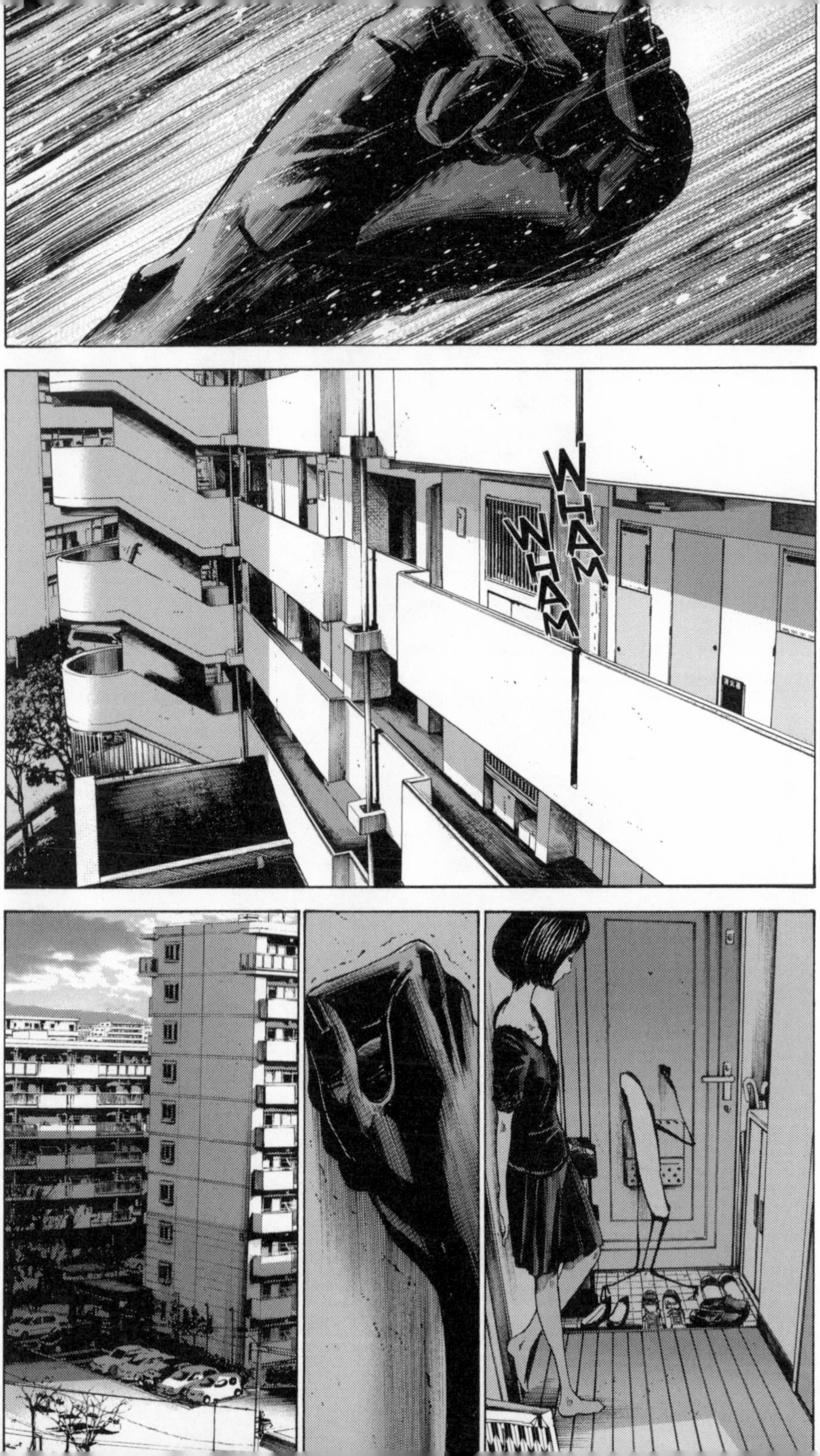
WHAM
WHAM

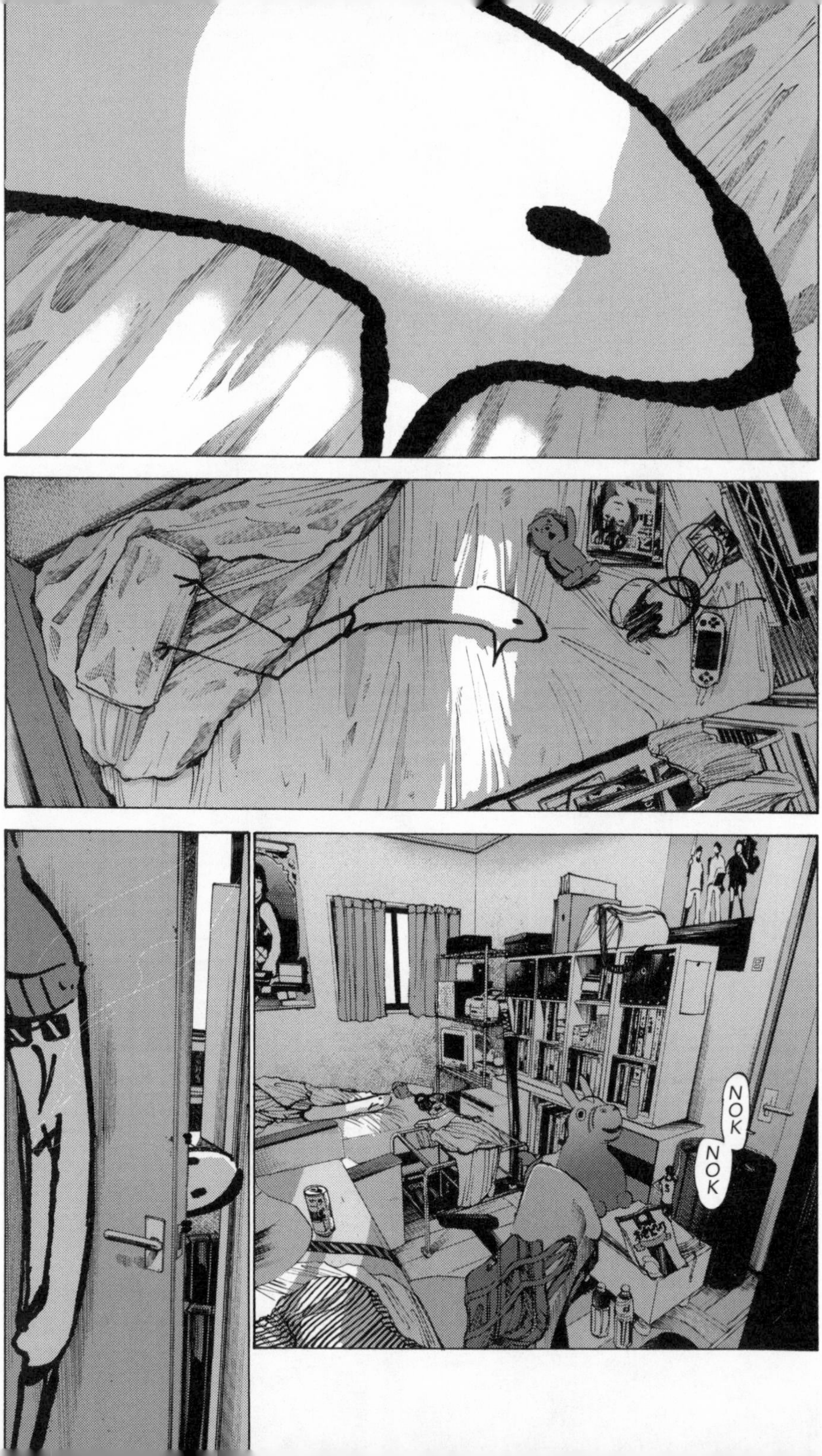
NOK NOK

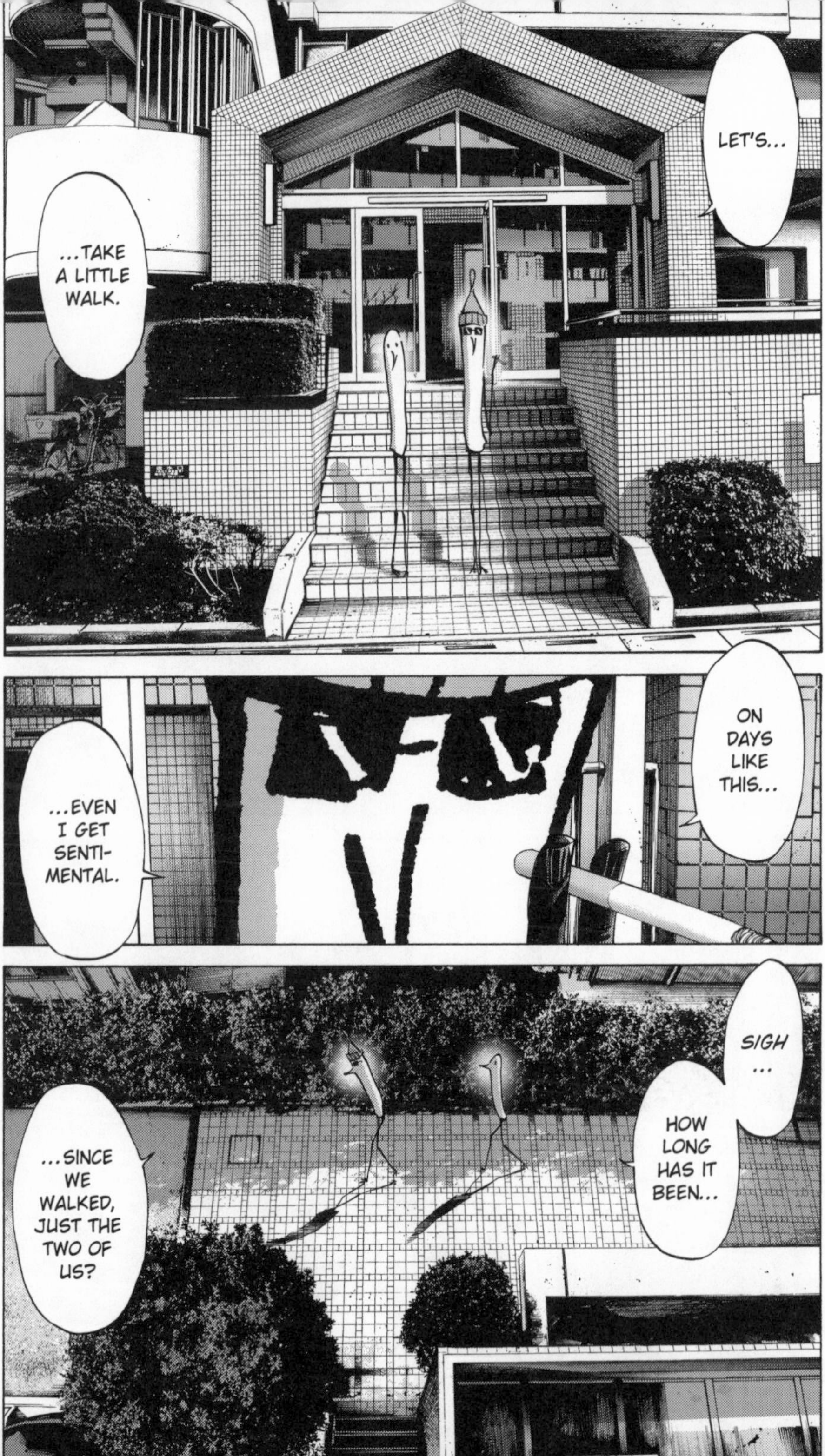
LET'S...
...TAKE A LITTLE WALK.
ON DAYS LIKE THIS...
...EVEN I GET SENTI-MENTAL.
SIGH...
HOW LONG HAS IT BEEN...
...SINCE WE WALKED, JUST THE TWO OF US?

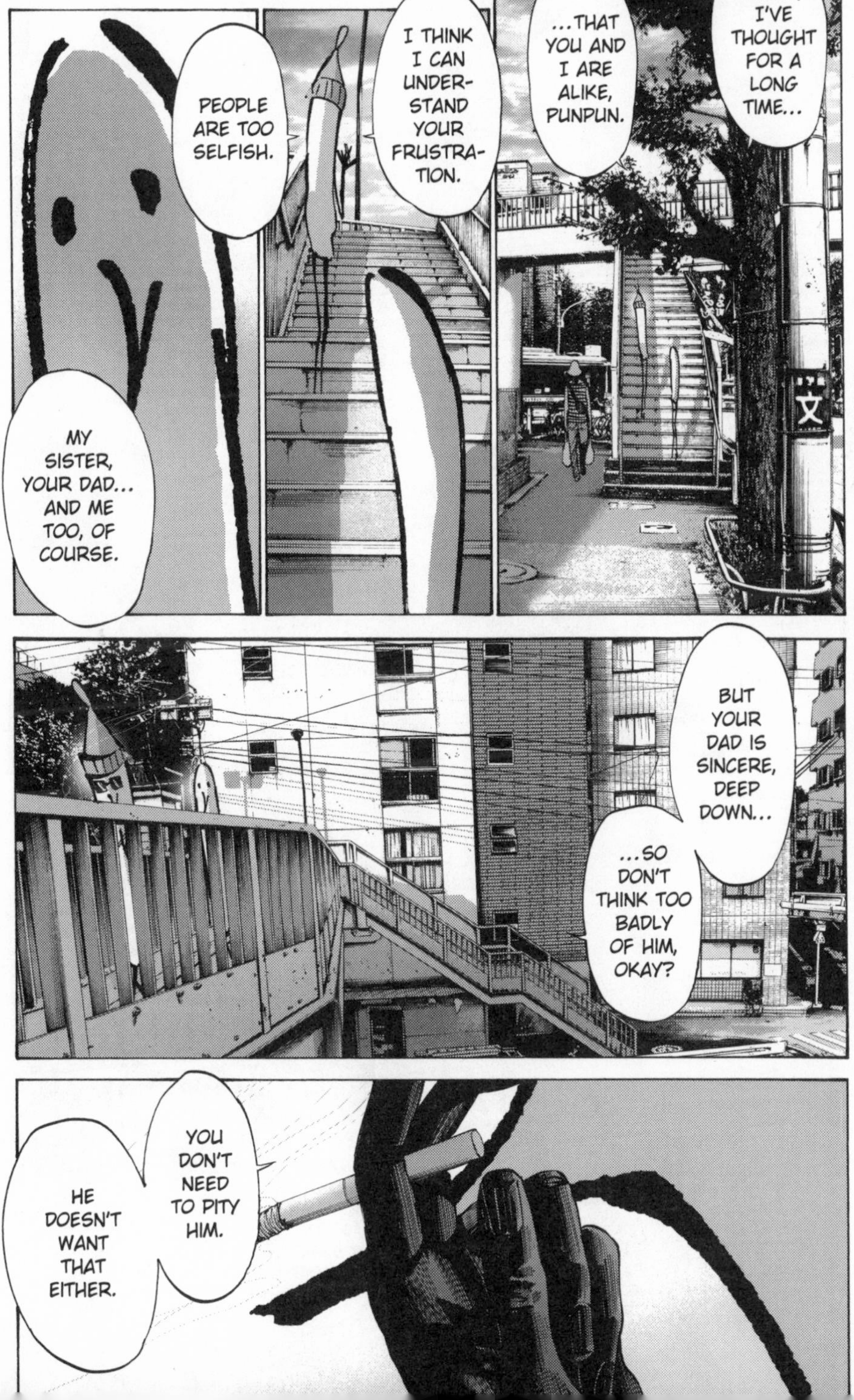
YOU KNOW, I'VE THOUGHT FOR A LONG TIME...
...THAT YOU AND I ARE ALIKE, PUNPUN.
I THINK I CAN UNDER-STAND YOUR FRUSTRA-TION.
PEOPLE ARE TOO SELFISH.
MY SISTER, YOUR DAD... AND ME TOO, OF COURSE.
BUT YOUR DAD IS SINCERE, DEEP DOWN...
...SO DON'T THINK TOO BADLY OF HIM, OKAY?
YOU DON'T NEED TO PITY HIM.
HE DOESN'T WANT THAT EITHER.

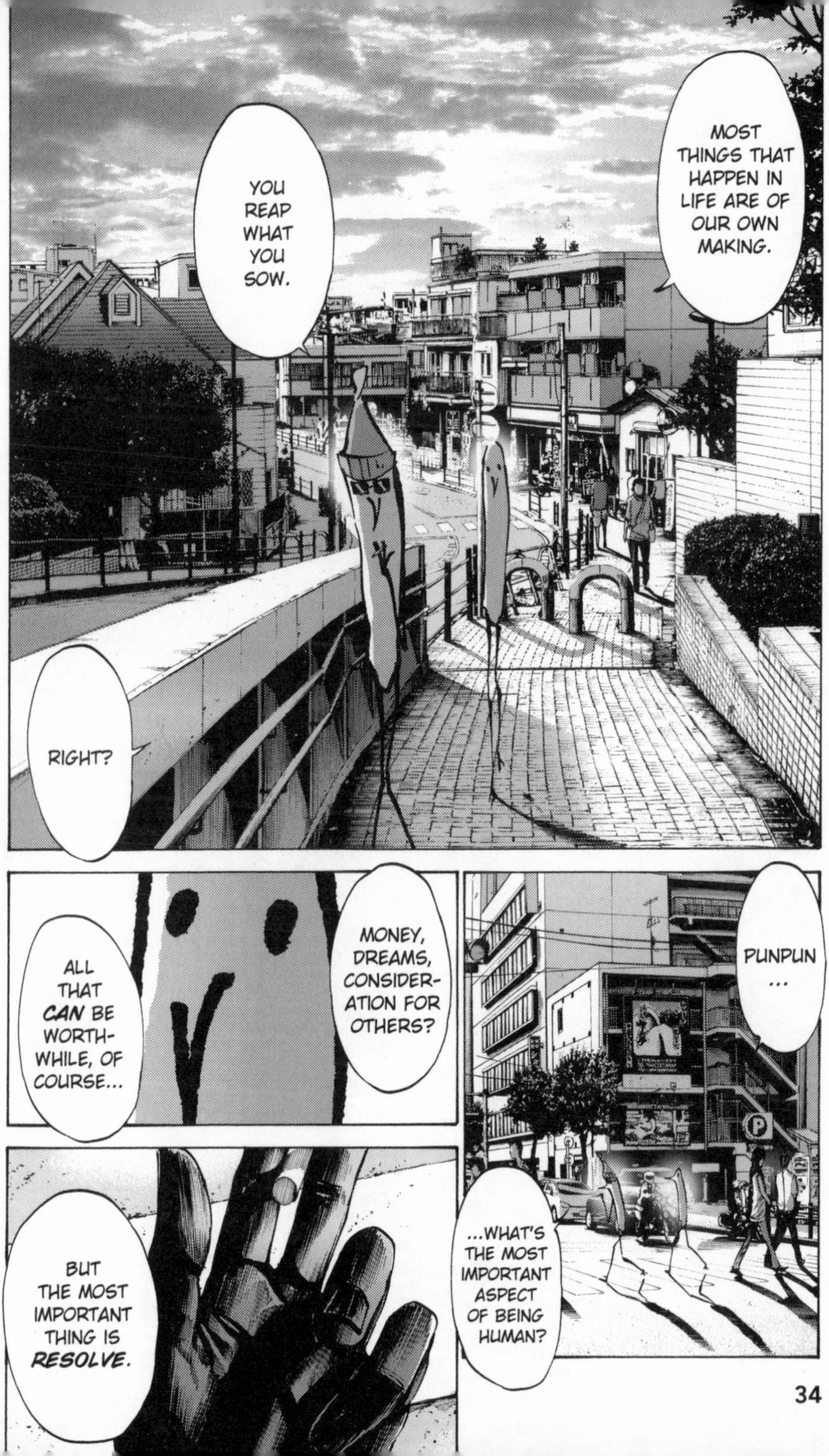
MOST THINGS THAT HAPPEN IN LIFE ARE OF OUR OWN MAKING.
YOU REAP WHAT YOU SOW.
RIGHT?
PUNPUN...
...WHAT'S THE MOST IMPORTANT ASPECT OF BEING HUMAN?
MONEY, DREAMS, CONSIDERATION FOR OTHERS?
ALL THAT CAN BE WORTHWHILE, OF COURSE...
BUT THE MOST IMPORTANT THING IS RESOLVE.

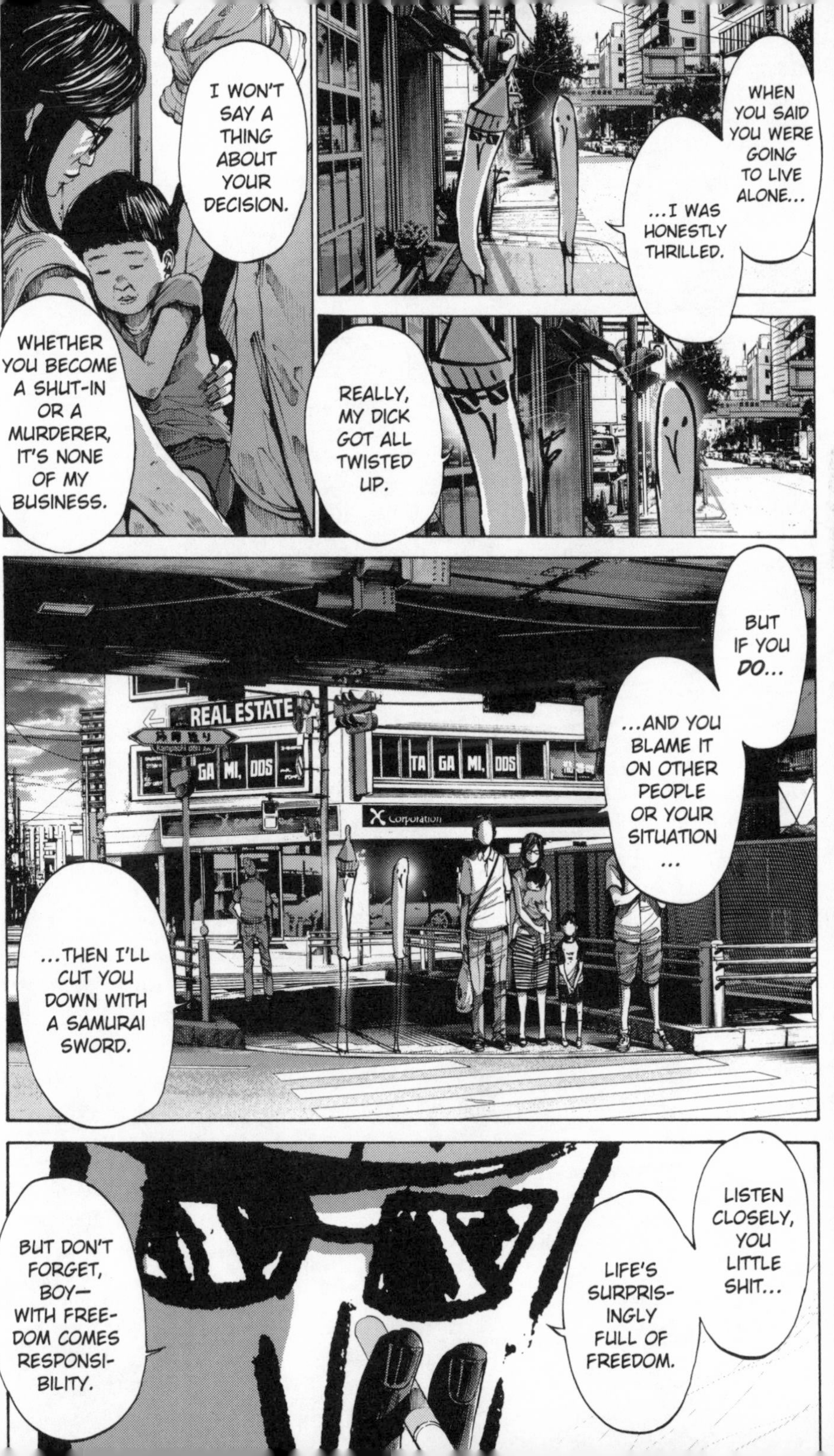
WHEN YOU SAID YOU WERE GOING TO LIVE ALONE...
...I WAS HONESTLY THRILLED.
REALLY, MY DICK GOT ALL TWISTED UP.
I WON'T SAY A THING ABOUT YOUR DECISION.
WHETHER YOU BECOME A SHUT-IN OR A MURDERER, IT'S NONE OF MY BUSINESS.
BUT IF YOU DO...
...AND YOU BLAME IT ON OTHER PEOPLE OR YOUR SITUATION ...
REAL ESTATE
Corporation
...THEN I'LL CUT YOU DOWN WITH A SAMURAI SWORD.
LISTEN CLOSELY, YOU LITTLE SHIT...
LIFE'S SURPRIS-INGLY FULL OF FREEDOM.
BUT DON'T FORGET, BOY—WITH FREE-DOM COMES RESPONSI-BILITY.

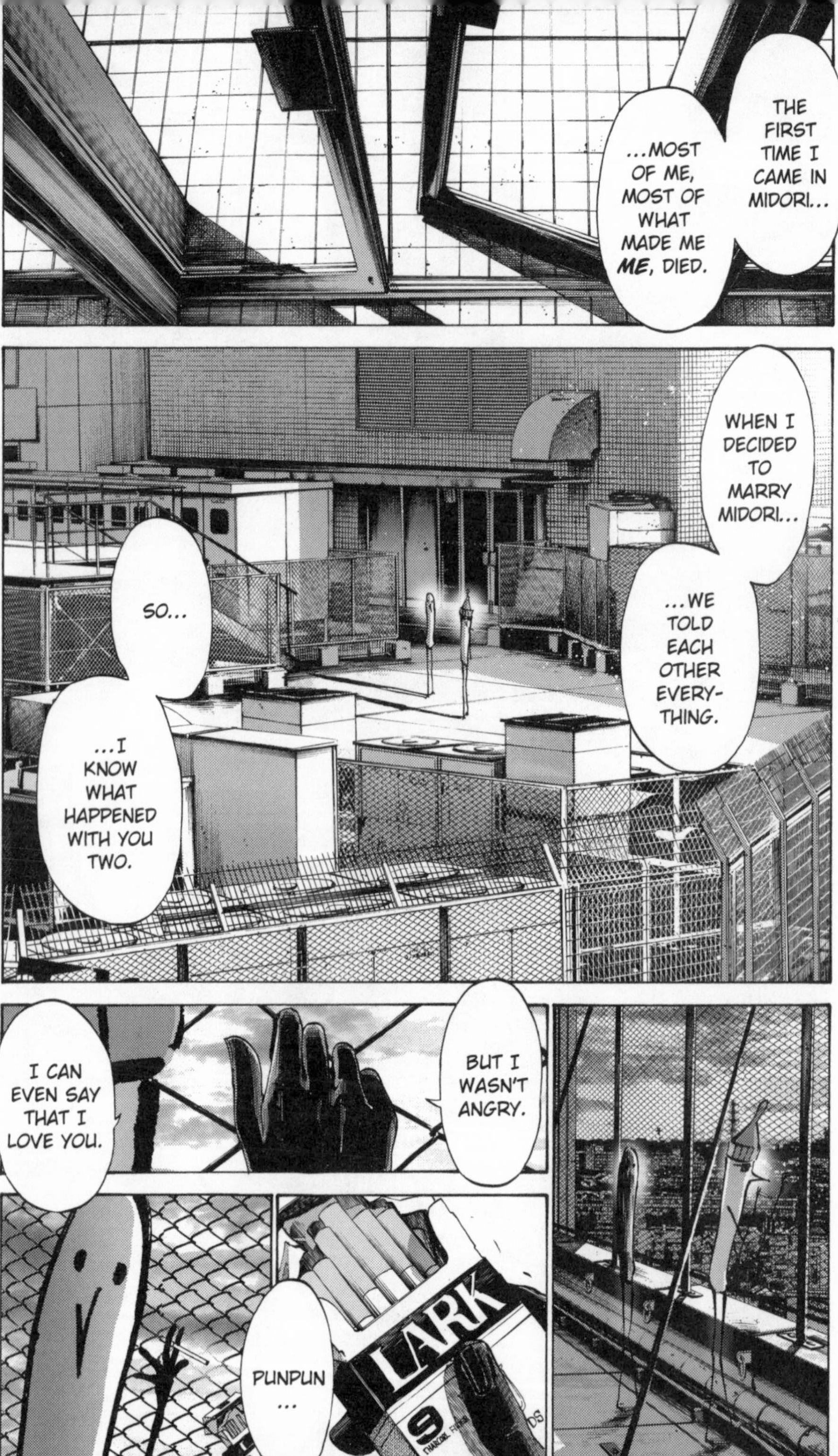
THE FIRST TIME I CAME IN MIDORI...
...MOST OF ME, MOST OF WHAT MADE ME *ME*, DIED.
WHEN I DECIDED TO MARRY MIDORI...
...WE TOLD EACH OTHER EVERYTHING.
SO...
...I KNOW WHAT HAPPENED WITH YOU TWO.
BUT I WASN'T ANGRY.
I CAN EVEN SAY THAT I LOVE YOU.
PUNPUN ...
LARK
9

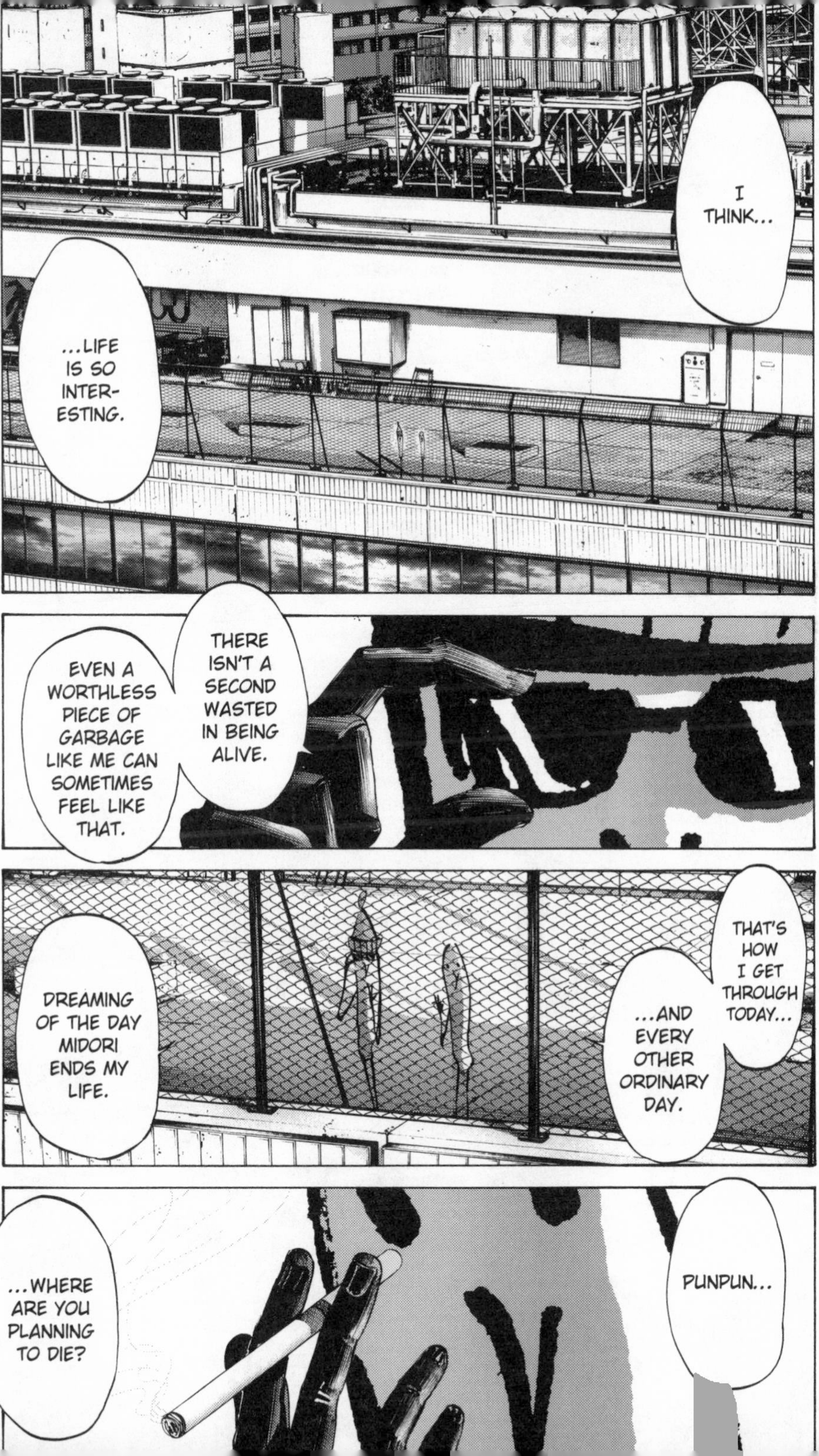
I THINK...
...LIFE IS SO INTERESTING.
THERE ISN'T A SECOND WASTED IN BEING ALIVE.
EVEN A WORTHLESS PIECE OF GARBAGE LIKE ME CAN SOMETIMES FEEL LIKE THAT.
THAT'S HOW I GET THROUGH TODAY...
...AND EVERY OTHER ORDINARY DAY.
DREAMING OF THE DAY MIDORI ENDS MY LIFE.
PUNPUN...
...WHERE ARE YOU PLANNING TO DIE?

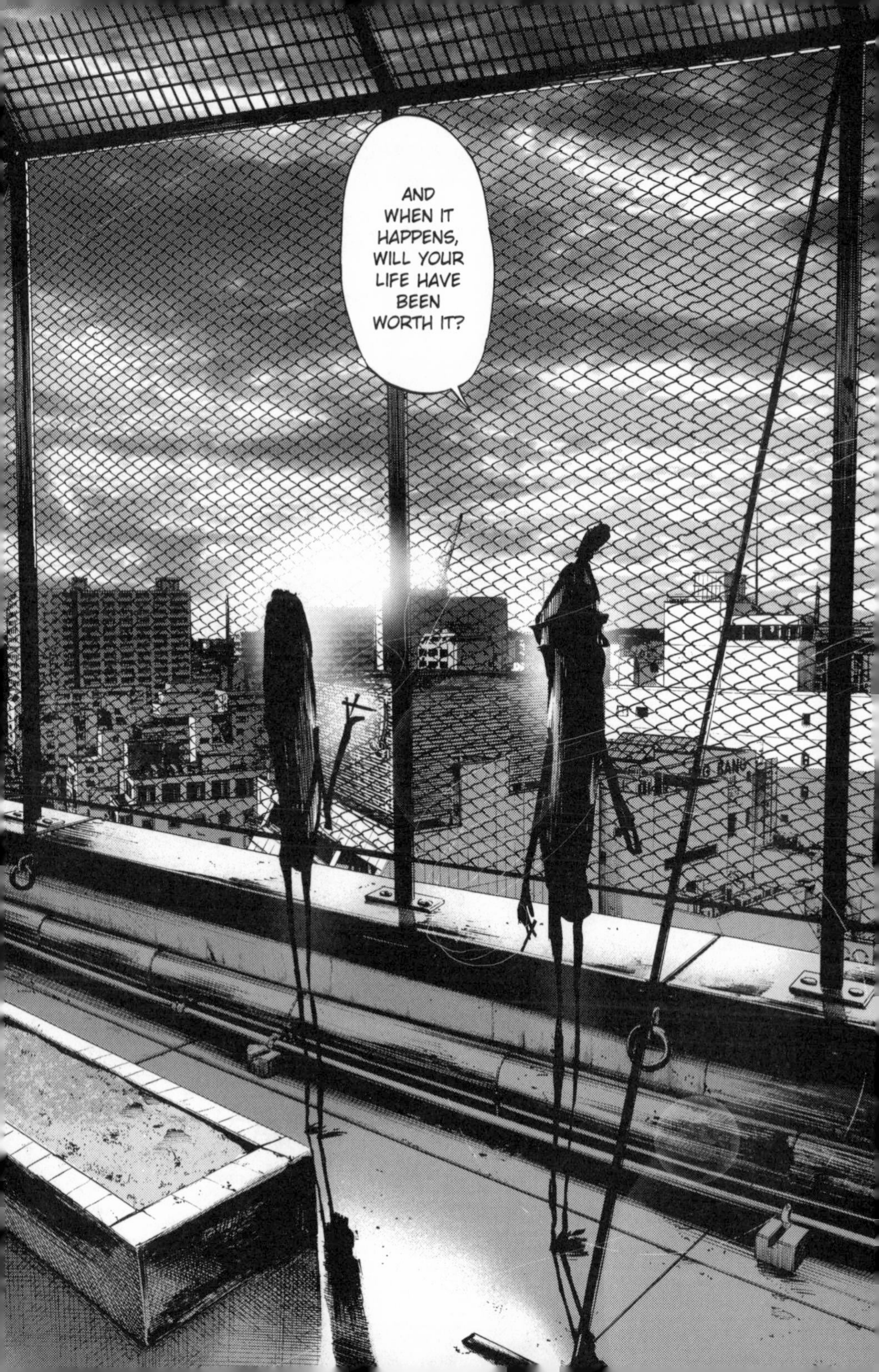
AND WHEN IT HAPPENS, WILL YOUR LIFE HAVE BEEN WORTH IT?

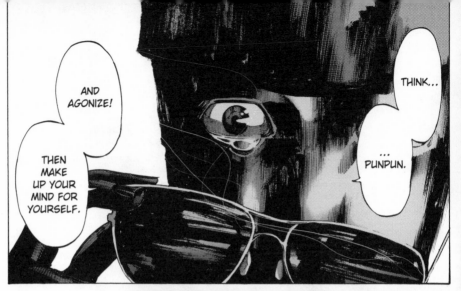

THINK...
...PUNPUN.
AND AGONIZE!
THEN MAKE UP YOUR MIND FOR YOURSELF.
EVEN IF YOU DON'T UNDER-STAND...
...AS LONG AS YOU STRIVE TO UNDER-STAND...
...YOU CAN JUST ABOUT HANG ON TO WHO YOU ARE.
THE BORING DAILY GRIND...
...THE USELESS SCENERY...
YOU'RE THE ONLY ONE WHO CAN CHANGE IT.
SO, PUNPUN ...
...AS LONG AS YOU REMAIN YOU...

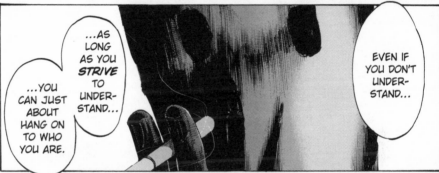

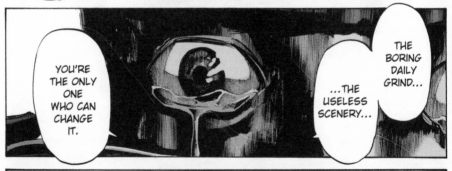

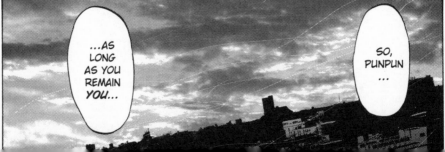

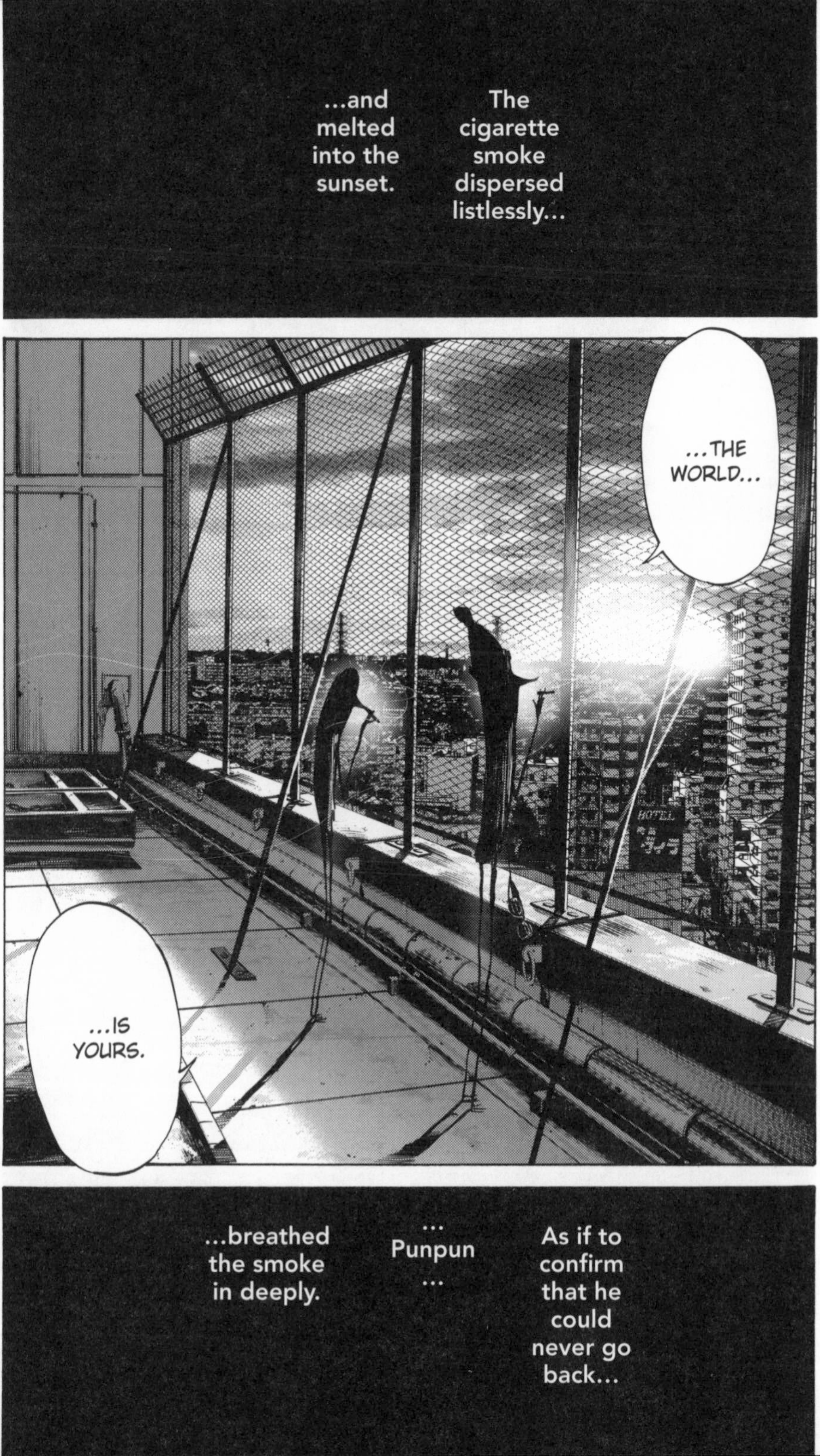
The cigarette smoke dispersed listlessly...
...and melted into the sunset.
...THE WORLD...
...IS YOURS.
As if to confirm that he could never go back...
...
Punpun
...
...breathed the smoke in deeply.

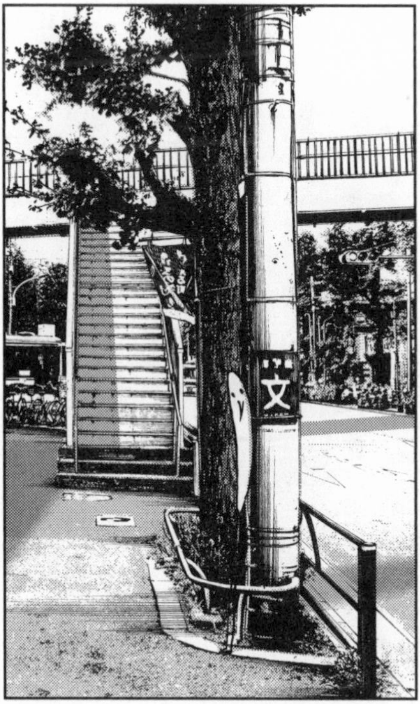
文

NEW!
RAINBOW
SUNTORY
COFFEE BOSS

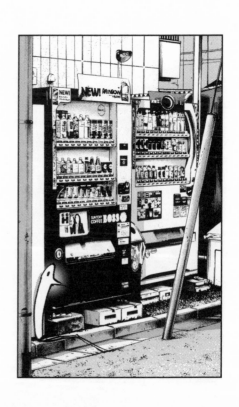

Chapter 70

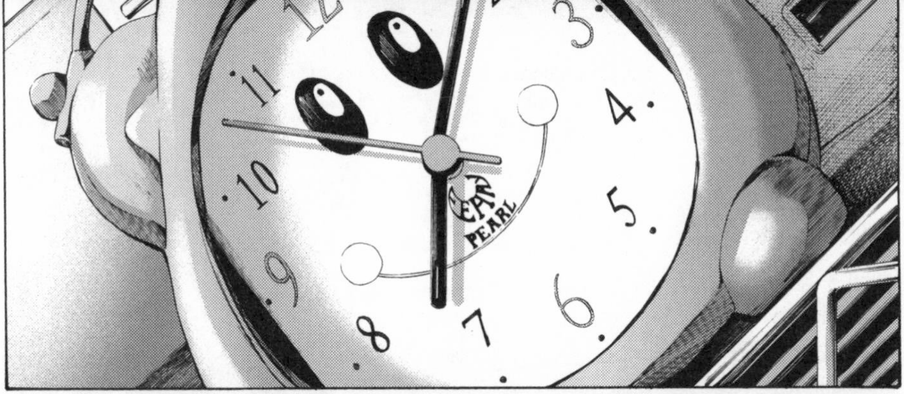
PEARL

The sound of the second hand ticking deep in his ear.

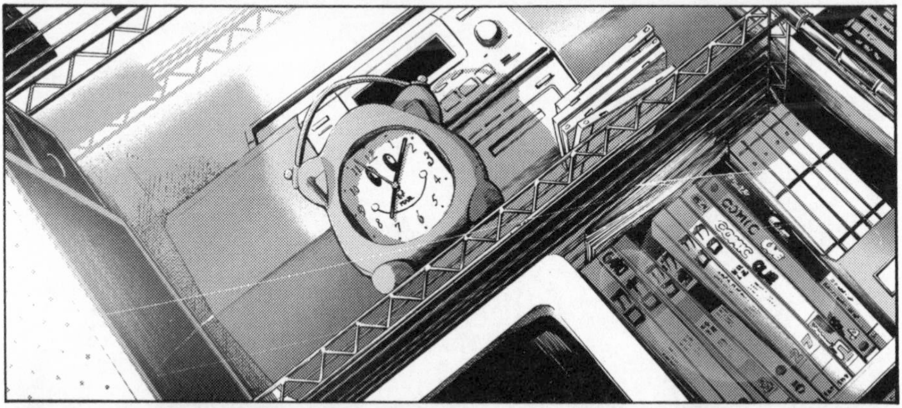

The alarm clock that would go off at 7:10.

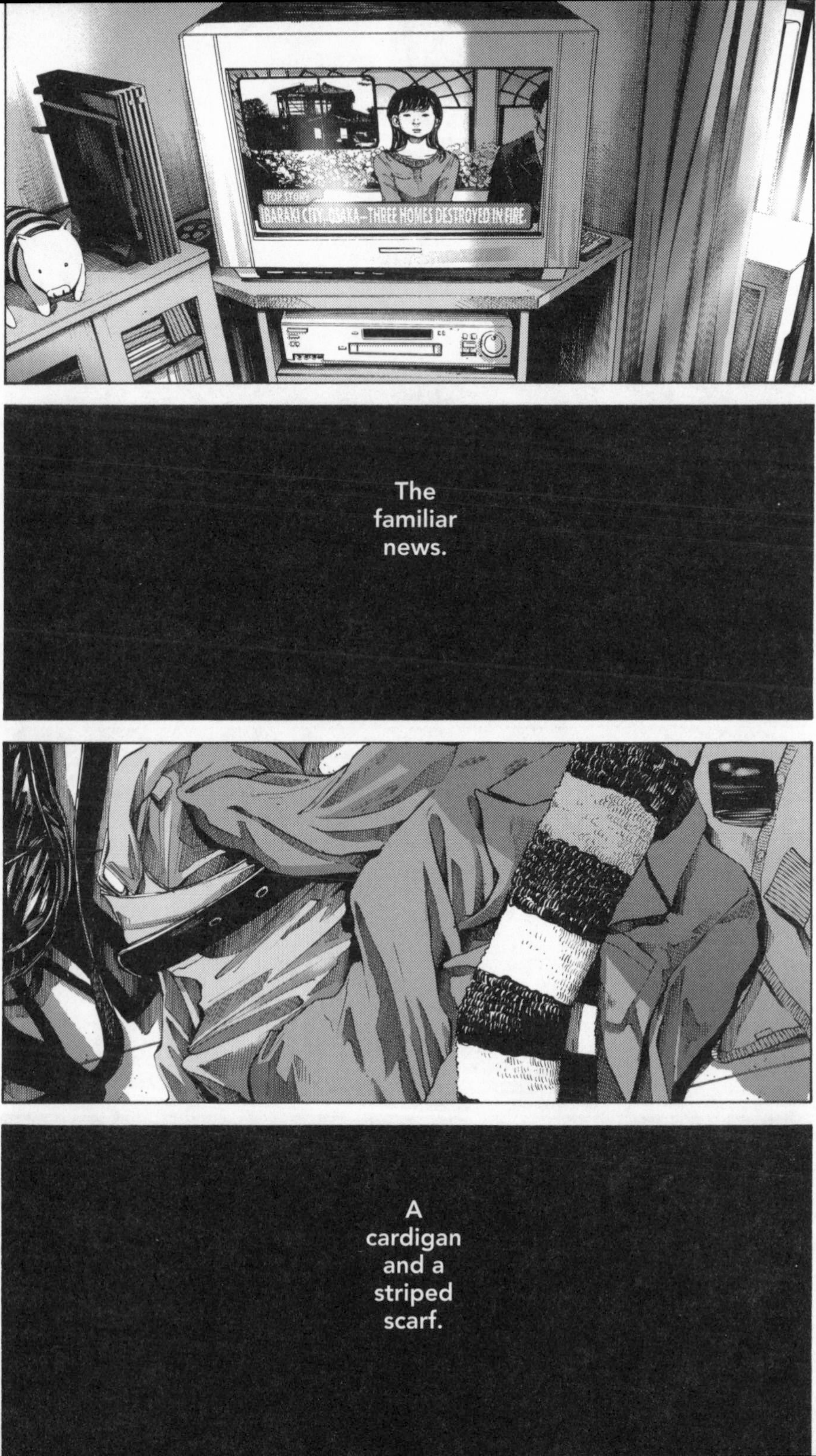
TOP STORY
IBARAKI CITY, OSAKA—THREE HOMES DESTROYED IN FIRE
The familiar news.
A cardigan and a striped scarf.

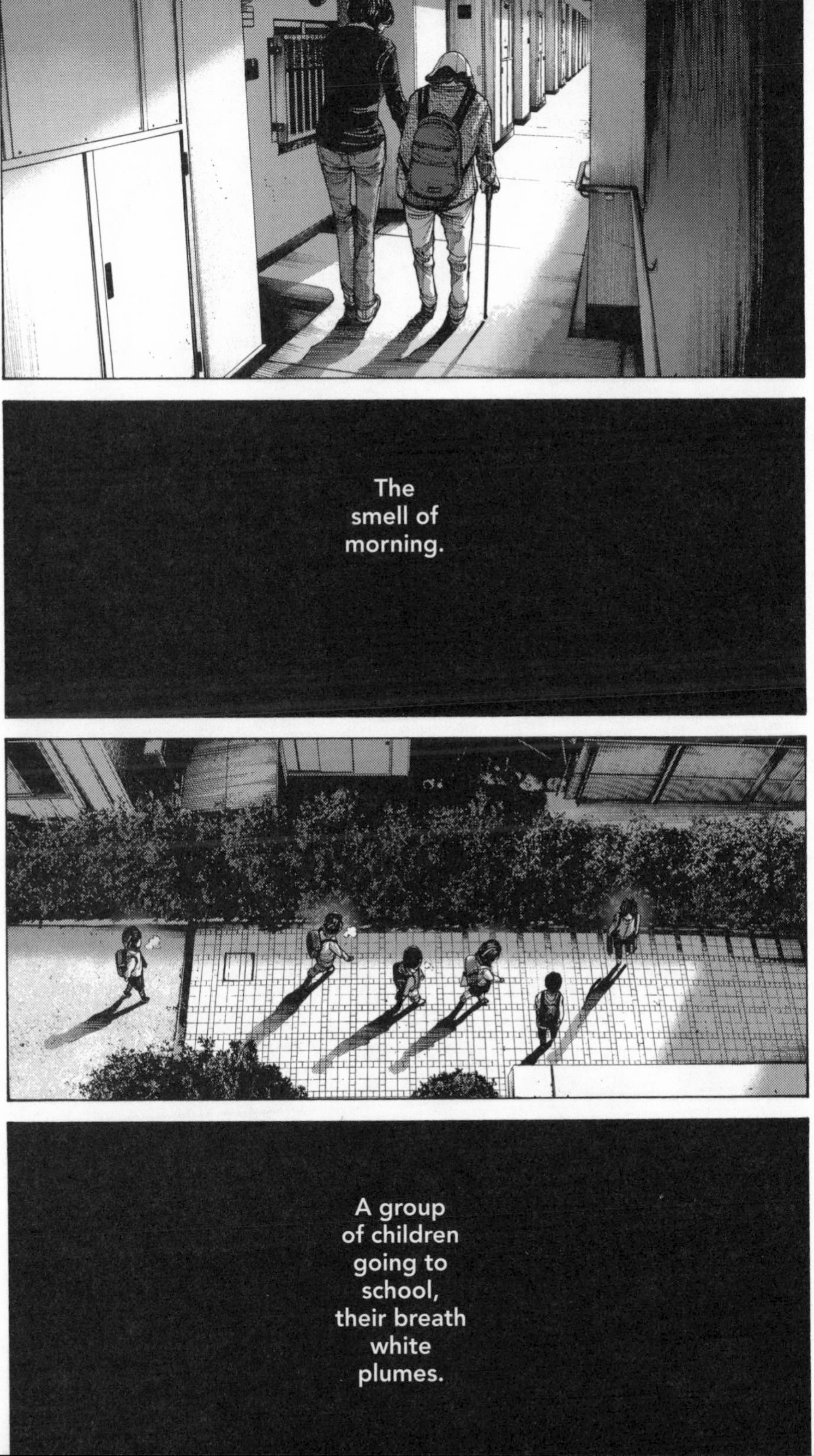
The smell of morning.
A group of children going to school, their breath white plumes.

The 7:45 local train.

The station platform, a mixture of yawns and sighs.

Conversations with no substance.

J-pop leaking from headphones.

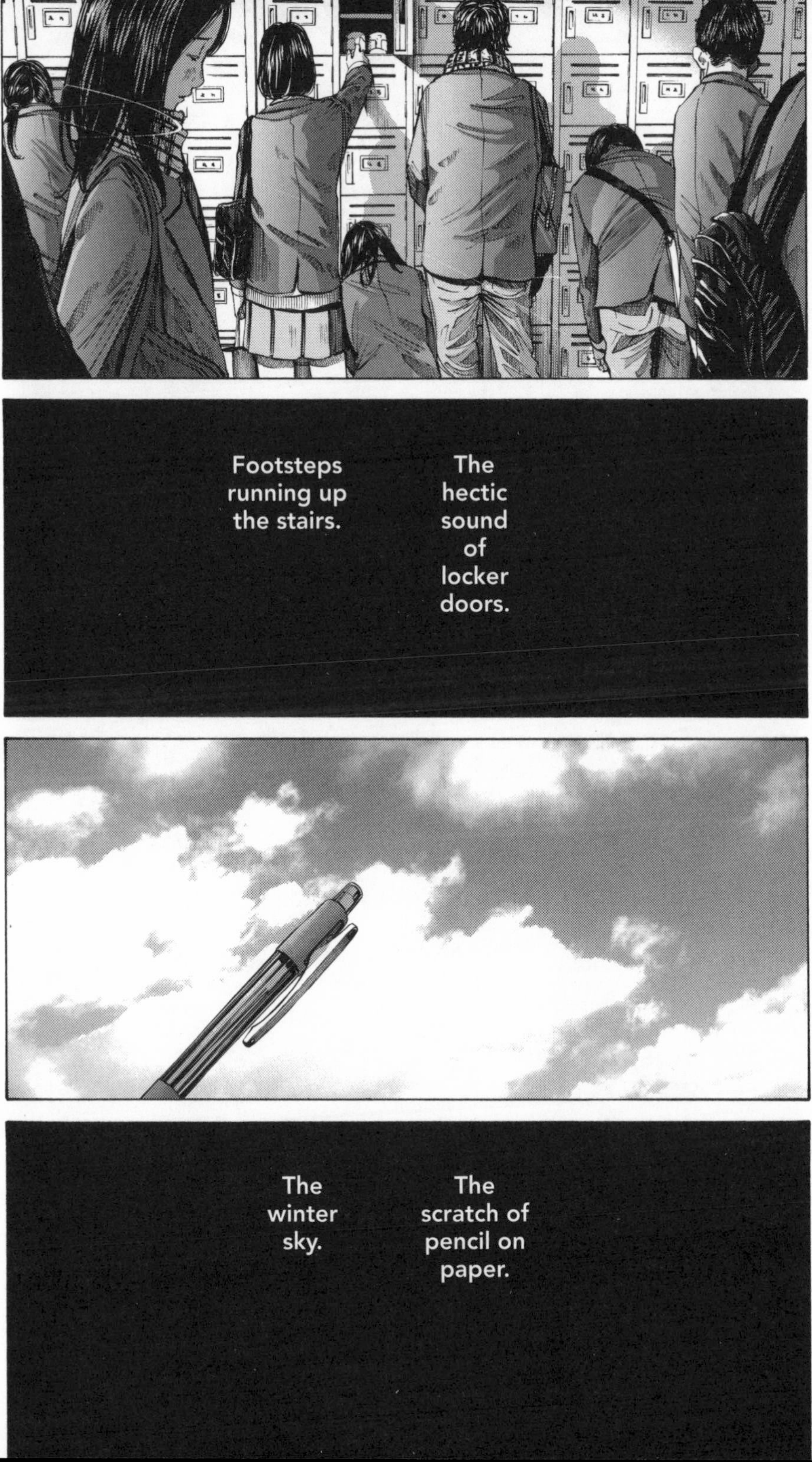
The hectic sound of locker doors.
Footsteps running up the stairs.
The scratch of pencil on paper.
The winter sky.

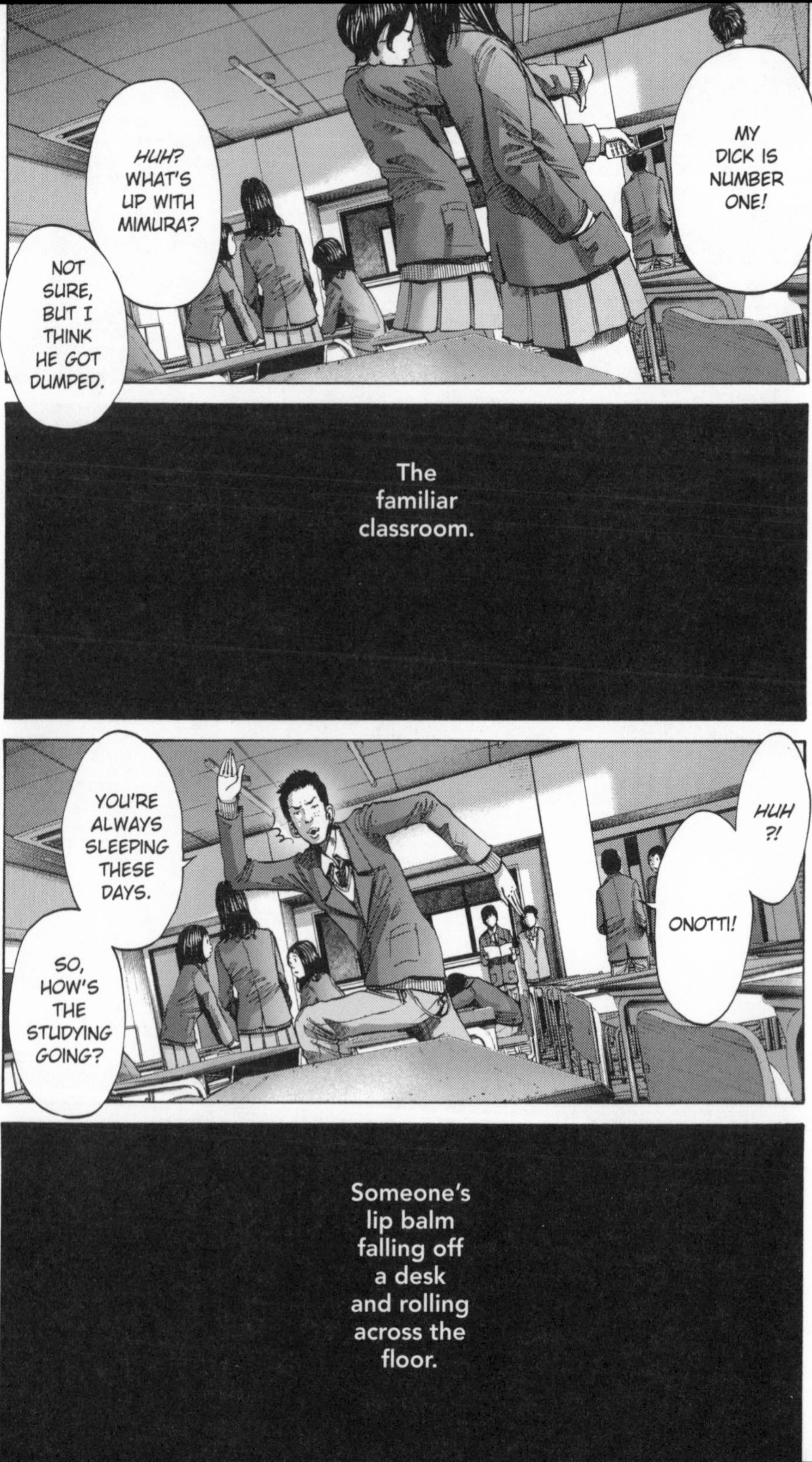
MY DICK IS NUMBER ONE!
HUH? WHAT'S UP WITH MIMURA?
NOT SURE, BUT I THINK HE GOT DUMPED.
The familiar classroom.
HUH ?!
ONOTTI!
YOU'RE ALWAYS SLEEPING THESE DAYS.
SO, HOW'S THE STUDYING GOING?
Someone's lip balm falling off a desk and rolling across the floor.

INDEED, AS SOMEONE WHO PICKED A COLLEGE THAT WOULD LET ME IN ON THE MERIT OF A HIGH SCHOOL RECOMMENDATION, I MAY SEEM SIMPLE TO YOU...
BUT...
...THIS IS JUST GROUND-WORK FOR MY MAGNIFICENT PLAN.

A comic book, in tatters from being shared around.

I'M GOING TO BUILD A PYRAMID IN SHIBUYA ...
PYUN!
SHUT UP, MIMURA!

An answer sheet, balled up and thrown in the trash.

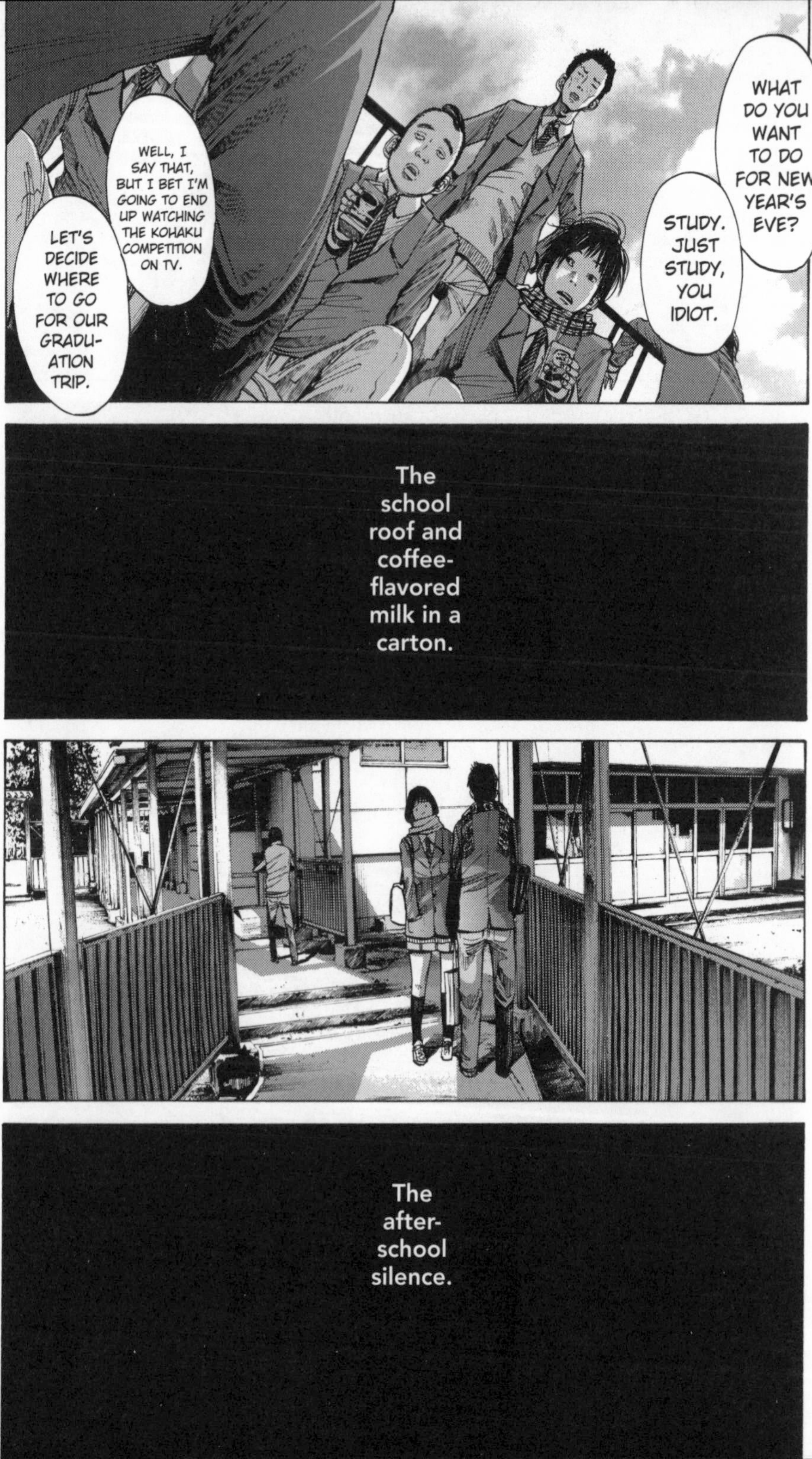
WHAT DO YOU WANT TO DO FOR NEW YEAR'S EVE?
STUDY. JUST STUDY, YOU IDIOT.
WELL, I SAY THAT, BUT I BET I'M GOING TO END UP WATCHING THE KOHAKU COMPETITION ON TV.
LET'S DECIDE WHERE TO GO FOR OUR GRADUATION TRIP.
The school roof and coffee-flavored milk in a carton.
The after-school silence.

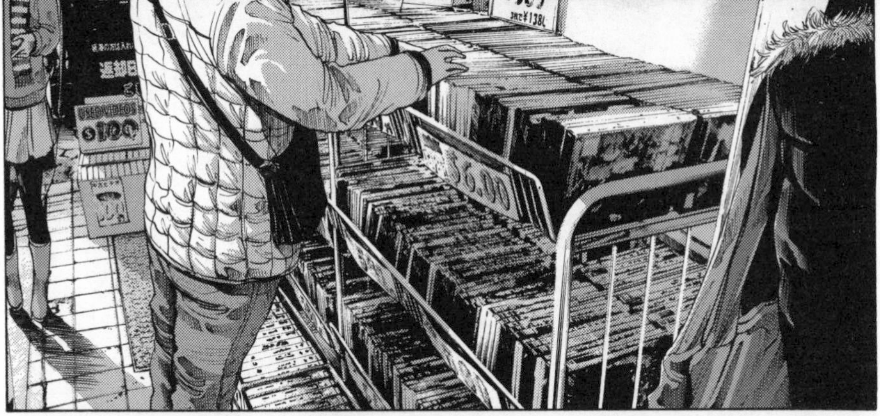
USED VIDEOS
$1.00
$6.00

The sale bin at the video store.

Christmas songs over the store loud-speakers.

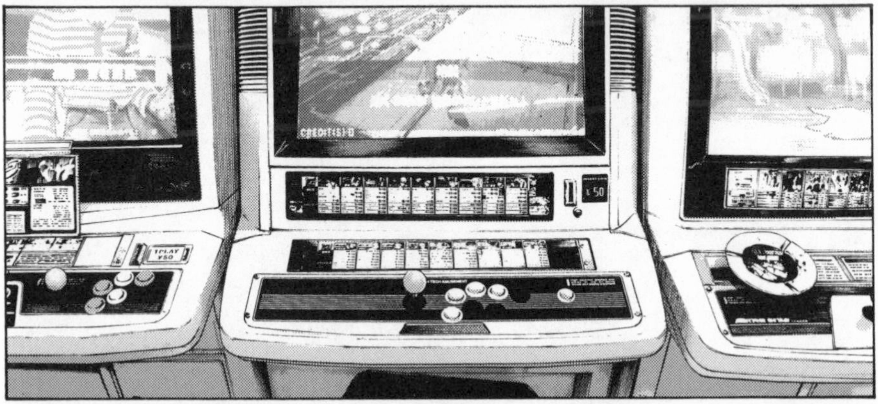
CREDIT(S) 0
1PLAY ¥50
¥50

The fifty-cent combat game at the arcade.

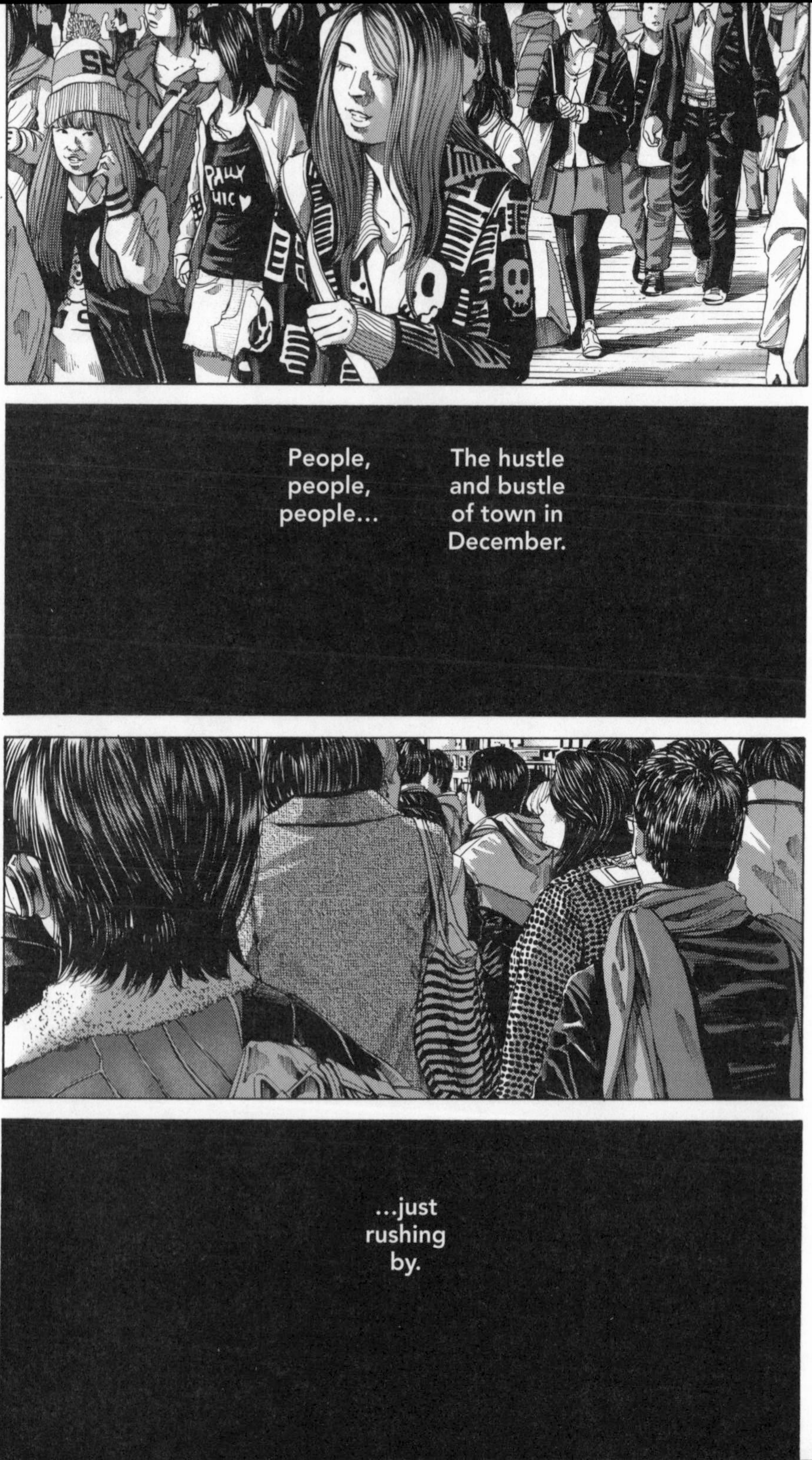
The hustle and bustle of town in December.
People, people, people...
...just rushing by.

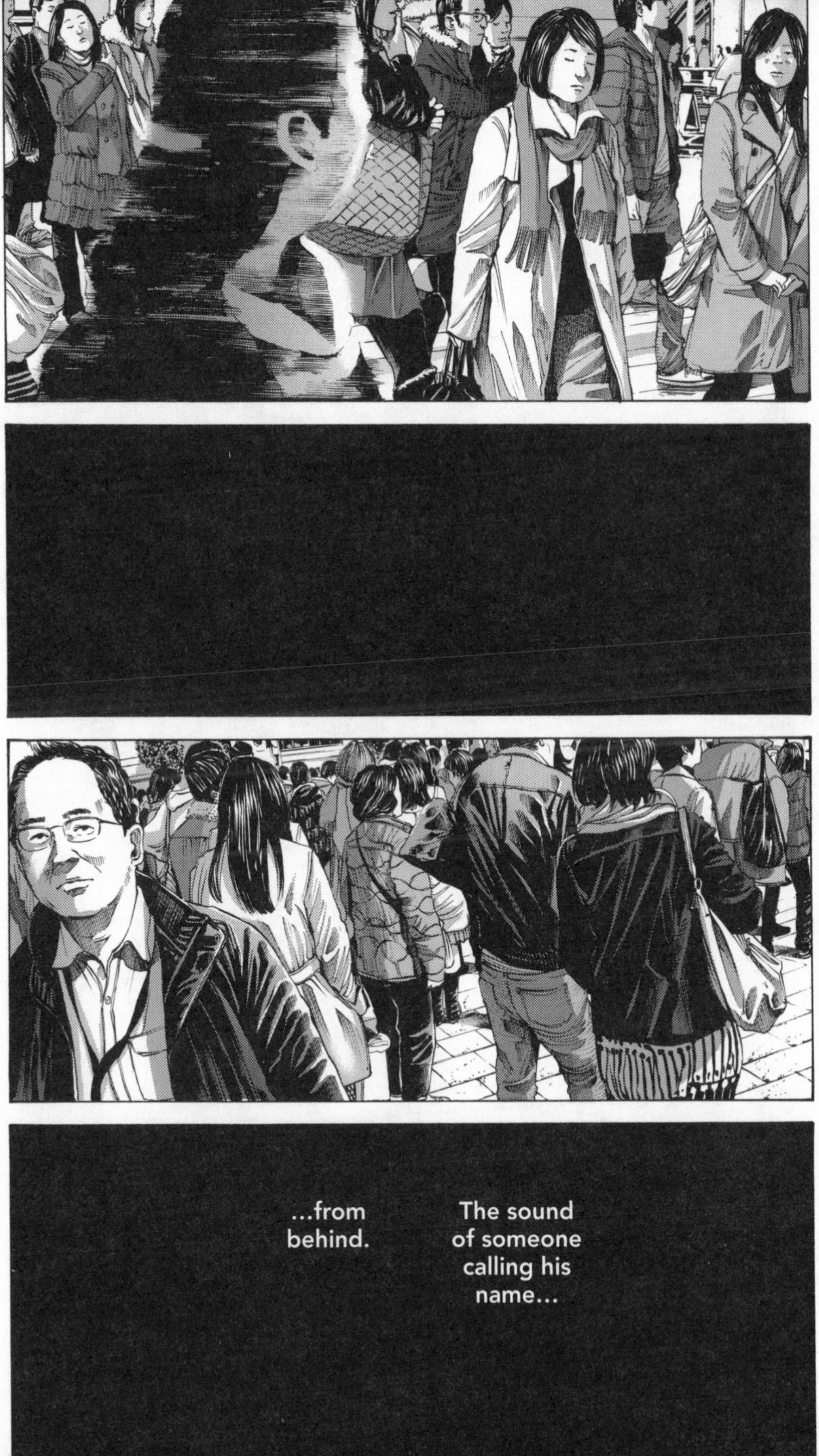
The sound of someone calling his name...
...from behind.

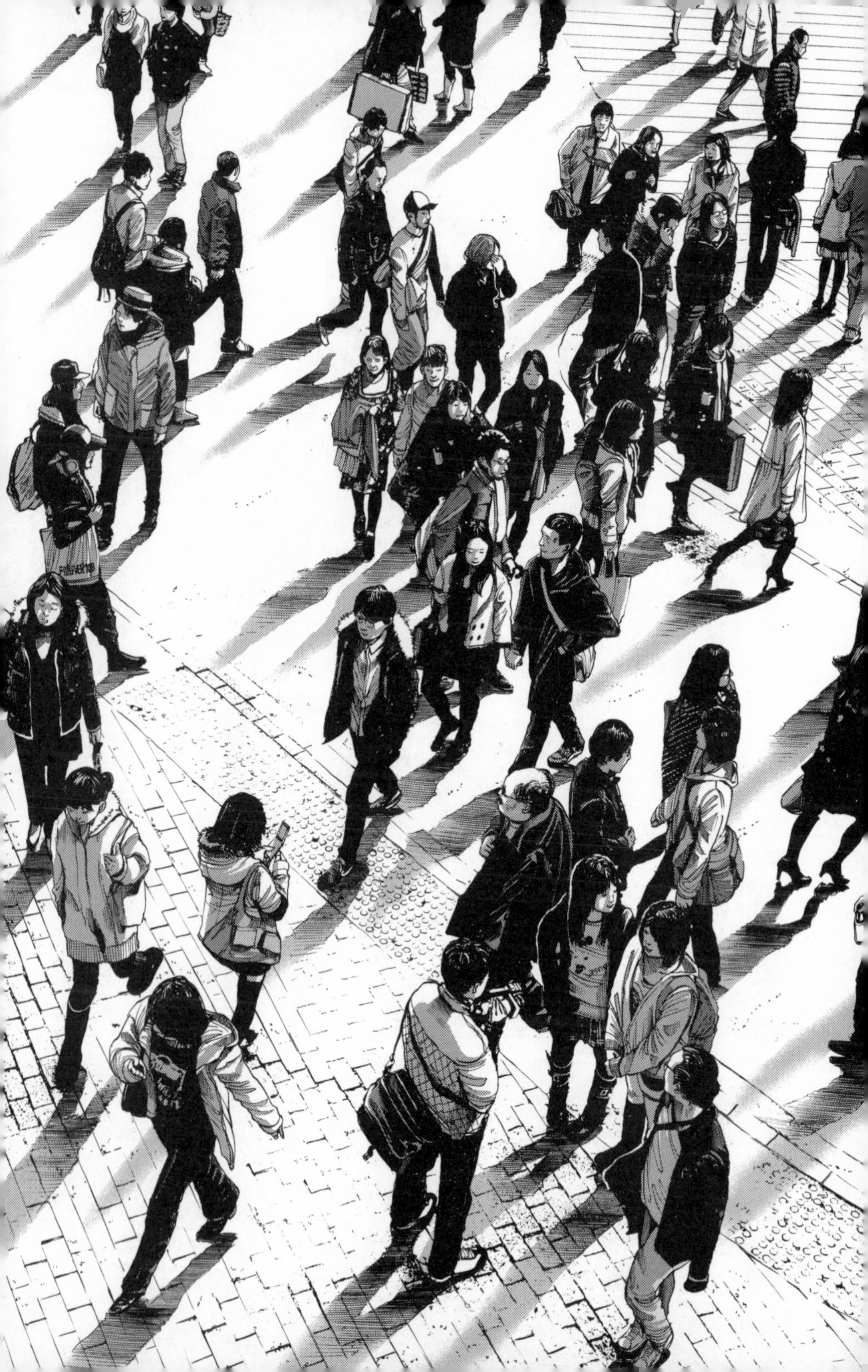

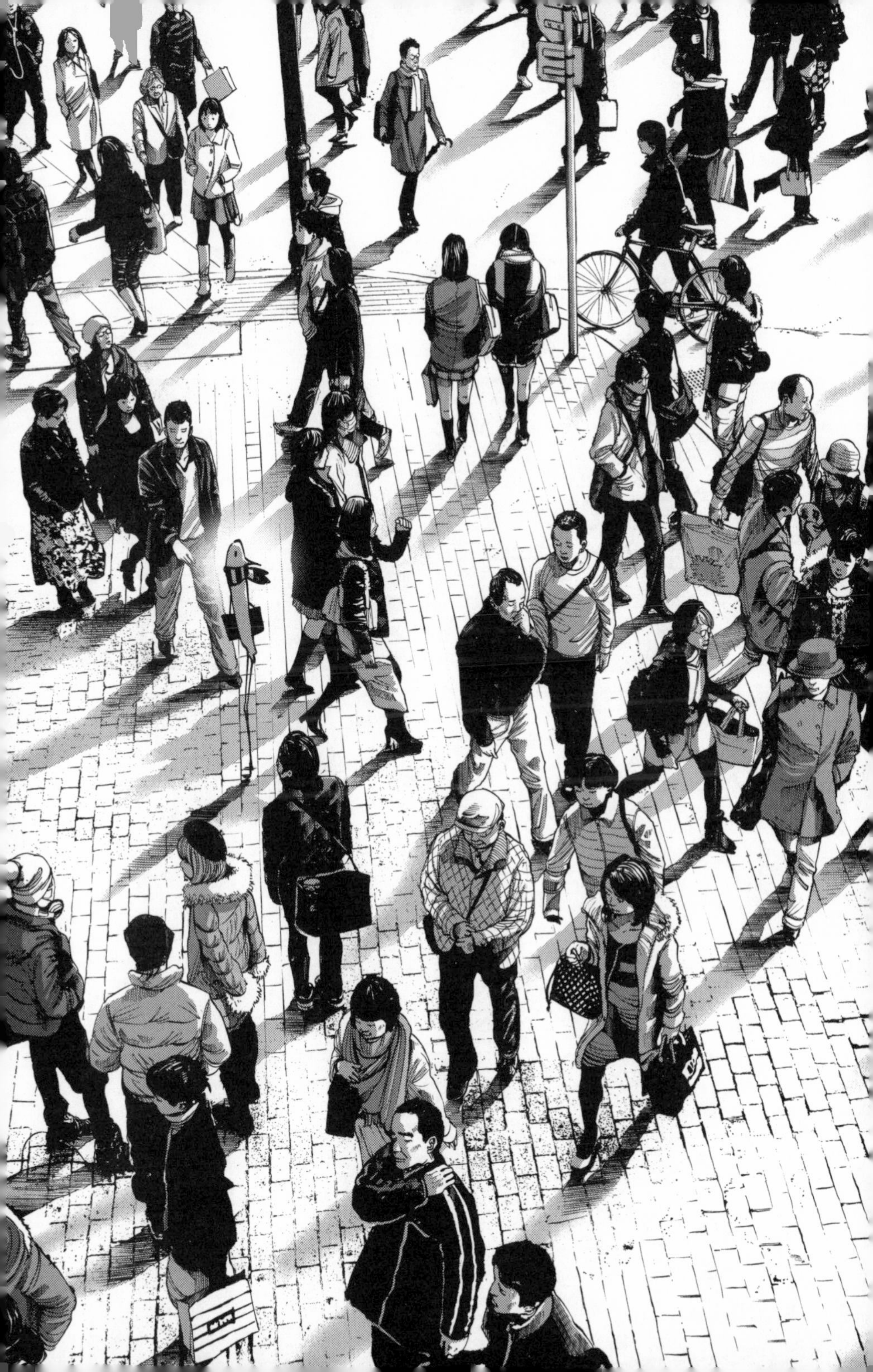

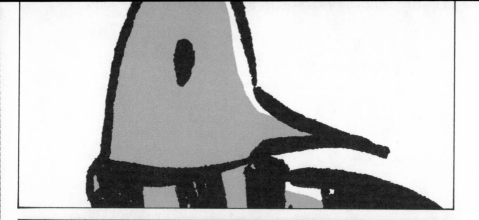

Loneliness.

Freedom.

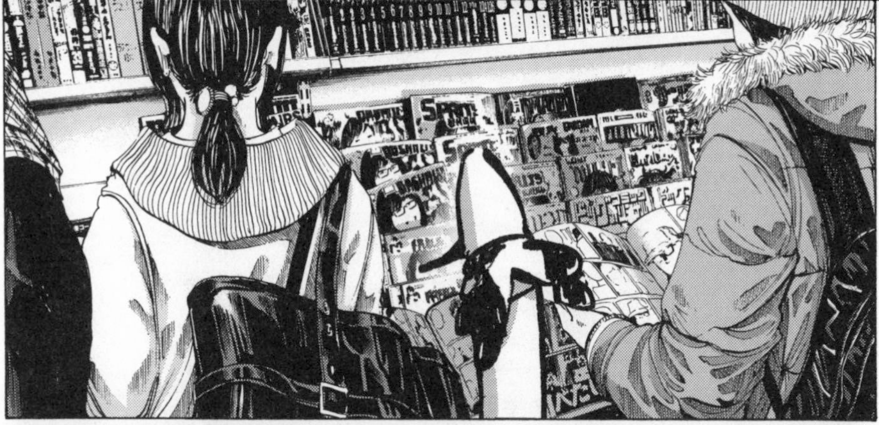

The manga section of the convenience store.

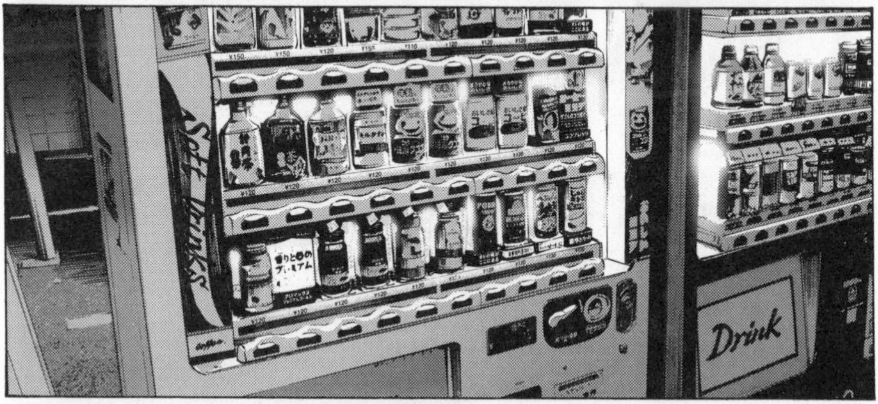
Drink

Canned coffee with just a little sugar.

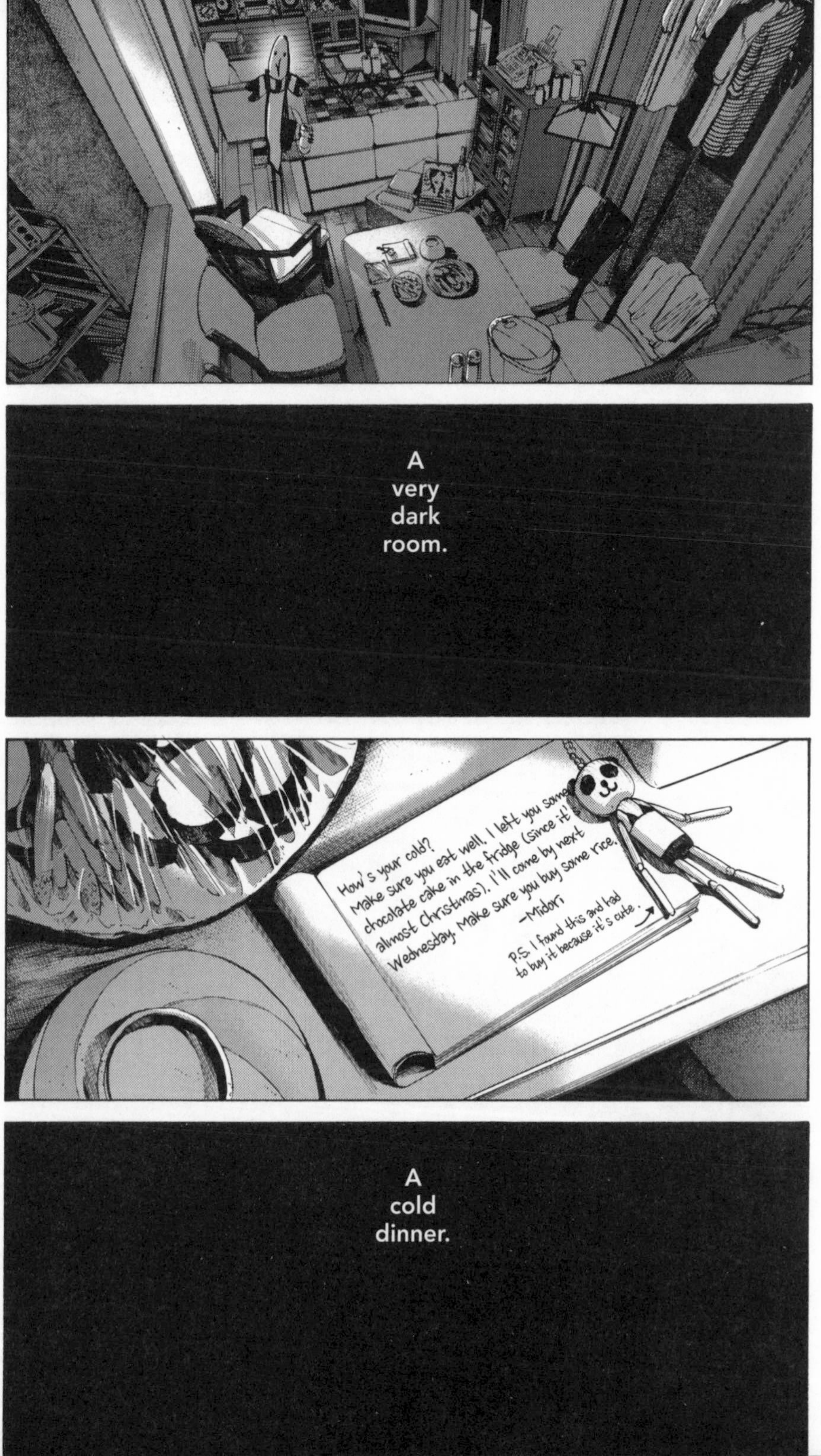
A very dark room.
How's your cold?
Make sure you eat well. I left you some
chocolate cake in the fridge (since it'
almost Christmas). I'll come by next
Wednesday. Make sure you buy some rice.
—Midori
P.S. I found this and had to buy it because it's cute.
A cold dinner.

COSMO HEALTH CENTER CULT HID EARNINGS

The
familiar
news.

The
alarm
clock
set to
7:10.

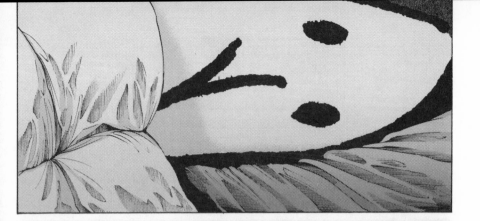

Punpun
was...

...doing
well
today.

GOODNIGHT PUNPUN

Part Seven

INIO ASANO

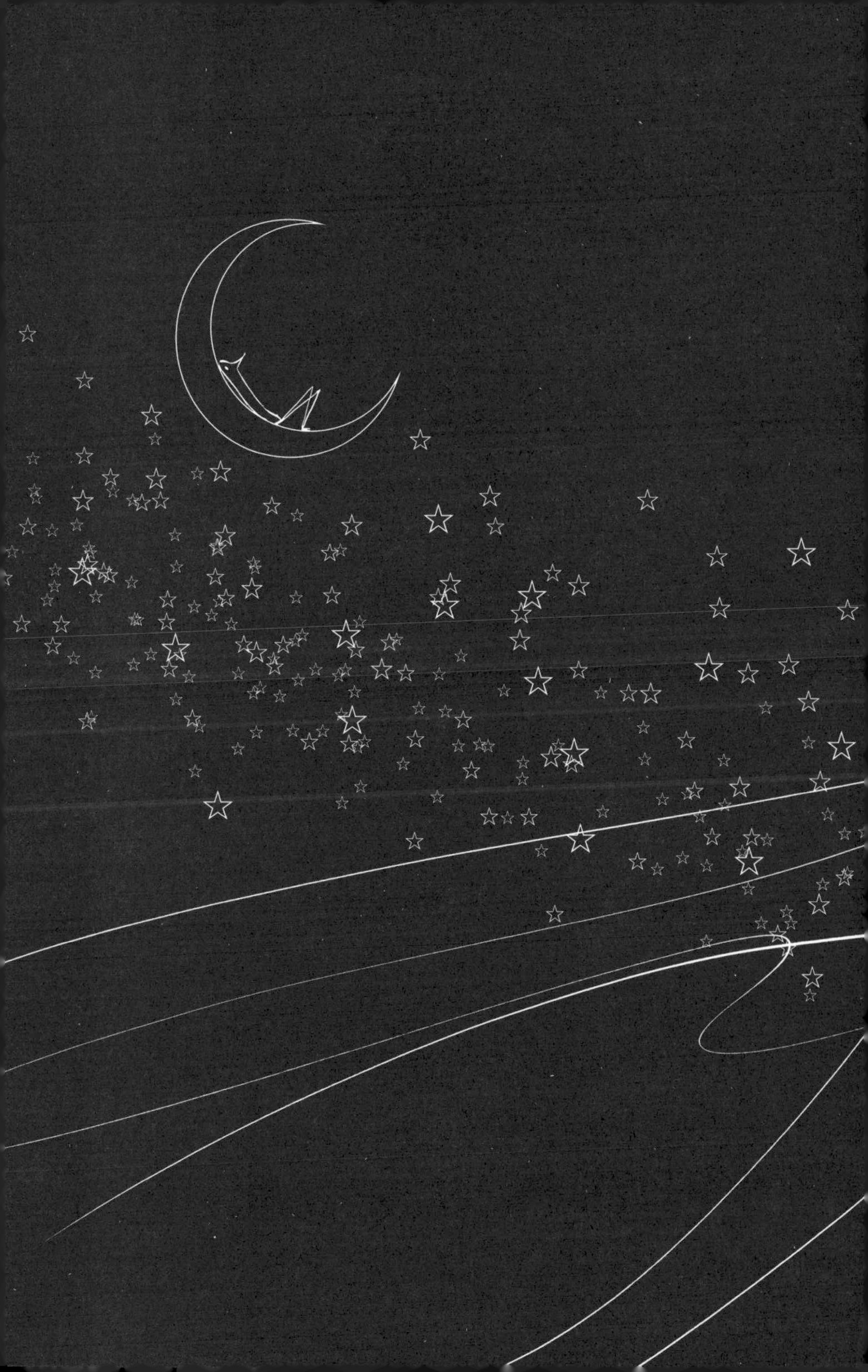

★ Chapter 71 ★

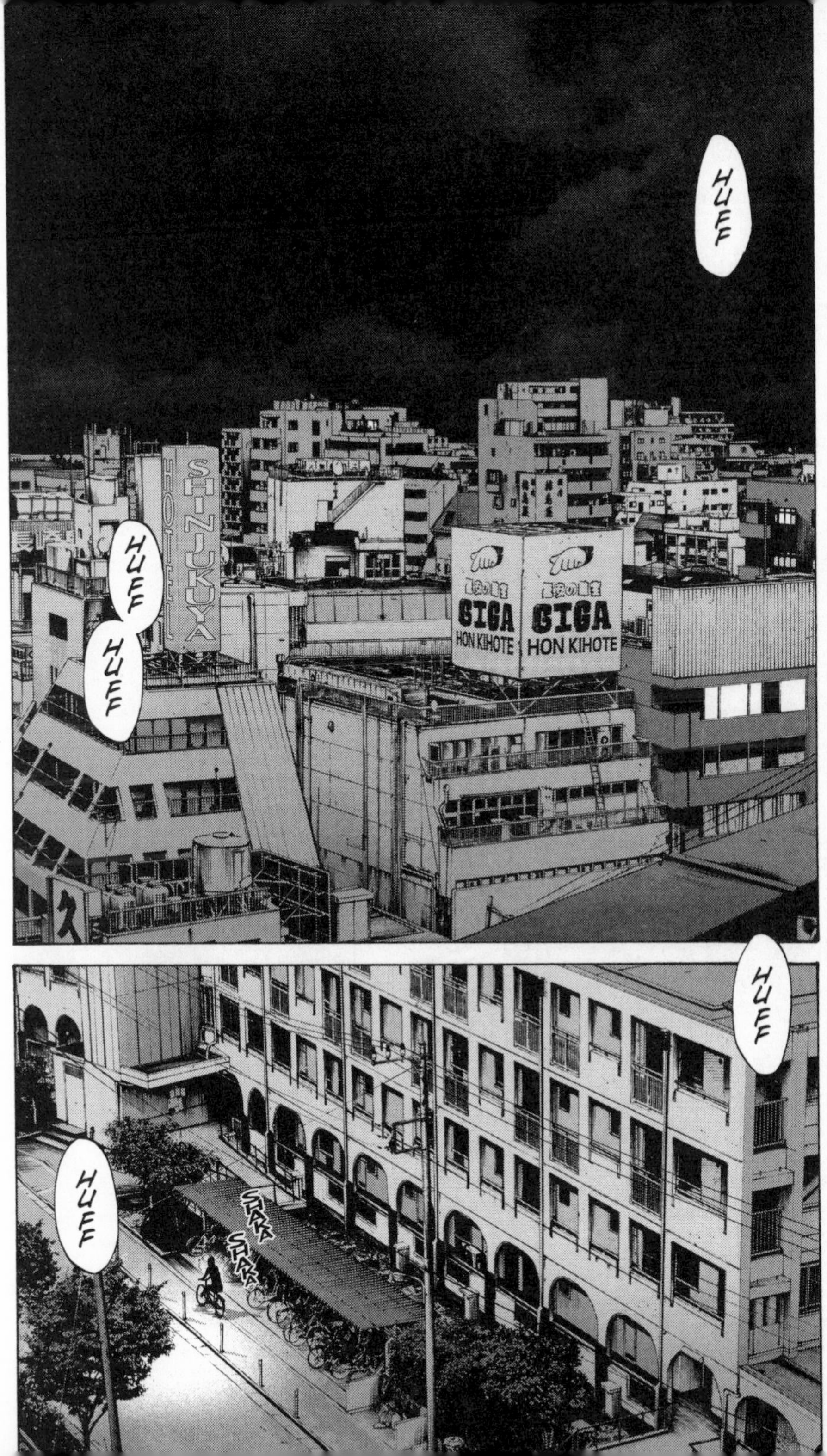
HUFF
HUFF
HUFF
SHINJUKUYA
HOTEL
GIGA
HON KIHOTE
GIGA
HON KIHOTE
HUFF
HUFF
SHAKA
SHAKA

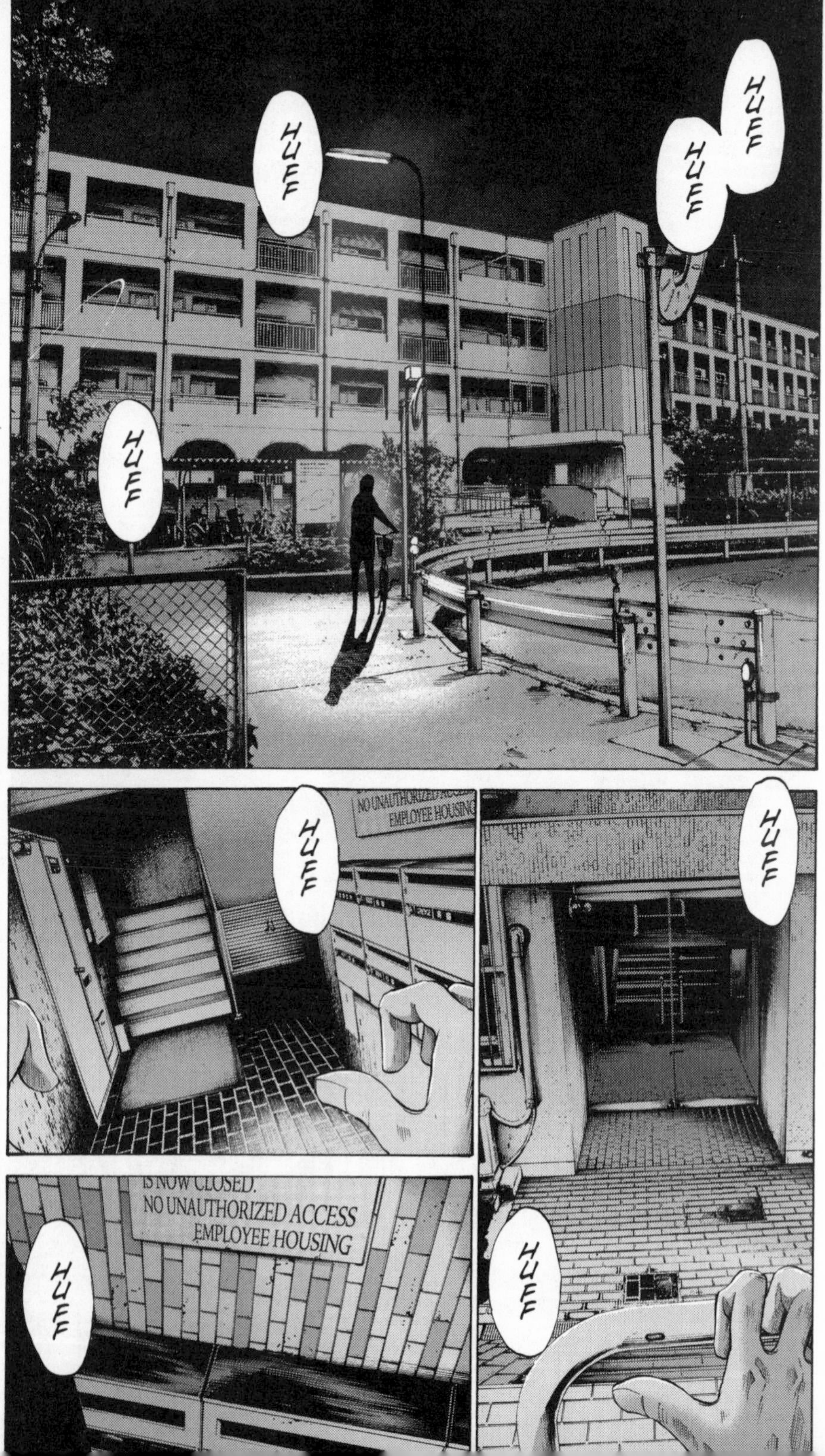
HUFF
HUFF
HUFF
HUFF
HUFF
HUFF
NO UNAUTHORIZED
EMPLOYEE HOUSING
HUFF
IS NOW CLOSED.
NO UNAUTHORIZED ACCESS
EMPLOYEE HOUSING
HUFF

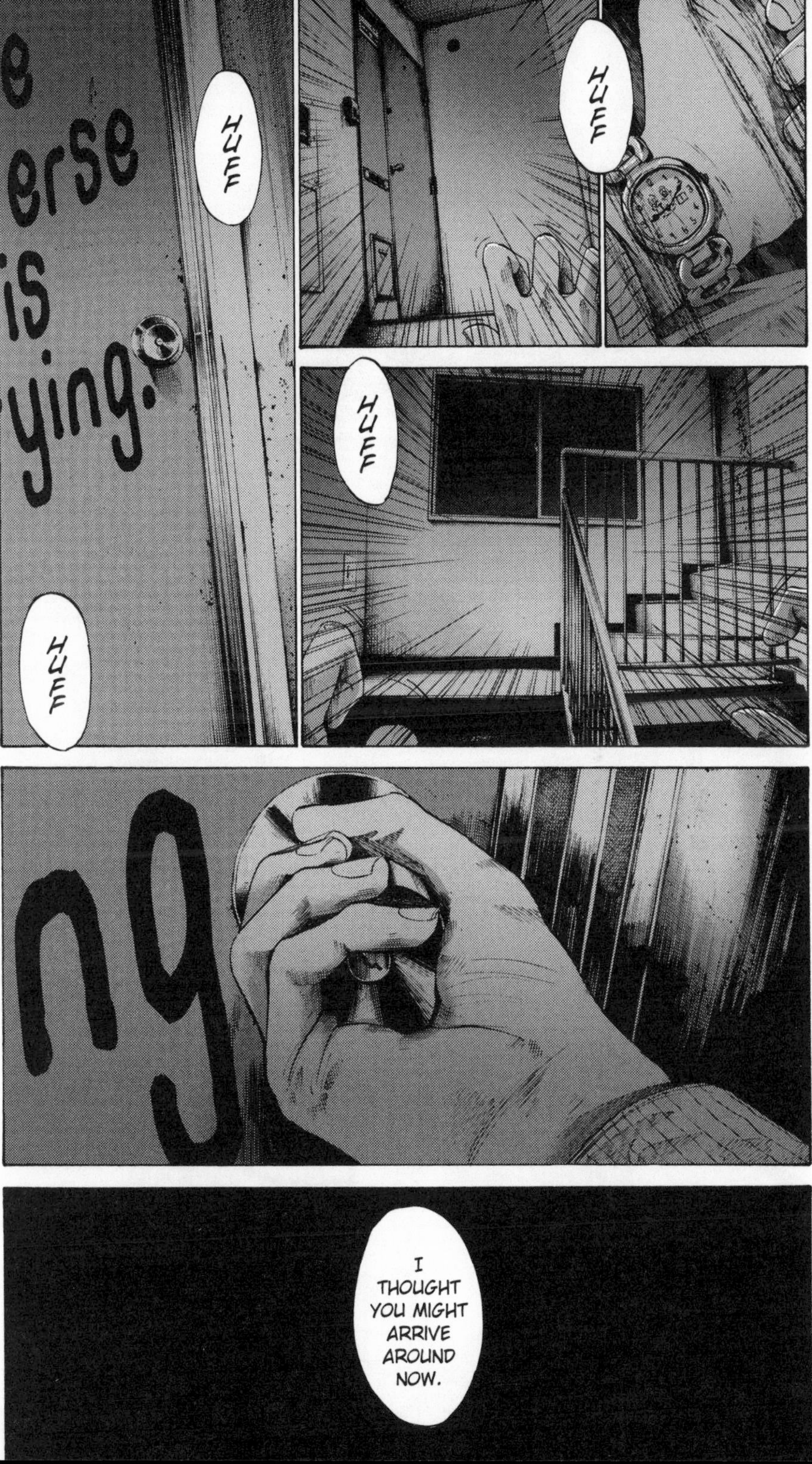
HUFF
HUFF
HUFF
HUFF
I THOUGHT YOU MIGHT ARRIVE AROUND NOW.

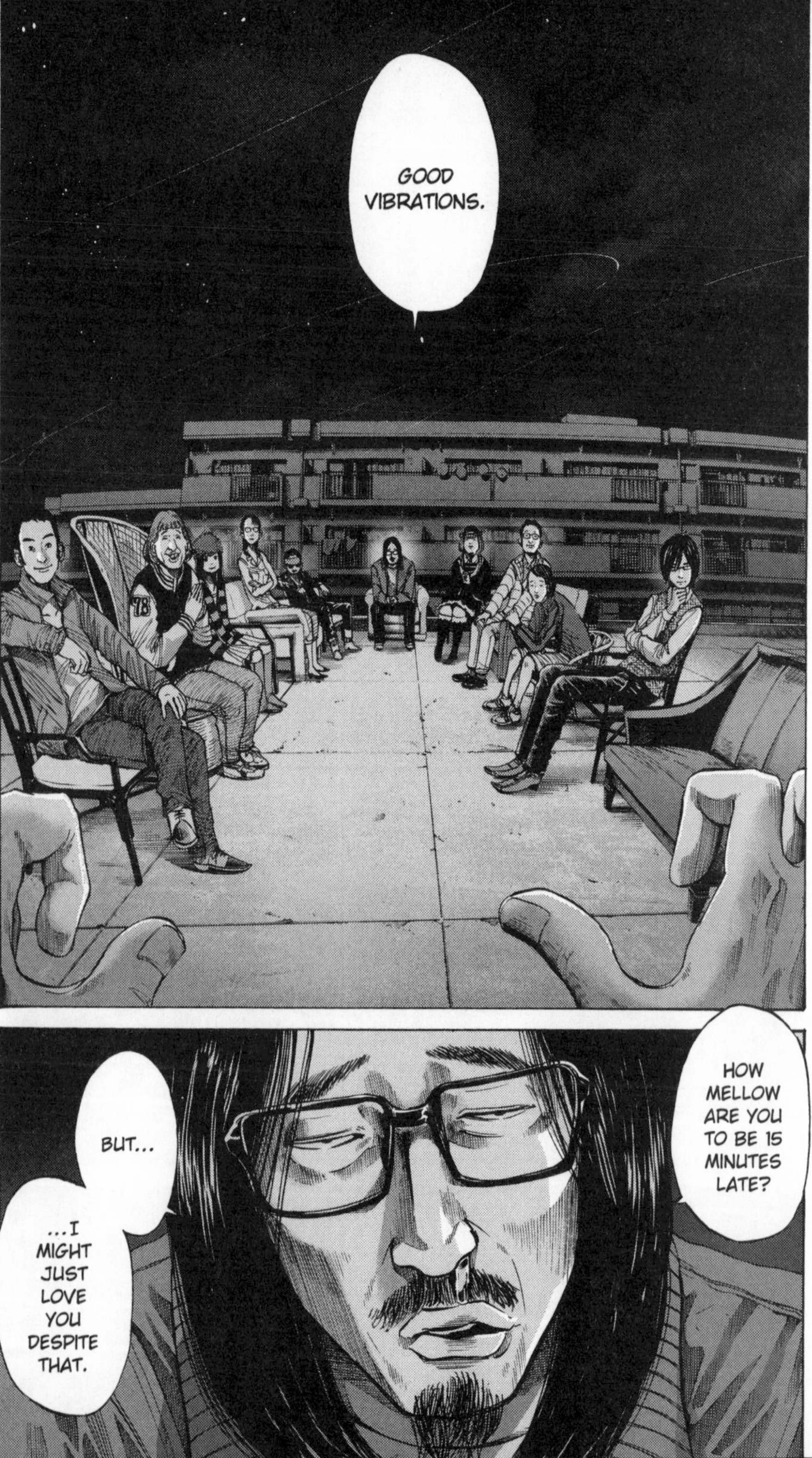
GOOD VIBRATIONS.
HOW MELLOW ARE YOU TO BE 15 MINUTES LATE?
BUT...
...I MIGHT JUST LOVE YOU DESPITE THAT.

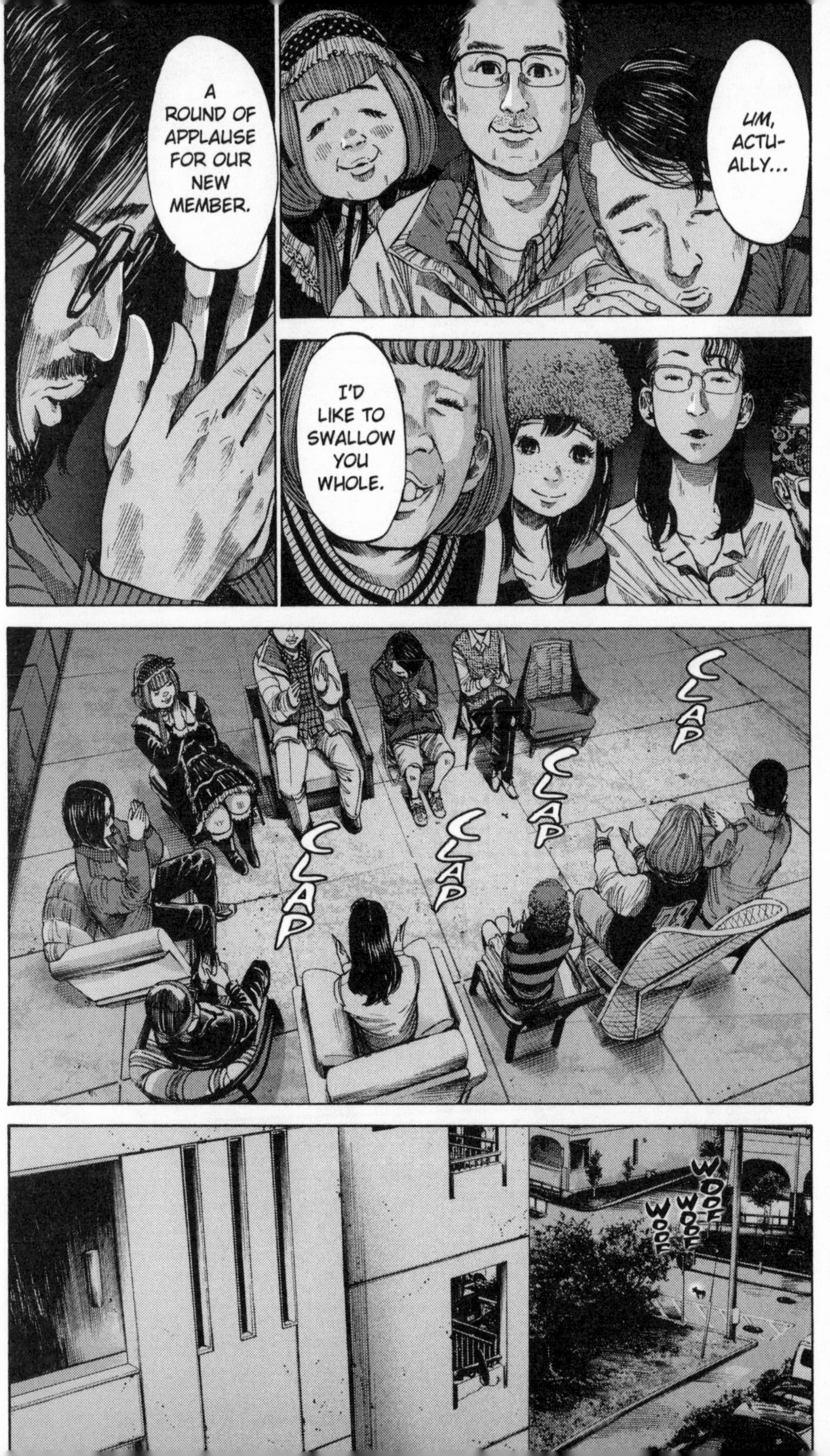
UM, ACTU-ALLY...
I'D LIKE TO SWALLOW YOU WHOLE.
A ROUND OF APPLAUSE FOR OUR NEW MEMBER.
CLAP
CLAP
CLAP
CLAP
WOOF
WOOF
WOOF

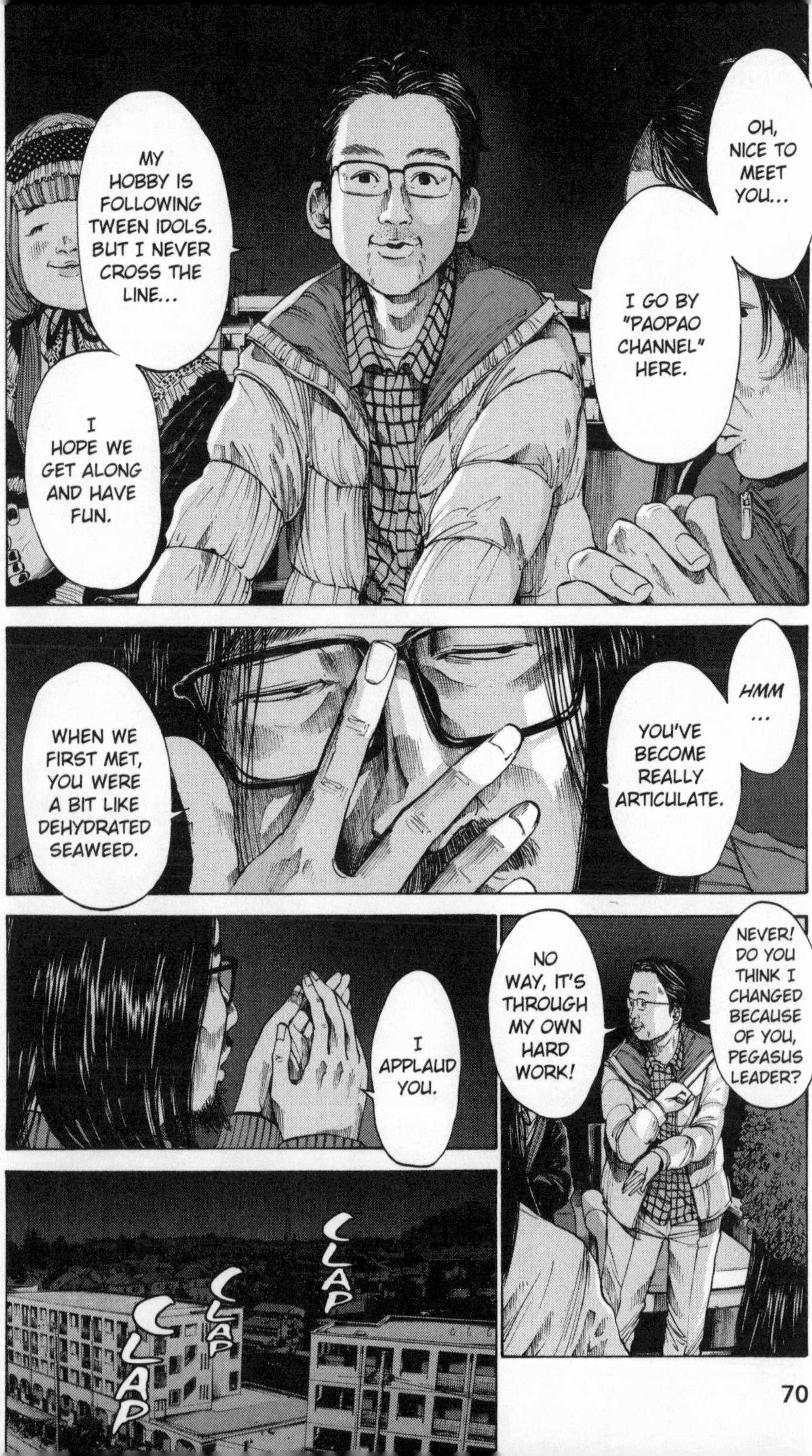
OH, NICE TO MEET YOU...
I GO BY "PAOPAO CHANNEL" HERE.
MY HOBBY IS FOLLOWING TWEEN IDOLS. BUT I NEVER CROSS THE LINE...
I HOPE WE GET ALONG AND HAVE FUN.
HMM...
YOU'VE BECOME REALLY ARTICULATE.
WHEN WE FIRST MET, YOU WERE A BIT LIKE DEHYDRATED SEAWEED.
NEVER! DO YOU THINK I CHANGED BECAUSE OF YOU, PEGASUS LEADER?
NO WAY, IT'S THROUGH MY OWN HARD WORK!
I APPLAUD YOU.
CLAP
CLAP
CLAP

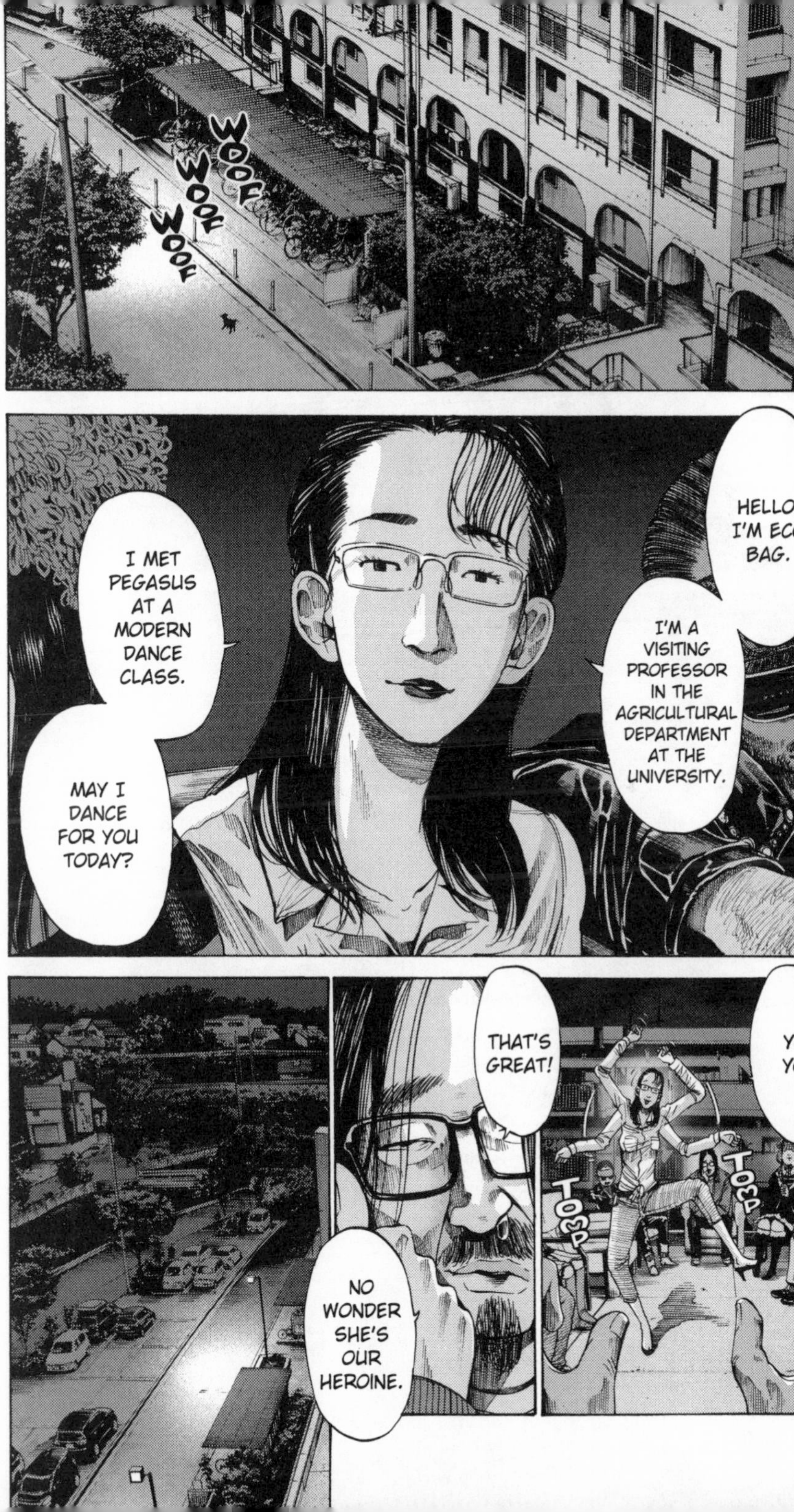
WOOF
WOOF
WOOF
HELLO, I'M ECO BAG.
I'M A VISITING PROFESSOR IN THE AGRICULTURAL DEPARTMENT AT THE UNIVERSITY.
I MET PEGASUS AT A MODERN DANCE CLASS.
MAY I DANCE FOR YOU TODAY?
YOI, YOI!
TOMP
TOMP
THAT'S GREAT!
NO WONDER SHE'S OUR HEROINE.

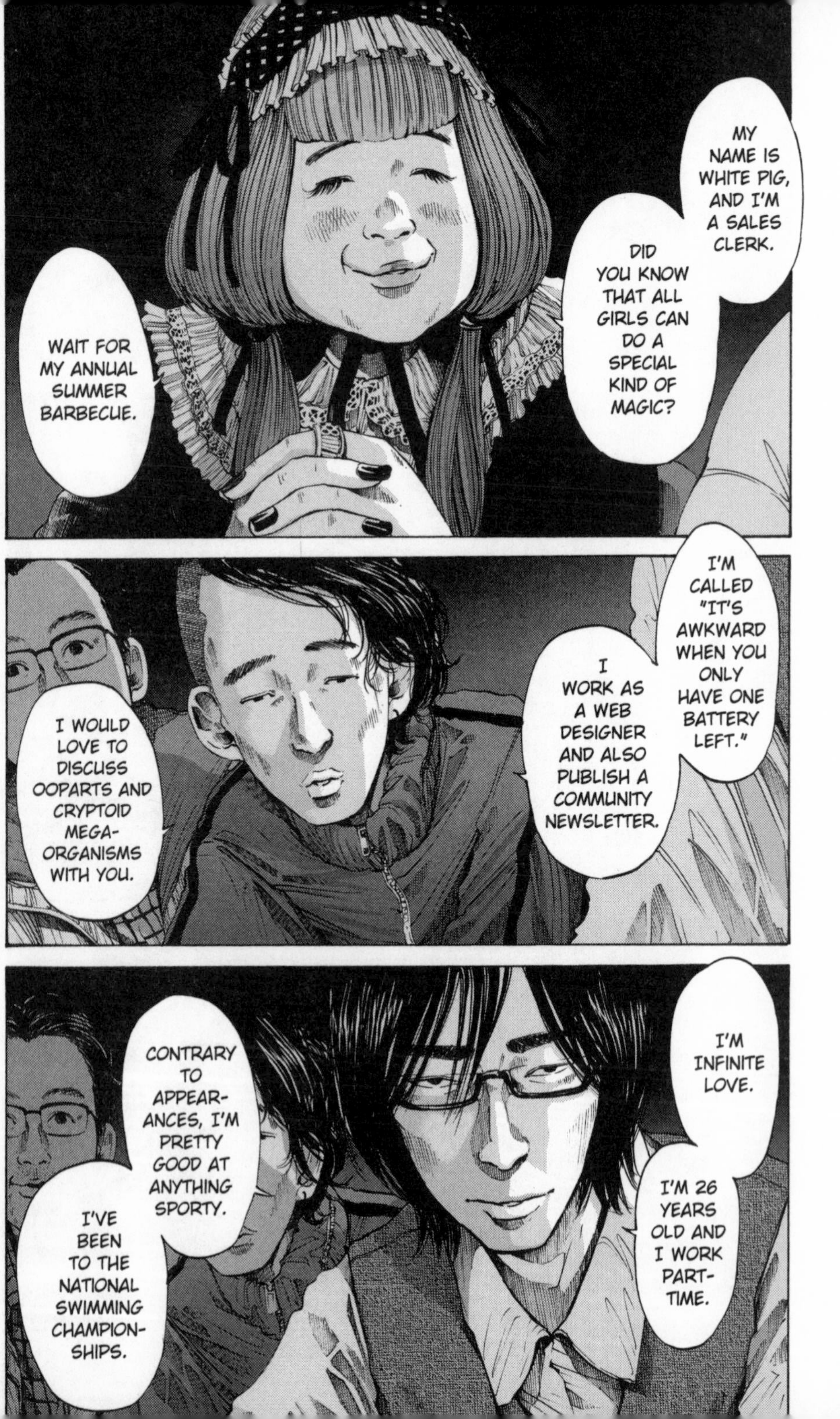
MY NAME IS WHITE PIG, AND I'M A SALES CLERK.
DID YOU KNOW THAT ALL GIRLS CAN DO A SPECIAL KIND OF MAGIC?
WAIT FOR MY ANNUAL SUMMER BARBECUE.
I'M CALLED "IT'S AWKWARD WHEN YOU ONLY HAVE ONE BATTERY LEFT."
I WORK AS A WEB DESIGNER AND ALSO PUBLISH A COMMUNITY NEWSLETTER.
I WOULD LOVE TO DISCUSS OOPARTS AND CRYPTOID MEGA-ORGANISMS WITH YOU.
I'M INFINITE LOVE.
I'M 26 YEARS OLD AND I WORK PART-TIME.
CONTRARY TO APPEARANCES, I'M PRETTY GOOD AT ANYTHING SPORTY.
I'VE BEEN TO THE NATIONAL SWIMMING CHAMPIONSHIPS.

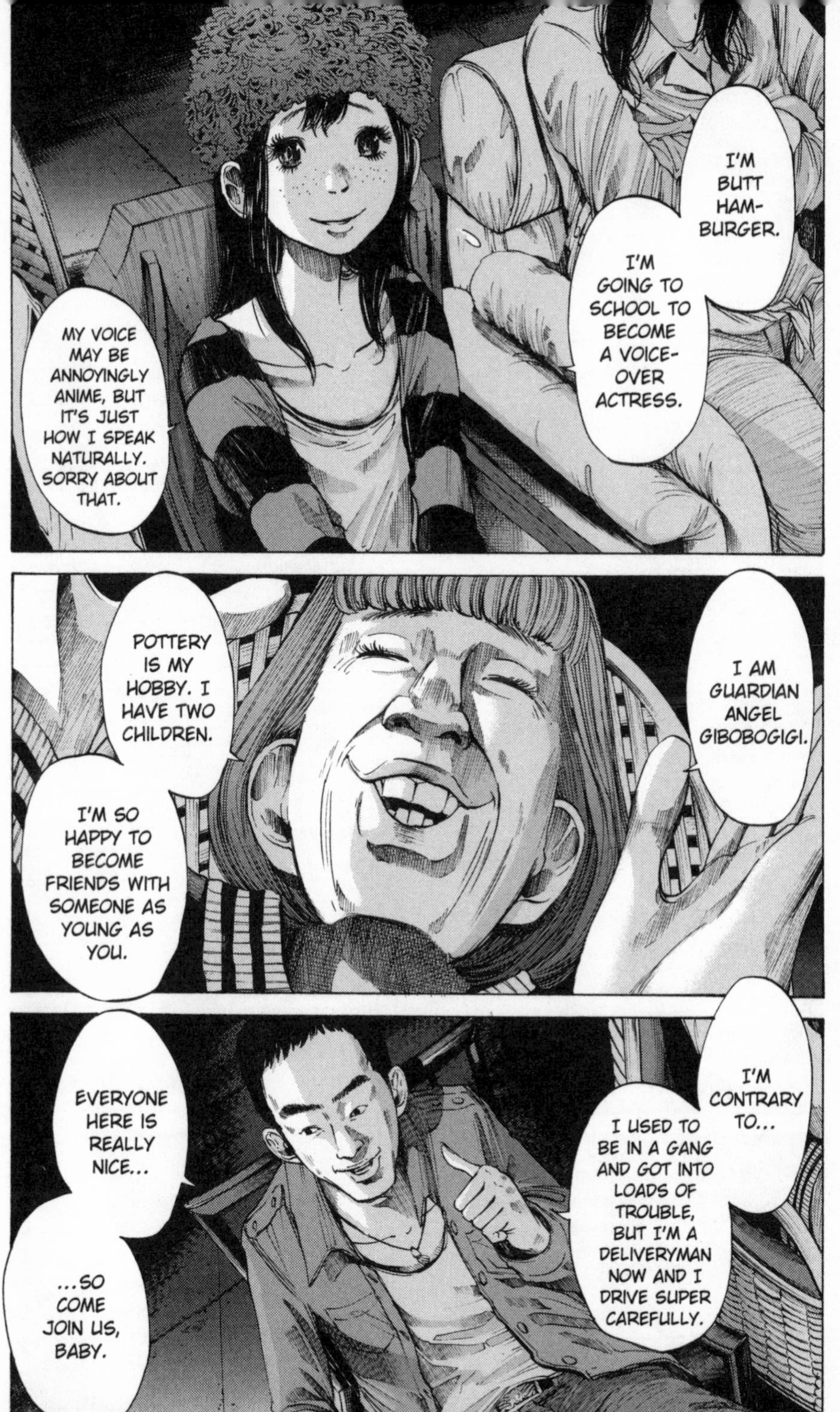
I'M BUTT HAM-BURGER.
I'M GOING TO SCHOOL TO BECOME A VOICE-OVER ACTRESS.
MY VOICE MAY BE ANNOYINGLY ANIME, BUT IT'S JUST HOW I SPEAK NATURALLY. SORRY ABOUT THAT.
I AM GUARDIAN ANGEL GIBOBOGIGI.
POTTERY IS MY HOBBY. I HAVE TWO CHILDREN.
I'M SO HAPPY TO BECOME FRIENDS WITH SOMEONE AS YOUNG AS YOU.
I'M CONTRARY TO...
I USED TO BE IN A GANG AND GOT INTO LOADS OF TROUBLE, BUT I'M A DELIVERYMAN NOW AND I DRIVE SUPER CAREFULLY.
EVERYONE HERE IS REALLY NICE...
...SO COME JOIN US, BABY.

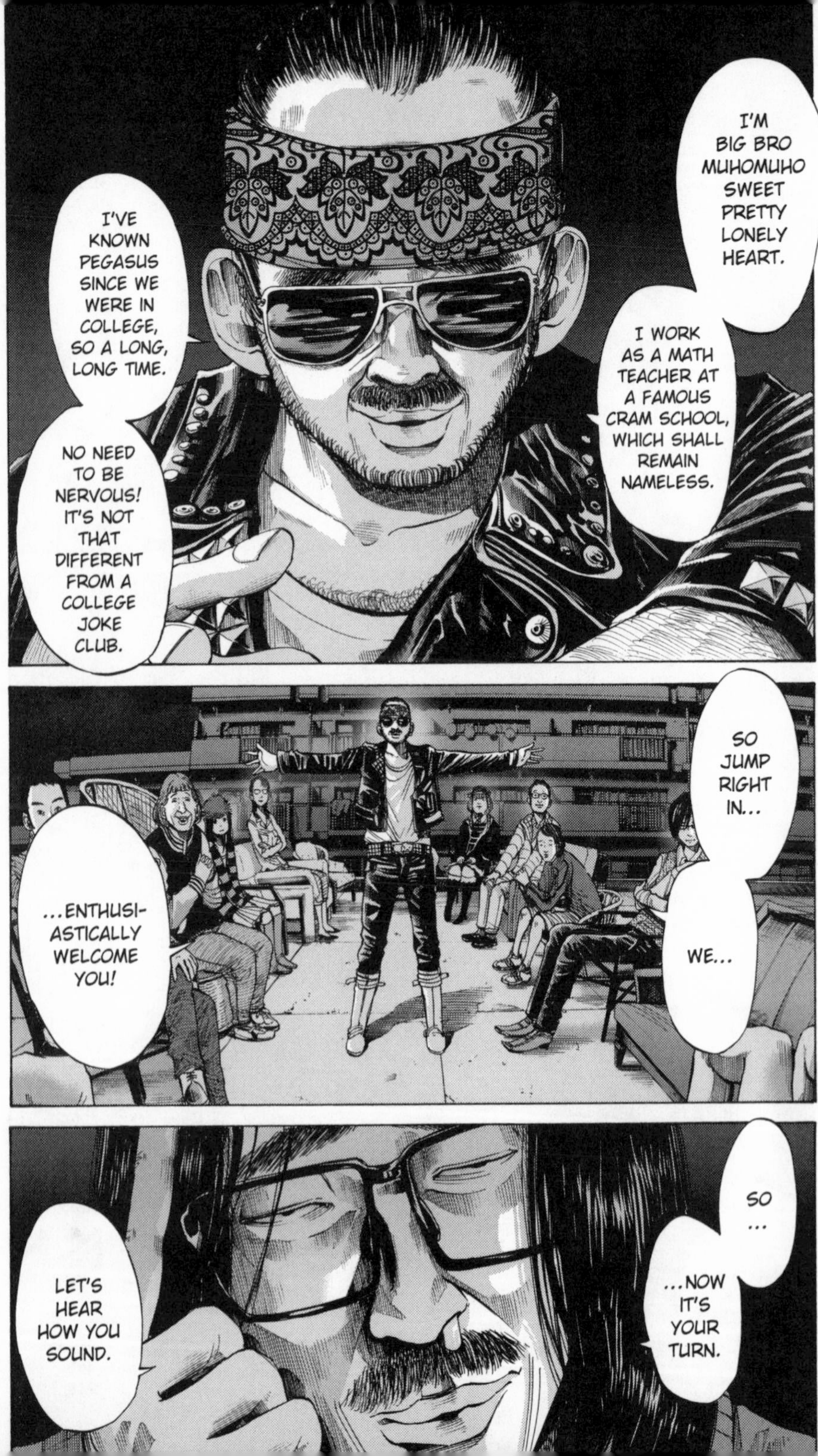
I'M BIG BRO MUHOMUHO SWEET PRETTY LONELY HEART.
I WORK AS A MATH TEACHER AT A FAMOUS CRAM SCHOOL, WHICH SHALL REMAIN NAMELESS.
I'VE KNOWN PEGASUS SINCE WE WERE IN COLLEGE, SO A LONG, LONG TIME.
NO NEED TO BE NERVOUS! IT'S NOT THAT DIFFERENT FROM A COLLEGE JOKE CLUB.
SO JUMP RIGHT IN...
WE...
...ENTHUSI-ASTICALLY WELCOME YOU!
SO ...
...NOW IT'S YOUR TURN.
LET'S HEAR HOW YOU SOUND.

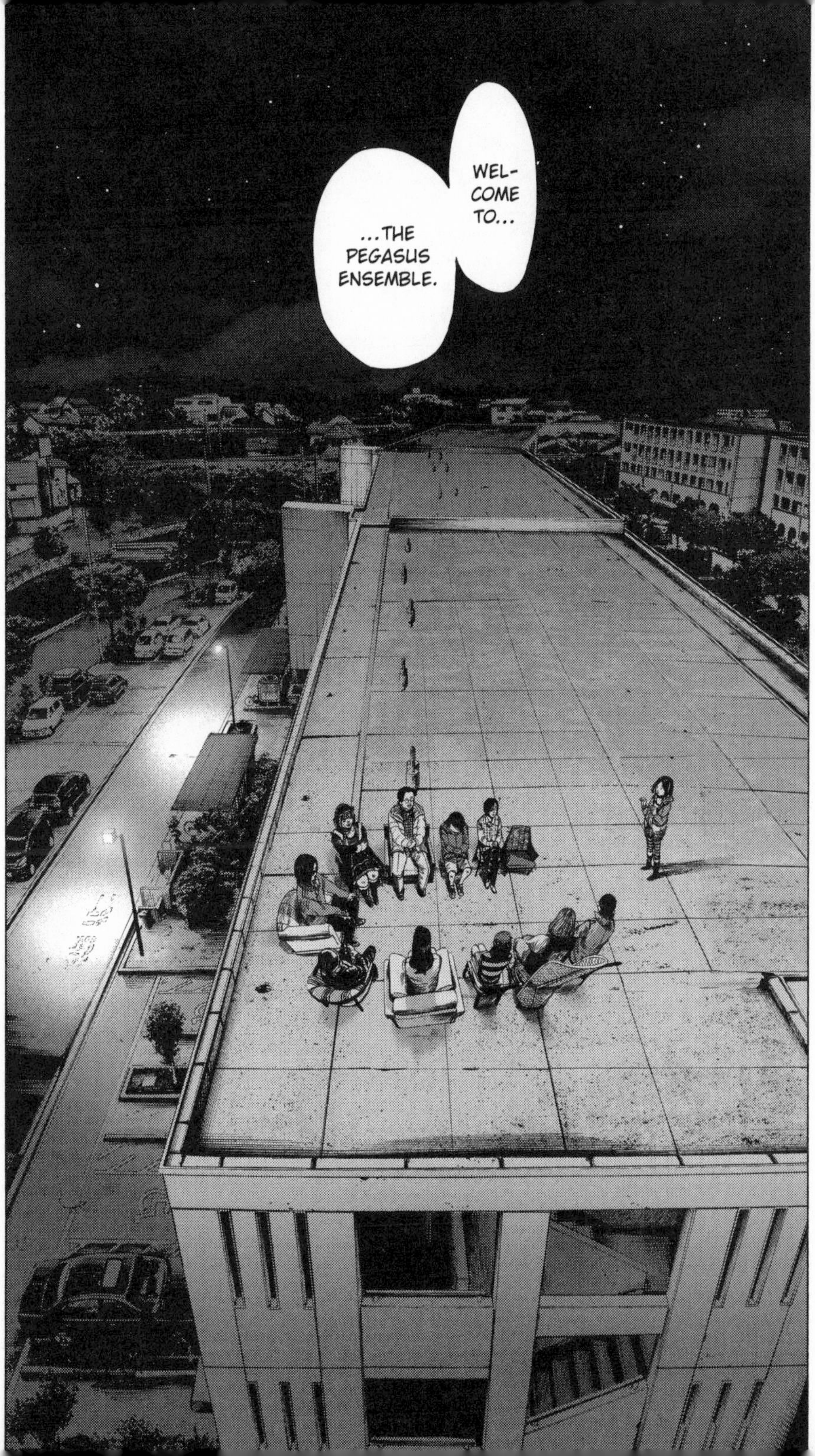
WEL-COME TO...
...THE PEGASUS ENSEMBLE.

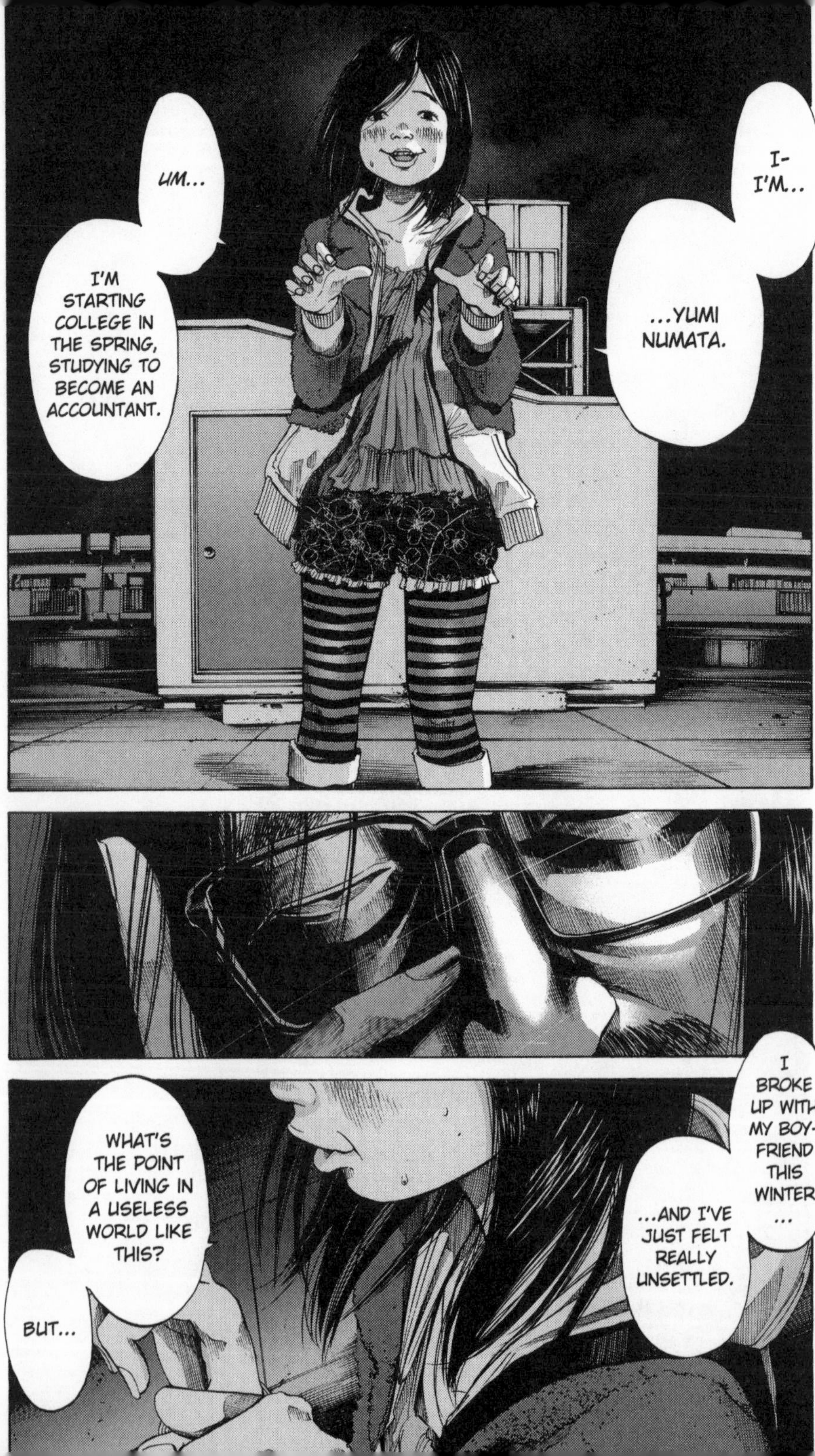
I- I'M...
...YUMI NUMATA.
UM...
I'M STARTING COLLEGE IN THE SPRING, STUDYING TO BECOME AN ACCOUNTANT.
I BROKE UP WITH MY BOY-FRIEND THIS WINTER...
...AND I'VE JUST FELT REALLY UNSETTLED.
WHAT'S THE POINT OF LIVING IN A USELESS WORLD LIKE THIS?
BUT...

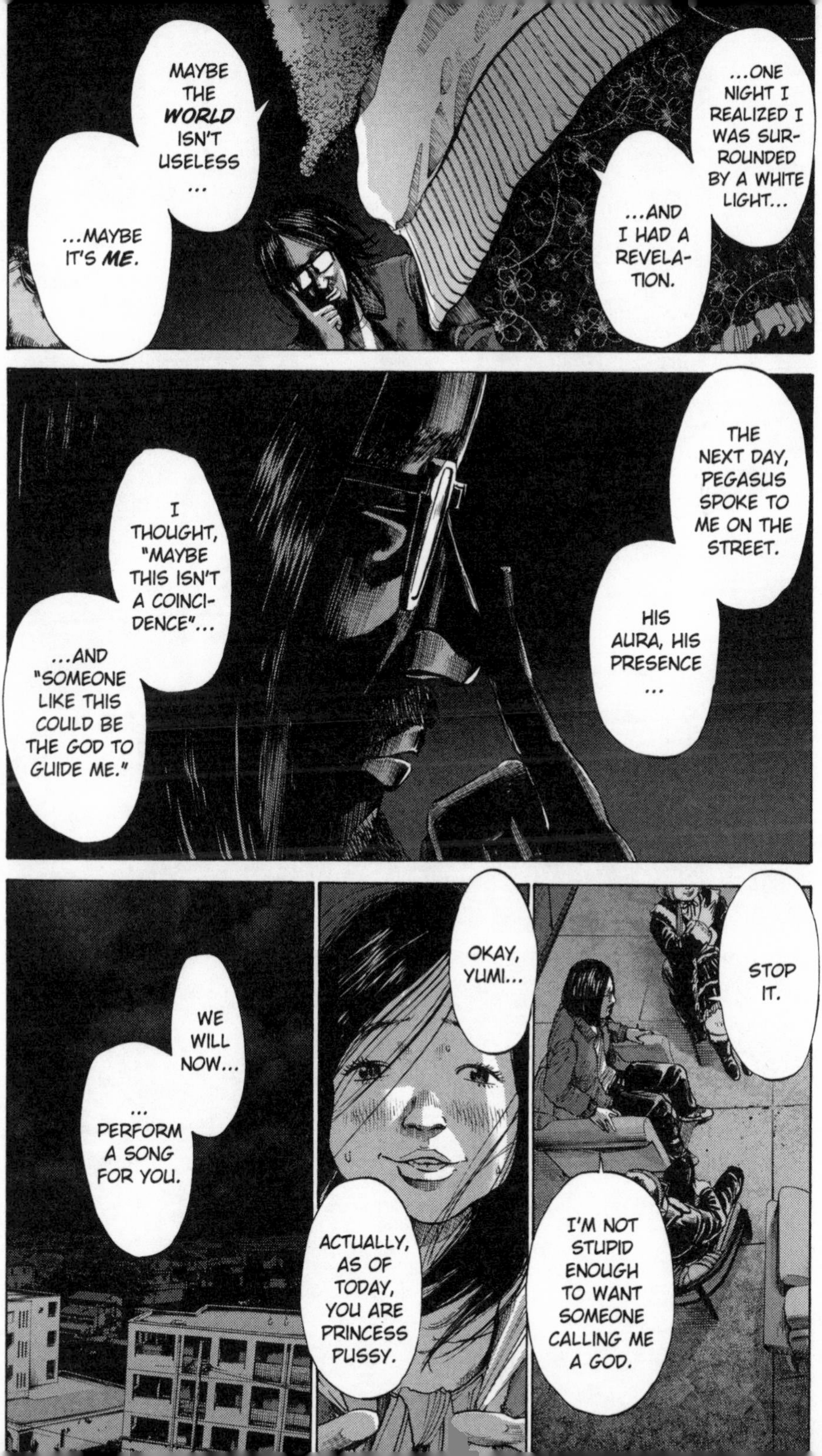
...ONE NIGHT I REALIZED I WAS SURROUNDED BY A WHITE LIGHT...
...AND I HAD A REVELATION.
MAYBE THE WORLD ISN'T USELESS...
...MAYBE IT'S ME.
THE NEXT DAY, PEGASUS SPOKE TO ME ON THE STREET.
HIS AURA, HIS PRESENCE...
I THOUGHT, "MAYBE THIS ISN'T A COINCIDENCE"...
...AND "SOMEONE LIKE THIS COULD BE THE GOD TO GUIDE ME."
STOP IT.
I'M NOT STUPID ENOUGH TO WANT SOMEONE CALLING ME A GOD.
OKAY, YUMI...
ACTUALLY, AS OF TODAY, YOU ARE PRINCESS PUSSY.
WE WILL NOW...
...PERFORM A SONG FOR YOU.

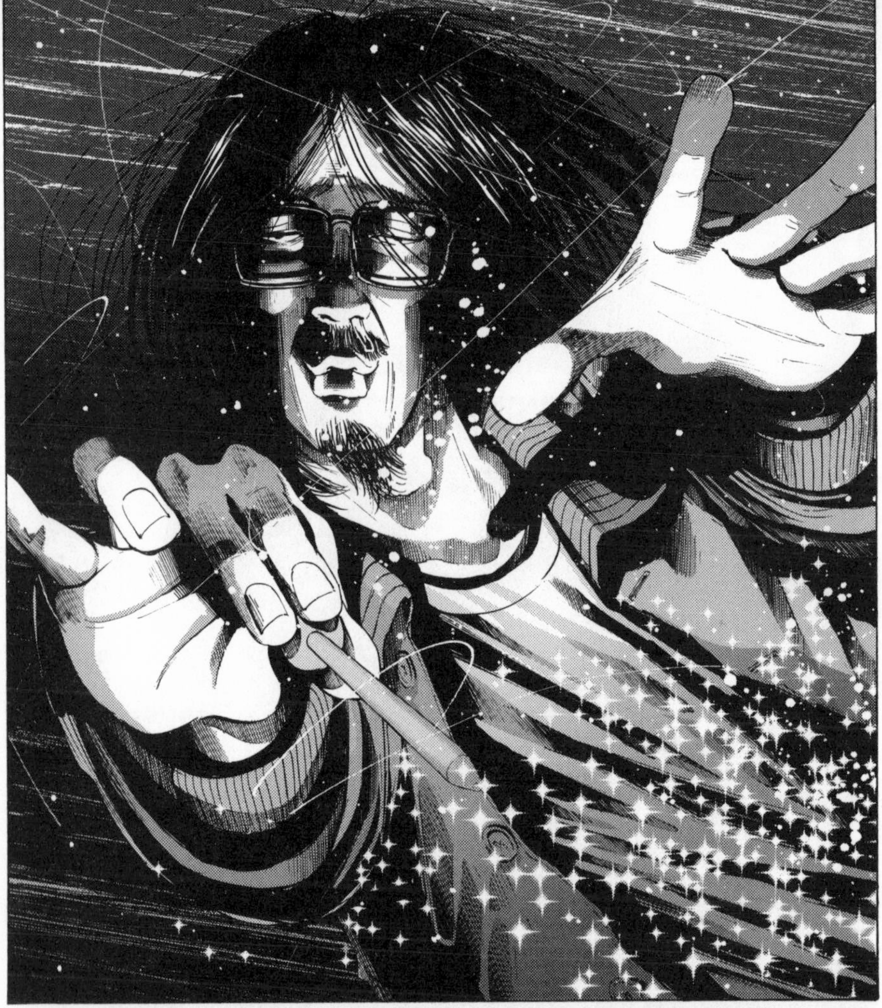
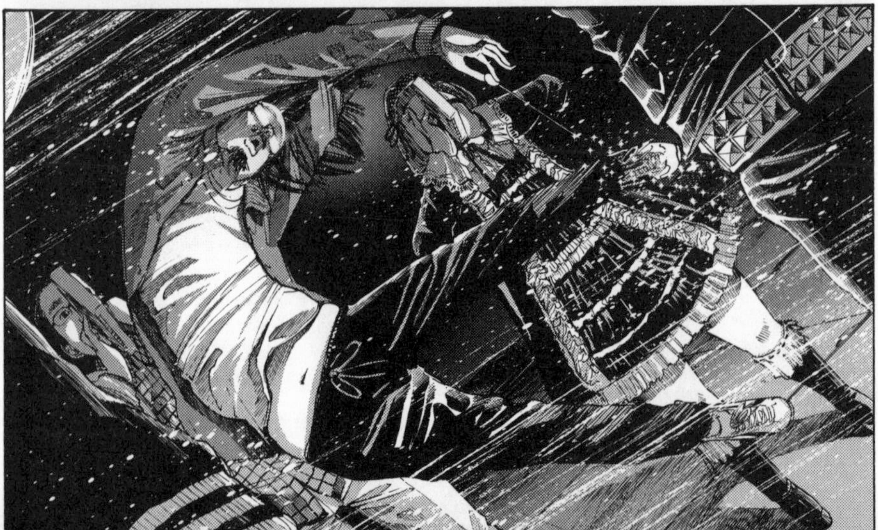

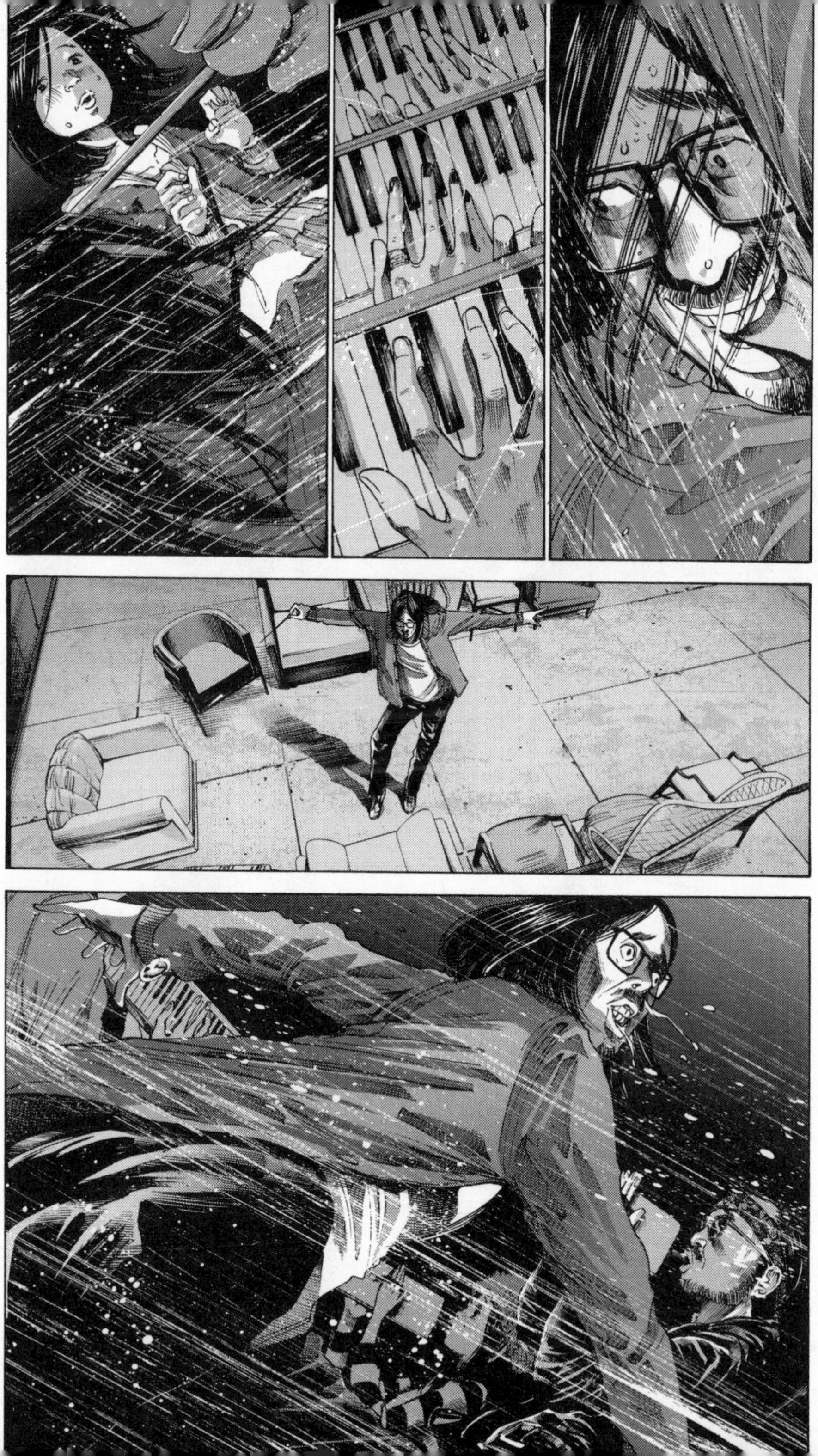

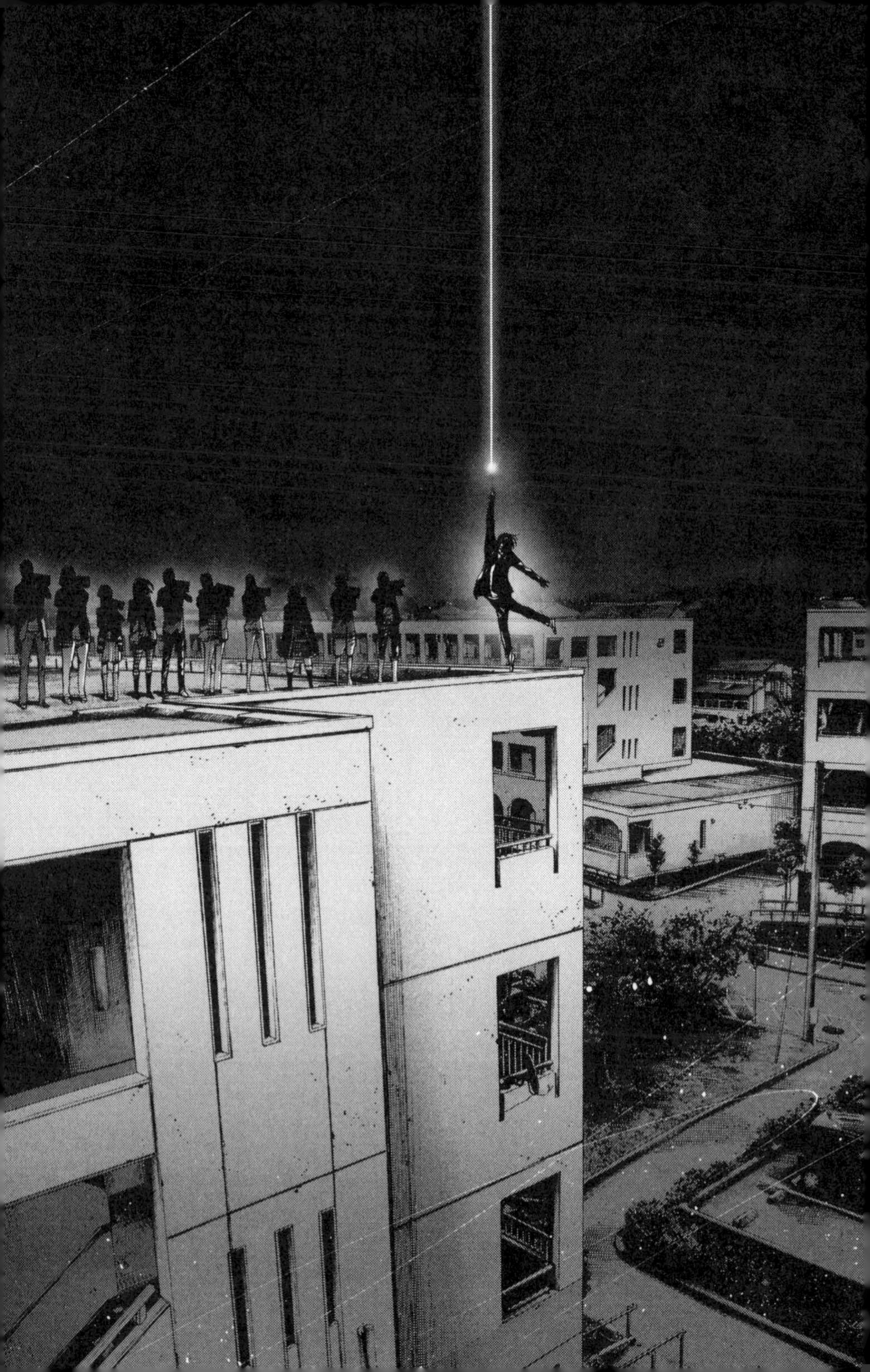

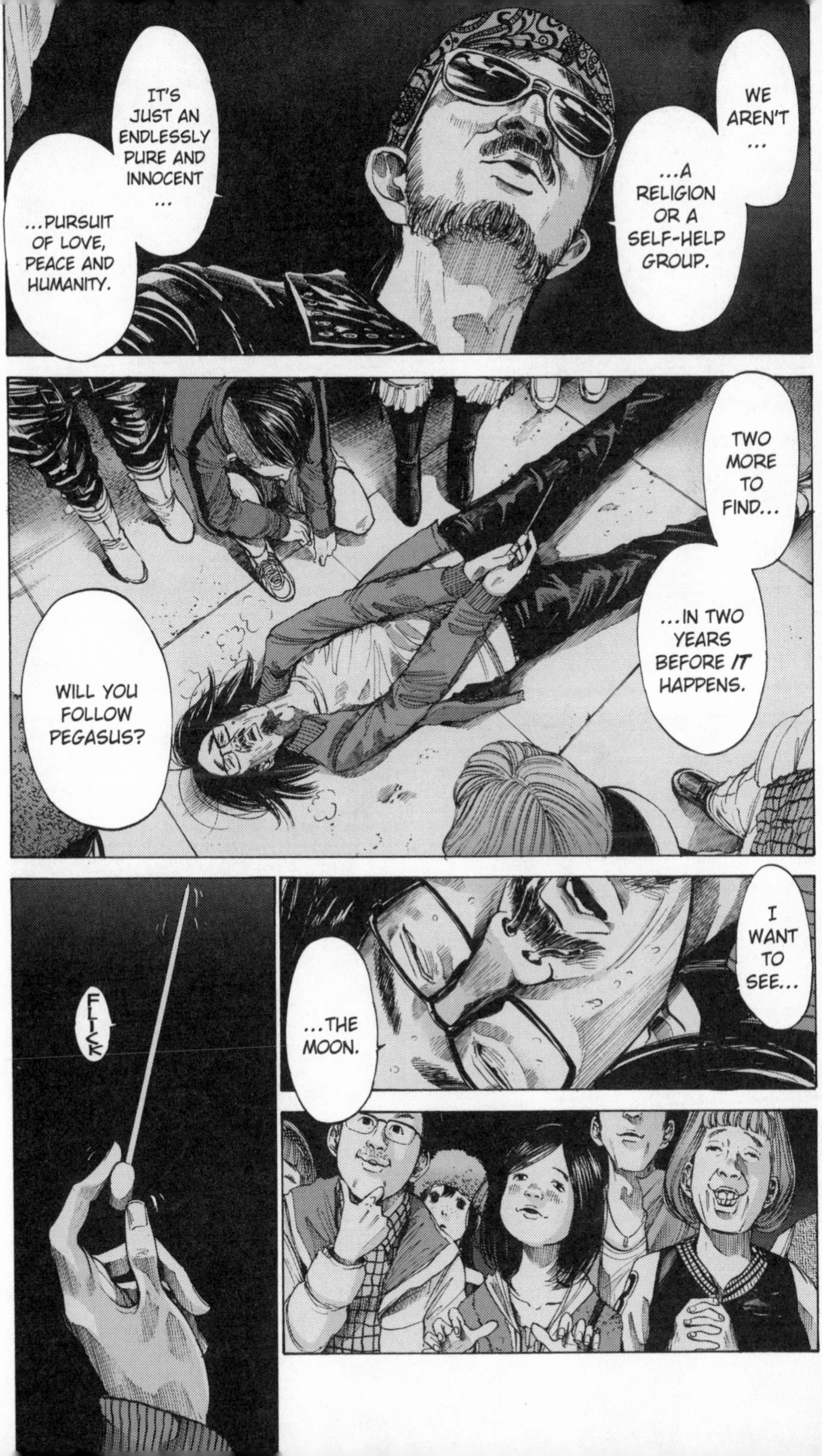
WE AREN'T ...
...A RELIGION OR A SELF-HELP GROUP.
IT'S JUST AN ENDLESSLY PURE AND INNOCENT ...
...PURSUIT OF LOVE, PEACE AND HUMANITY.
TWO MORE TO FIND...
...IN TWO YEARS BEFORE *IT* HAPPENS.
WILL YOU FOLLOW PEGASUS?
I WANT TO SEE...
...THE MOON.
FLICK

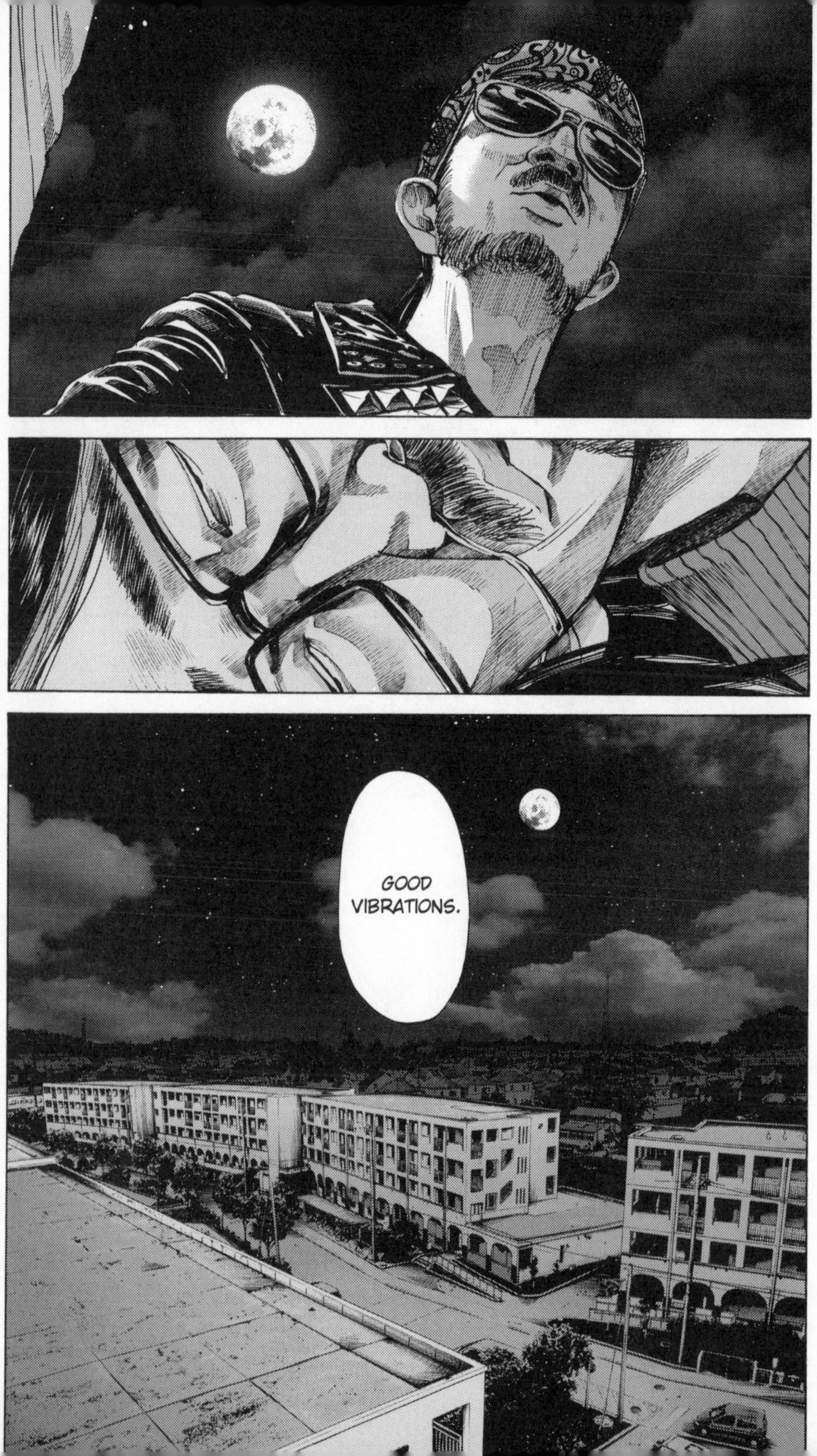
GOOD VIBRATIONS.

Chapter 72

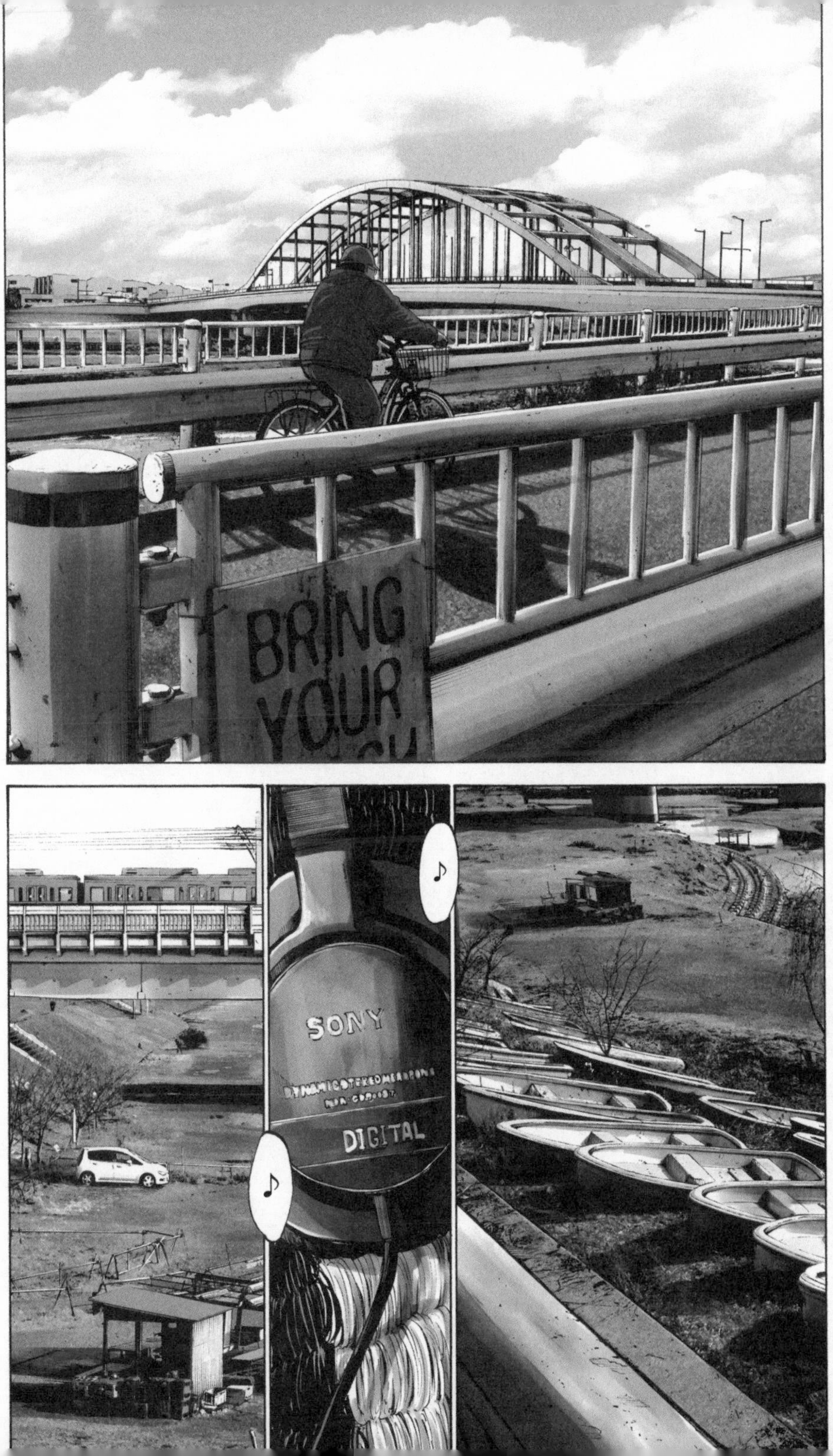
BRING YOUR
♪
SONY
DIGITAL
♪

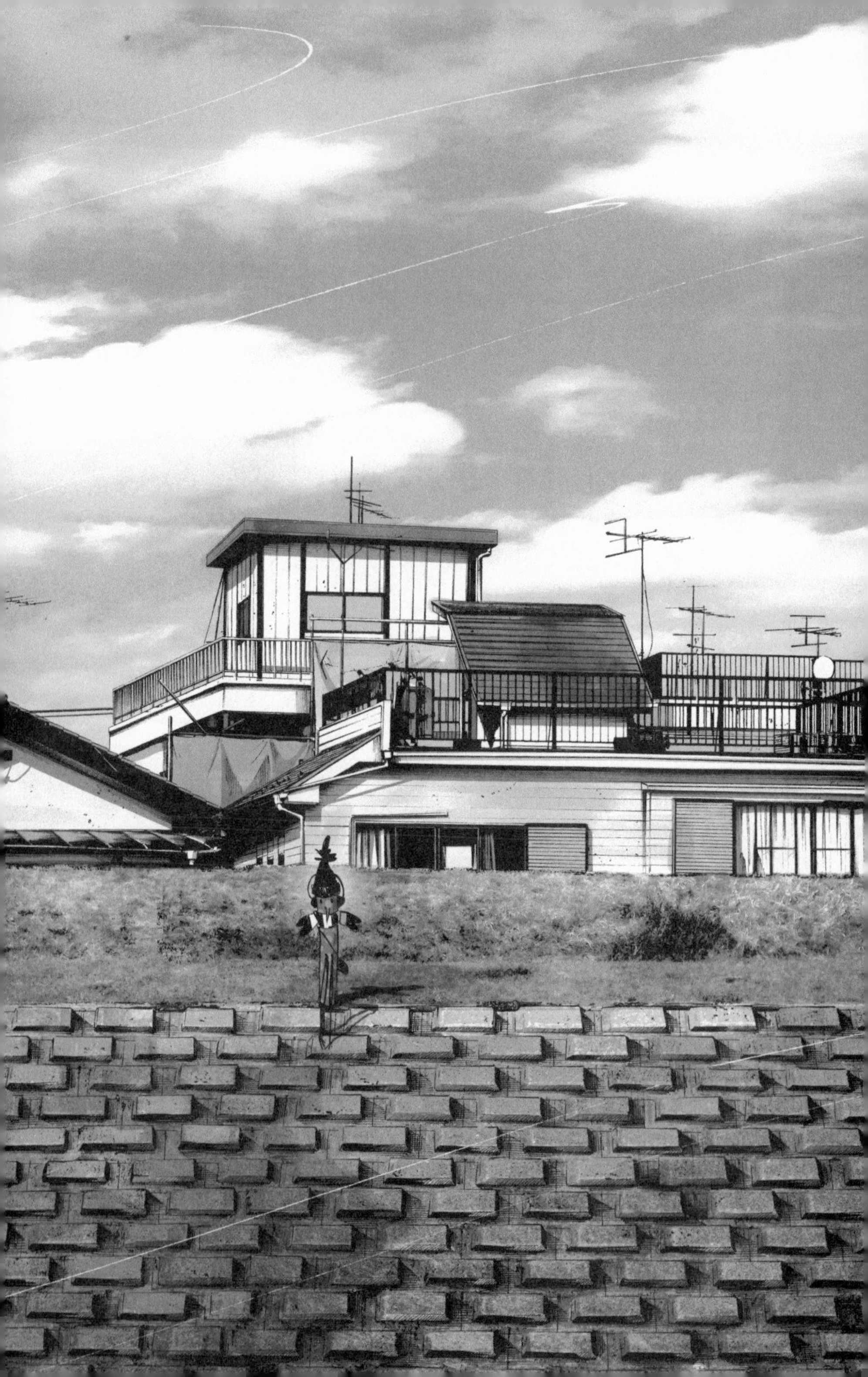

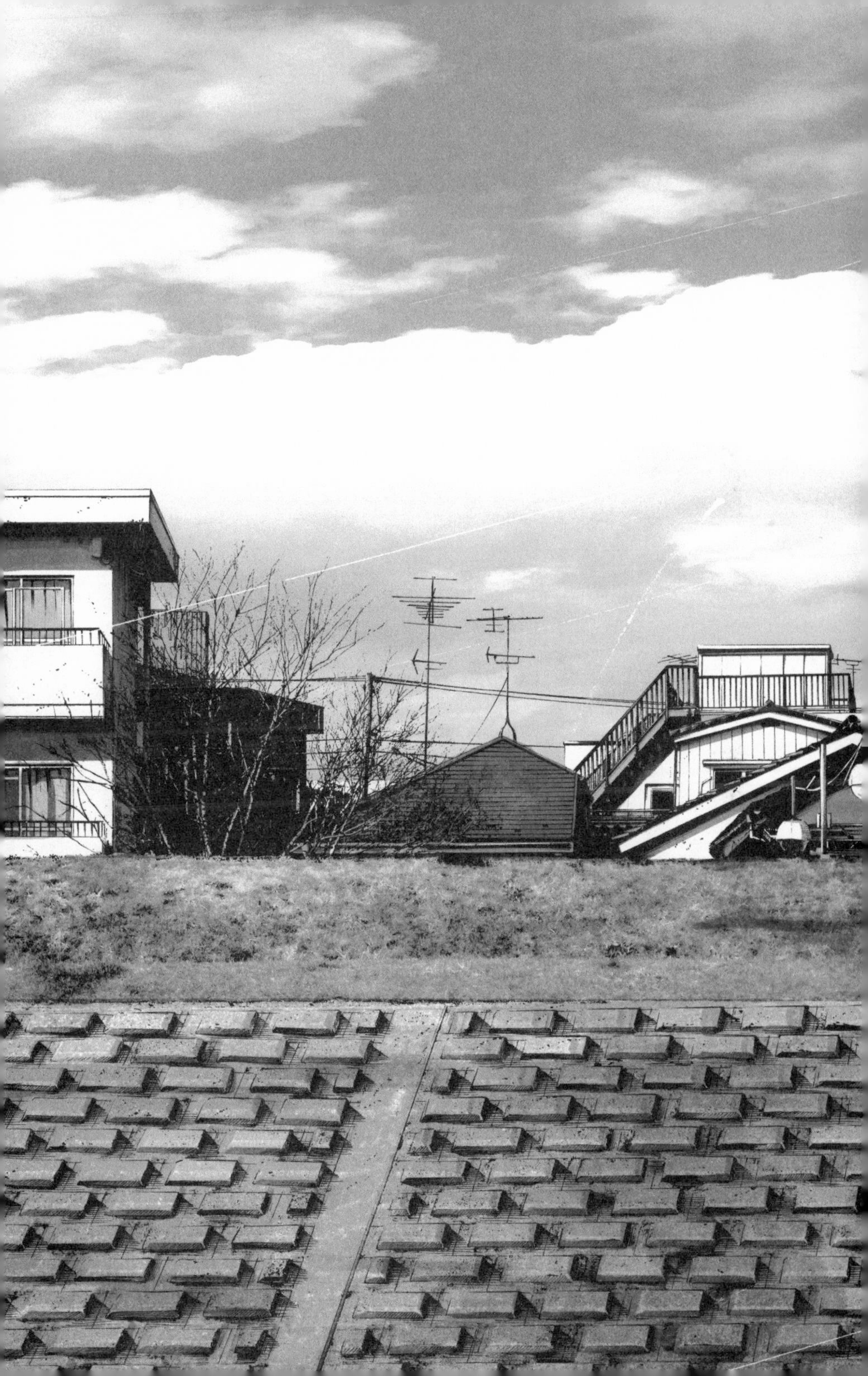

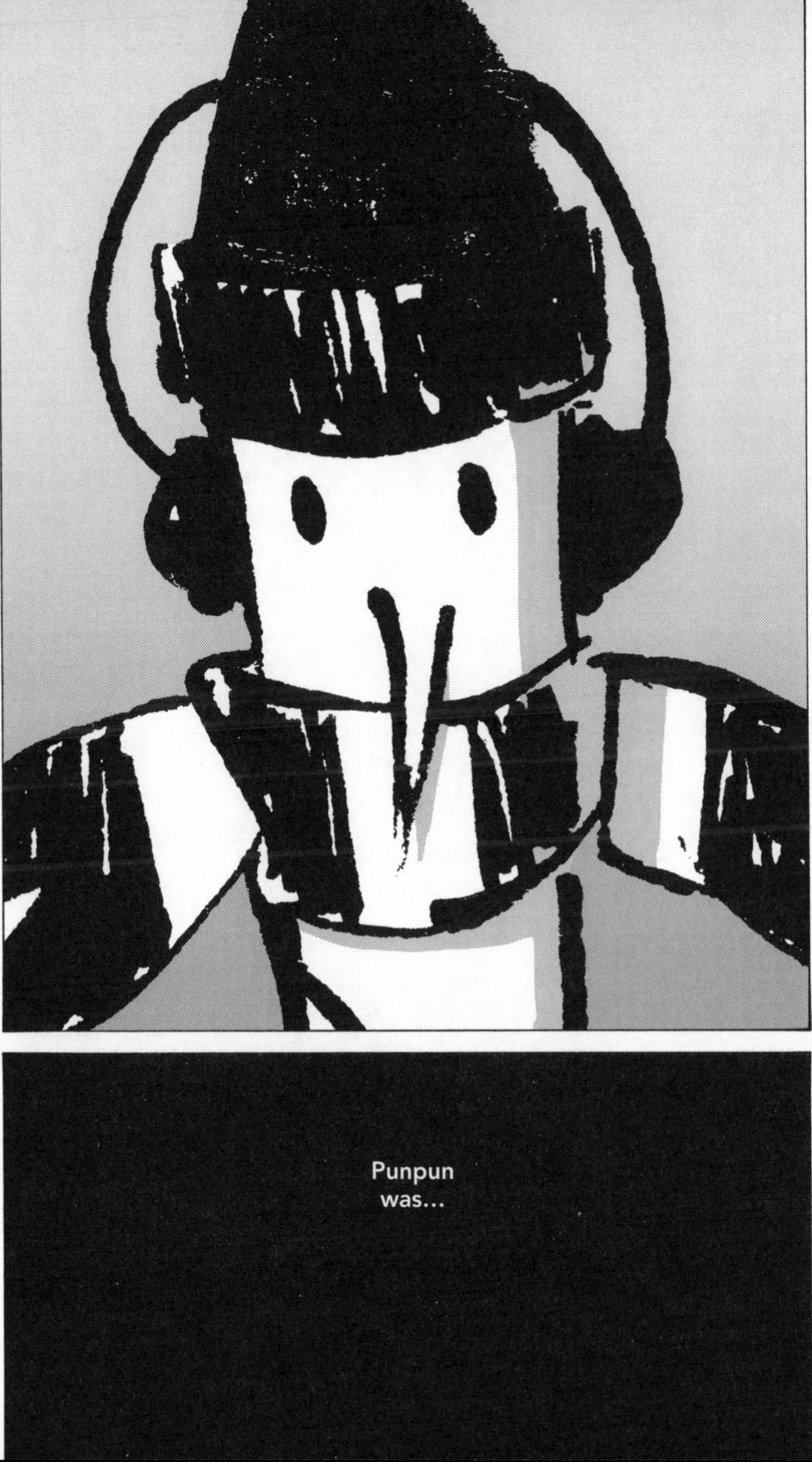
Punpun was...

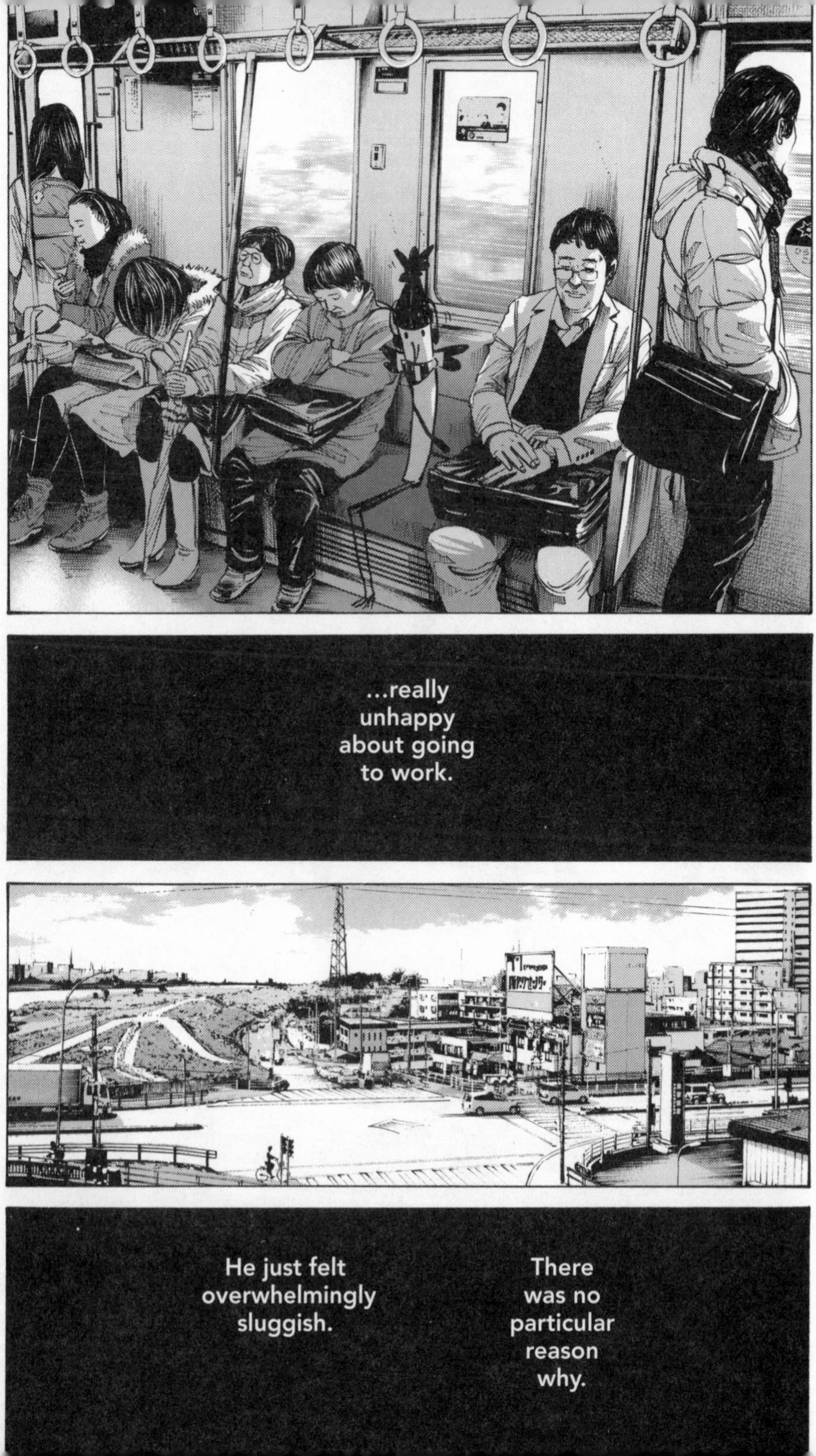
...really unhappy about going to work.
There was no particular reason why.
He just felt overwhelmingly sluggish.

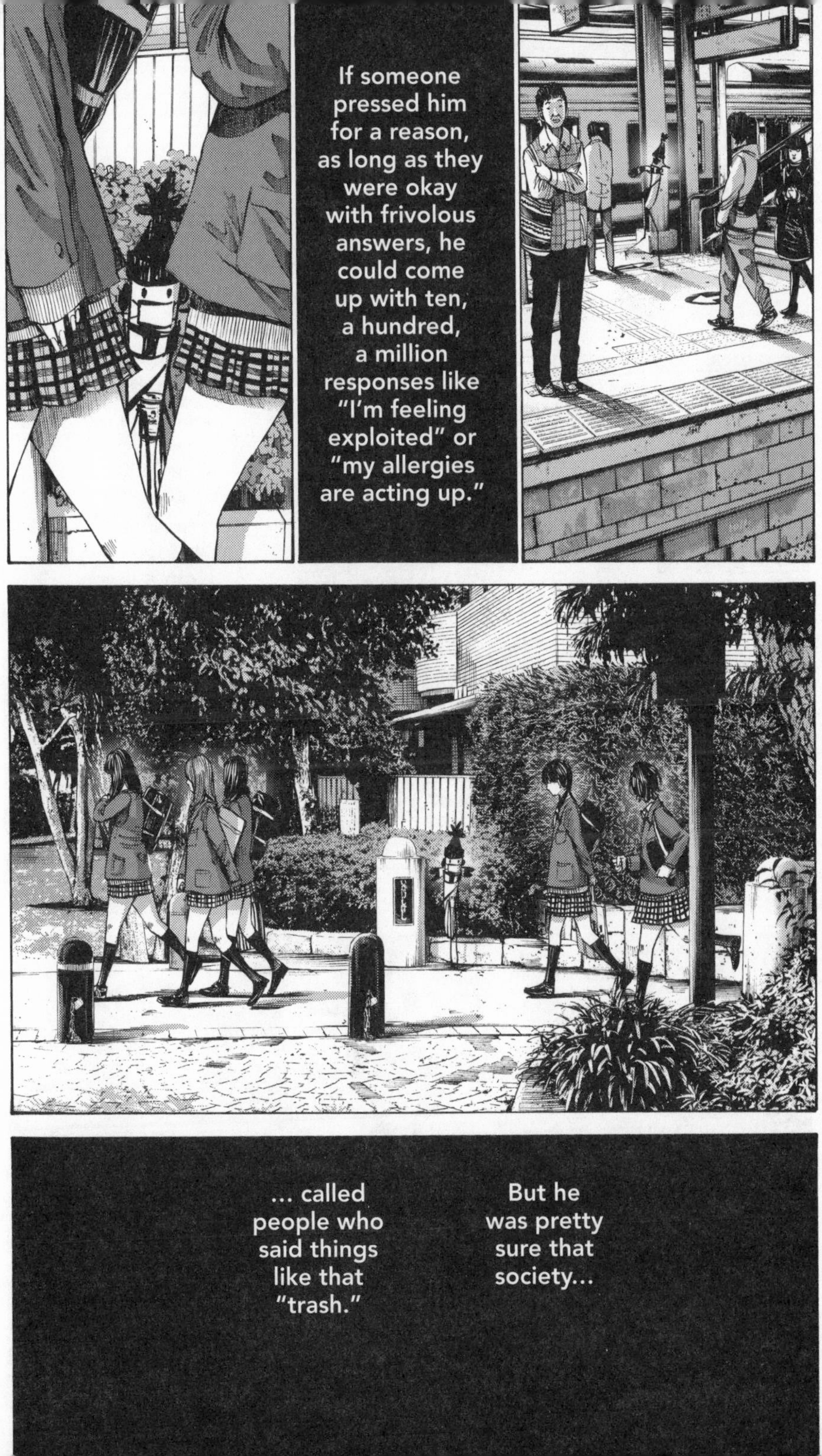
If someone pressed him for a reason, as long as they were okay with frivolous answers, he could come up with ten, a hundred, a million responses like "I'm feeling exploited" or "my allergies are acting up."
But he was pretty sure that society...
... called people who said things like that "trash."

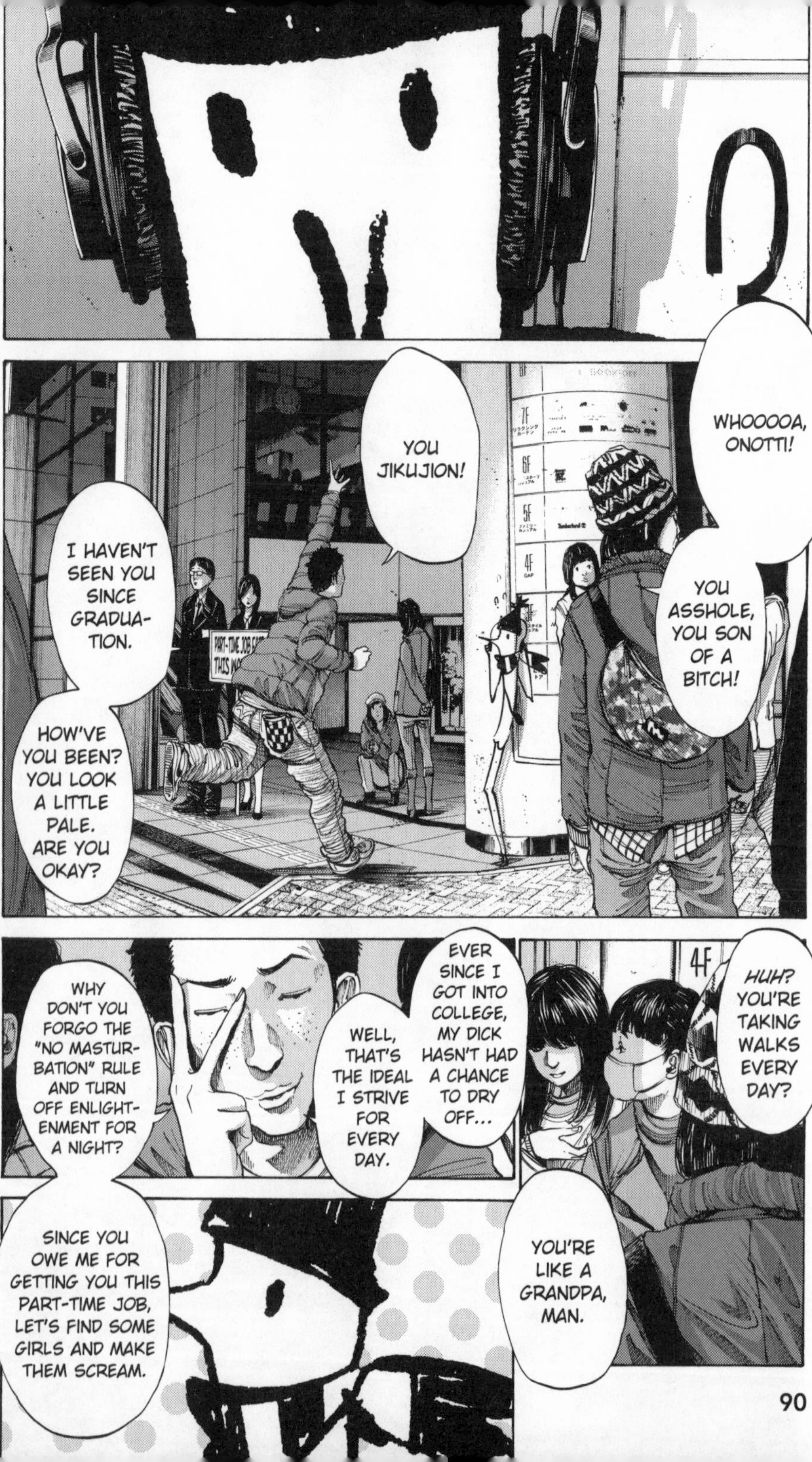
WHOOOOA, ONOTTI!
YOU ASSHOLE, YOU SON OF A BITCH!
YOU JIKUJION!
I HAVEN'T SEEN YOU SINCE GRADUATION.
HOW'VE YOU BEEN? YOU LOOK A LITTLE PALE. ARE YOU OKAY?
HUH? YOU'RE TAKING WALKS EVERY DAY?
EVER SINCE I GOT INTO COLLEGE, MY DICK HASN'T HAD A CHANCE TO DRY OFF...
WELL, THAT'S THE IDEAL I STRIVE FOR EVERY DAY.
WHY DON'T YOU FORGO THE "NO MASTURBATION" RULE AND TURN OFF ENLIGHTENMENT FOR A NIGHT?
YOU'RE LIKE A GRANDPA, MAN.
SINCE YOU OWE ME FOR GETTING YOU THIS PART-TIME JOB, LET'S FIND SOME GIRLS AND MAKE THEM SCREAM.

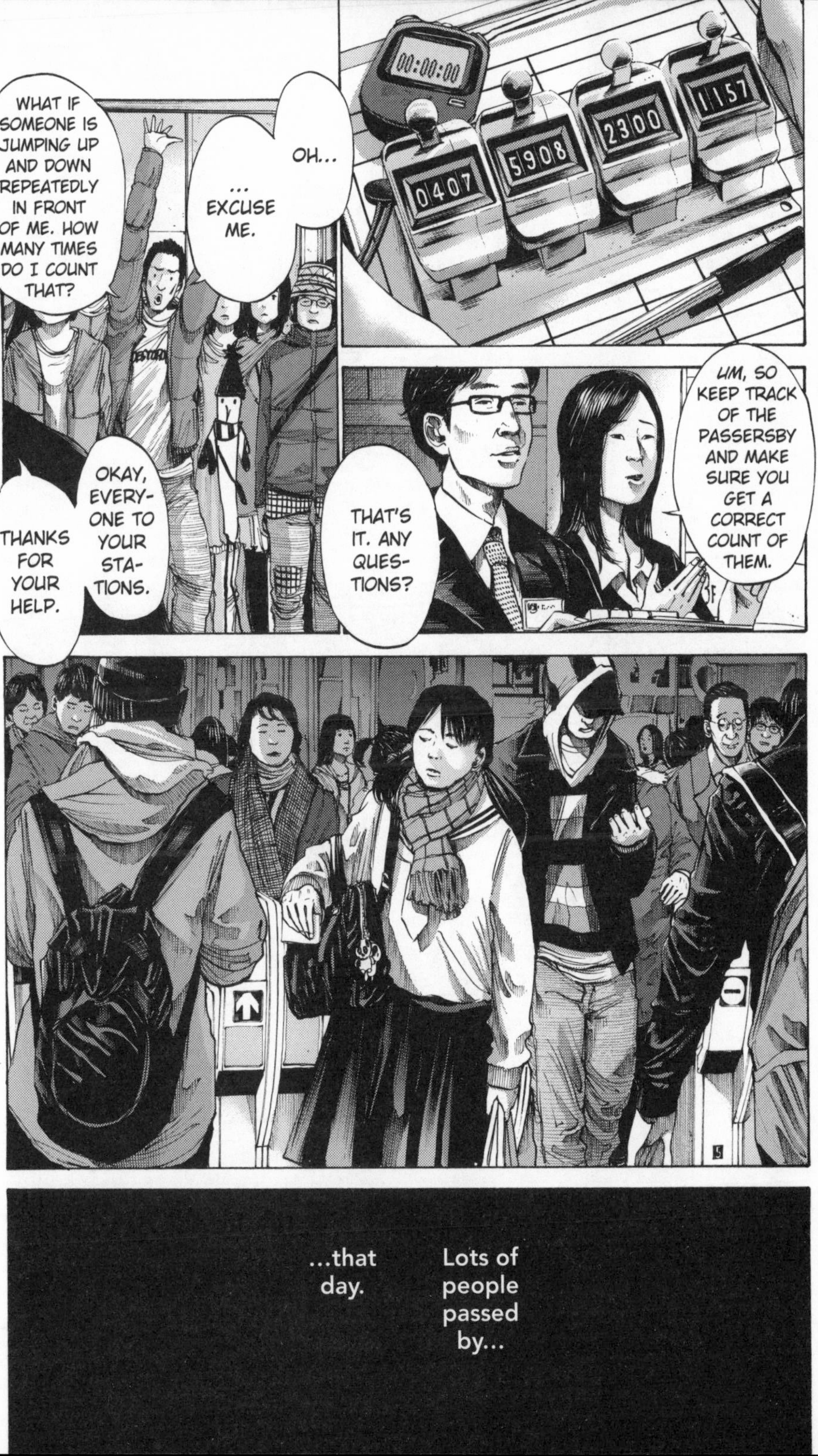
00:00:00
0407
5908
2300
1157
UM, SO KEEP TRACK OF THE PASSERSBY AND MAKE SURE YOU GET A CORRECT COUNT OF THEM.
THAT'S IT. ANY QUES-TIONS?
OH...
...EXCUSE ME.
WHAT IF SOMEONE IS JUMPING UP AND DOWN REPEATEDLY IN FRONT OF ME. HOW MANY TIMES DO I COUNT THAT?
OKAY, EVERY-ONE TO YOUR STA-TIONS.
THANKS FOR YOUR HELP.
Lots of people passed by...
...that day.

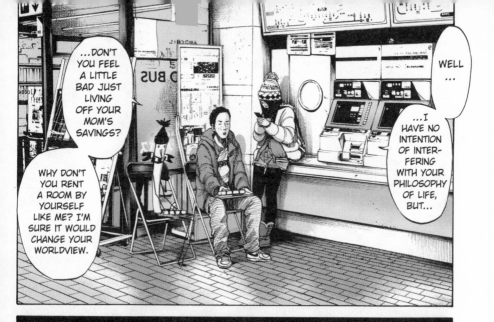

WELL...
...I HAVE NO INTENTION OF INTER-FERING WITH YOUR PHILOSOPHY OF LIFE, BUT...
...DON'T YOU FEEL A LITTLE BAD JUST LIVING OFF YOUR MOM'S SAVINGS?
WHY DON'T YOU RENT A ROOM BY YOURSELF LIKE ME? I'M SURE IT WOULD CHANGE YOUR WORLDVIEW.
Among the pedestrians passing by were bound to be...
...some with major problems at home...
...some with serious illnesses...
...or some depressed by irrevocable guilt.
WOO!
I JUST SPOTTED A TOTAL HARD-ON BABE.
OKAY, I'LL GIVE HER TWO POINTS.
THE ONES ON EITHER SIDE OF HER ARE ABOUT HALF A POINT EACH, SO TOGETHER THEY'RE A POINT.

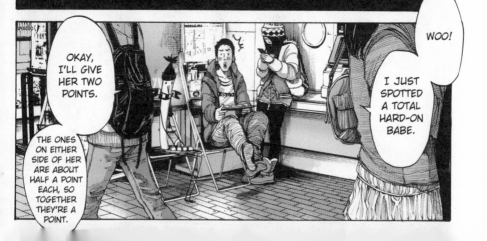

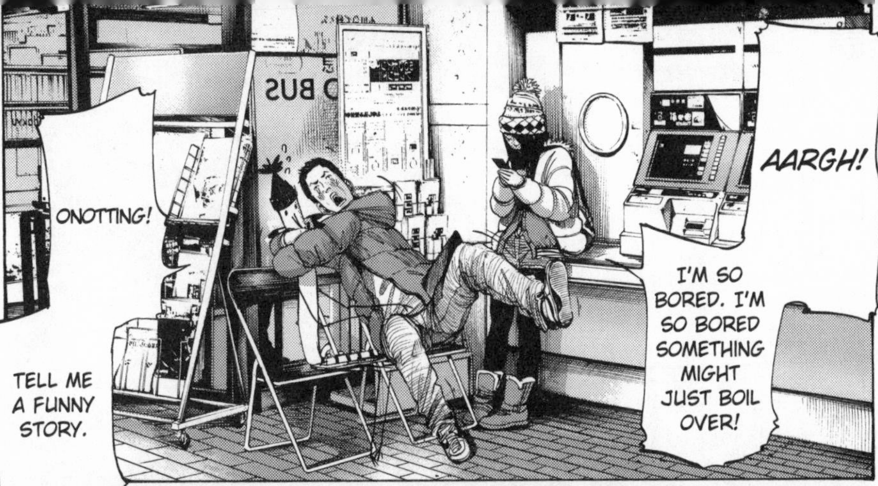
AARGH!
I'M SO BORED. I'M SO BORED SOMETHING MIGHT JUST BOIL OVER!
ONOTTING!
TELL ME A FUNNY STORY.

For some reason, Punpun was following them as they went back and forth, as if he was clinging to something.

Who was he looking for?

No one would help him. No one would meet his gaze.

Well, of course not. They were all confidently moving forward.

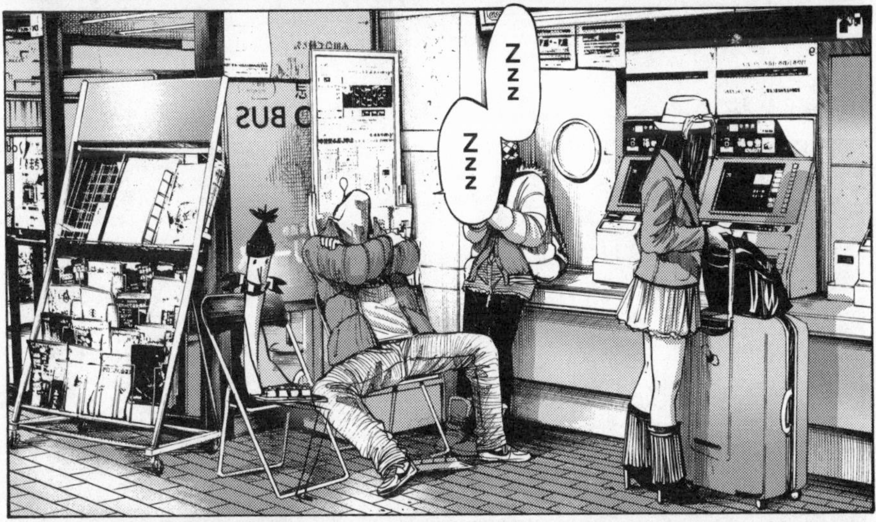
Zzz
Zzz

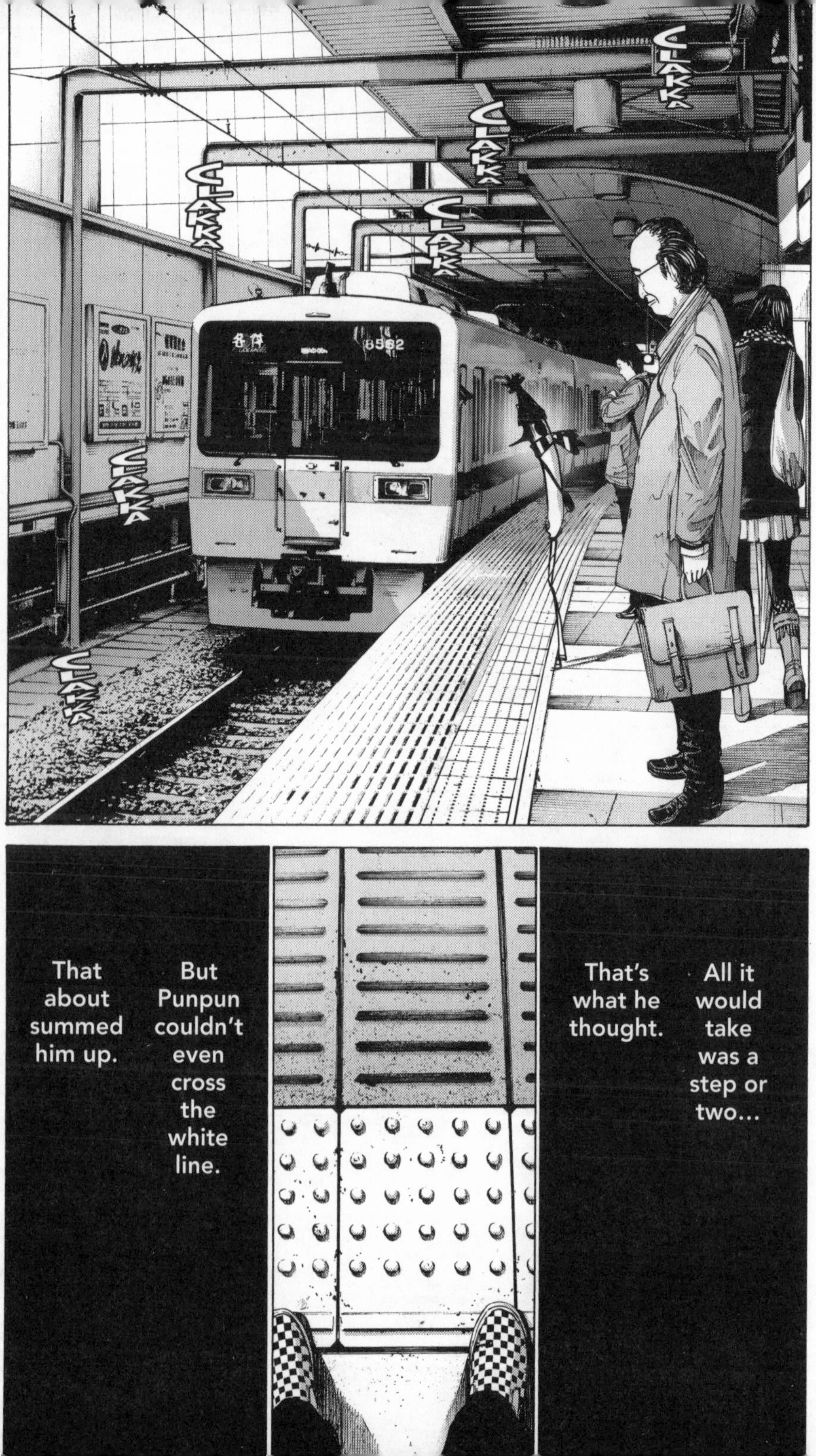
CLAKKA
CLAKKA
CLAKKA
CLAKKA
CLAKKA
CLAKKA
All it would take was a step or two...
That's what he thought.
But Punpun couldn't even cross the white line.
That about summed him up.

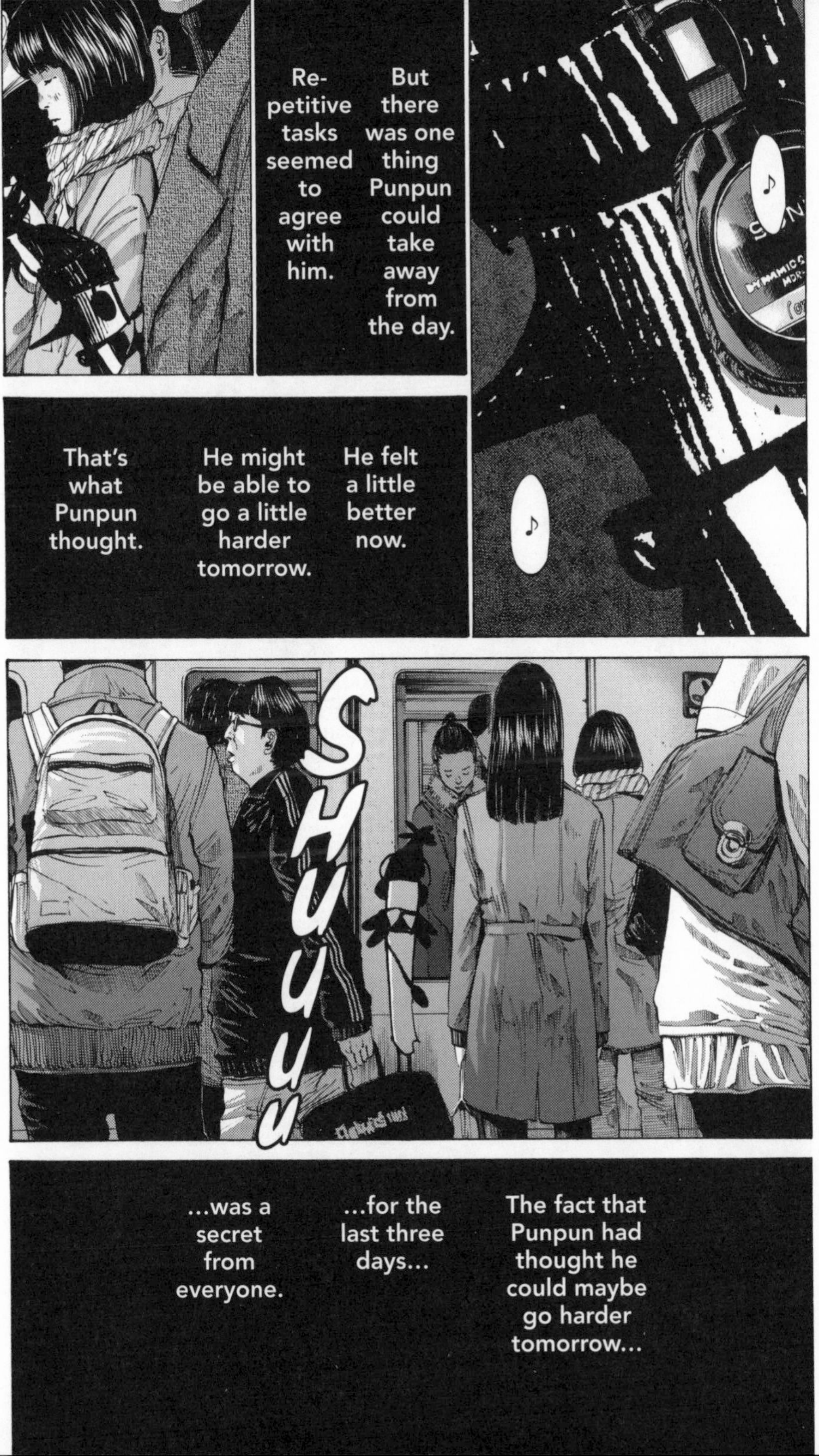
♪
♪
But there was one thing Punpun could take away from the day.
Re-petitive tasks seemed to agree with him.
He felt a little better now.
He might be able to go a little harder tomorrow.
That's what Punpun thought.
SHUUUUU
The fact that Punpun had thought he could maybe go harder tomorrow...
...for the last three days...
...was a secret from everyone.

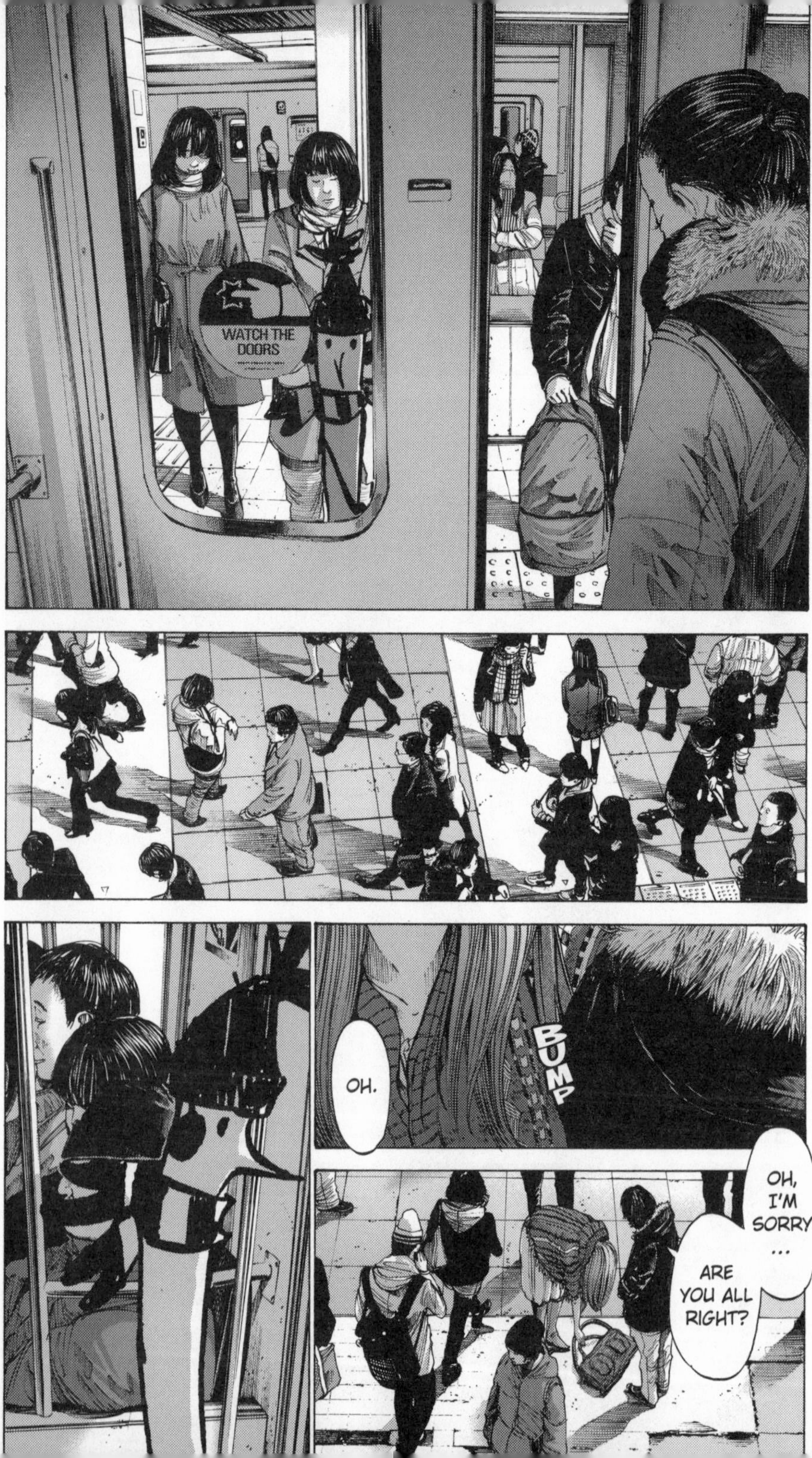
WATCH THE DOORS
OH.
BUMP
OH, I'M SORRY ...
ARE YOU ALL RIGHT?

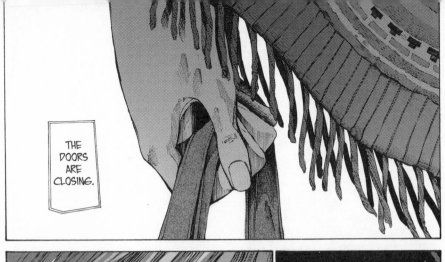

THE DOORS ARE CLOSING.

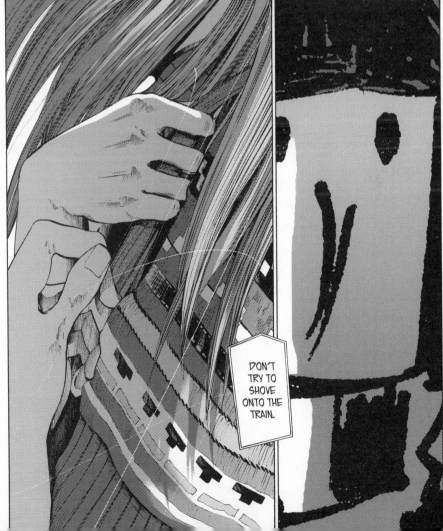

DON'T TRY TO SHOVE ONTO THE TRAIN.

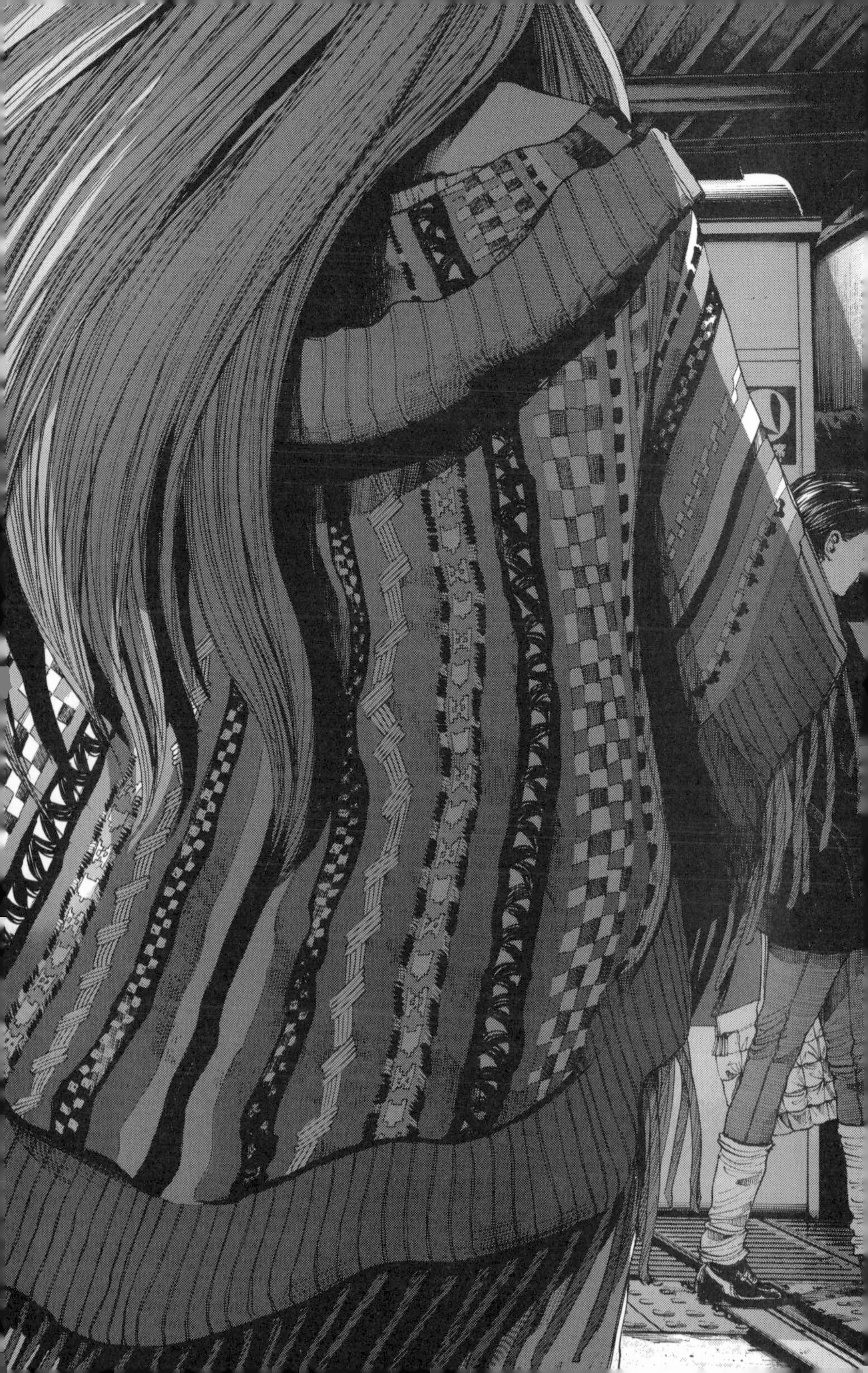

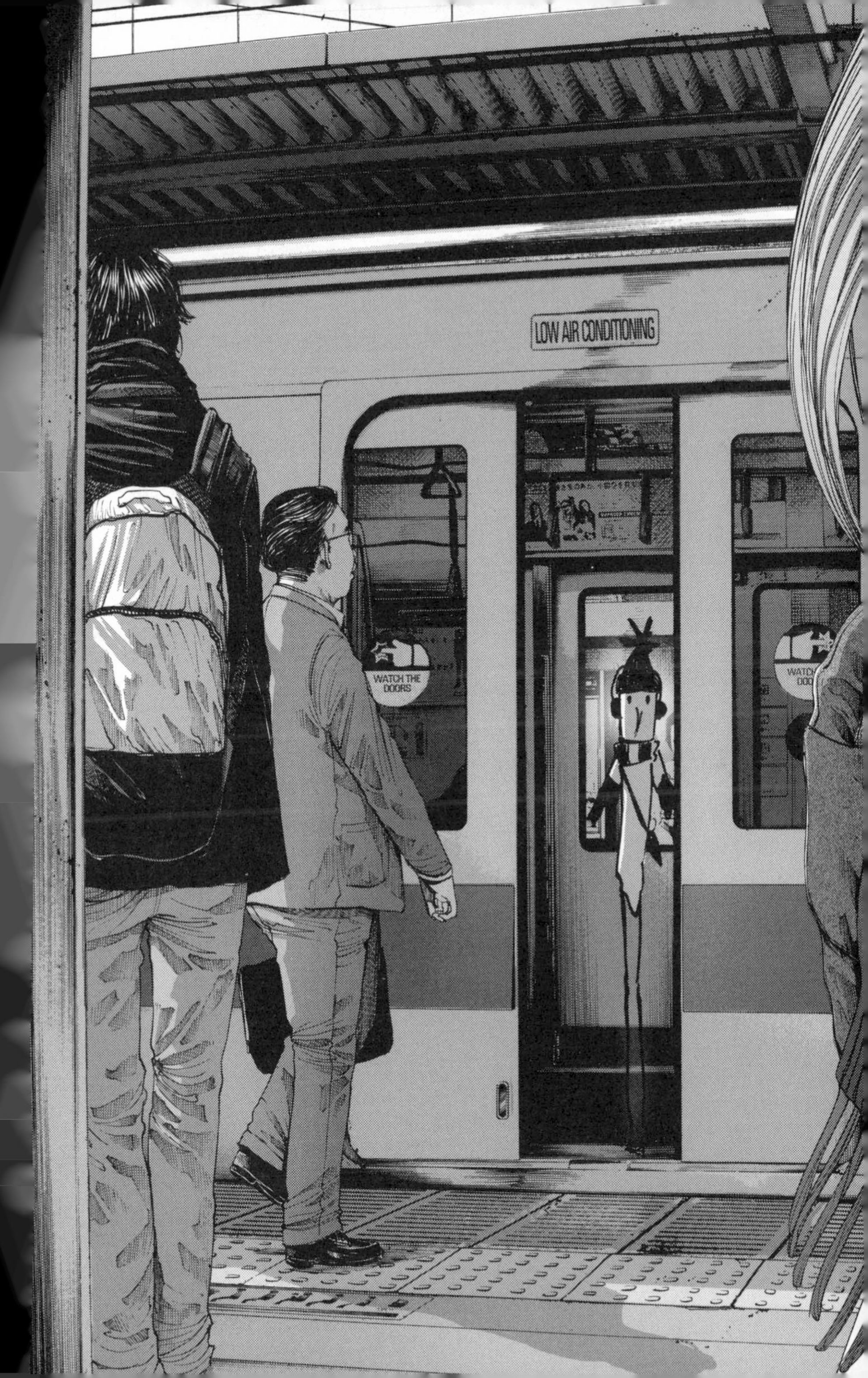
LOW AIR CONDITIONING
WATCH THE DOORS
WATCH THE DOORS

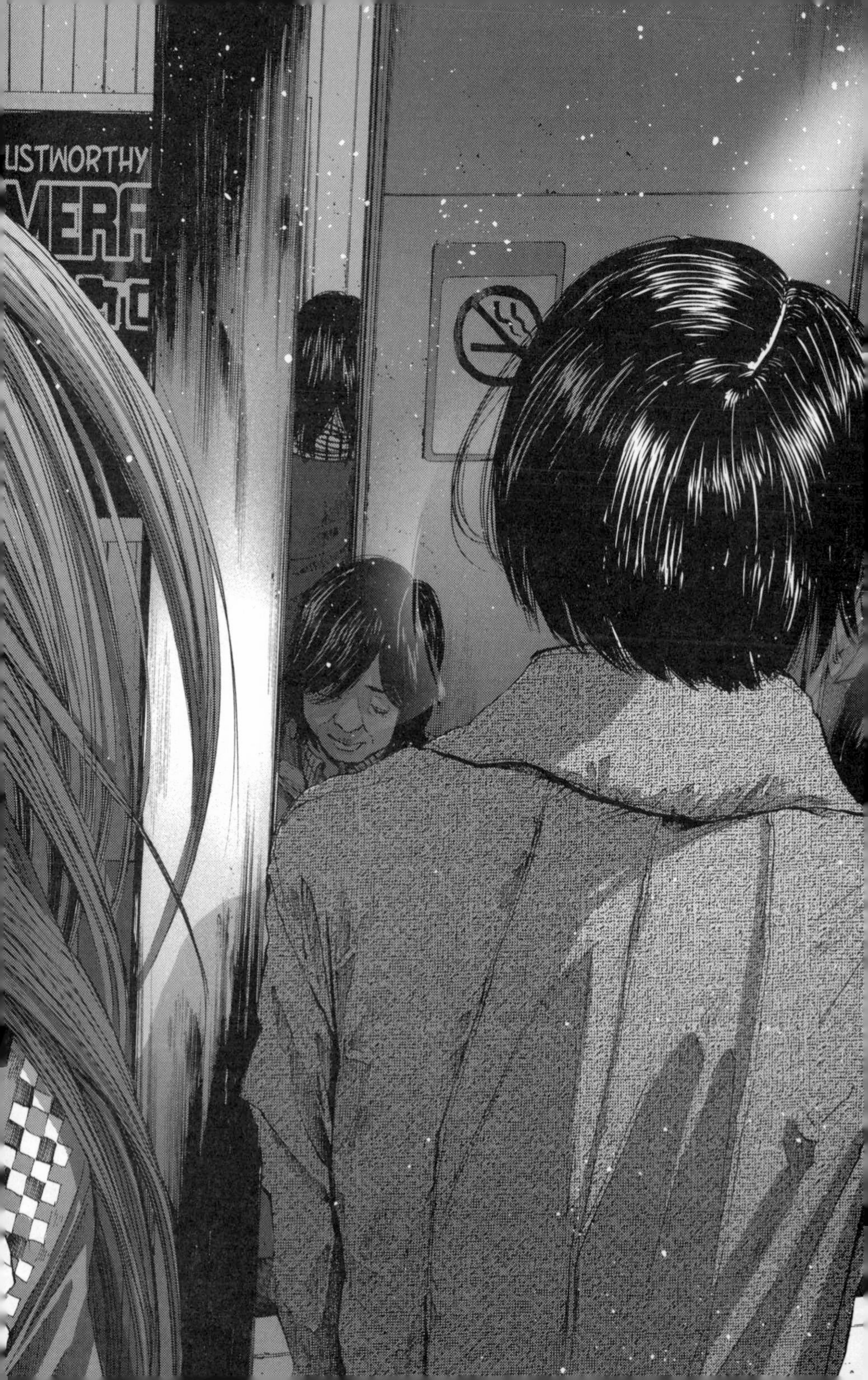
USTWORTHY

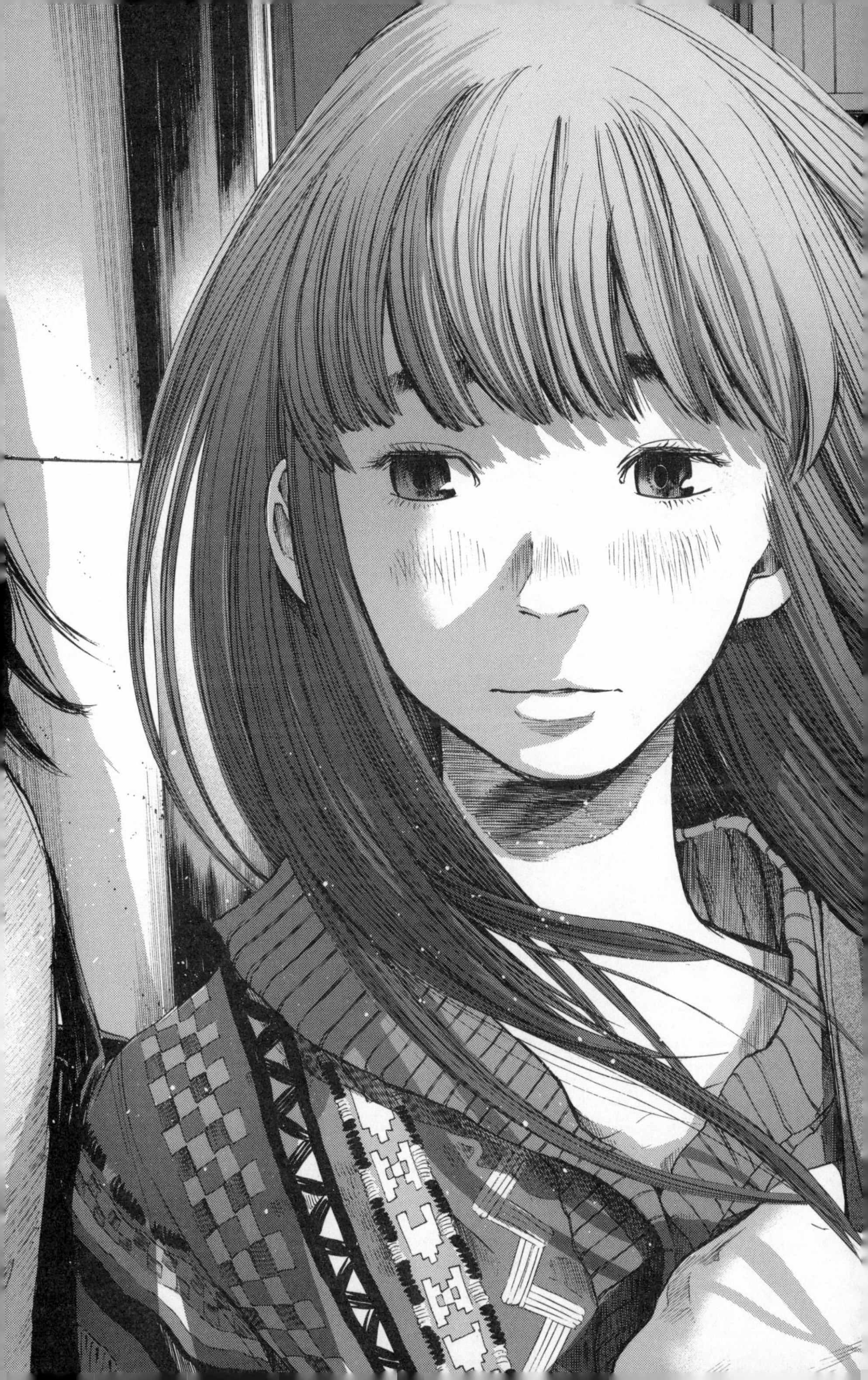

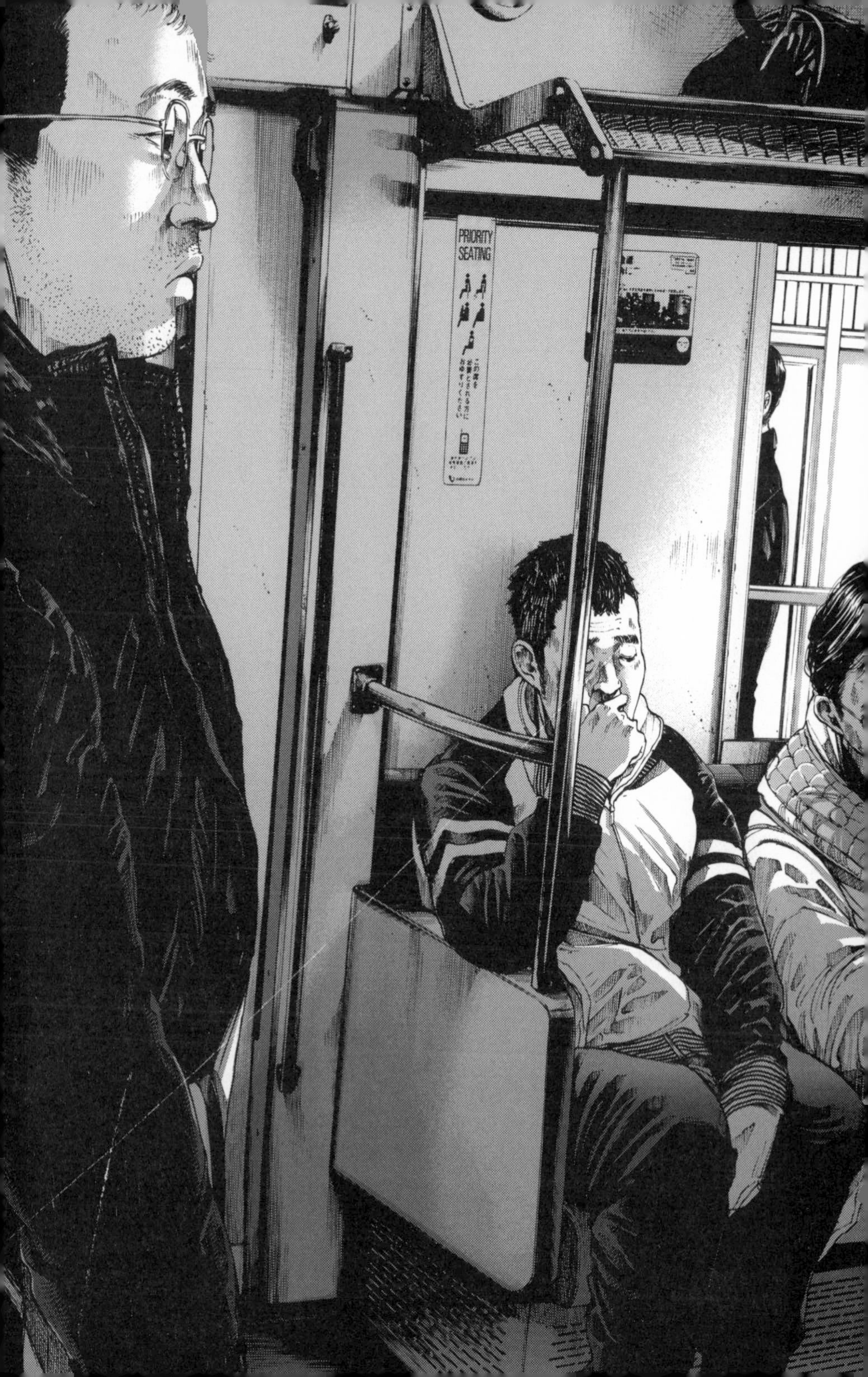
PRIORITY SEATING
この席を必要とされる方におゆずりください

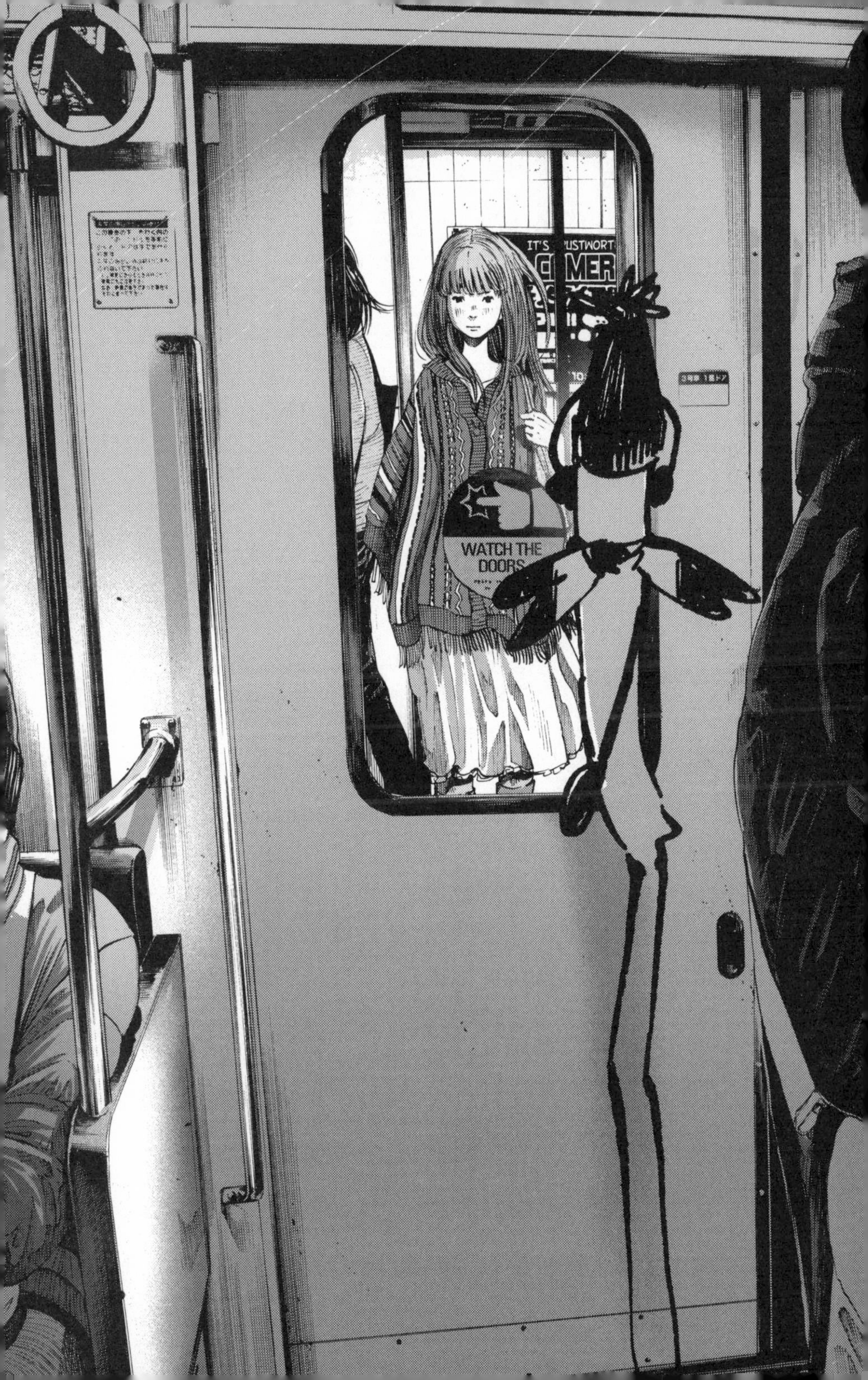
WATCH THE DOORS

It's
Aiko.

Chapter 73

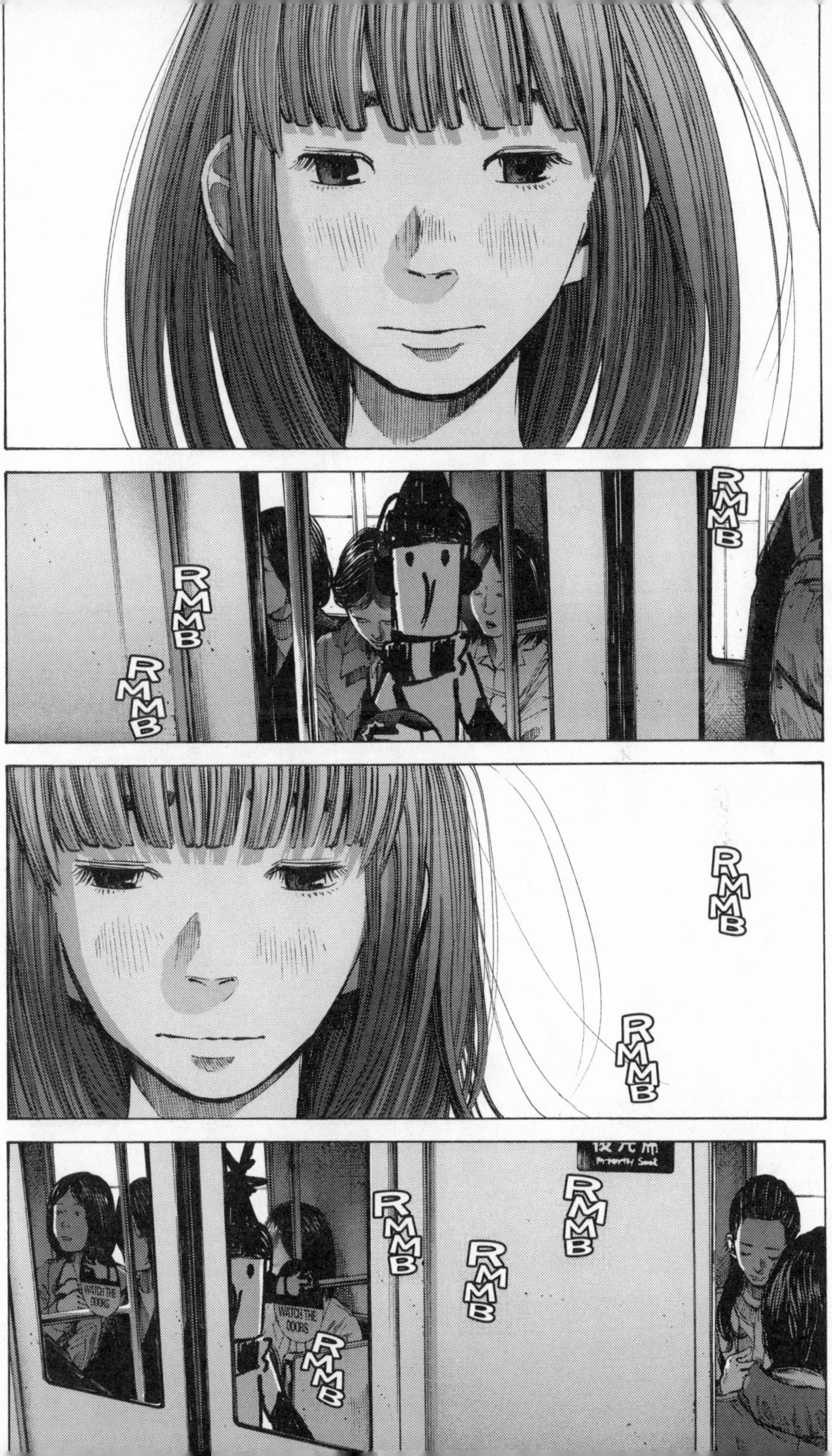
RMMB
RMMB
RMMB
RMMB
RMMB
RMMB
RMMB
RMMB
WATCH THE DOORS
WATCH THE DOORS
RMMB

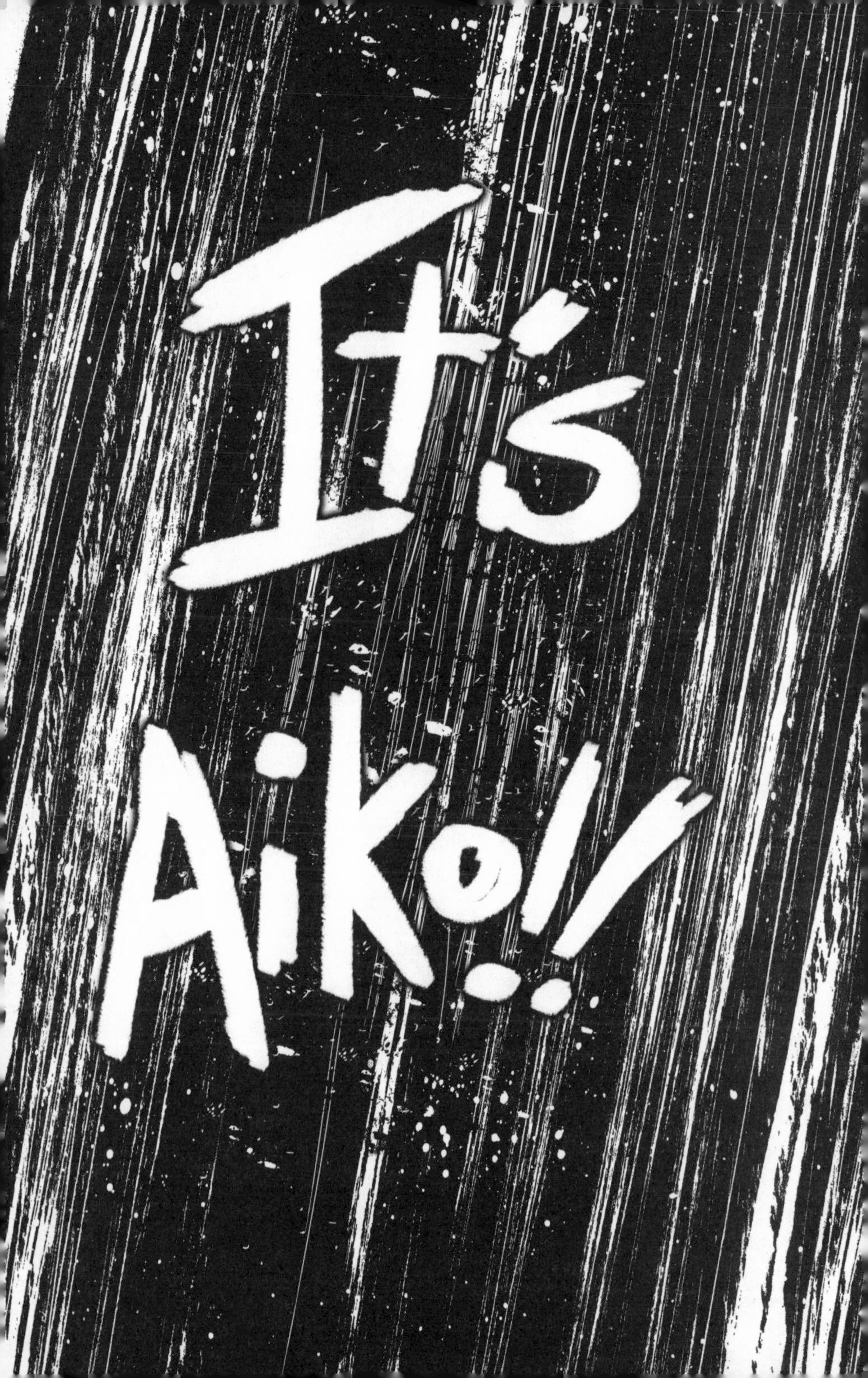
It's Aiko!!

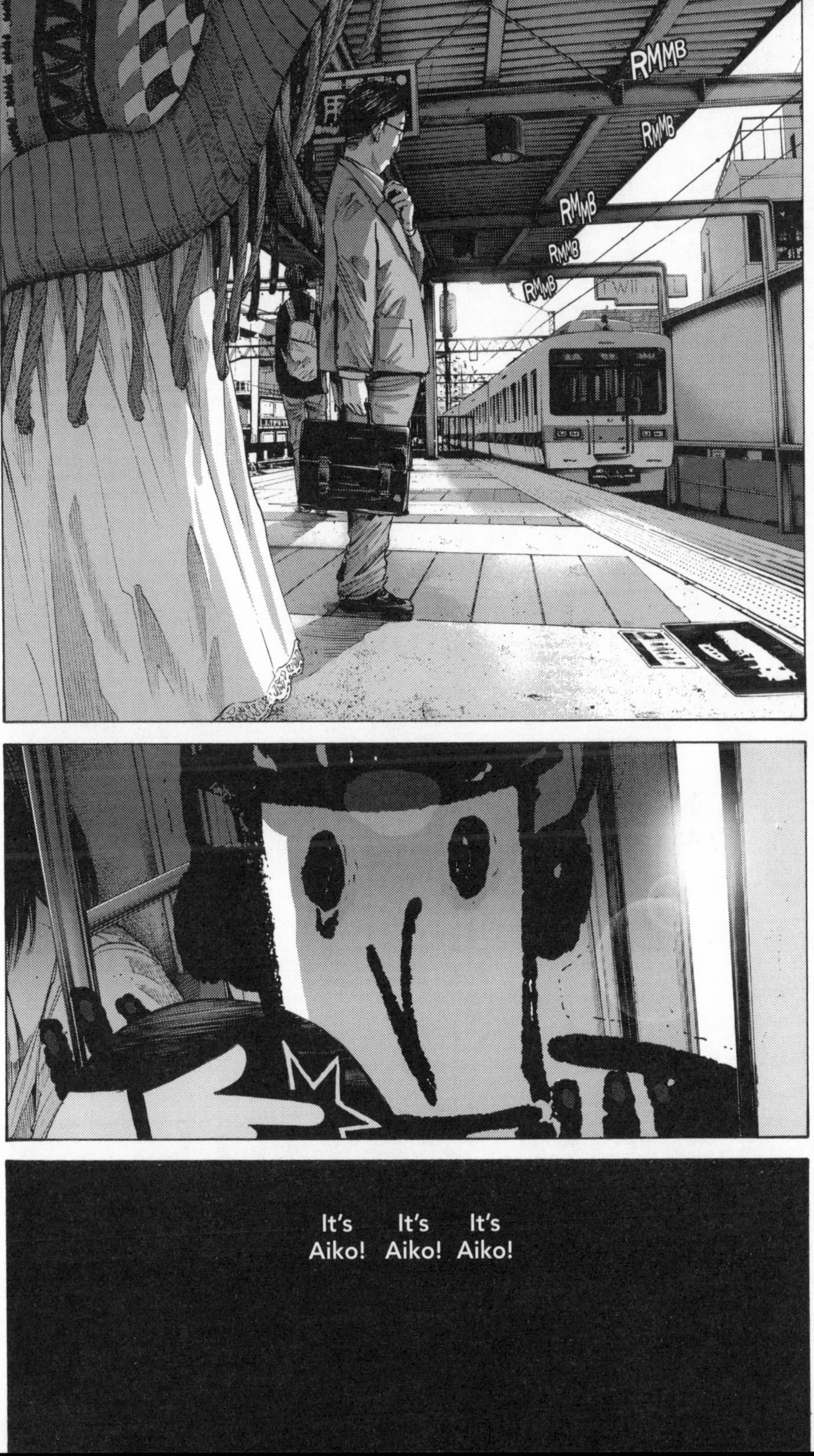
RMMB
RMMB
RMMB
RMMB
RMMB
It's Aiko! It's Aiko! It's Aiko!

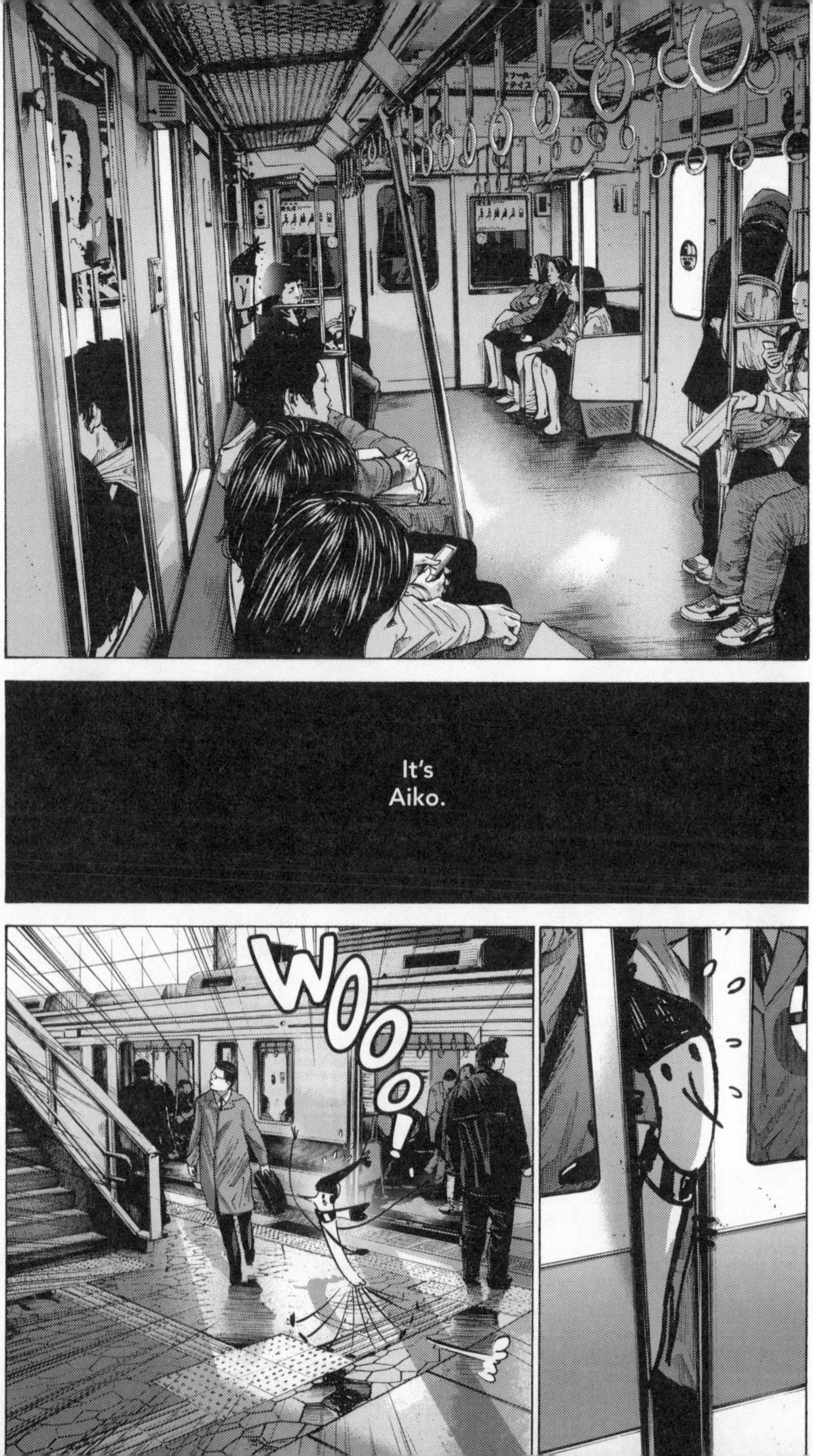
It's
Aiko.
WOOO!

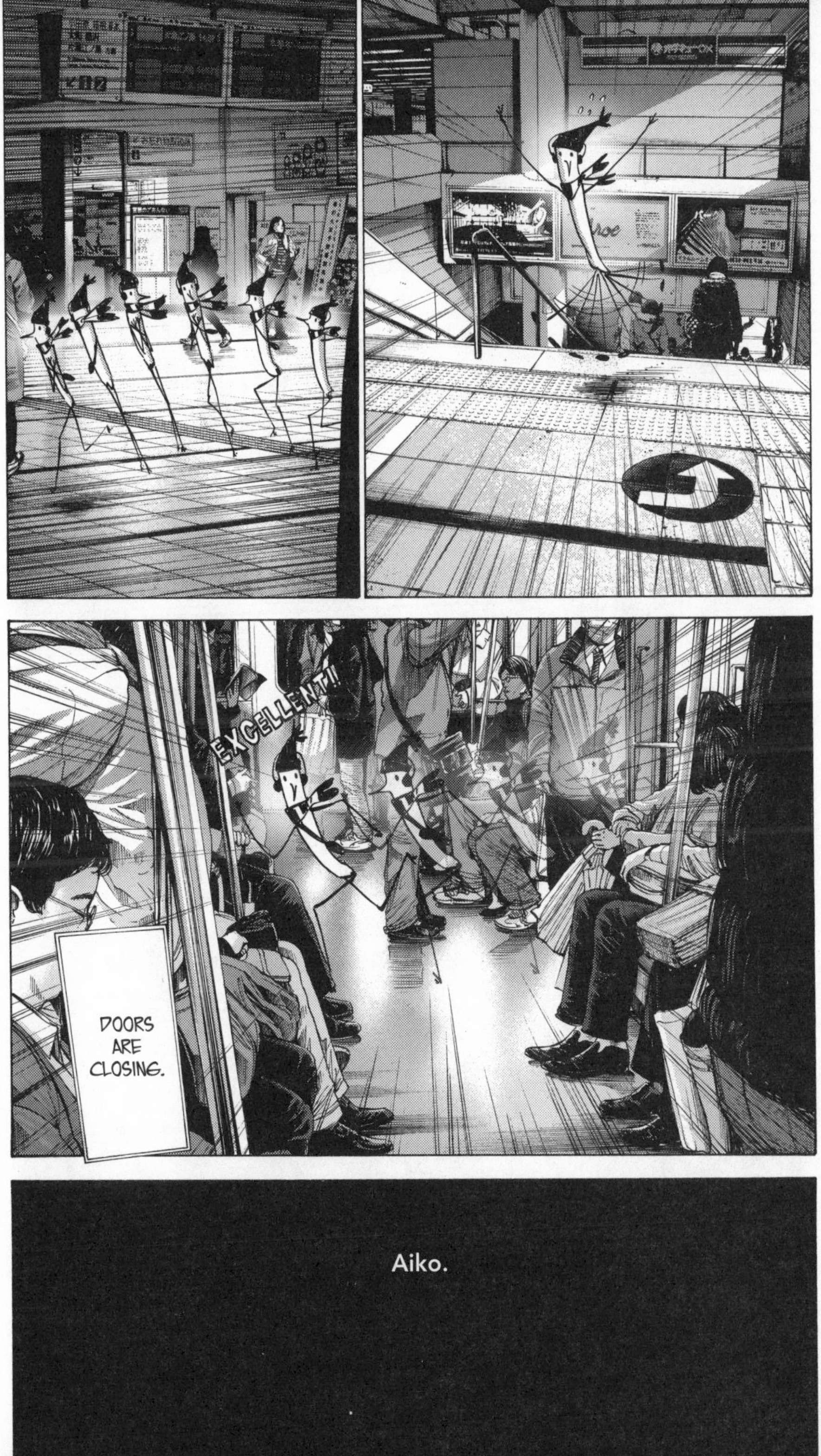
EXCELLENT!!
DOORS ARE CLOSING.
Aiko.

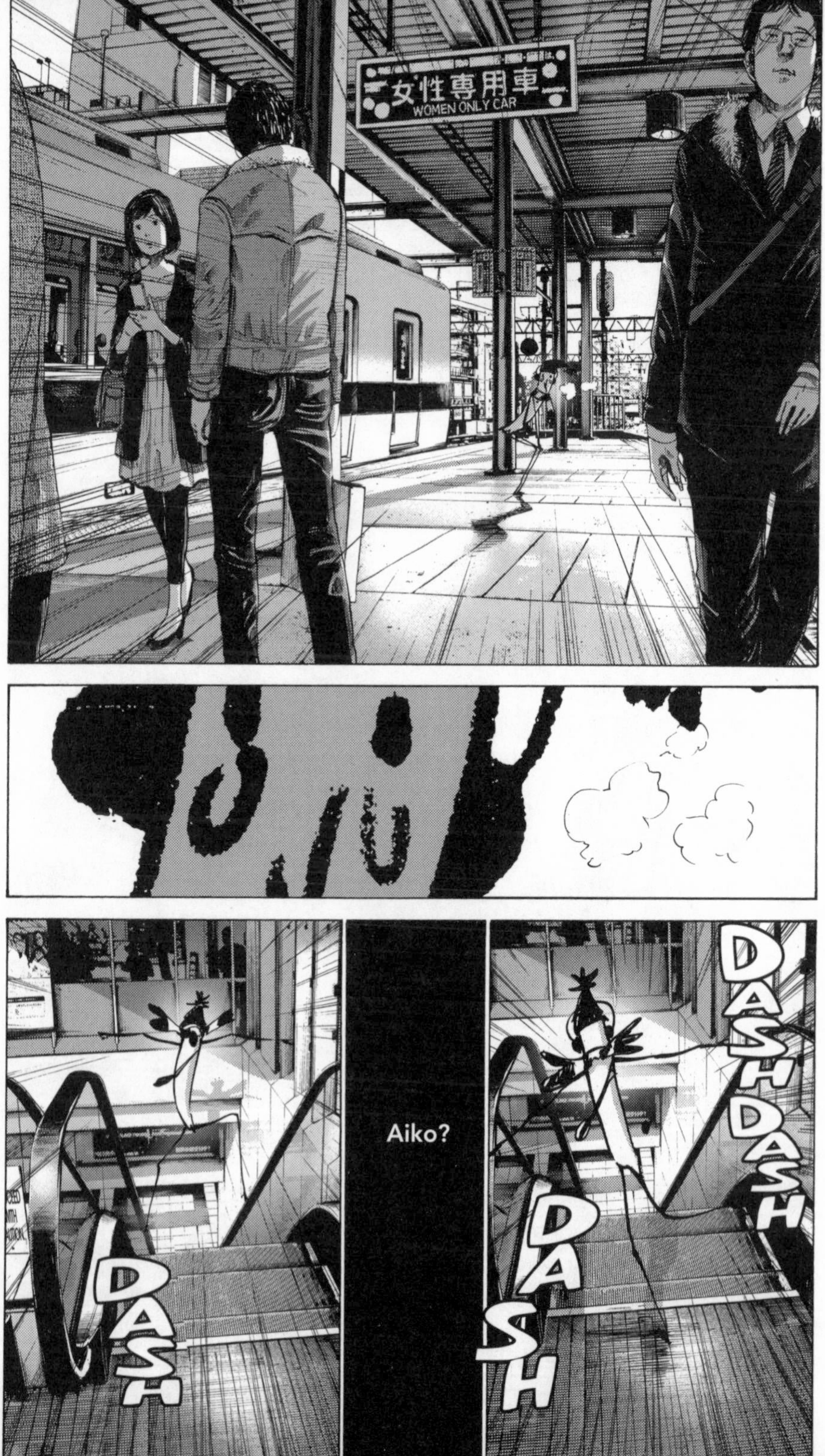
女性専用車
WOMEN ONLY CAR
DASHDASH
DASH
Aiko?
DASH

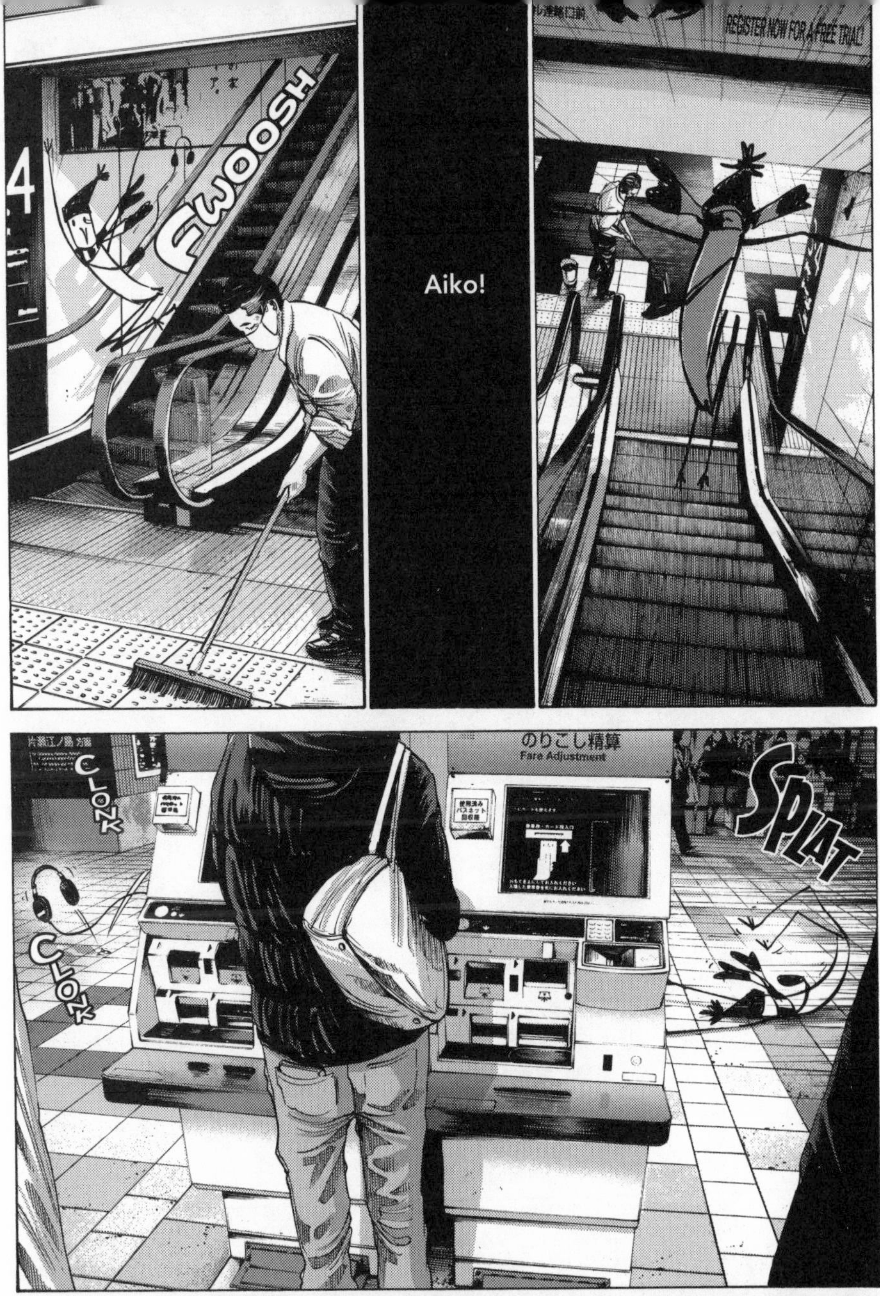
REGISTER NOW FOR A FREE TRIAL!
Aiko!
FWOOSH
SPLAT
のりこし精算
Fare Adjustment
CLONK
CLONK

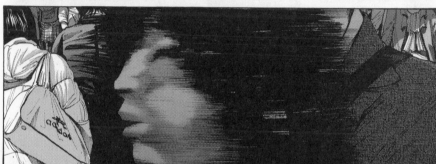

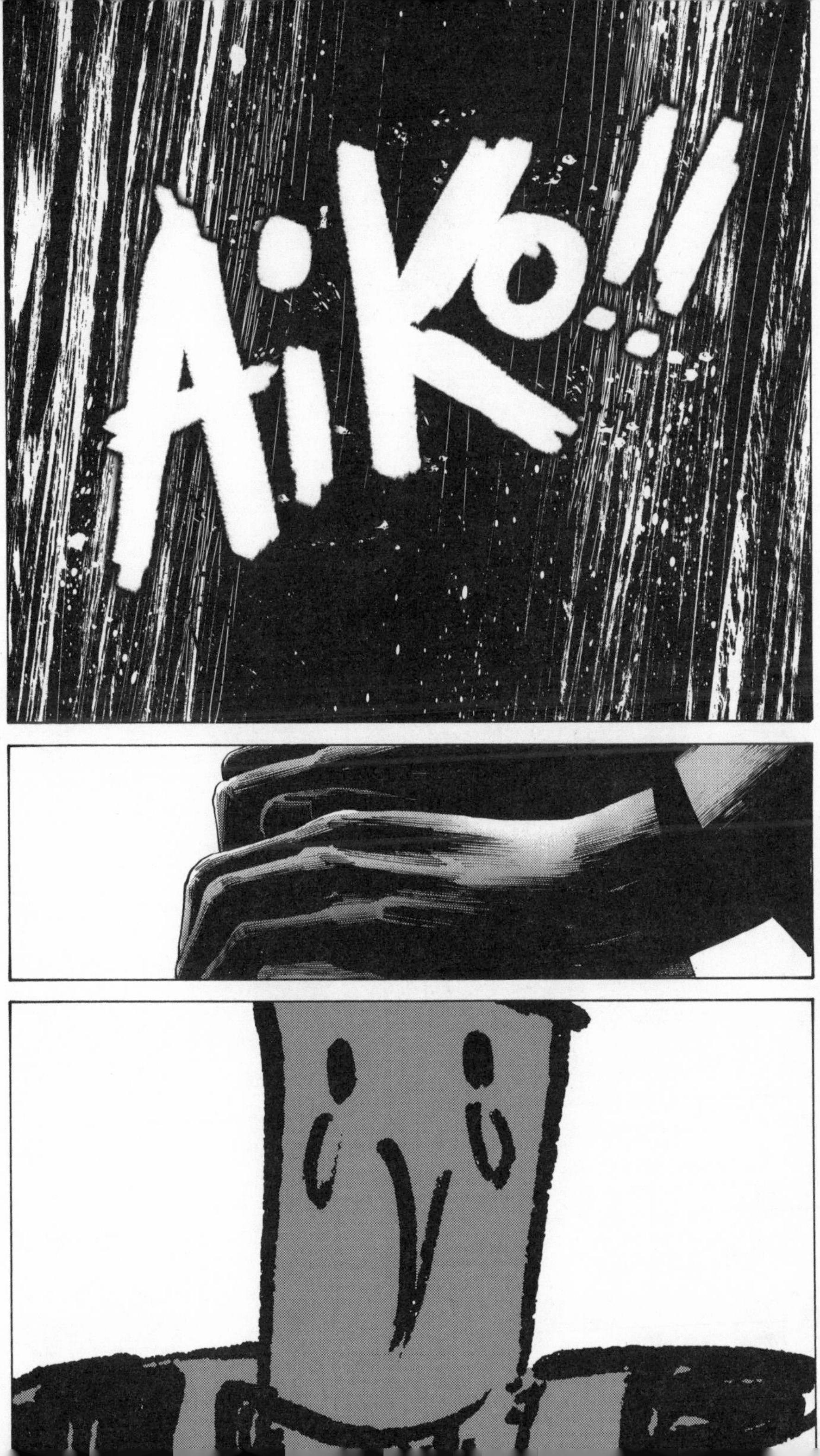
AiKo!!

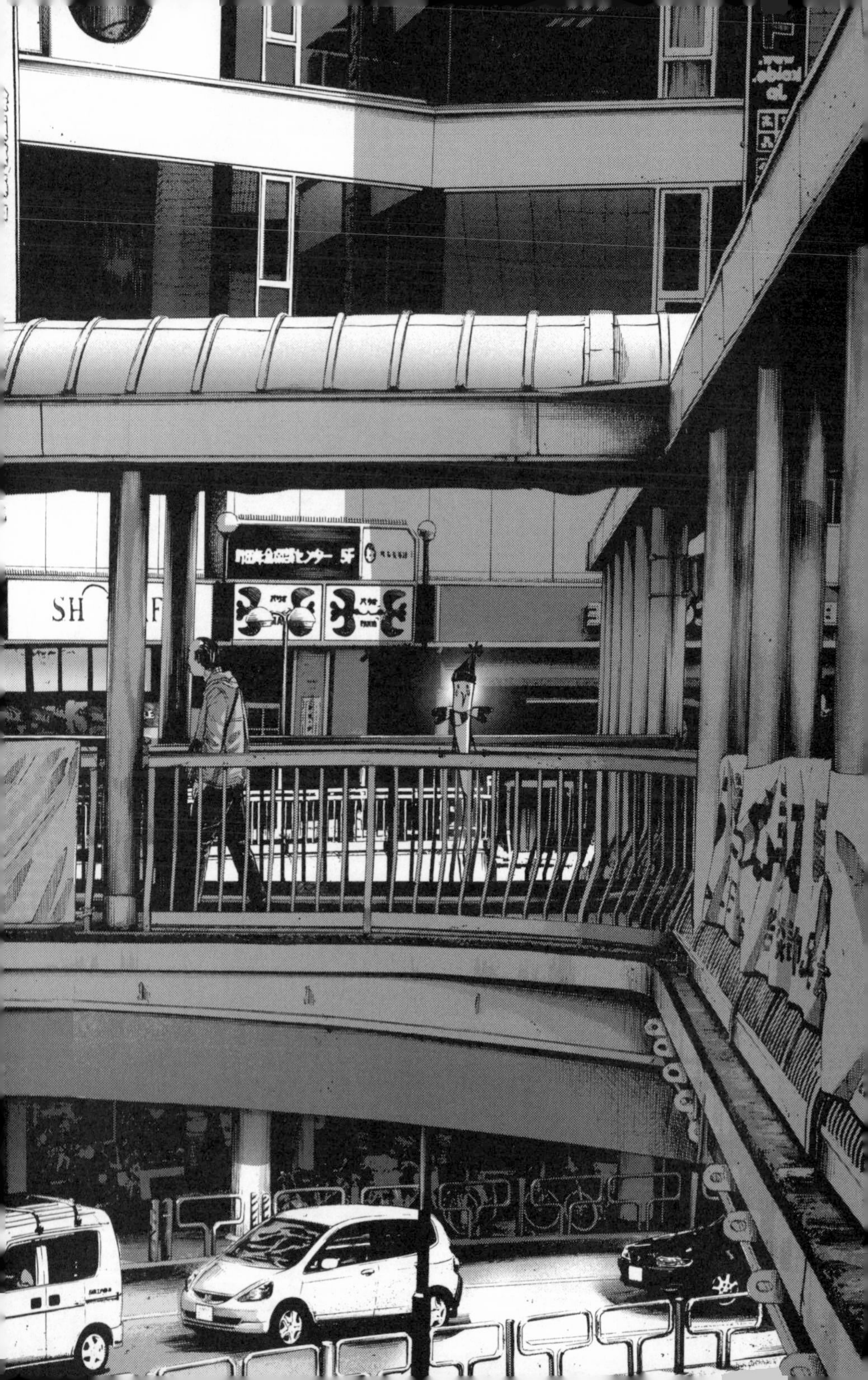

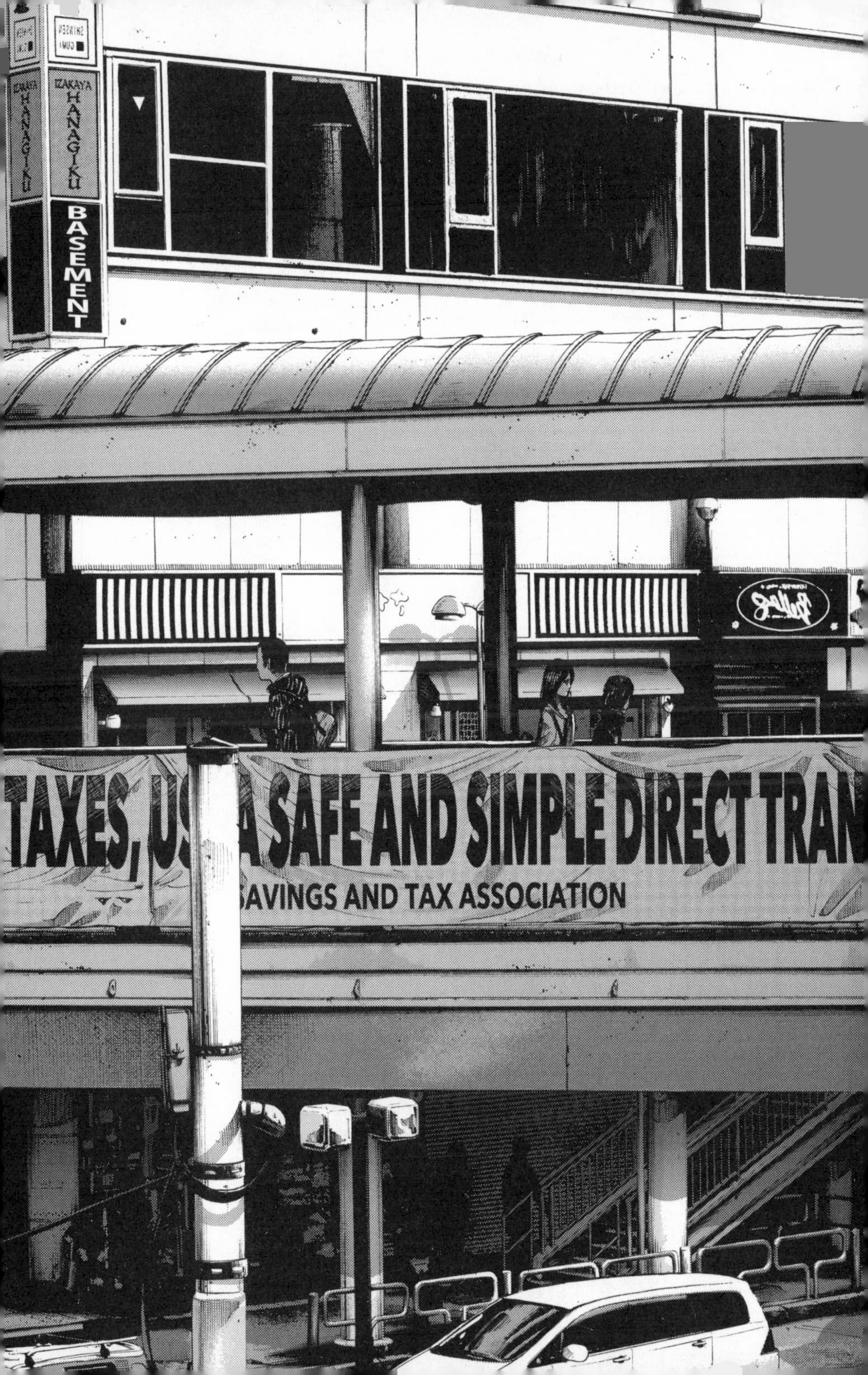
IZAKAYA HANAGIKU
BASEMENT
TAXES, US A SAFE AND SIMPLE DIRECT TRAN
SAVINGS AND TAX ASSOCIATION

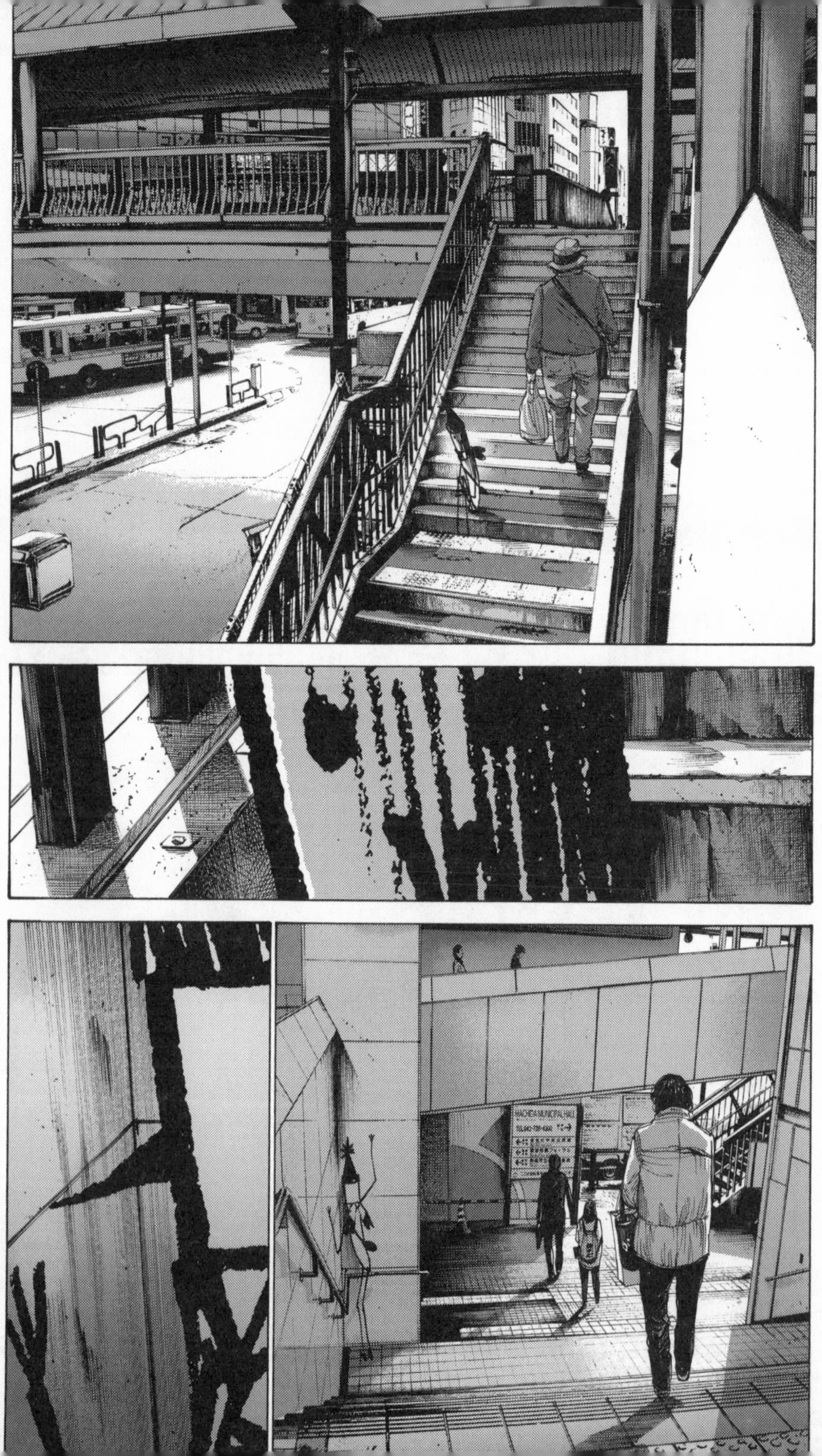
MACHIDA MUNICIPAL HALL

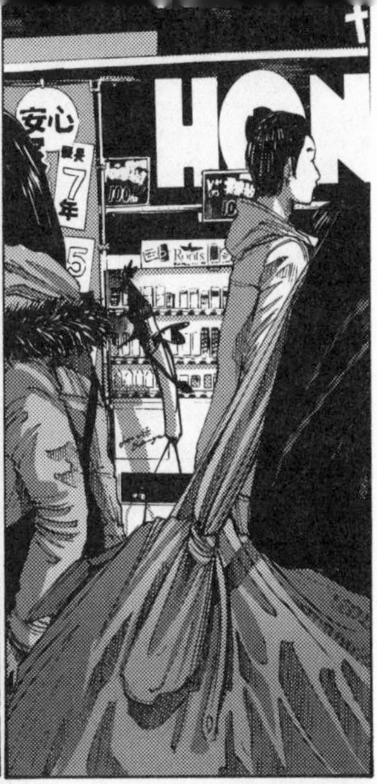
安心
7年
HON
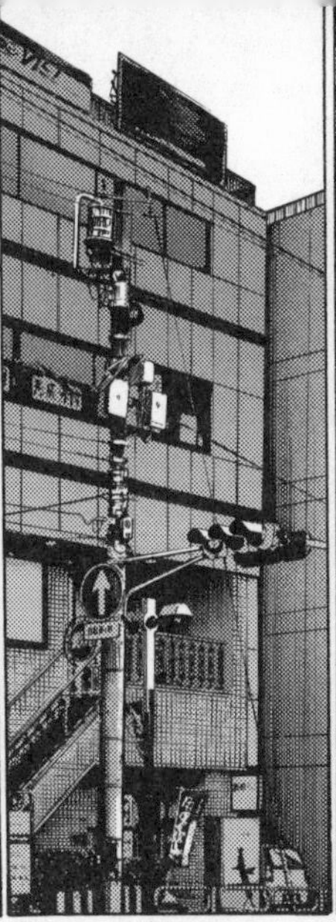
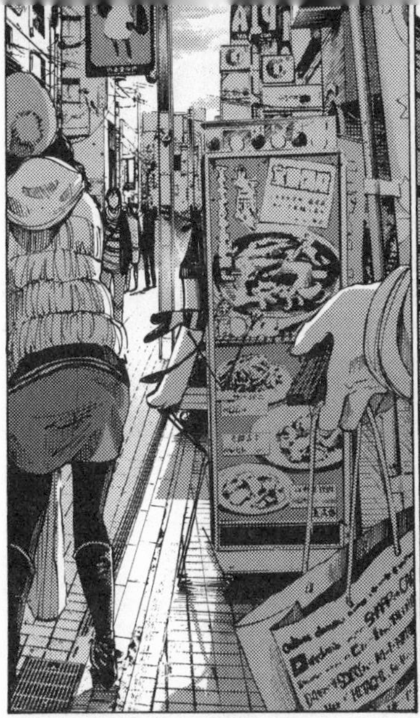
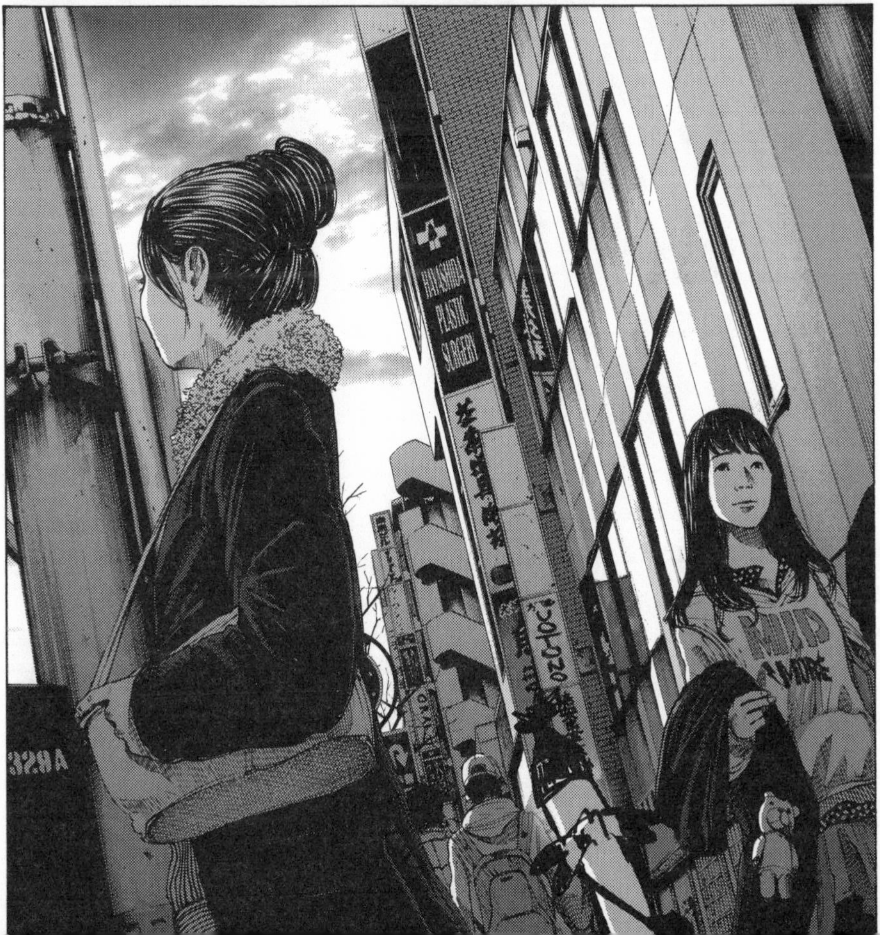
HAYASHIDA
PLASTIC
SURGERY

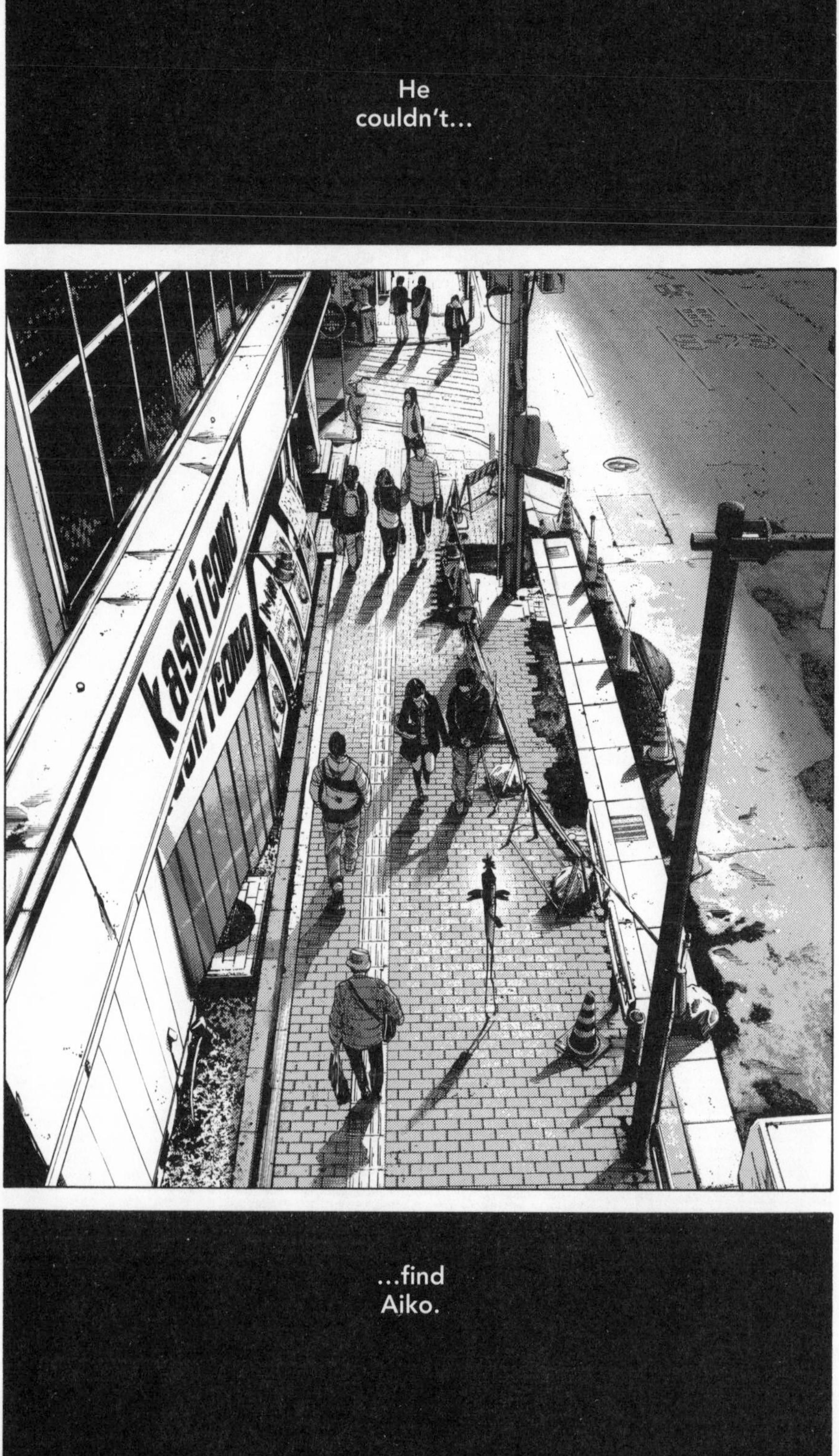
He couldn't...
kashicomo
...find Aiko.

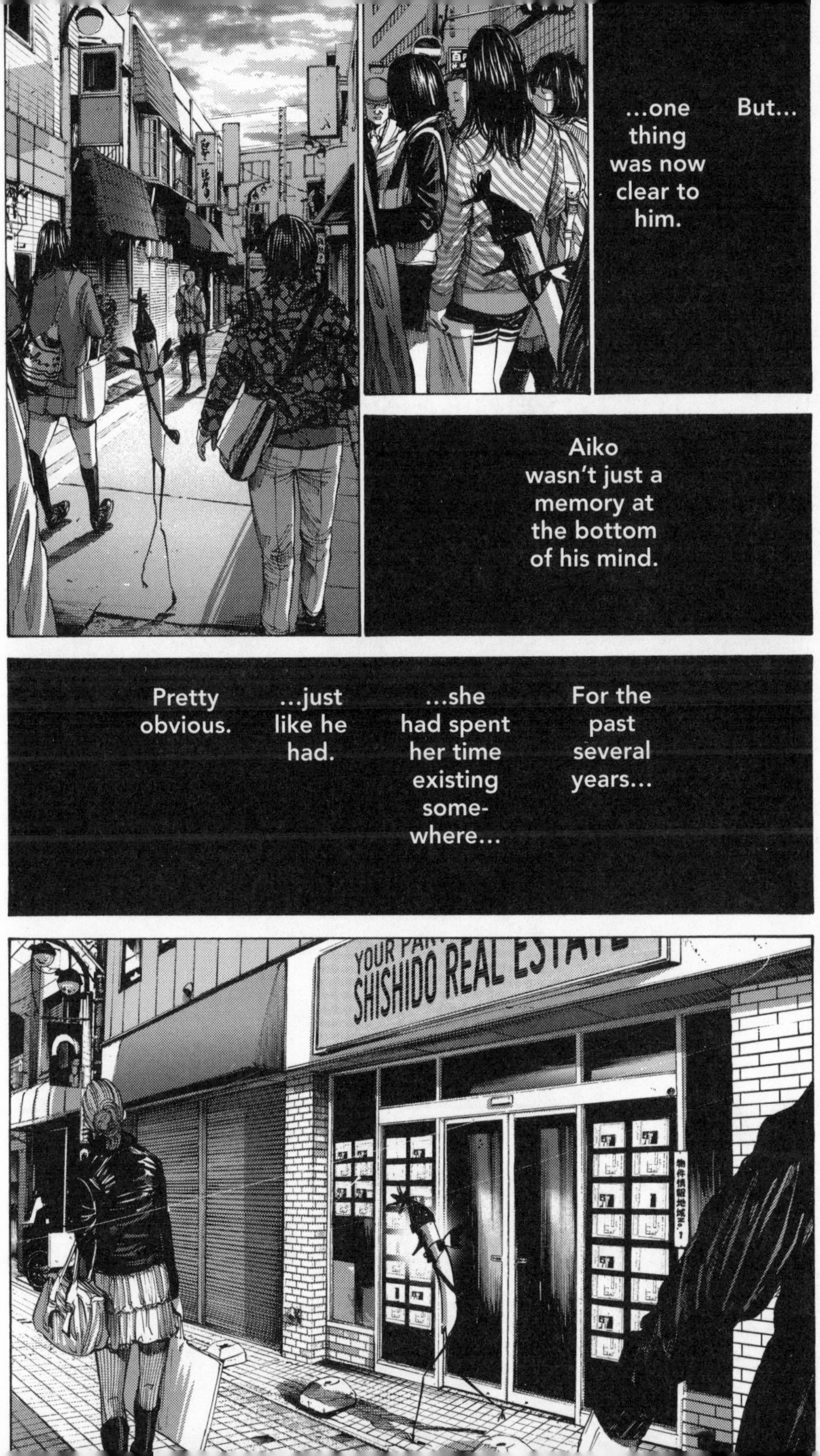
But...
...one thing was now clear to him.
Aiko wasn't just a memory at the bottom of his mind.
For the past several years...
...she had spent her time existing some-where...
...just like he had.
Pretty obvious.
SHISHIDO REAL ESTATE

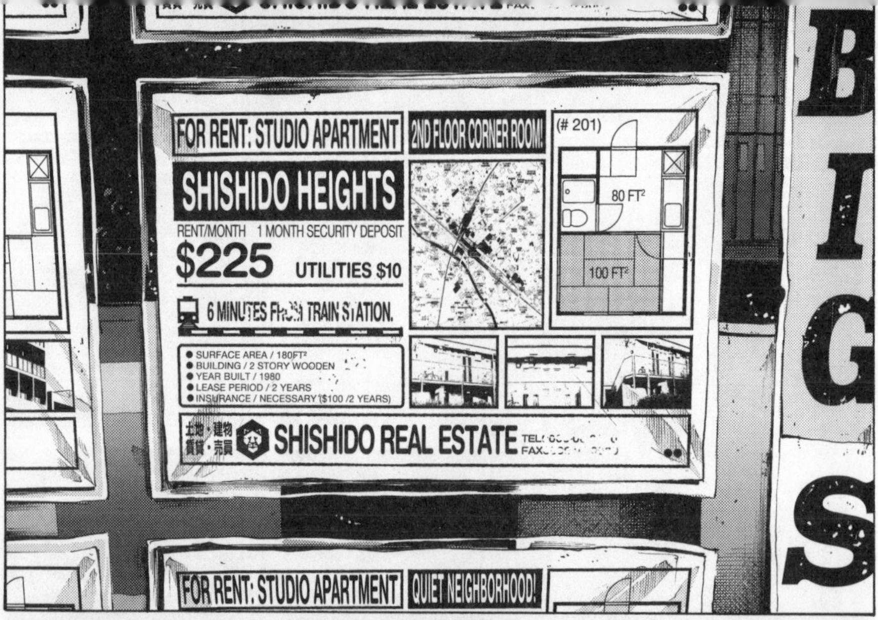
FOR RENT: STUDIO APARTMENT
2ND FLOOR CORNER ROOM!
(# 201)
SHISHIDO HEIGHTS
RENT/MONTH 1 MONTH SECURITY DEPOSIT
$225
UTILITIES $10
80 FT²
100 FT²
SURFACE AREA / 180FT²
BUILDING / 2 STORY WOODEN
YEAR BUILT / 1980
LEASE PERIOD / 2 YEARS
INSURANCE / NECESSARY ($100 /2 YEARS)
土地・建物
賃貸・売買
SHISHIDO REAL ESTATE
FOR RENT: STUDIO APARTMENT
QUIET NEIGHBORHOOD!

Aiko...

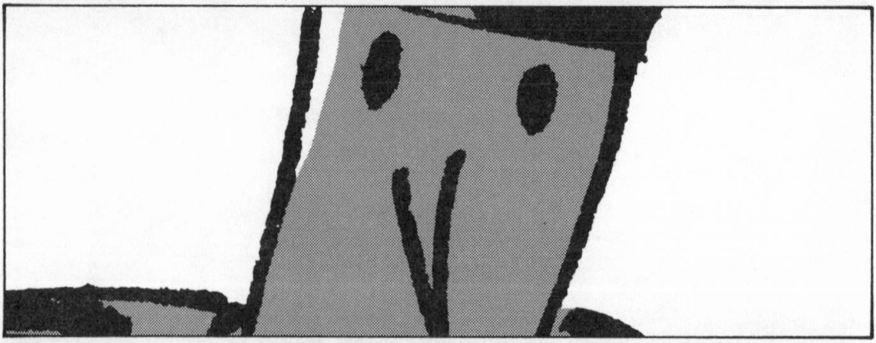

...must be a proper grown-up now...

(unlike someone else Punpun knew)

...and live somewhere in town.

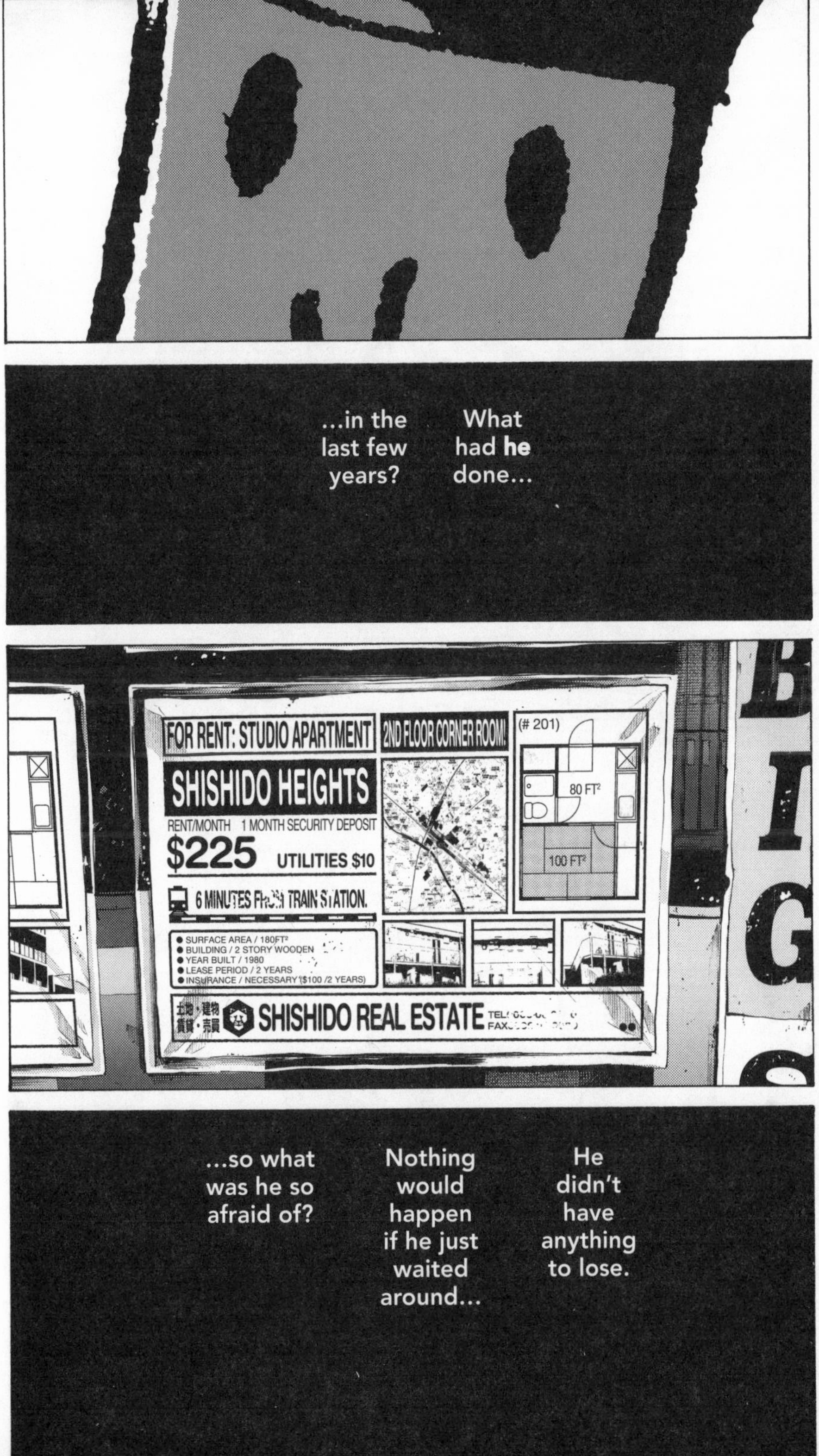
What had he done...
...in the last few years?
FOR RENT: STUDIO APARTMENT
SHISHIDO HEIGHTS
RENT/MONTH 1 MONTH SECURITY DEPOSIT
$225
UTILITIES $10
2ND FLOOR CORNER ROOM!
(# 201)
80 FT²
100 FT²
SURFACE AREA / 180FT²
BUILDING / 2 STORY WOODEN
YEAR BUILT / 1980
LEASE PERIOD / 2 YEARS
INSURANCE / NECESSARY ($100 /2 YEARS)
土地・建物
賃貸・売買
SHISHIDO REAL ESTATE
He didn't have anything to lose.
Nothing would happen if he just waited around...
...so what was he so afraid of?

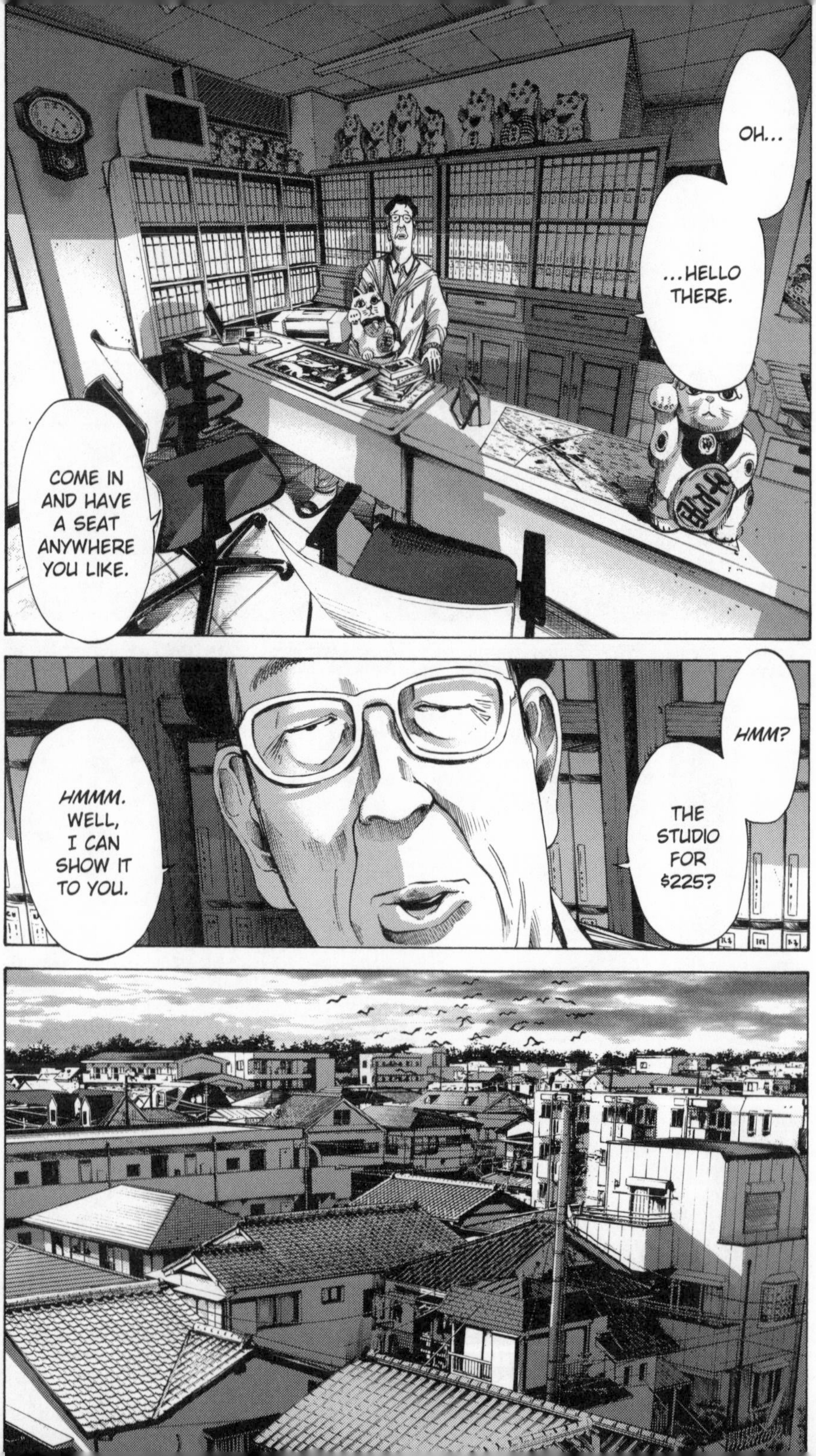
OH...
...HELLO THERE.
COME IN AND HAVE A SEAT ANYWHERE YOU LIKE.
HMM?
THE STUDIO FOR $225?
HMMM. WELL, I CAN SHOW IT TO YOU.

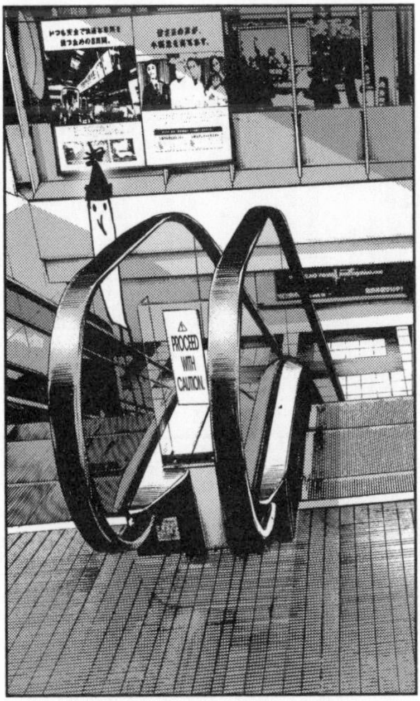
PROCEED
WITH
CAUTION.

Chapter 74

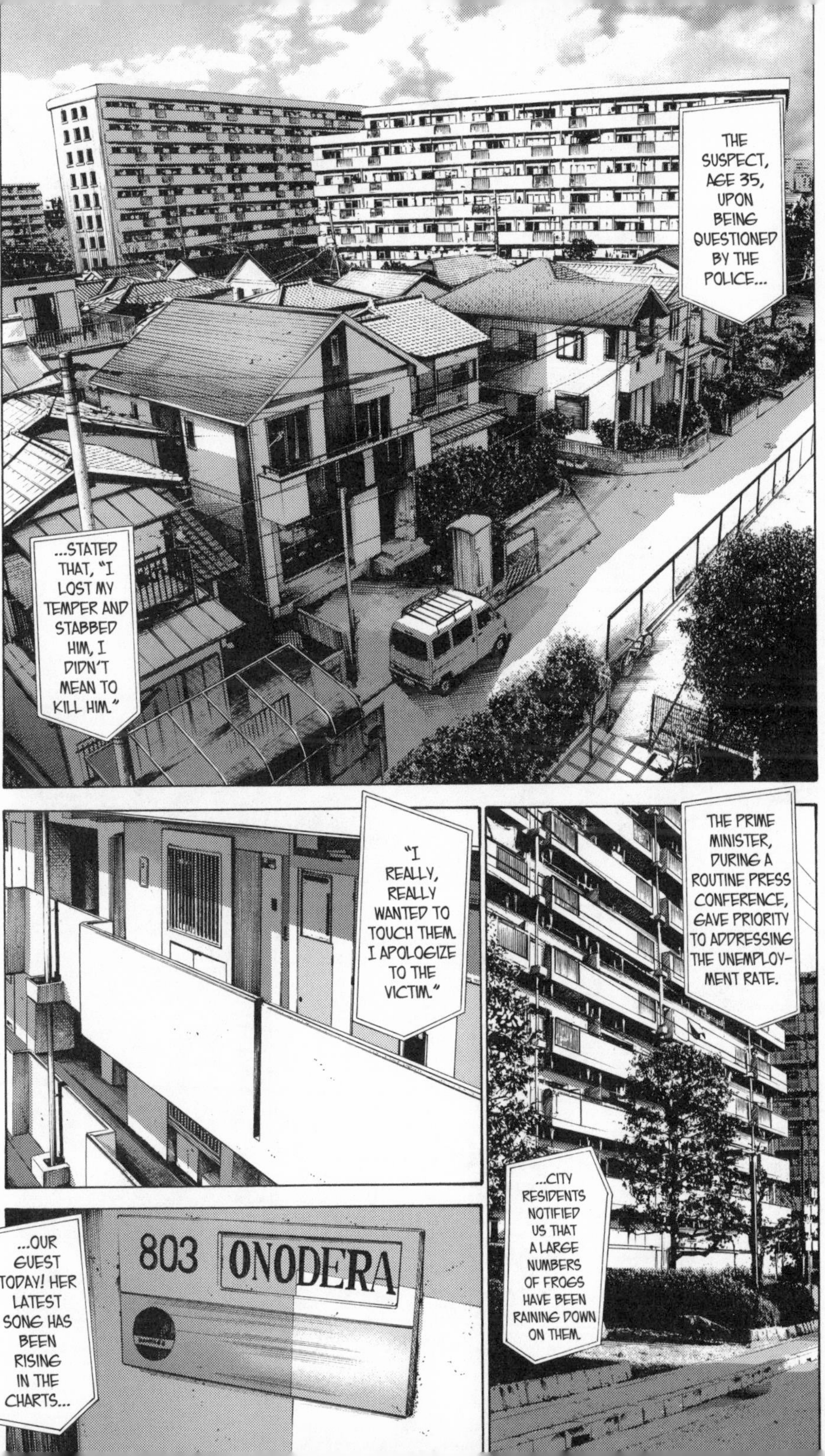
THE SUSPECT, AGE 35, UPON BEING QUESTIONED BY THE POLICE...
...STATED THAT, "I LOST MY TEMPER AND STABBED HIM, I DIDN'T MEAN TO KILL HIM."
THE PRIME MINISTER, DURING A ROUTINE PRESS CONFERENCE, GAVE PRIORITY TO ADDRESSING THE UNEMPLOYMENT RATE.
...CITY RESIDENTS NOTIFIED US THAT A LARGE NUMBERS OF FROGS HAVE BEEN RAINING DOWN ON THEM.
"I REALLY, REALLY WANTED TO TOUCH THEM. I APOLOGIZE TO THE VICTIM."
803 ONODERA
...OUR GUEST TODAY! HER LATEST SONG HAS BEEN RISING IN THE CHARTS...

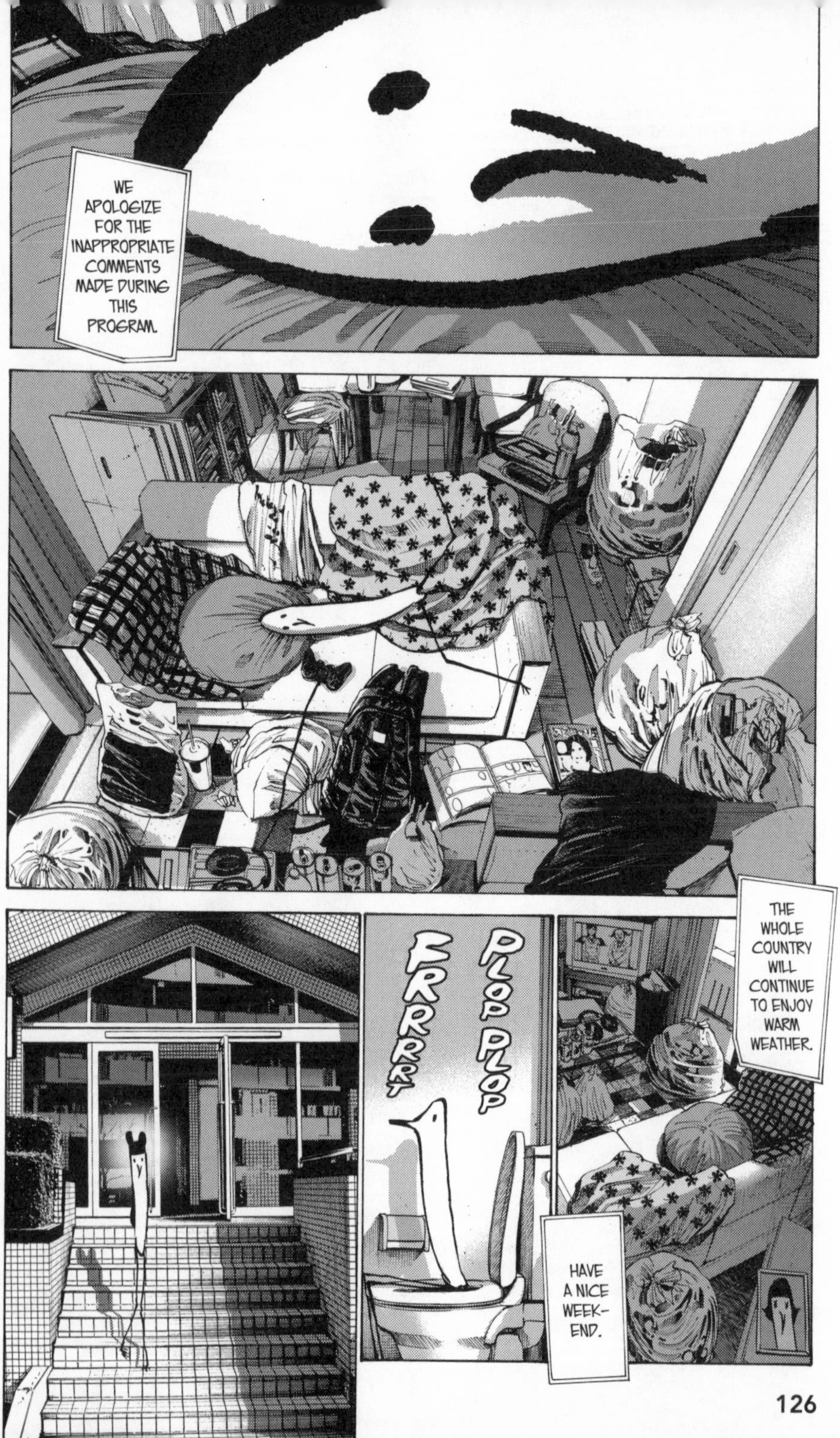
WE APOLOGIZE FOR THE INAPPROPRIATE COMMENTS MADE DURING THIS PROGRAM.
THE WHOLE COUNTRY WILL CONTINUE TO ENJOY WARM WEATHER.
HAVE A NICE WEEK-END.
PLOP PLOP
FRRRRT

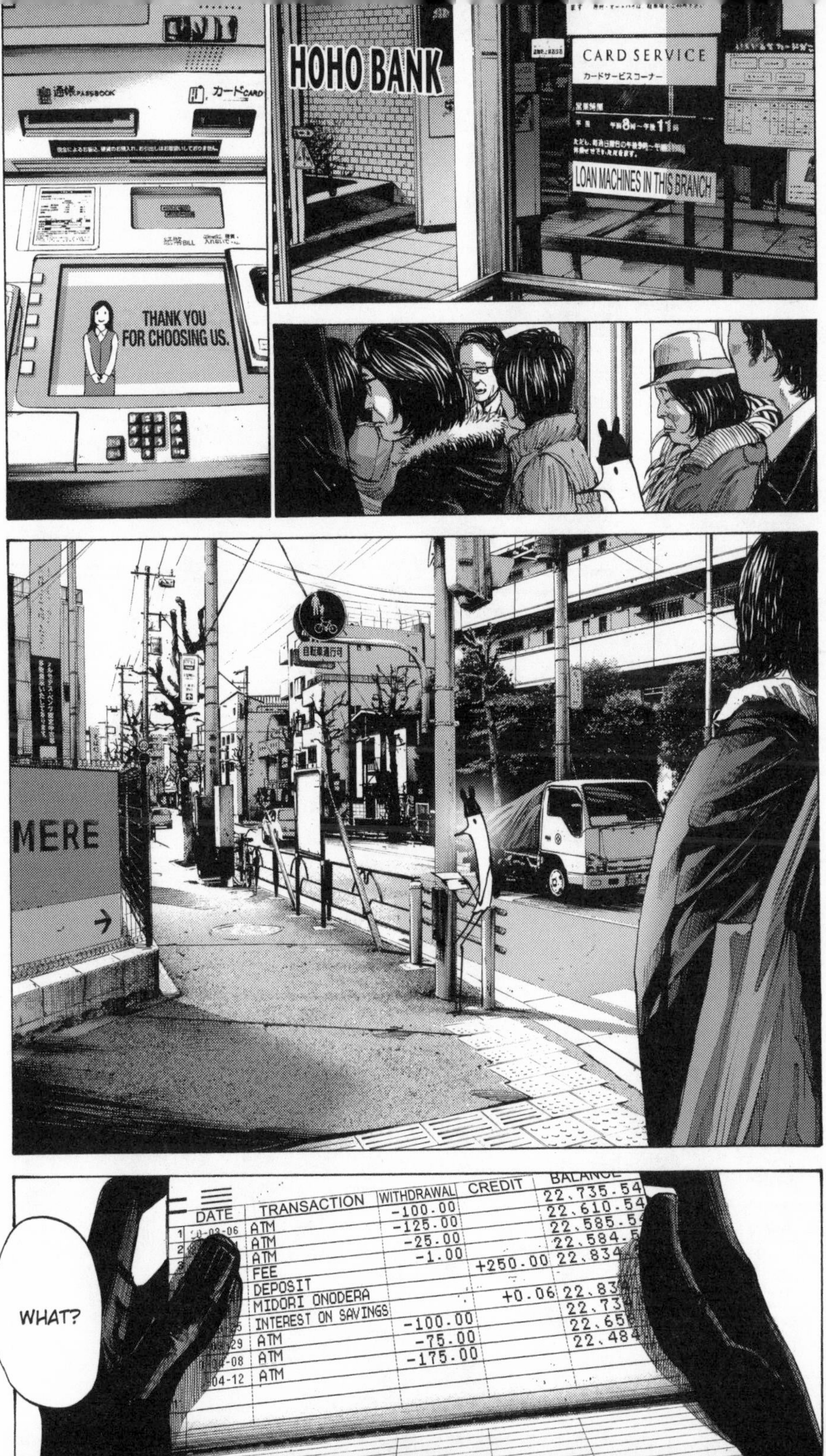
HOHO BANK
CARD SERVICE
カードサービスコーナー
LOAN MACHINES IN THIS BRANCH
通帳 PASSBOOK
カード CARD
THANK YOU FOR CHOOSING US.
自転車通行可
MERE
DATE
TRANSACTION
WITHDRAWAL
CREDIT
BALANCE
ATM -100.00 22,735.54
ATM -125.00 22,610.54
ATM -25.00 22,585.54
FEE -1.00
DEPOSIT MIDORI ONODERA +250.00
INTEREST ON SAVINGS +0.06
ATM -100.00
ATM -75.00
ATM -175.00
WHAT?

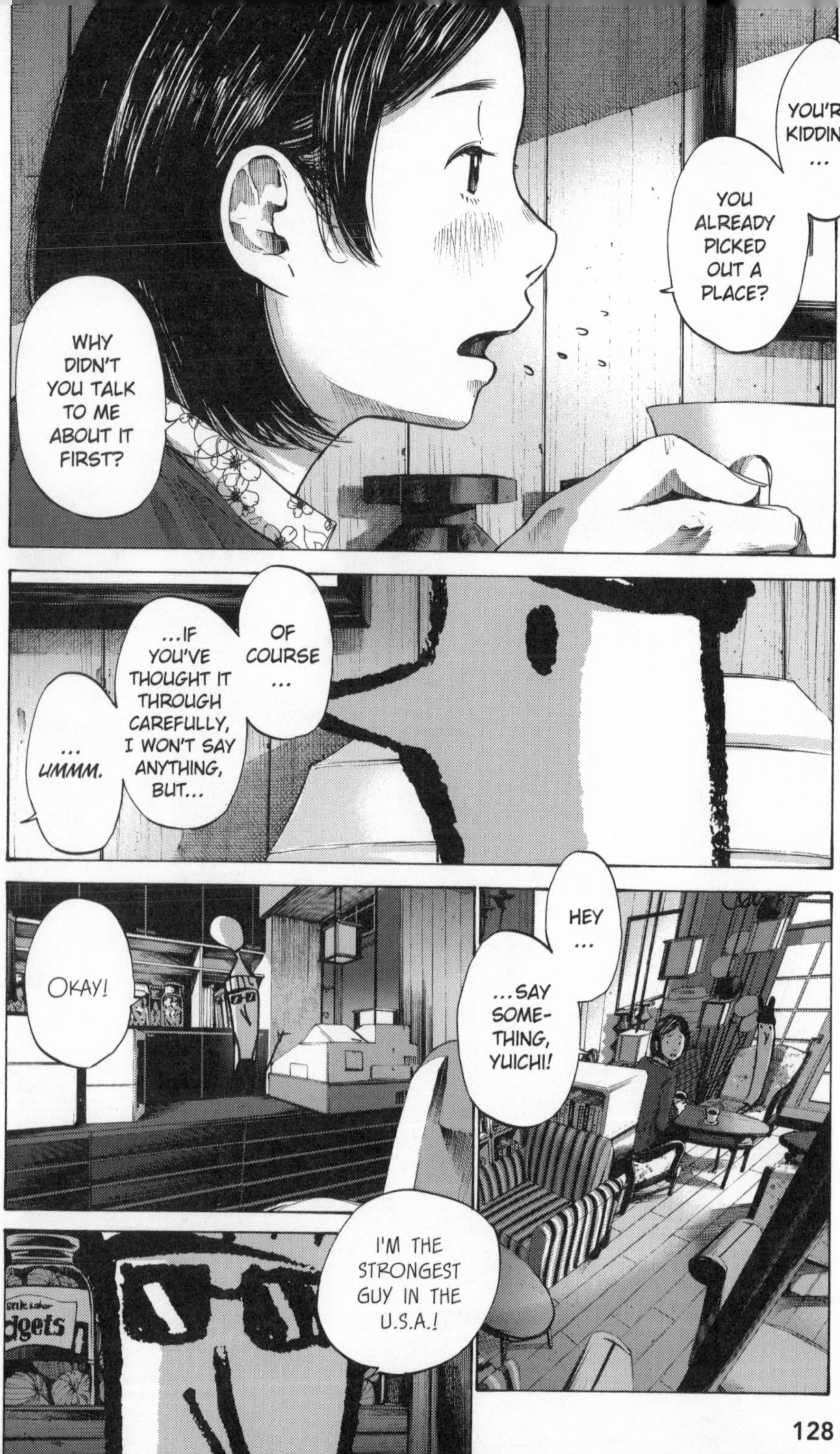
YOU'RE KIDDING ...
YOU ALREADY PICKED OUT A PLACE?
WHY DIDN'T YOU TALK TO ME ABOUT IT FIRST?
OF COURSE ...
...IF YOU'VE THOUGHT IT THROUGH CAREFULLY, I WON'T SAY ANYTHING, BUT...
... UMMM.
HEY ...
...SAY SOME-THING, YUICHI!
OKAY!
I'M THE STRONGEST GUY IN THE U.S.A.!

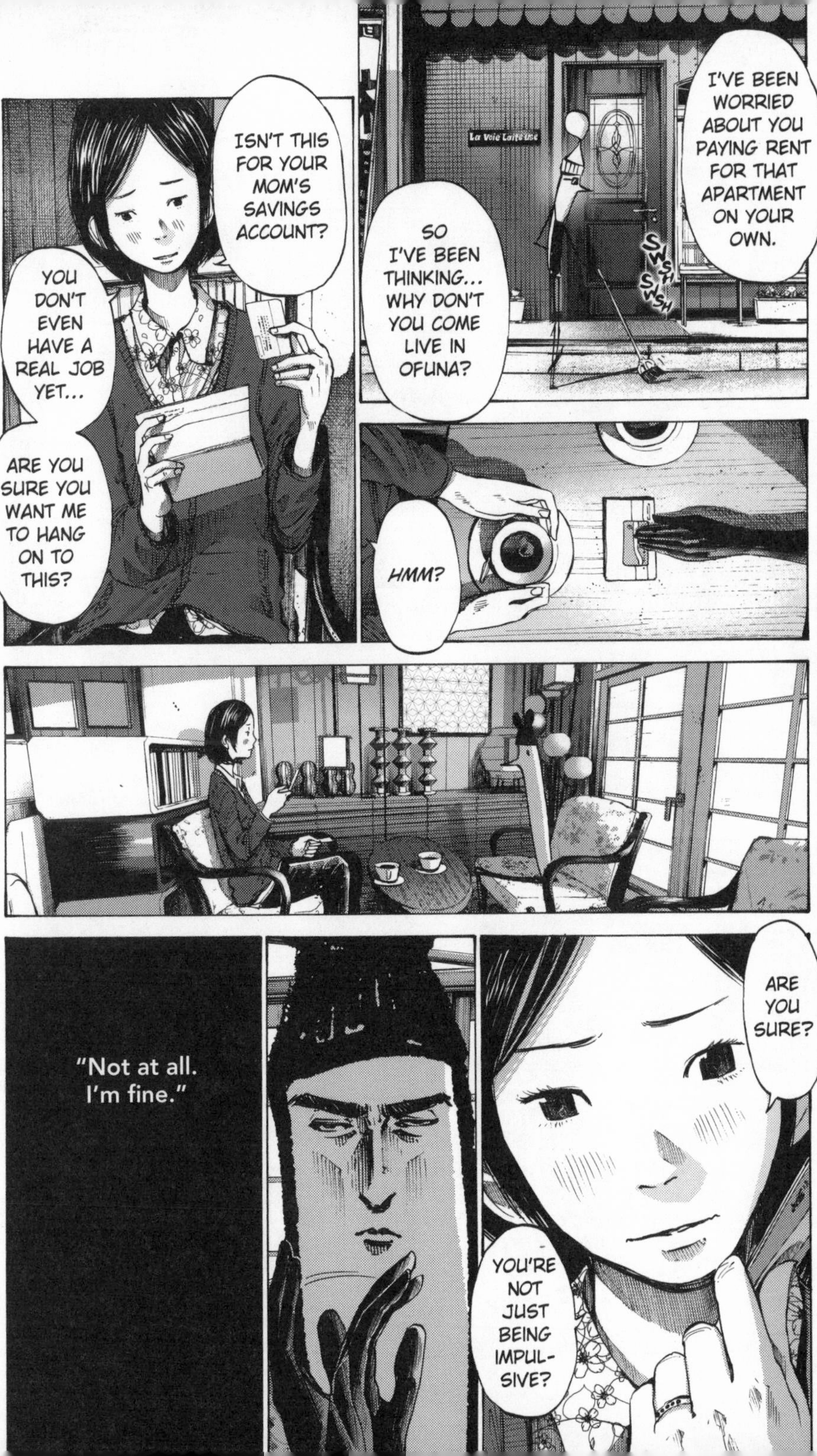
I'VE BEEN WORRIED ABOUT YOU PAYING RENT FOR THAT APARTMENT ON YOUR OWN.
SWSH SWSH
SO I'VE BEEN THINKING... WHY DON'T YOU COME LIVE IN OFUNA?
HMM?
ISN'T THIS FOR YOUR MOM'S SAVINGS ACCOUNT?
YOU DON'T EVEN HAVE A REAL JOB YET...
ARE YOU SURE YOU WANT ME TO HANG ON TO THIS?
ARE YOU SURE?
YOU'RE NOT JUST BEING IMPUL-SIVE?
"Not at all. I'm fine."

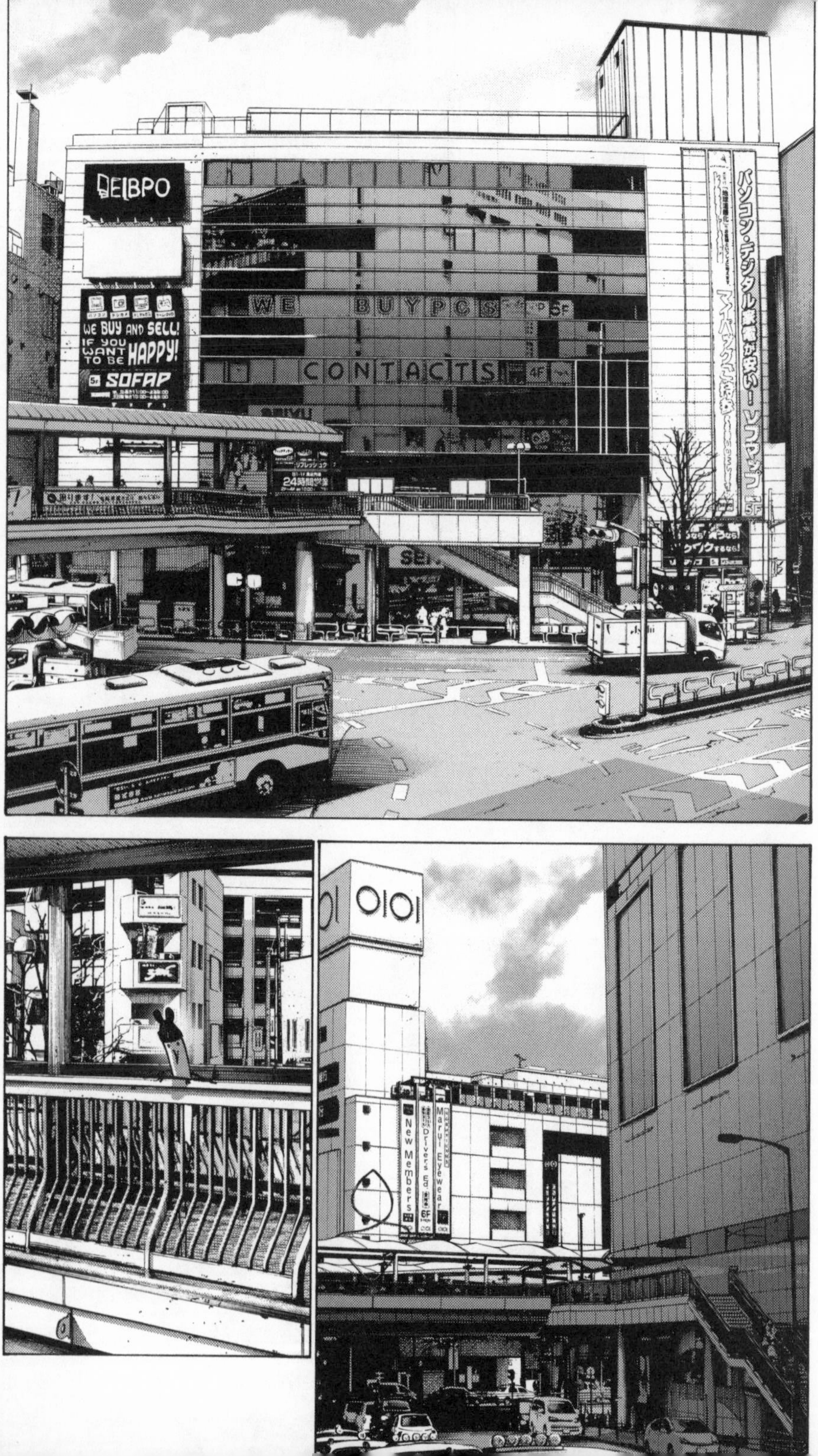
DELBPO
WE BUY AND SELL!
IF YOU WANT TO BE HAPPY!
5F SOFAP
WE BUYPCS 5F
CONTACTS 4F
パソコン・デジタル家電が安い！ソフマップ
5F
24時間営業
リフレッシュ
OIOI
New Members
Driver's Ed.
6F
Marui Eyewear

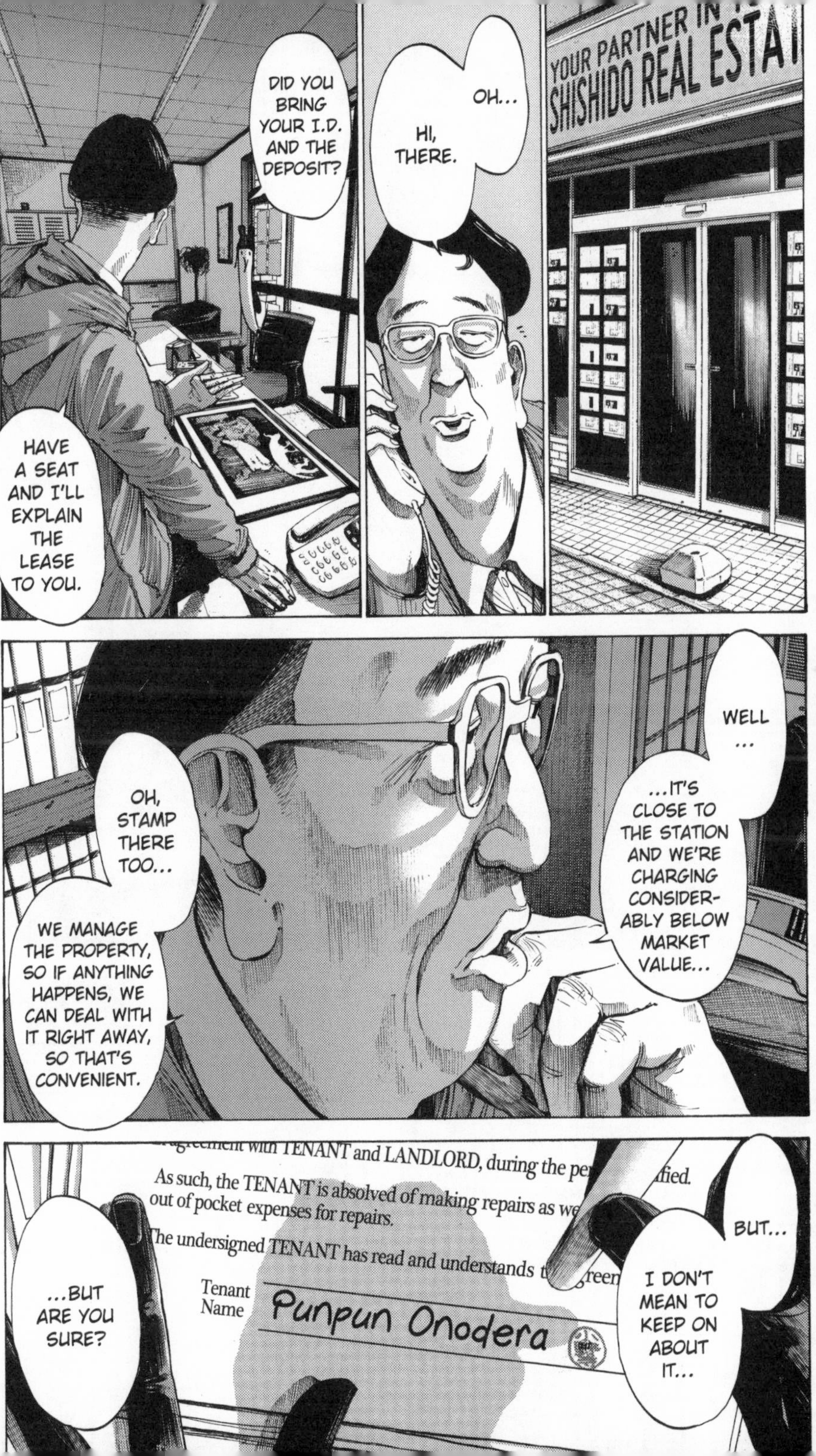
YOUR PARTNER IN
SHISHIDO REAL ESTA
OH...
HI, THERE.
DID YOU BRING YOUR I.D. AND THE DEPOSIT?
HAVE A SEAT AND I'LL EXPLAIN THE LEASE TO YOU.
WELL...
...IT'S CLOSE TO THE STATION AND WE'RE CHARGING CONSIDER-ABLY BELOW MARKET VALUE...
OH, STAMP THERE TOO...
WE MANAGE THE PROPERTY, SO IF ANYTHING HAPPENS, WE CAN DEAL WITH IT RIGHT AWAY, SO THAT'S CONVENIENT.
agreement with TENANT and LANDLORD, during the pe ified.
As such, the TENANT is absolved of making repairs as we
out of pocket expenses for repairs.
The undersigned TENANT has read and understands t green
Tenant Name
Punpun Onodera
BUT...
I DON'T MEAN TO KEEP ON ABOUT IT...
...BUT ARE YOU SURE?

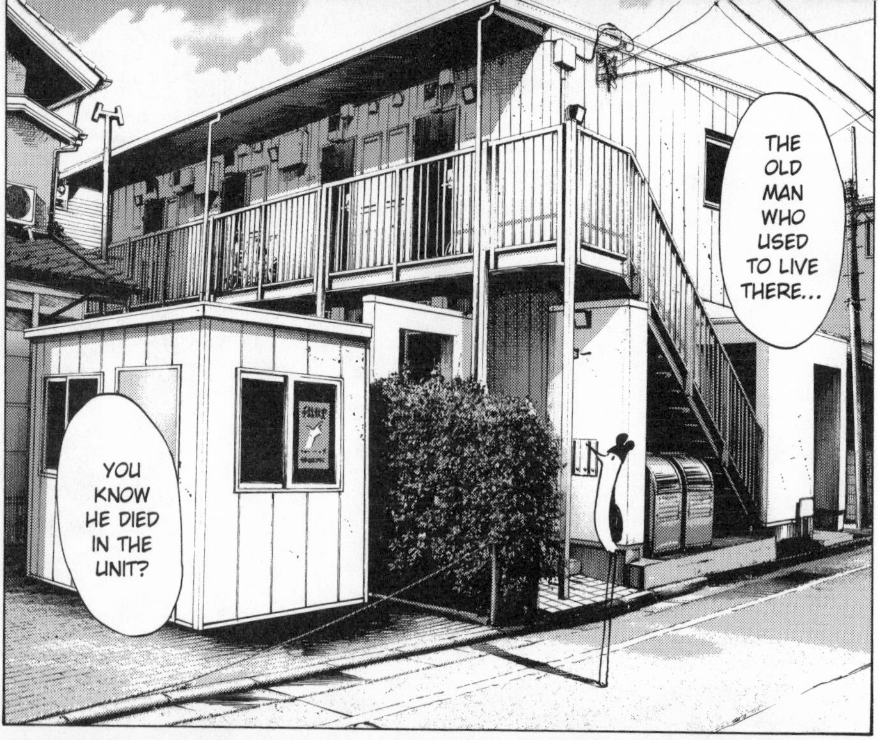
THE OLD MAN WHO USED TO LIVE THERE...
YOU KNOW HE DIED IN THE UNIT?

That was the first time Punpun had signed a contract.

It was such a simple thing, but it made him feel a little more grown-up.

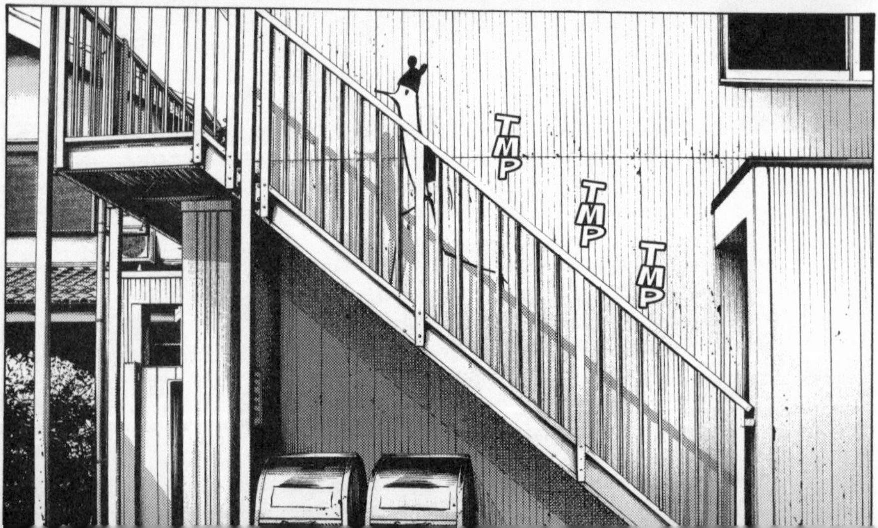
TMP
TMP
TMP

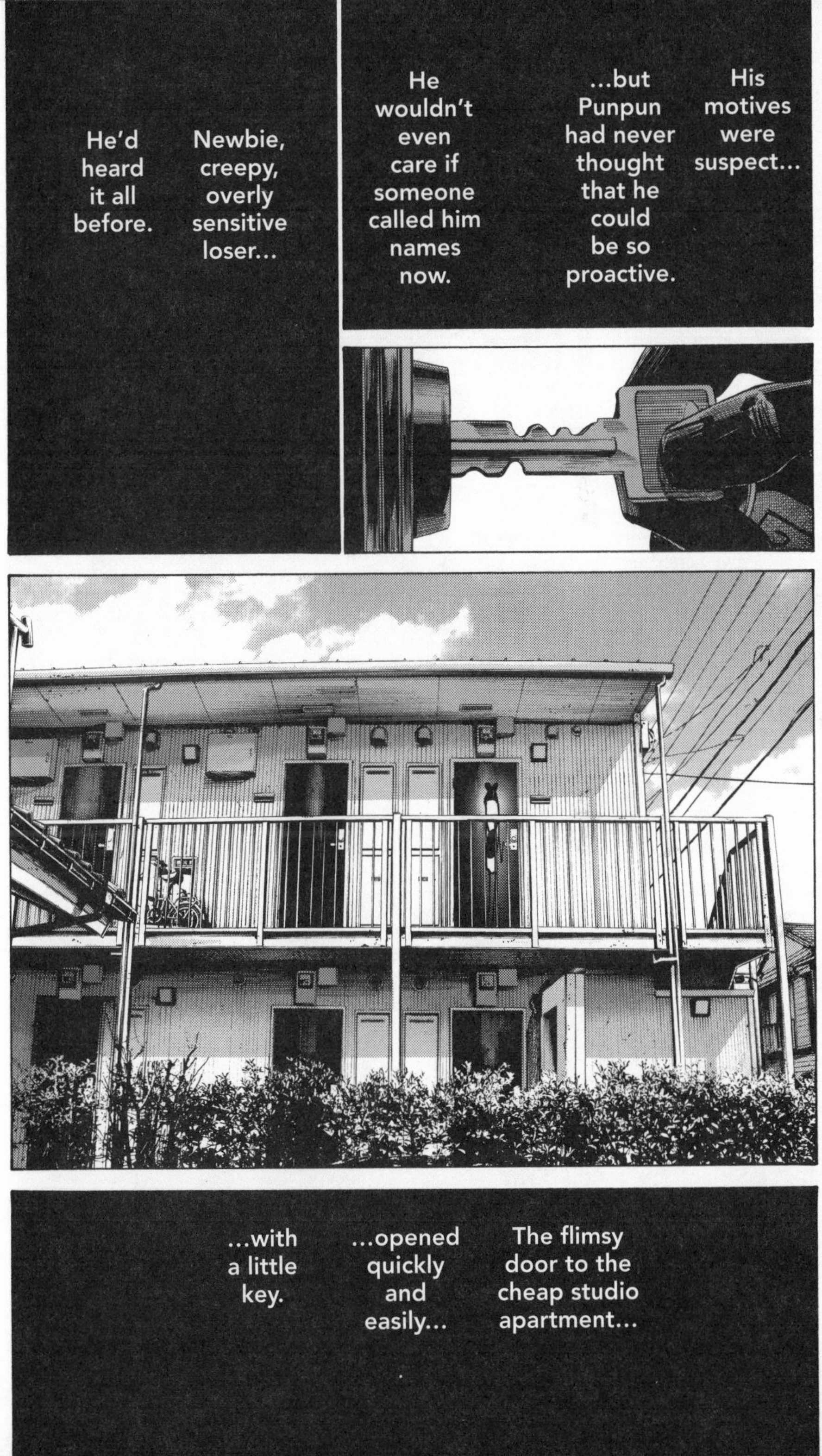
His motives were suspect...
...but Punpun had never thought that he could be so proactive.
He wouldn't even care if someone called him names now.
Newbie, creepy, overly sensitive loser...
He'd heard it all before.
The flimsy door to the cheap studio apartment...
...opened quickly and easily...
...with a little key.

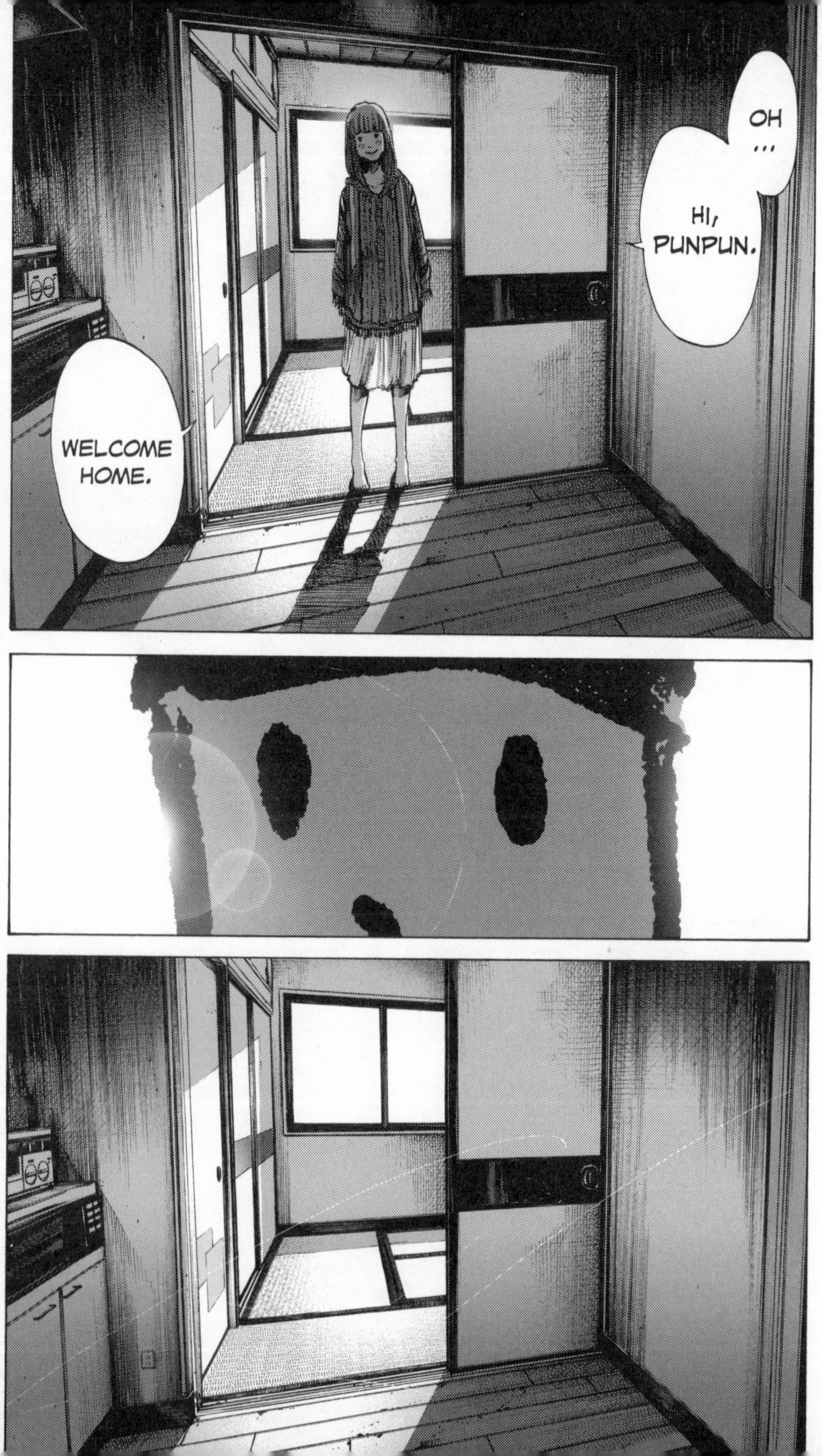
OH...
HI, PUNPUN.
WELCOME HOME.

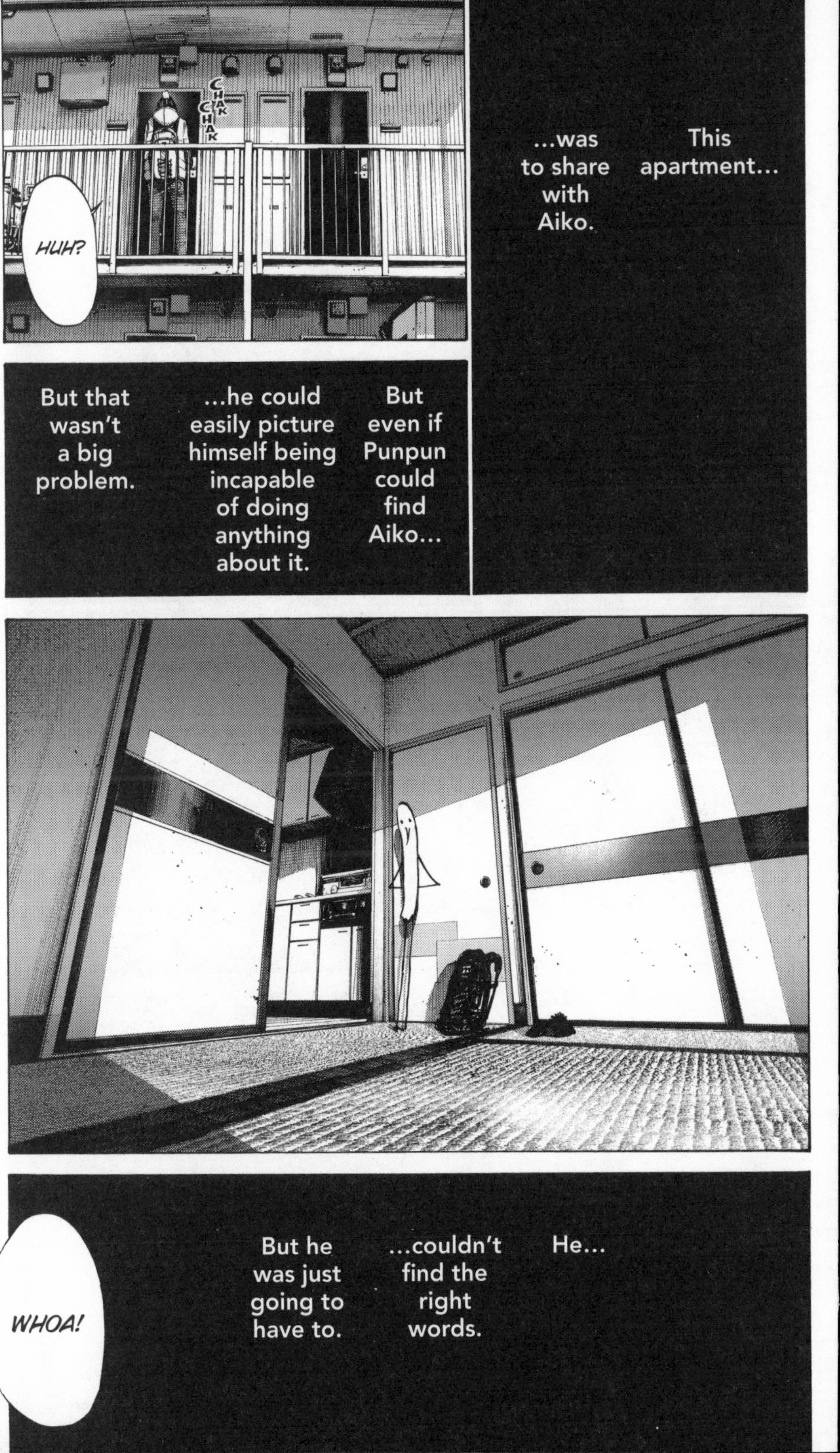
This apartment...
...was to share with Aiko.
CHAK CHAK
HUH?
But even if Punpun could find Aiko...
...he could easily picture himself being incapable of doing anything about it.
But that wasn't a big problem.
He...
...couldn't find the right words.
But he was just going to have to.
WHOA!

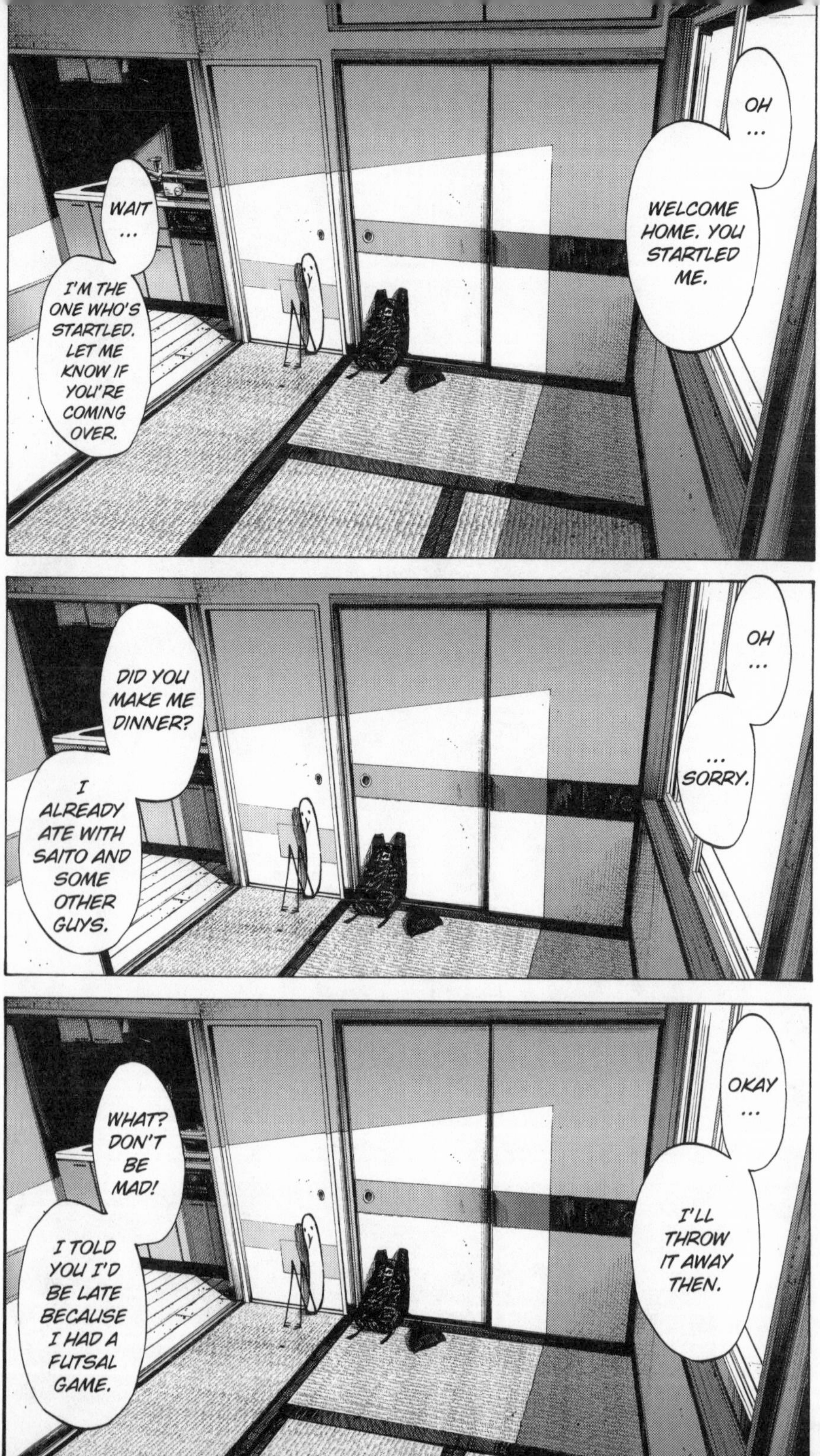
OH ...
WELCOME HOME. YOU STARTLED ME.
WAIT ...
I'M THE ONE WHO'S STARTLED. LET ME KNOW IF YOU'RE COMING OVER.
OH ...
... SORRY.
DID YOU MAKE ME DINNER?
I ALREADY ATE WITH SAITO AND SOME OTHER GUYS.
OKAY ...
I'LL THROW IT AWAY THEN.
WHAT? DON'T BE MAD!
I TOLD YOU I'D BE LATE BECAUSE I HAD A FUTSAL GAME.

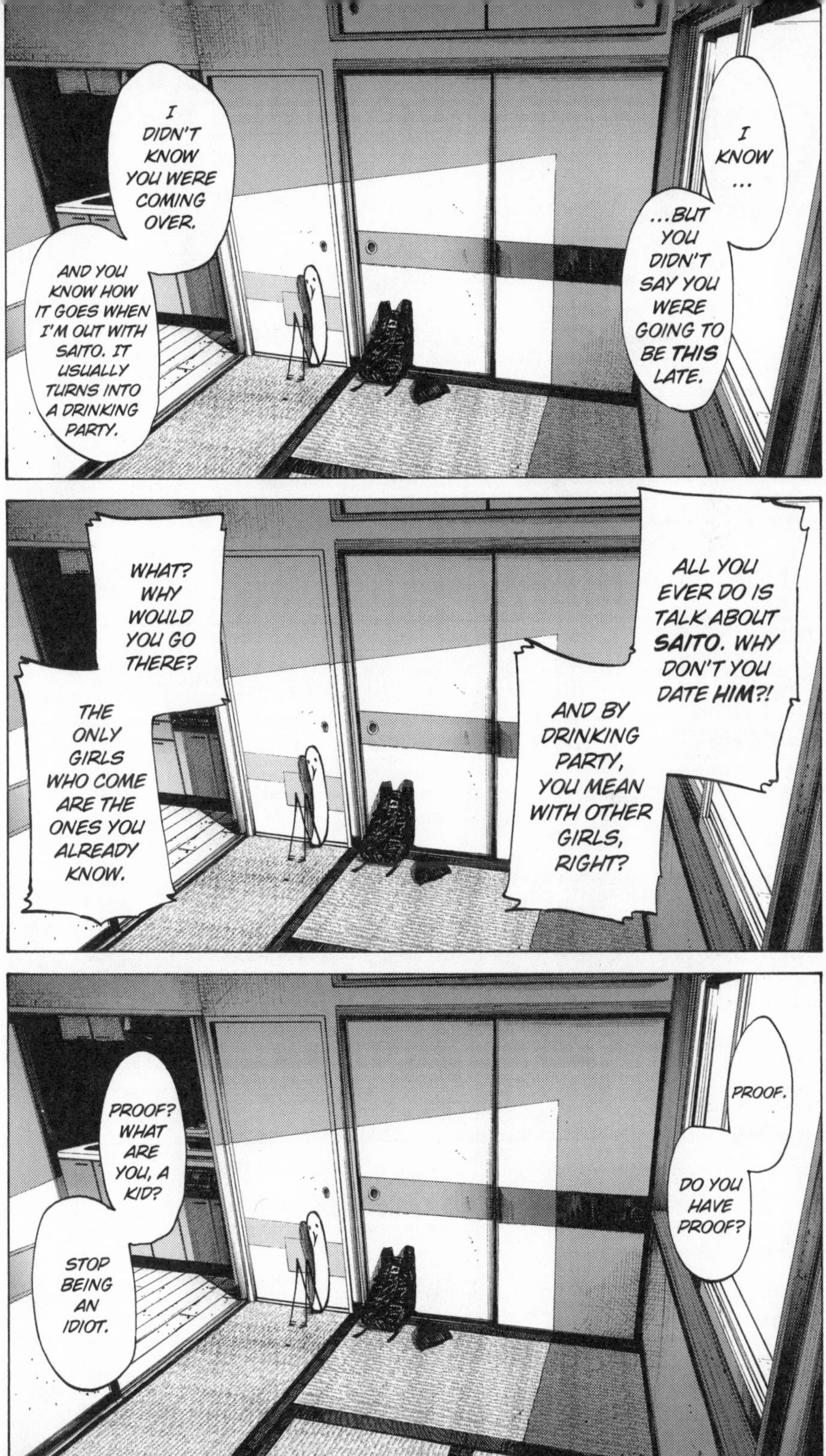
I KNOW...
...BUT YOU DIDN'T SAY YOU WERE GOING TO BE THIS LATE.
I DIDN'T KNOW YOU WERE COMING OVER.
AND YOU KNOW HOW IT GOES WHEN I'M OUT WITH SAITO. IT USUALLY TURNS INTO A DRINKING PARTY.
ALL YOU EVER DO IS TALK ABOUT SAITO. WHY DON'T YOU DATE HIM?!
AND BY DRINKING PARTY, YOU MEAN WITH OTHER GIRLS, RIGHT?
WHAT? WHY WOULD YOU GO THERE?
THE ONLY GIRLS WHO COME ARE THE ONES YOU ALREADY KNOW.
PROOF.
DO YOU HAVE PROOF?
PROOF? WHAT ARE YOU, A KID?
STOP BEING AN IDIOT.

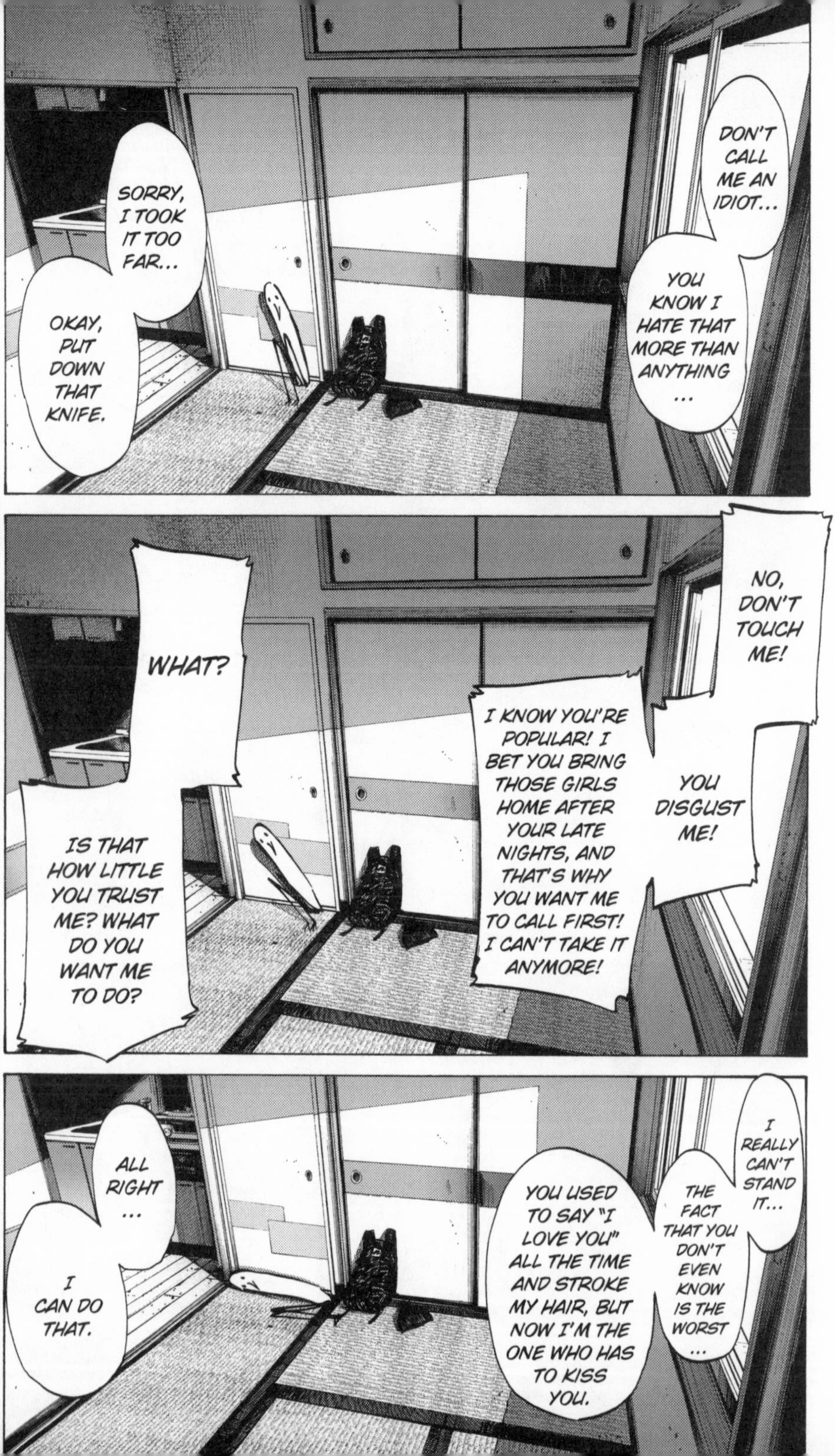
DON'T CALL ME AN IDIOT...
YOU KNOW I HATE THAT MORE THAN ANYTHING ...
SORRY, I TOOK IT TOO FAR...
OKAY, PUT DOWN THAT KNIFE.
NO, DON'T TOUCH ME!
YOU DISGUST ME!
I KNOW YOU'RE POPULAR! I BET YOU BRING THOSE GIRLS HOME AFTER YOUR LATE NIGHTS, AND THAT'S WHY YOU WANT ME TO CALL FIRST! I CAN'T TAKE IT ANYMORE!
WHAT?
IS THAT HOW LITTLE YOU TRUST ME? WHAT DO YOU WANT ME TO DO?
I REALLY CAN'T STAND IT...
THE FACT THAT YOU DON'T EVEN KNOW IS THE WORST ...
YOU USED TO SAY "I LOVE YOU" ALL THE TIME AND STROKE MY HAIR, BUT NOW I'M THE ONE WHO HAS TO KISS YOU.
ALL RIGHT ...
I CAN DO THAT.

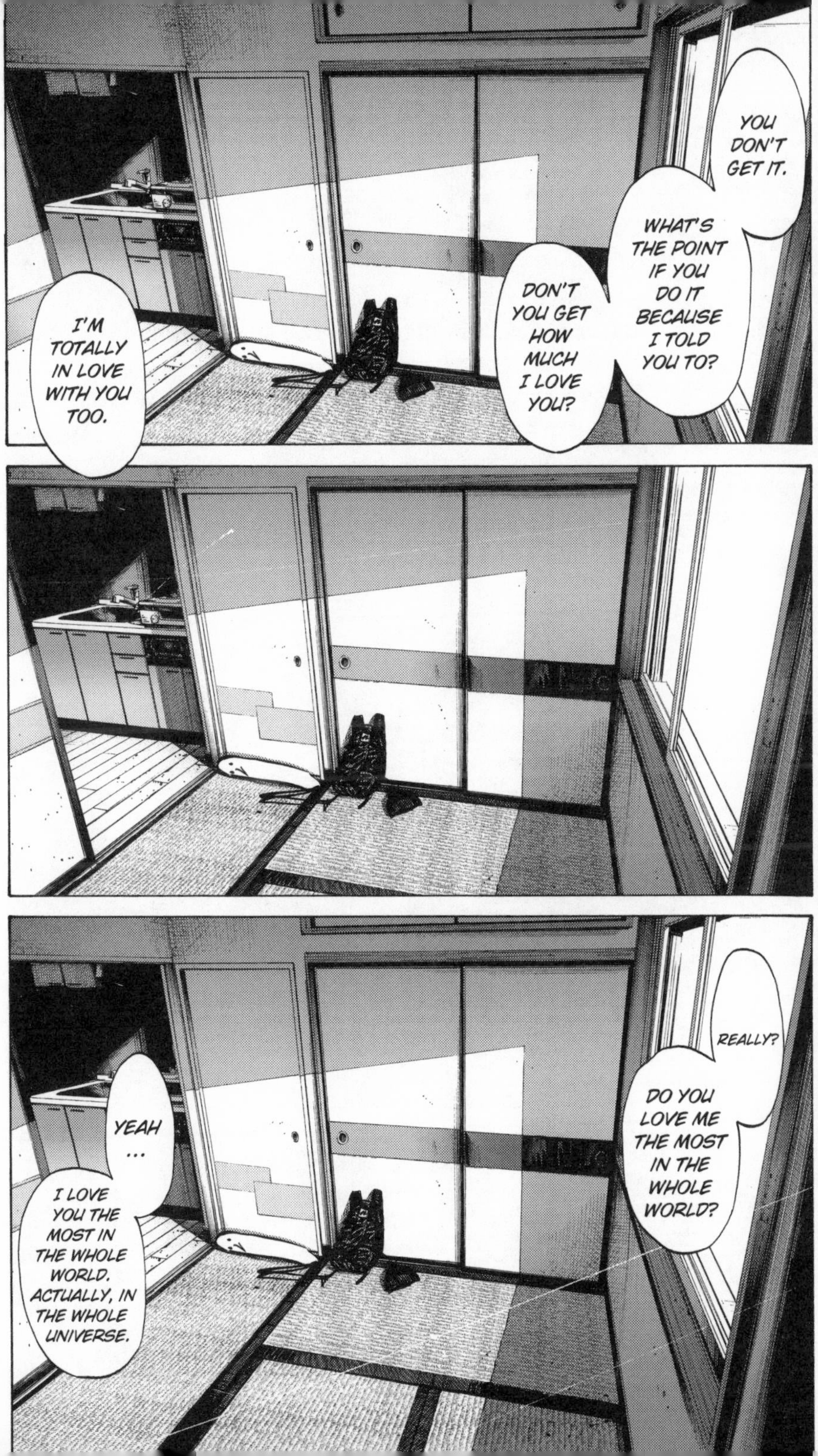
YOU DON'T GET IT.
WHAT'S THE POINT IF YOU DO IT BECAUSE I TOLD YOU TO?
DON'T YOU GET HOW MUCH I LOVE YOU?
I'M TOTALLY IN LOVE WITH YOU TOO.
REALLY?
DO YOU LOVE ME THE MOST IN THE WHOLE WORLD?
YEAH ...
I LOVE YOU THE MOST IN THE WHOLE WORLD. ACTUALLY, IN THE WHOLE UNIVERSE.

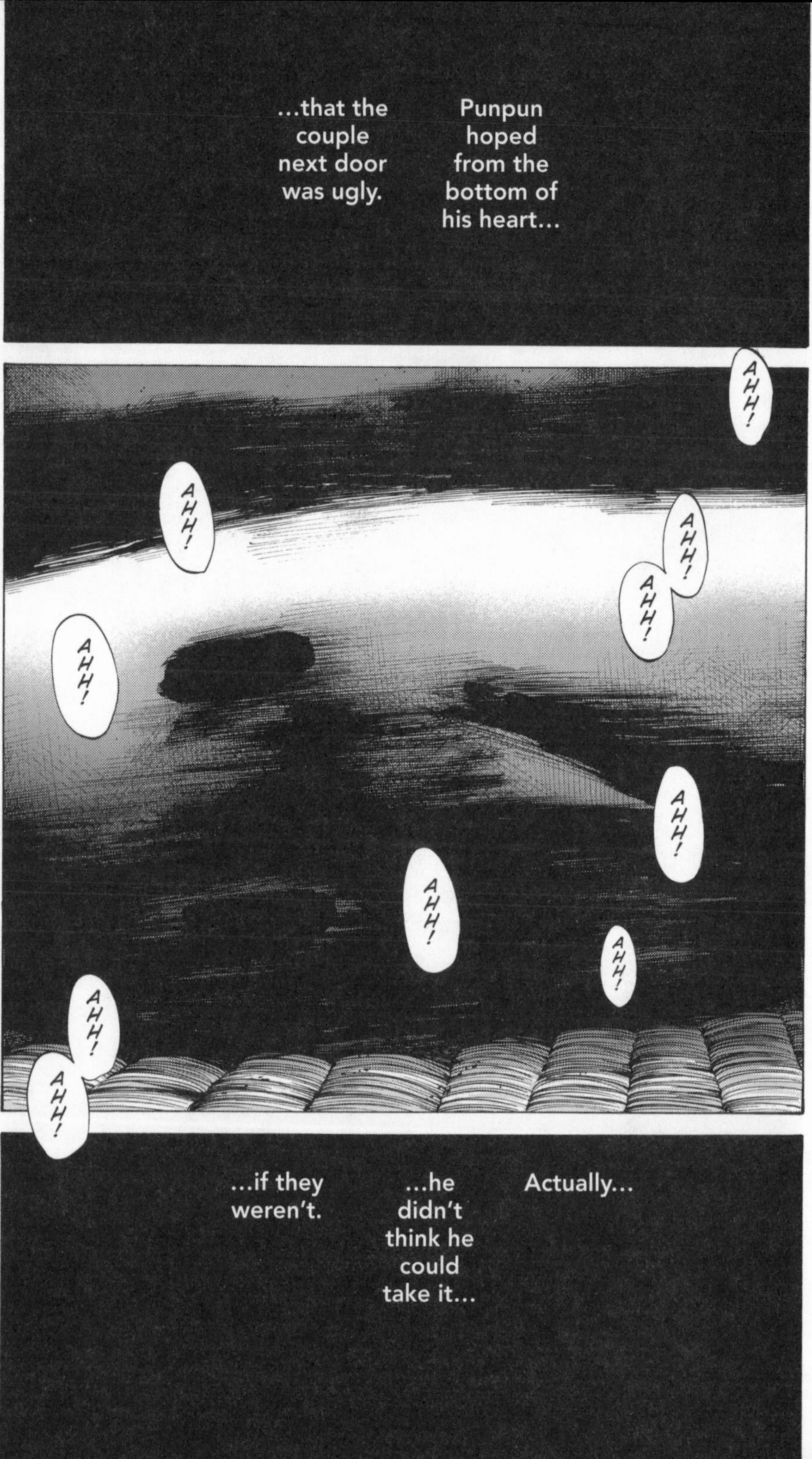
Punpun hoped from the bottom of his heart...
...that the couple next door was ugly.
AHH!
AHH!
AHH!
AHH!
AHH!
AHH!
AHH!
AHH!
AHH!
AHH!
Actually...
...he didn't think he could take it...
...if they weren't.

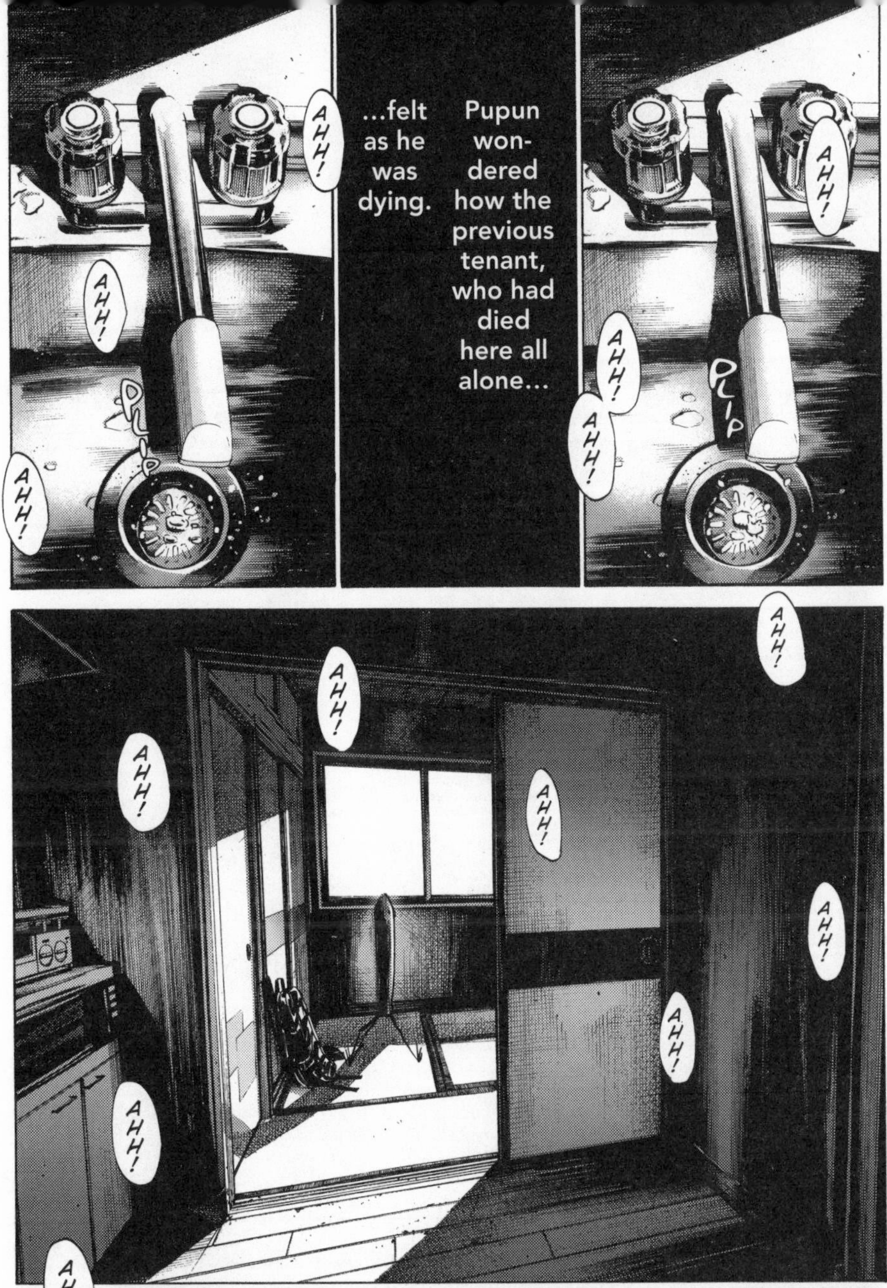
AHH!
AHH!
AHH!
PLIP
Pupun wondered how the previous tenant, who had died here all alone...
...felt as he was dying.
AHH!
AHH!
AHH!
PLIP
AHH!
AHH!
AHH!
AHH!
AHH!
AHH!
AHH!

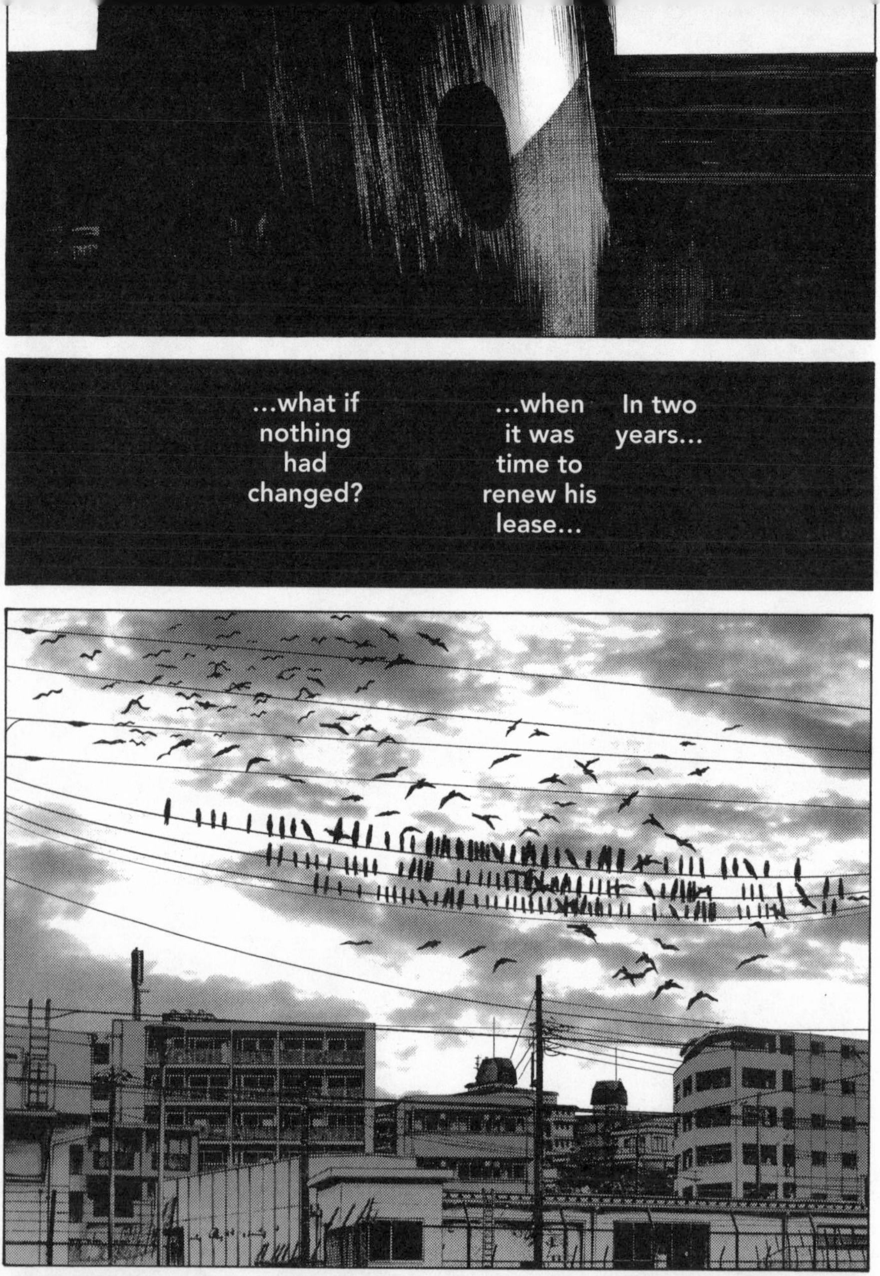
In two years...
...when it was time to renew his lease...
...what if nothing had changed?

Chapter 75

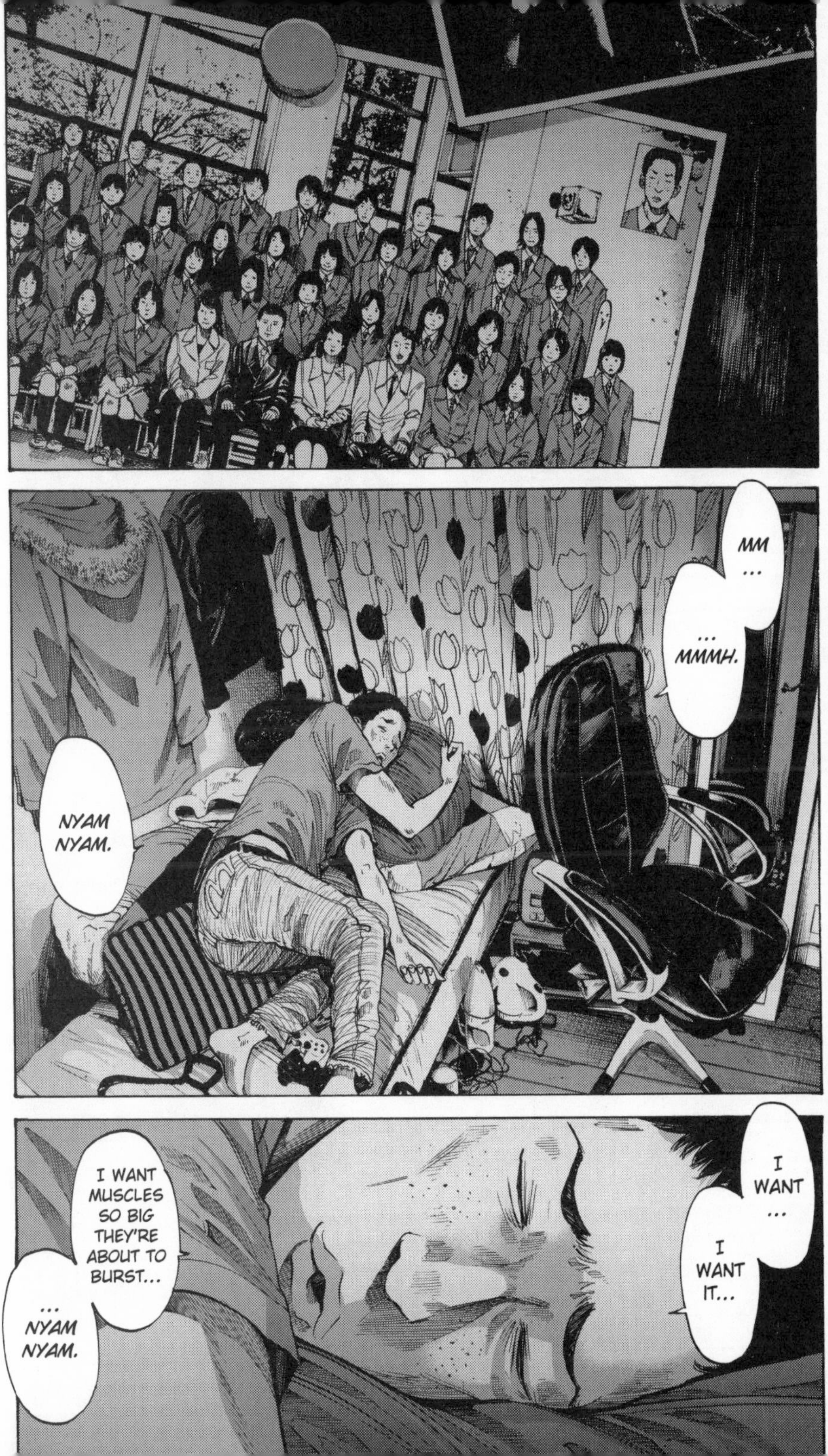
MM ...
... MMMH.
NYAM NYAM.
I WANT ...
I WANT IT...
I WANT MUSCLES SO BIG THEY'RE ABOUT TO BURST...
... NYAM NYAM.

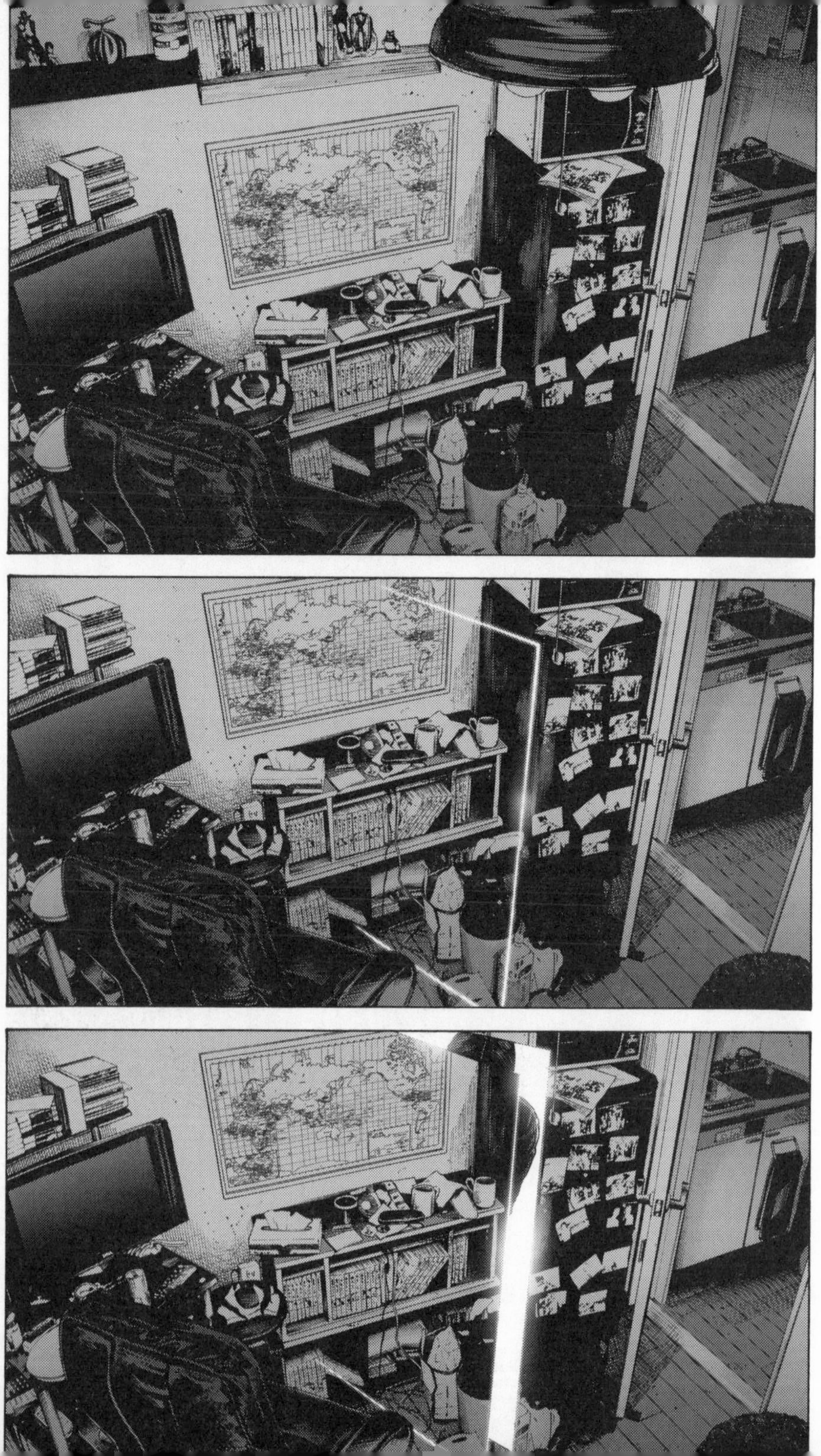

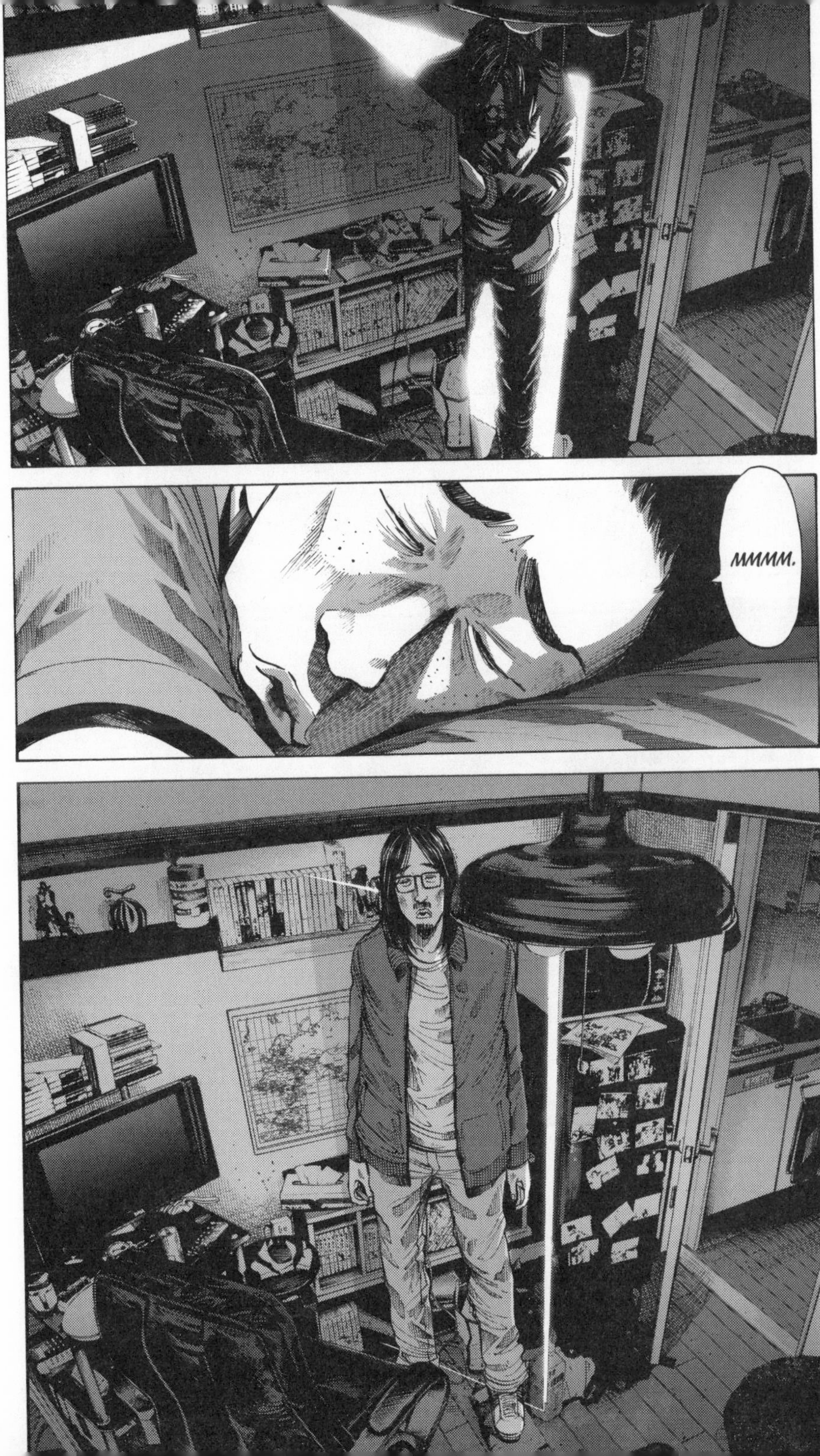
MMMM.

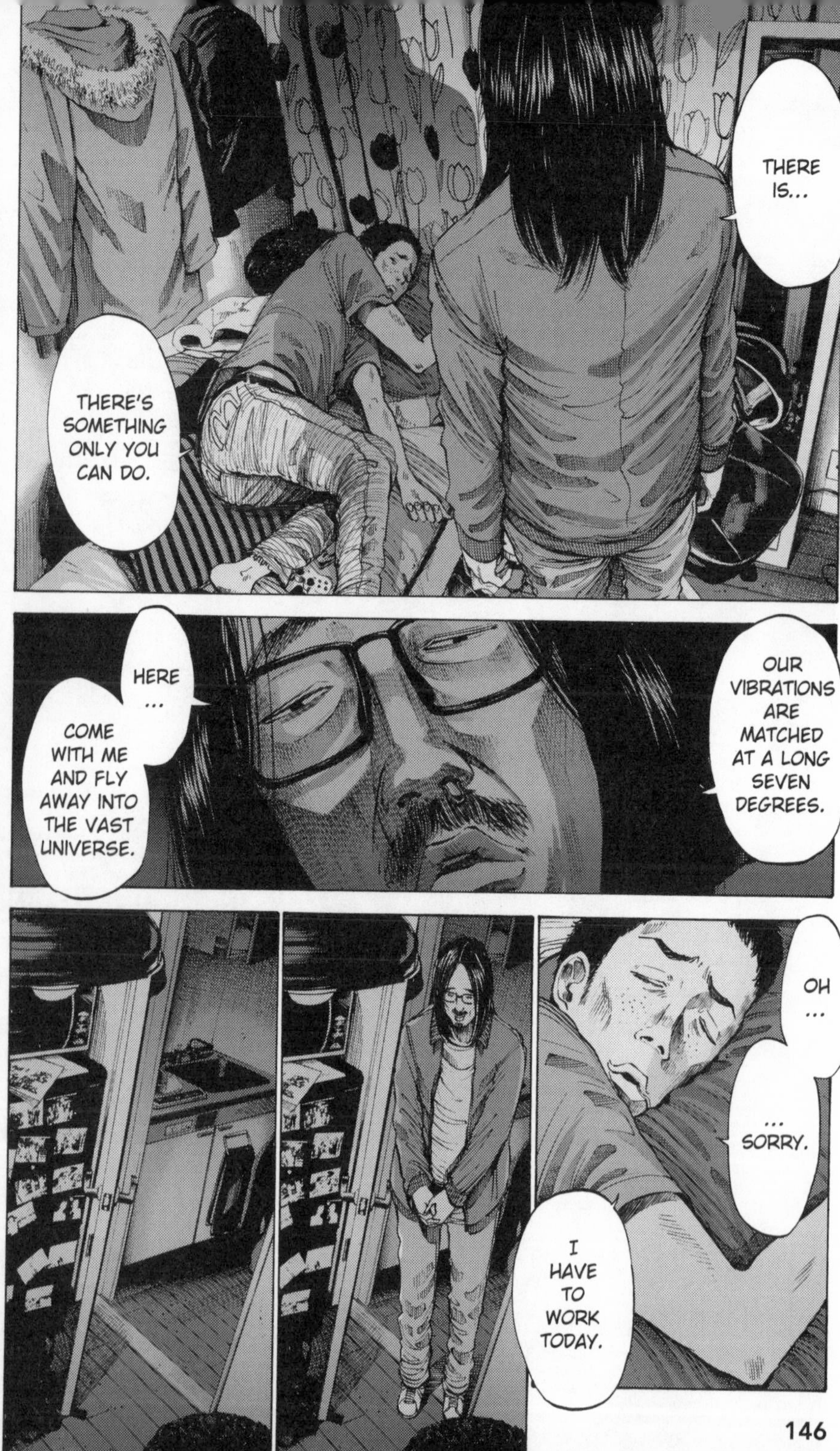
THERE IS...
THERE'S SOMETHING ONLY YOU CAN DO.
OUR VIBRATIONS ARE MATCHED AT A LONG SEVEN DEGREES.
HERE ...
COME WITH ME AND FLY AWAY INTO THE VAST UNIVERSE.
OH ...
... SORRY.
I HAVE TO WORK TODAY.

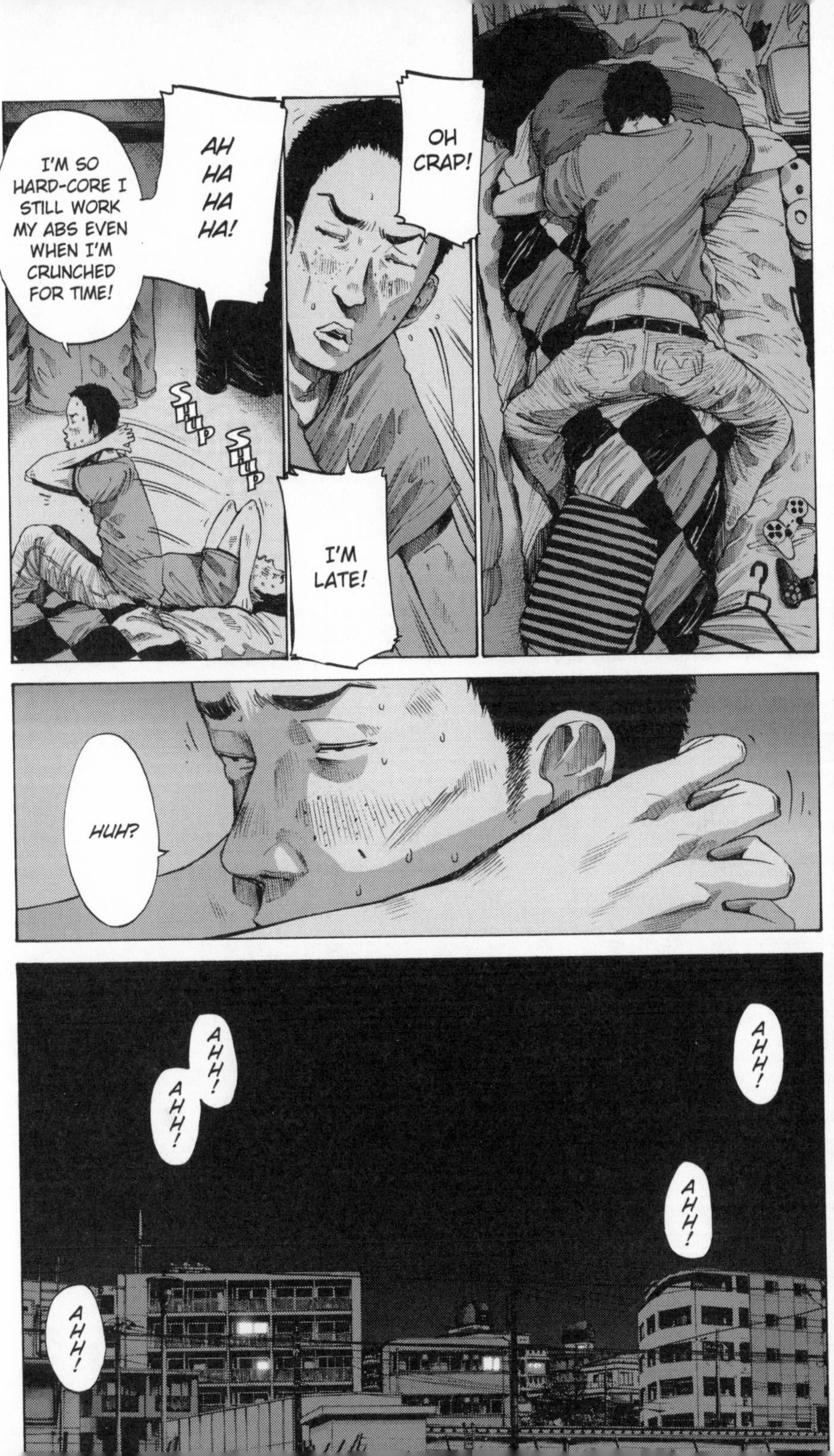
OH CRAP!
I'M LATE!
AH HA HA HA!
I'M SO HARD-CORE I STILL WORK MY ABS EVEN WHEN I'M CRUNCHED FOR TIME!
SHUP
SHUP
HUH?
AHH!
AHH!
AHH!
AHH!
AHH!

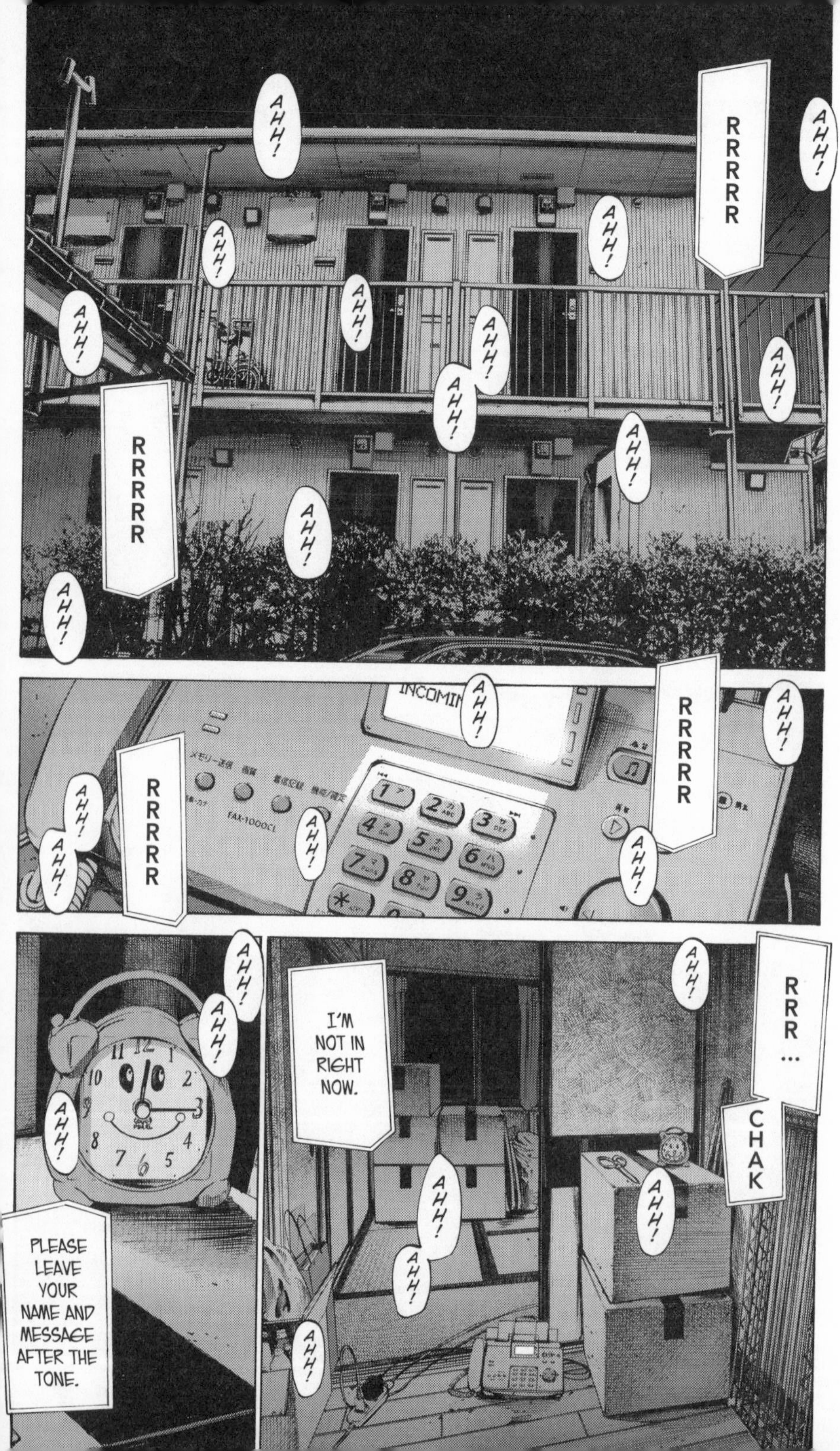
AHH!
RRRRR
AHH!
AHH!
AHH!
AHH!
AHH!
AHH!
AHH!
AHH!
AHH!
AHH!
RRRRR
AHH!
AHH!
AHH!
RRRRR
INCOMIN
AHH!
AHH!
AHH!
RRRRR
AHH!
AHH!
RRR...
CHAK
AHH!
I'M NOT IN RIGHT NOW.
AHH!
AHH!
AHH!
AHH!
AHH!
AHH!
AHH!
PLEASE LEAVE YOUR NAME AND MESSAGE AFTER THE TONE.

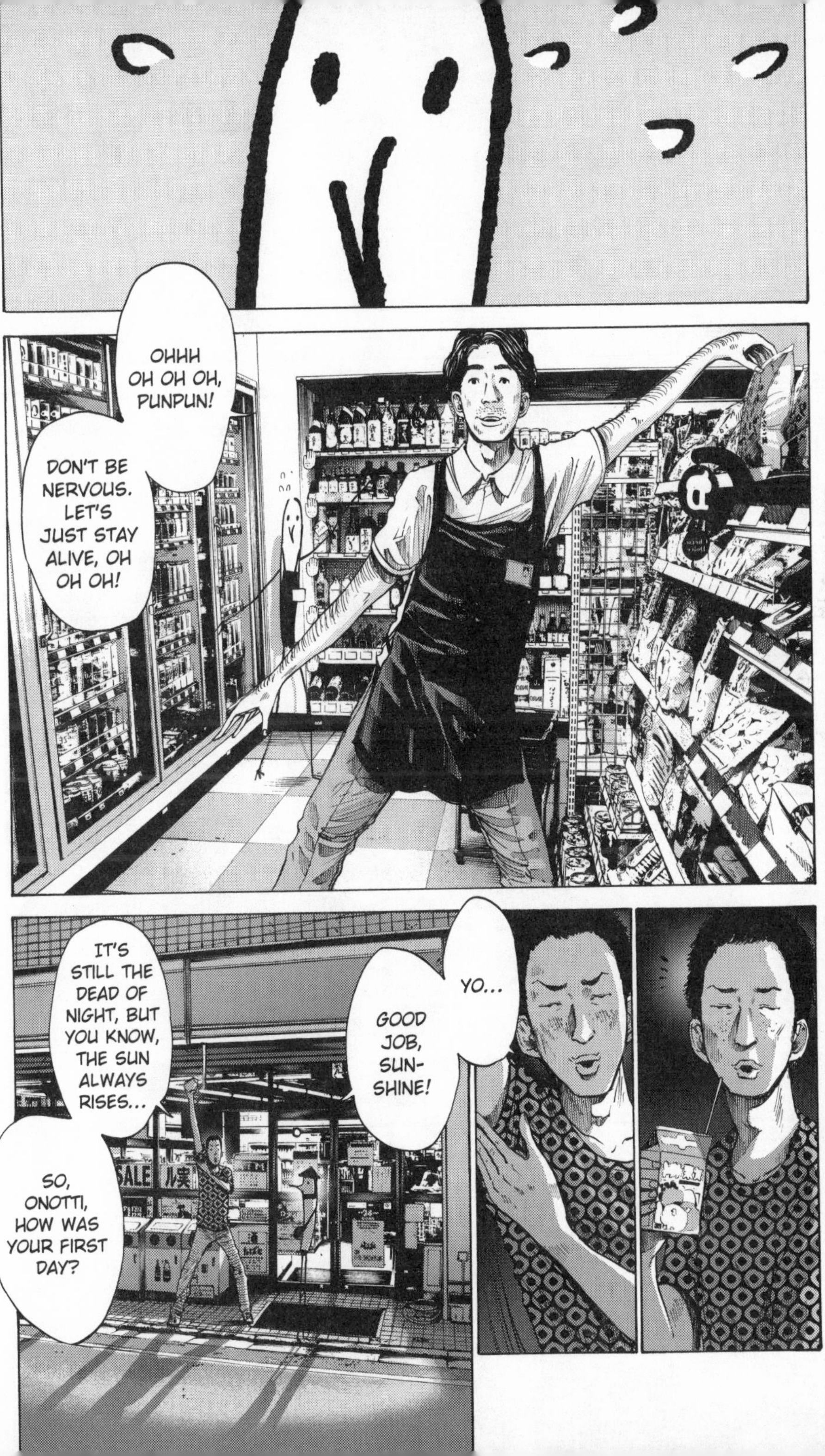
OHHH OH OH OH, PUNPUN!
DON'T BE NERVOUS. LET'S JUST STAY ALIVE, OH OH OH!
YO...
GOOD JOB, SUN-SHINE!
IT'S STILL THE DEAD OF NIGHT, BUT YOU KNOW, THE SUN ALWAYS RISES...
SO, ONOTTI, HOW WAS YOUR FIRST DAY?
SALE

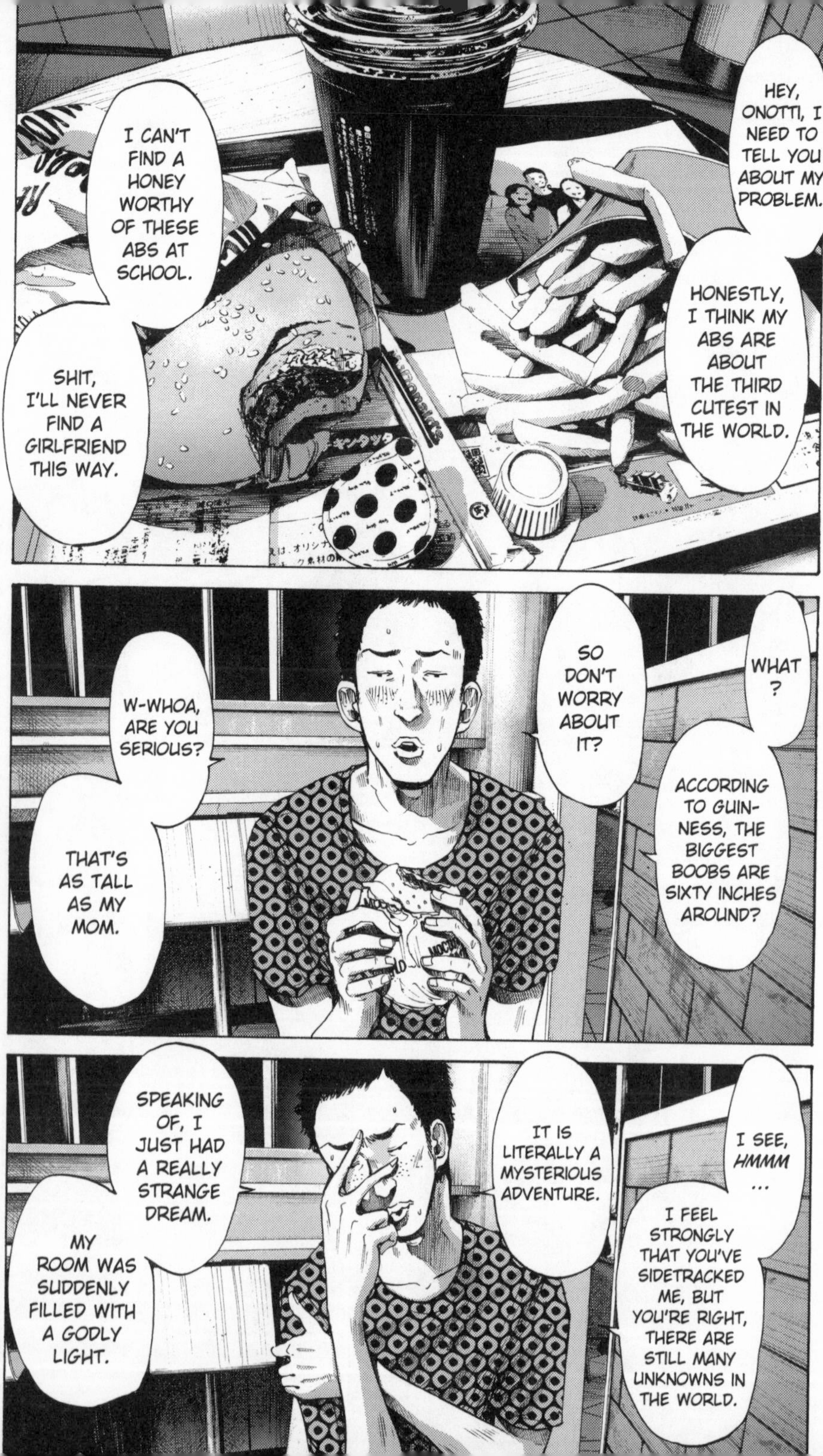
HEY, ONOTTI, I NEED TO TELL YOU ABOUT MY PROBLEM.
HONESTLY, I THINK MY ABS ARE ABOUT THE THIRD CUTEST IN THE WORLD.
I CAN'T FIND A HONEY WORTHY OF THESE ABS AT SCHOOL.
SHIT, I'LL NEVER FIND A GIRLFRIEND THIS WAY.
WHAT?
SO DON'T WORRY ABOUT IT?
ACCORDING TO GUINNESS, THE BIGGEST BOOBS ARE SIXTY INCHES AROUND?
W-WHOA, ARE YOU SERIOUS?
THAT'S AS TALL AS MY MOM.
I SEE, *HMMM*...
I FEEL STRONGLY THAT YOU'VE SIDETRACKED ME, BUT YOU'RE RIGHT, THERE ARE STILL MANY UNKNOWNS IN THE WORLD.
IT IS LITERALLY A MYSTERIOUS ADVENTURE.
SPEAKING OF, I JUST HAD A REALLY STRANGE DREAM.
MY ROOM WAS SUDDENLY FILLED WITH A GODLY LIGHT.

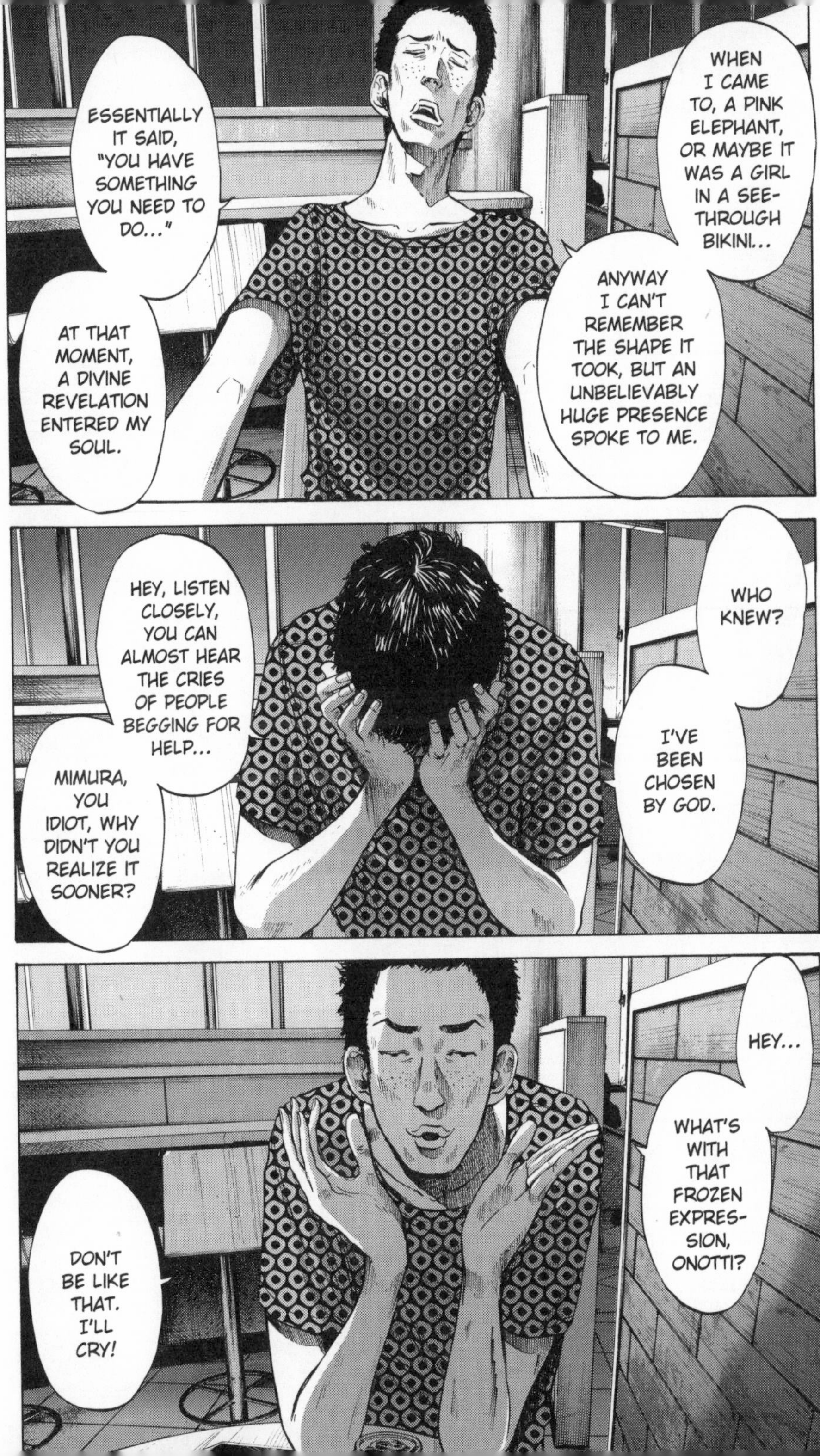
WHEN I CAME TO, A PINK ELEPHANT, OR MAYBE IT WAS A GIRL IN A SEE-THROUGH BIKINI...
ANYWAY I CAN'T REMEMBER THE SHAPE IT TOOK, BUT AN UNBELIEVABLY HUGE PRESENCE SPOKE TO ME.
ESSENTIALLY IT SAID, "YOU HAVE SOMETHING YOU NEED TO DO..."
AT THAT MOMENT, A DIVINE REVELATION ENTERED MY SOUL.
WHO KNEW?
I'VE BEEN CHOSEN BY GOD.
HEY, LISTEN CLOSELY, YOU CAN ALMOST HEAR THE CRIES OF PEOPLE BEGGING FOR HELP...
MIMURA, YOU IDIOT, WHY DIDN'T YOU REALIZE IT SOONER?
HEY...
WHAT'S WITH THAT FROZEN EXPRES-SION, ONOTTI?
DON'T BE LIKE THAT. I'LL CRY!

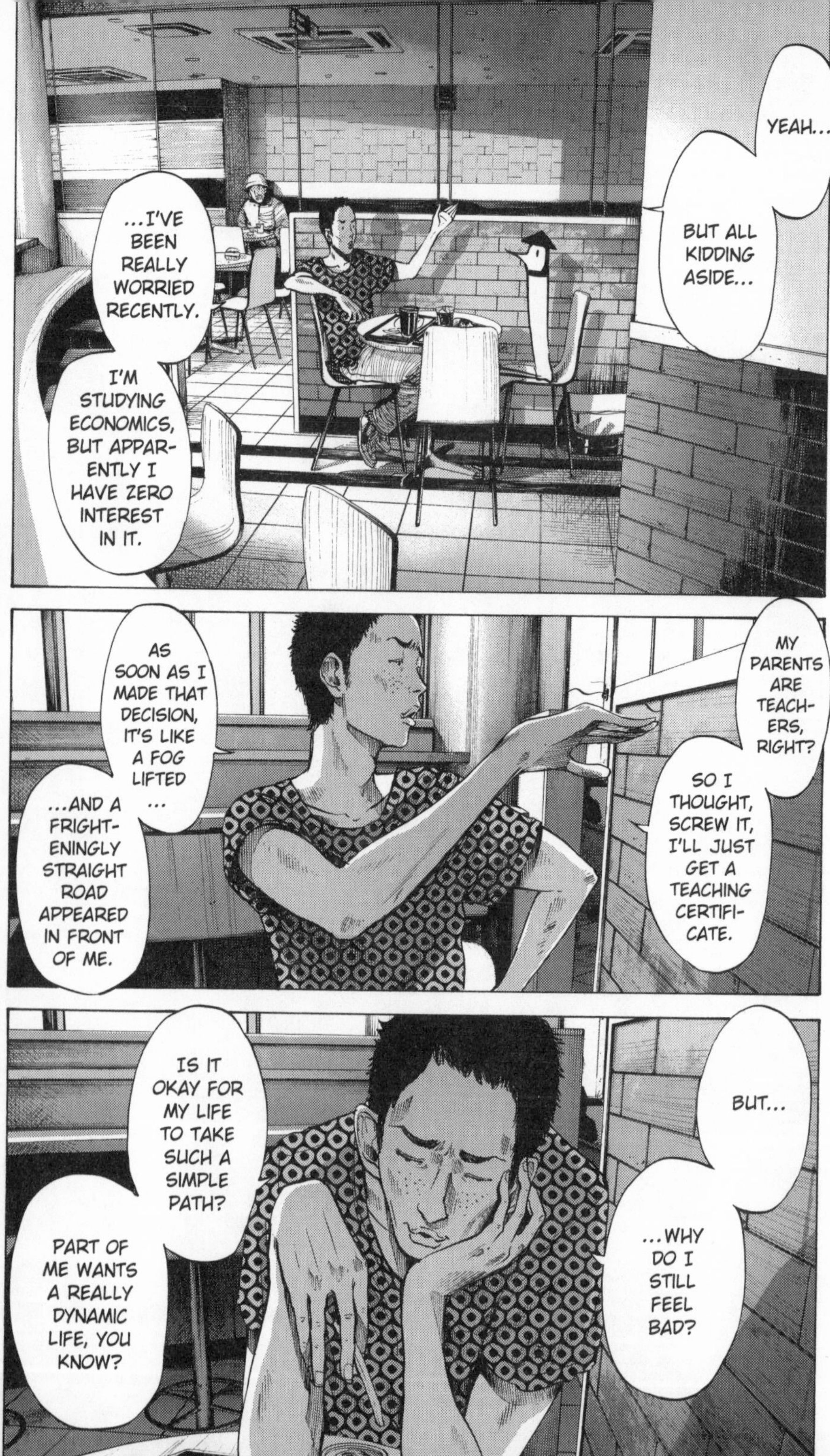
YEAH...
BUT ALL KIDDING ASIDE...
...I'VE BEEN REALLY WORRIED RECENTLY.
I'M STUDYING ECONOMICS, BUT APPAR-ENTLY I HAVE ZERO INTEREST IN IT.
MY PARENTS ARE TEACH-ERS, RIGHT?
SO I THOUGHT, SCREW IT, I'LL JUST GET A TEACHING CERTIFI-CATE.
AS SOON AS I MADE THAT DECISION, IT'S LIKE A FOG LIFTED ...
...AND A FRIGHT-ENINGLY STRAIGHT ROAD APPEARED IN FRONT OF ME.
BUT...
...WHY DO I STILL FEEL BAD?
IS IT OKAY FOR MY LIFE TO TAKE SUCH A SIMPLE PATH?
PART OF ME WANTS A REALLY DYNAMIC LIFE, YOU KNOW?

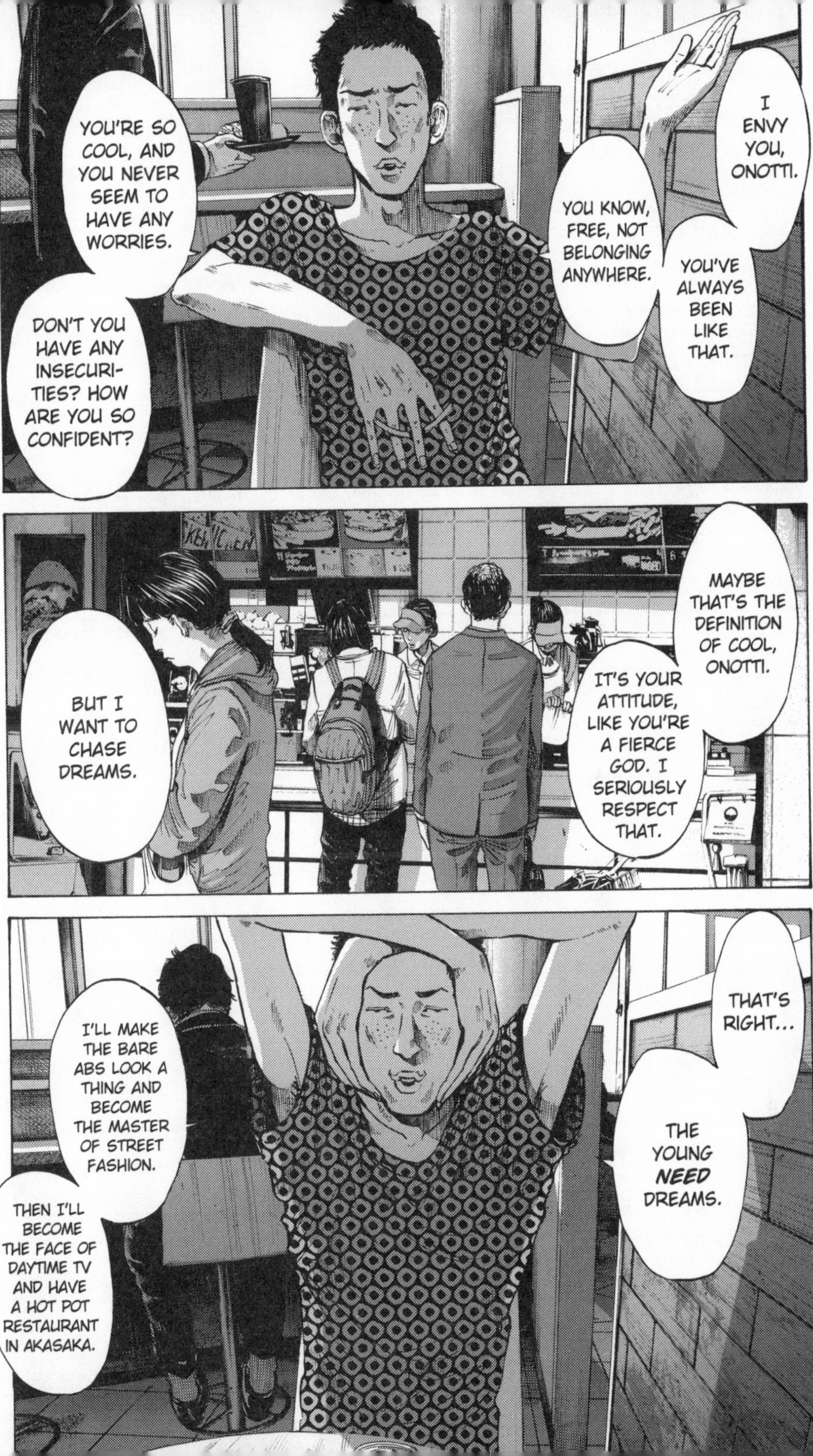
I ENVY YOU, ONOTTI.
YOU'VE ALWAYS BEEN LIKE THAT.
YOU KNOW, FREE, NOT BELONGING ANYWHERE.
YOU'RE SO COOL, AND YOU NEVER SEEM TO HAVE ANY WORRIES.
DON'T YOU HAVE ANY INSECURITIES? HOW ARE YOU SO CONFIDENT?
MAYBE THAT'S THE DEFINITION OF COOL, ONOTTI.
IT'S YOUR ATTITUDE, LIKE YOU'RE A FIERCE GOD. I SERIOUSLY RESPECT THAT.
BUT I WANT TO CHASE DREAMS.
THAT'S RIGHT...
THE YOUNG **NEED** DREAMS.
I'LL MAKE THE BARE ABS LOOK A THING AND BECOME THE MASTER OF STREET FASHION.
THEN I'LL BECOME THE FACE OF DAYTIME TV AND HAVE A HOT POT RESTAURANT IN AKASAKA.

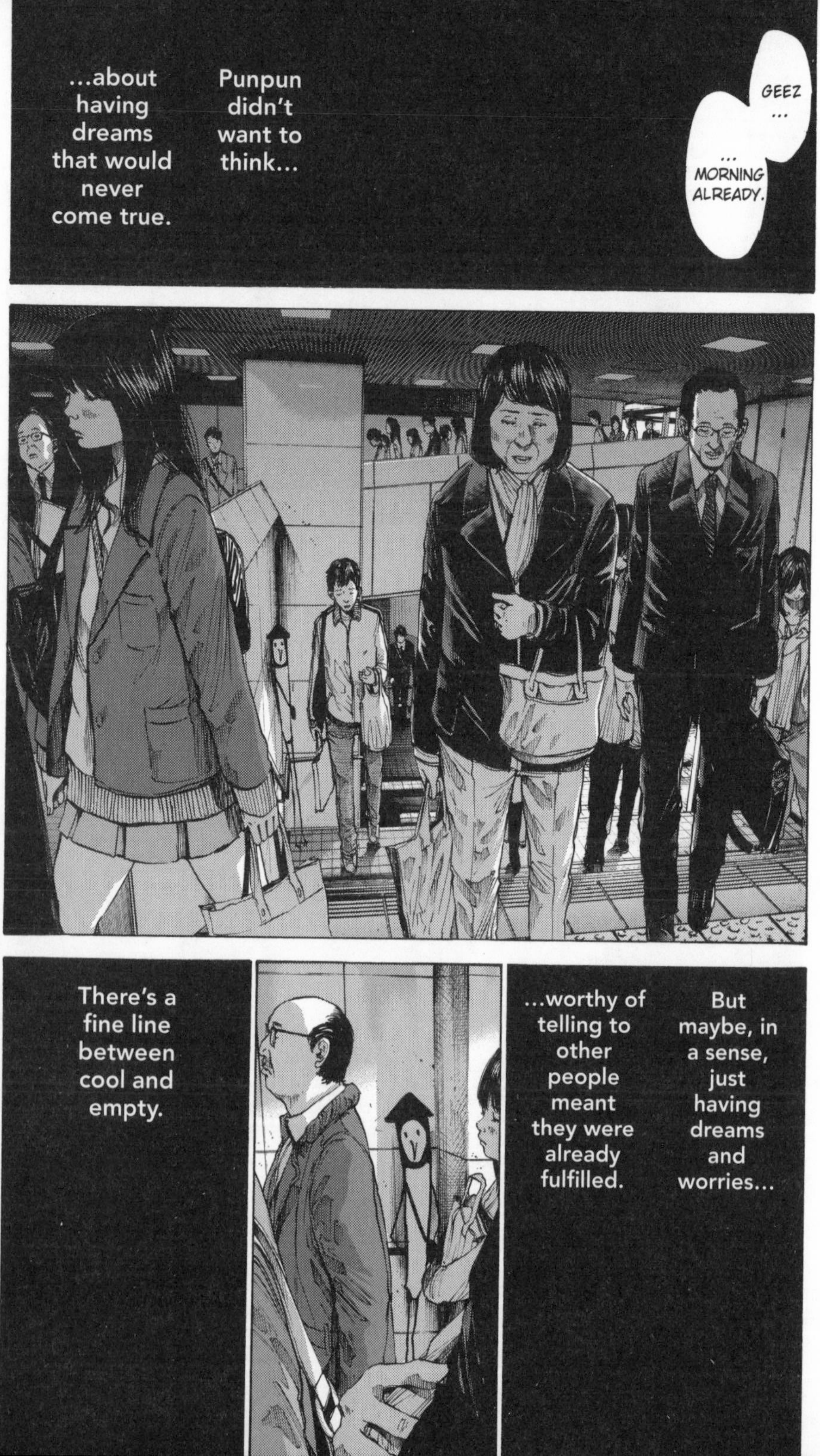
GEEZ...
...MORNING ALREADY.
Punpun didn't want to think...
...about having dreams that would never come true.
But maybe, in a sense, just having dreams and worries...
...worthy of telling to other people meant they were already fulfilled.
There's a fine line between cool and empty.

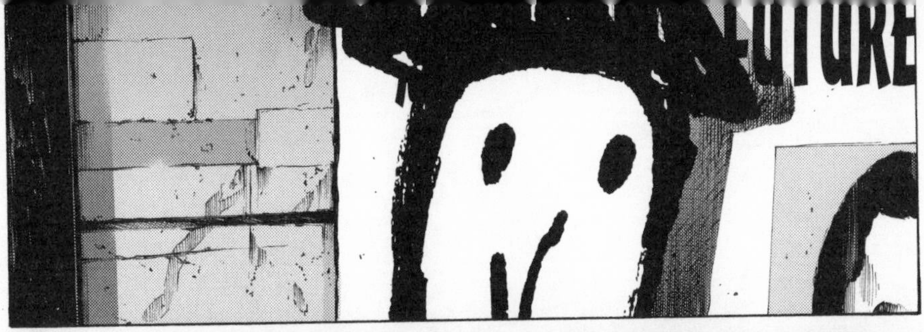

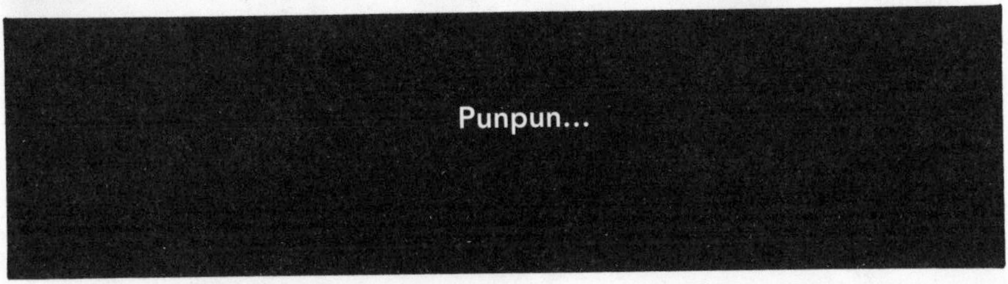
Punpun...

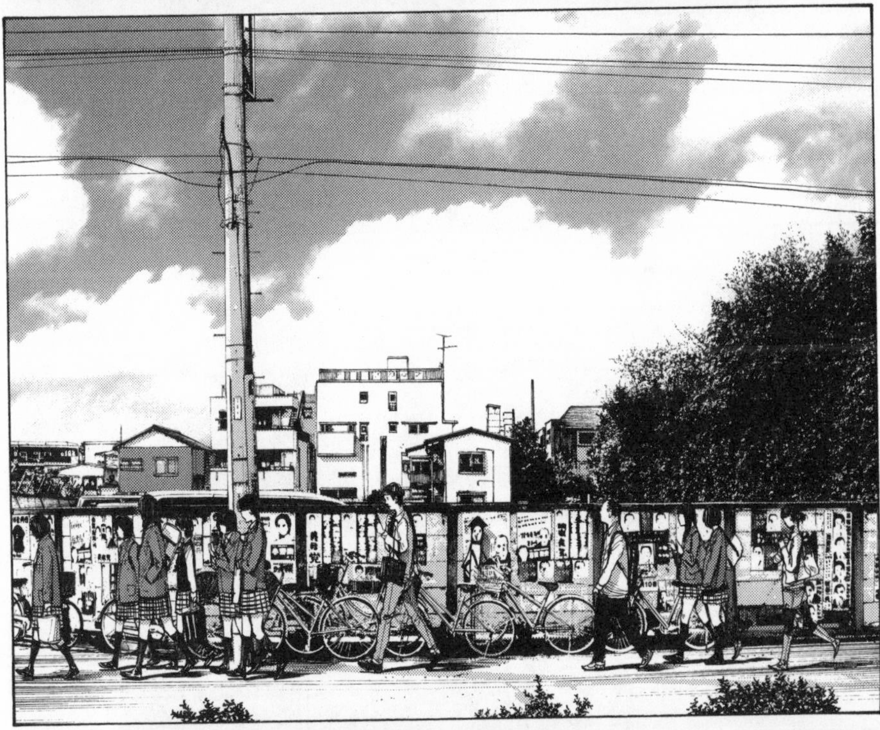

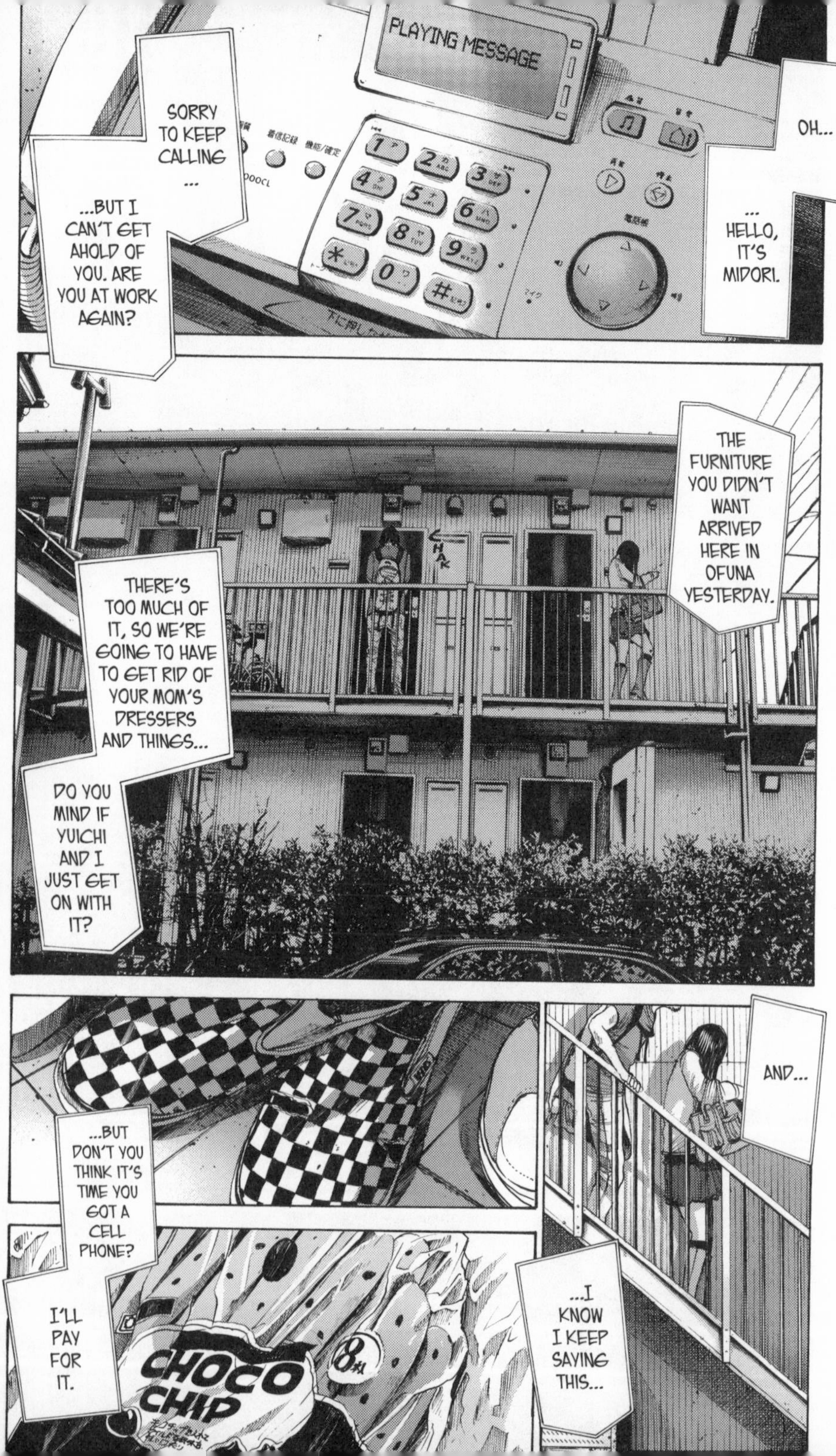
PLAYING MESSAGE
OH...
...HELLO, IT'S MIDORI.
SORRY TO KEEP CALLING...
...BUT I CAN'T GET AHOLD OF YOU. ARE YOU AT WORK AGAIN?
THE FURNITURE YOU DIDN'T WANT ARRIVED HERE IN OFUNA YESTERDAY.
CHAK
THERE'S TOO MUCH OF IT, SO WE'RE GOING TO HAVE TO GET RID OF YOUR MOM'S DRESSERS AND THINGS...
DO YOU MIND IF YUICHI AND I JUST GET ON WITH IT?
AND...
...I KNOW I KEEP SAYING THIS...
...BUT DON'T YOU THINK IT'S TIME YOU GOT A CELL PHONE?
I'LL PAY FOR IT.
CHOCO CHIP

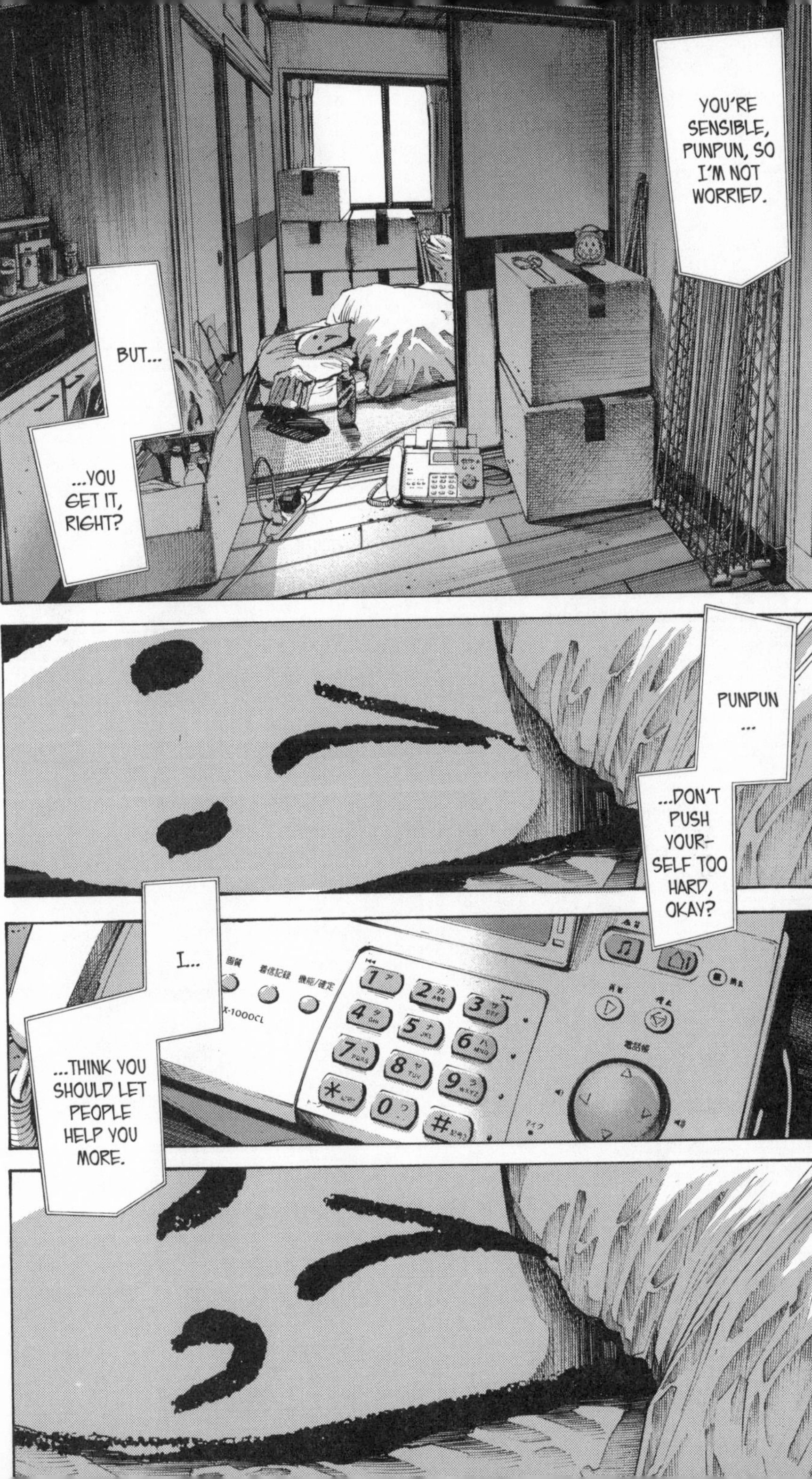
YOU'RE SENSIBLE, PUNPUN, SO I'M NOT WORRIED.
BUT...
...YOU GET IT, RIGHT?
PUNPUN ...
...DON'T PUSH YOUR-SELF TOO HARD, OKAY?
I...
...THINK YOU SHOULD LET PEOPLE HELP YOU MORE.

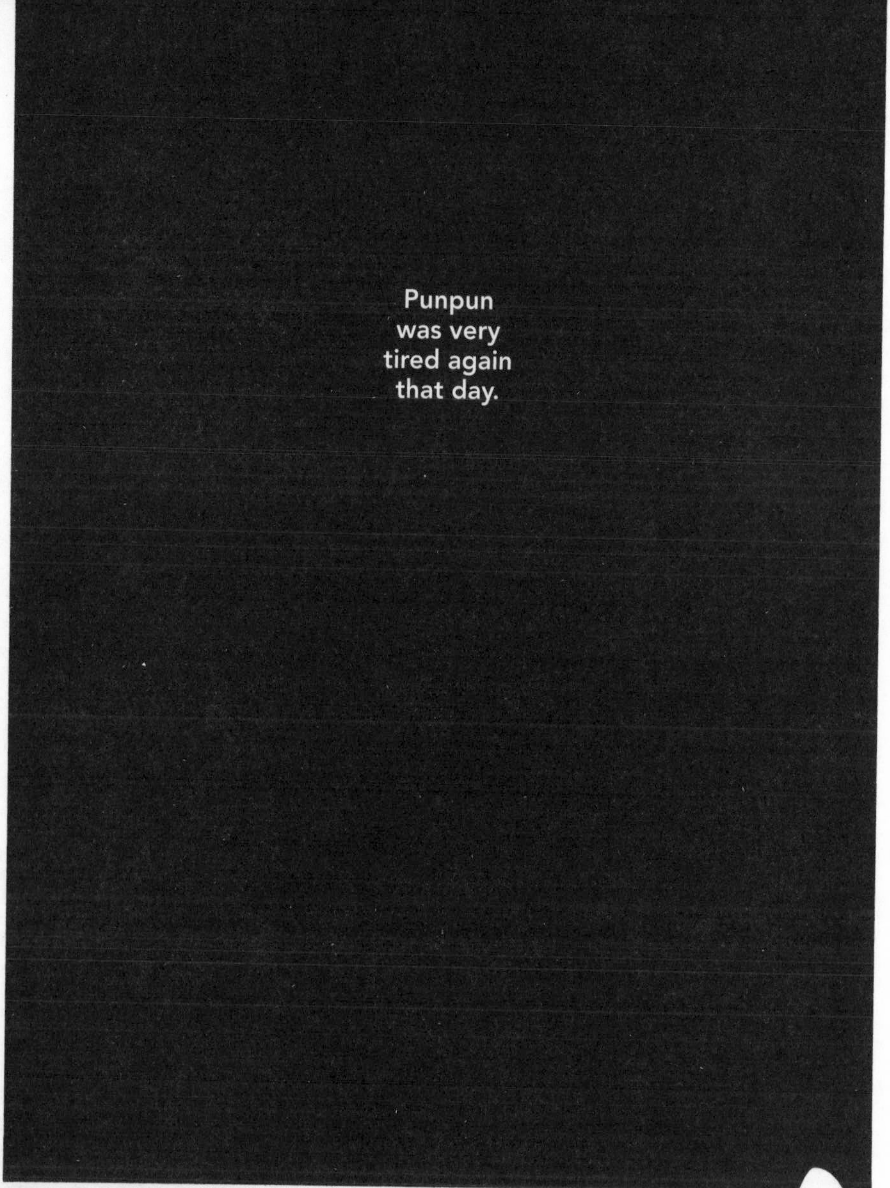
Punpun was very tired again that day.

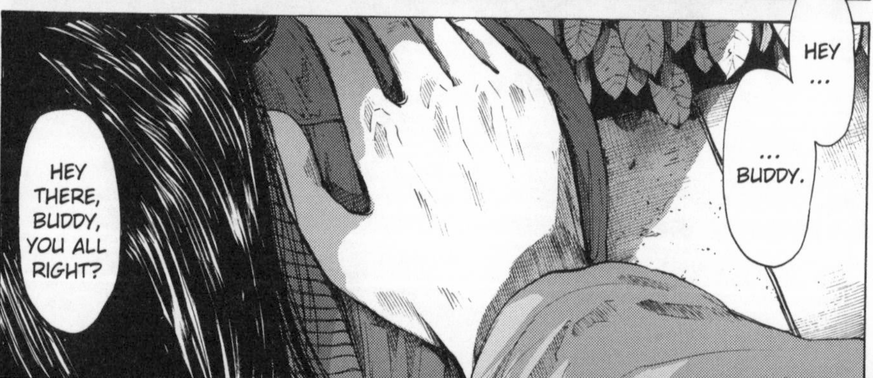
HEY ...
... BUDDY.
HEY THERE, BUDDY, YOU ALL RIGHT?

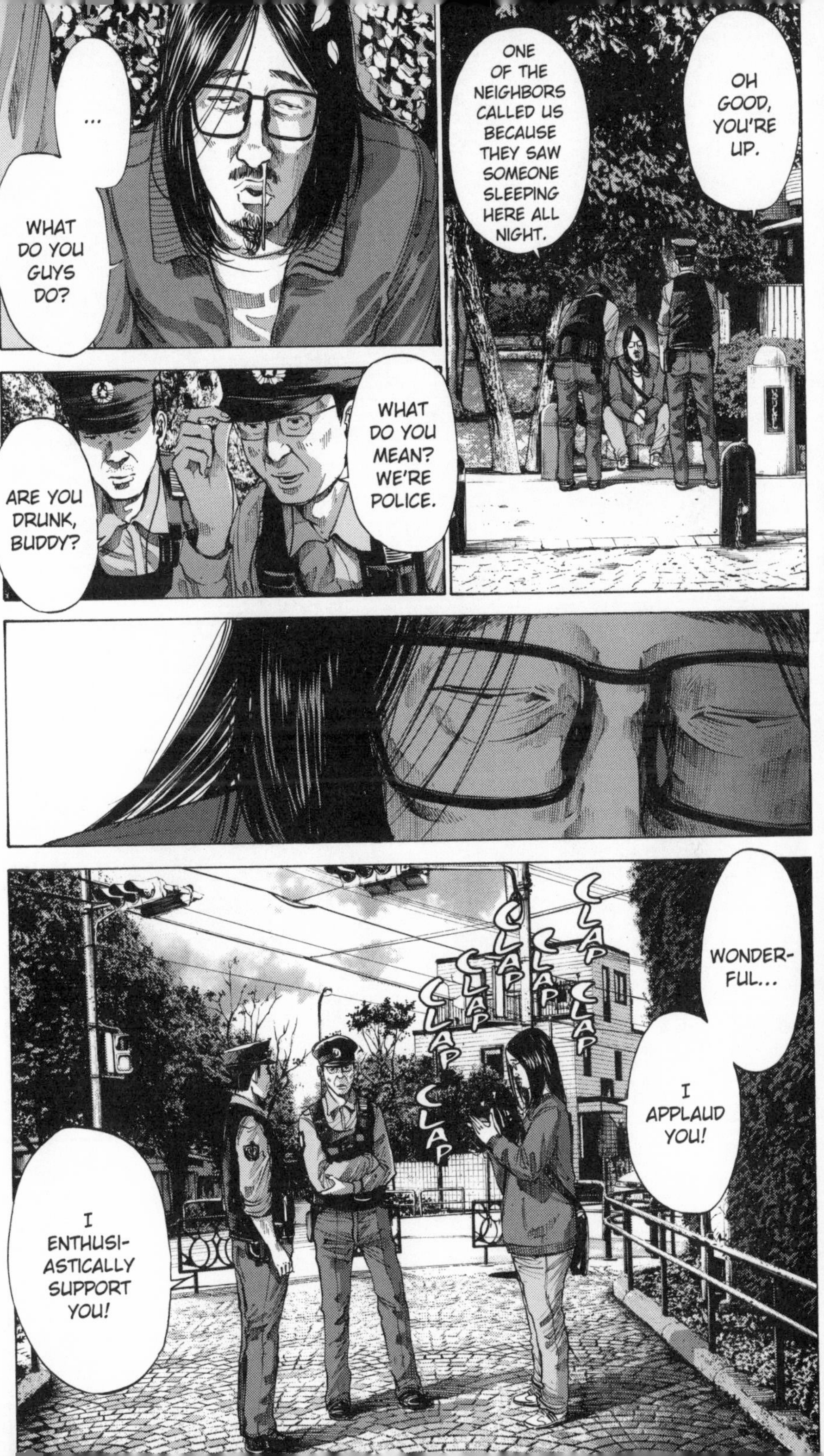
OH GOOD, YOU'RE UP.
ONE OF THE NEIGHBORS CALLED US BECAUSE THEY SAW SOMEONE SLEEPING HERE ALL NIGHT.
...
WHAT DO YOU GUYS DO?
WHAT DO YOU MEAN? WE'RE POLICE.
ARE YOU DRUNK, BUDDY?
WONDERFUL...
I APPLAUD YOU!
CLAP CLAP CLAP CLAP CLAP CLAP CLAP CLAP
I ENTHUSI-ASTICALLY SUPPORT YOU!

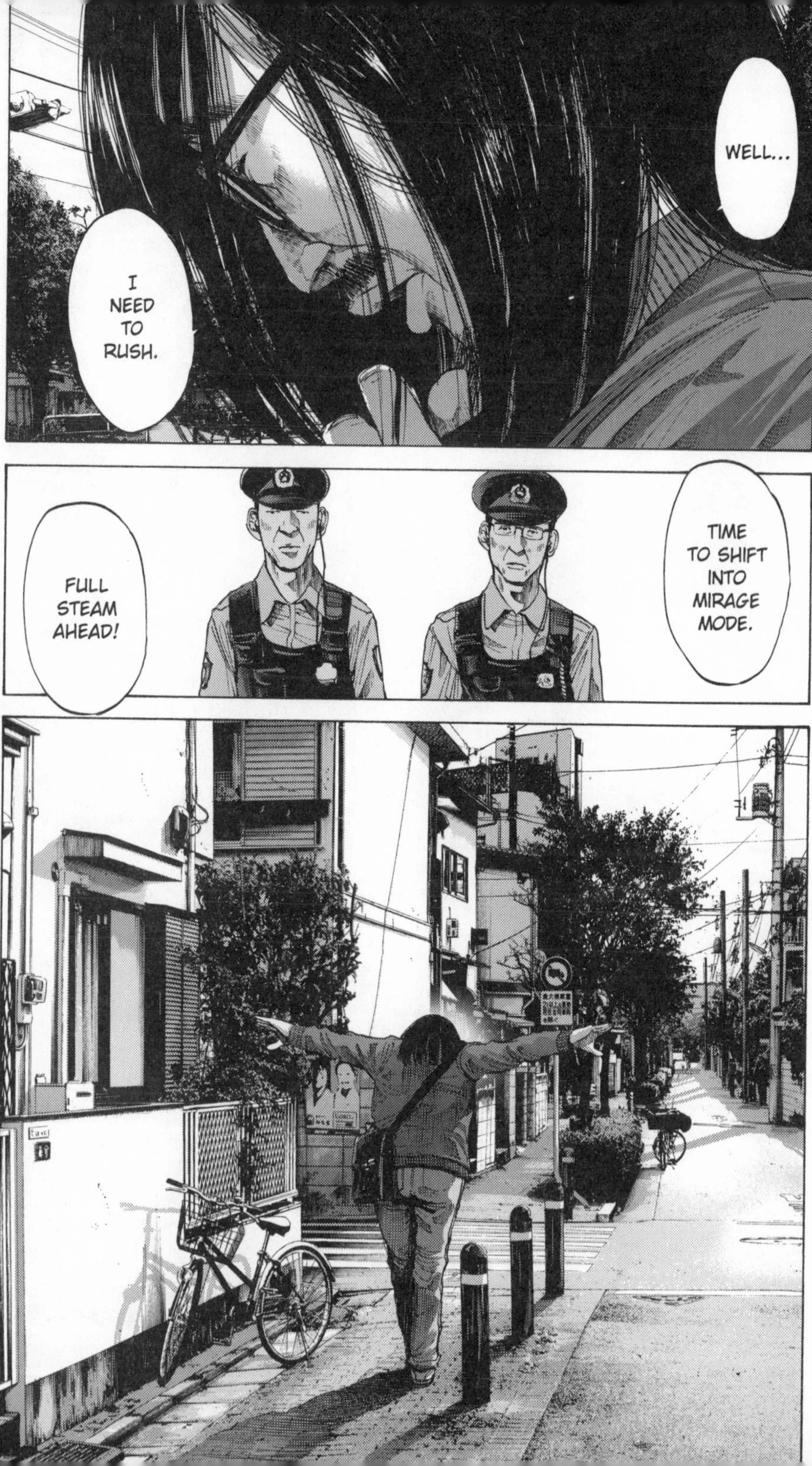
WELL...
I NEED TO RUSH.
TIME TO SHIFT INTO MIRAGE MODE.
FULL STEAM AHEAD!

Chapter 76 ☆

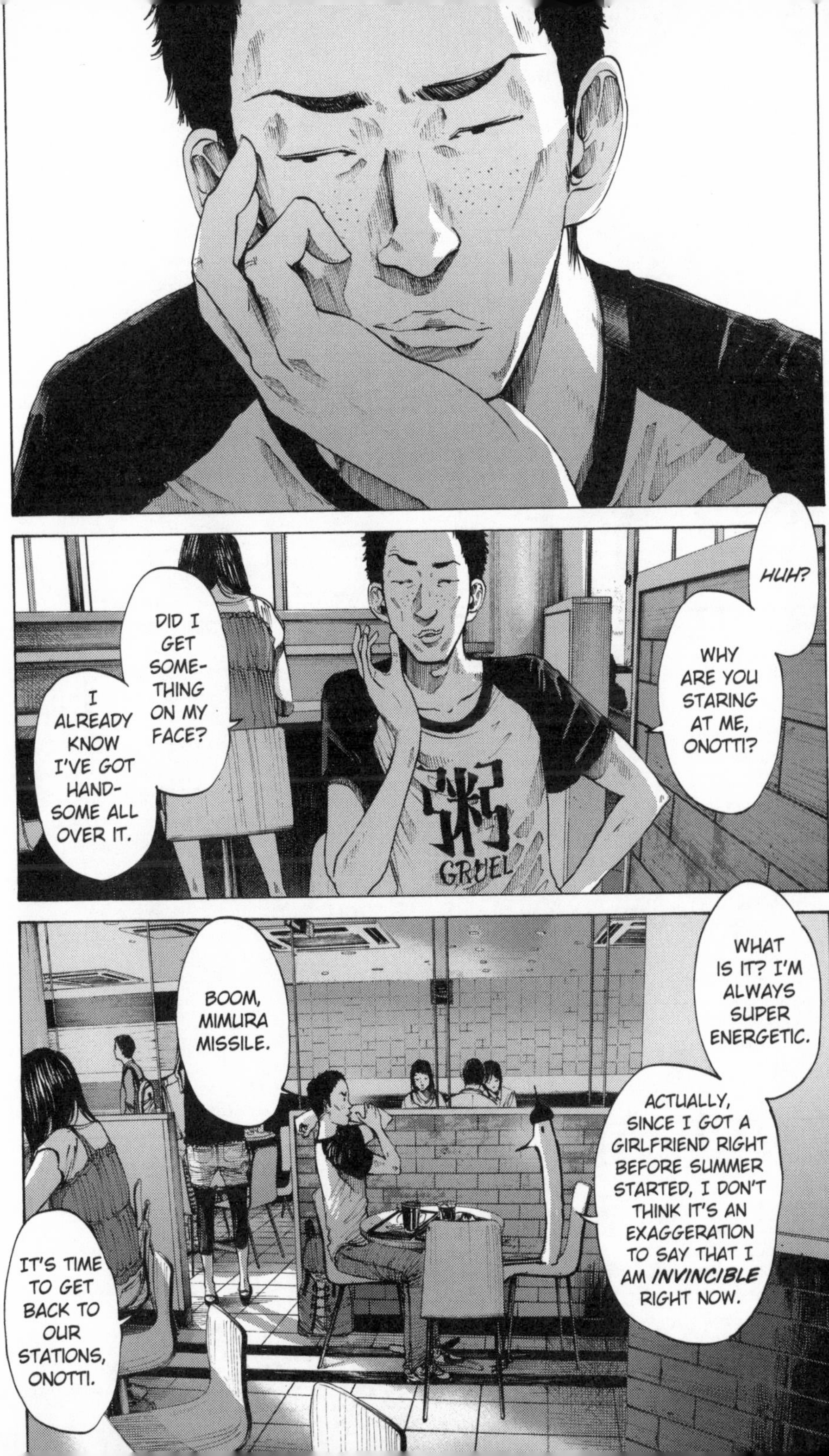

HUH?
WHY ARE YOU STARING AT ME, ONOTTI?
DID I GET SOMETHING ON MY FACE?
I ALREADY KNOW I'VE GOT HANDSOME ALL OVER IT.
GRUEL
WHAT IS IT? I'M ALWAYS SUPER ENERGETIC.
BOOM, MIMURA MISSILE.
ACTUALLY, SINCE I GOT A GIRLFRIEND RIGHT BEFORE SUMMER STARTED, I DON'T THINK IT'S AN EXAGGERATION TO SAY THAT I AM *INVINCIBLE* RIGHT NOW.
IT'S TIME TO GET BACK TO OUR STATIONS, ONOTTI.

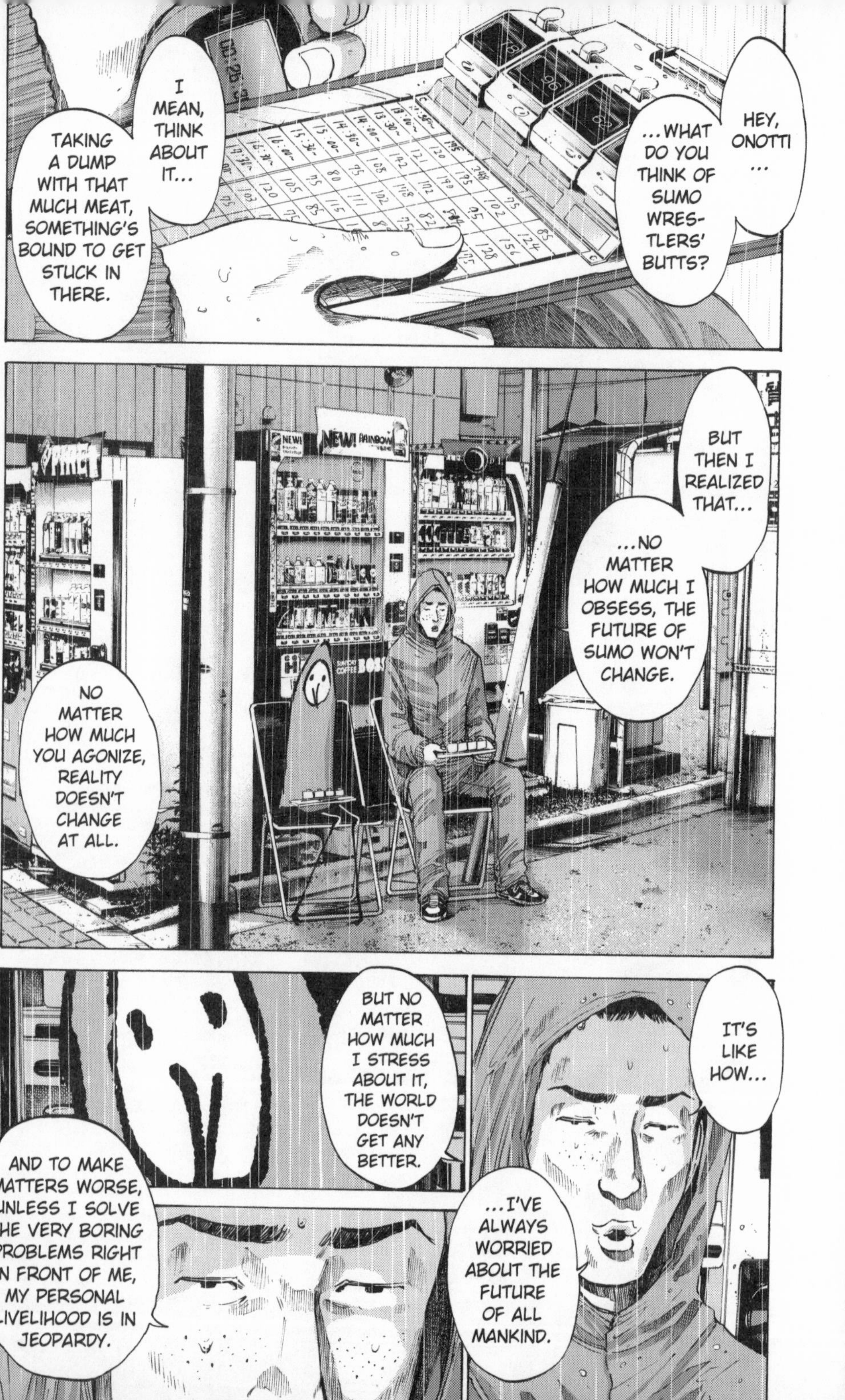
HEY, ONOTTI ...
...WHAT DO YOU THINK OF SUMO WRESTLERS' BUTTS?
I MEAN, THINK ABOUT IT...
TAKING A DUMP WITH THAT MUCH MEAT, SOMETHING'S BOUND TO GET STUCK IN THERE.
BUT THEN I REALIZED THAT...
...NO MATTER HOW MUCH I OBSESS, THE FUTURE OF SUMO WON'T CHANGE.
NO MATTER HOW MUCH YOU AGONIZE, REALITY DOESN'T CHANGE AT ALL.
IT'S LIKE HOW...
...I'VE ALWAYS WORRIED ABOUT THE FUTURE OF ALL MANKIND.
BUT NO MATTER HOW MUCH I STRESS ABOUT IT, THE WORLD DOESN'T GET ANY BETTER.
AND TO MAKE MATTERS WORSE, UNLESS I SOLVE THE VERY BORING PROBLEMS RIGHT IN FRONT OF ME, MY PERSONAL LIVELIHOOD IS IN JEOPARDY.

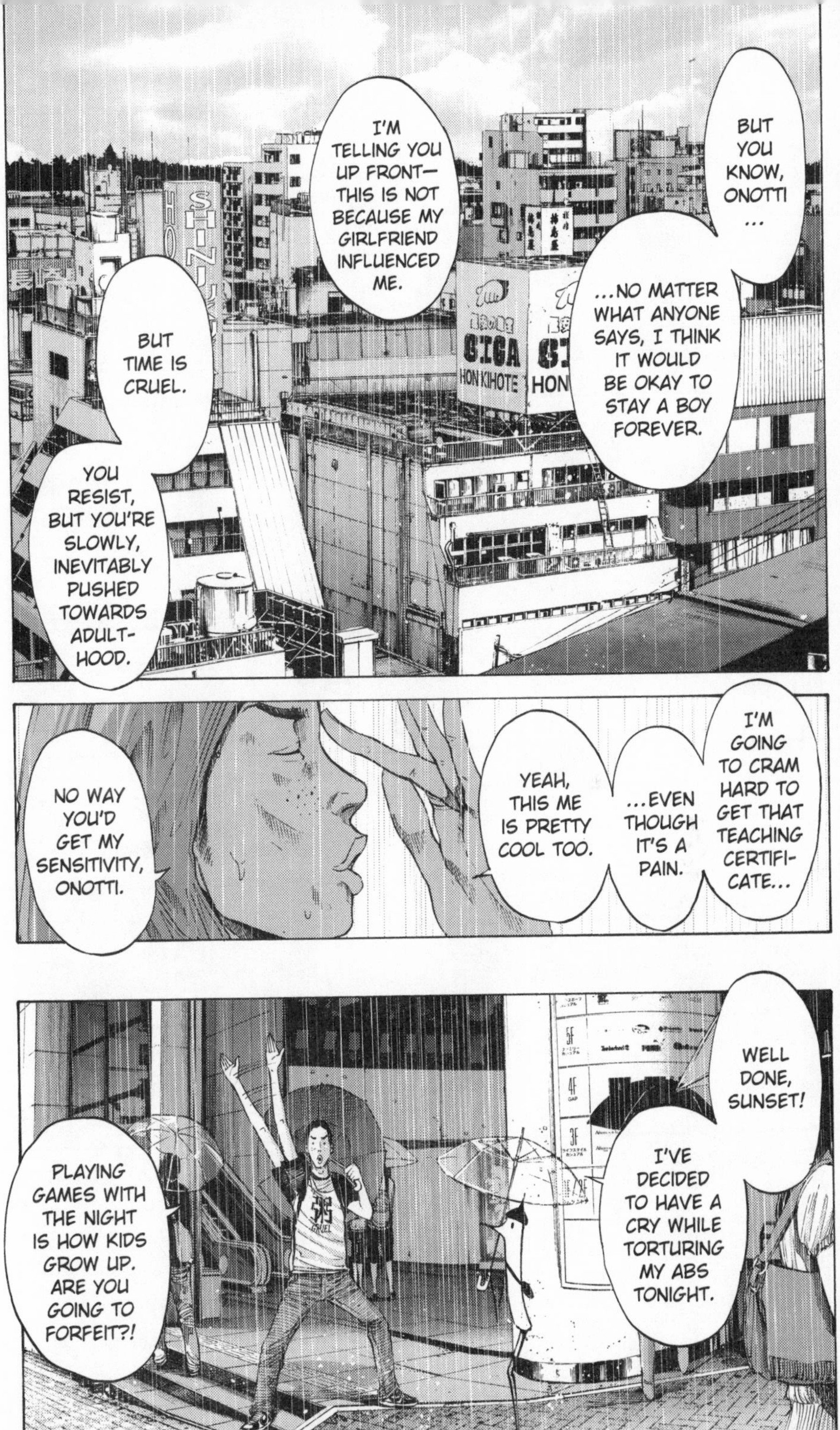
BUT YOU KNOW, ONOTTI...
...NO MATTER WHAT ANYONE SAYS, I THINK IT WOULD BE OKAY TO STAY A BOY FOREVER.
I'M TELLING YOU UP FRONT—THIS IS NOT BECAUSE MY GIRLFRIEND INFLUENCED ME.
GIGA
HON KIHOTE
BUT TIME IS CRUEL.
YOU RESIST, BUT YOU'RE SLOWLY, INEVITABLY PUSHED TOWARDS ADULT-HOOD.
I'M GOING TO CRAM HARD TO GET THAT TEACHING CERTIFI-CATE...
...EVEN THOUGH IT'S A PAIN.
YEAH, THIS ME IS PRETTY COOL TOO.
NO WAY YOU'D GET MY SENSITIVITY, ONOTTI.
WELL DONE, SUNSET!
I'VE DECIDED TO HAVE A CRY WHILE TORTURING MY ABS TONIGHT.
PLAYING GAMES WITH THE NIGHT IS HOW KIDS GROW UP. ARE YOU GOING TO FORFEIT?!

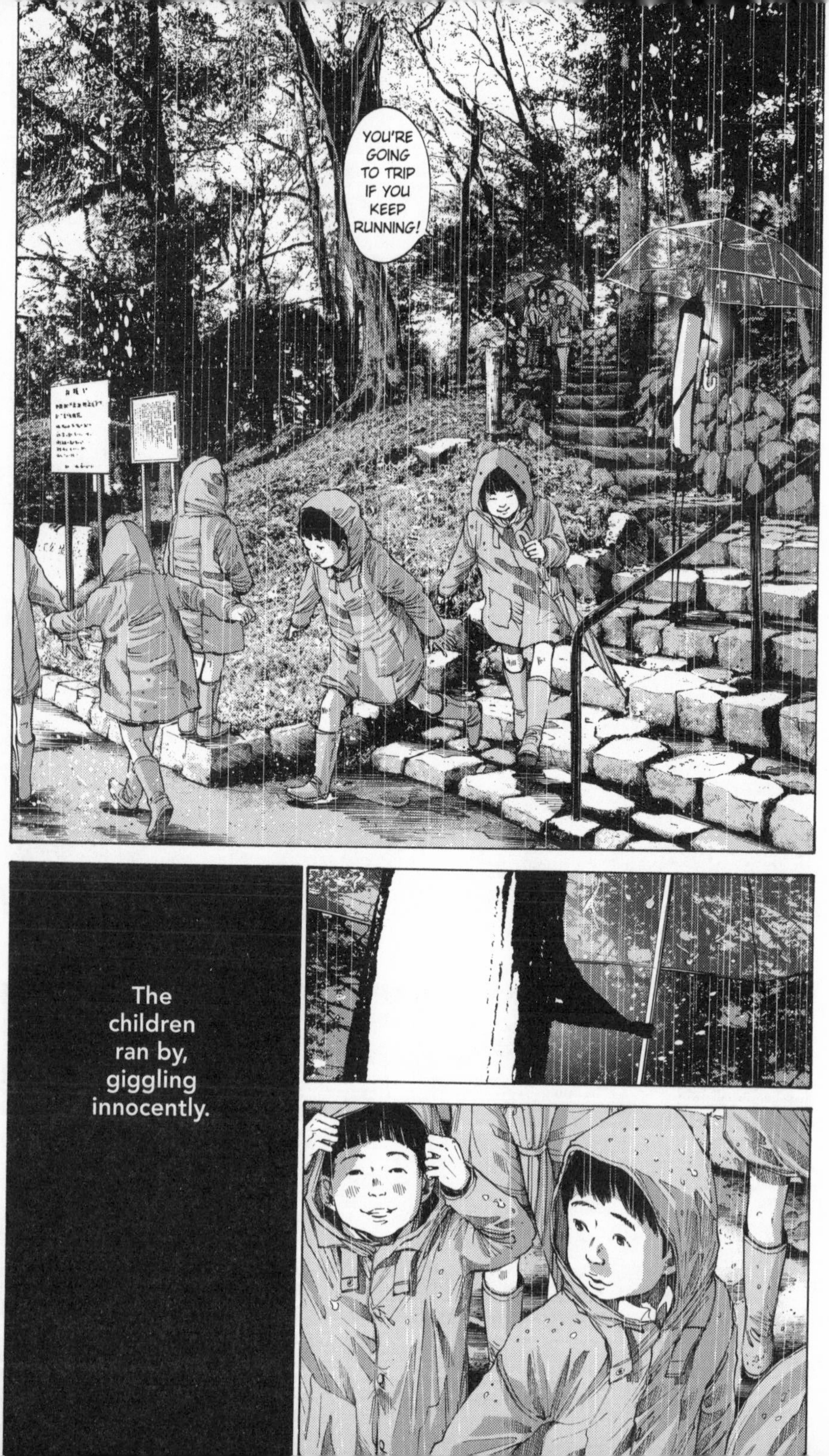
YOU'RE GOING TO TRIP IF YOU KEEP RUNNING!
The children ran by, giggling innocently.

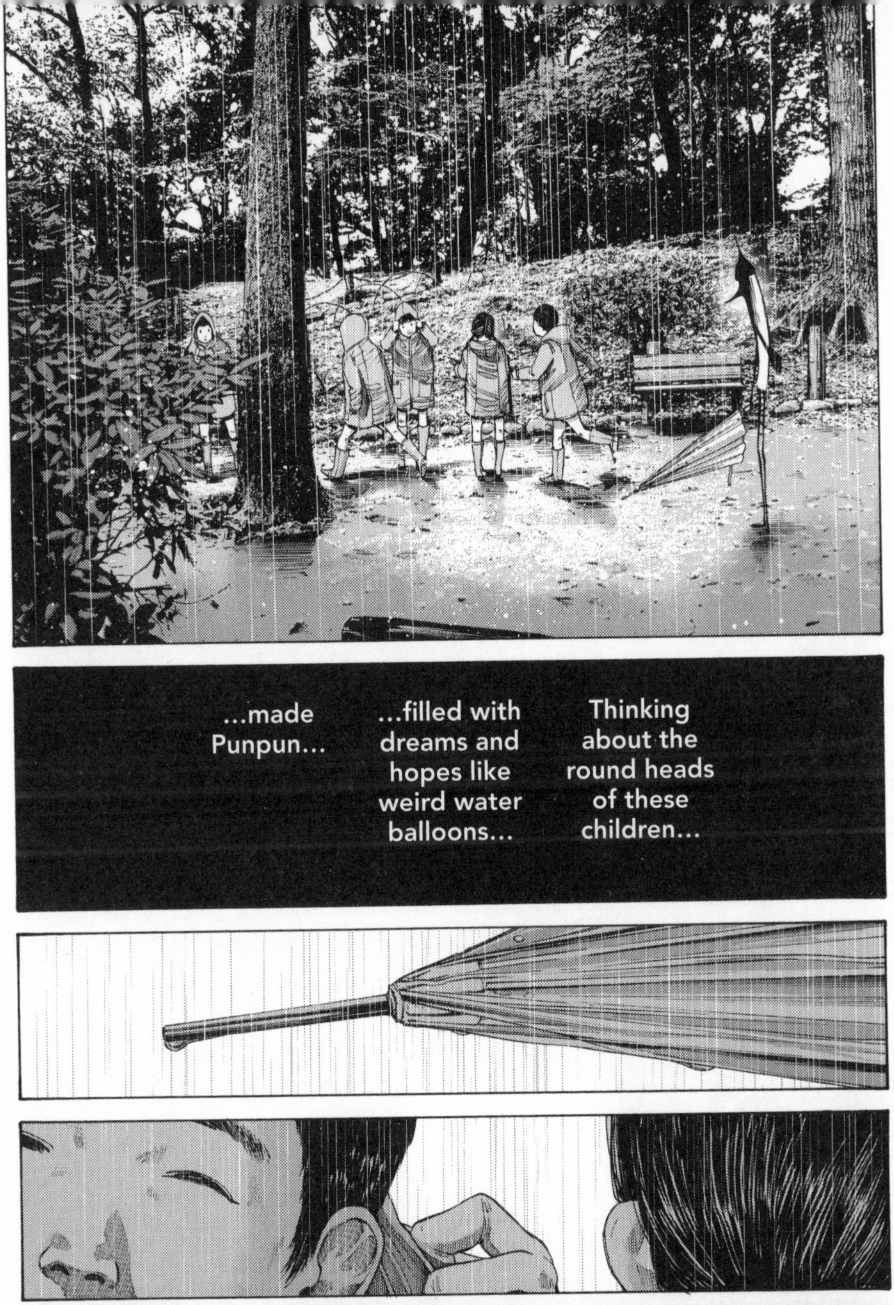
Thinking about the round heads of these children...
...filled with dreams and hopes like weird water balloons...
...made Punpun...

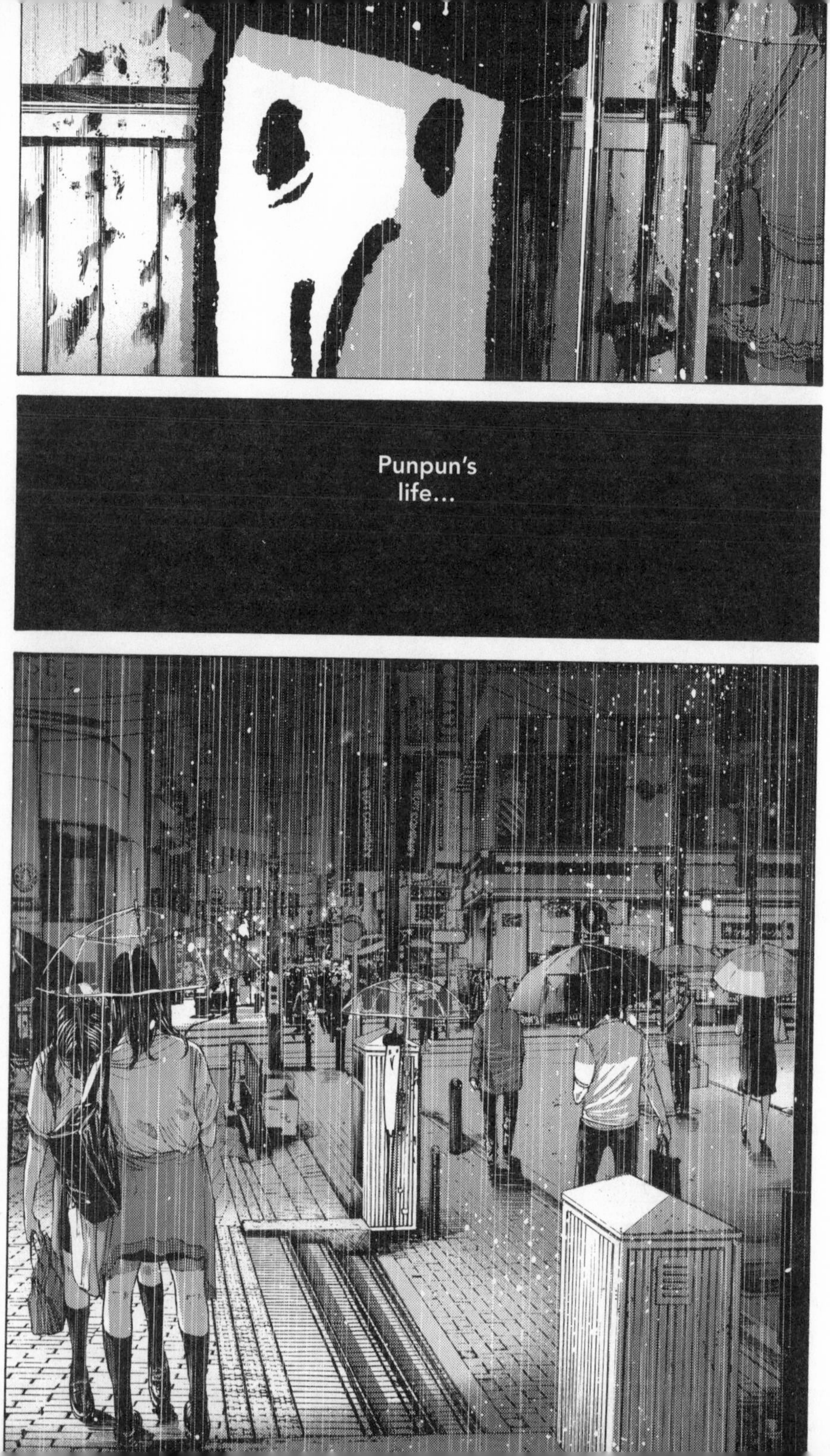
Punpun's life...

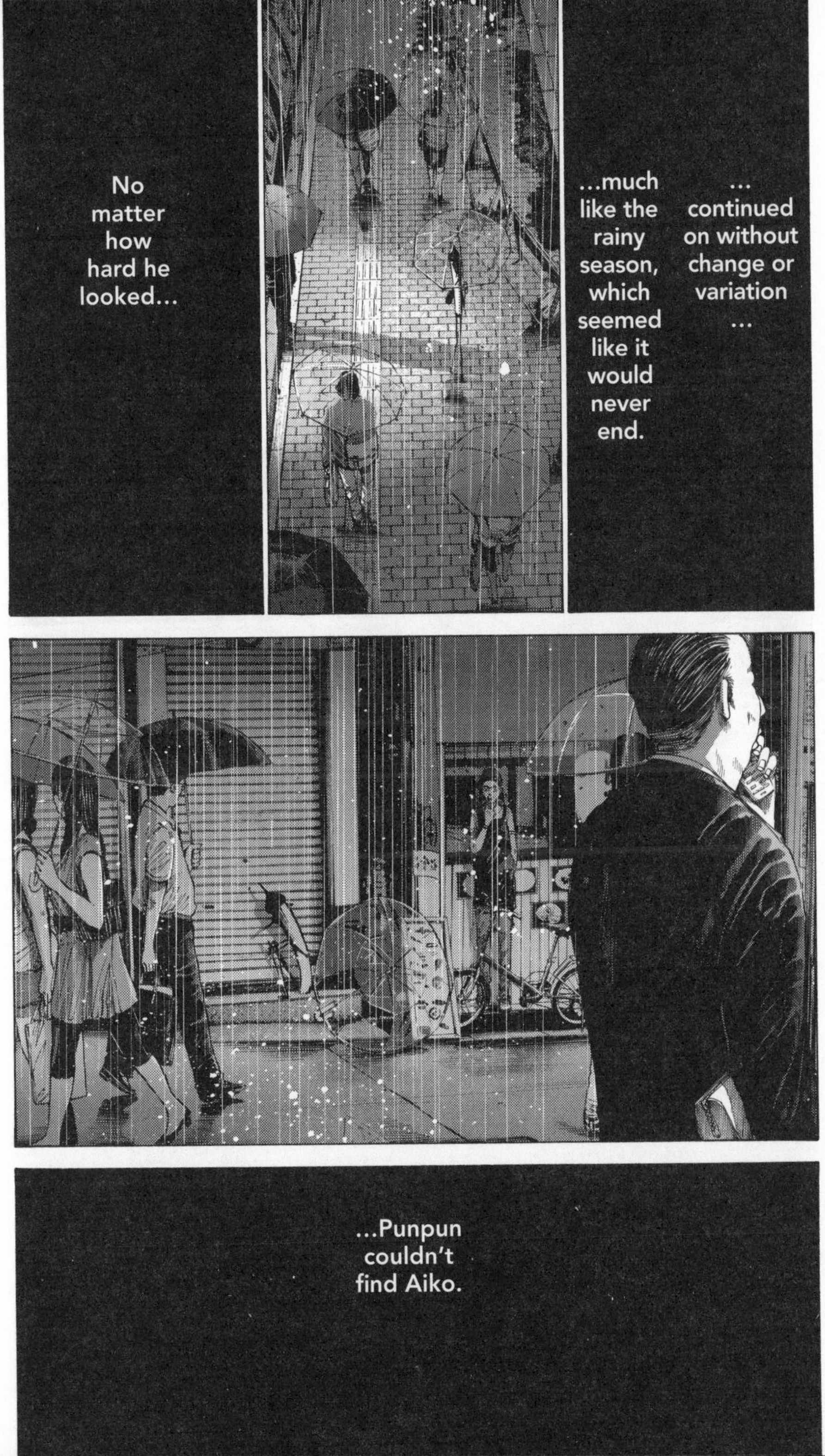
...continued on without change or variation...
...much like the rainy season, which seemed like it would never end.
No matter how hard he looked...
...Punpun couldn't find Aiko.

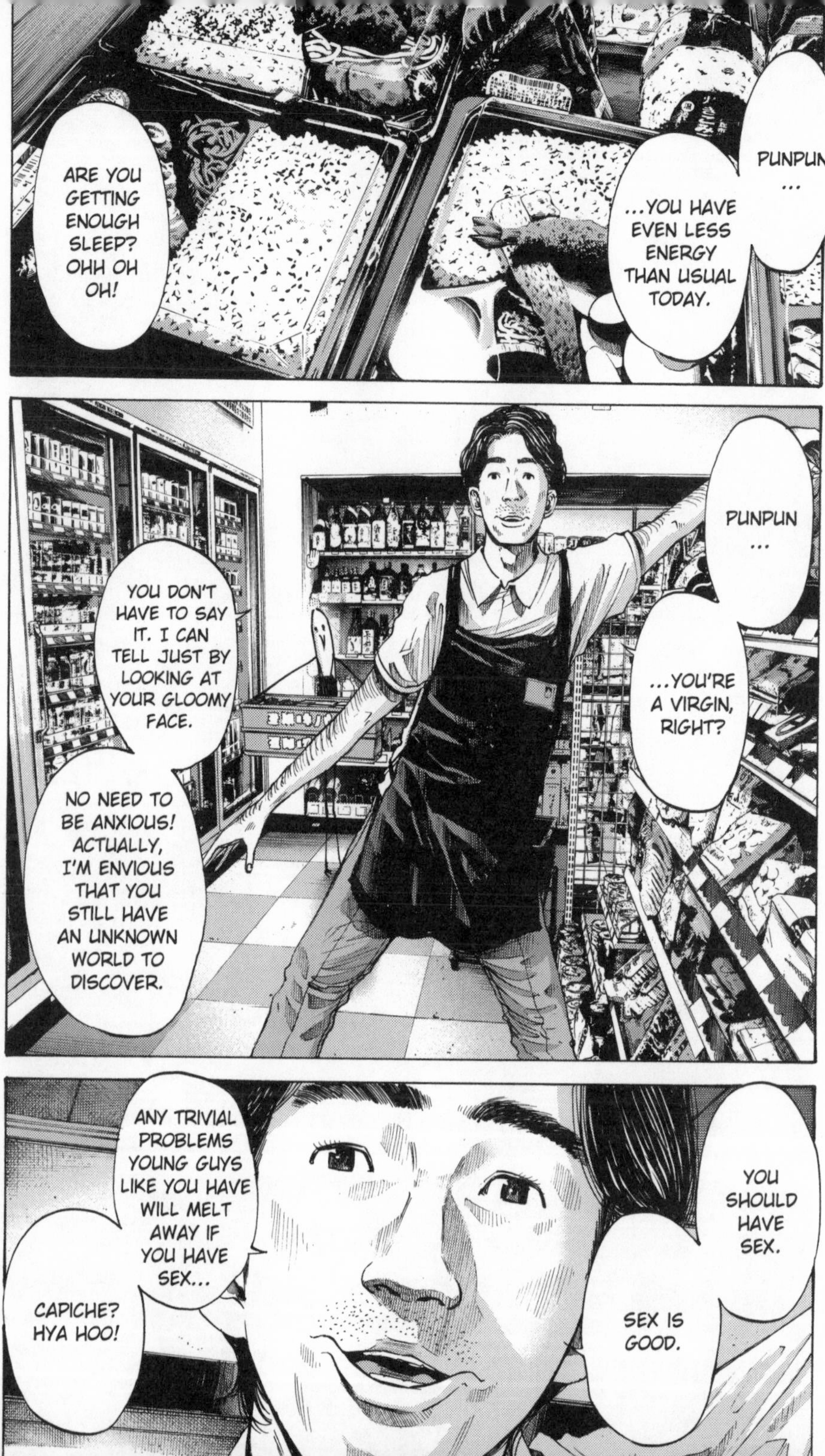
PUNPUN ...
...YOU HAVE EVEN LESS ENERGY THAN USUAL TODAY.
ARE YOU GETTING ENOUGH SLEEP? OHH OH OH!
PUNPUN ...
...YOU'RE A VIRGIN, RIGHT?
YOU DON'T HAVE TO SAY IT. I CAN TELL JUST BY LOOKING AT YOUR GLOOMY FACE.
NO NEED TO BE ANXIOUS! ACTUALLY, I'M ENVIOUS THAT YOU STILL HAVE AN UNKNOWN WORLD TO DISCOVER.
YOU SHOULD HAVE SEX.
SEX IS GOOD.
ANY TRIVIAL PROBLEMS YOUNG GUYS LIKE YOU HAVE WILL MELT AWAY IF YOU HAVE SEX...
CAPICHE? HYA HOO!

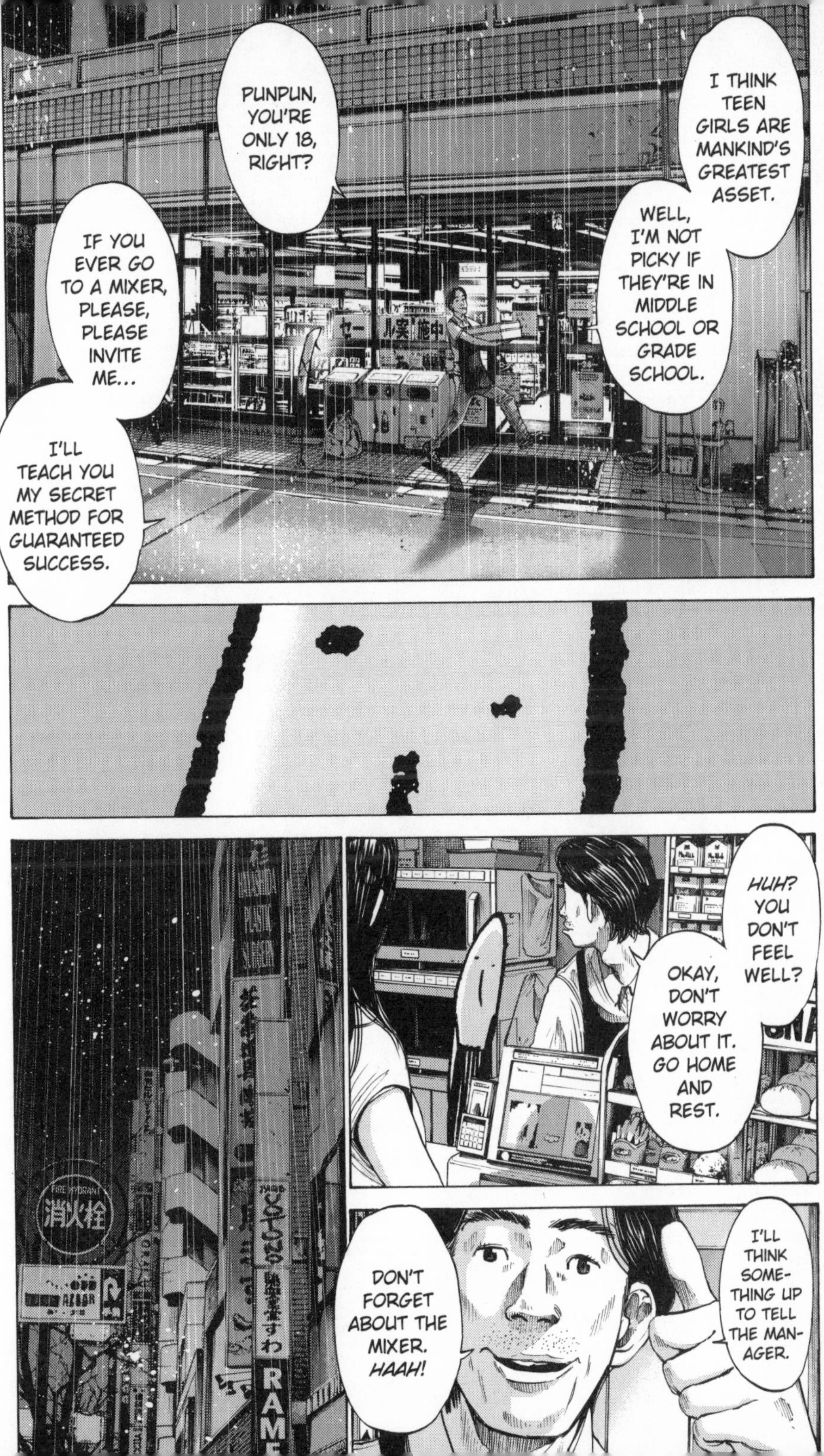
I THINK TEEN GIRLS ARE MANKIND'S GREATEST ASSET.
WELL, I'M NOT PICKY IF THEY'RE IN MIDDLE SCHOOL OR GRADE SCHOOL.
PUNPUN, YOU'RE ONLY 18, RIGHT?
IF YOU EVER GO TO A MIXER, PLEASE, PLEASE INVITE ME...
I'LL TEACH YOU MY SECRET METHOD FOR GUARANTEED SUCCESS.
HUH? YOU DON'T FEEL WELL?
OKAY, DON'T WORRY ABOUT IT. GO HOME AND REST.
I'LL THINK SOME-THING UP TO TELL THE MAN-AGER.
DON'T FORGET ABOUT THE MIXER. *HAAH!*
FIRE HYDRANT
消火栓
RAM

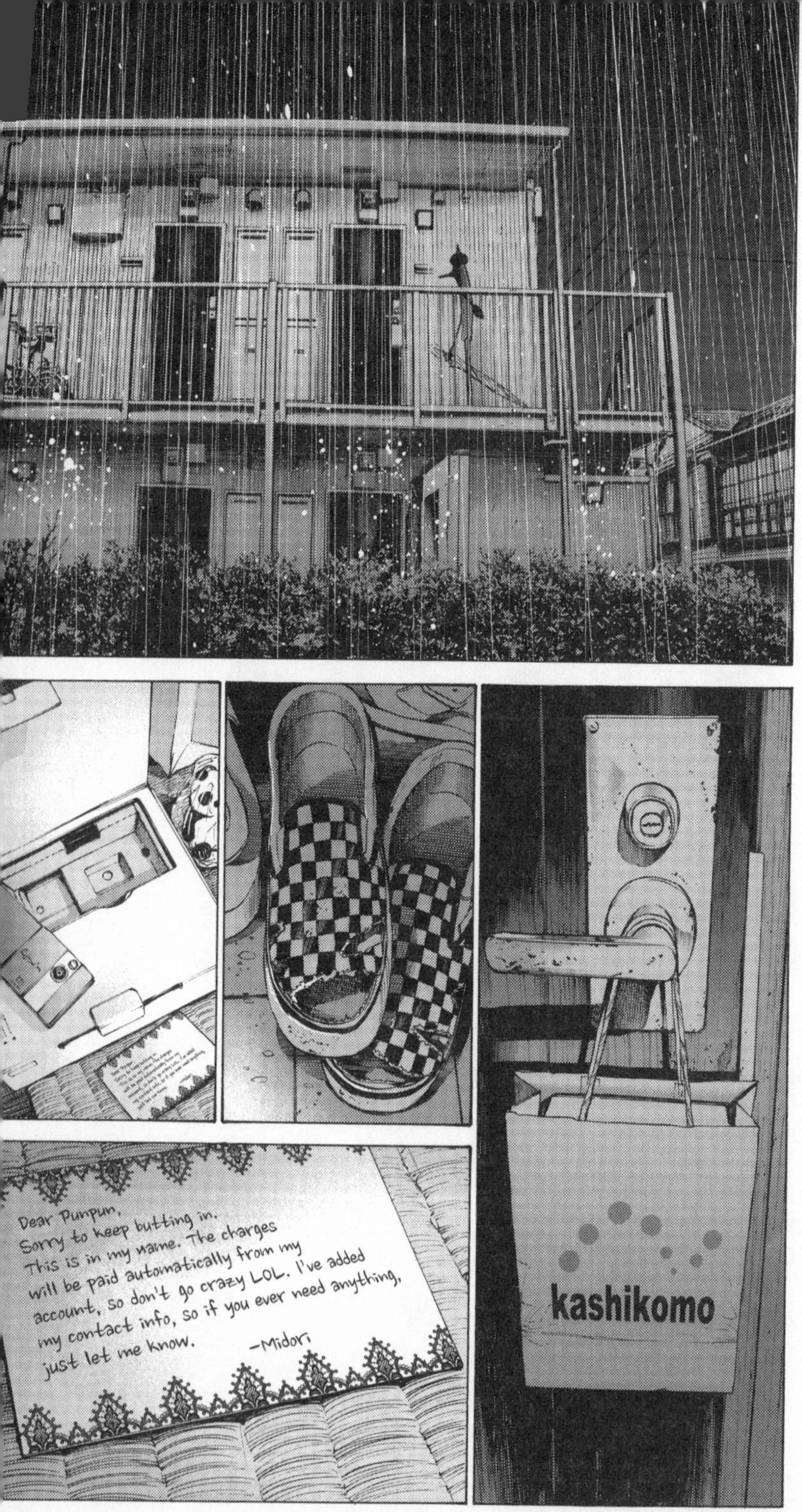
kashikomo
Dear Punpun,
Sorry to keep butting in.
This is in my name. The charges
will be paid automatically from my
account, so don't go crazy LOL. I've added
my contact info, so if you ever need anything,
just let me know.
—Midori

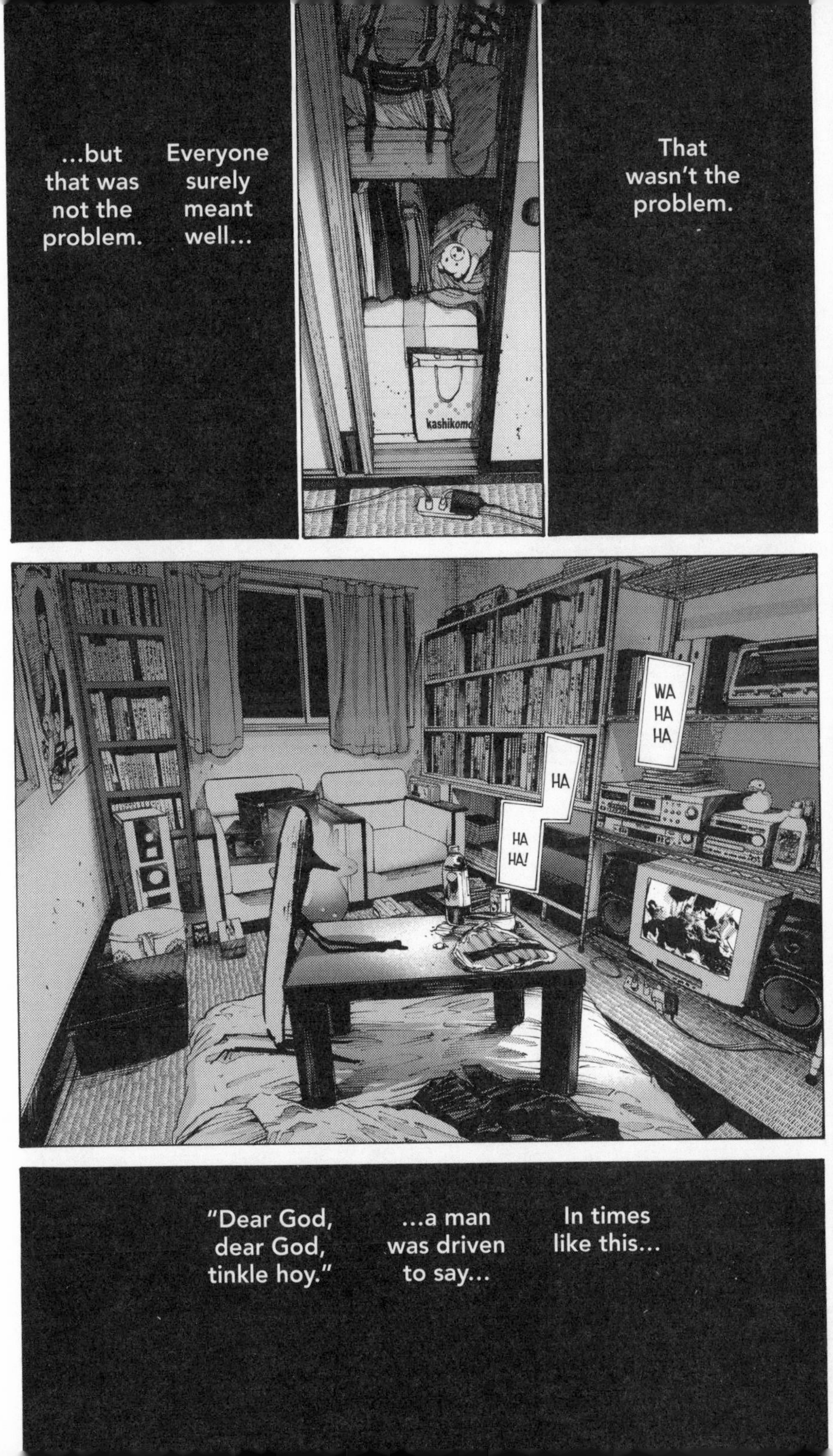
That wasn't the problem.
Everyone surely meant well...
...but that was not the problem.
WA HA HA
HA
HA HA!
In times like this...
...a man was driven to say...
"Dear God, dear God, tinkle hoy."

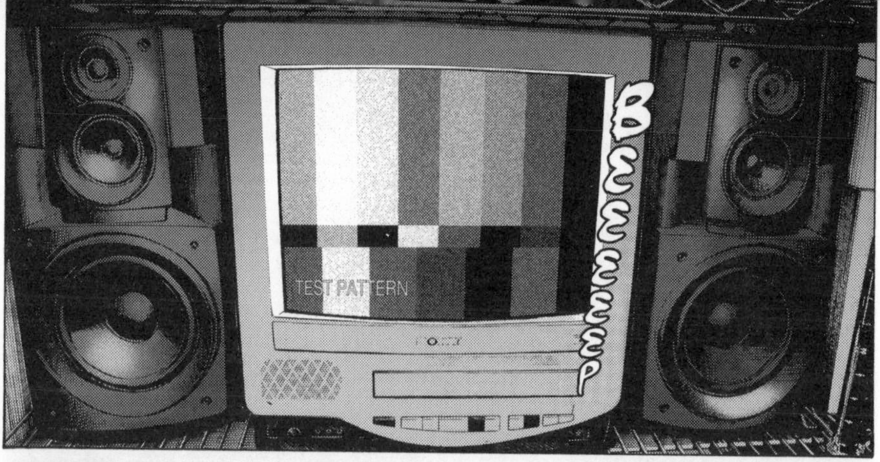
BEEEEEEP
TEST PATTERN
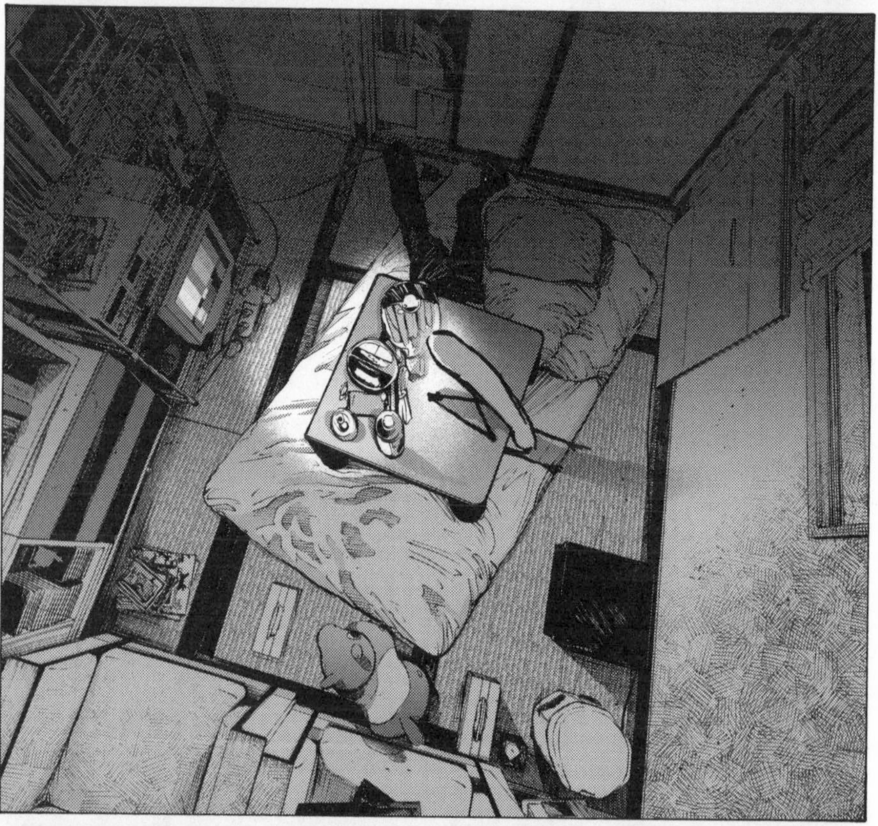

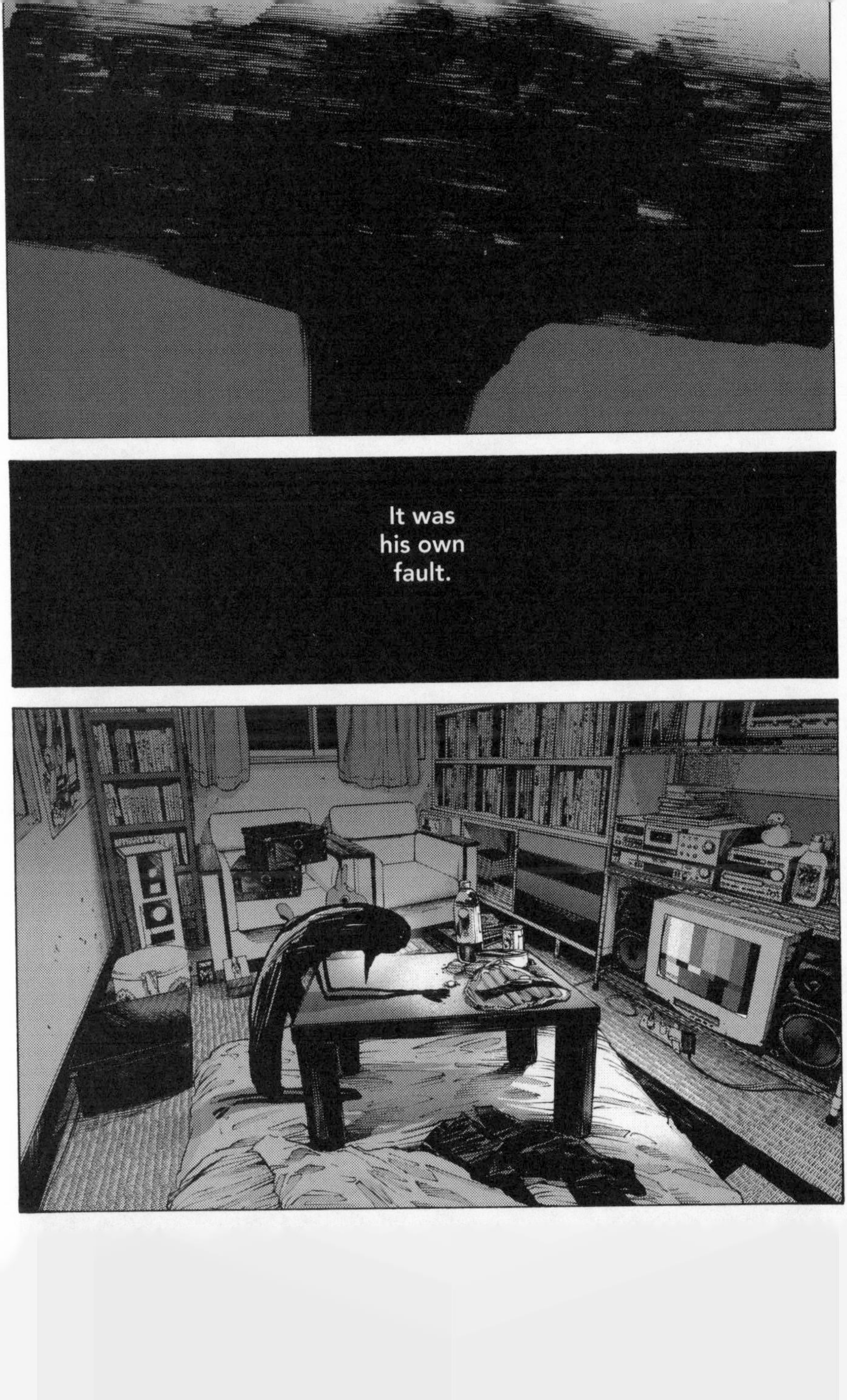
It was
his own
fault.

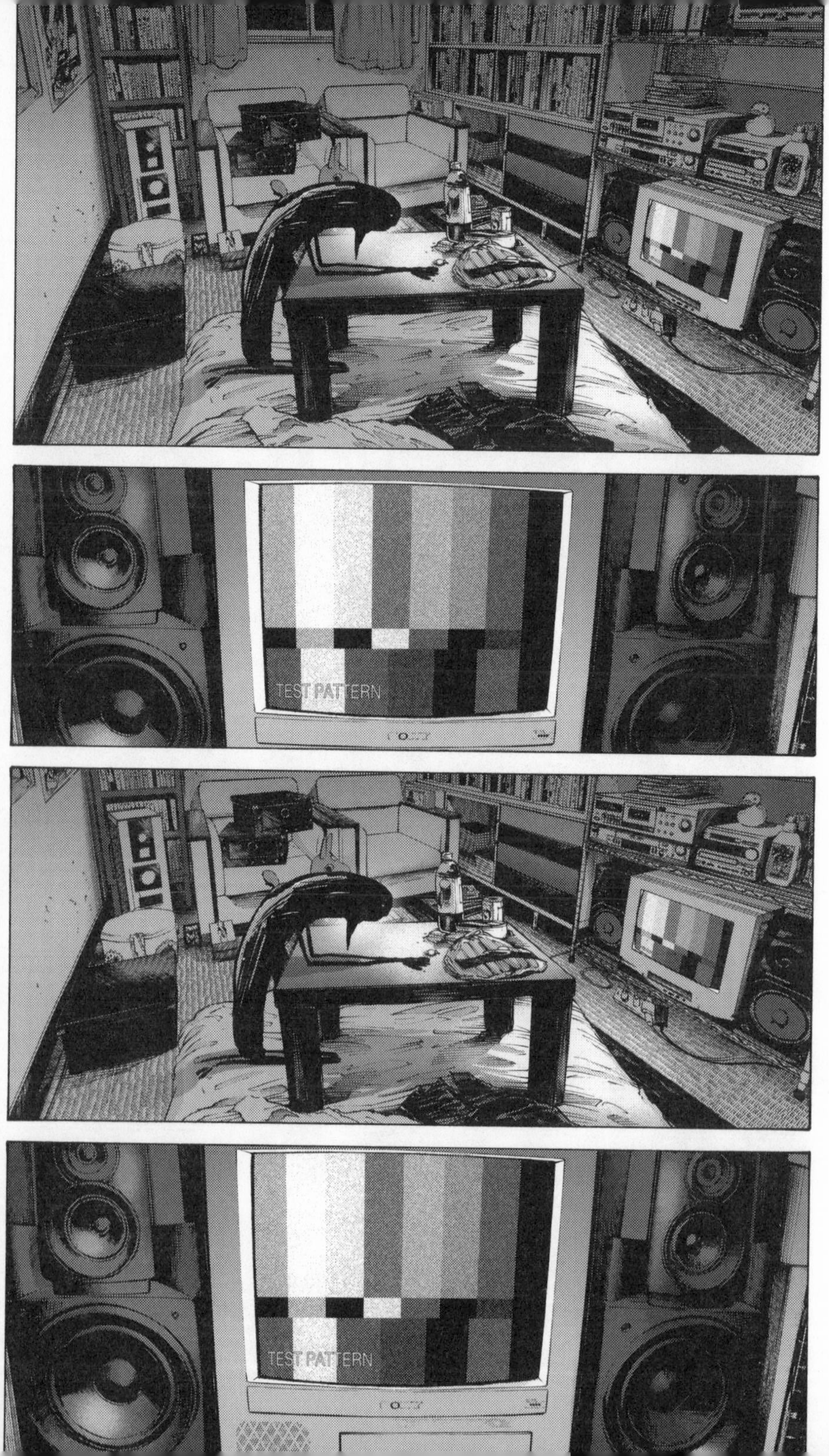
TEST PATTERN
TEST PATTERN

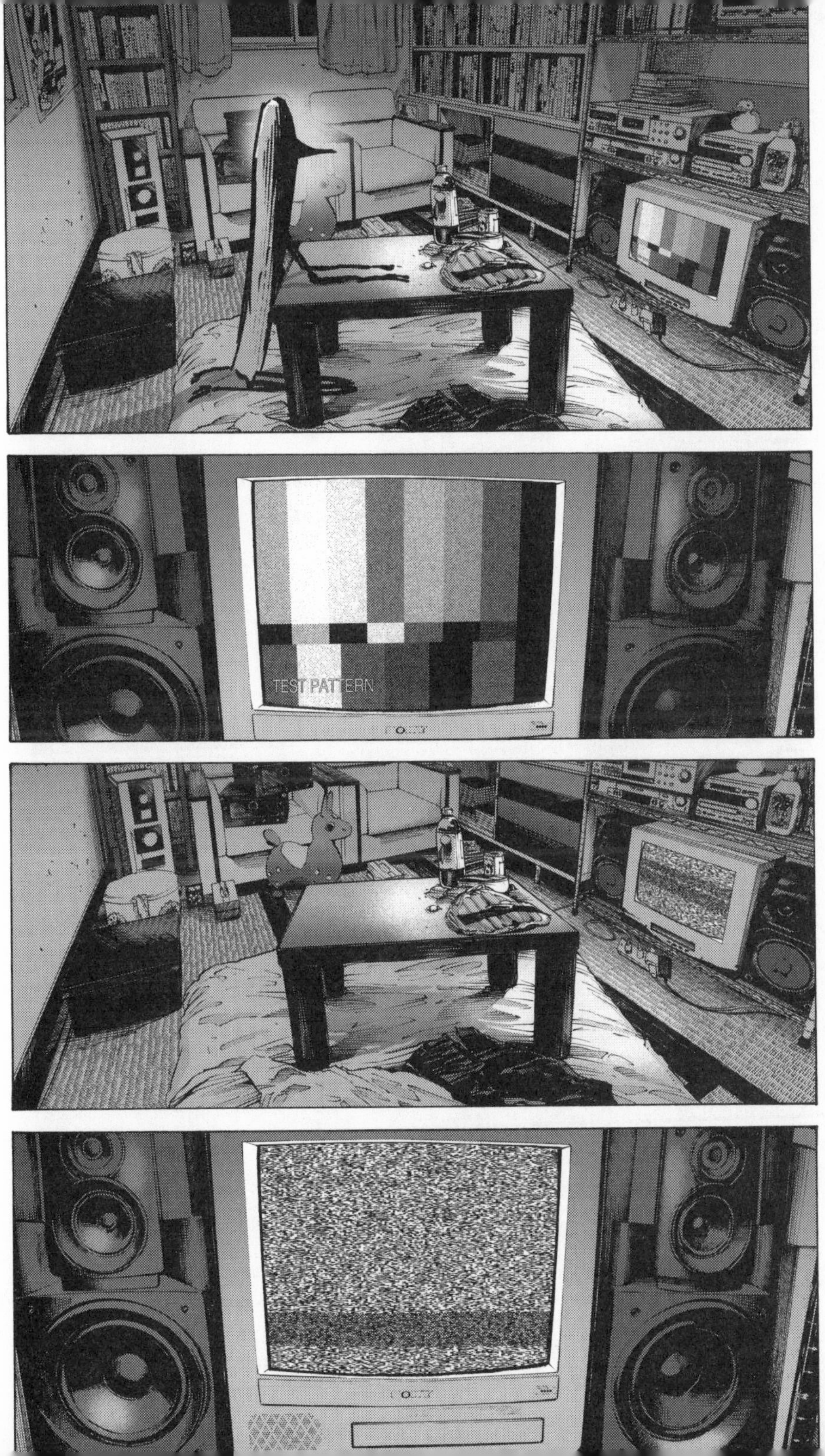
TEST PATTERN

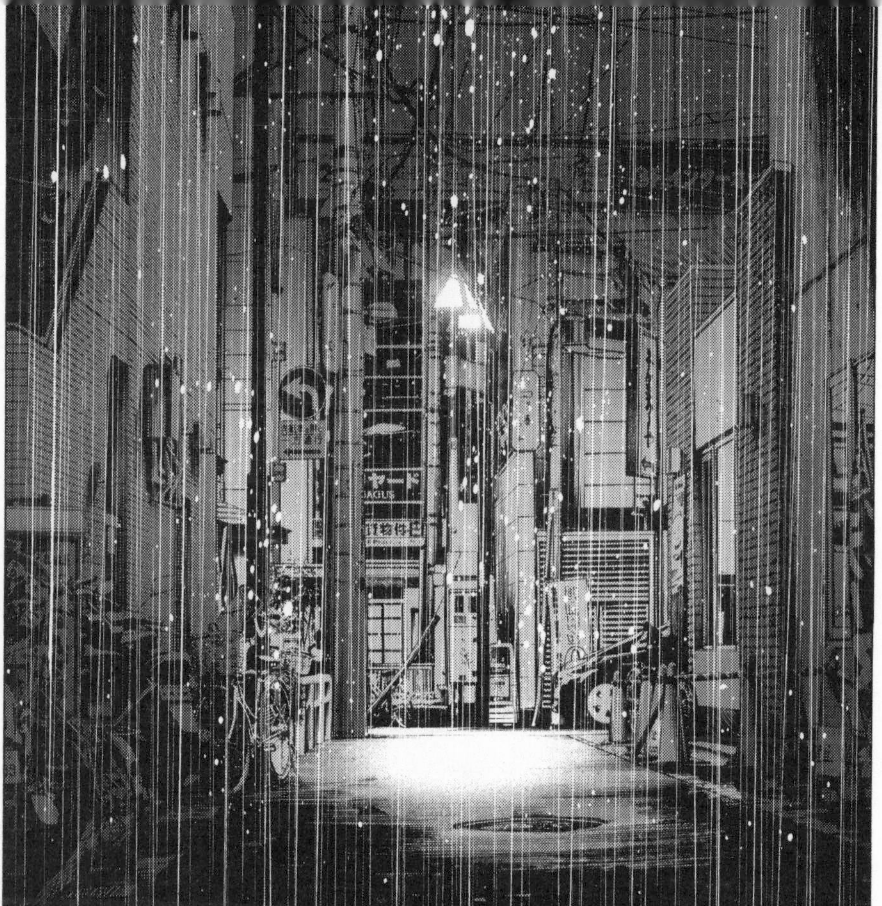

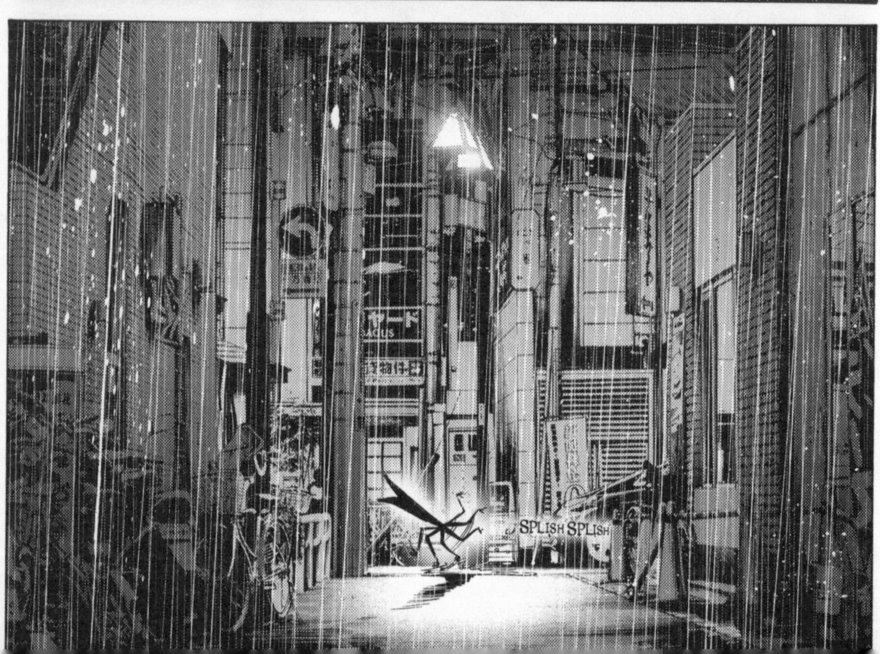
SPLISH SPLISH

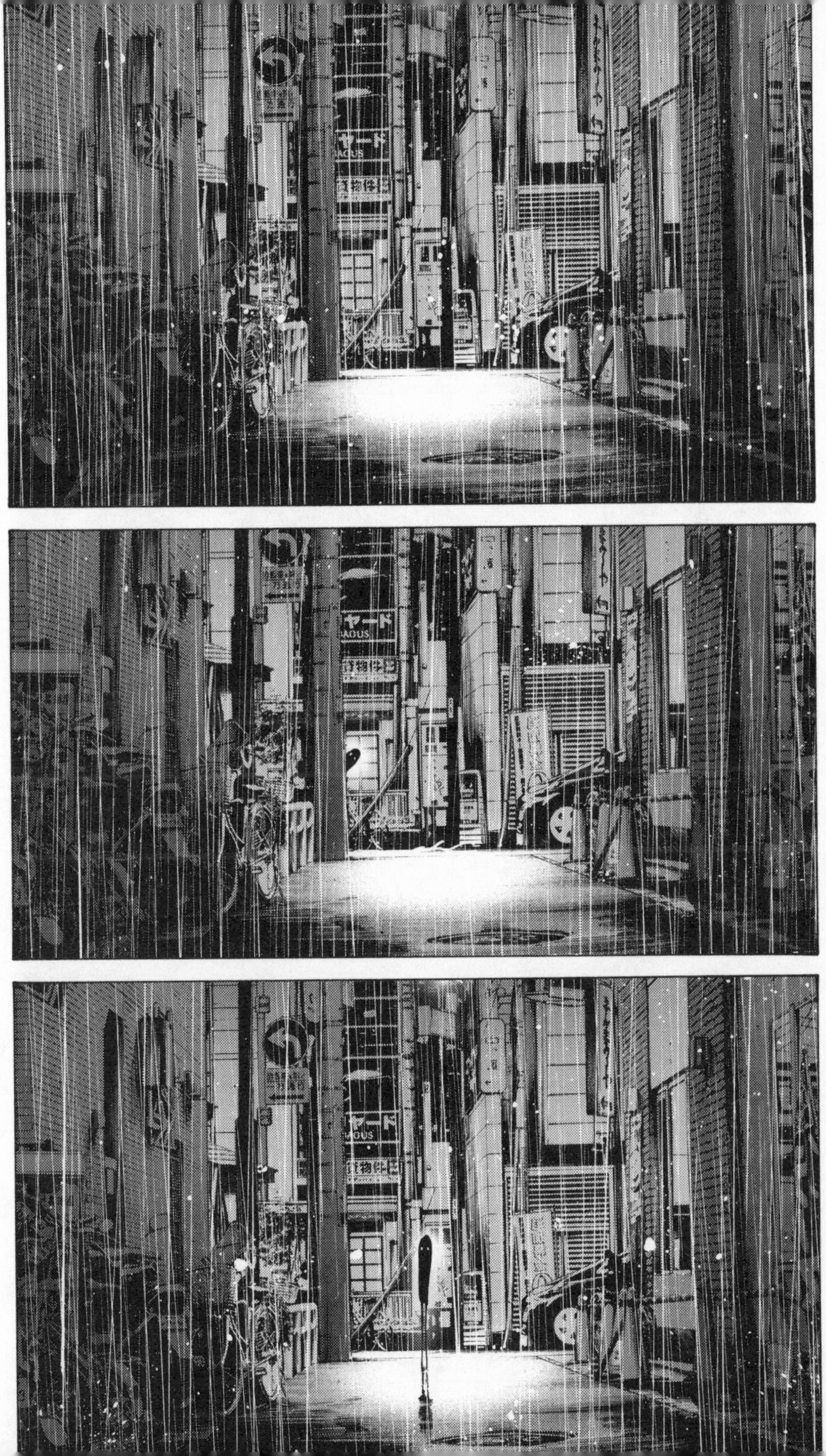

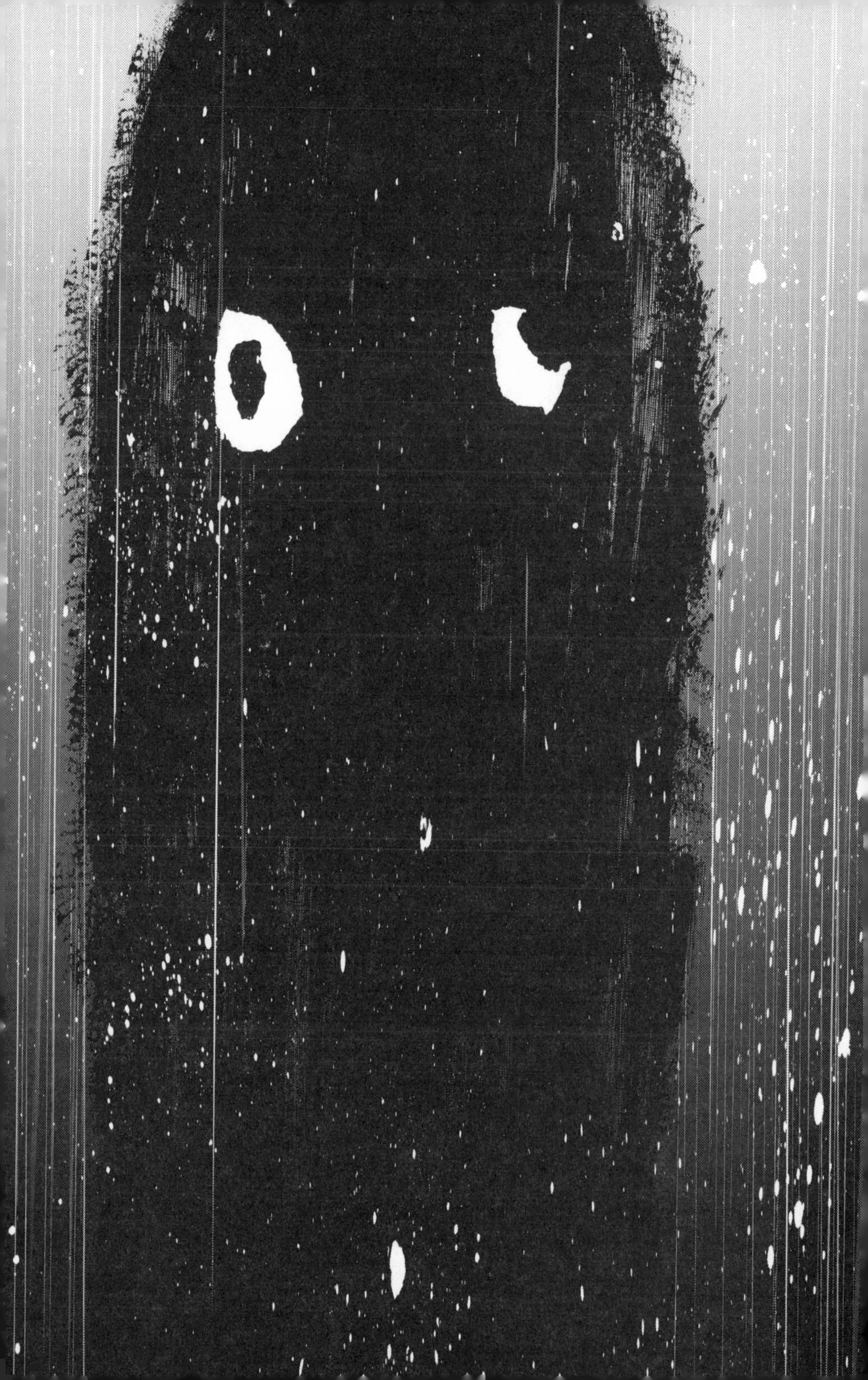

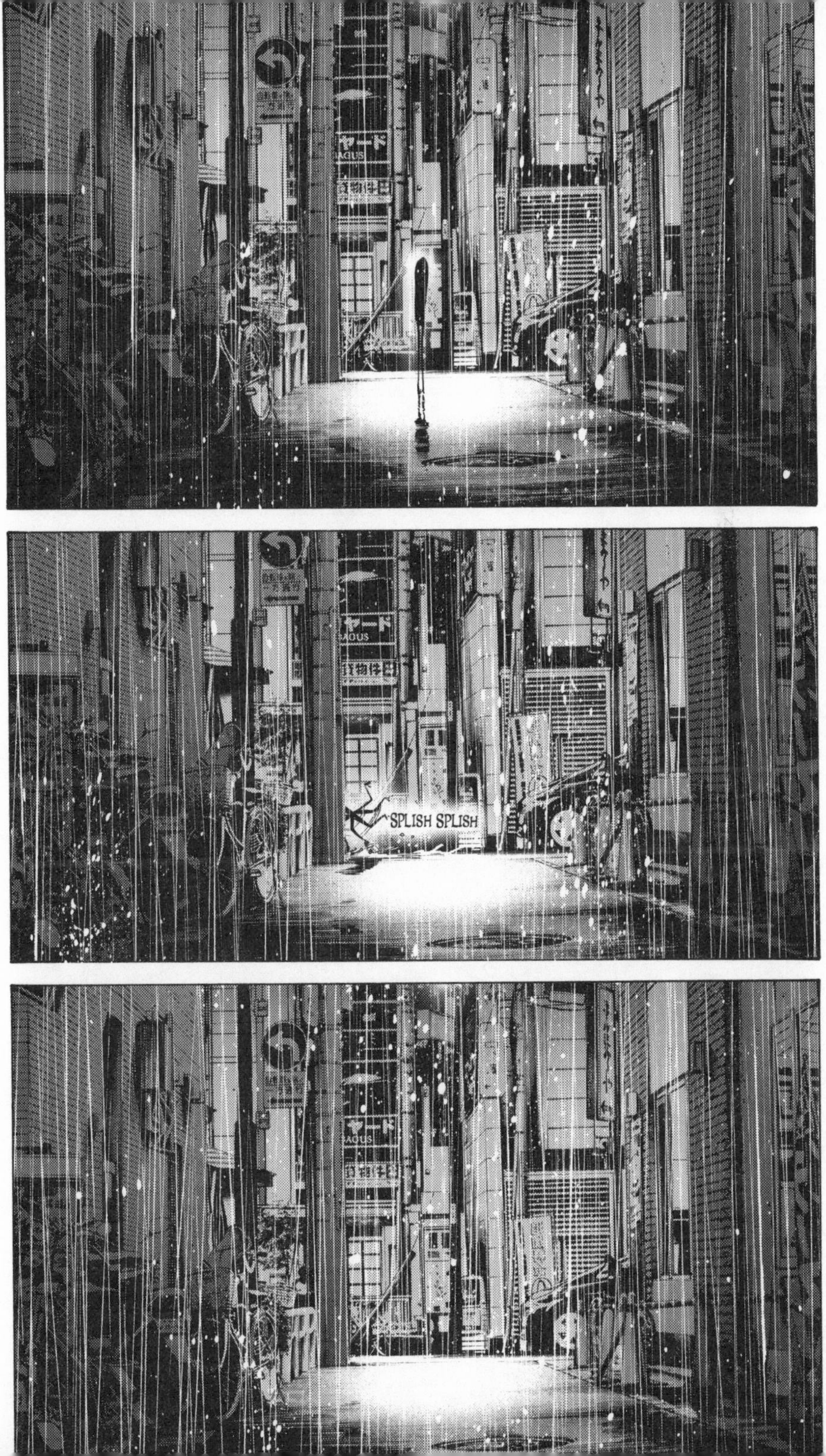
SPLISH SPLISH

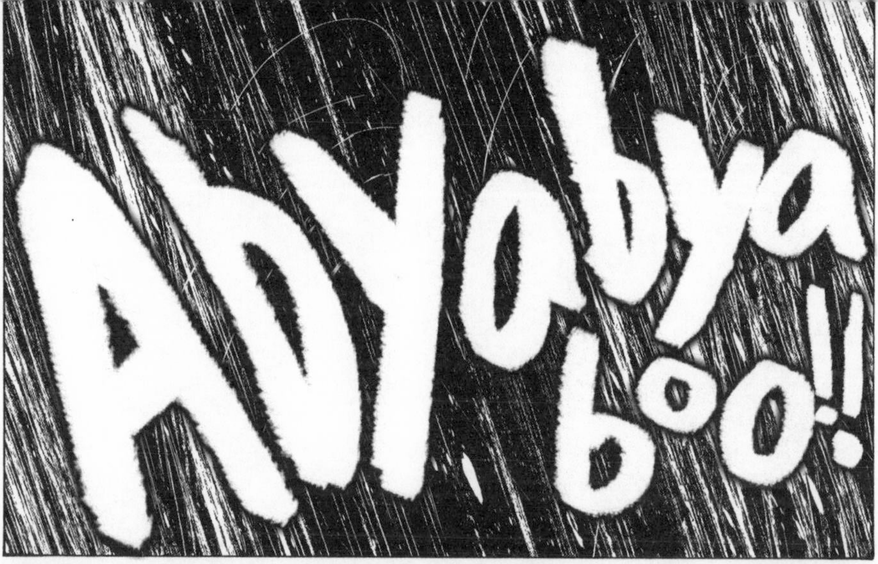
ADYobya boo!!
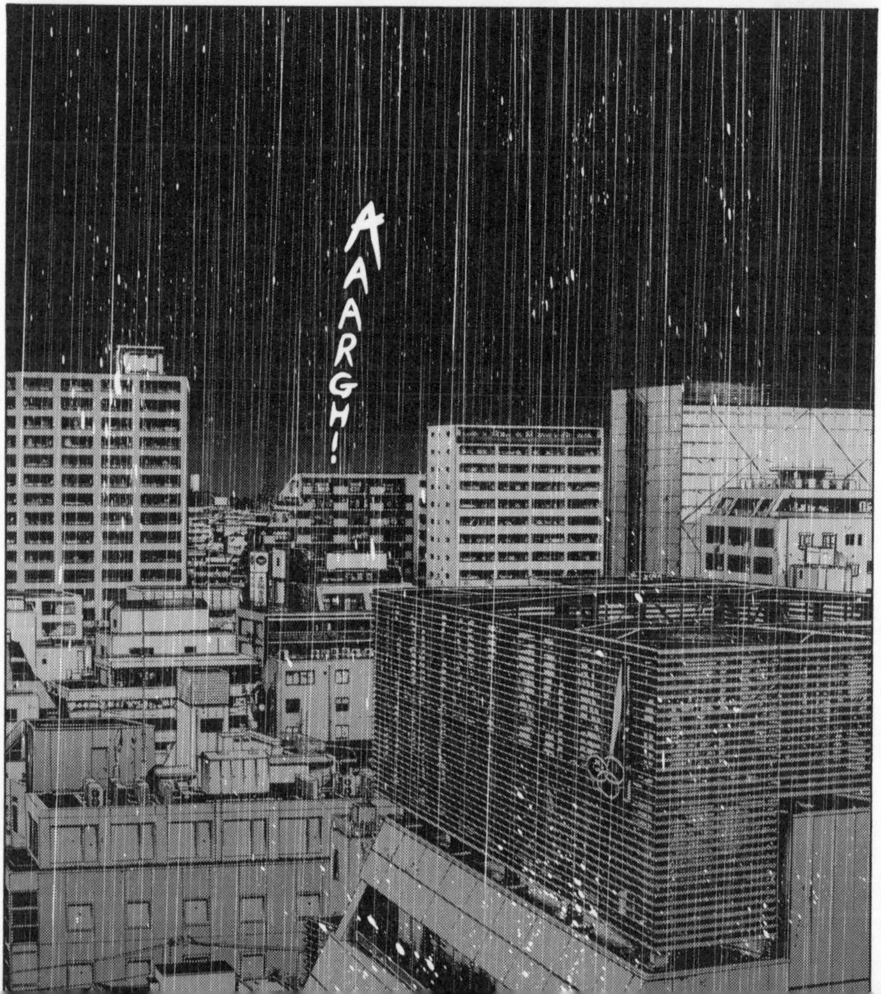
AAAARGH!

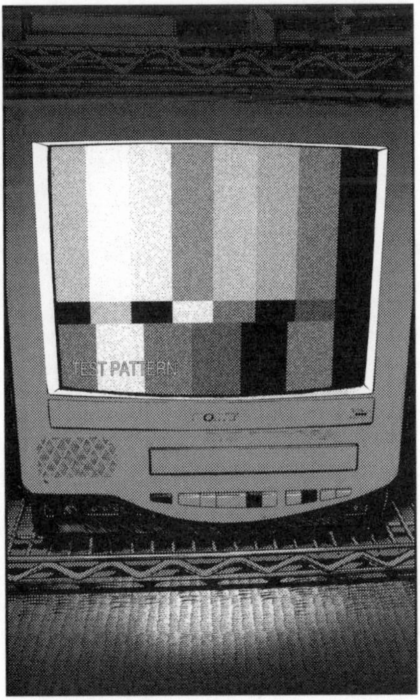
TEST PATTERN

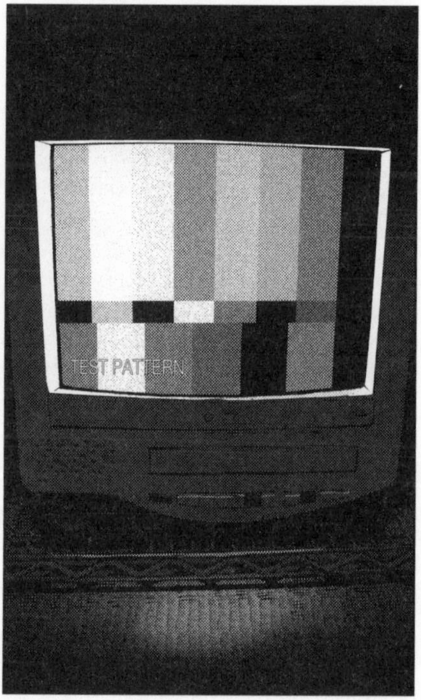
TEST PATTERN

Chapter 77

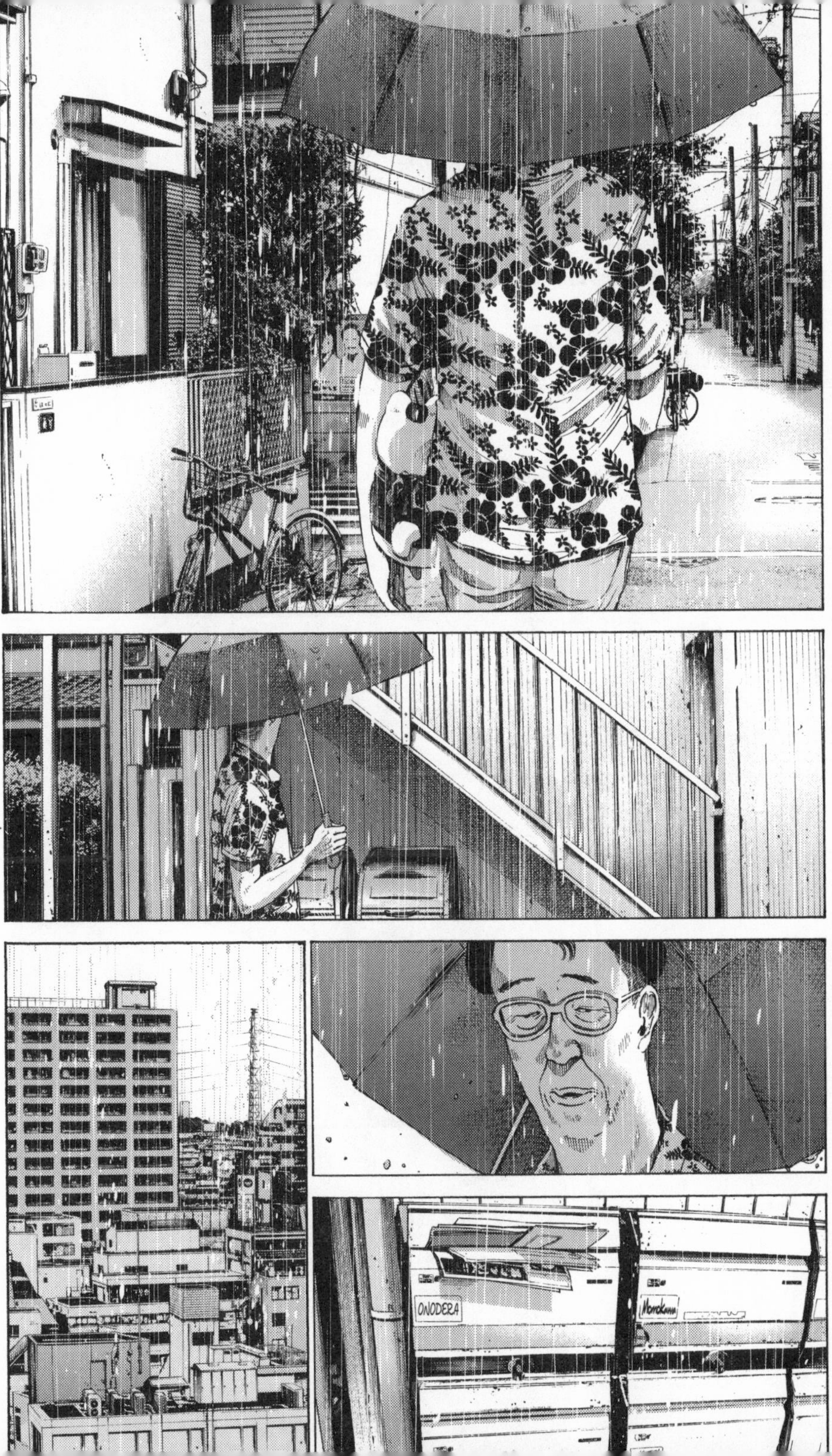
ONODERA

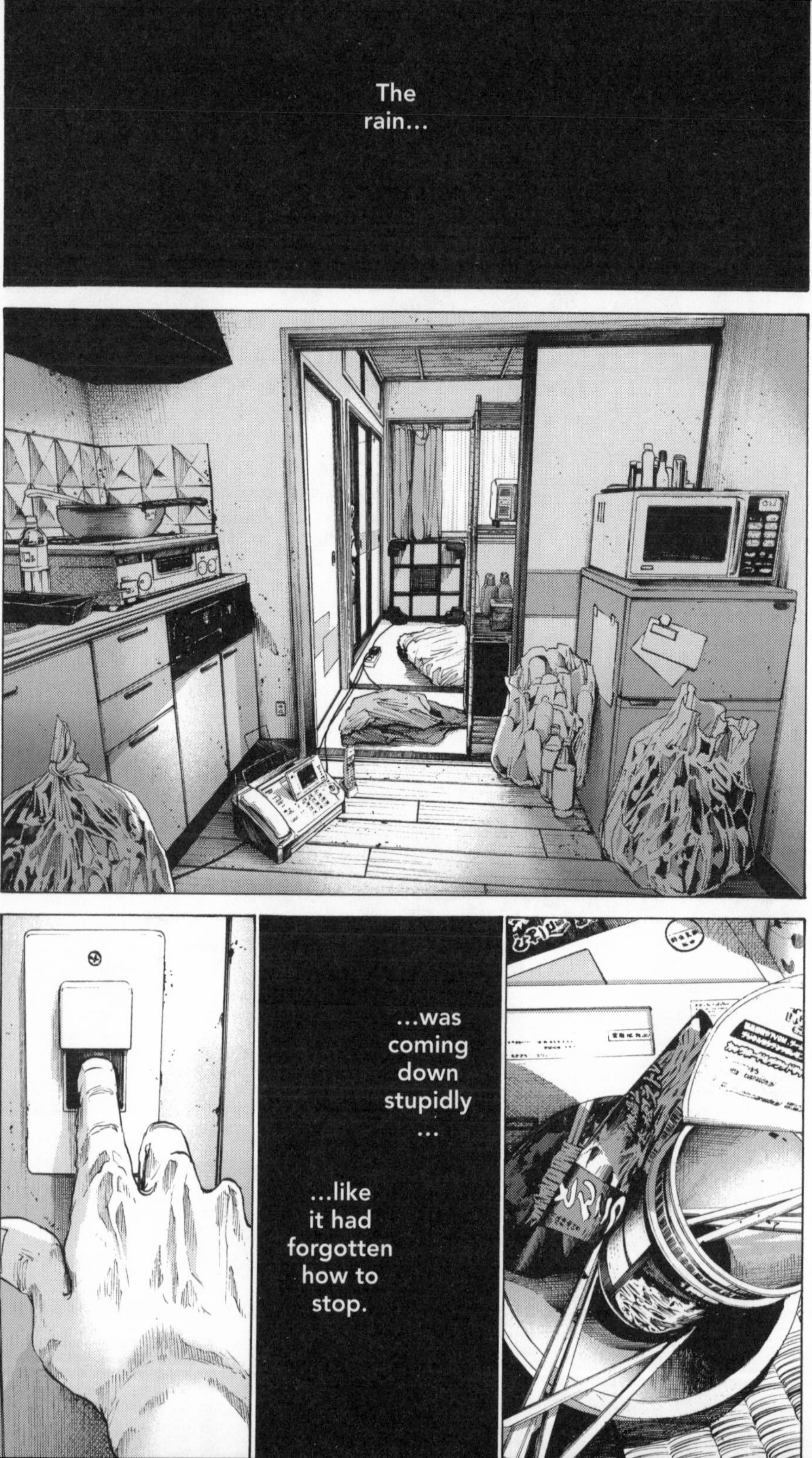
The rain...
...was coming down stupidly...
...like it had forgotten how to stop.

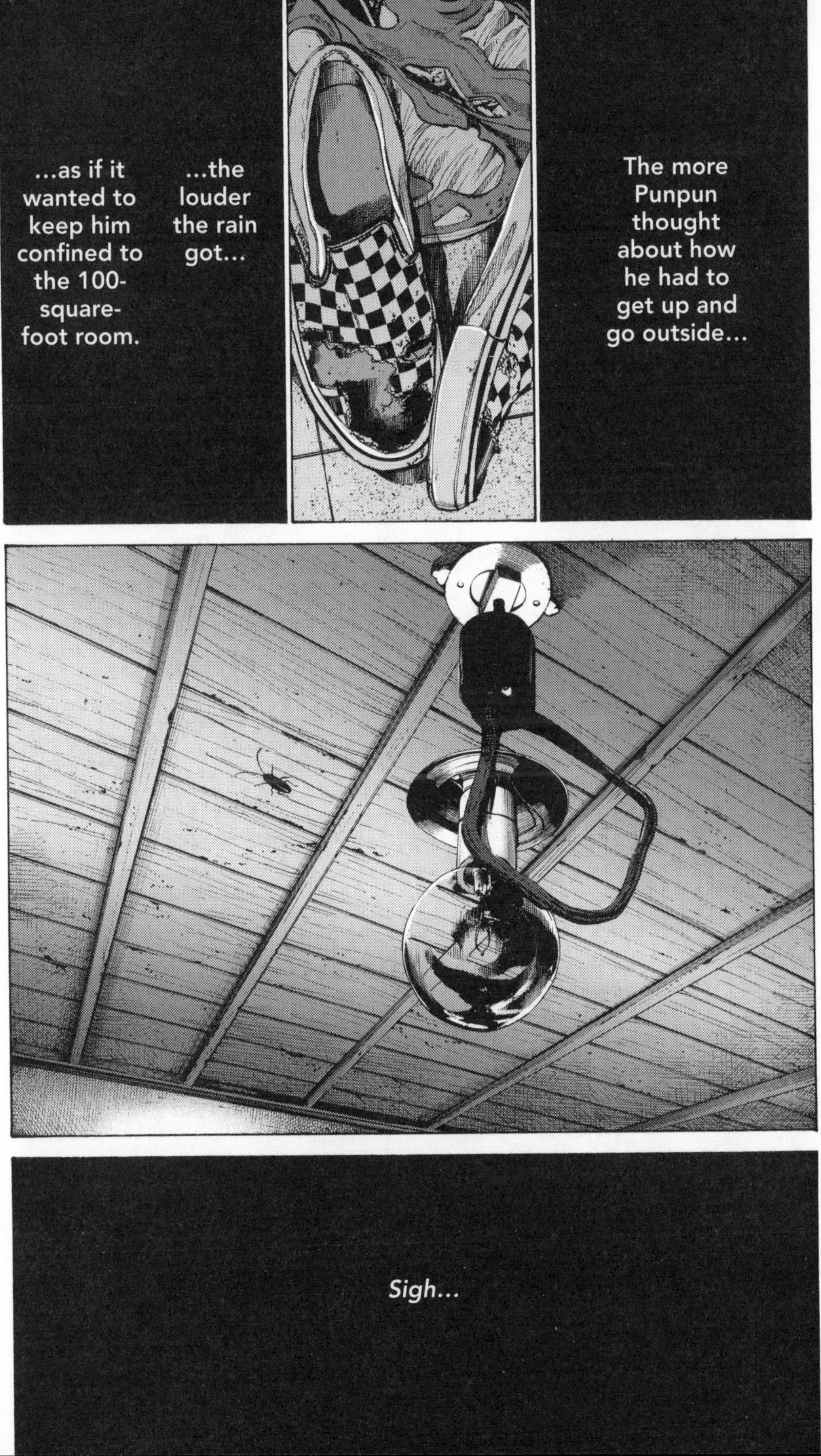
The more Punpun thought about how he had to get up and go outside...
...the louder the rain got...
...as if it wanted to keep him confined to the 100-square-foot room.
Sigh...

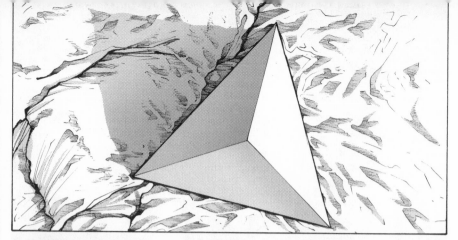

DING DONG

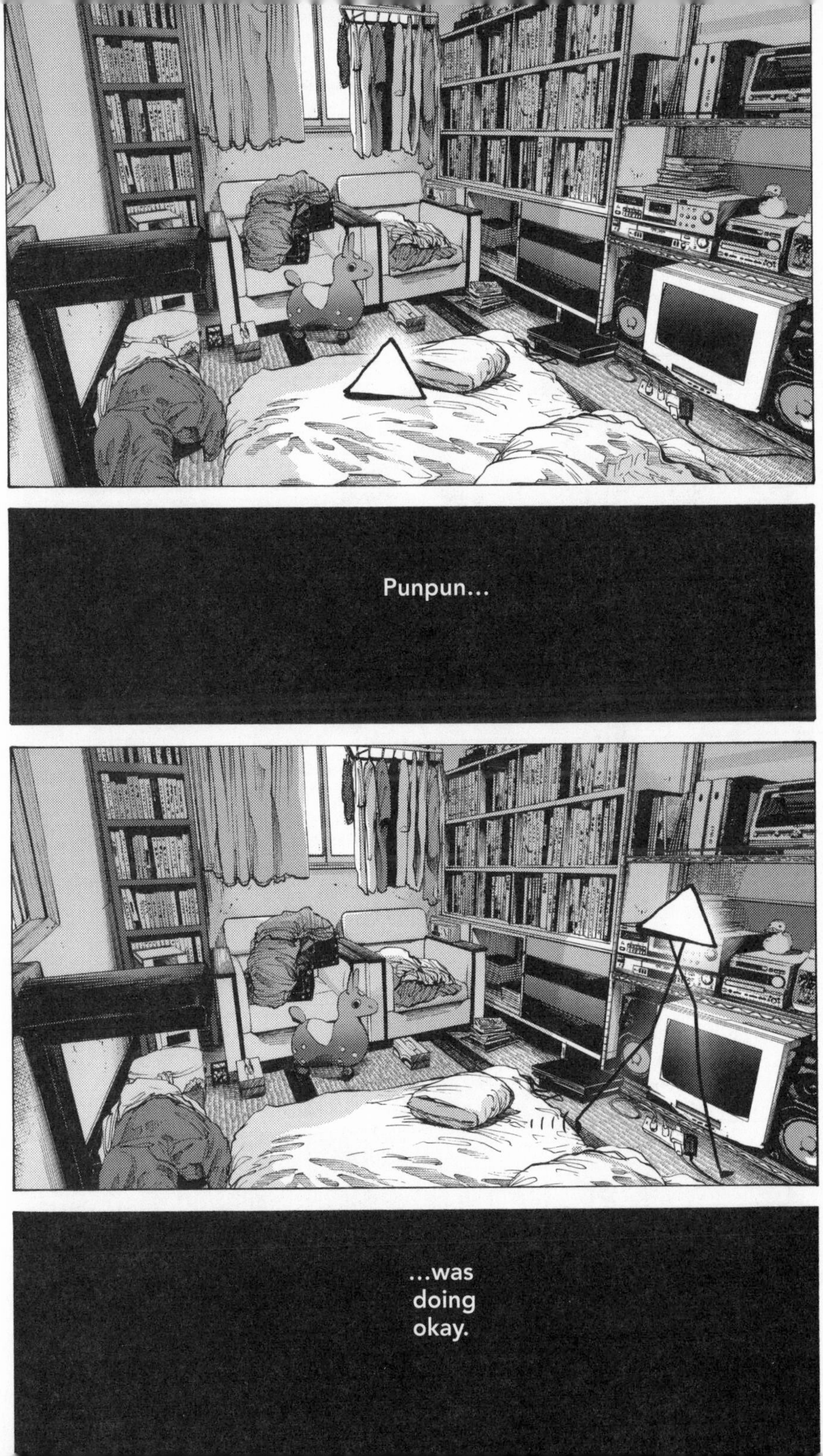
Punpun...
...was doing okay.

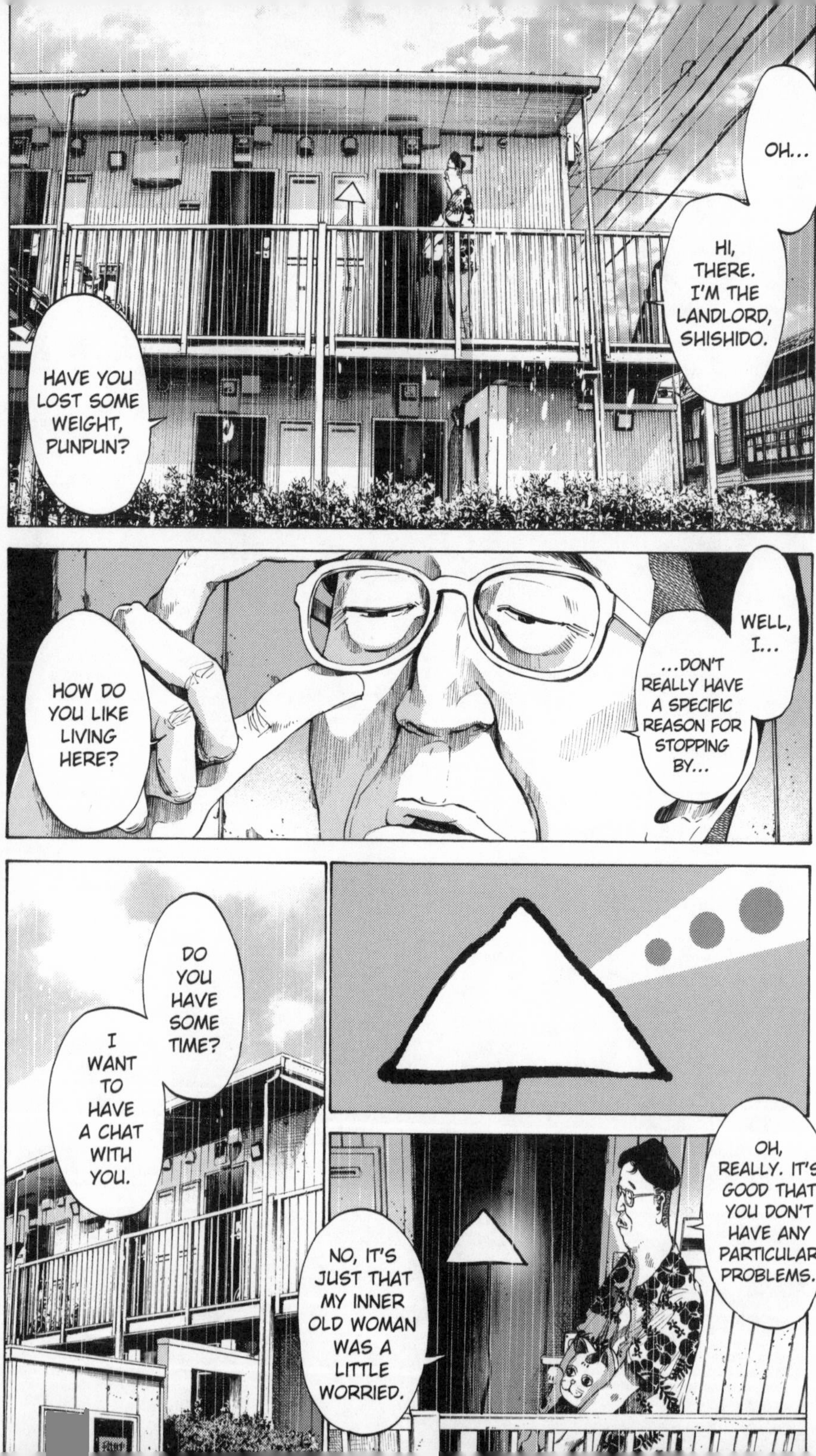
OH...
HI, THERE. I'M THE LANDLORD, SHISHIDO.
HAVE YOU LOST SOME WEIGHT, PUNPUN?
WELL, I...
...DON'T REALLY HAVE A SPECIFIC REASON FOR STOPPING BY...
HOW DO YOU LIKE LIVING HERE?
OH, REALLY. IT'S GOOD THAT YOU DON'T HAVE ANY PARTICULAR PROBLEMS.
NO, IT'S JUST THAT MY INNER OLD WOMAN WAS A LITTLE WORRIED.
DO YOU HAVE SOME TIME?
I WANT TO HAVE A CHAT WITH YOU.

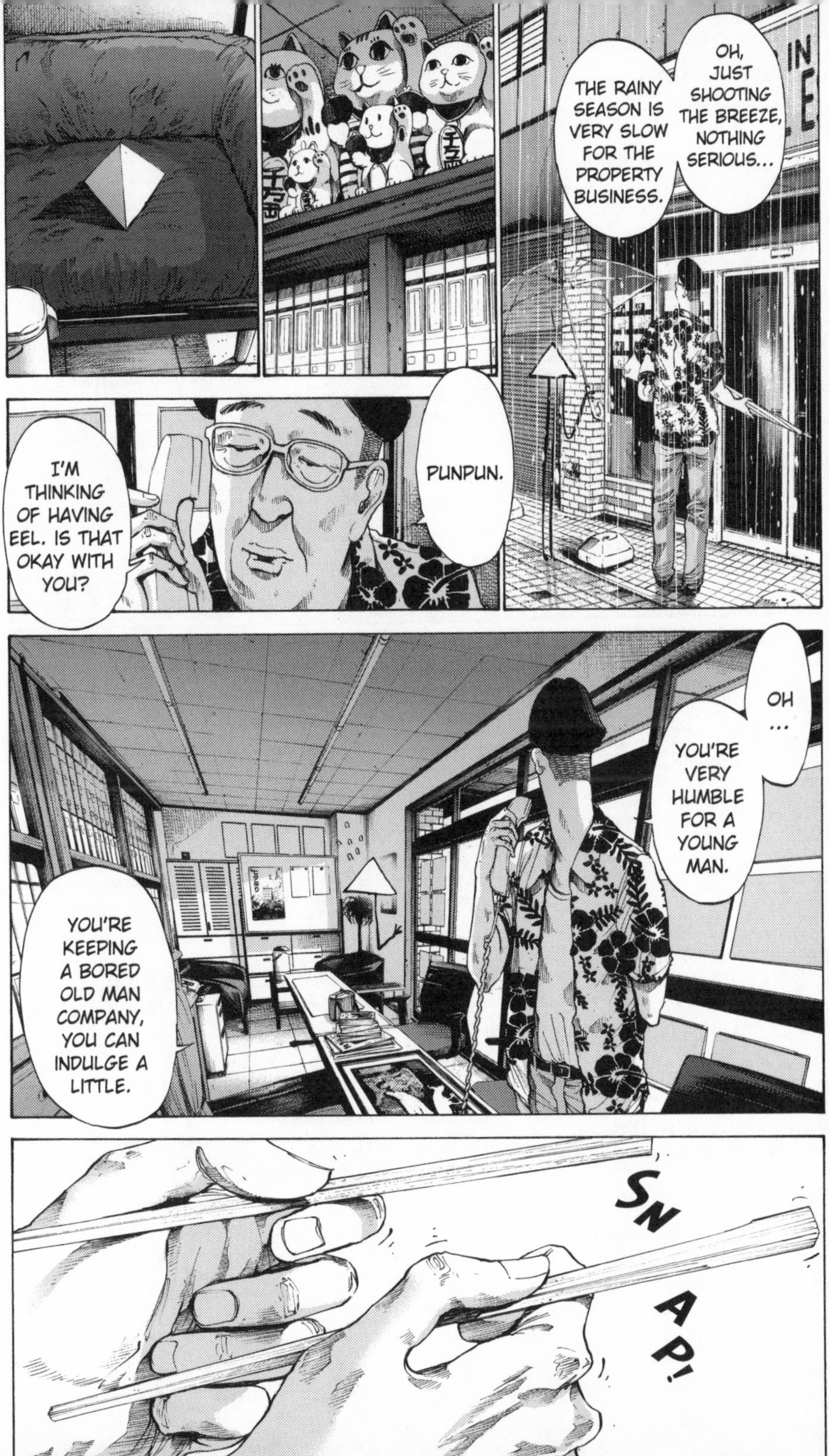
OH, JUST SHOOTING THE BREEZE, NOTHING SERIOUS...
THE RAINY SEASON IS VERY SLOW FOR THE PROPERTY BUSINESS.
PUNPUN.
I'M THINKING OF HAVING EEL. IS THAT OKAY WITH YOU?
OH ...
YOU'RE VERY HUMBLE FOR A YOUNG MAN.
YOU'RE KEEPING A BORED OLD MAN COMPANY, YOU CAN INDULGE A LITTLE.
SNAP!

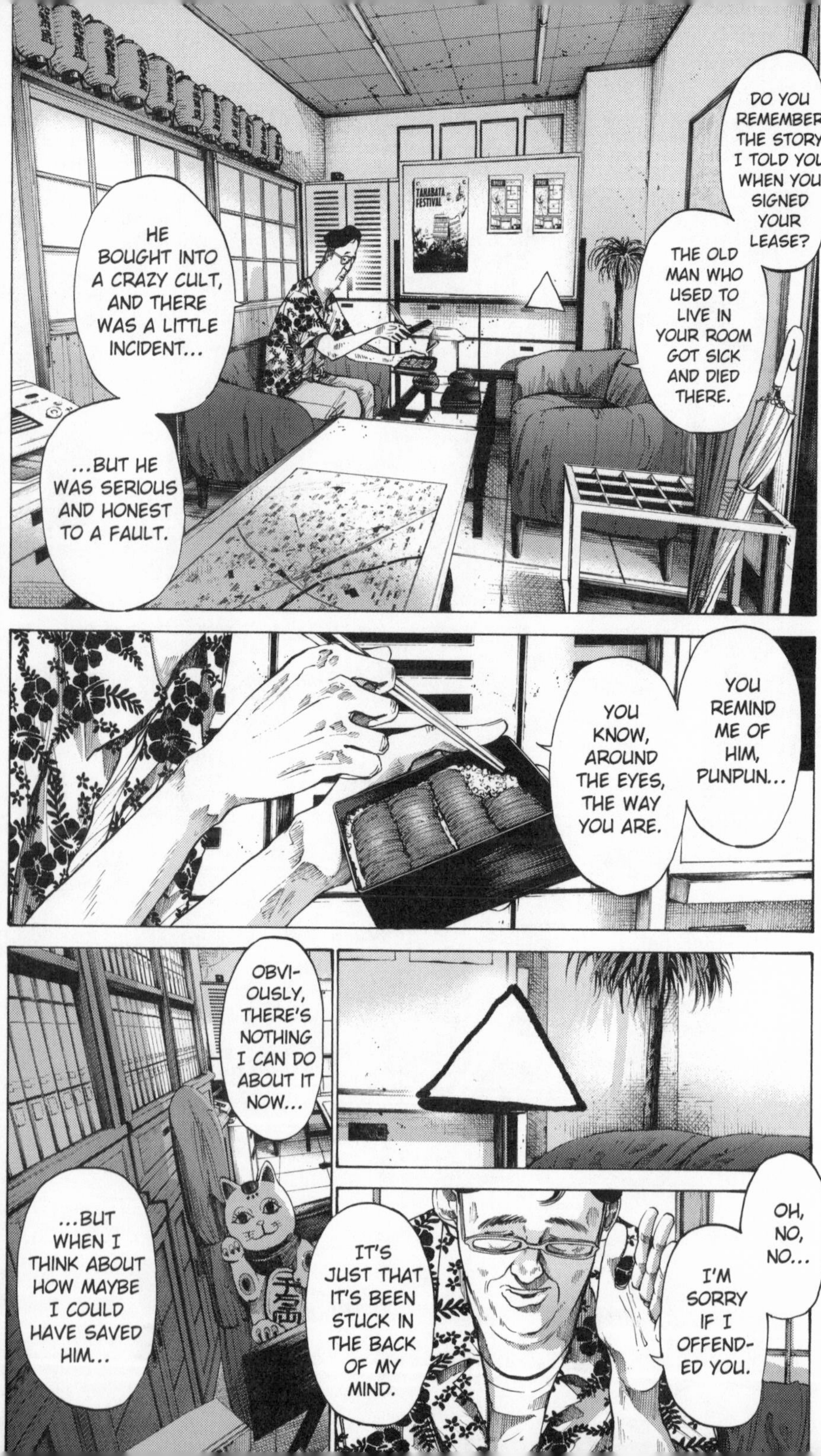
DO YOU REMEMBER THE STORY I TOLD YOU WHEN YOU SIGNED YOUR LEASE?
THE OLD MAN WHO USED TO LIVE IN YOUR ROOM GOT SICK AND DIED THERE.
TANABATA FESTIVAL
HE BOUGHT INTO A CRAZY CULT, AND THERE WAS A LITTLE INCIDENT...
...BUT HE WAS SERIOUS AND HONEST TO A FAULT.
YOU REMIND ME OF HIM, PUNPUN...
YOU KNOW, AROUND THE EYES, THE WAY YOU ARE.
OH, NO, NO...
I'M SORRY IF I OFFENDED YOU.
IT'S JUST THAT IT'S BEEN STUCK IN THE BACK OF MY MIND.
OBVIOUSLY, THERE'S NOTHING I CAN DO ABOUT IT NOW...
...BUT WHEN I THINK ABOUT HOW MAYBE I COULD HAVE SAVED HIM...

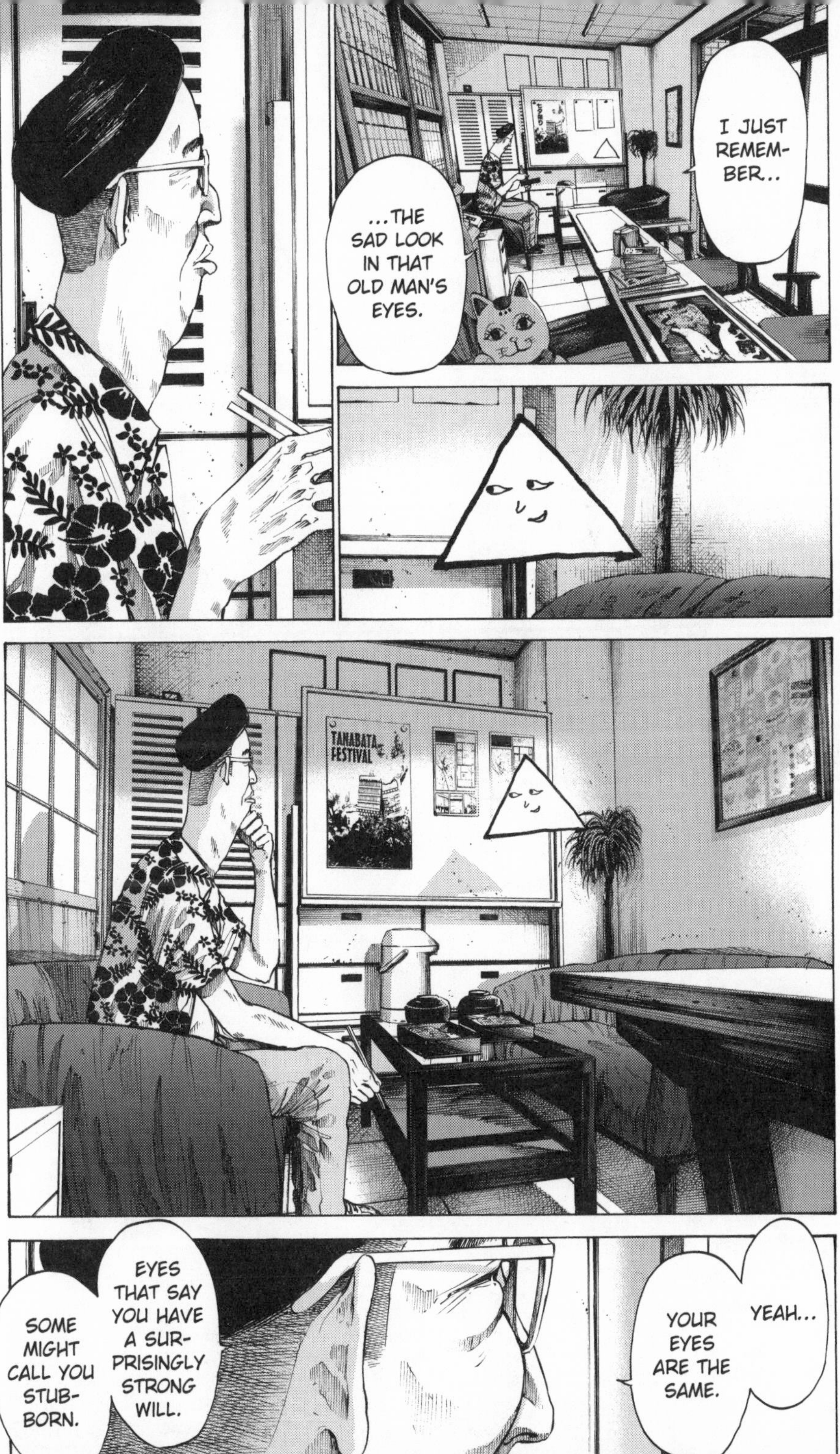
I JUST REMEMBER..
...THE SAD LOOK IN THAT OLD MAN'S EYES.
TANABATA FESTIVAL
YEAH...
YOUR EYES ARE THE SAME.
EYES THAT SAY YOU HAVE A SURPRISINGLY STRONG WILL.
SOME MIGHT CALL YOU STUBBORN.

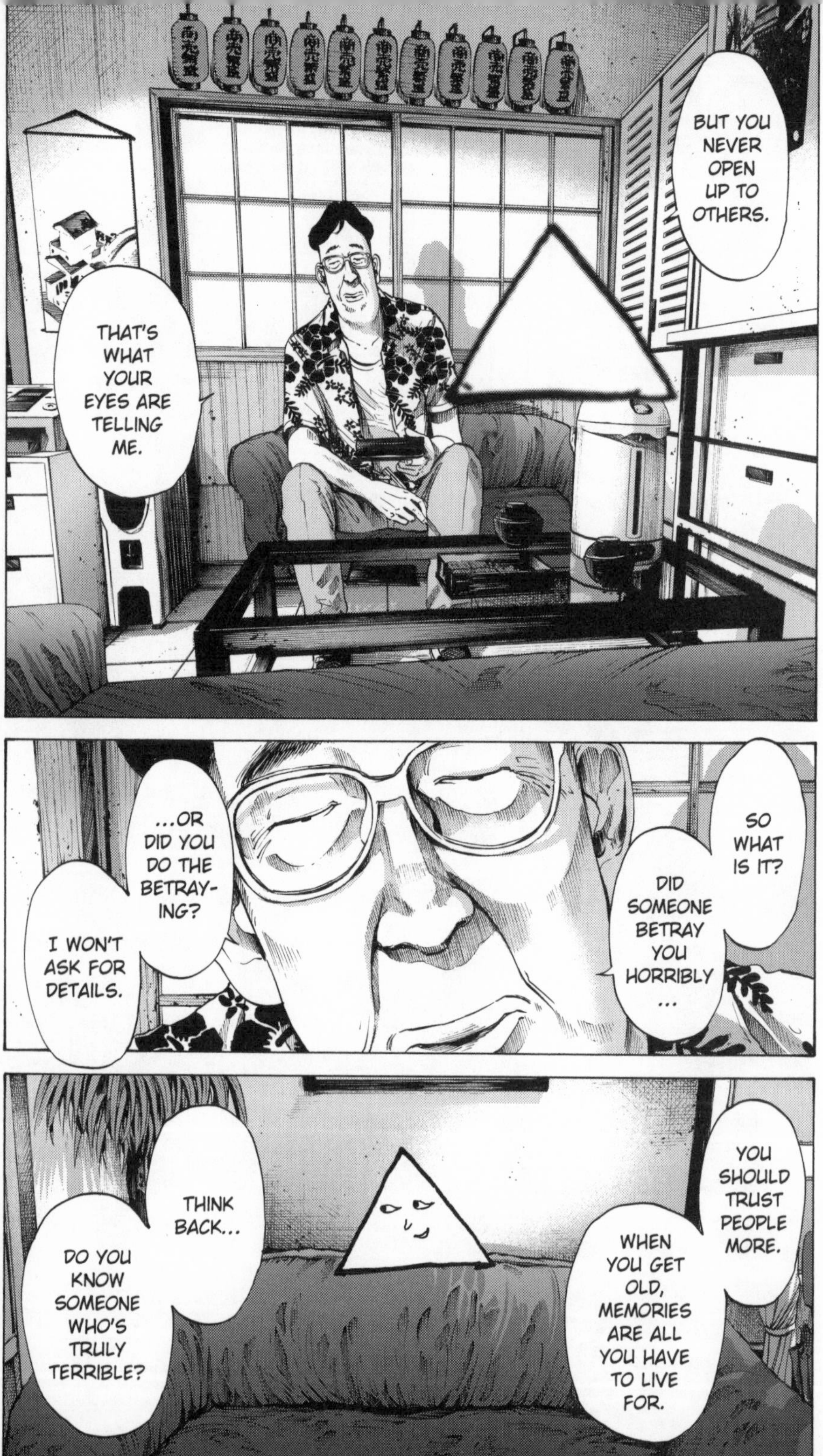
BUT YOU NEVER OPEN UP TO OTHERS.
THAT'S WHAT YOUR EYES ARE TELLING ME.
SO WHAT IS IT?
DID SOMEONE BETRAY YOU HORRIBLY ...
...OR DID YOU DO THE BETRAYING?
I WON'T ASK FOR DETAILS.
YOU SHOULD TRUST PEOPLE MORE.
WHEN YOU GET OLD, MEMORIES ARE ALL YOU HAVE TO LIVE FOR.
THINK BACK...
DO YOU KNOW SOMEONE WHO'S TRULY TERRIBLE?

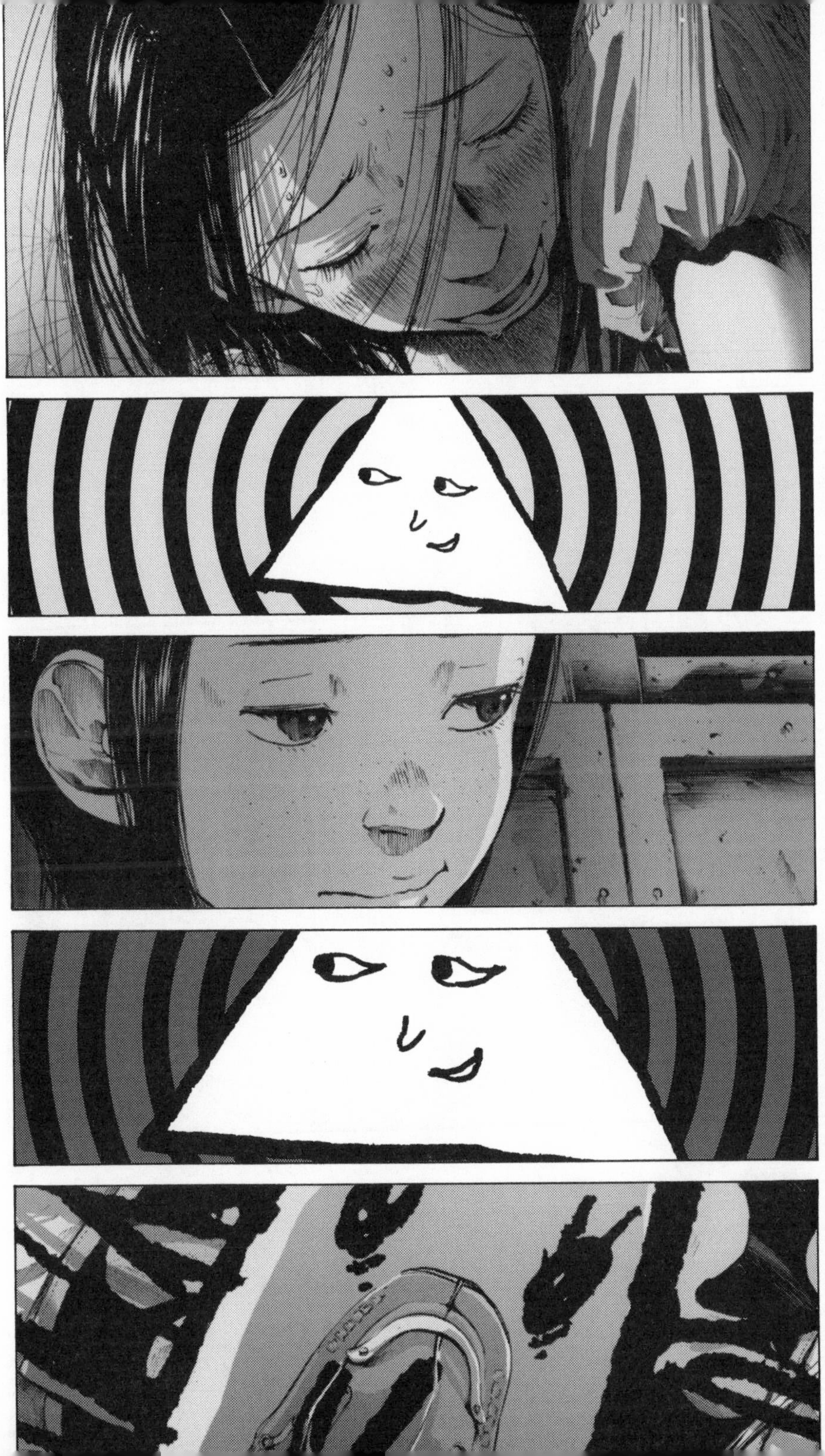

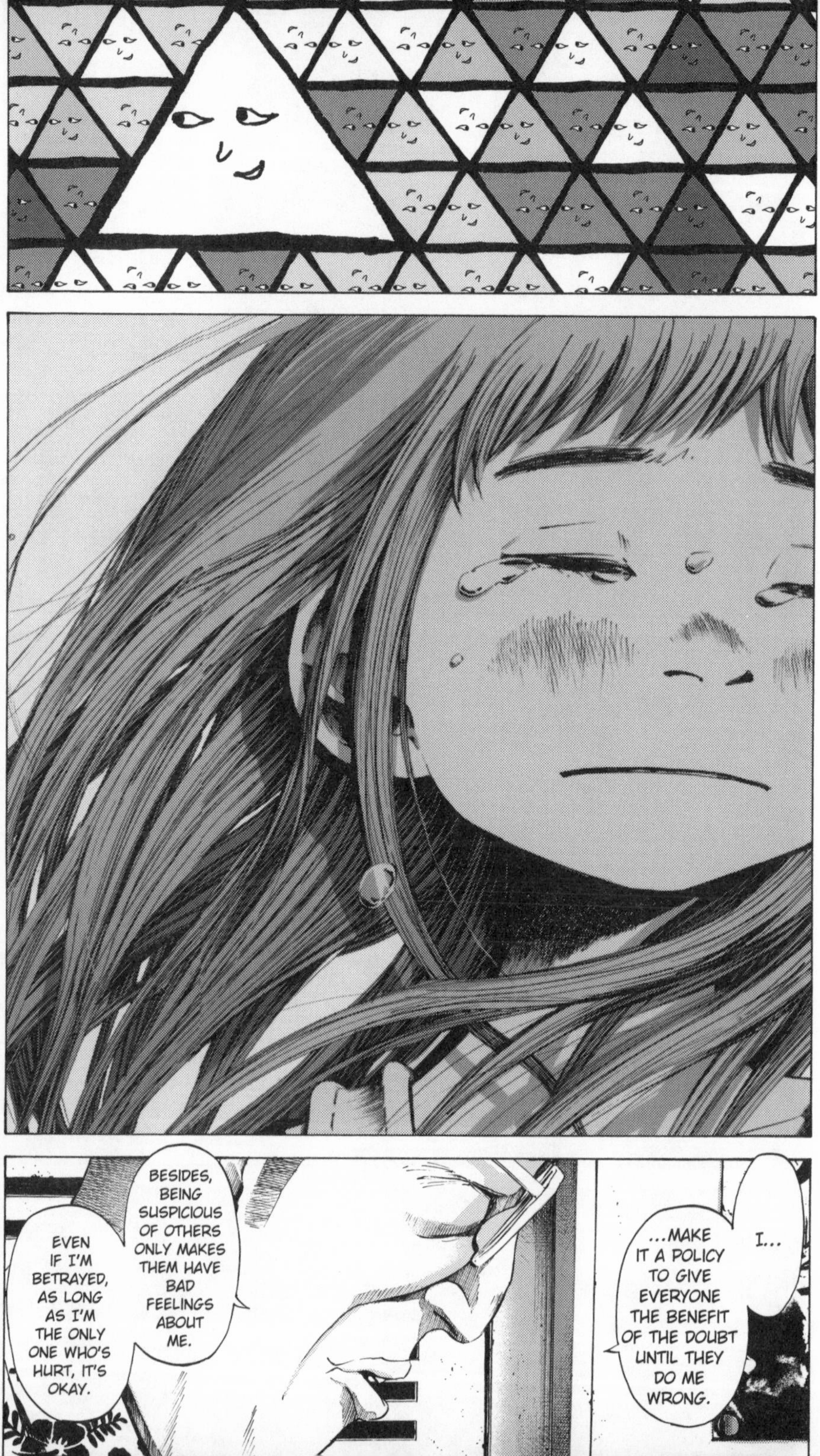
I...
...MAKE IT A POLICY TO GIVE EVERYONE THE BENEFIT OF THE DOUBT UNTIL THEY DO ME WRONG.
BESIDES, BEING SUSPICIOUS OF OTHERS ONLY MAKES THEM HAVE BAD FEELINGS ABOUT ME.
EVEN IF I'M BETRAYED, AS LONG AS I'M THE ONLY ONE WHO'S HURT, IT'S OKAY.

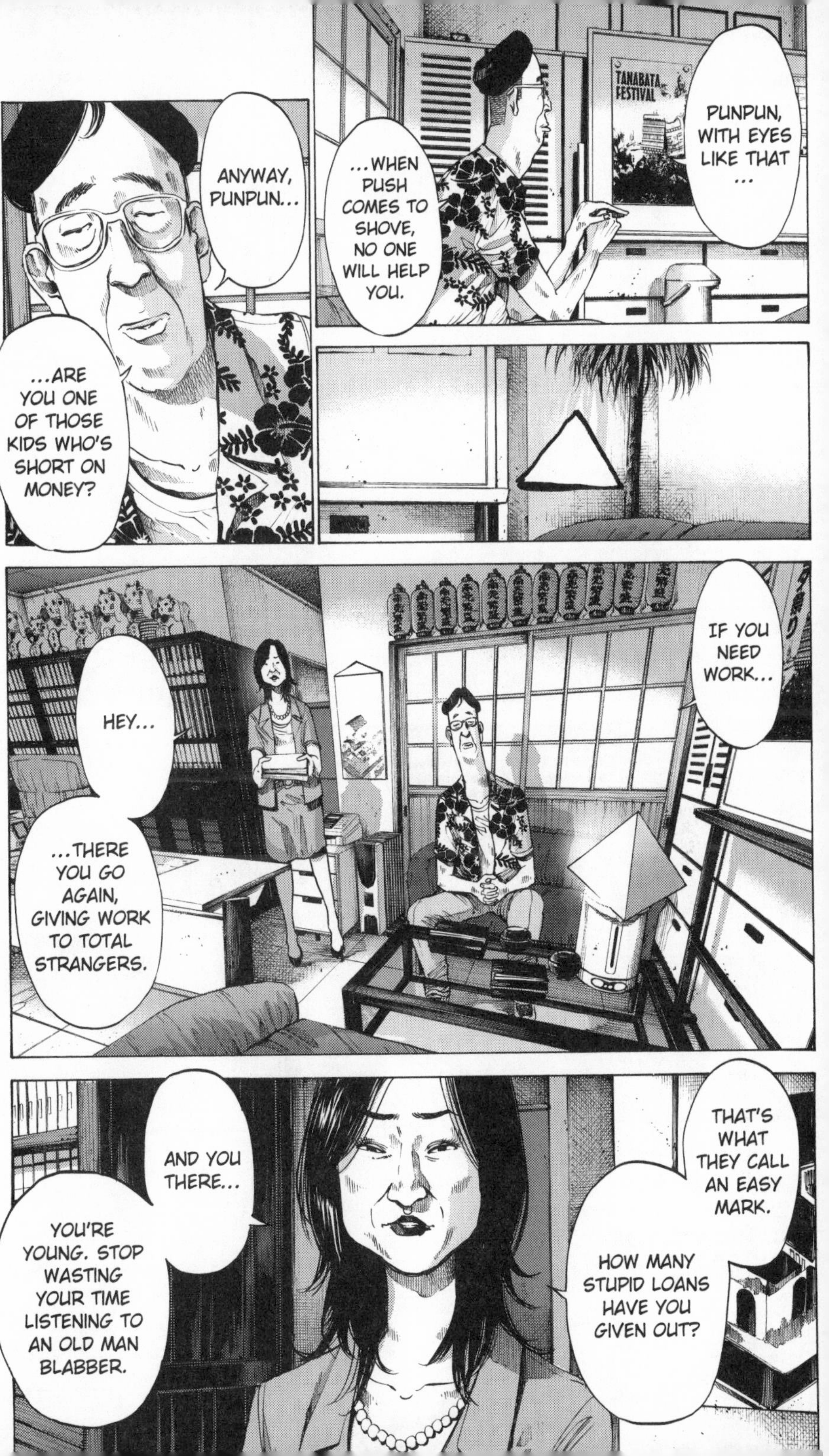
TANABATA FESTIVAL
PUNPUN, WITH EYES LIKE THAT ...
...WHEN PUSH COMES TO SHOVE, NO ONE WILL HELP YOU.
ANYWAY, PUNPUN...
...ARE YOU ONE OF THOSE KIDS WHO'S SHORT ON MONEY?
IF YOU NEED WORK...
HEY...
...THERE YOU GO AGAIN, GIVING WORK TO TOTAL STRANGERS.
THAT'S WHAT THEY CALL AN EASY MARK.
HOW MANY STUPID LOANS HAVE YOU GIVEN OUT?
AND YOU THERE...
YOU'RE YOUNG. STOP WASTING YOUR TIME LISTENING TO AN OLD MAN BLABBER.

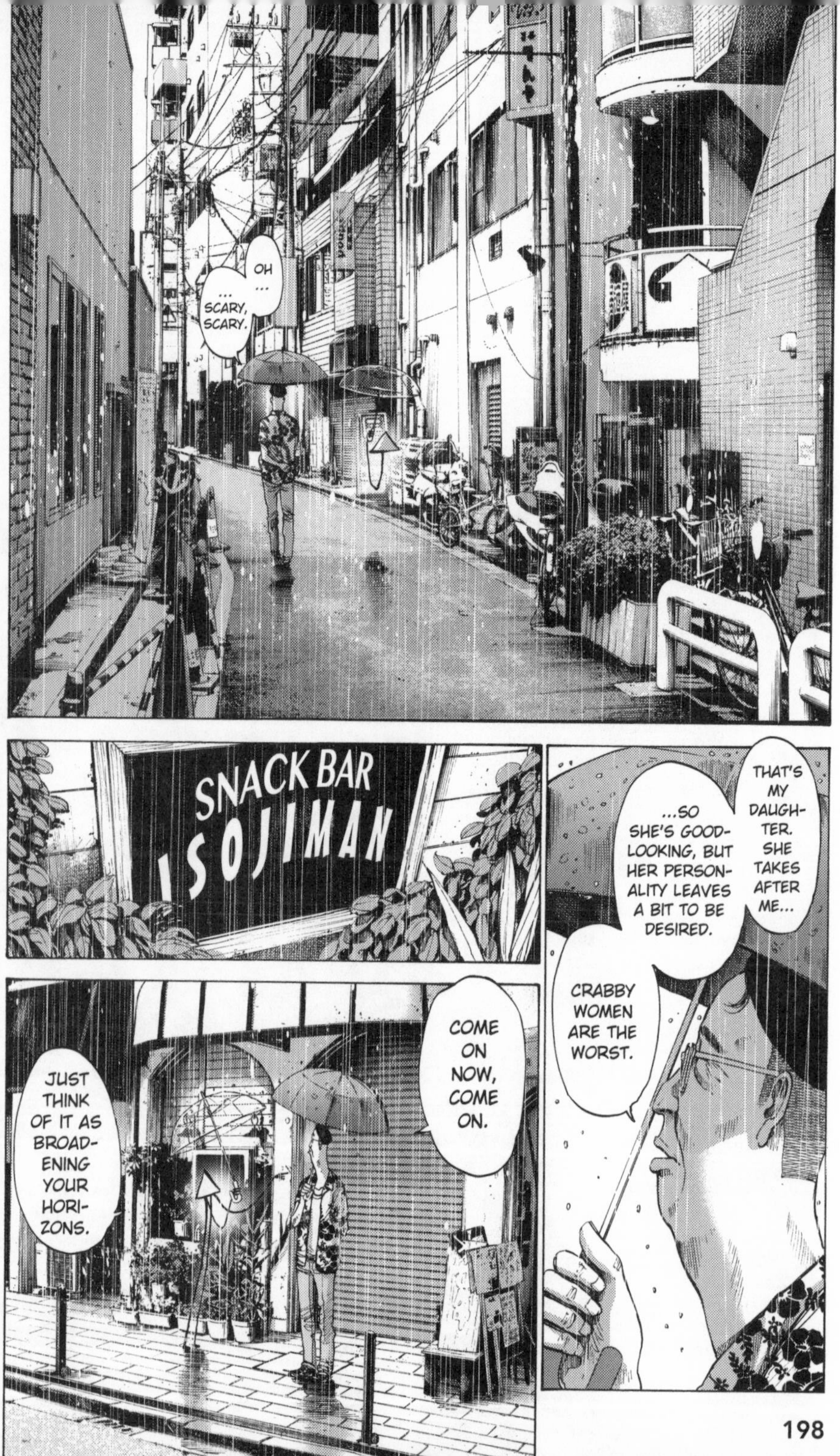
OH ... ... SCARY, SCARY.
THAT'S MY DAUGH-TER. SHE TAKES AFTER ME...
...SO SHE'S GOOD-LOOKING, BUT HER PERSON-ALITY LEAVES A BIT TO BE DESIRED.
CRABBY WOMEN ARE THE WORST.
SNACK BAR ISOJIMAN
COME ON NOW, COME ON.
JUST THINK OF IT AS BROAD-ENING YOUR HORI-ZONS.

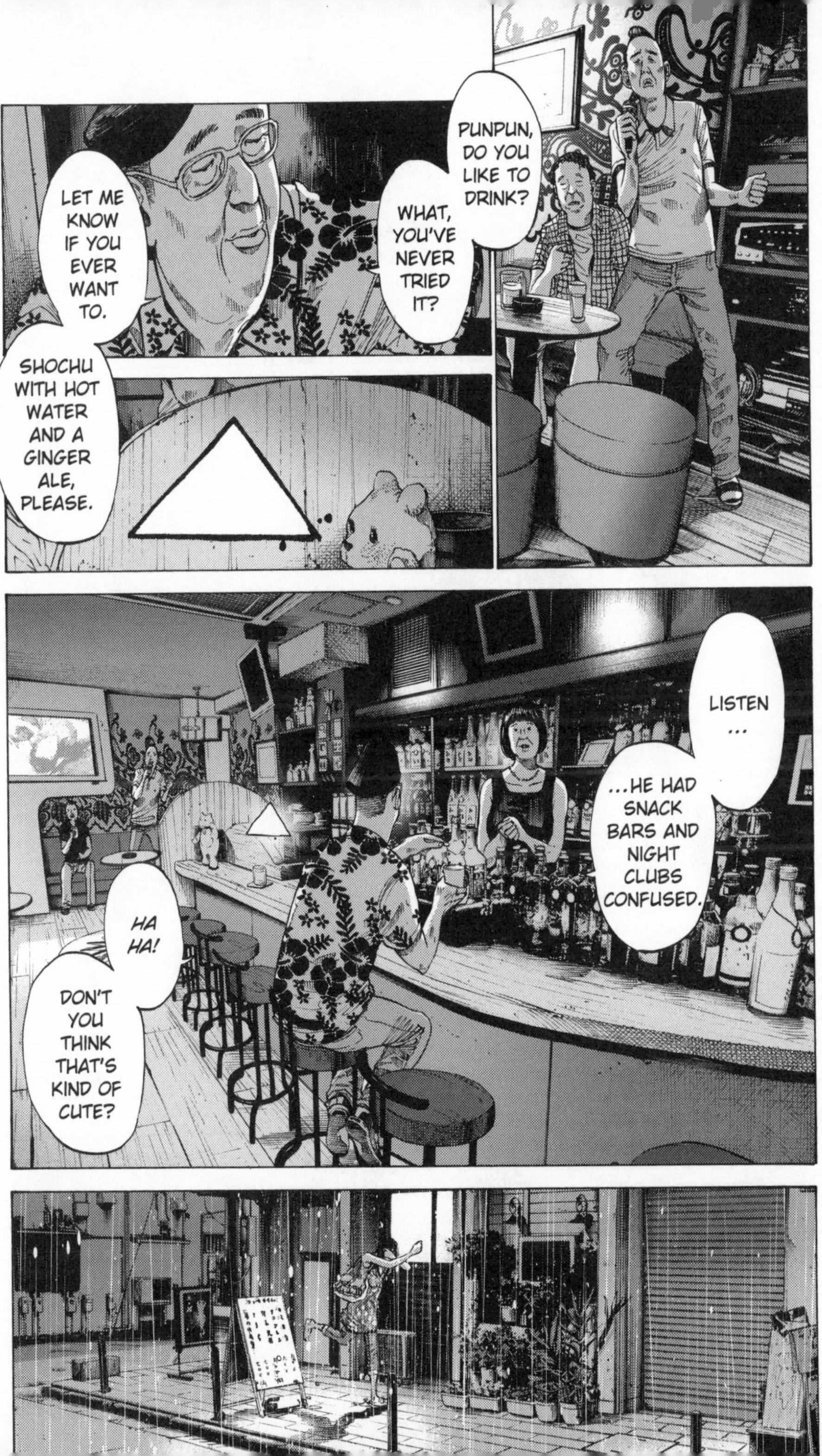
PUNPUN, DO YOU LIKE TO DRINK?
WHAT, YOU'VE NEVER TRIED IT?
LET ME KNOW IF YOU EVER WANT TO.
SHOCHU WITH HOT WATER AND A GINGER ALE, PLEASE.
LISTEN ...
...HE HAD SNACK BARS AND NIGHT CLUBS CONFUSED.
HA HA!
DON'T YOU THINK THAT'S KIND OF CUTE?

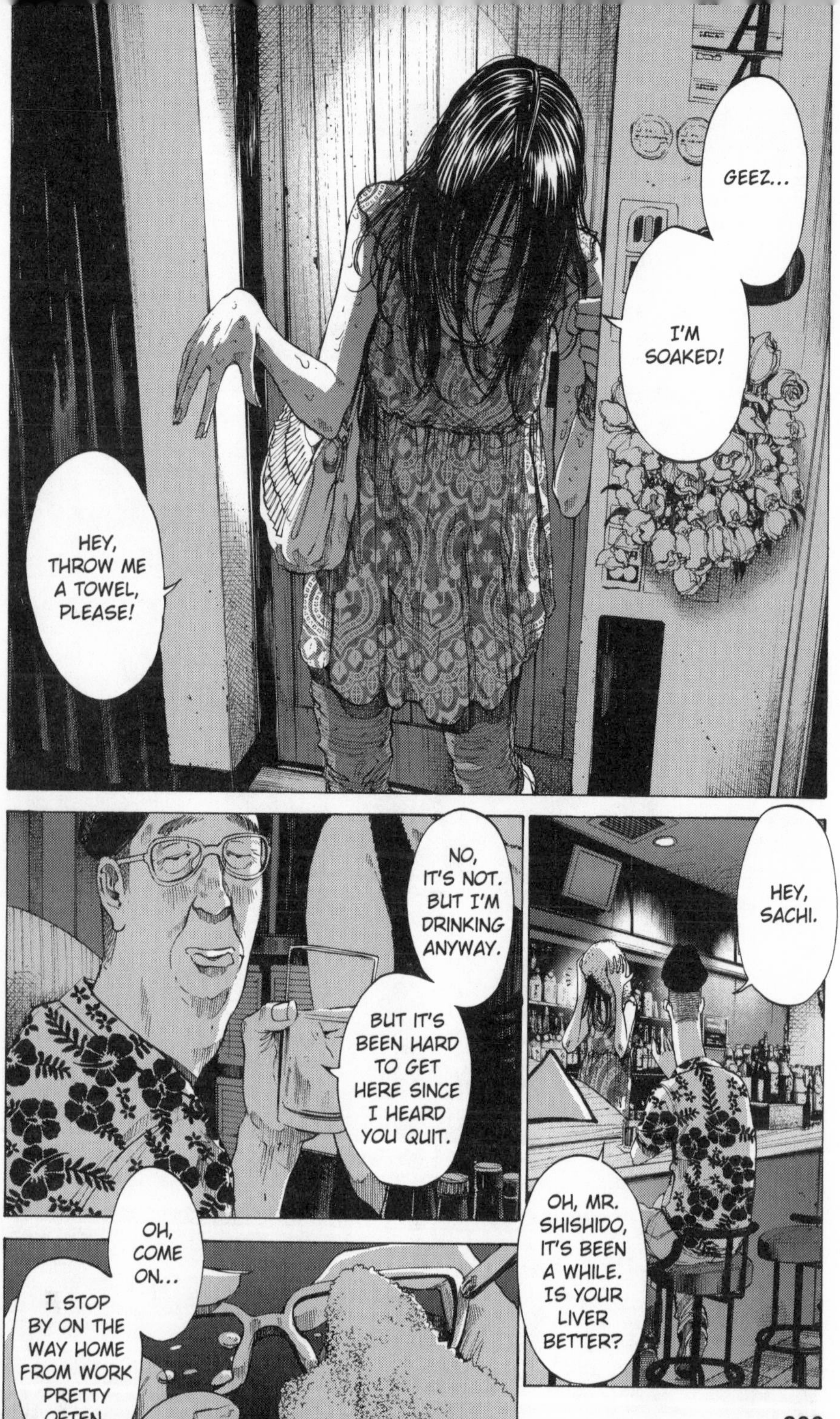
GEEZ...
I'M SOAKED!
HEY, THROW ME A TOWEL, PLEASE!
HEY, SACHI.
OH, MR. SHISHIDO, IT'S BEEN A WHILE. IS YOUR LIVER BETTER?
NO, IT'S NOT. BUT I'M DRINKING ANYWAY.
BUT IT'S BEEN HARD TO GET HERE SINCE I HEARD YOU QUIT.
OH, COME ON...
I STOP BY ON THE WAY HOME FROM WORK PRETTY OFTEN.

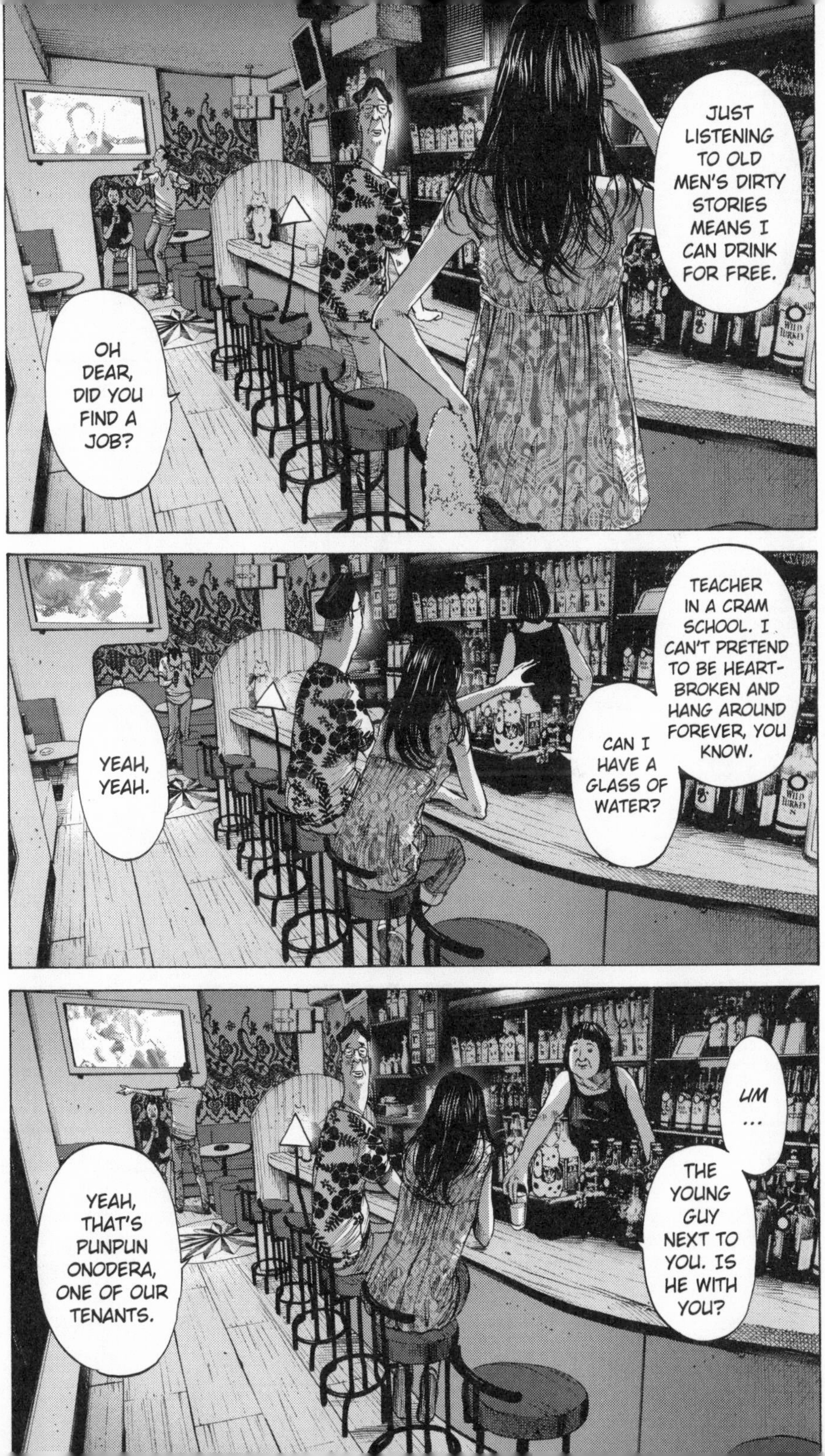
JUST LISTENING TO OLD MEN'S DIRTY STORIES MEANS I CAN DRINK FOR FREE.
OH DEAR, DID YOU FIND A JOB?
TEACHER IN A CRAM SCHOOL. I CAN'T PRETEND TO BE HEART-BROKEN AND HANG AROUND FOREVER, YOU KNOW.
CAN I HAVE A GLASS OF WATER?
YEAH, YEAH.
UM ...
THE YOUNG GUY NEXT TO YOU. IS HE WITH YOU?
YEAH, THAT'S PUNPUN ONODERA, ONE OF OUR TENANTS.

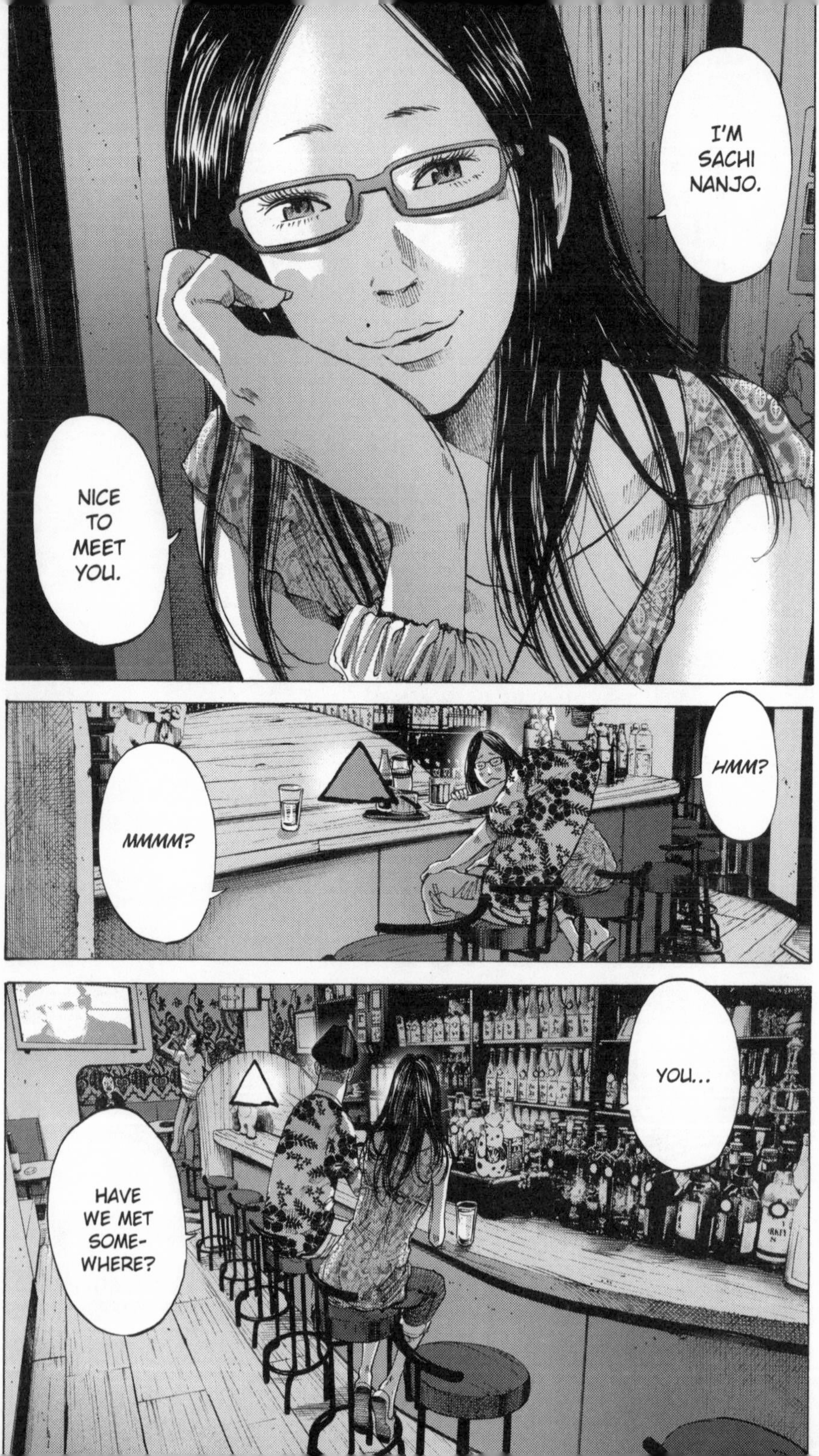
I'M SACHI NANJO.
NICE TO MEET YOU.
HMM?
MMMM?
YOU...
HAVE WE MET SOME-WHERE?

Chapter 78

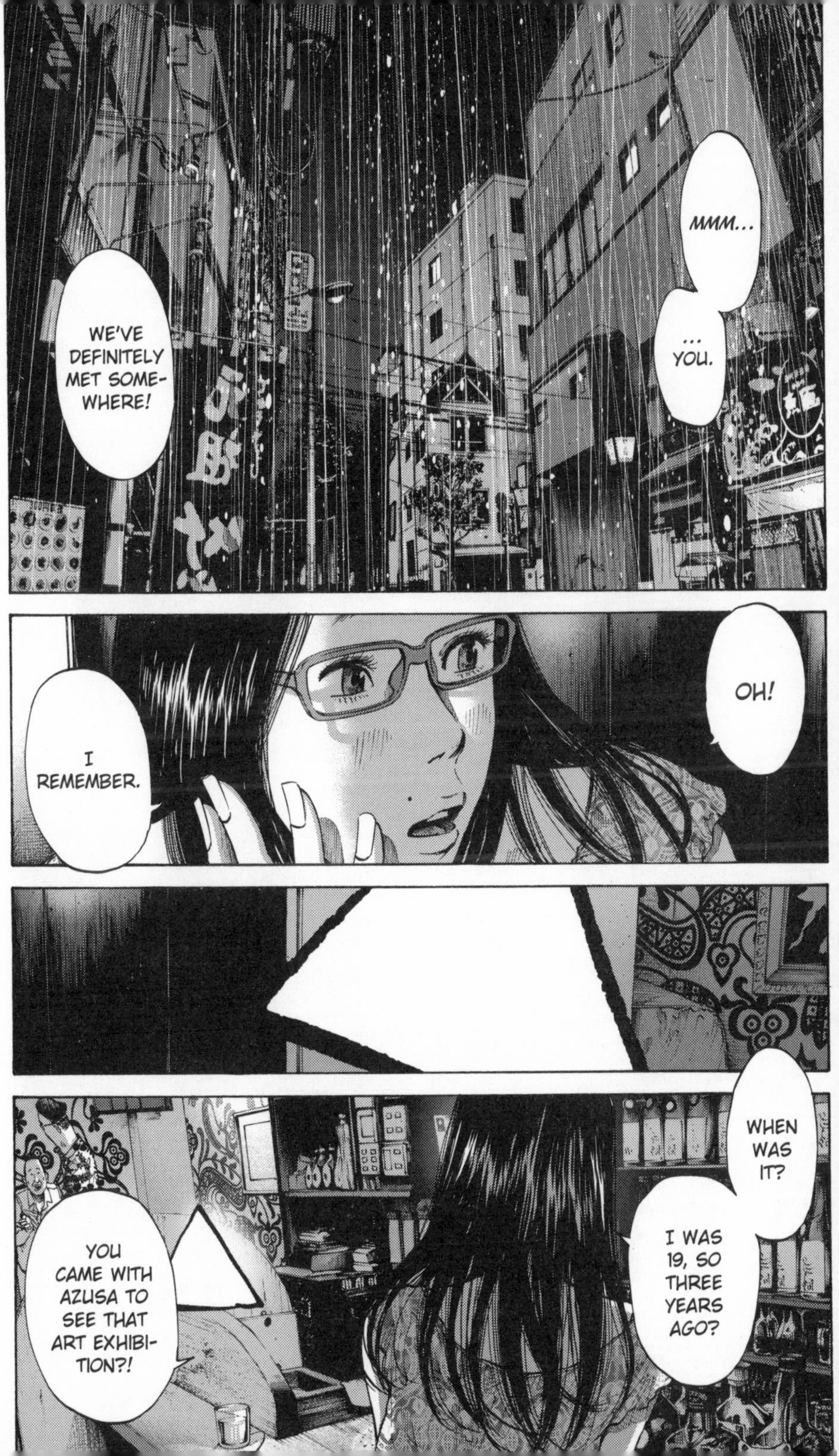
MMM...
... YOU.
WE'VE DEFINITELY MET SOME-WHERE!
OH!
I REMEMBER.
WHEN WAS IT?
I WAS 19, SO THREE YEARS AGO?
YOU CAME WITH AZUSA TO SEE THAT ART EXHIBI-TION?!

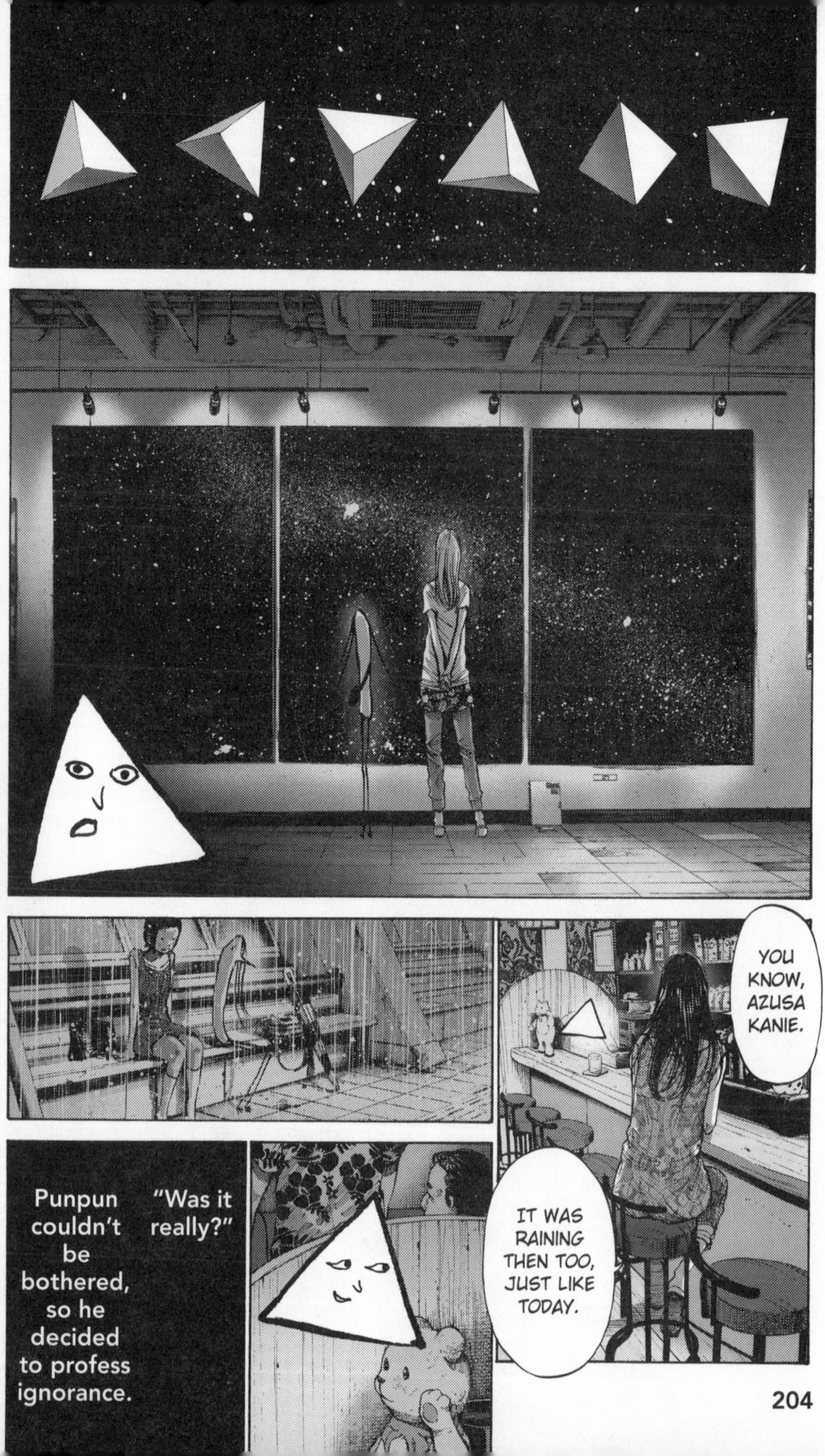
YOU KNOW, AZUSA KANIE.
IT WAS RAINING THEN TOO, JUST LIKE TODAY.
"Was it really?"
Punpun couldn't be bothered, so he decided to profess ignorance.

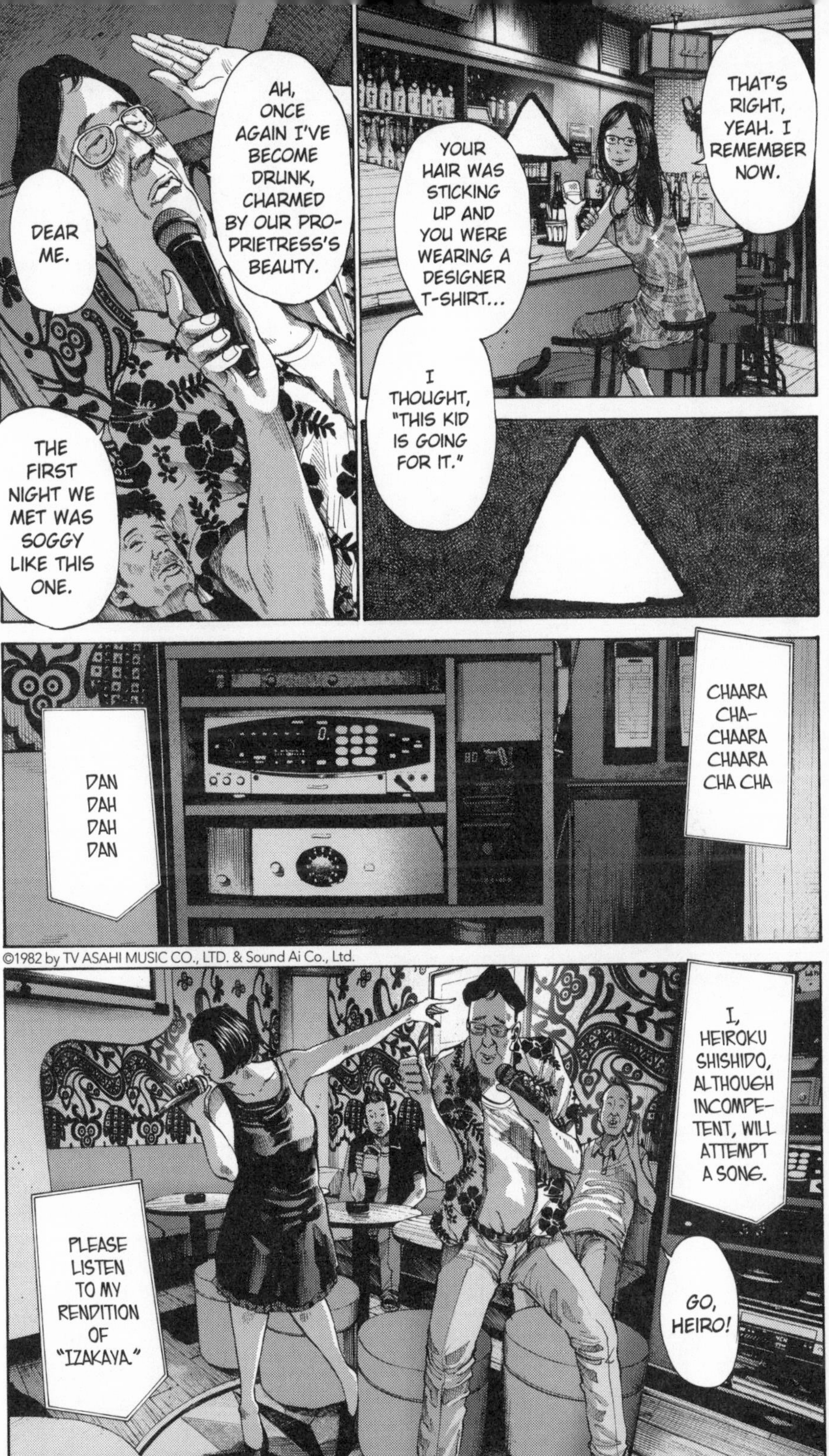
THAT'S RIGHT, YEAH. I REMEMBER NOW.
YOUR HAIR WAS STICKING UP AND YOU WERE WEARING A DESIGNER T-SHIRT...
I THOUGHT, "THIS KID IS GOING FOR IT."
AH, ONCE AGAIN I'VE BECOME DRUNK, CHARMED BY OUR PRO-PRIETRESS'S BEAUTY.
DEAR ME.
THE FIRST NIGHT WE MET WAS SOGGY LIKE THIS ONE.
CHAARA CHA-CHAARA CHAARA CHA CHA
DAN DAH DAH DAN
I, HEIROKU SHISHIDO, ALTHOUGH INCOMPE-TENT, WILL ATTEMPT A SONG.
GO, HEIRO!
PLEASE LISTEN TO MY RENDITION OF "IZAKAYA."

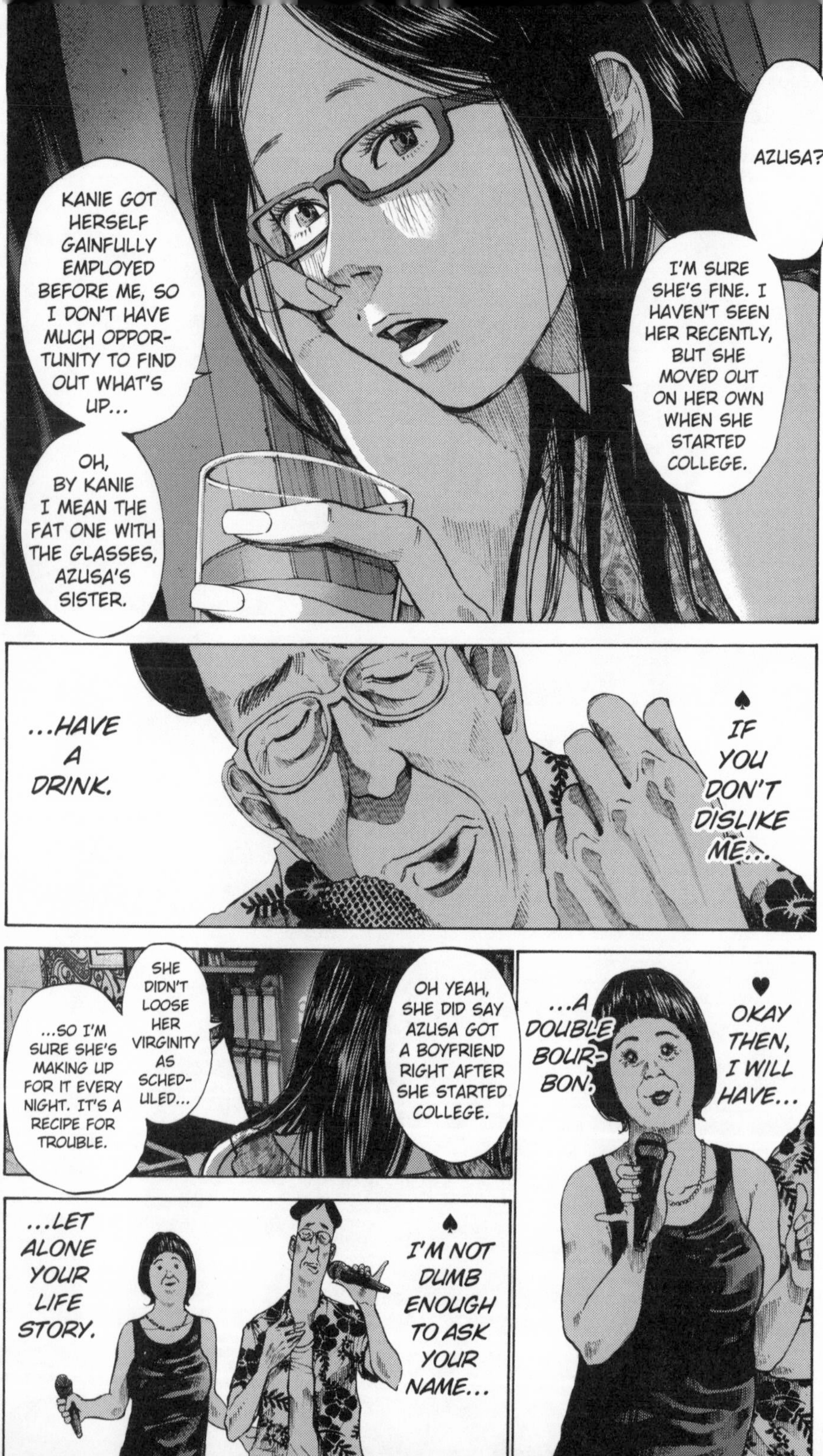
AZUSA?
I'M SURE SHE'S FINE. I HAVEN'T SEEN HER RECENTLY, BUT SHE MOVED OUT ON HER OWN WHEN SHE STARTED COLLEGE.
KANIE GOT HERSELF GAINFULLY EMPLOYED BEFORE ME, SO I DON'T HAVE MUCH OPPOR-TUNITY TO FIND OUT WHAT'S UP...
OH, BY KANIE I MEAN THE FAT ONE WITH THE GLASSES, AZUSA'S SISTER.
♠ IF YOU DON'T DISLIKE ME...
...HAVE A DRINK.
♥ OKAY THEN, I WILL HAVE...
...A DOUBLE BOUR-BON.
OH YEAH, SHE DID SAY AZUSA GOT A BOYFRIEND RIGHT AFTER SHE STARTED COLLEGE.
SHE DIDN'T LOOSE HER VIRGINITY AS SCHED-ULED...
...SO I'M SURE SHE'S MAKING UP FOR IT EVERY NIGHT. IT'S A RECIPE FOR TROUBLE.
♠ I'M NOT DUMB ENOUGH TO ASK YOUR NAME...
...LET ALONE YOUR LIFE STORY.

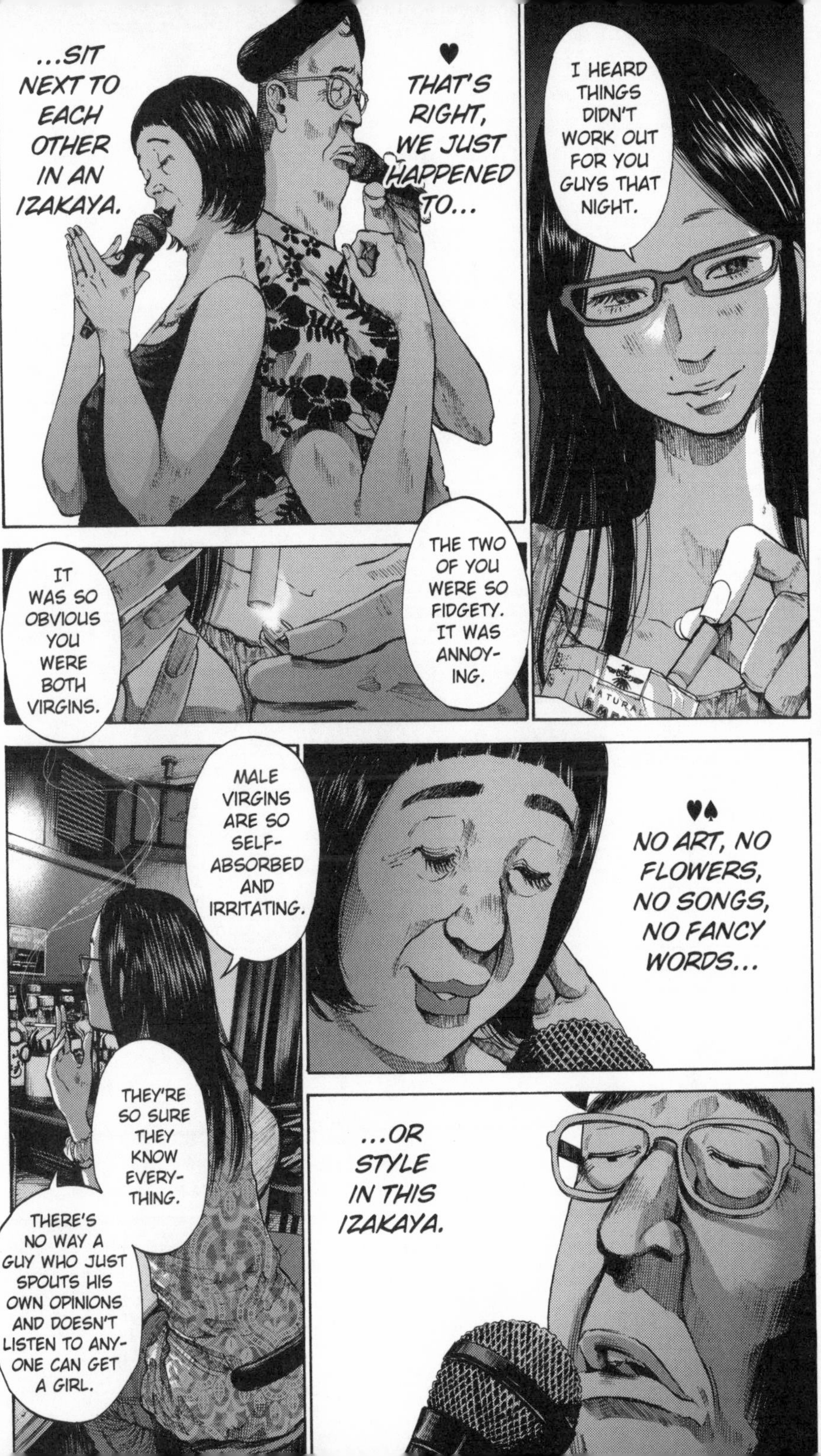
I HEARD THINGS DIDN'T WORK OUT FOR YOU GUYS THAT NIGHT.
♥ THAT'S RIGHT, WE JUST HAPPENED TO...
...SIT NEXT TO EACH OTHER IN AN IZAKAYA.
THE TWO OF YOU WERE SO FIDGETY. IT WAS ANNOY-ING.
IT WAS SO OBVIOUS YOU WERE BOTH VIRGINS.
♥♠ NO ART, NO FLOWERS, NO SONGS, NO FANCY WORDS...
...OR STYLE IN THIS IZAKAYA.
MALE VIRGINS ARE SO SELF-ABSORBED AND IRRITATING.
THEY'RE SO SURE THEY KNOW EVERY-THING.
THERE'S NO WAY A GUY WHO JUST SPOUTS HIS OWN OPINIONS AND DOESN'T LISTEN TO ANY-ONE CAN GET A GIRL.

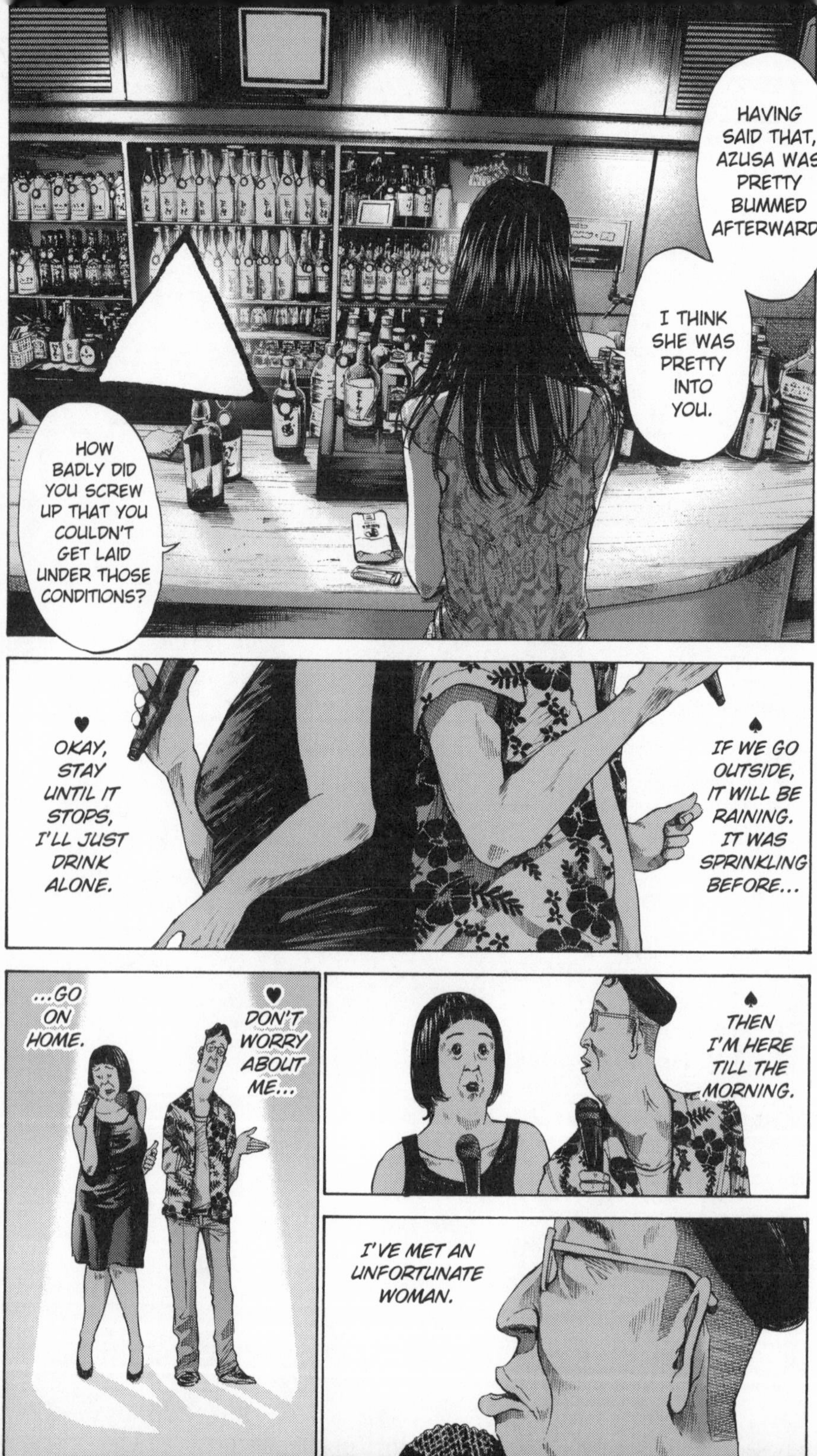
HAVING SAID THAT, AZUSA WAS PRETTY BUMMED AFTERWARD.
I THINK SHE WAS PRETTY INTO YOU.
HOW BADLY DID YOU SCREW UP THAT YOU COULDN'T GET LAID UNDER THOSE CONDITIONS?
♠ IF WE GO OUTSIDE, IT WILL BE RAINING. IT WAS SPRINKLING BEFORE...
♥ OKAY, STAY UNTIL IT STOPS, I'LL JUST DRINK ALONE.
♠ THEN I'M HERE TILL THE MORNING.
I'VE MET AN UNFORTUNATE WOMAN.
♥ DON'T WORRY ABOUT ME...
...GO ON HOME.

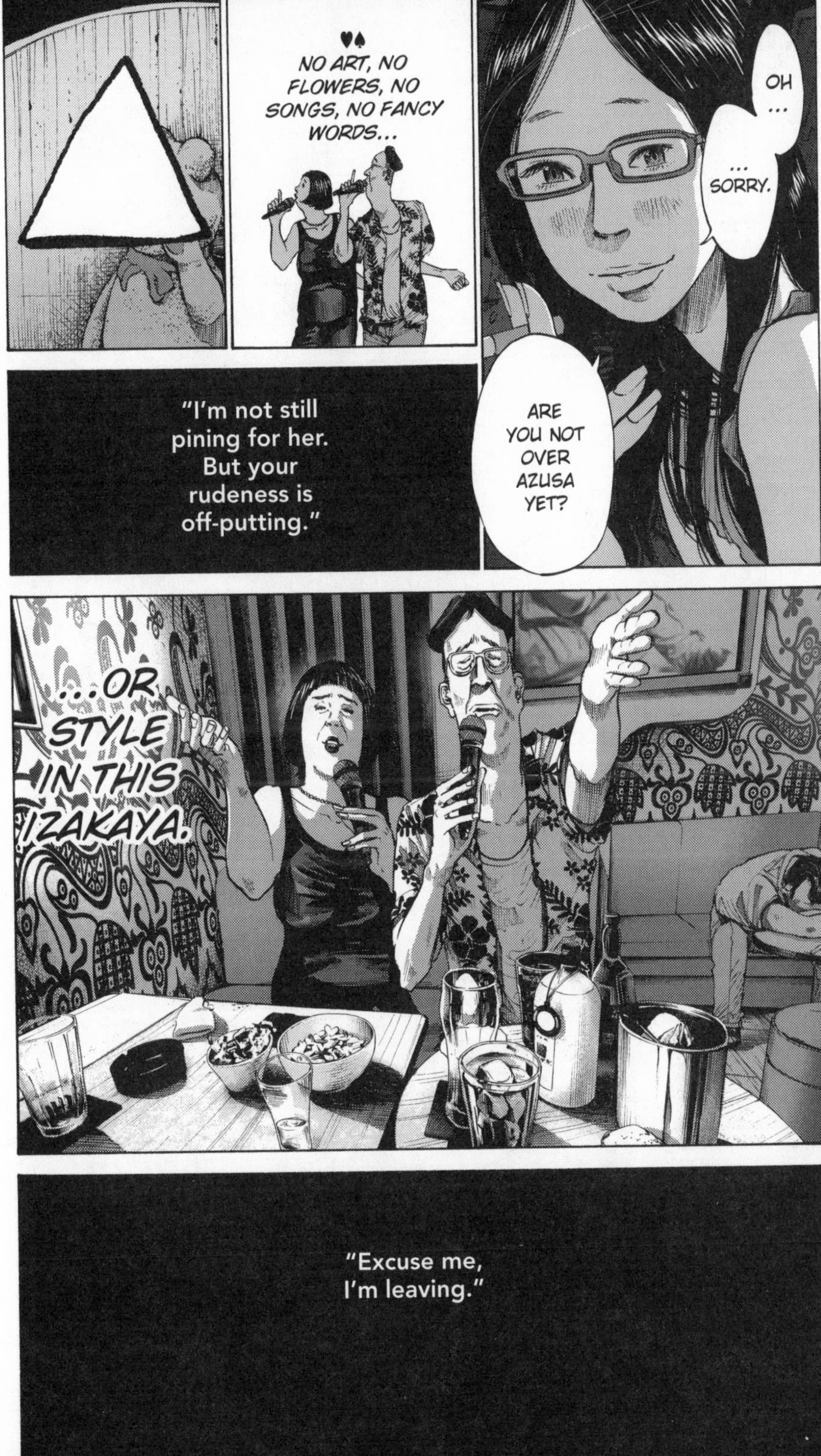
OH ...
... SORRY.
ARE YOU NOT OVER AZUSA YET?
NO ART, NO FLOWERS, NO SONGS, NO FANCY WORDS...
"I'm not still pining for her. But your rudeness is off-putting."
...OR STYLE IN THIS IZAKAYA.
"Excuse me, I'm leaving."

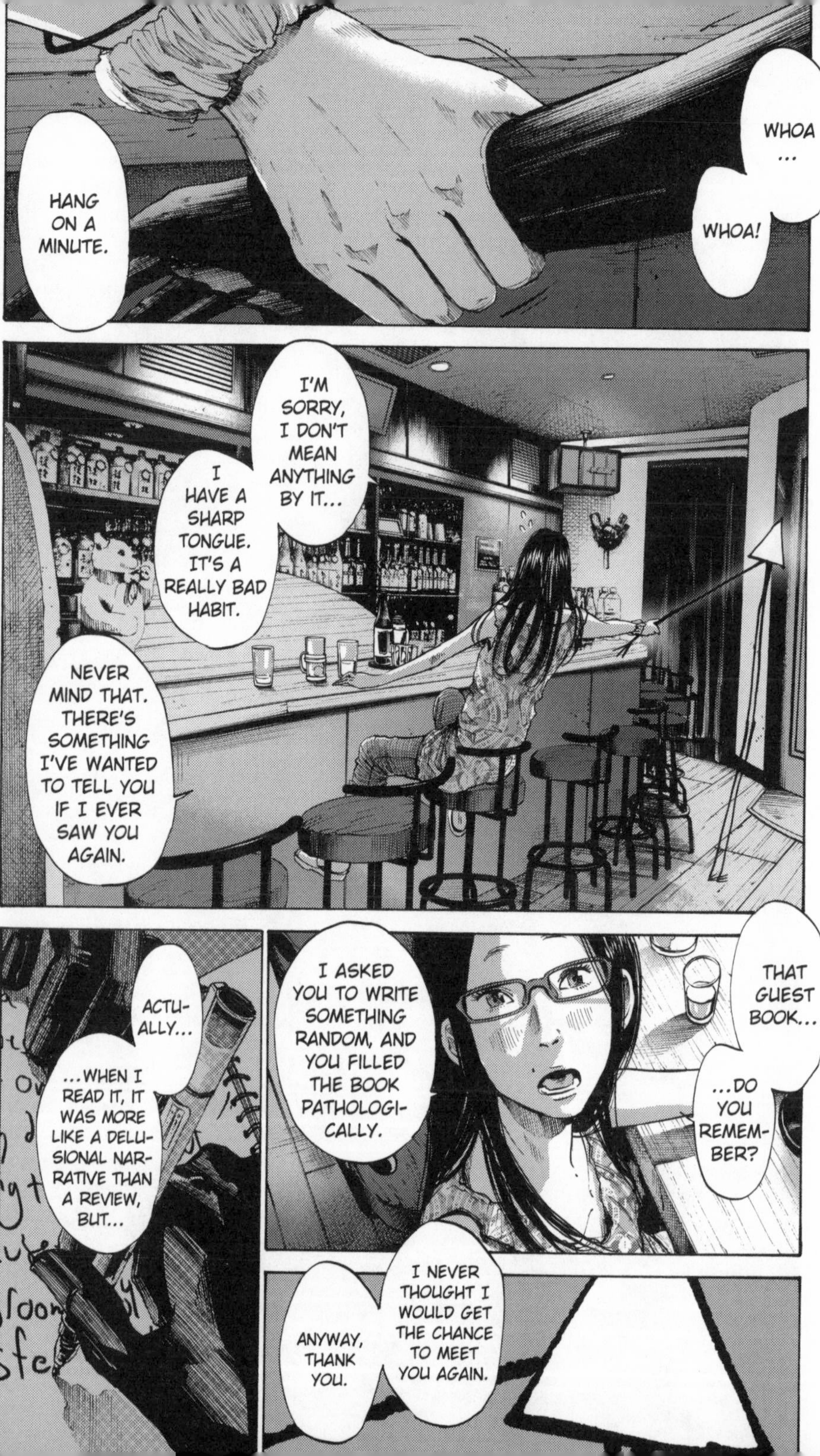
WHOA ... WHOA!
HANG ON A MINUTE.
I'M SORRY, I DON'T MEAN ANYTHING BY IT...
I HAVE A SHARP TONGUE. IT'S A REALLY BAD HABIT.
NEVER MIND THAT. THERE'S SOMETHING I'VE WANTED TO TELL YOU IF I EVER SAW YOU AGAIN.
THAT GUEST BOOK...
...DO YOU REMEMBER?
I ASKED YOU TO WRITE SOMETHING RANDOM, AND YOU FILLED THE BOOK PATHOLOGICALLY.
I NEVER THOUGHT I WOULD GET THE CHANCE TO MEET YOU AGAIN.
ANYWAY, THANK YOU.
ACTUALLY...
...WHEN I READ IT, IT WAS MORE LIKE A DELUSIONAL NARRATIVE THAN A REVIEW, BUT...

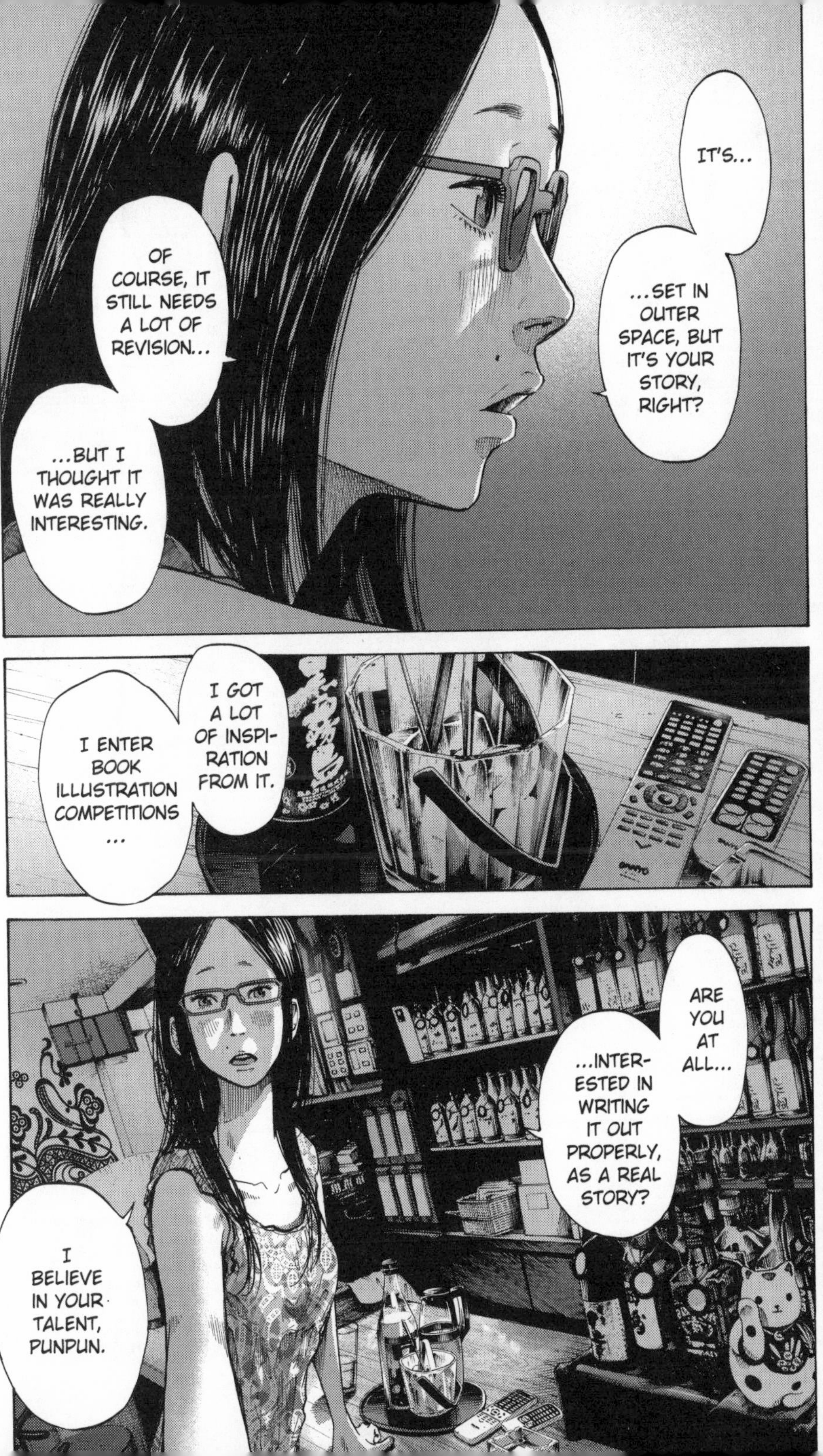
IT'S...
...SET IN OUTER SPACE, BUT IT'S YOUR STORY, RIGHT?
OF COURSE, IT STILL NEEDS A LOT OF REVISION...
...BUT I THOUGHT IT WAS REALLY INTERESTING.
I GOT A LOT OF INSPIRATION FROM IT.
I ENTER BOOK ILLUSTRATION COMPETITIONS...
ARE YOU AT ALL...
...INTERESTED IN WRITING IT OUT PROPERLY, AS A REAL STORY?
I BELIEVE IN YOUR TALENT, PUNPUN.

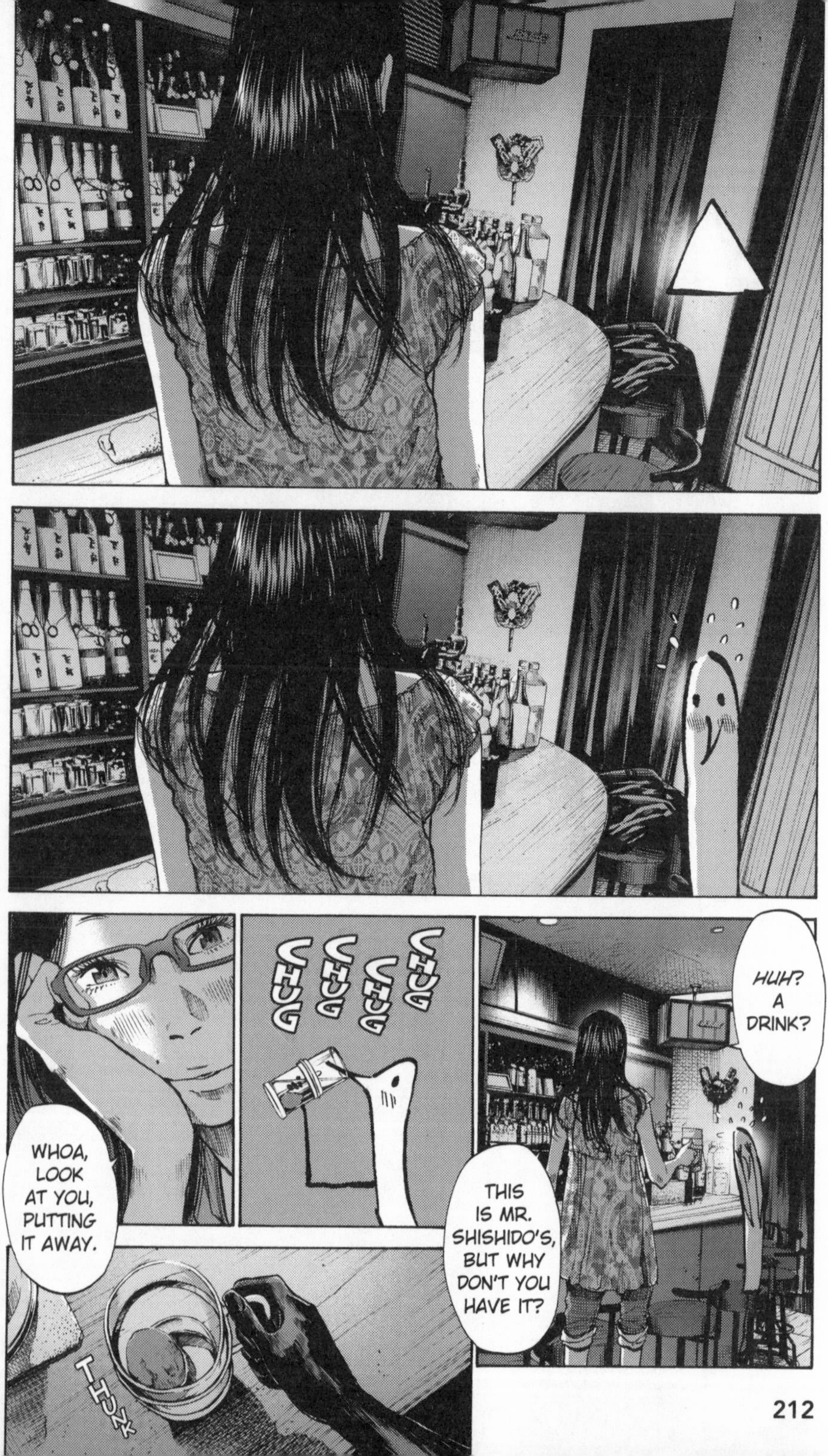
HUH? A DRINK?
THIS IS MR. SHISHIDO'S, BUT WHY DON'T YOU HAVE IT?
CHUG CHUG CHUG CHUG
WHOA, LOOK AT YOU, PUTTING IT AWAY.
THUNK

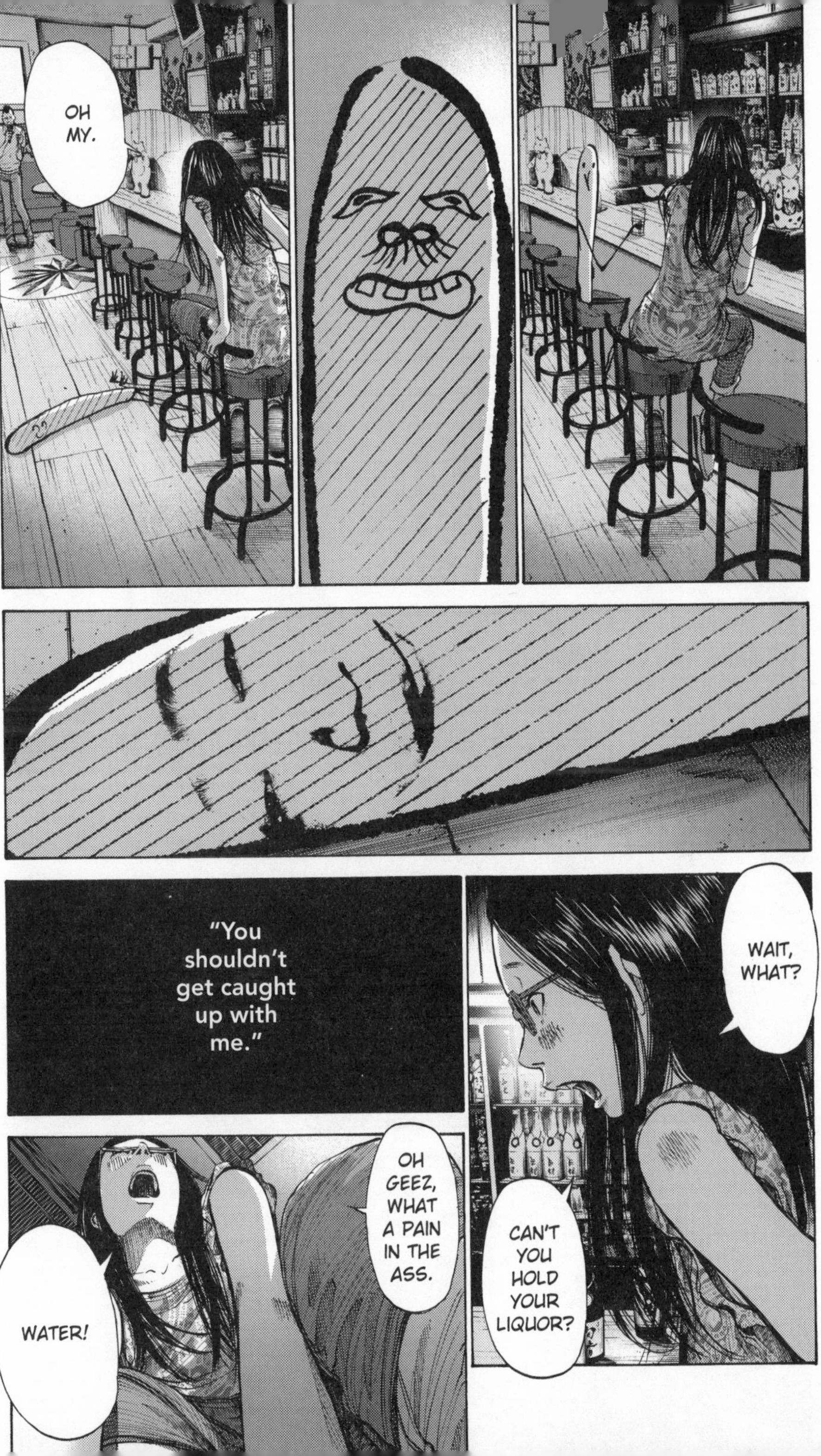
OH MY.
WAIT, WHAT?
CAN'T YOU HOLD YOUR LIQUOR?
"You shouldn't get caught up with me."
OH GEEZ, WHAT A PAIN IN THE ASS.
WATER!

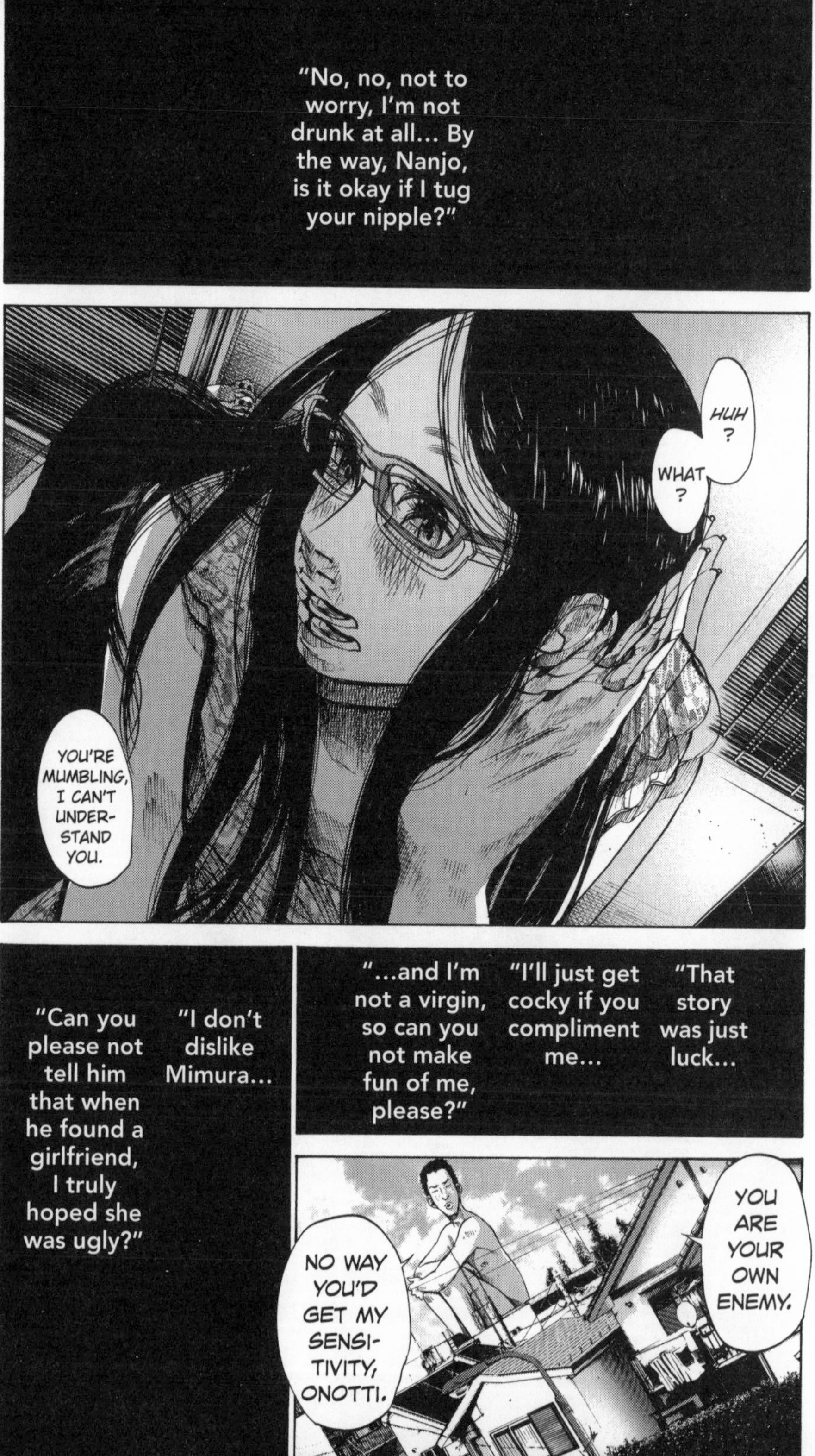
"No, no, not to worry, I'm not drunk at all... By the way, Nanjo, is it okay if I tug your nipple?"
HUH? WHAT?
YOU'RE MUMBLING, I CAN'T UNDER-STAND YOU.
"That story was just luck...
"I'll just get cocky if you compliment me...
"...and I'm not a virgin, so can you not make fun of me, please?"
YOU ARE YOUR OWN ENEMY.
NO WAY YOU'D GET MY SENSI-TIVITY, ONOTTI.
"I don't dislike Mimura...
"Can you please not tell him that when he found a girlfriend, I truly hoped she was ugly?"

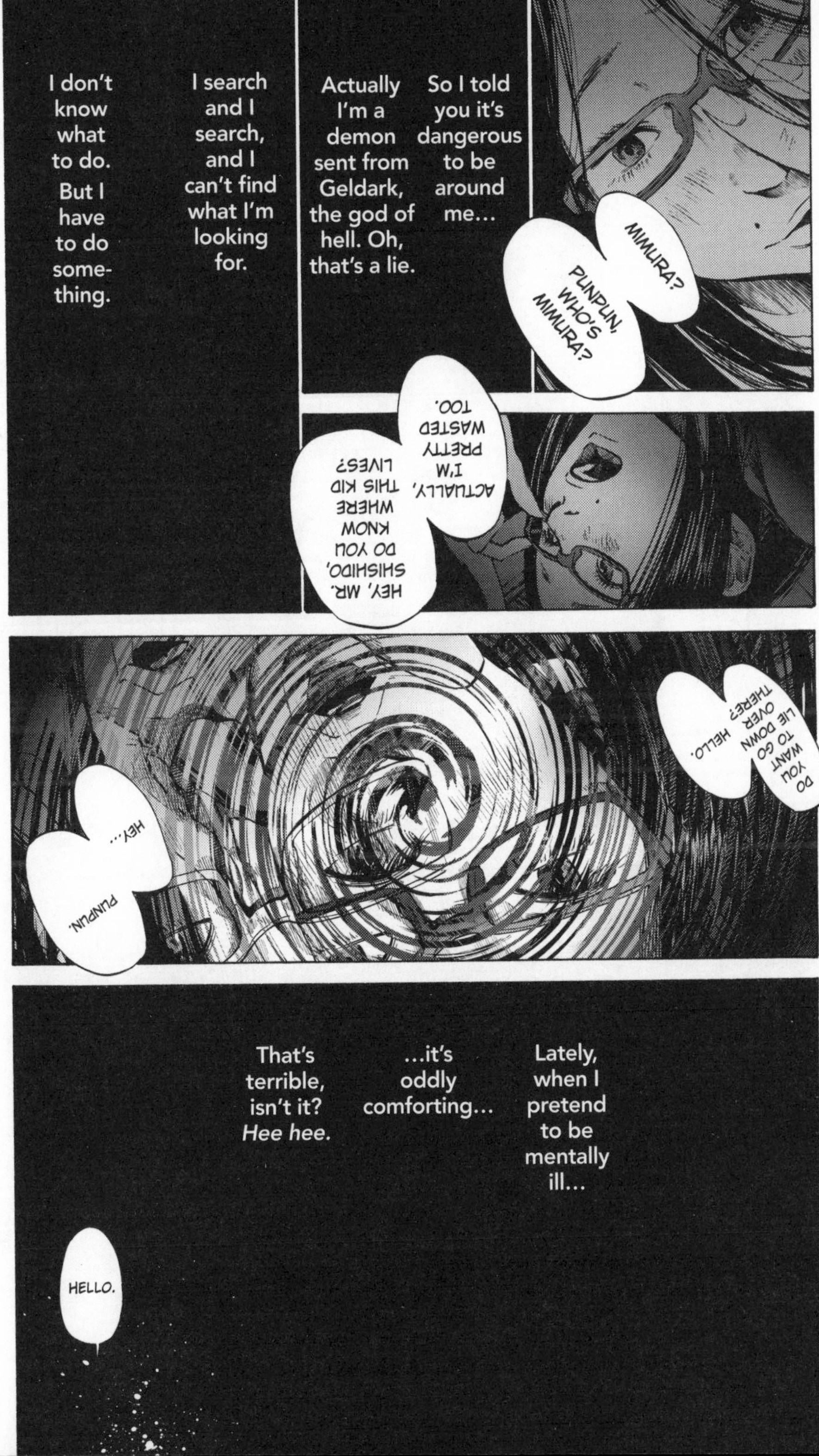
So I told you it's dangerous to be around me…
Actually I'm a demon sent from Geldark, the god of hell. Oh, that's a lie.
I search and I search, and I can't find what I'm looking for.
I don't know what to do.
But I have to do something.
MIMURA?
PUNPUN, WHO'S MIMURA?
ACTUALLY, I'M PRETTY WASTED TOO.
HEY, MR. SHISHIDO, DO YOU KNOW WHERE THIS KID LIVES?
HELLO.
DO YOU WANT TO GO LIE DOWN OVER THERE?
PUNPUN.
HEY…
Lately, when I pretend to be mentally ill…
…it's oddly comforting…
That's terrible, isn't it? *Hee hee.*
HELLO.

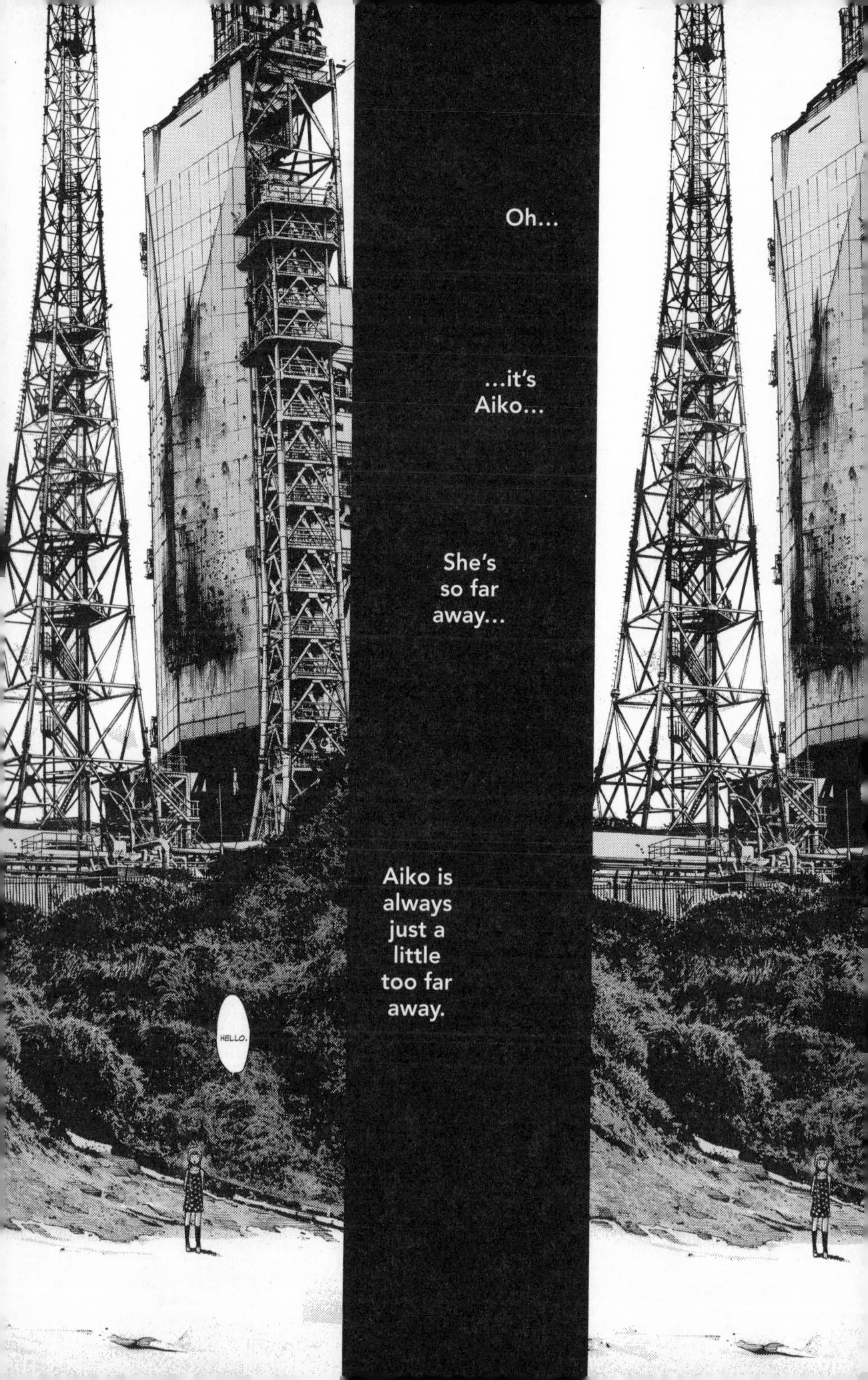
Oh...
...it's Aiko...
She's so far away...
Aiko is always just a little too far away.
HELLO.

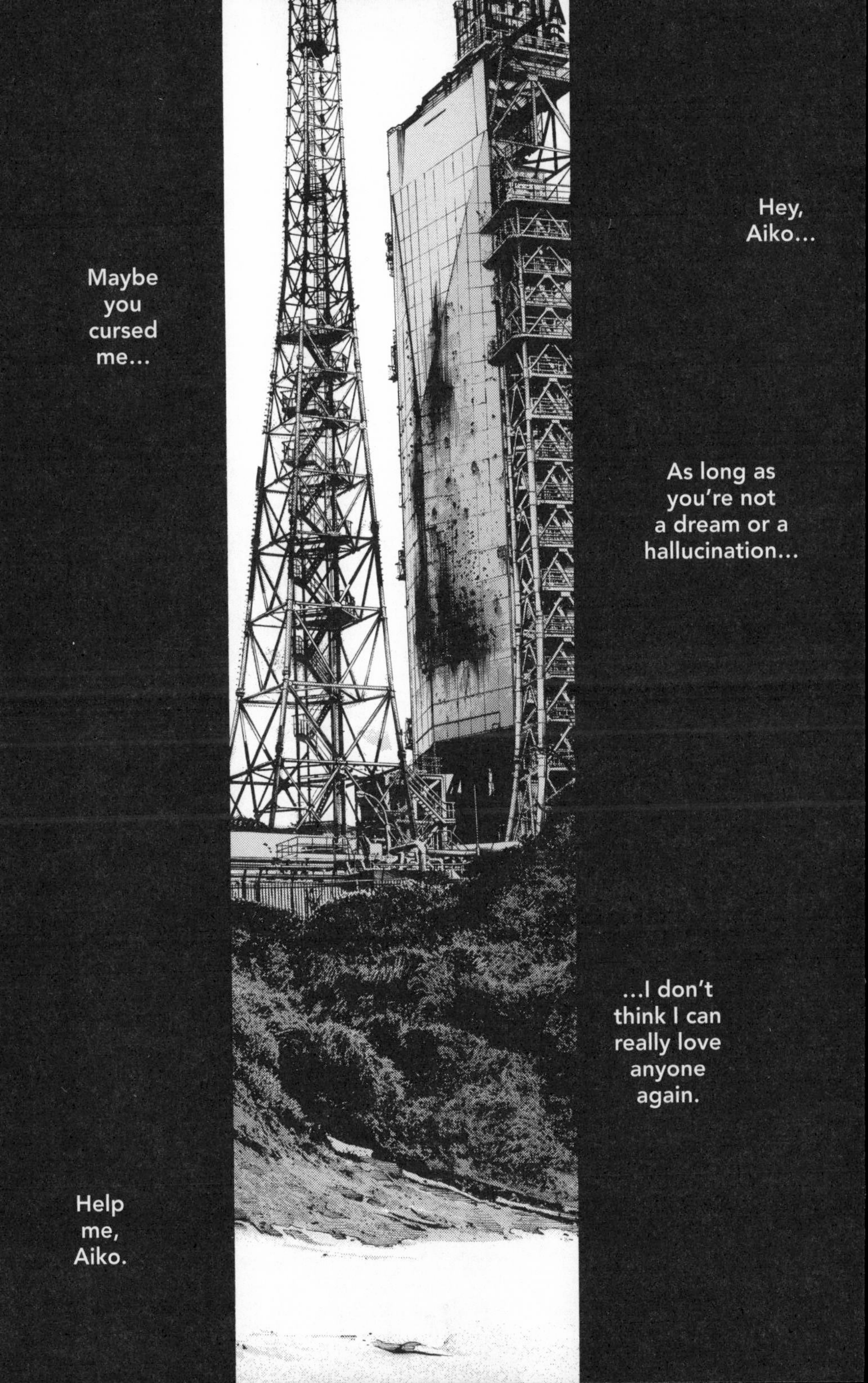
Hey, Aiko...
As long as you're not a dream or a hallucination...
...I don't think I can really love anyone again.
Maybe you cursed me...
Help me, Aiko.

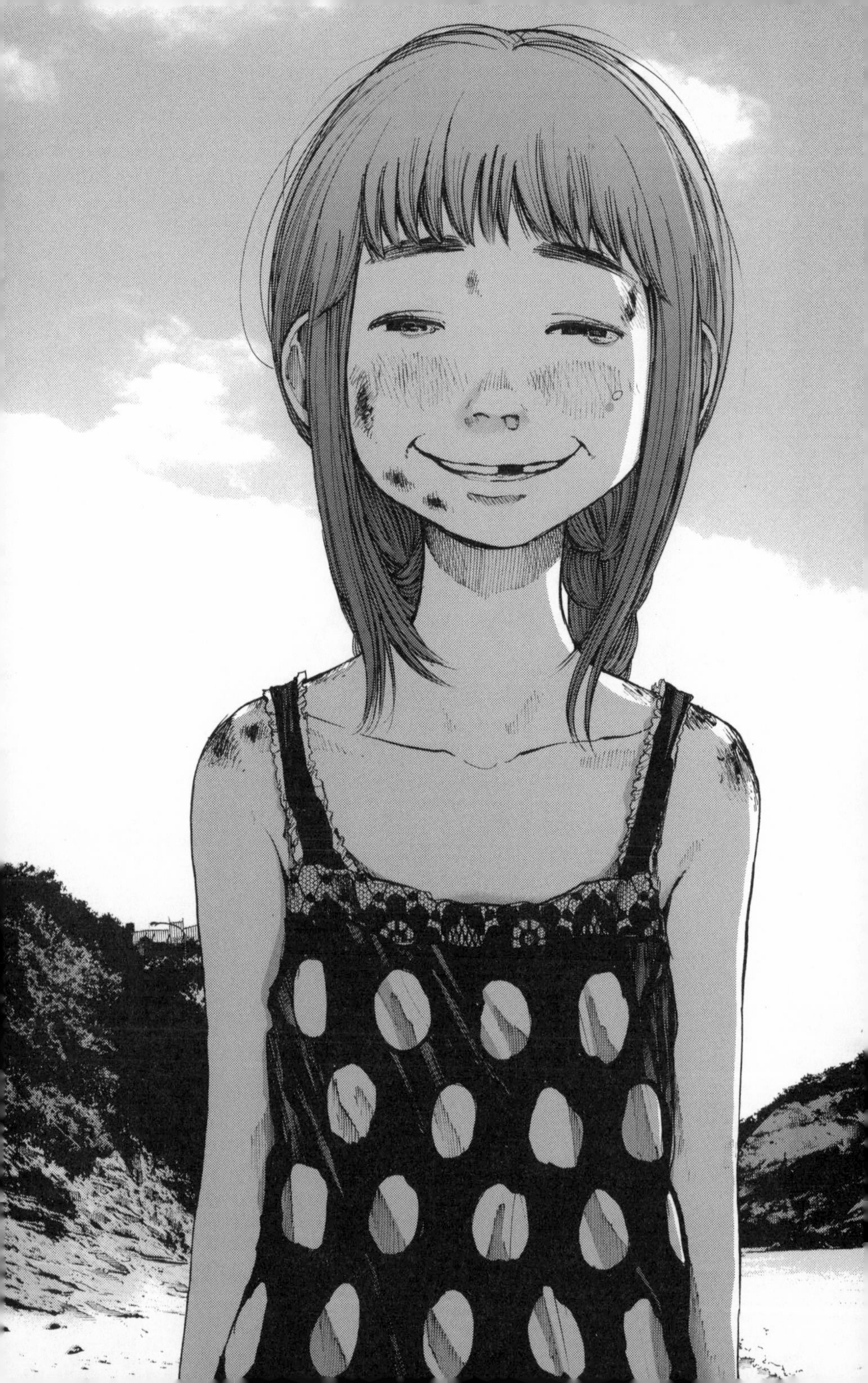

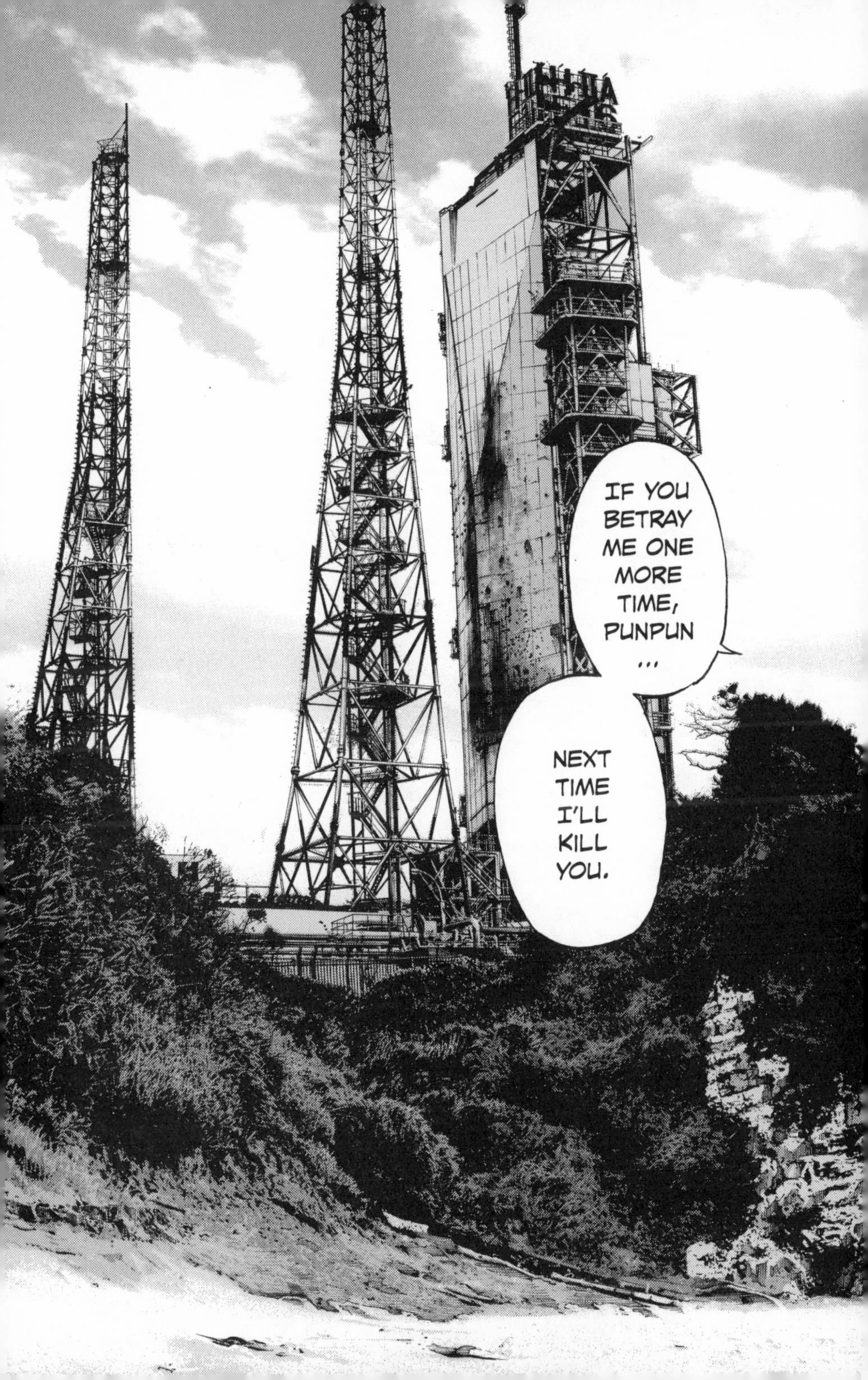
IF YOU BETRAY ME ONE MORE TIME, PUNPUN ...
NEXT TIME I'LL KILL YOU.

SEIKO
MMMM.

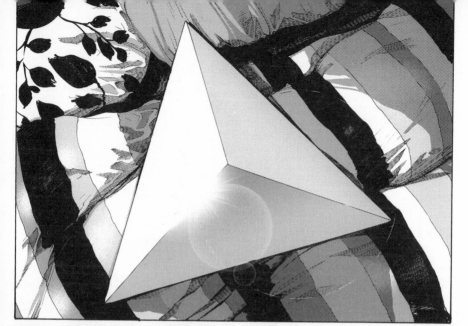

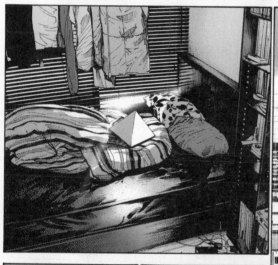

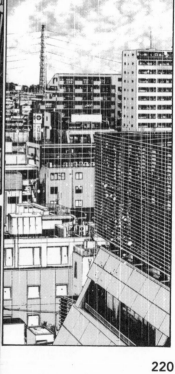

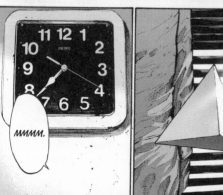

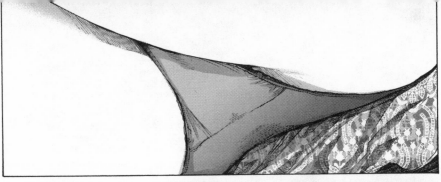

Huh?

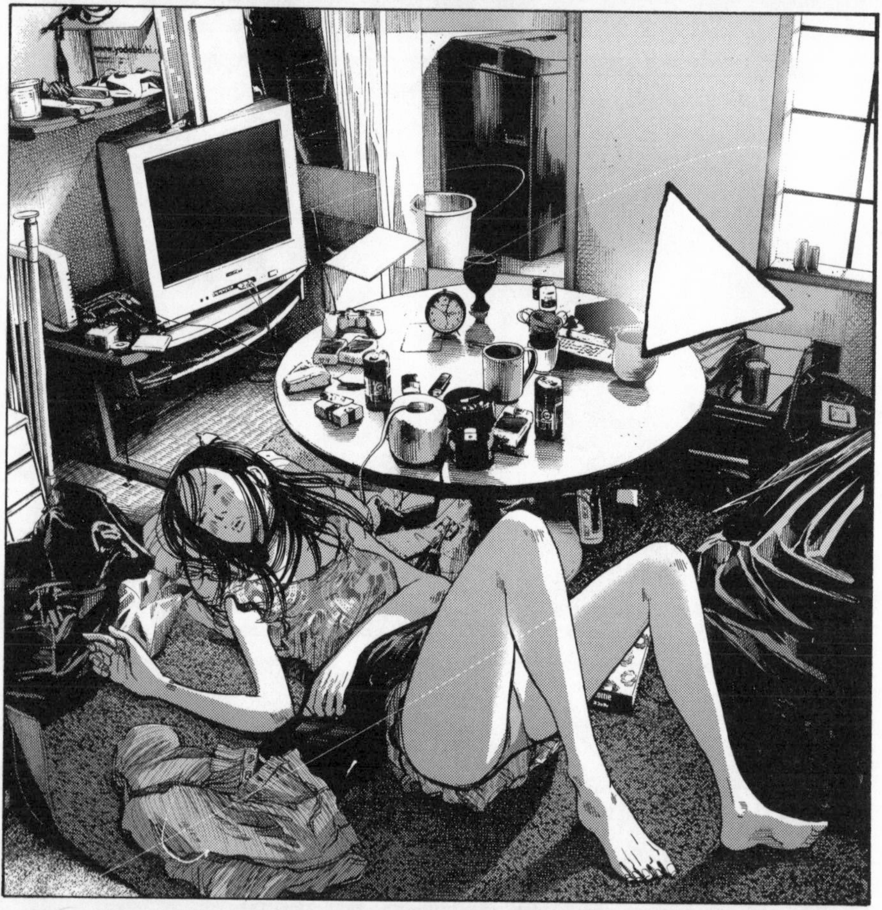

Huh?

GOODNIGHT PUNPUN INIO ASANO
Part Seven

BACKGROUND ASSISTANTS: Yuki Toribuchi
Satsuki Sato
CG ASSISTANT: Hisashi Saito
COOPERATION: Kumatsuto
Yu Uehara

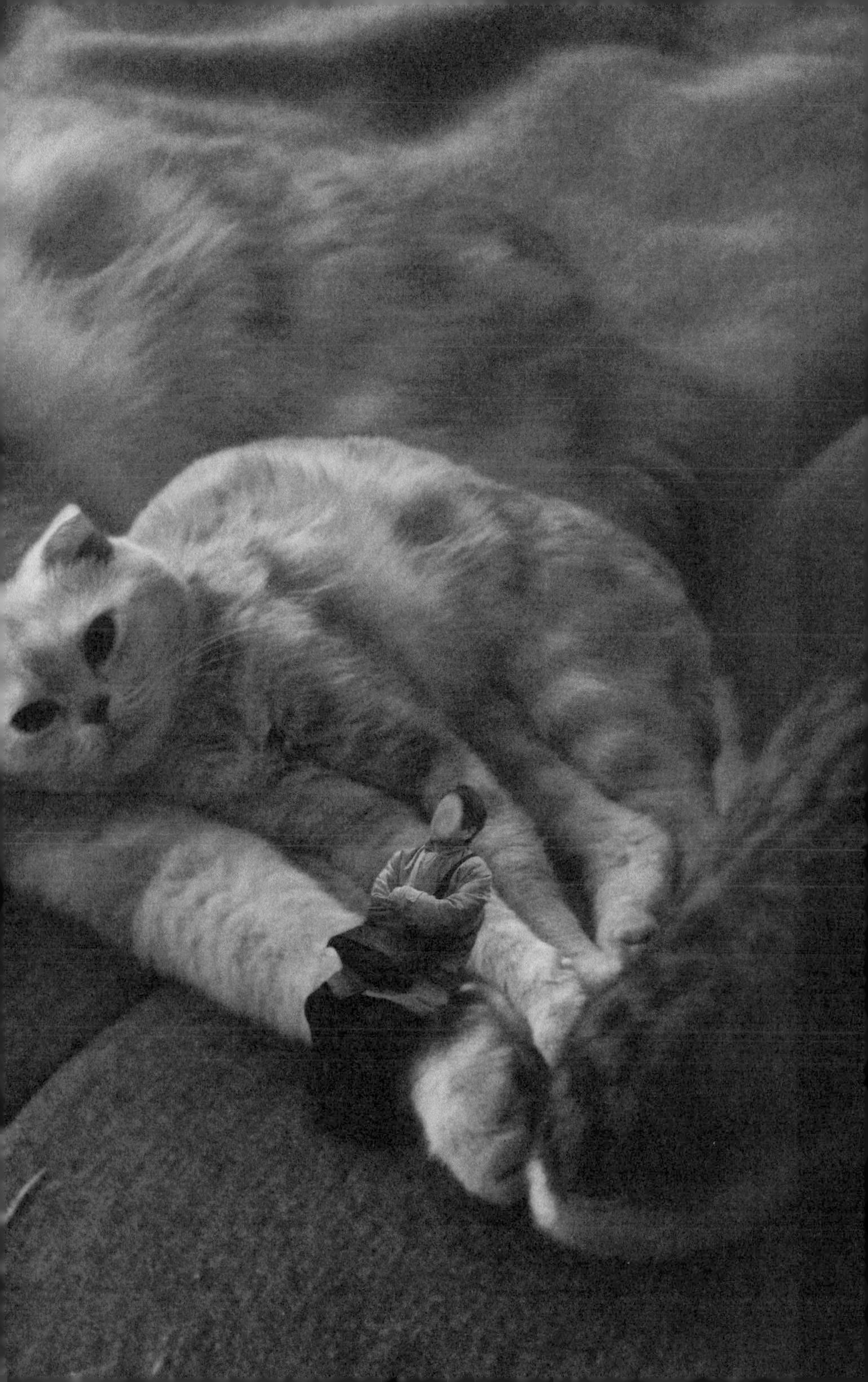

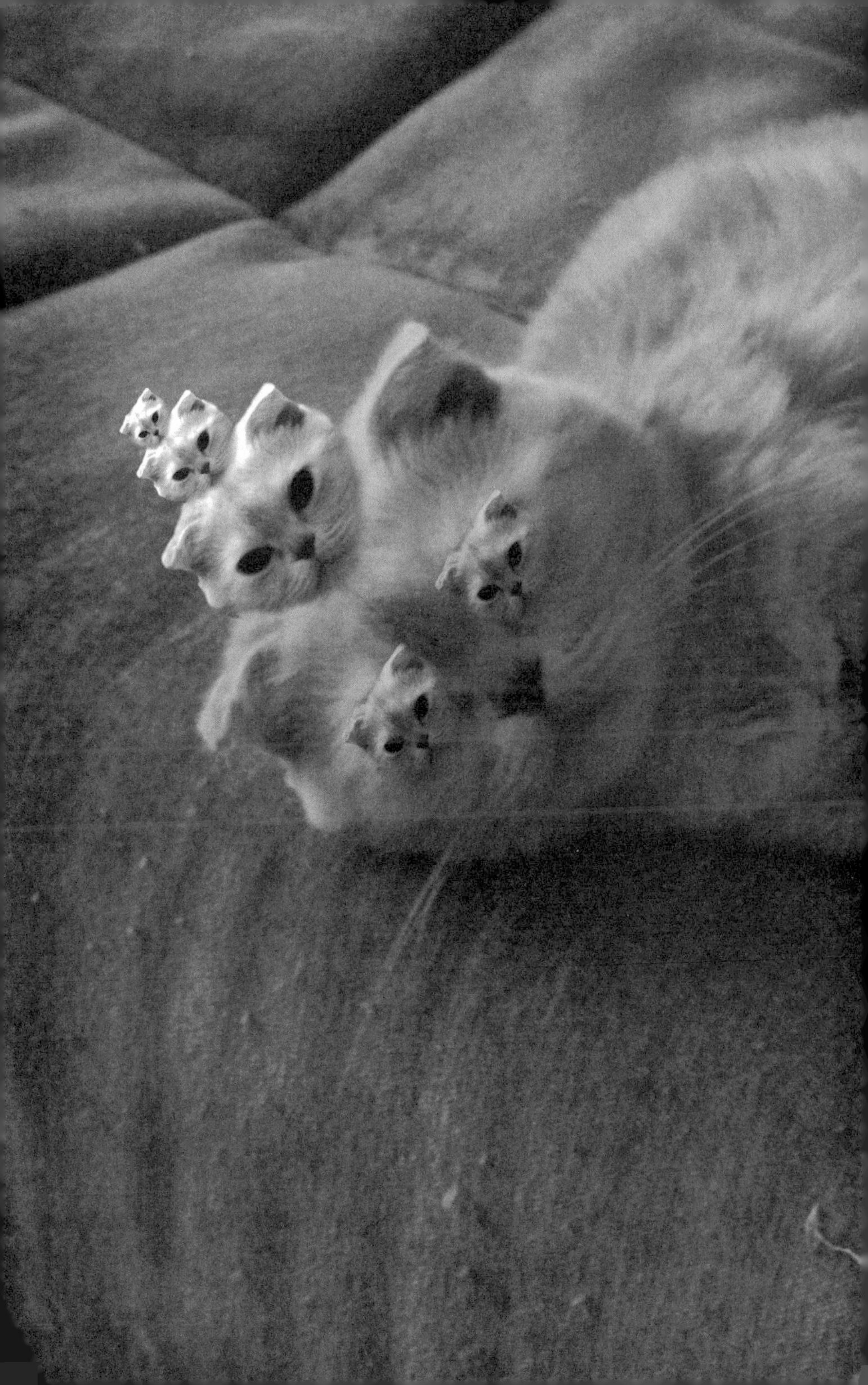

GOODNIGHT PUNPUN

Part Eight

CONTENTS

STORY THUS FAR...

Having mistaken ulterior motive for motivation. Punpun moves out on his own. He later meets up again with the dark-haired artist with the center part. She then comes on to him big-time. Punpun is in a tizzy.

CAST OF CHARACTERS

PUNPUN ONODERA
An 18-year-old part-timer. He is invincible.

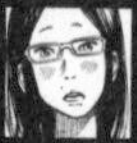

SACHI NANJO
A 22-year-old cram school teacher. Her glasses are the core of her being, so she dies if they come off.

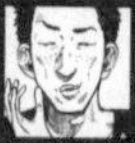

YUKINOSHIN MIMURA
An 18-year-old college student.
"The moon will be dyed red again tonight...!"

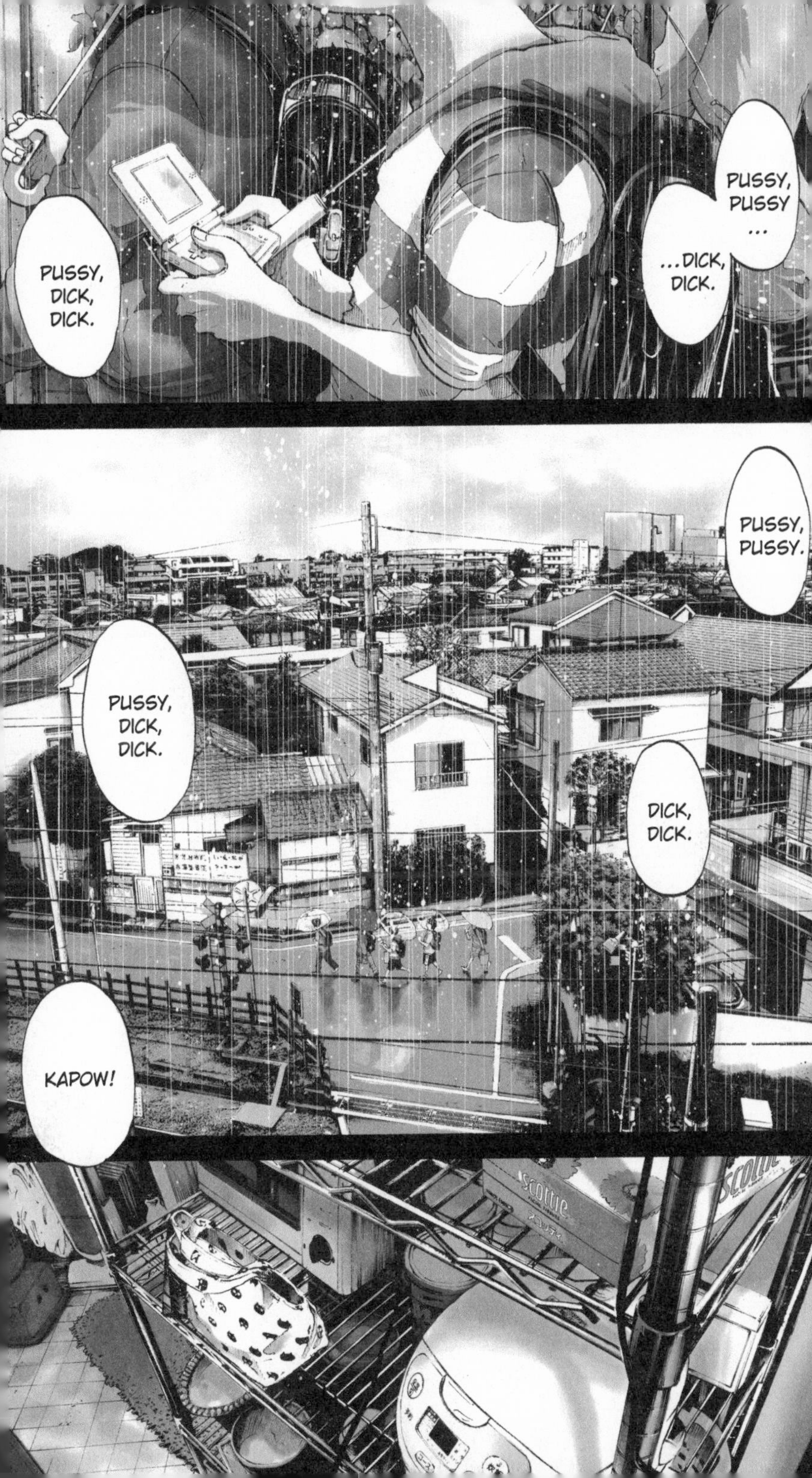
PUSSY, PUSSY ...
...DICK, DICK.
PUSSY, DICK, DICK.
PUSSY, PUSSY.
PUSSY, DICK, DICK.
DICK, DICK.
KAPOW!

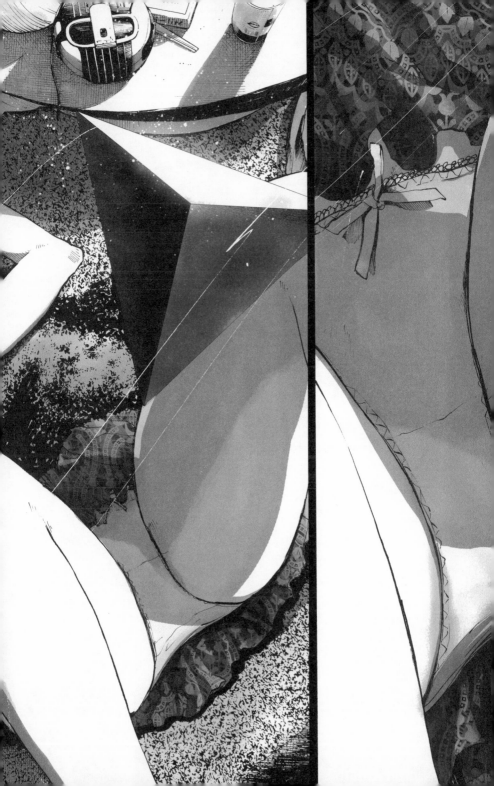

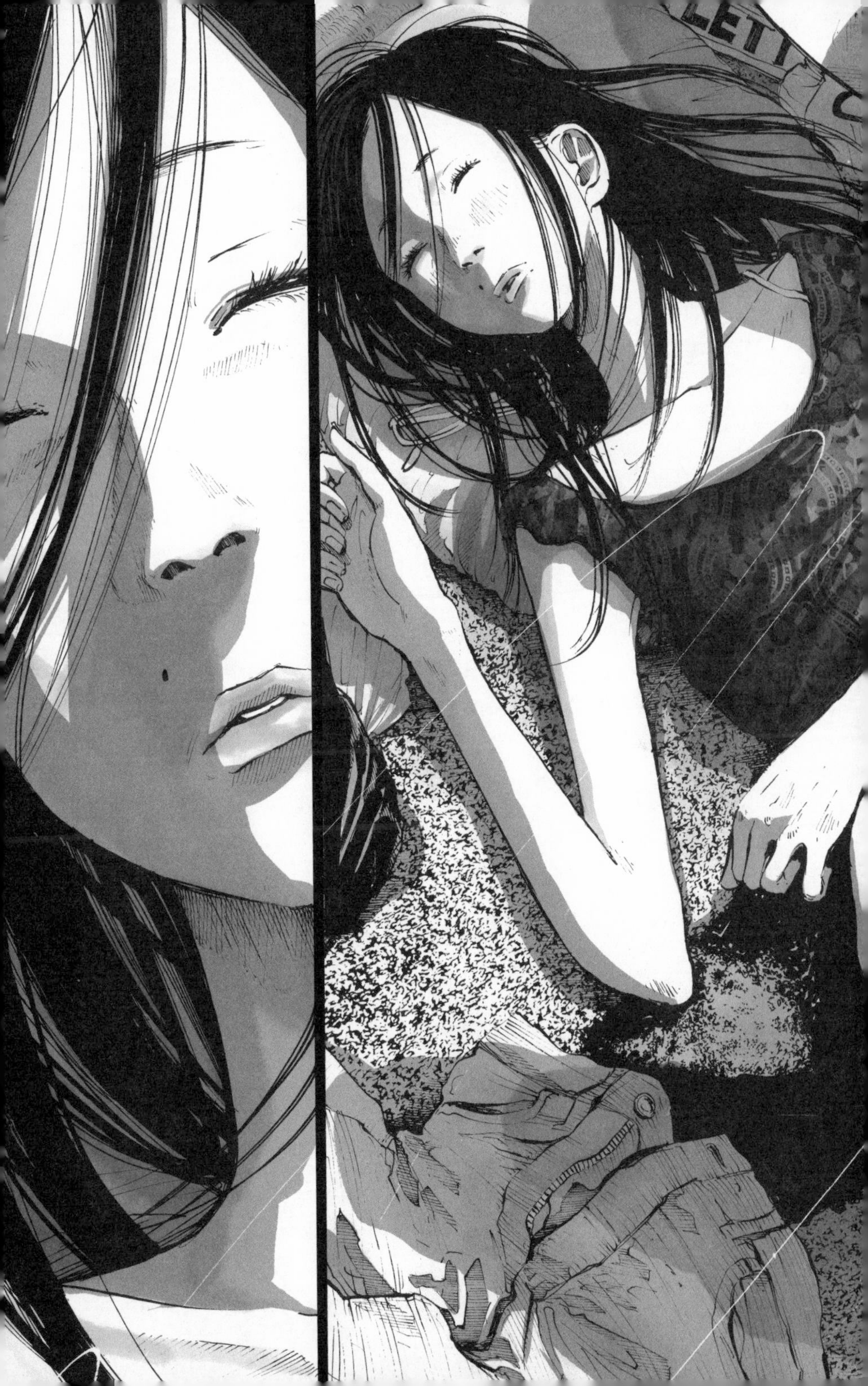

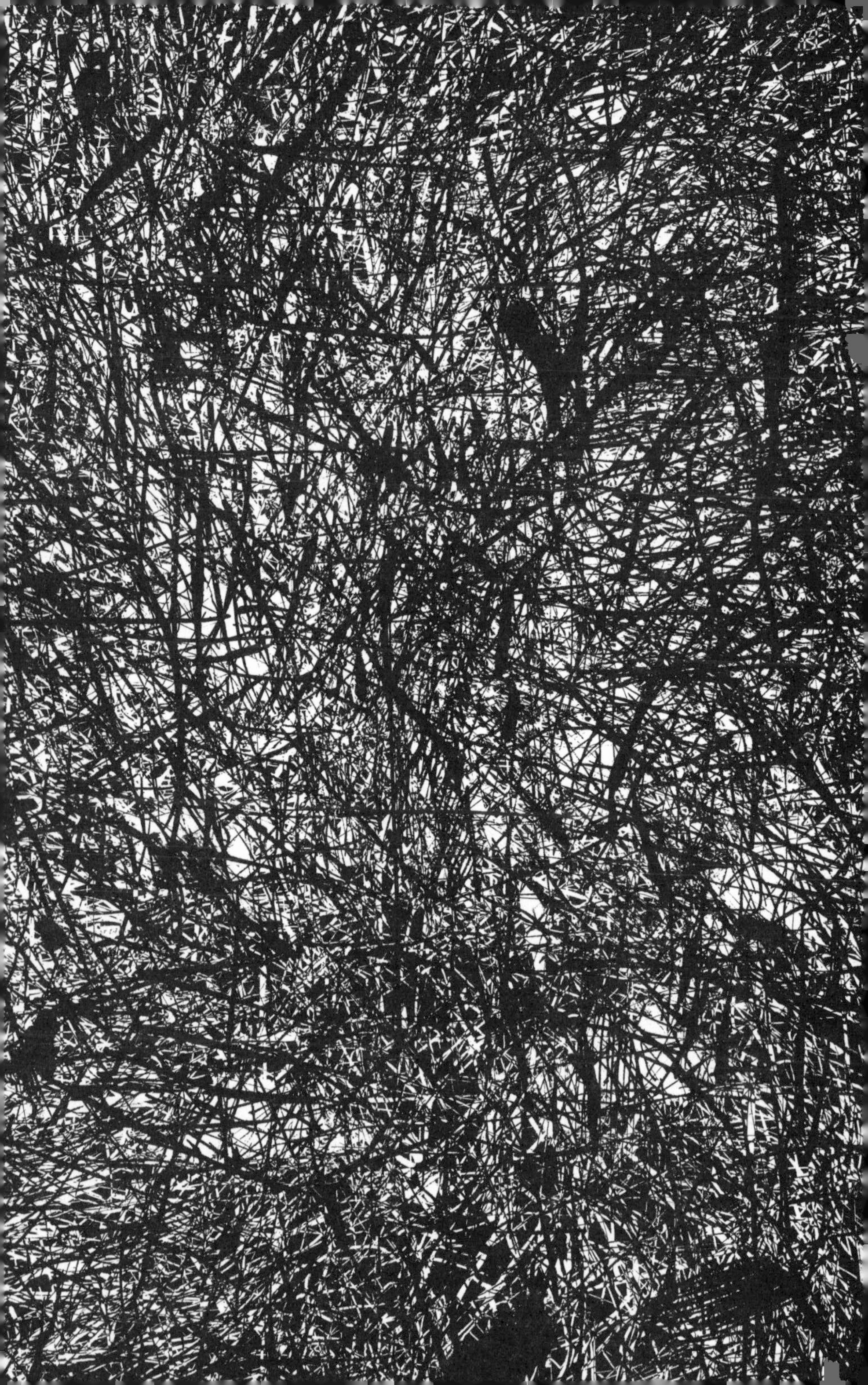

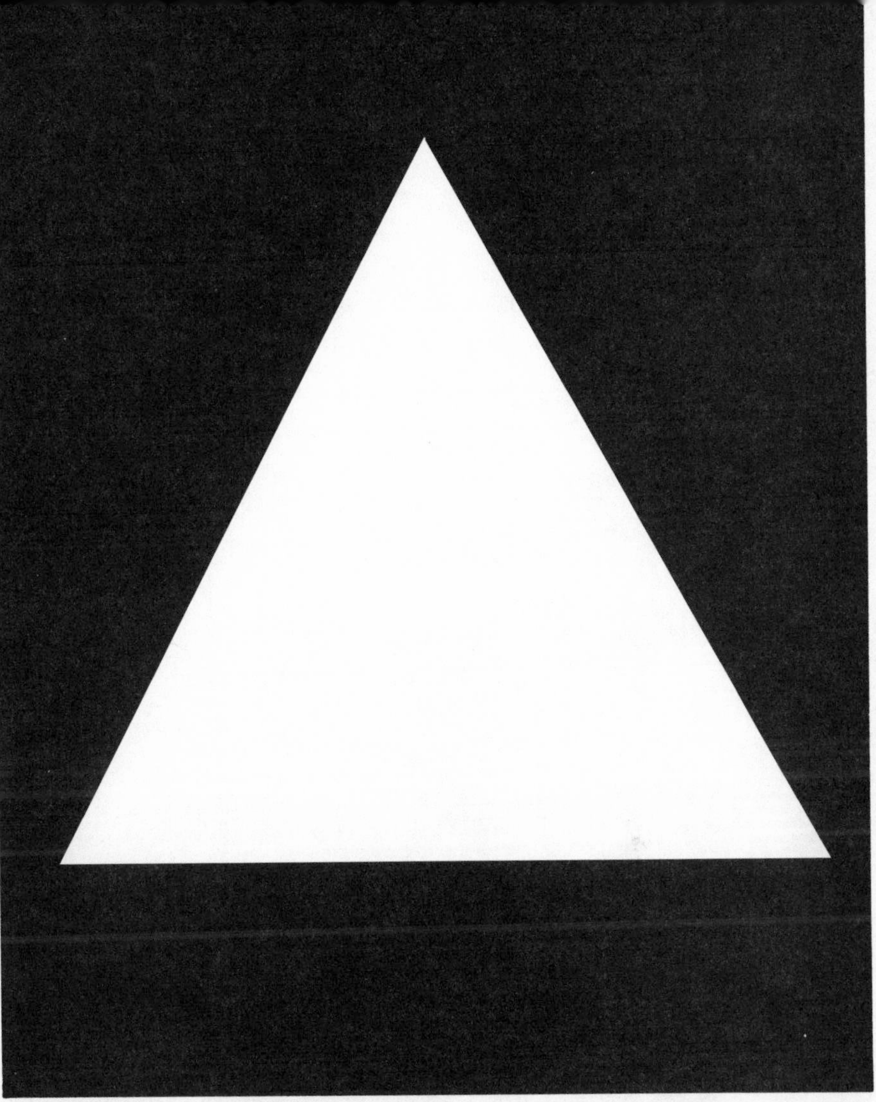

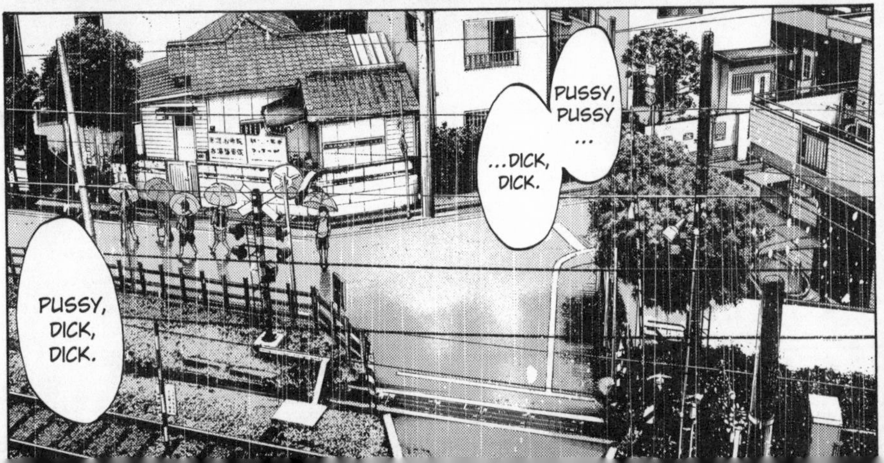
PUSSY, PUSSY ...
...DICK, DICK.
PUSSY, DICK, DICK.

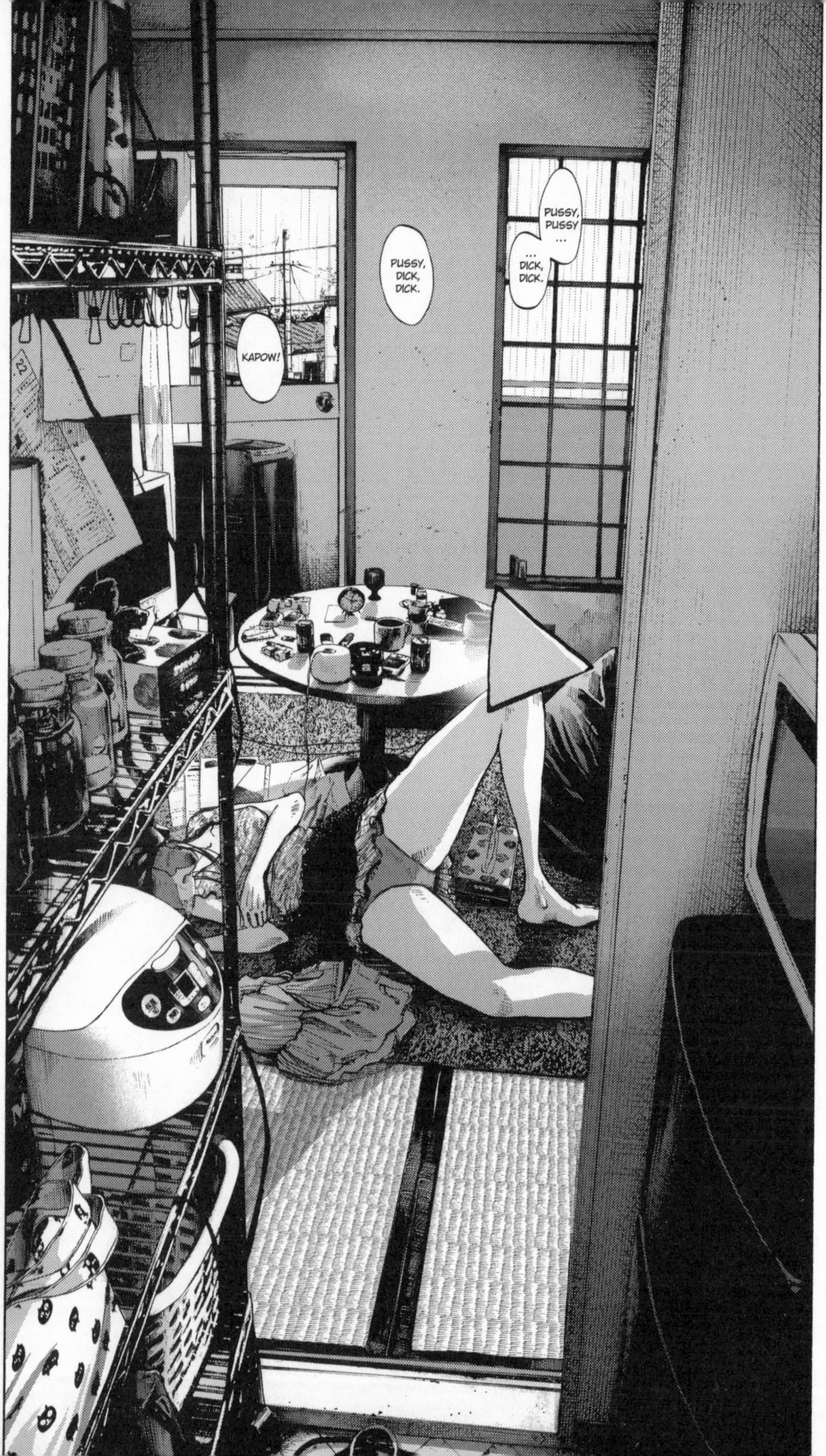
PUSSY, PUSSY ...
... DICK, DICK.
PUSSY, DICK, DICK.
KAPOW!

Oh.

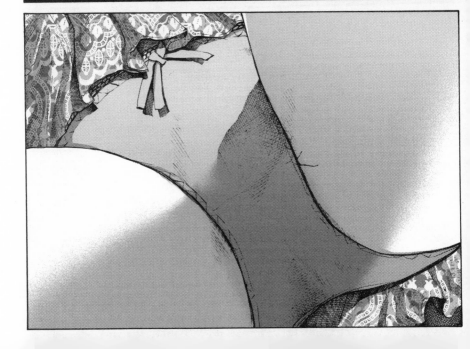

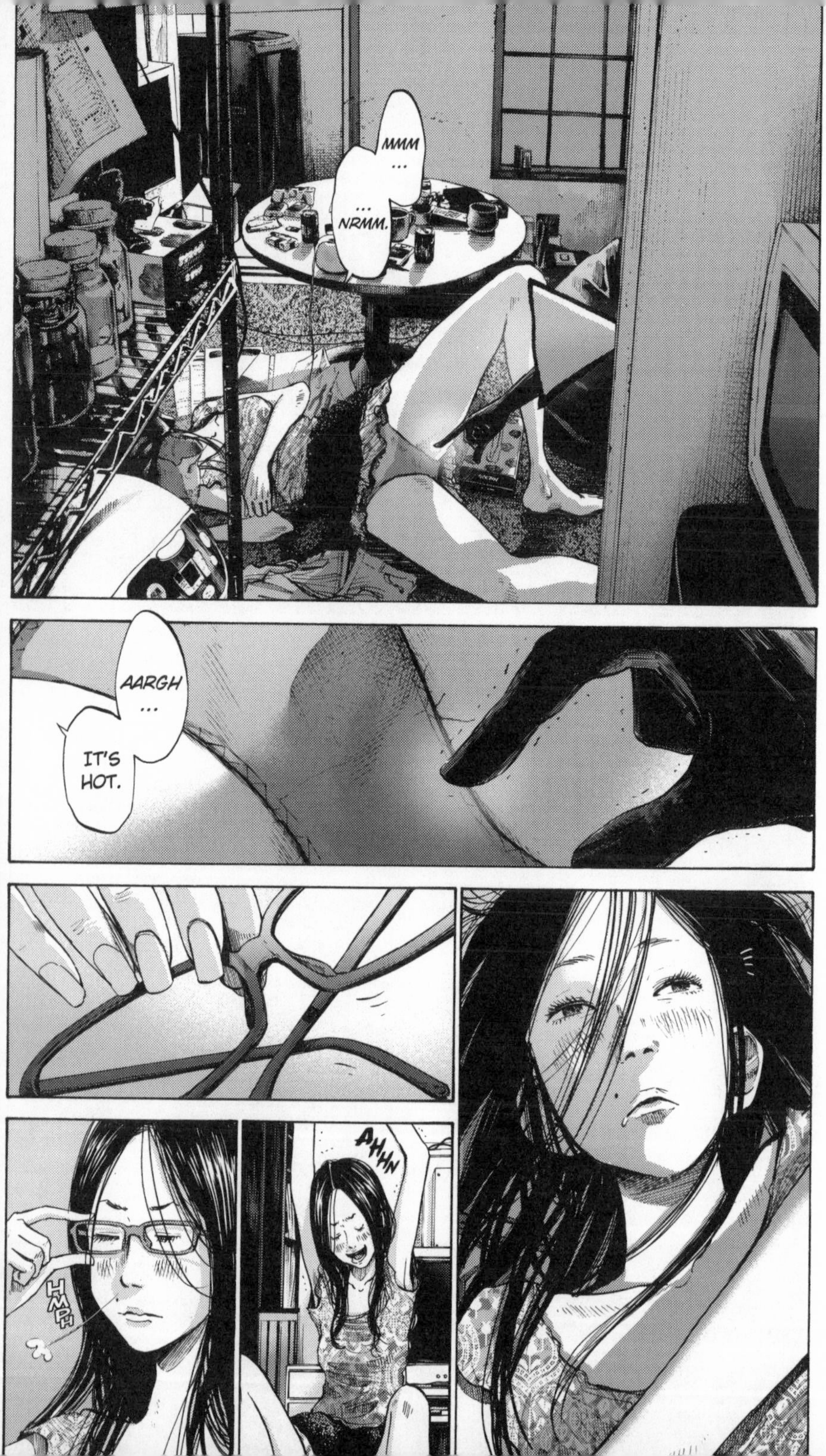
MMM ...
... NRMM.
AARGH ...
IT'S HOT.
AHHN
HMPH

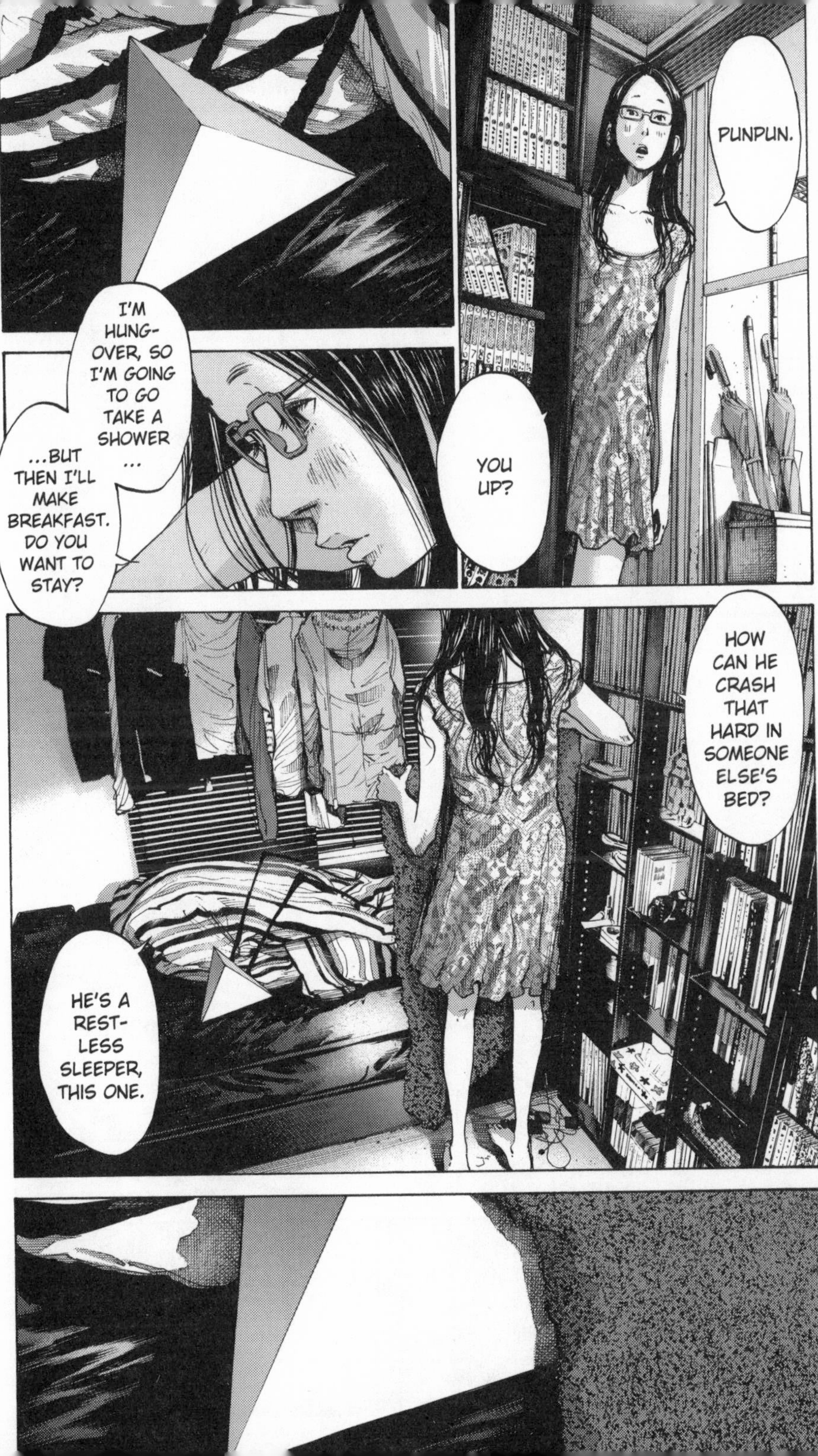
PUNPUN.
YOU UP?
I'M HUNG-OVER, SO I'M GOING TO GO TAKE A SHOWER...
...BUT THEN I'LL MAKE BREAKFAST. DO YOU WANT TO STAY?
HOW CAN HE CRASH THAT HARD IN SOMEONE ELSE'S BED?
HE'S A REST-LESS SLEEPER, THIS ONE.

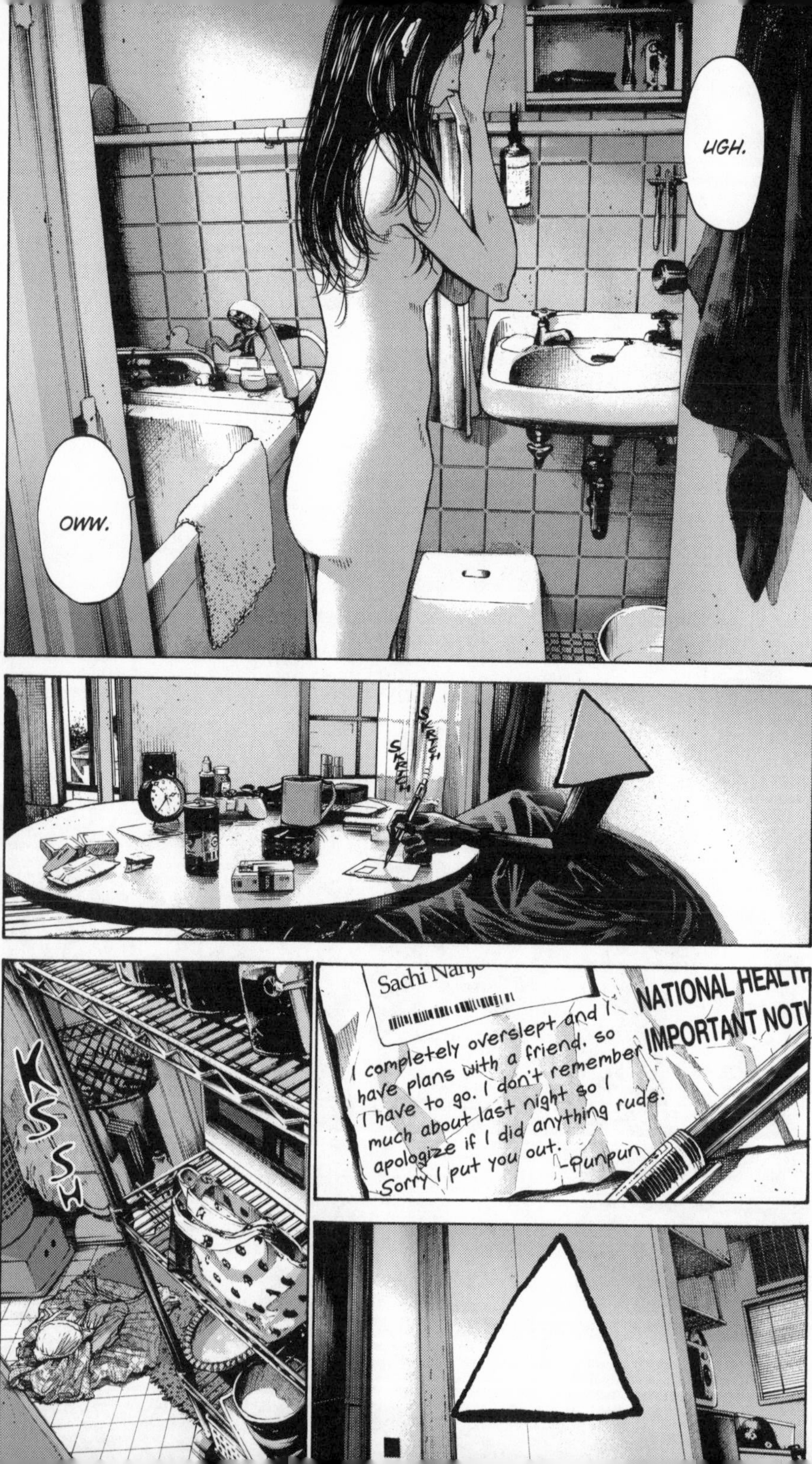

UGH.
OWW.
SKRTCH
SKRTCH
Sachi Nanj
NATIONAL HEAL
IMPORTANT NOT
I completely overslept and I have plans with a friend. so I have to go. I don't remember much about last night so I apologize if I did anything rude. Sorry I put you out.
-Punpun
KSSH

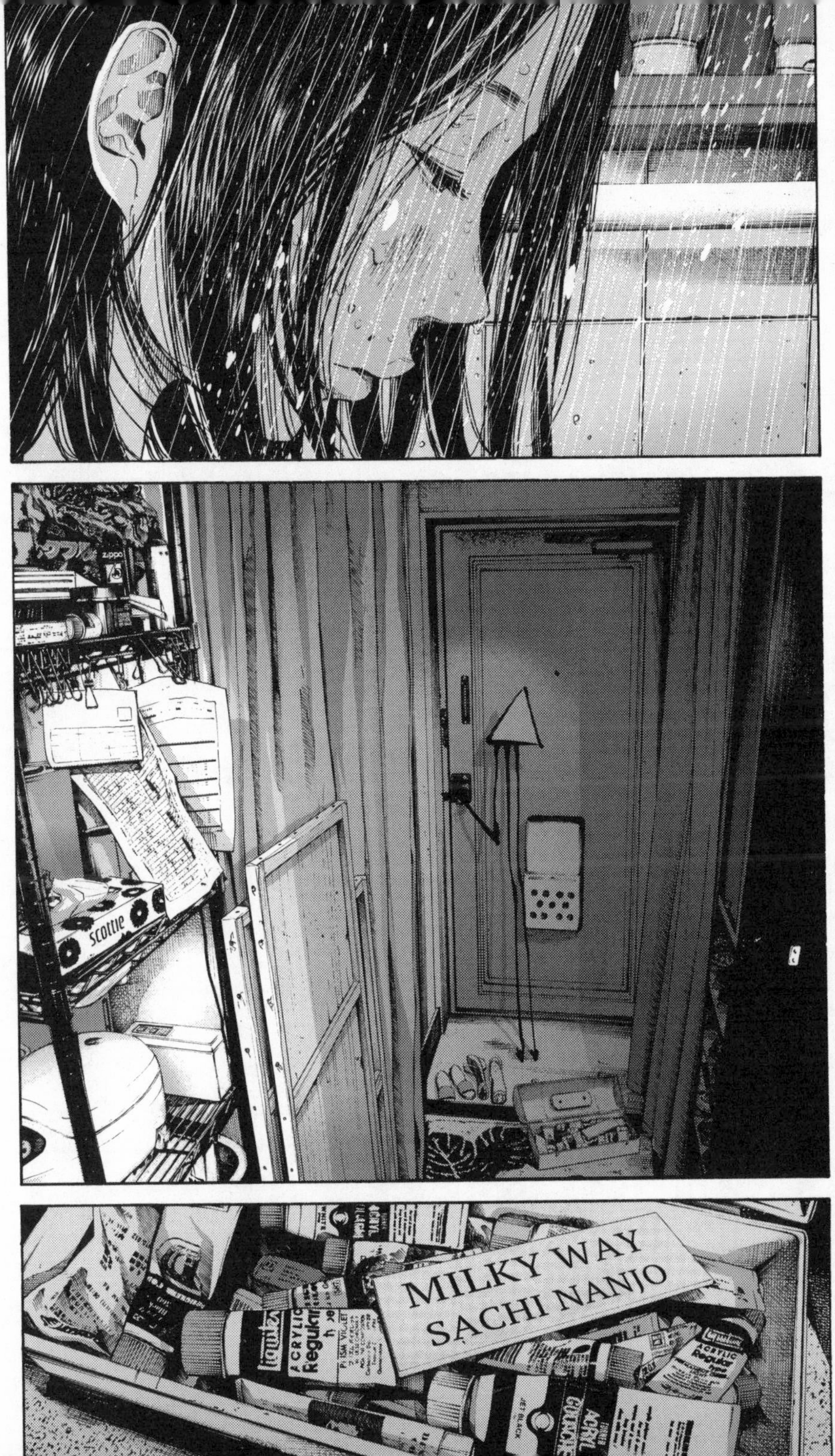

zippo
scottie
MILKY WAY
SACHI NANJO
ACRYLIC
Regular

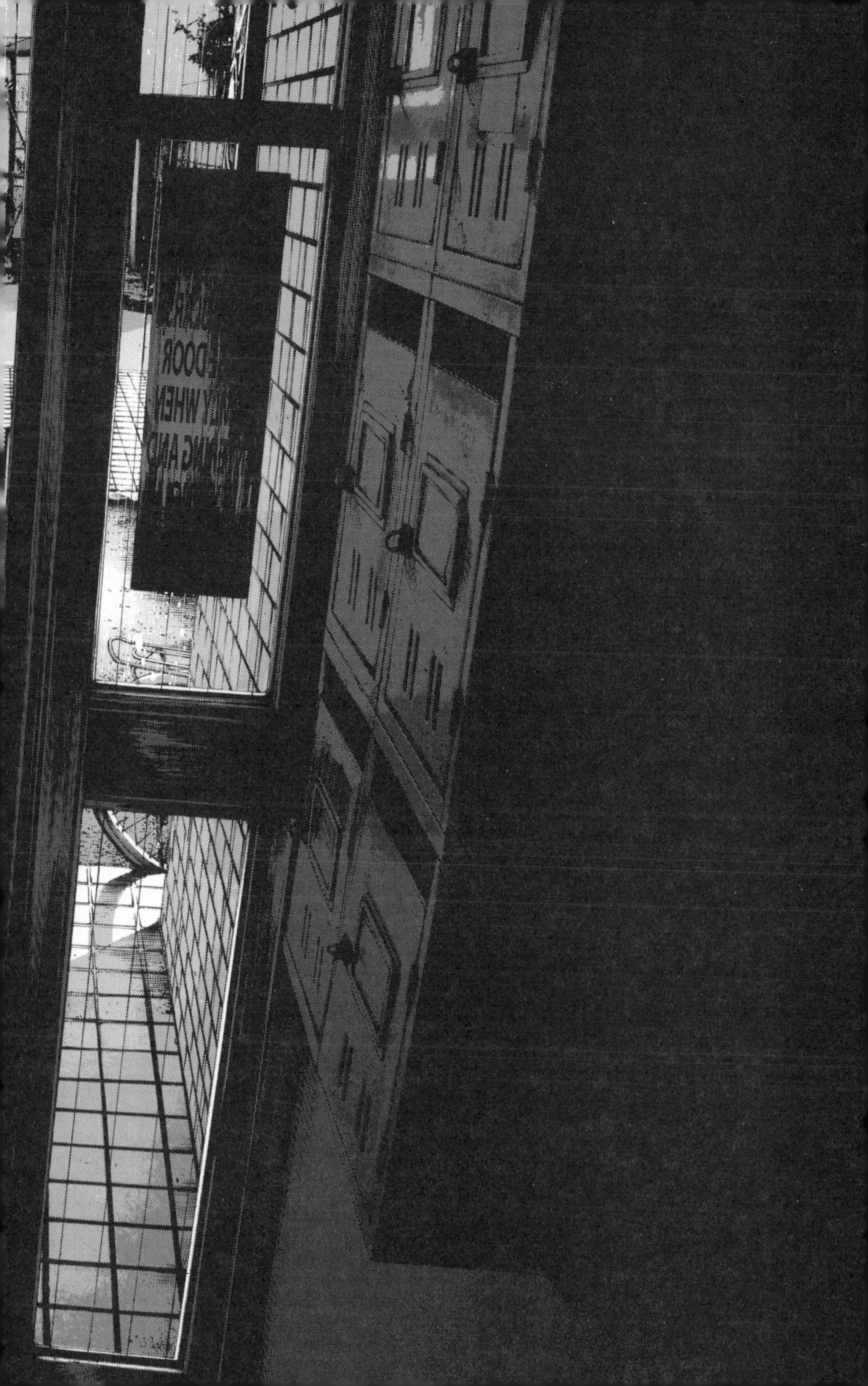

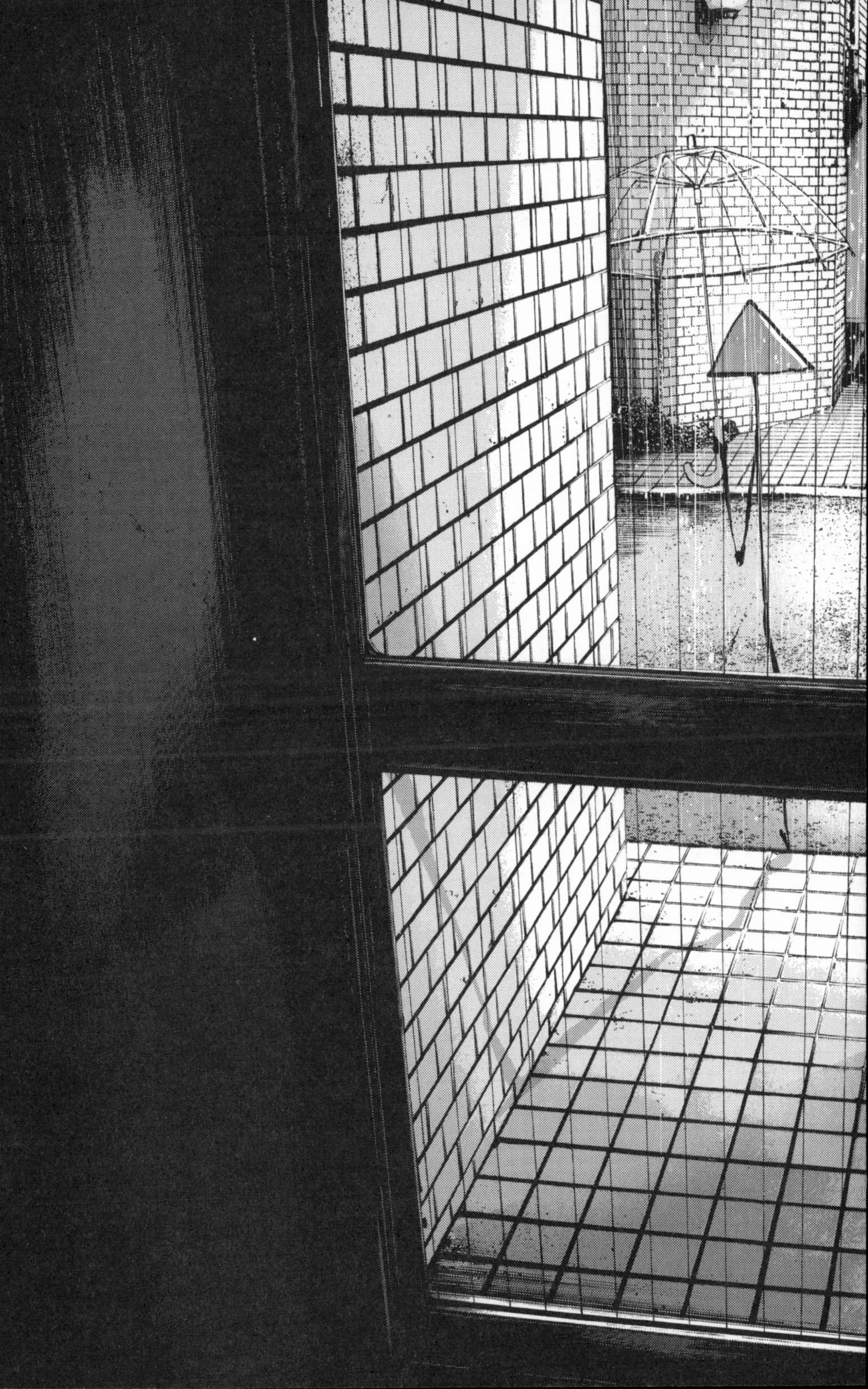

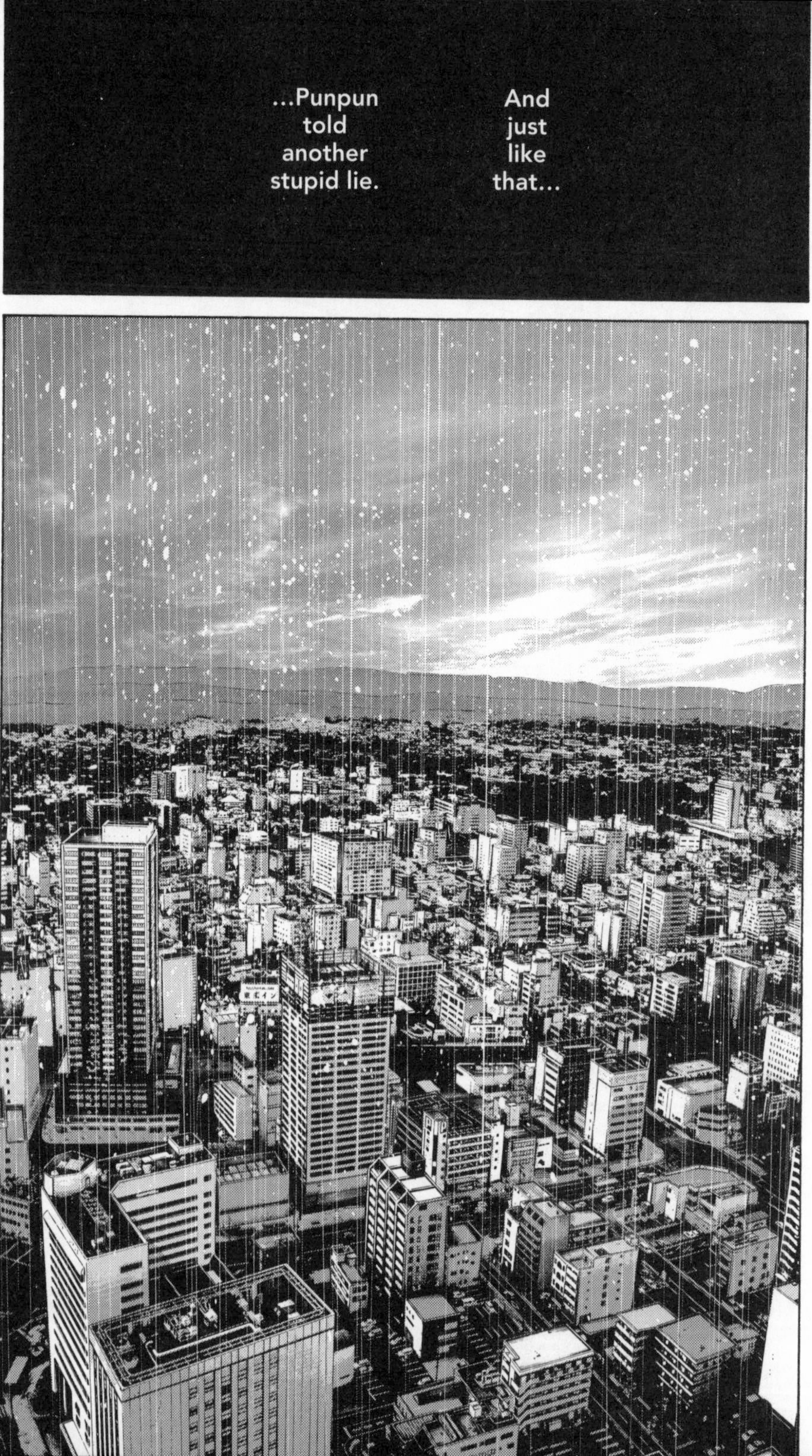
And just like that...
...Punpun told another stupid lie.

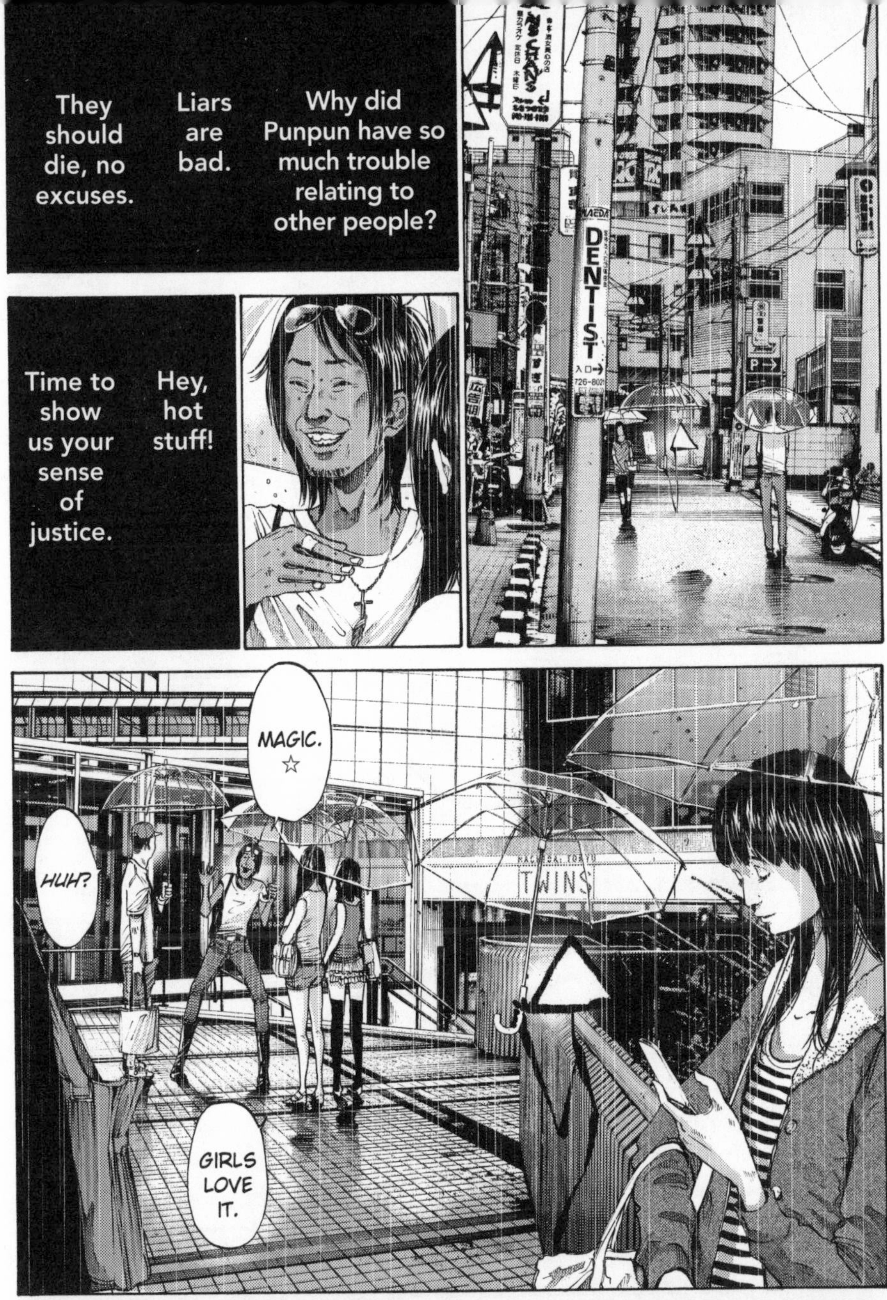
DENTIST
Why did Punpun have so much trouble relating to other people?
Liars are bad.
They should die, no excuses.
Hey, hot stuff!
Time to show us your sense of justice.
TWINS
MAGIC. ☆
HUH?
GIRLS LOVE IT.

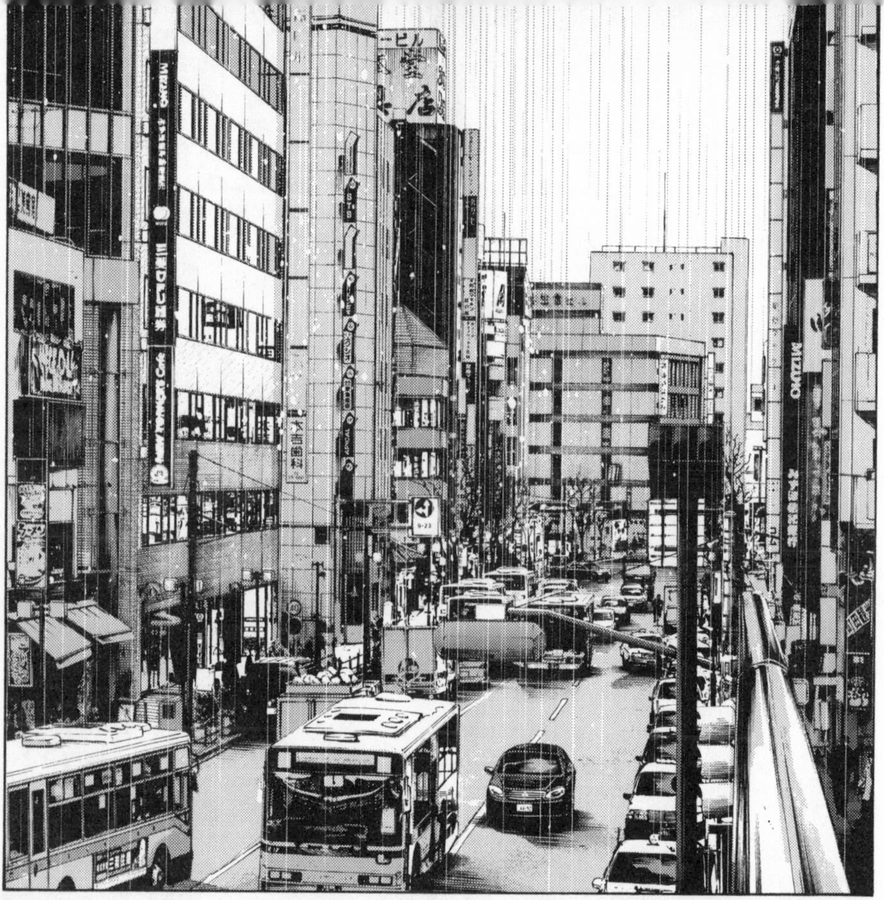

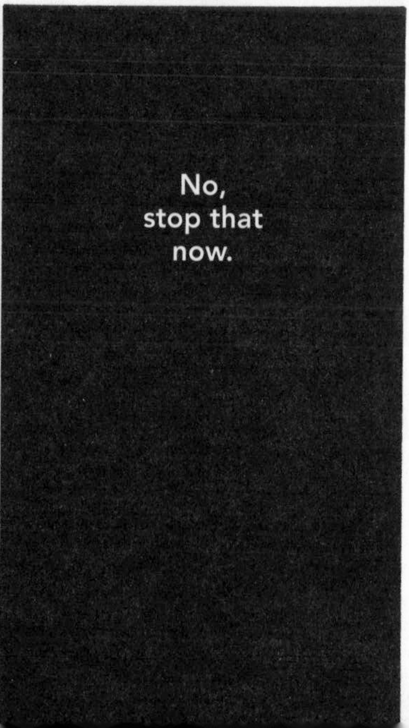
No, stop that now.

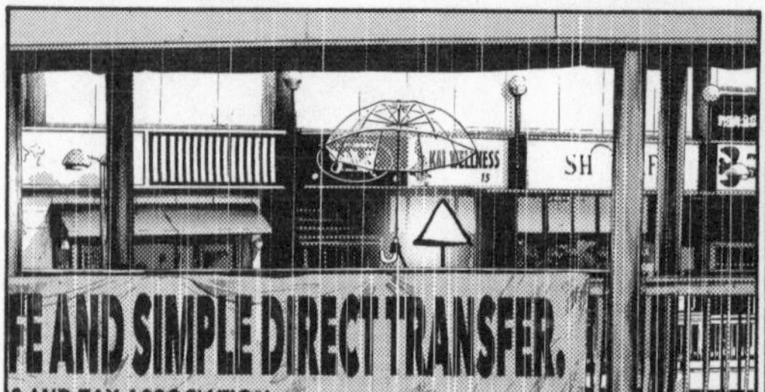
FE AND SIMPLE DIRECT TRANSFER.
S AND TAX ASSOCIATION

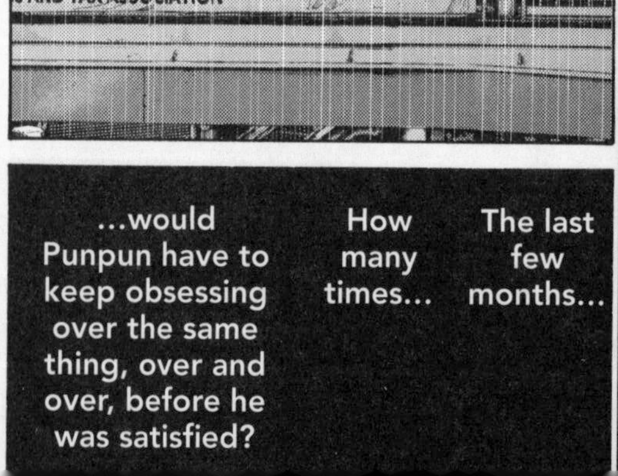
The last few months...
How many times...
...would Punpun have to keep obsessing over the same thing, over and over, before he was satisfied?

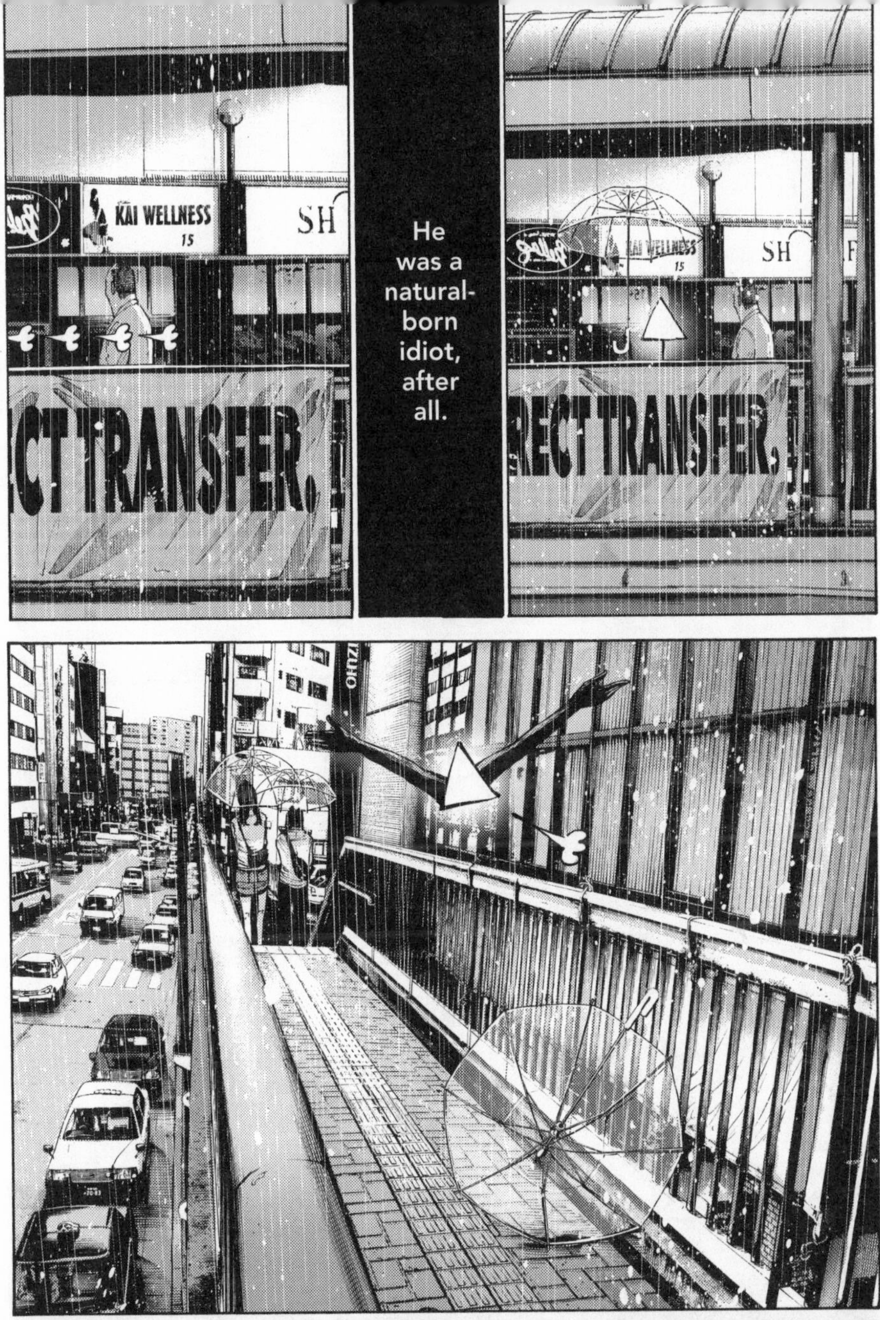
KAI WELLNESS
15
SH
RECT TRANSFER.
He was a natural-born idiot, after all.
KAI WELLNESS
15
SH
ECT TRANSFER.
OHZU

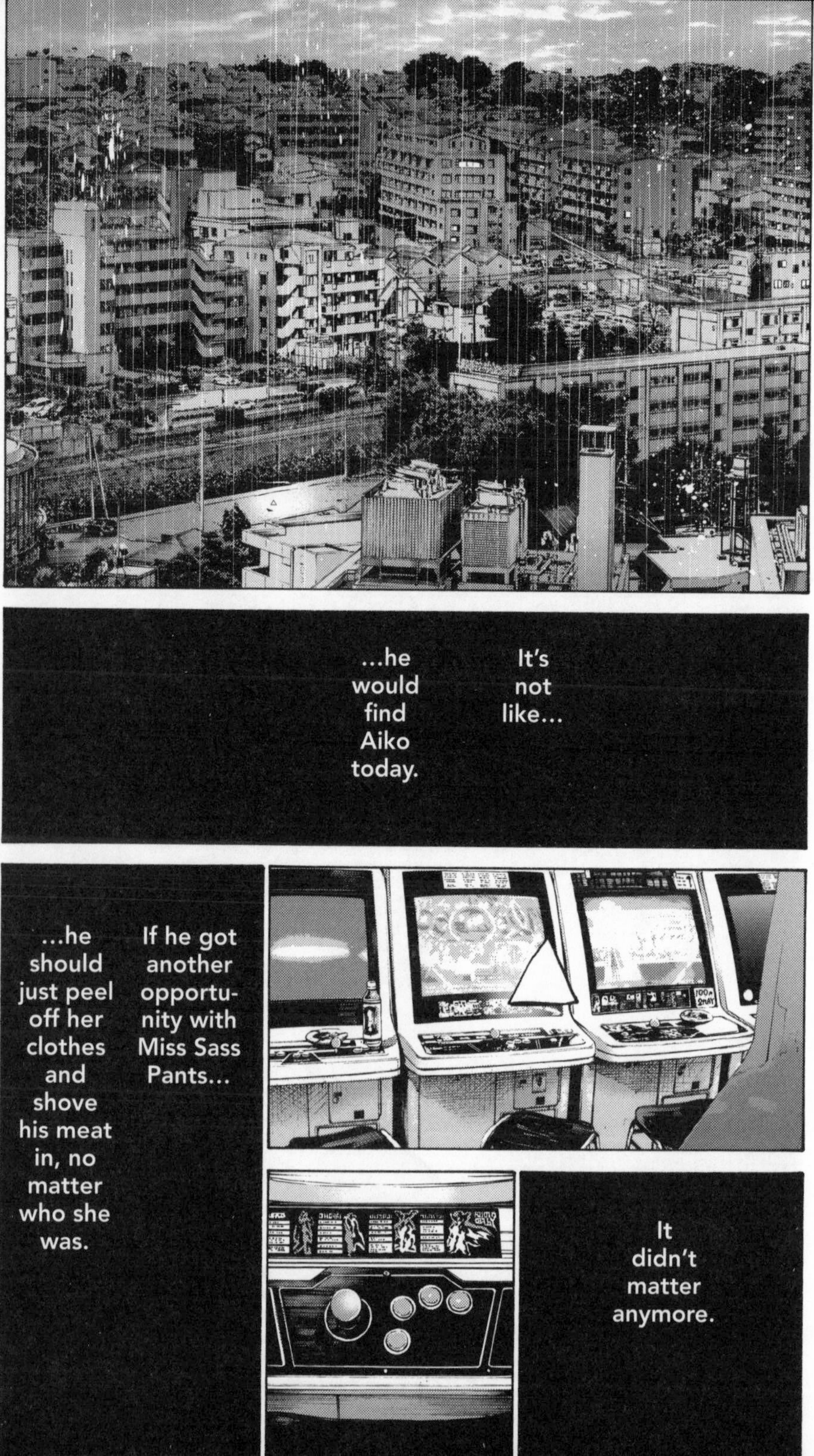
It's not like...
...he would find Aiko today.
It didn't matter anymore.
If he got another opportunity with Miss Sass Pants...
...he should just peel off her clothes and shove his meat in, no matter who she was.

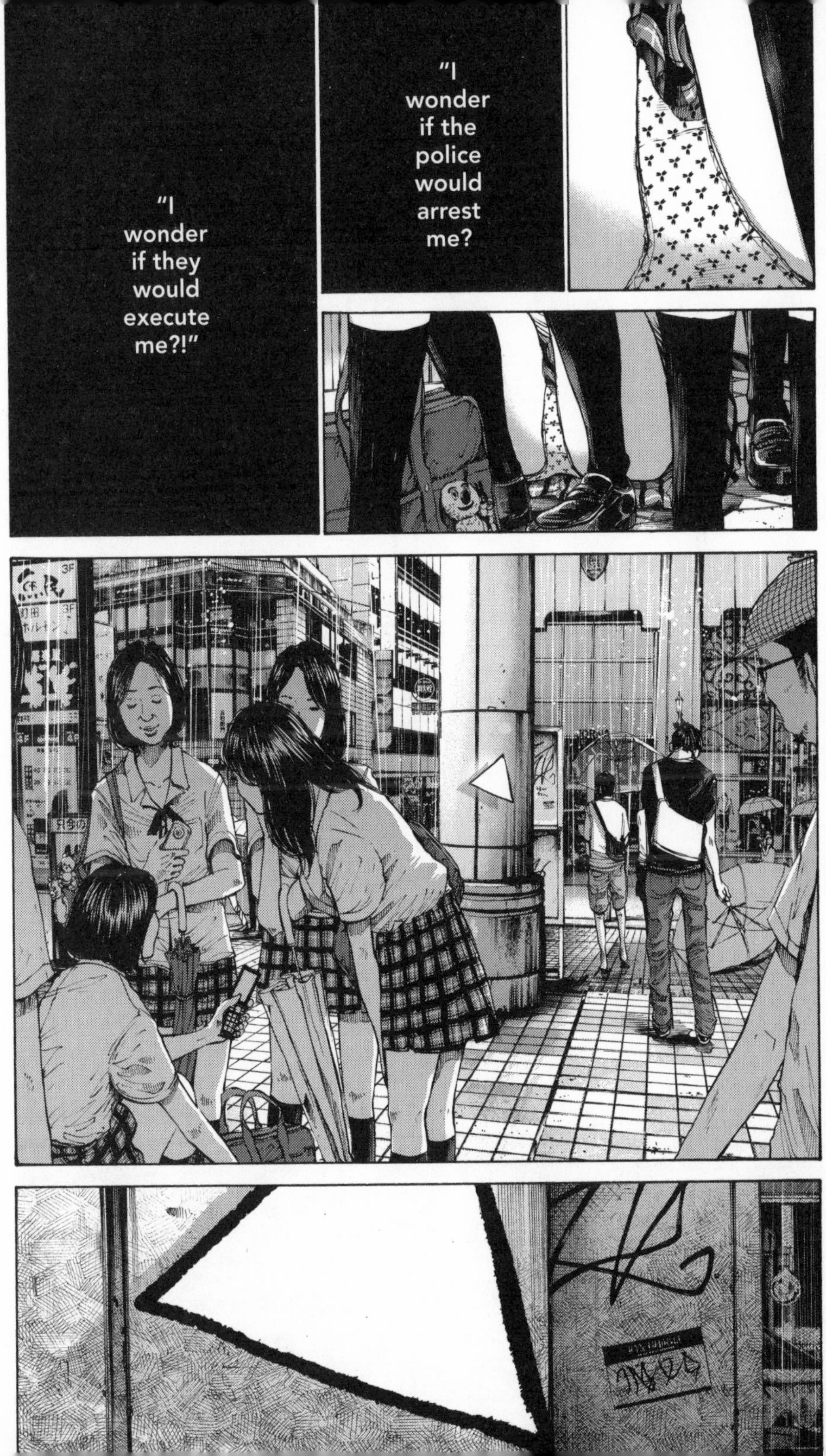
"I wonder if the police would arrest me?
"I wonder if they would execute me?!"

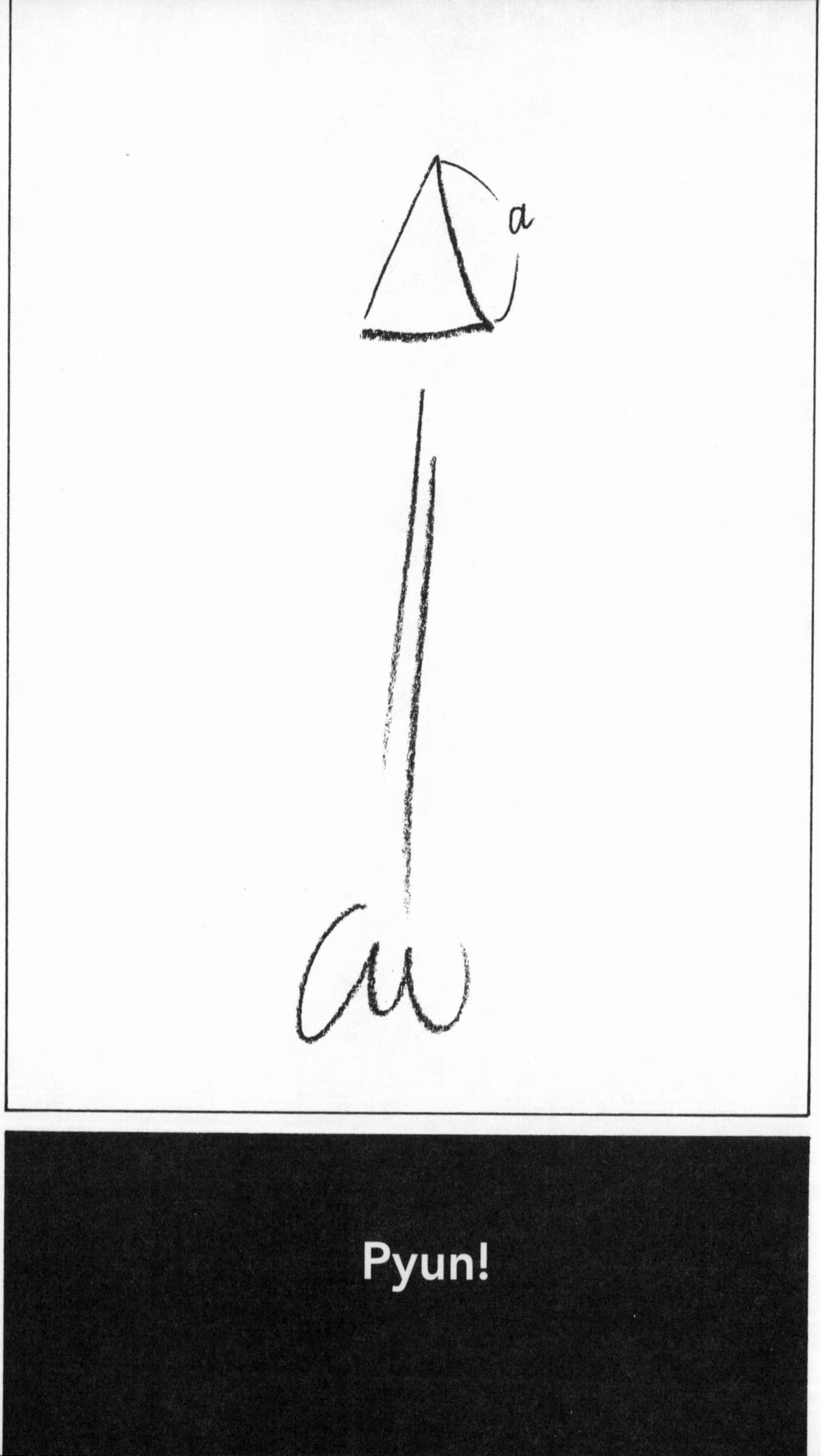
Pyun!

Chapter 80

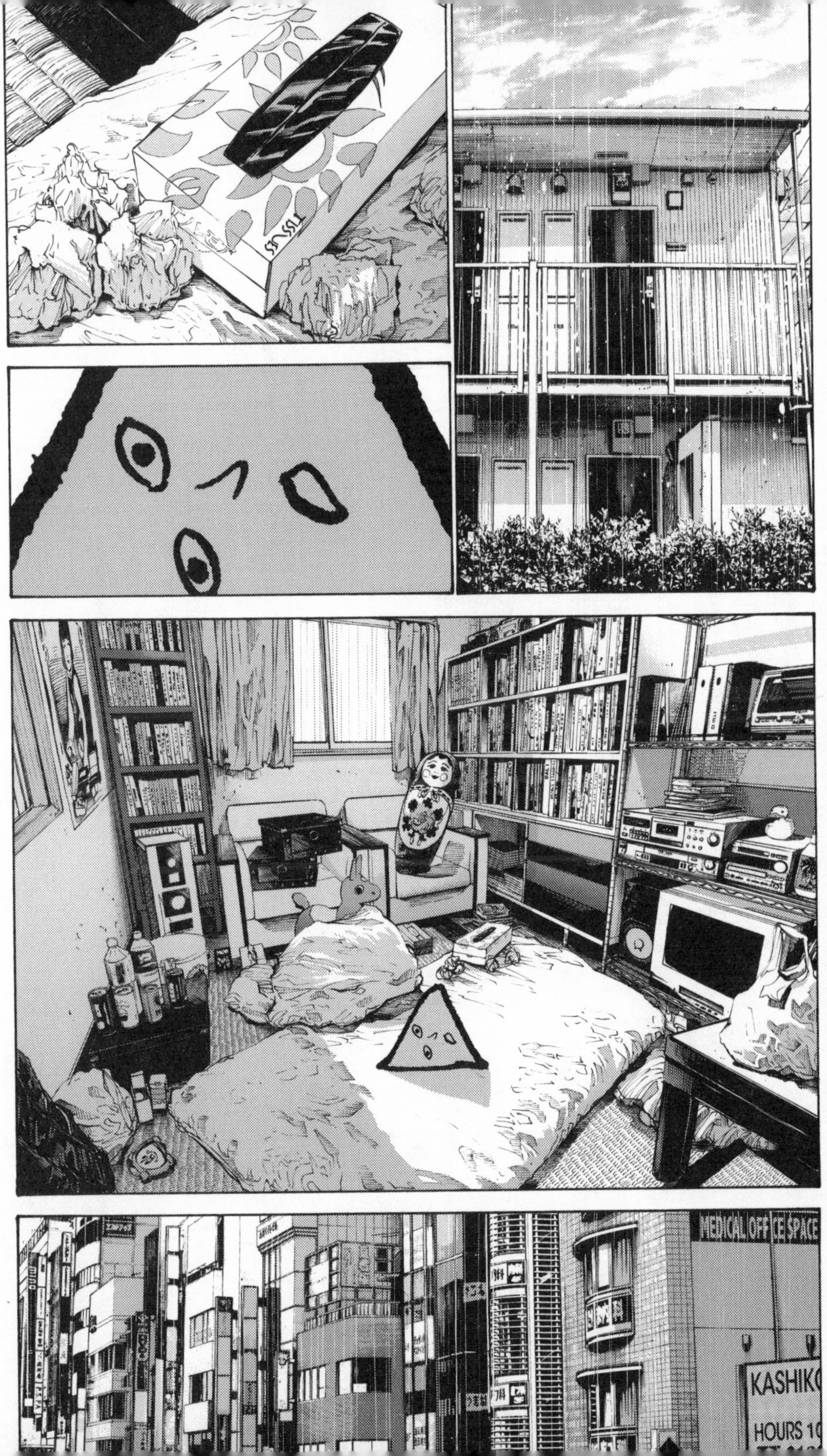
MEDICAL OFFICE SPACE
KASHIKO

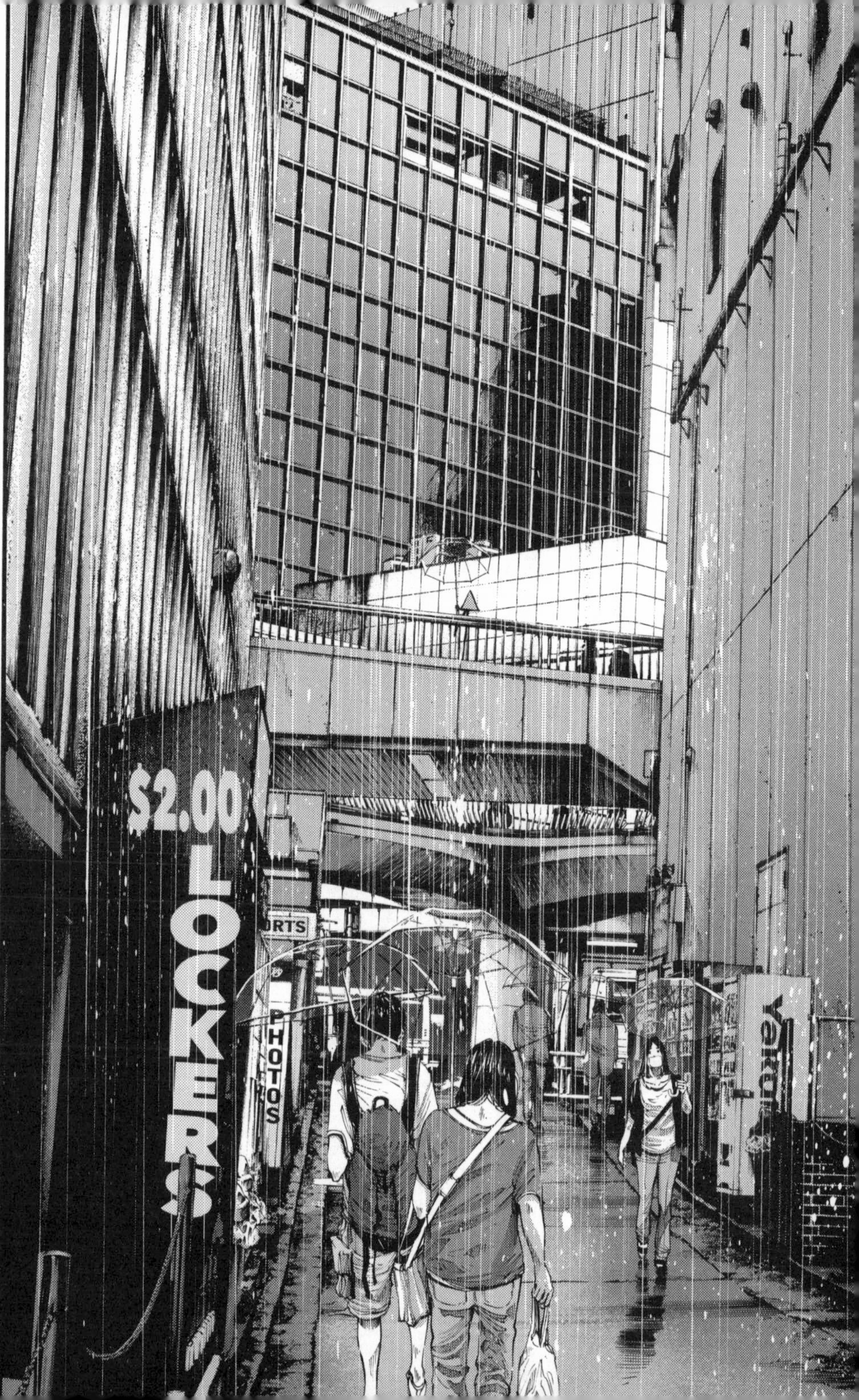
$2.00
LOCKERS
PHOTOS

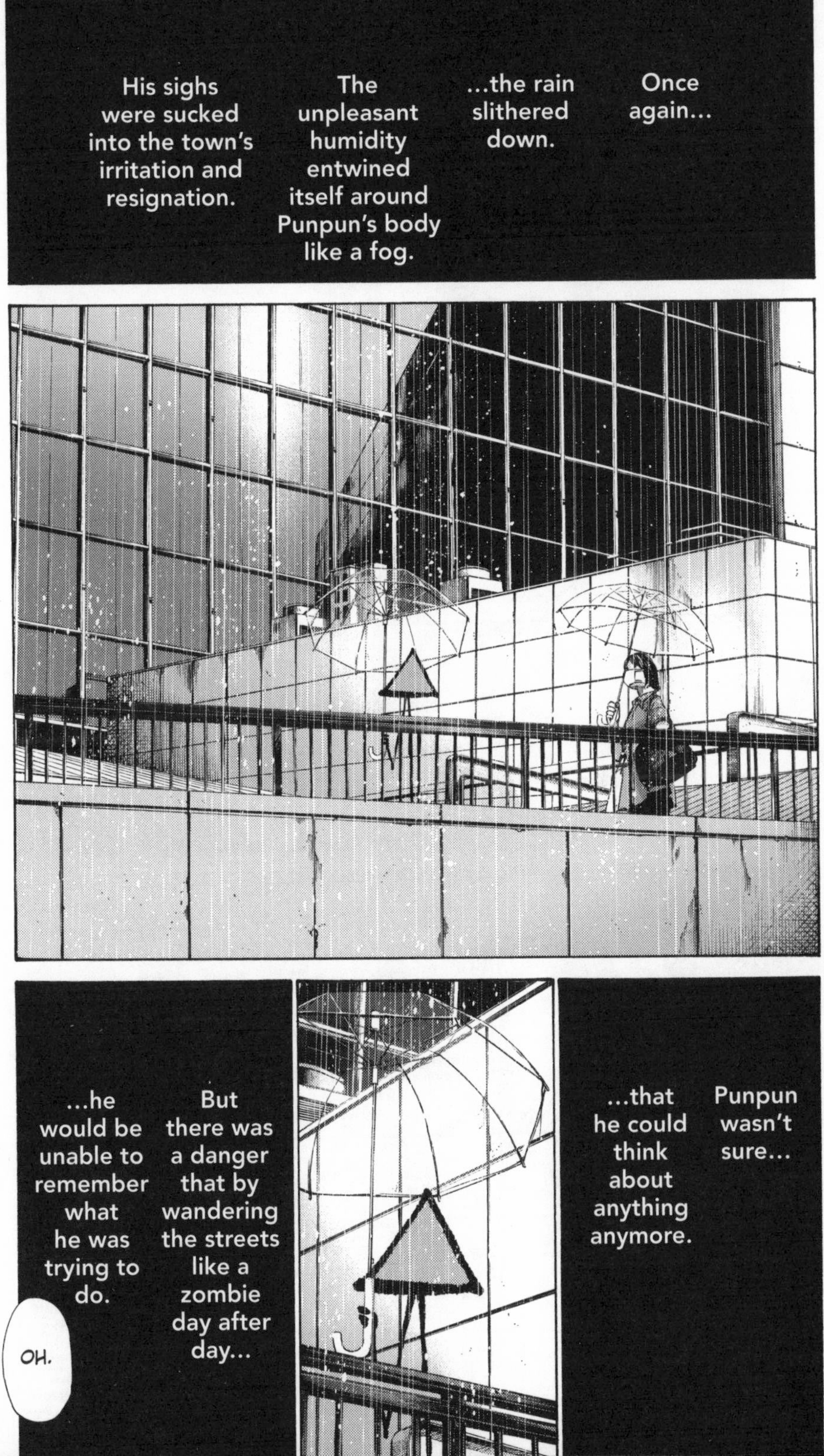
Once again...
...the rain slithered down.
The unpleasant humidity entwined itself around Punpun's body like a fog.
His sighs were sucked into the town's irritation and resignation.
Punpun wasn't sure...
...that he could think about anything anymore.
But there was a danger that by wandering the streets like a zombie day after day...
...he would be unable to remember what he was trying to do.
OH.

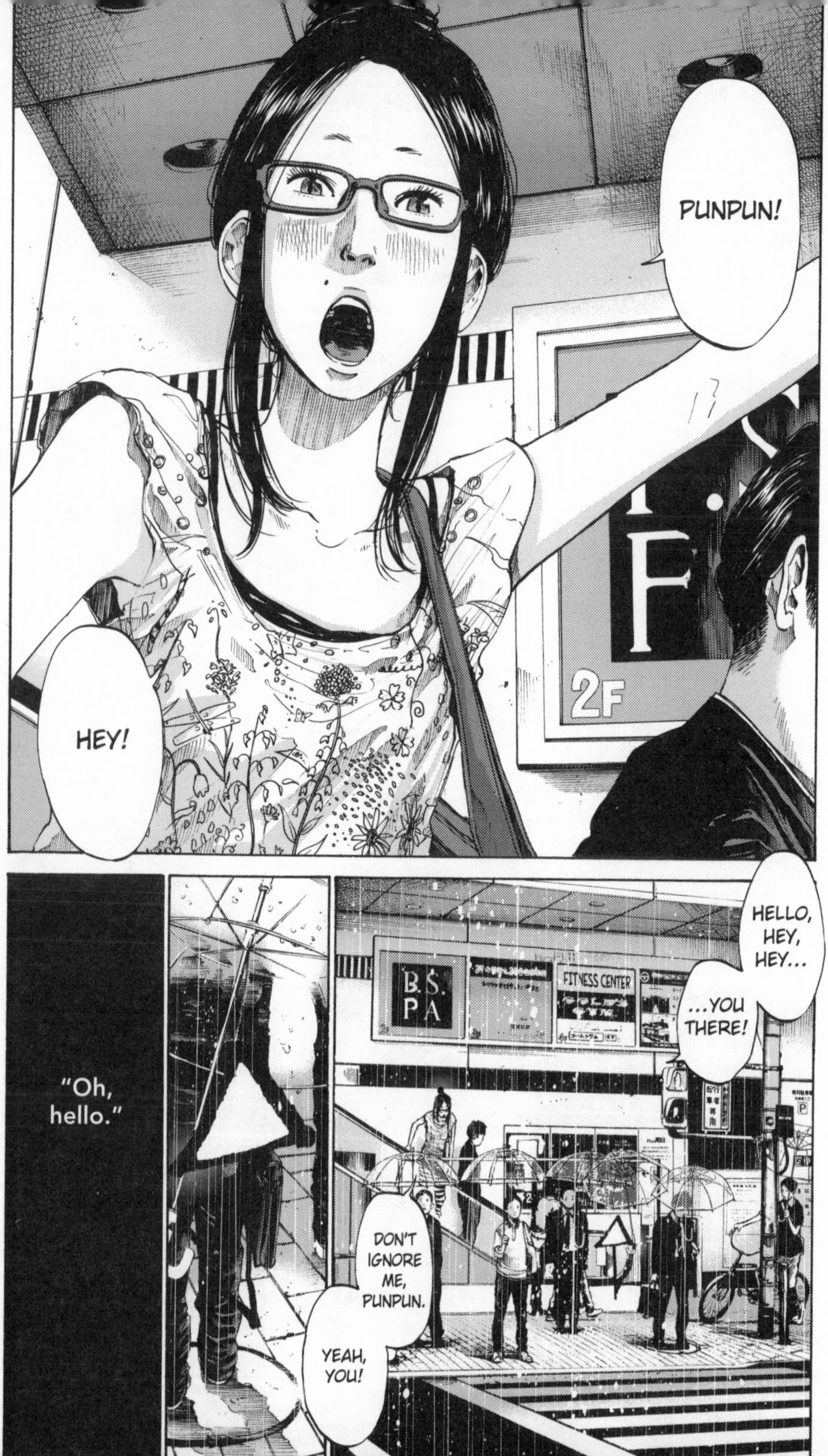
PUNPUN!
HEY!
2F
HELLO, HEY, HEY…
…YOU THERE!
B.S. PA
FITNESS CENTER
DON'T IGNORE ME, PUNPUN.
YEAH, YOU!
"Oh, hello."

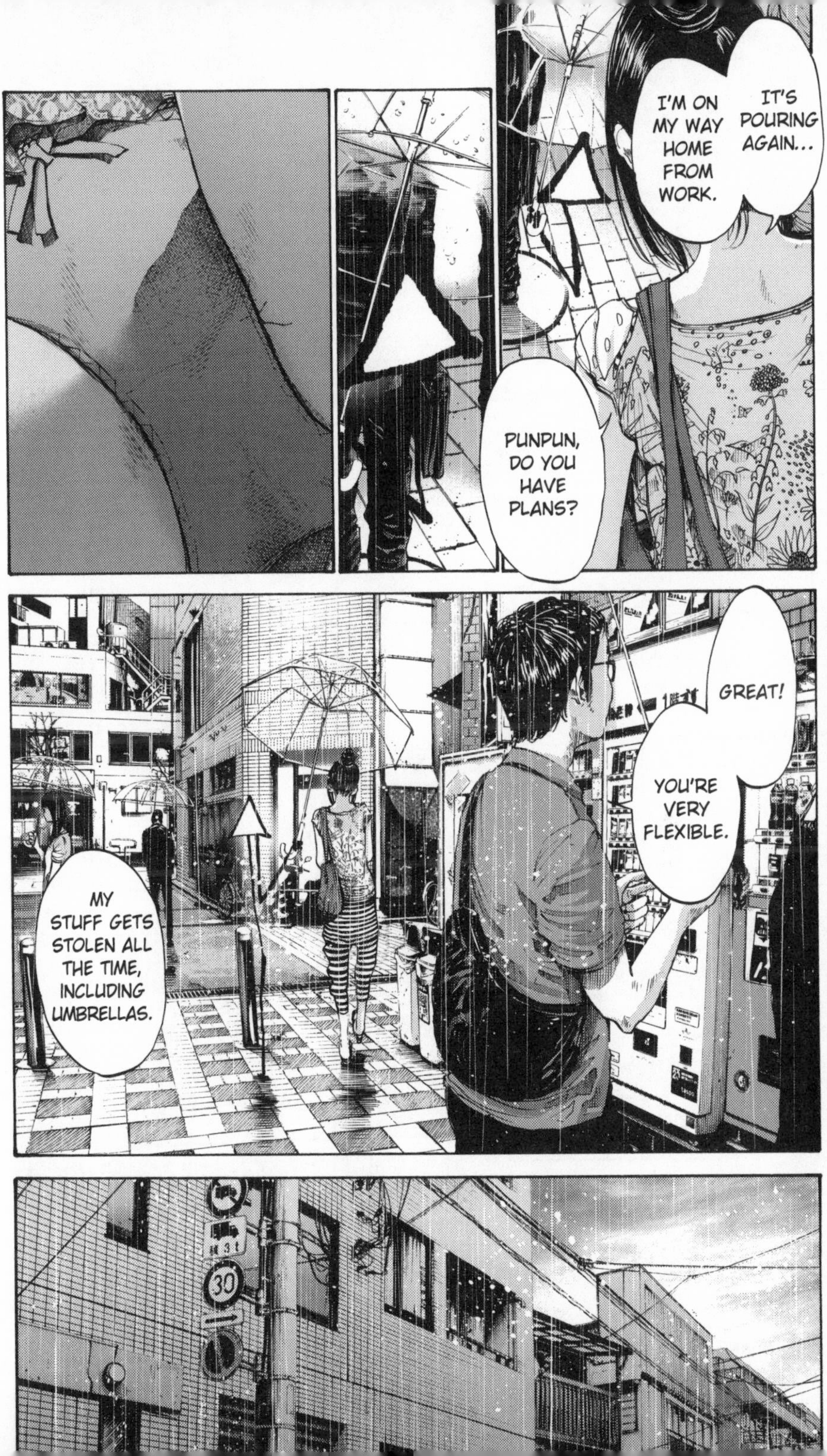
IT'S POURING AGAIN...
I'M ON MY WAY HOME FROM WORK.
PUNPUN, DO YOU HAVE PLANS?
GREAT!
YOU'RE VERY FLEXIBLE.
MY STUFF GETS STOLEN ALL THE TIME, INCLUDING UMBRELLAS.
30

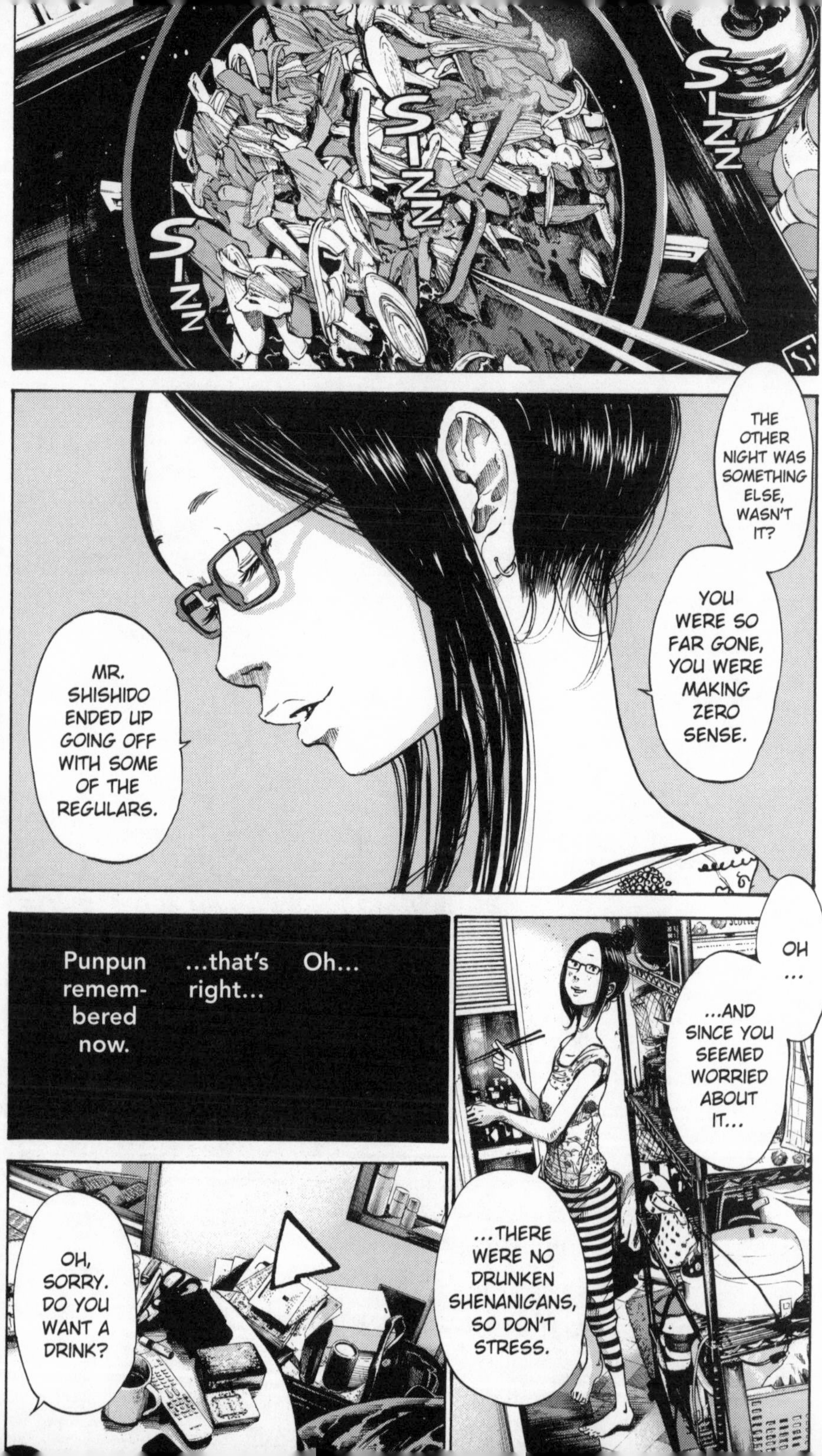
SIZZ
SIZZ
SIZZ
THE OTHER NIGHT WAS SOMETHING ELSE, WASN'T IT?
YOU WERE SO FAR GONE, YOU WERE MAKING ZERO SENSE.
MR. SHISHIDO ENDED UP GOING OFF WITH SOME OF THE REGULARS.
OH ...
...AND SINCE YOU SEEMED WORRIED ABOUT IT...
...THERE WERE NO DRUNKEN SHENANIGANS, SO DON'T STRESS.
Oh...
...that's right...
Punpun remem-bered now.
OH, SORRY. DO YOU WANT A DRINK?

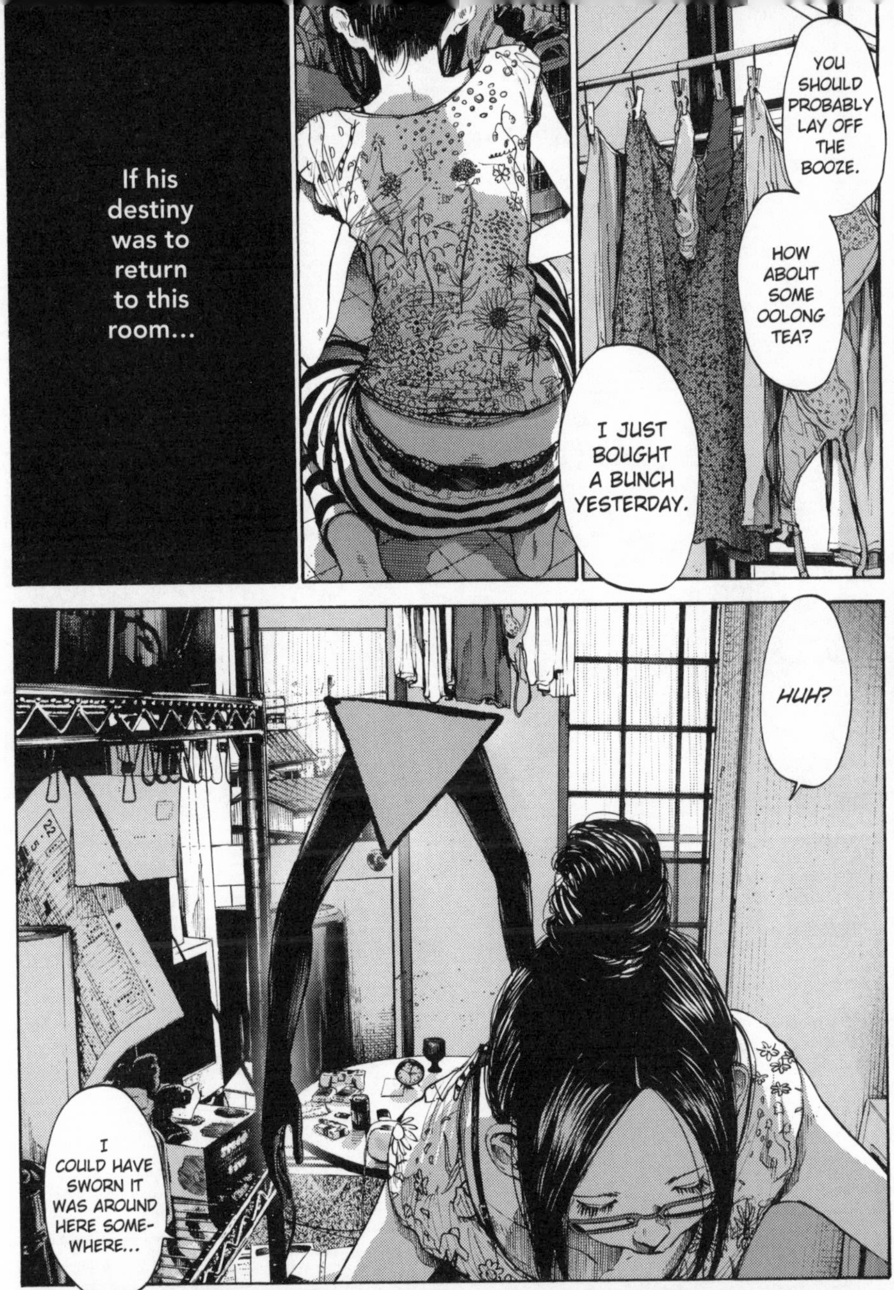
YOU SHOULD PROBABLY LAY OFF THE BOOZE.
HOW ABOUT SOME OOLONG TEA?
I JUST BOUGHT A BUNCH YESTERDAY.
If his destiny was to return to this room...
HUH?
I COULD HAVE SWORN IT WAS AROUND HERE SOME-WHERE...

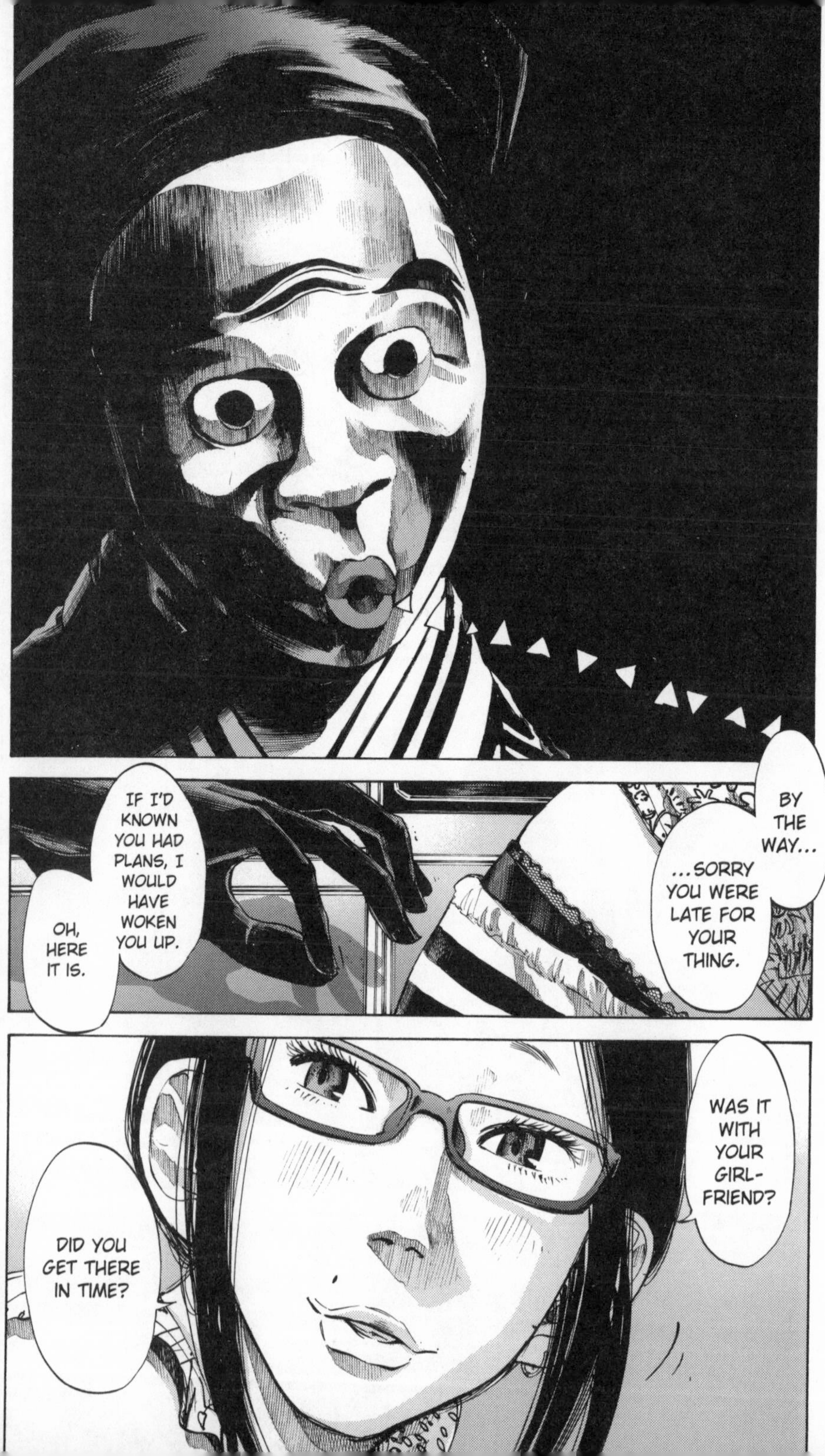
BY THE WAY...
...SORRY YOU WERE LATE FOR YOUR THING.
IF I'D KNOWN YOU HAD PLANS, I WOULD HAVE WOKEN YOU UP.
OH, HERE IT IS.
WAS IT WITH YOUR GIRL-FRIEND?
DID YOU GET THERE IN TIME?

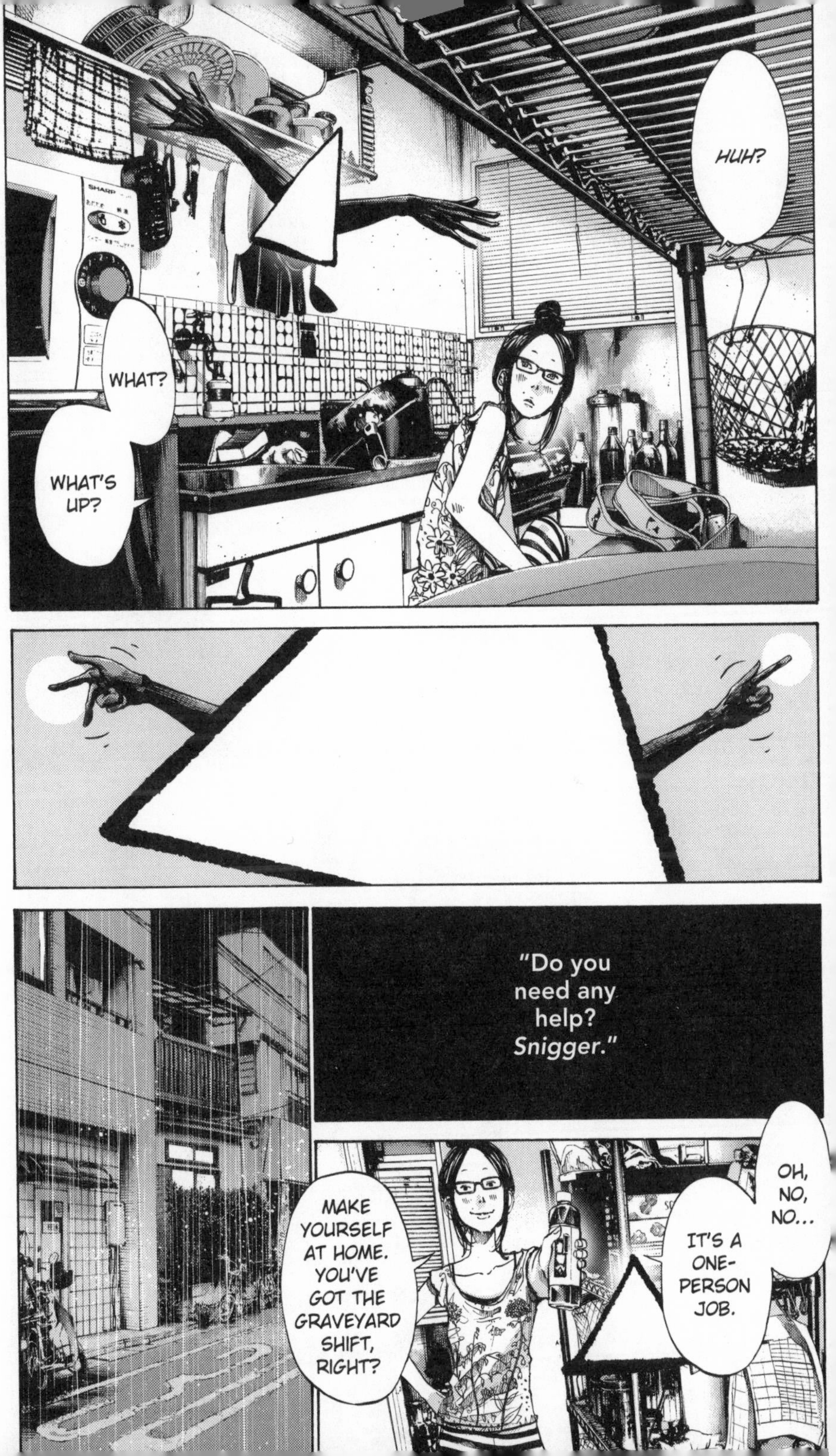
HUH?
WHAT?
WHAT'S UP?
"Do you need any help? *Snigger.*"
OH, NO, NO...
IT'S A ONE-PERSON JOB.
MAKE YOURSELF AT HOME. YOU'VE GOT THE GRAVEYARD SHIFT, RIGHT?

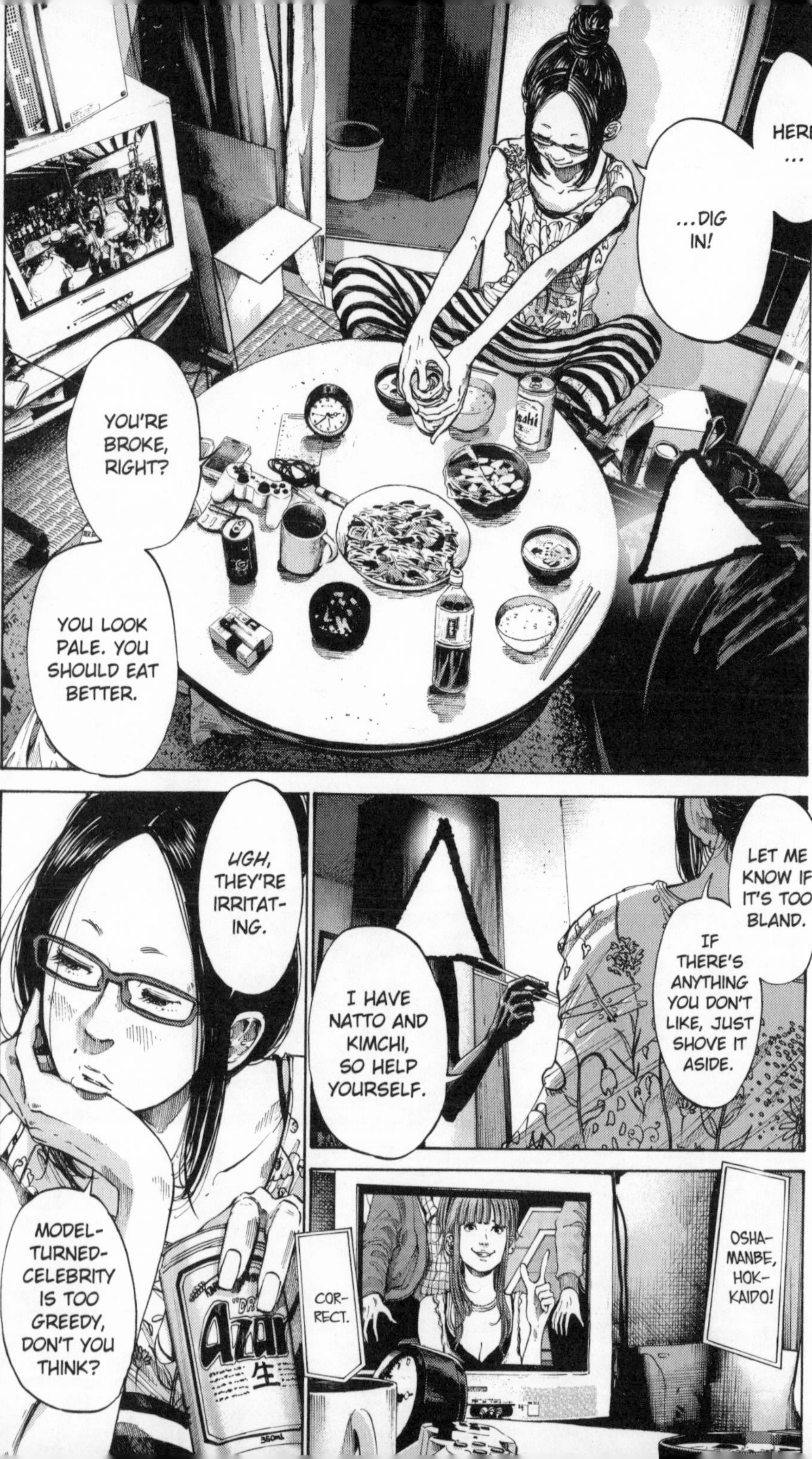
HERE ...
...DIG IN!
YOU'RE BROKE, RIGHT?
YOU LOOK PALE. YOU SHOULD EAT BETTER.
LET ME KNOW IF IT'S TOO BLAND.
IF THERE'S ANYTHING YOU DON'T LIKE, JUST SHOVE IT ASIDE.
I HAVE NATTO AND KIMCHI, SO HELP YOURSELF.
OSHA-MANBE, HOK-KAIDO!
COR-RECT.
UGH, THEY'RE IRRITAT-ING.
MODEL-TURNED-CELEBRITY IS TOO GREEDY, DON'T YOU THINK?

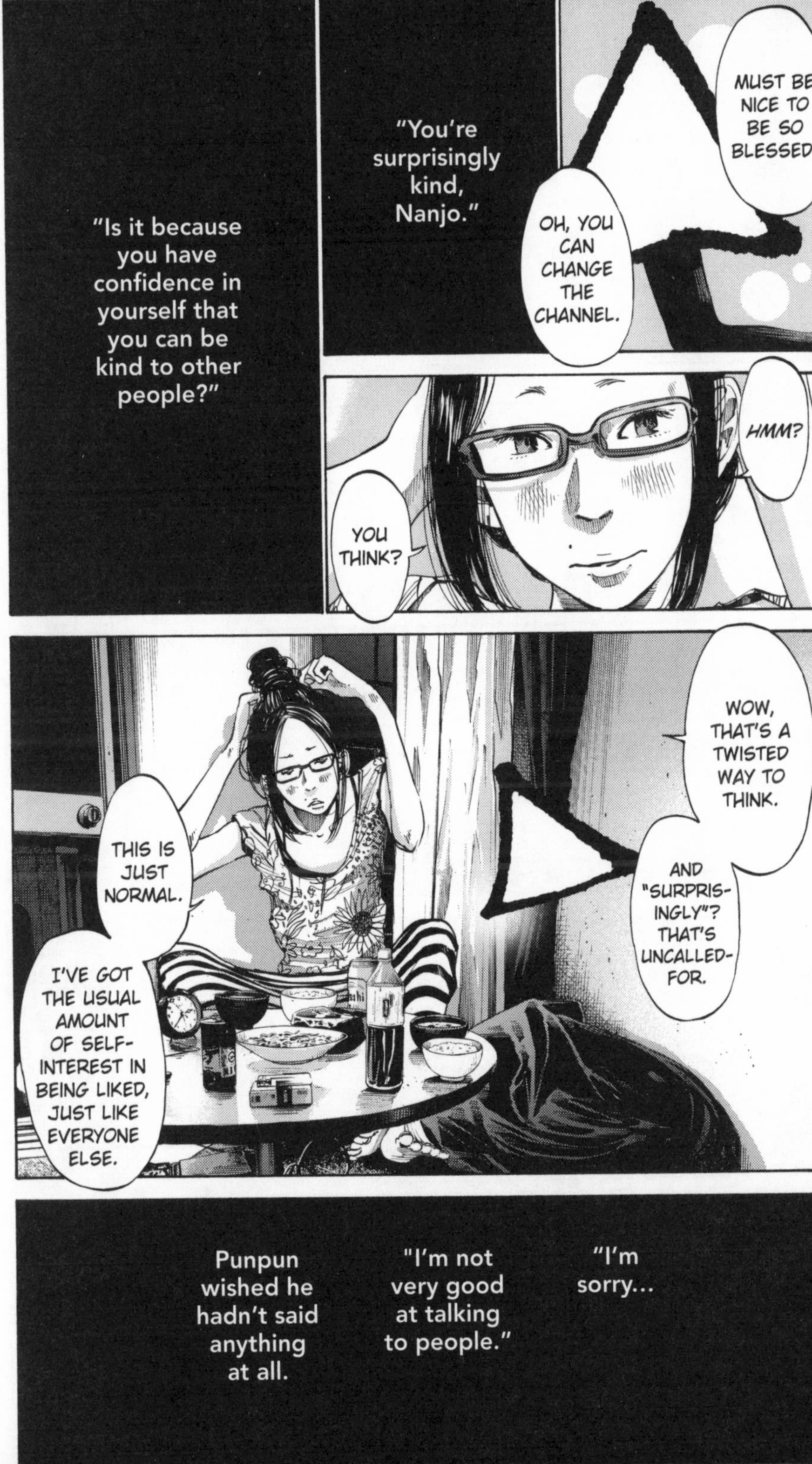
MUST BE NICE TO BE SO BLESSED.
OH, YOU CAN CHANGE THE CHANNEL.
"You're surprisingly kind, Nanjo."
HMM?
YOU THINK?
"Is it because you have confidence in yourself that you can be kind to other people?"
WOW, THAT'S A TWISTED WAY TO THINK.
AND "SURPRIS-INGLY"? THAT'S UNCALLED-FOR.
THIS IS JUST NORMAL.
I'VE GOT THE USUAL AMOUNT OF SELF-INTEREST IN BEING LIKED, JUST LIKE EVERYONE ELSE.
"I'm sorry...
"I'm not very good at talking to people."
Punpun wished he hadn't said anything at all.

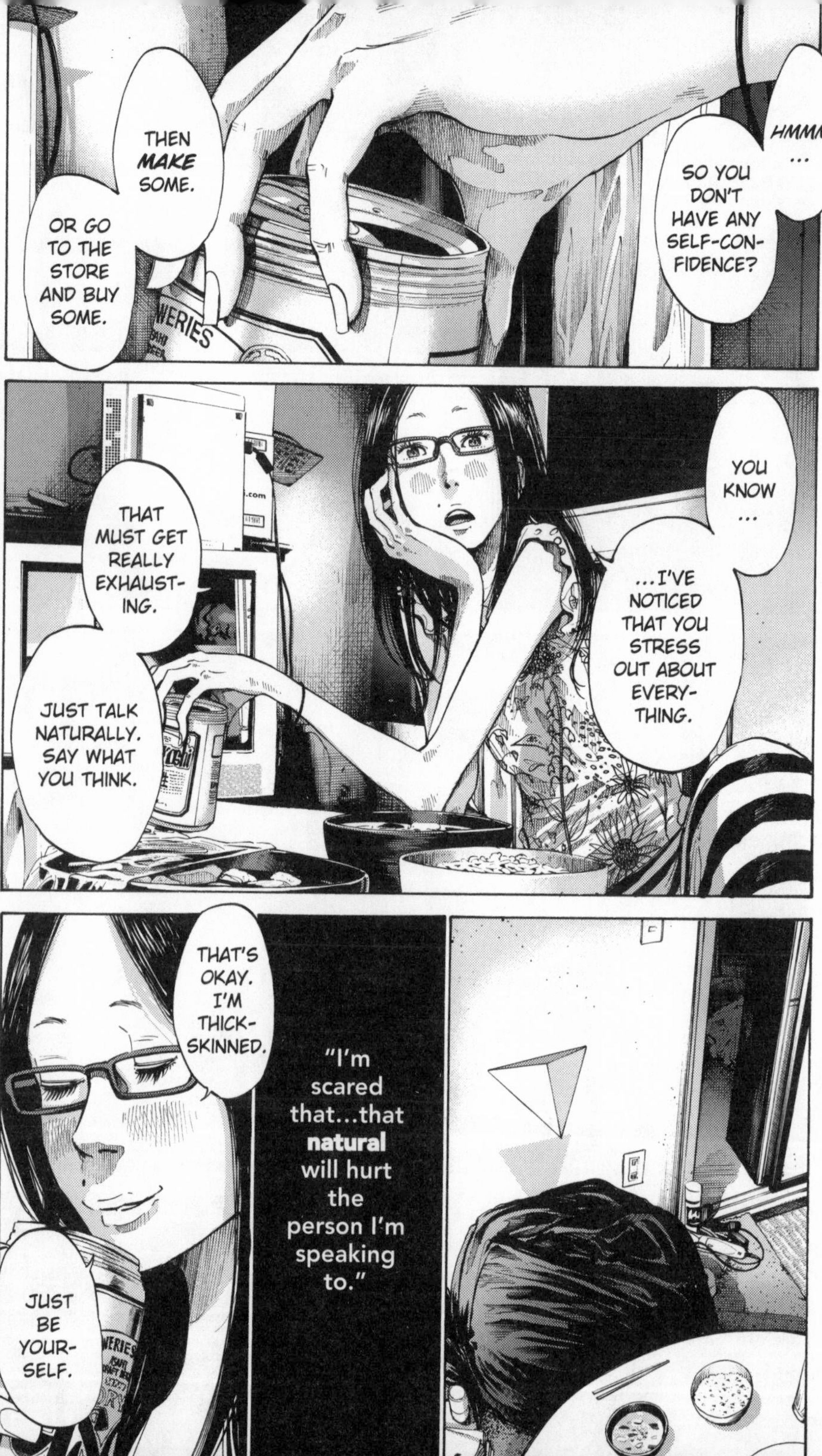
HMMM ...
SO YOU DON'T HAVE ANY SELF-CON-FIDENCE?
THEN MAKE SOME.
OR GO TO THE STORE AND BUY SOME.
YOU KNOW ...
...I'VE NOTICED THAT YOU STRESS OUT ABOUT EVERY-THING.
THAT MUST GET REALLY EXHAUST-ING.
JUST TALK NATURALLY. SAY WHAT YOU THINK.
"I'm scared that...that natural will hurt the person I'm speaking to."
THAT'S OKAY. I'M THICK-SKINNED.
JUST BE YOUR-SELF.

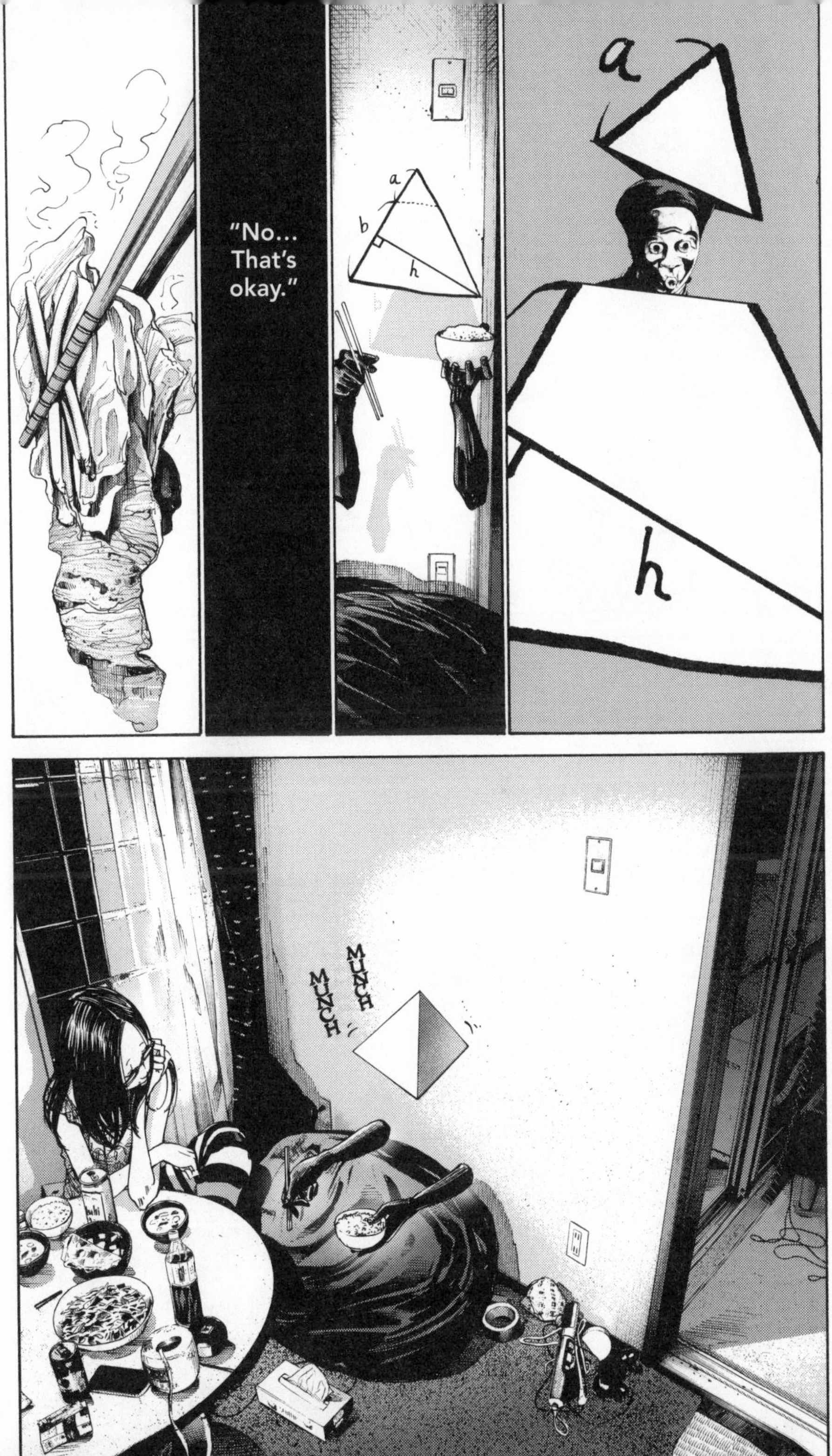
a
h
a
b
h
"No... That's okay."
MUNCH
MUNCH

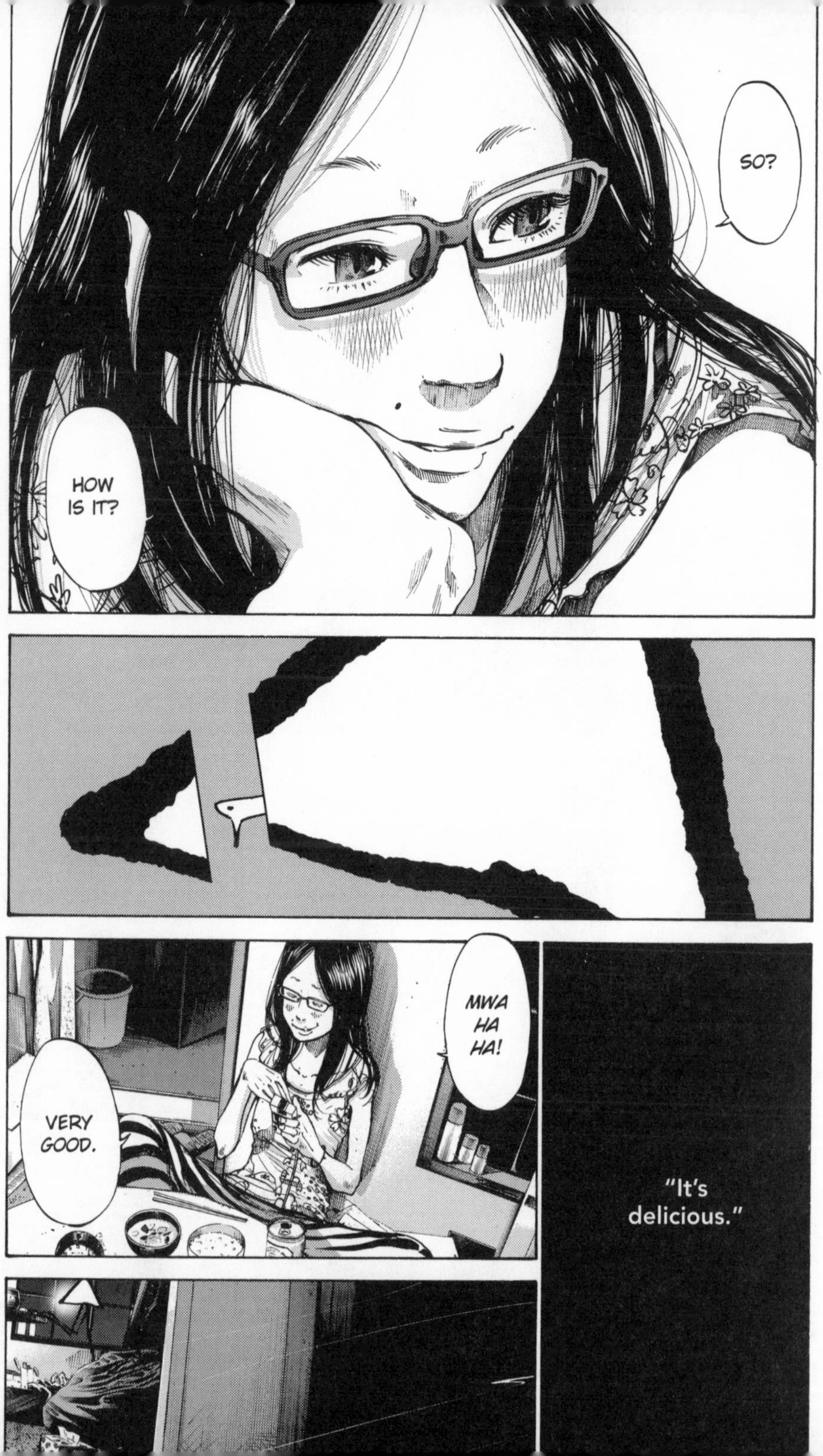
SO?
HOW IS IT?
"It's delicious."
MWA HA HA!
VERY GOOD.

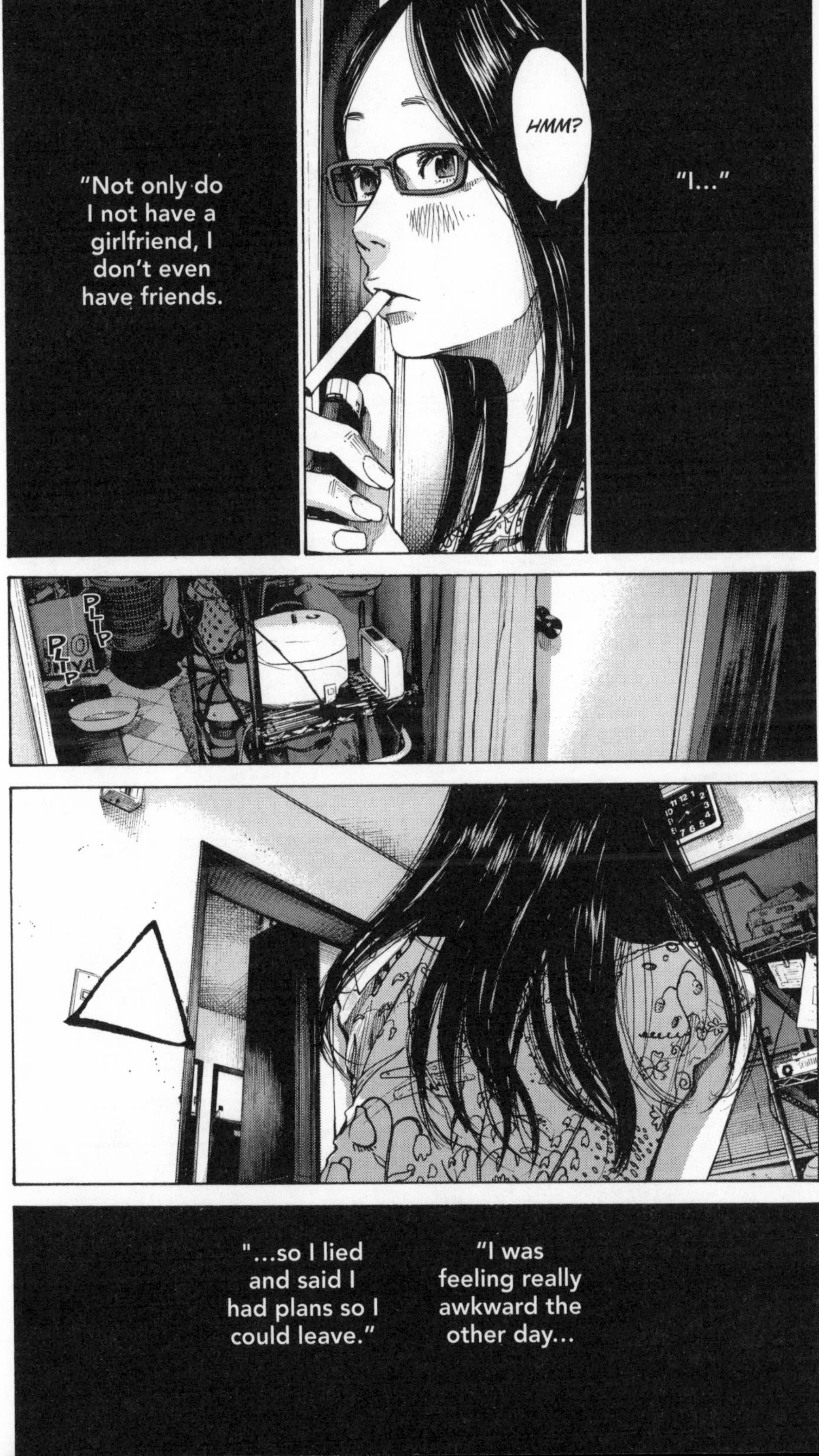
"I..."
HMM?
"Not only do I not have a girlfriend, I don't even have friends.
PLIP
PLIP
"I was feeling really awkward the other day...
"...so I lied and said I had plans so I could leave."

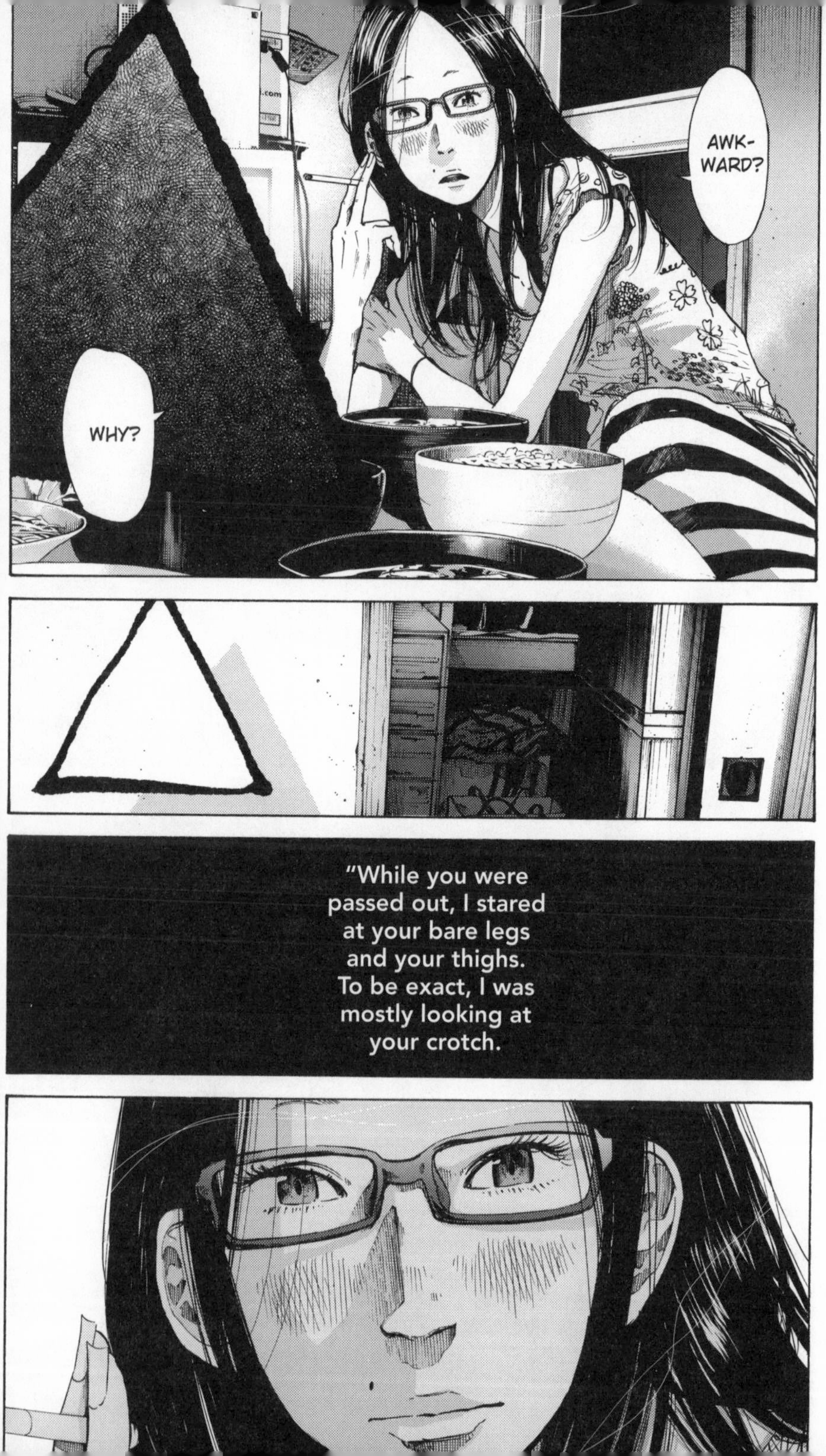
AWK-WARD?
WHY?
"While you were passed out, I stared at your bare legs and your thighs. To be exact, I was mostly looking at your crotch.

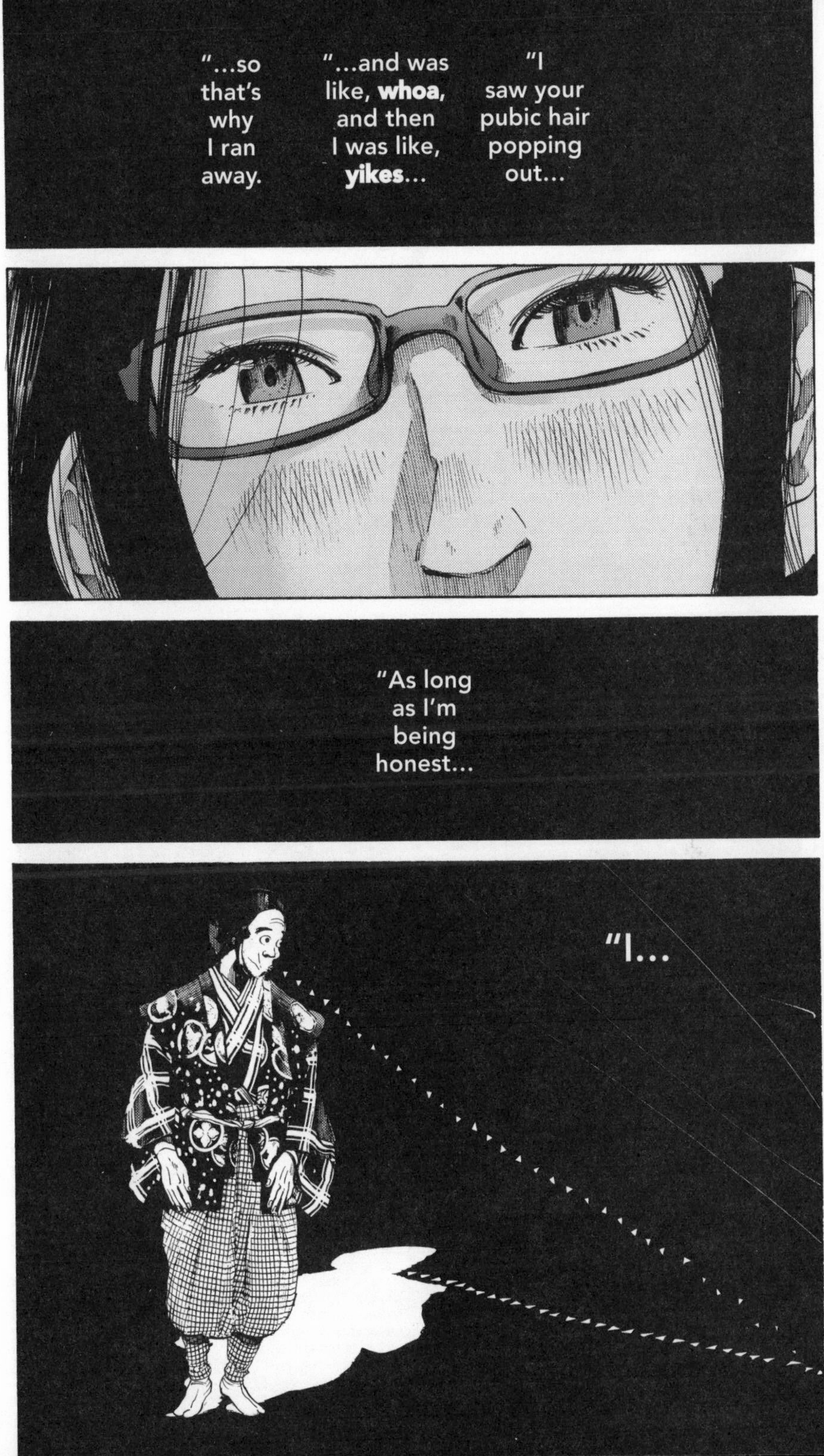
"I saw your pubic hair popping out...
"...and was like, **whoa,** and then I was like, **yikes**...
"...so that's why I ran away.
"As long as I'm being honest...
"I...

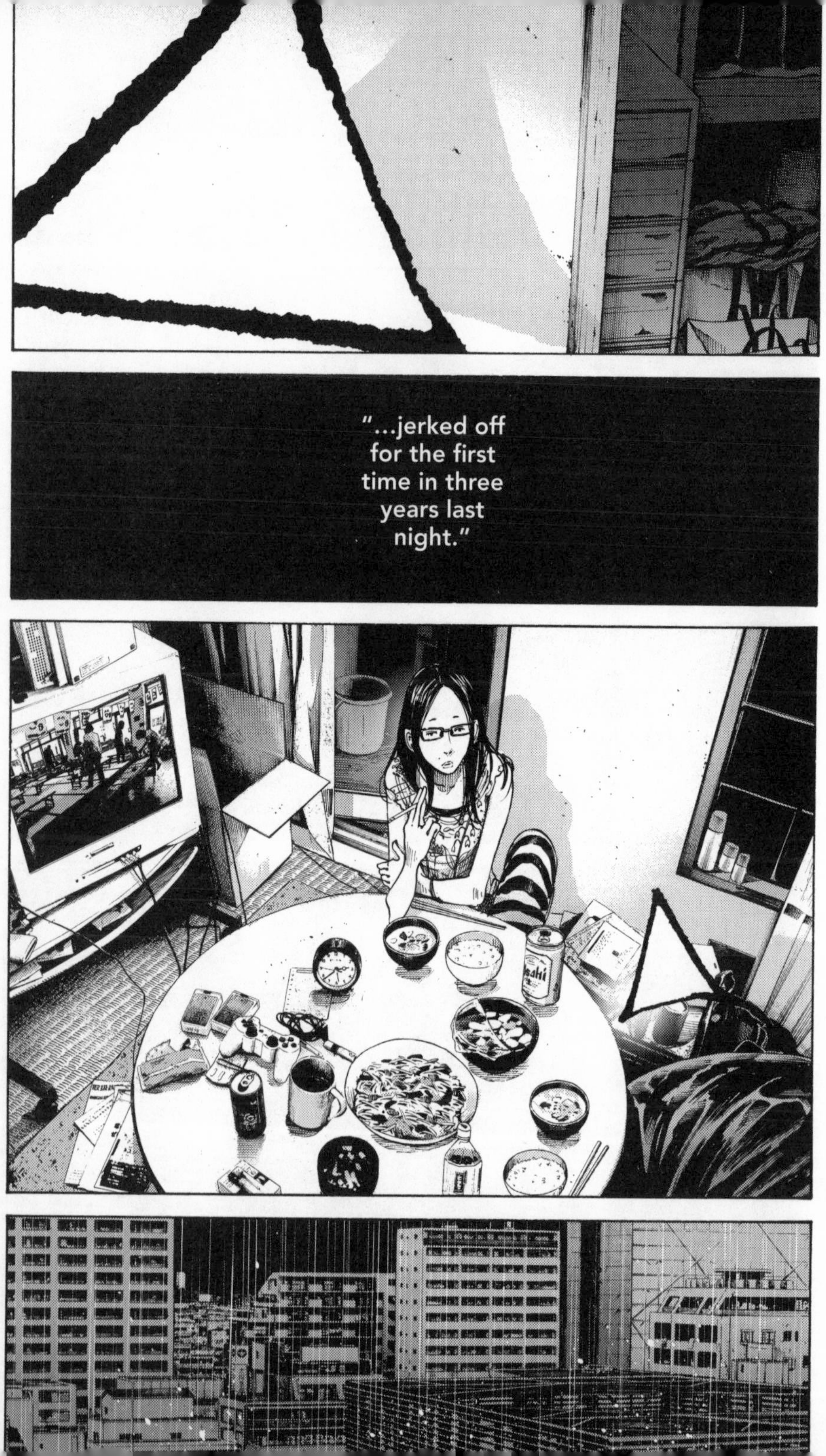
"...jerked off for the first time in three years last night."

Chapter 81

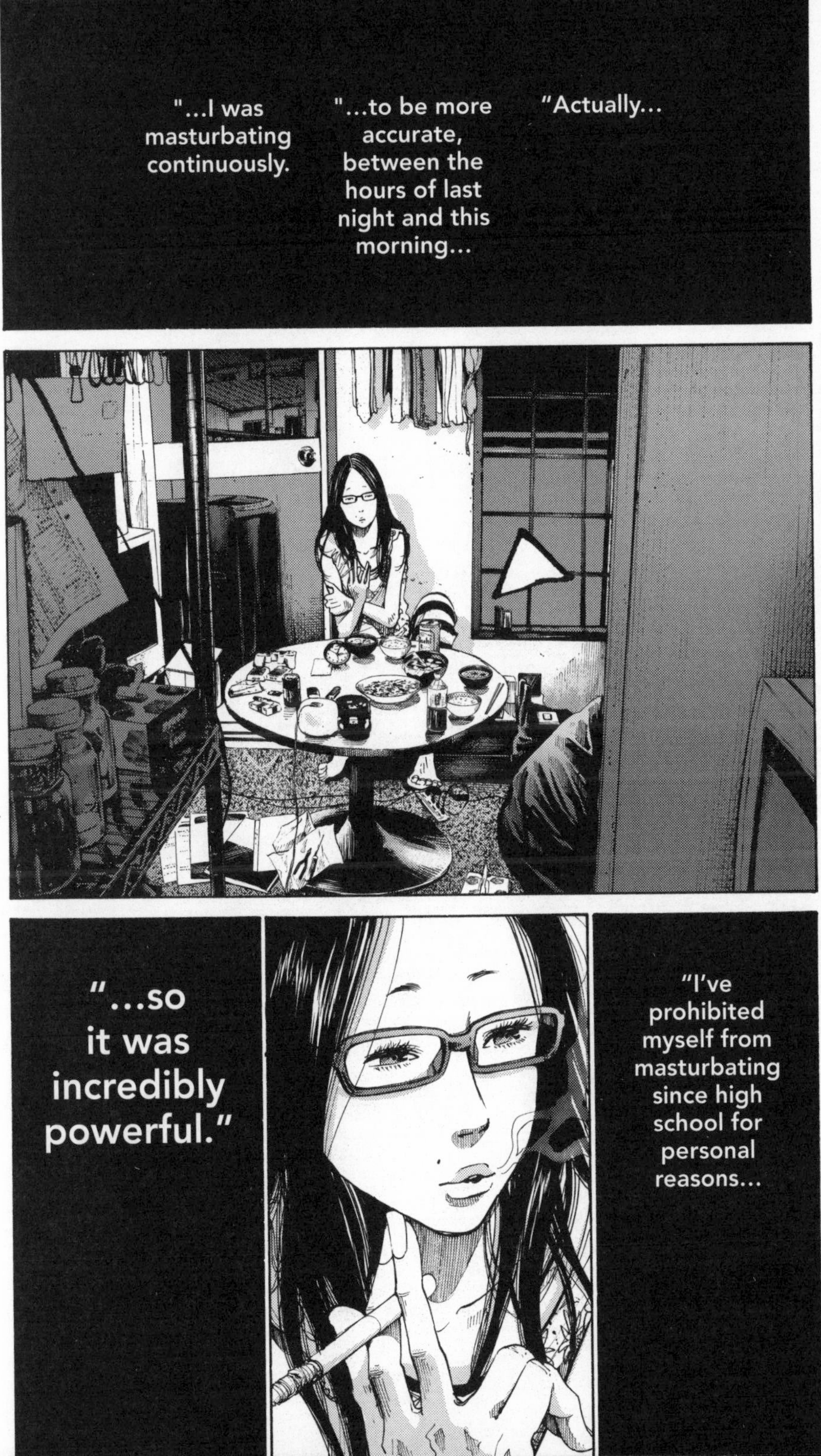
"Actually...
"...to be more accurate, between the hours of last night and this morning...
"...I was masturbating continuously.
"I've prohibited myself from masturbating since high school for personal reasons...
"...so it was incredibly powerful."

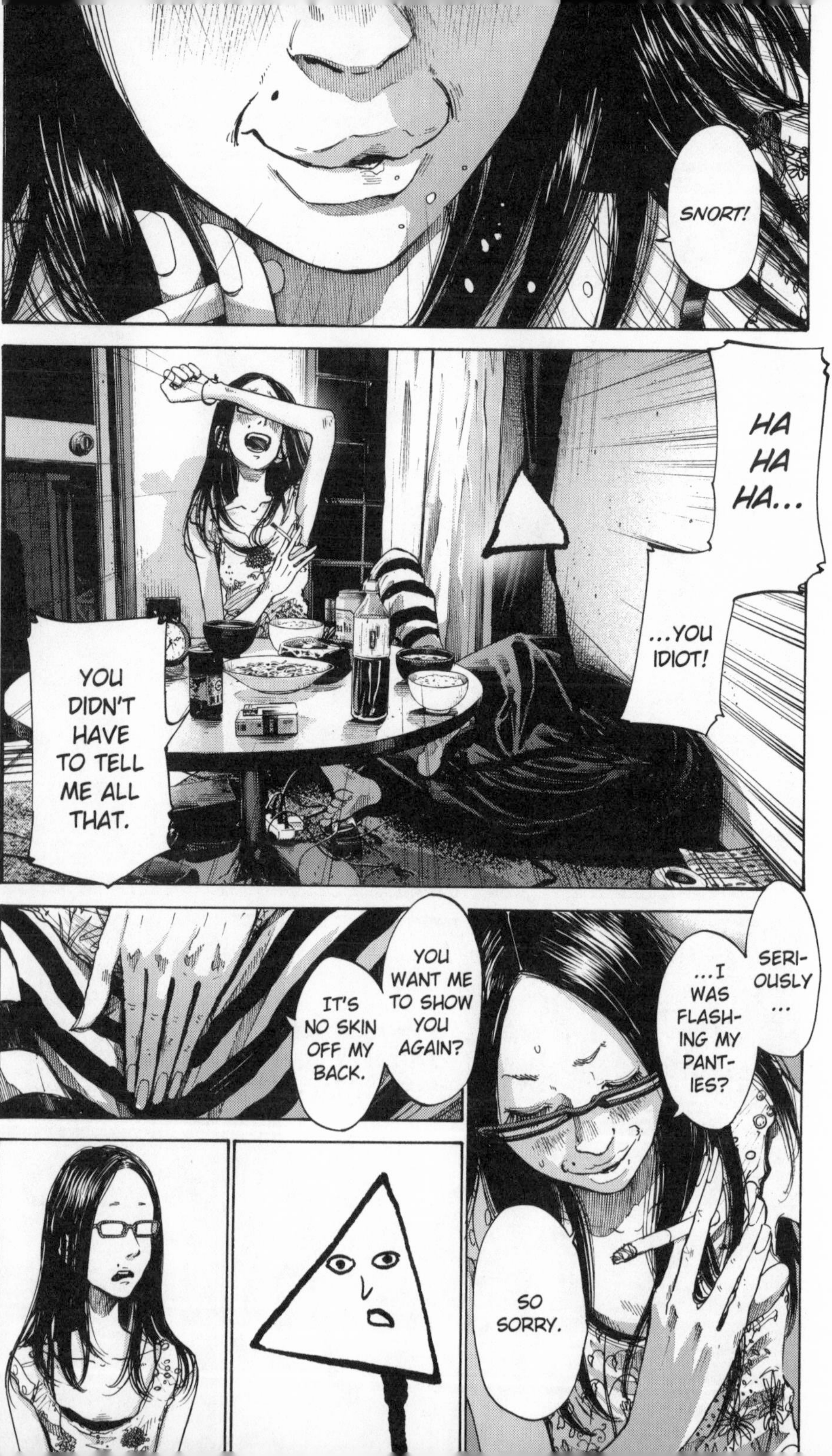
SNORT!
HA HA HA...
...YOU IDIOT!
YOU DIDN'T HAVE TO TELL ME ALL THAT.
SERI-OUSLY...
...I WAS FLASH-ING MY PANT-IES?
SO SORRY.
YOU WANT ME TO SHOW YOU AGAIN?
IT'S NO SKIN OFF MY BACK.

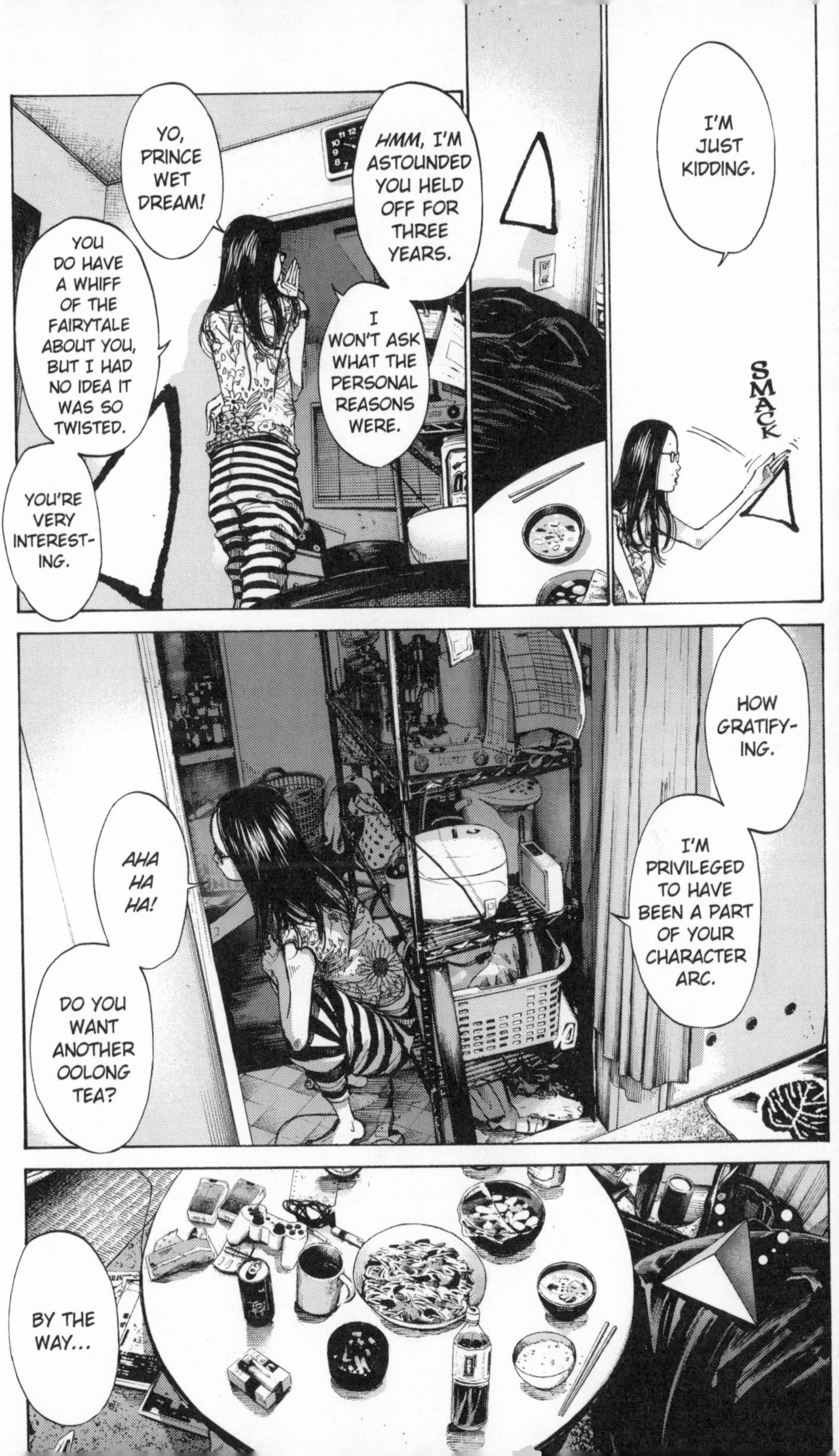
I'M JUST KIDDING.
SMACK
HMM, I'M ASTOUNDED YOU HELD OFF FOR THREE YEARS.
YO, PRINCE WET DREAM!
I WON'T ASK WHAT THE PERSONAL REASONS WERE.
YOU DO HAVE A WHIFF OF THE FAIRYTALE ABOUT YOU, BUT I HAD NO IDEA IT WAS SO TWISTED.
YOU'RE VERY INTEREST-ING.
HOW GRATIFY-ING.
I'M PRIVILEGED TO HAVE BEEN A PART OF YOUR CHARACTER ARC.
AHA HA HA!
DO YOU WANT ANOTHER OOLONG TEA?
BY THE WAY...

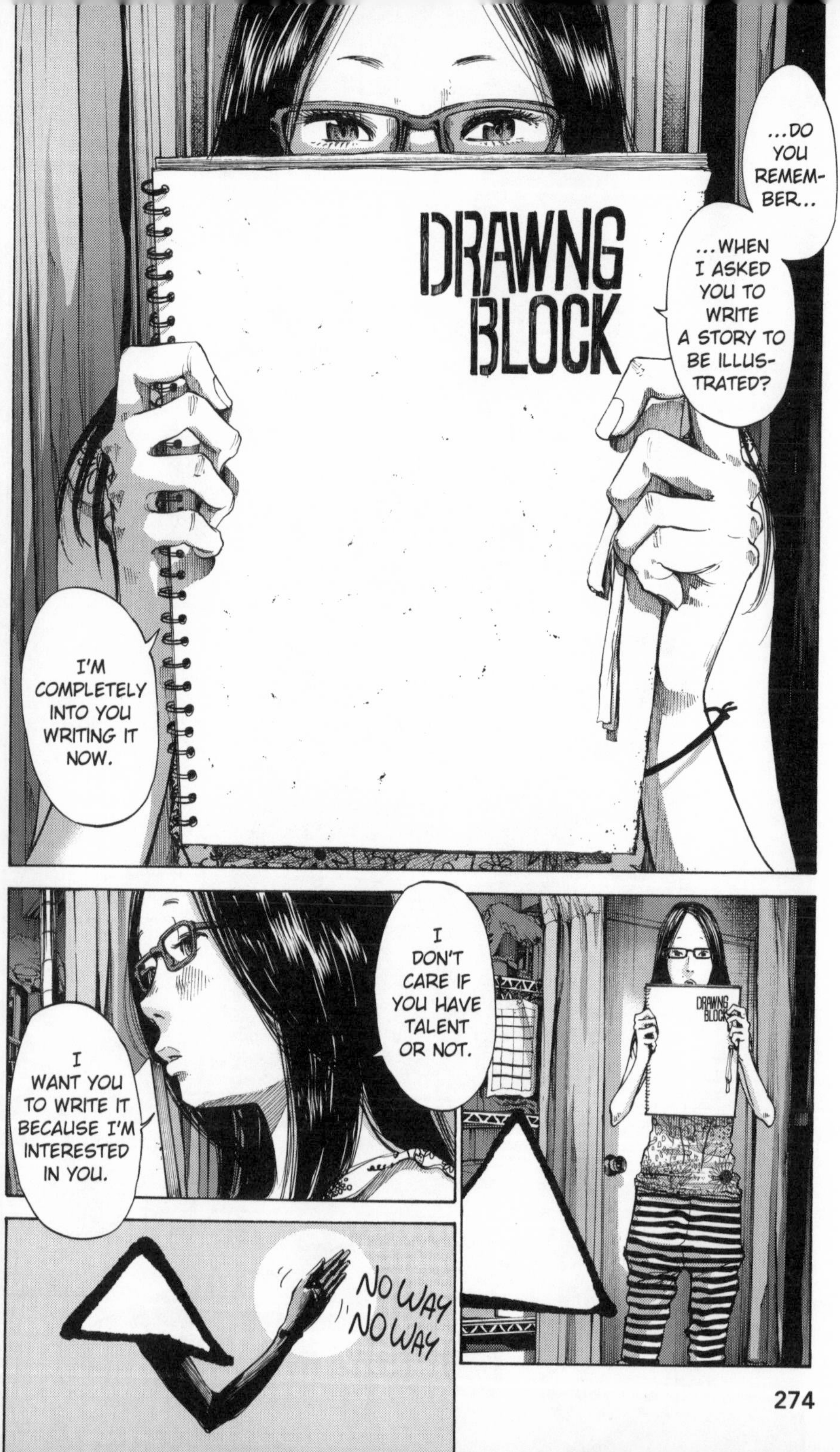
...DO YOU REMEMBER...
...WHEN I ASKED YOU TO WRITE A STORY TO BE ILLUSTRATED?
DRAWNG BLOCK
I'M COMPLETELY INTO YOU WRITING IT NOW.
DRAWNG BLOCK
I DON'T CARE IF YOU HAVE TALENT OR NOT.
I WANT YOU TO WRITE IT BECAUSE I'M INTERESTED IN YOU.
NO WAY NO WAY

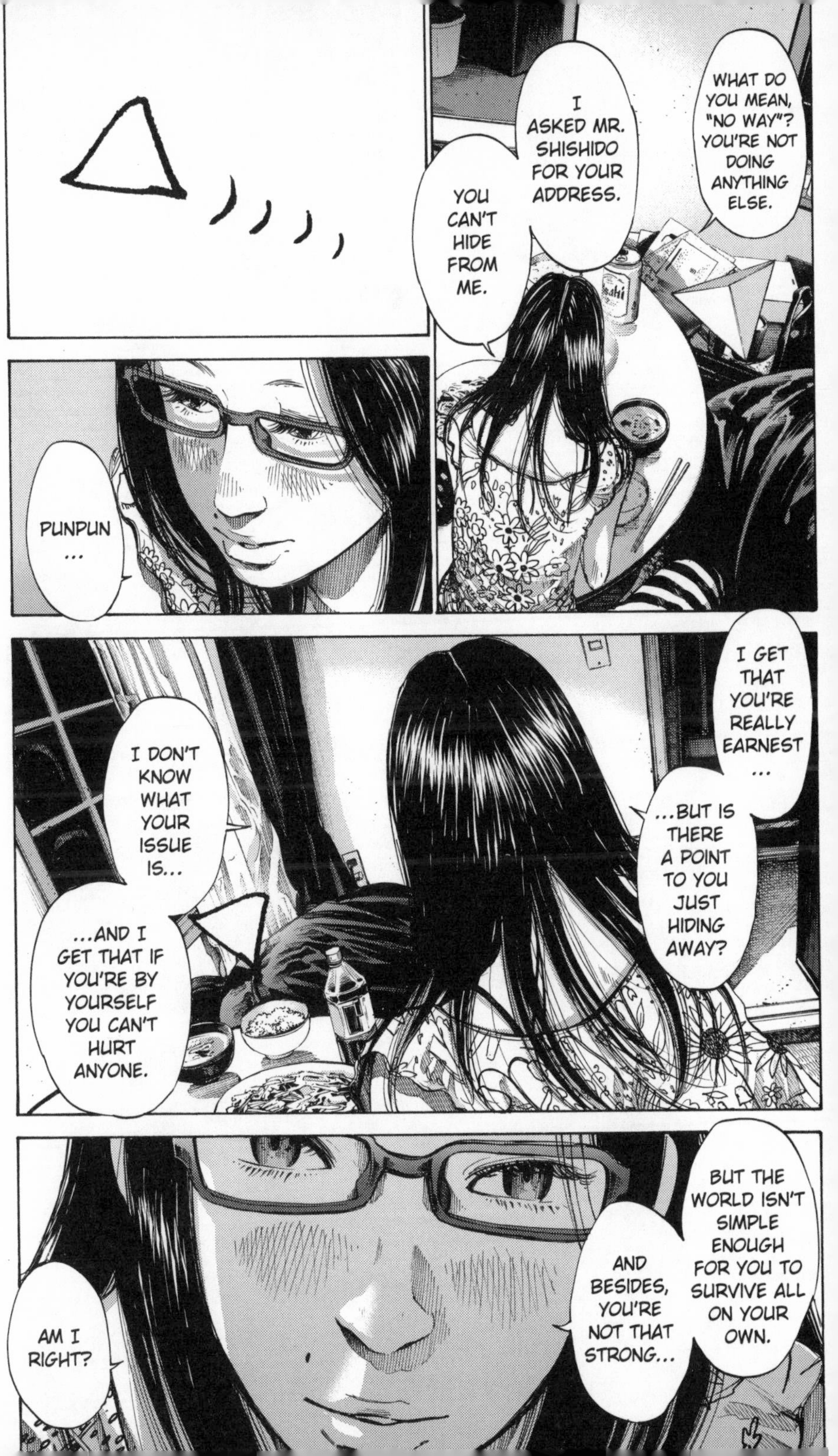
WHAT DO YOU MEAN, "NO WAY"? YOU'RE NOT DOING ANYTHING ELSE.
I ASKED MR. SHISHIDO FOR YOUR ADDRESS.
YOU CAN'T HIDE FROM ME.
PUNPUN ...
I GET THAT YOU'RE REALLY EARNEST ...
...BUT IS THERE A POINT TO YOU JUST HIDING AWAY?
I DON'T KNOW WHAT YOUR ISSUE IS...
...AND I GET THAT IF YOU'RE BY YOURSELF YOU CAN'T HURT ANYONE.
BUT THE WORLD ISN'T SIMPLE ENOUGH FOR YOU TO SURVIVE ALL ON YOUR OWN.
AND BESIDES, YOU'RE NOT THAT STRONG...
AM I RIGHT?

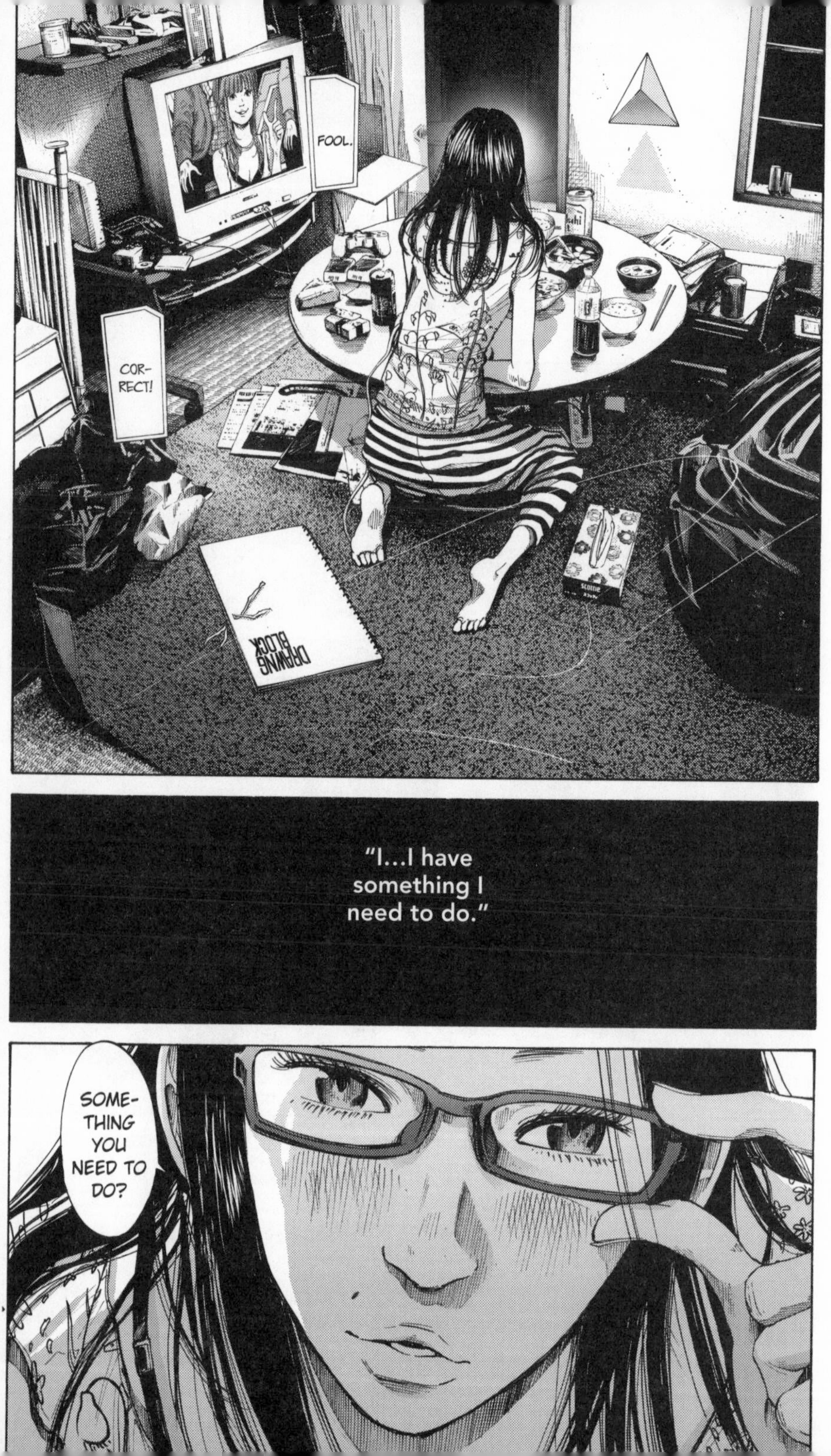
FOOL.
COR-RECT!
DRAWING BLOCK
"I...I have something I need to do."
SOME-THING YOU NEED TO DO?

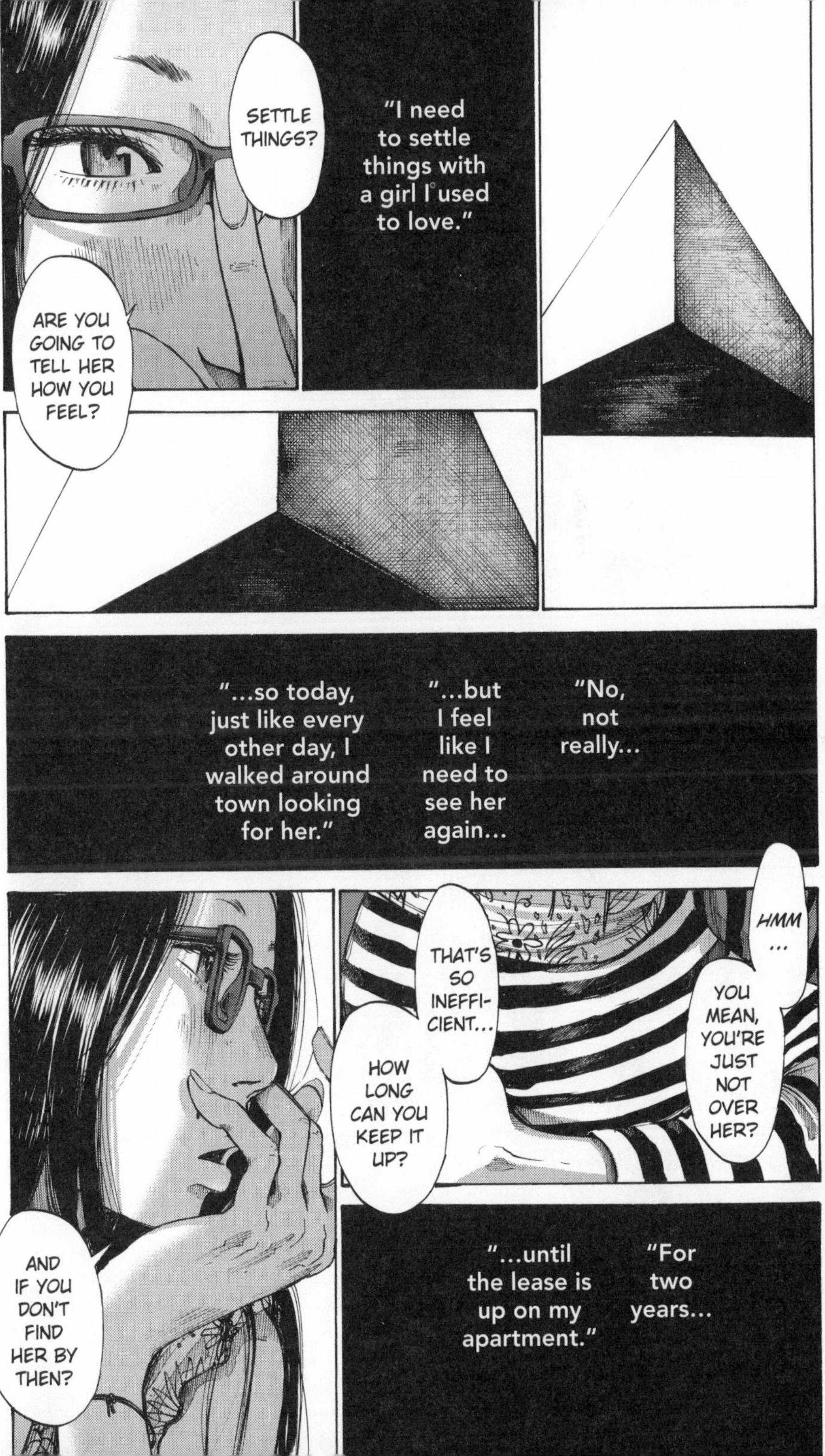
"I need to settle things with a girl I used to love."
SETTLE THINGS?
ARE YOU GOING TO TELL HER HOW YOU FEEL?
"No, not really...
"...but I feel like I need to see her again...
"...so today, just like every other day, I walked around town looking for her."
HMM...
YOU MEAN, YOU'RE JUST NOT OVER HER?
THAT'S SO INEFFI-CIENT...
HOW LONG CAN YOU KEEP IT UP?
"For two years...
"...until the lease is up on my apartment."
AND IF YOU DON'T FIND HER BY THEN?

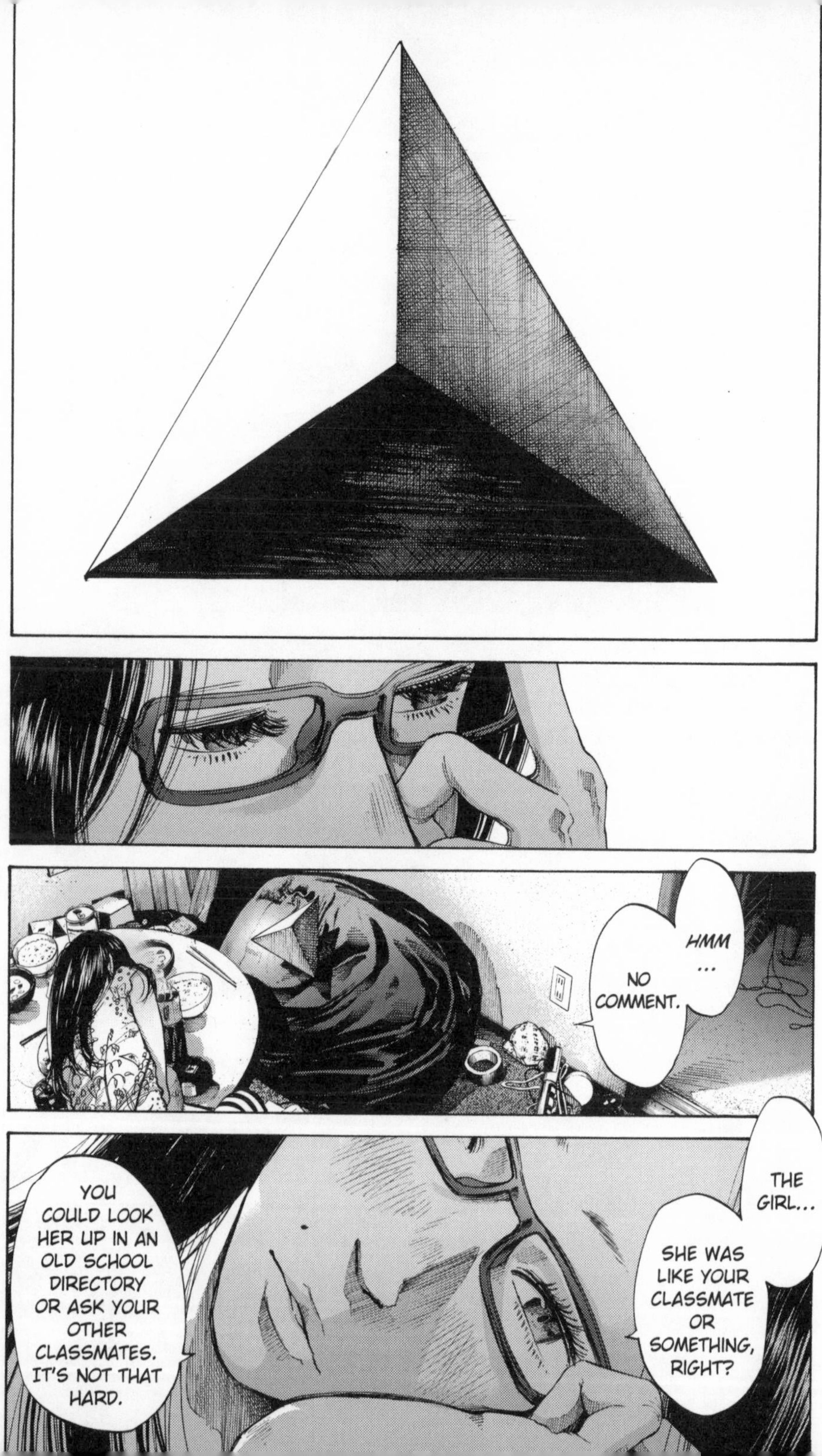
HMM ...
NO COMMENT.
THE GIRL...
SHE WAS LIKE YOUR CLASSMATE OR SOMETHING, RIGHT?
YOU COULD LOOK HER UP IN AN OLD SCHOOL DIRECTORY OR ASK YOUR OTHER CLASSMATES. IT'S NOT THAT HARD.

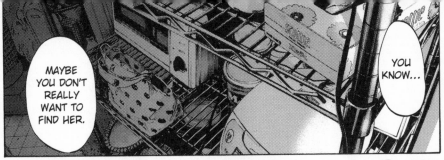

YOU KNOW...
MAYBE YOU DON'T REALLY WANT TO FIND HER.
MAYBE YOU **ARE** LOOKING FORWARD TO A MOMENTOUS REUNION...
...BUT WHAT'S THE POINT?
IT SEEMS LIKE...
...YOU'RE JUST MAKING EXCUSES AND PUTTING OFF MAKING A DECISION.
I SUSPECT IT WON'T BE JUST TWO YEARS.
I THINK IN TEN YEARS YOU'LL STILL BE LOOKING FOR EXCUSES.
YOU'LL APPEAR CONFLICTED...
...BUT IN REALITY YOU'LL BE LIVING AN UNPRODUCTIVE LIFE WITHOUT THINKING OR DOING A THING.
I DON'T MIND.
LOTS OF PEOPLE ARE SATISFIED PLAYING THE DESPAIR GAME.
BUT I THINK YOUR DESPAIR IS POINTLESS.
BECAUSE YOU'RE LOOKING FOR SOLITUDE TOO, WHICH MEANS THERE'S NO ONE TO SHARE YOUR DESPAIR WITH.

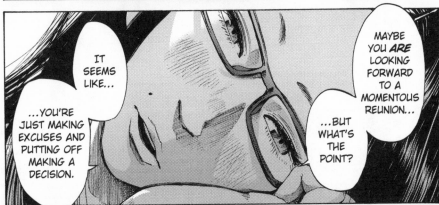

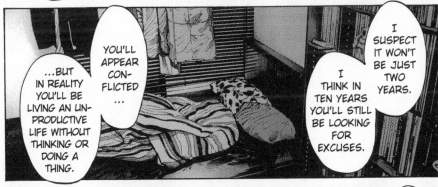

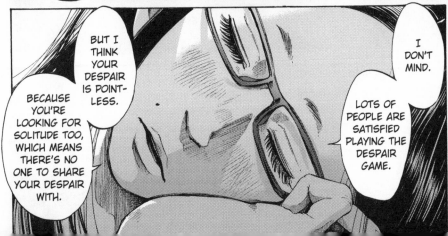

SO,
PUNPUN
...

I THINK
BUMPING
INTO ME
AGAIN WAS
LIKE FATE.

BUT
WHETHER YOU
ACCEPT IT AS
FATE OR A MERE
COINCIDENCE IS
UP TO YOU.

SO,
WHAT'LL
YOU
DO...?

DO YOU
WANT ME
TO FIND
THAT GIRL
FOR YOU?

I'M
INTERESTED
IN WHAT YOU
MEAN BY
"SETTLING
THINGS."

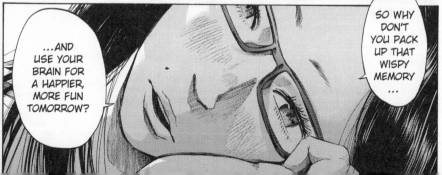

SO WHY
DON'T
YOU PACK
UP THAT
WISPY
MEMORY
...

...AND
USE YOUR
BRAIN FOR
A HAPPIER,
MORE FUN
TOMORROW?

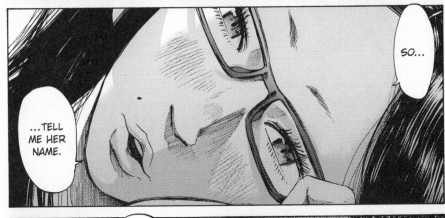

SO...

...TELL ME HER NAME.

I'LL BRING HER TO YOU IN THREE DAYS.

S-stop it!

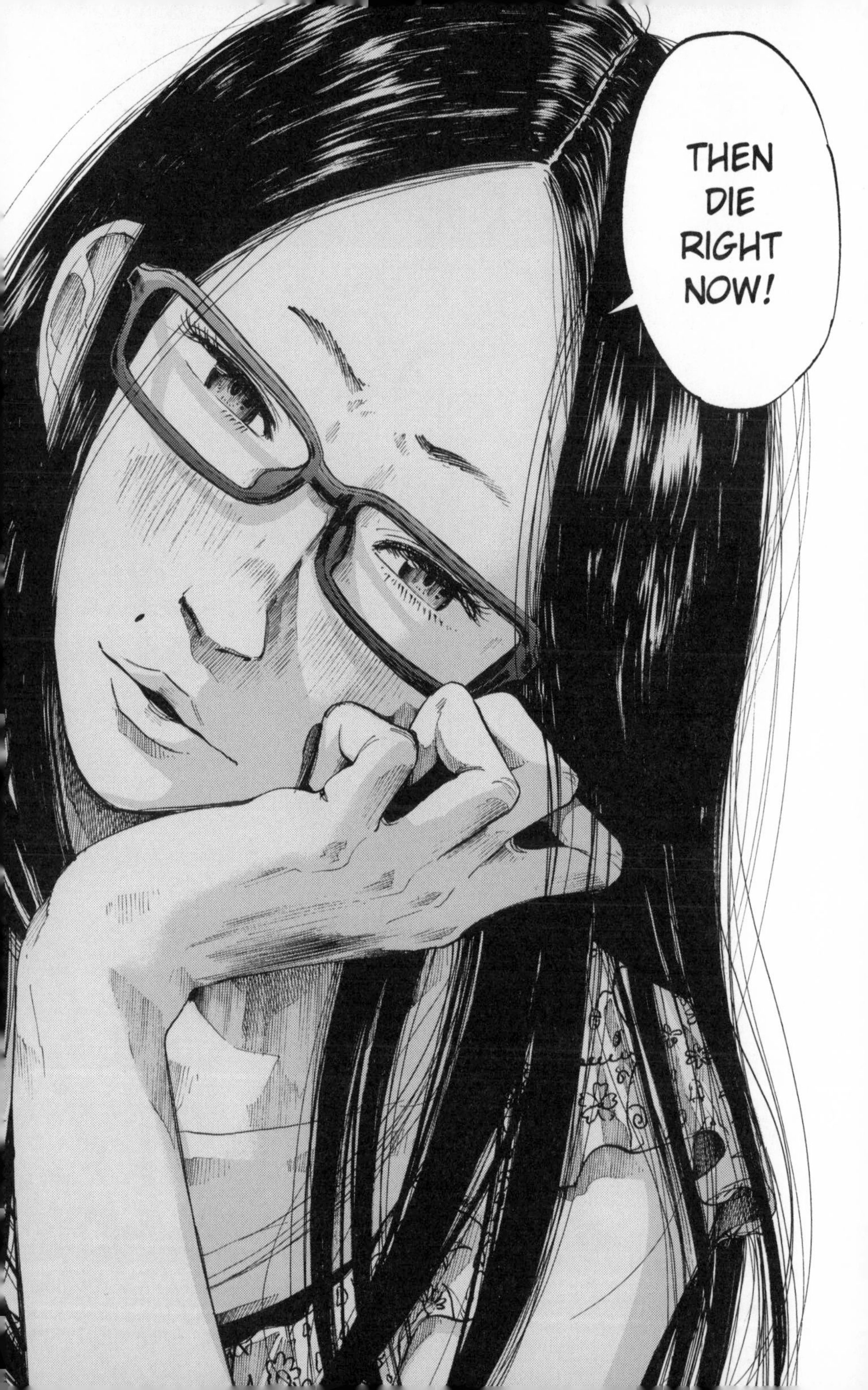
THEN DIE RIGHT NOW!

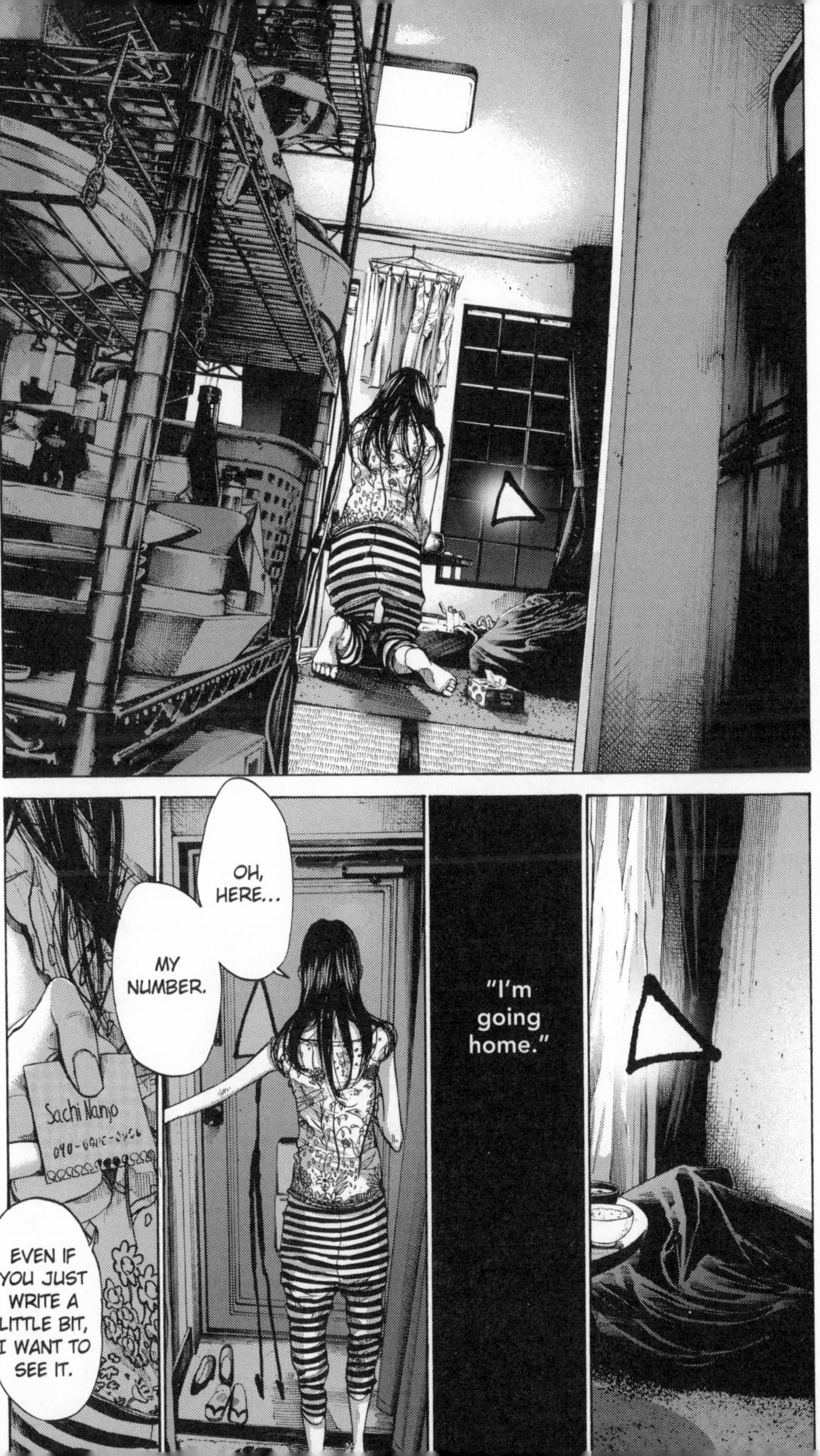
"I'm going home."
OH, HERE...
MY NUMBER.
EVEN IF YOU JUST WRITE A LITTLE BIT, I WANT TO SEE IT.

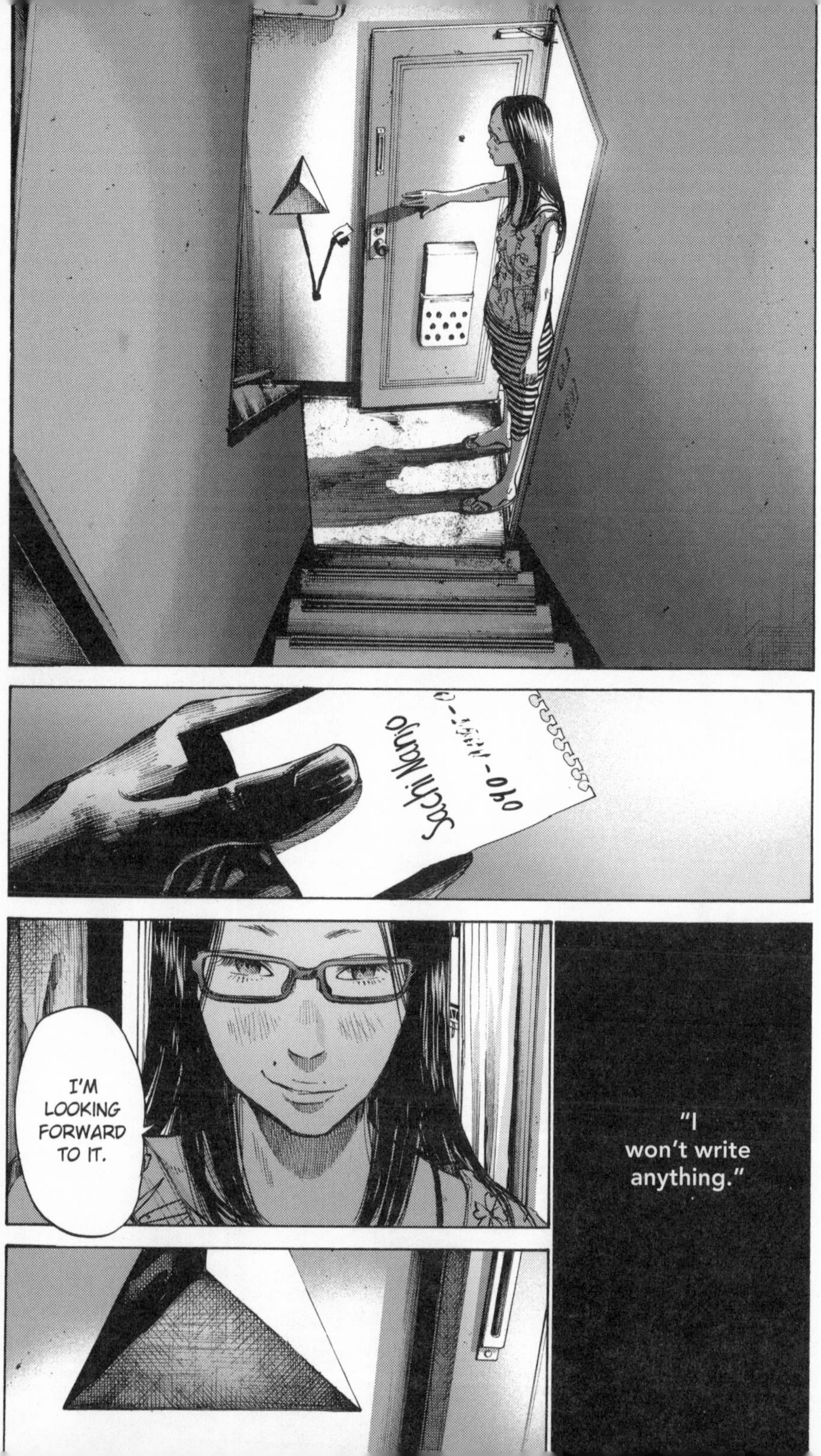
"I won't write anything."
I'M LOOKING FORWARD TO IT.

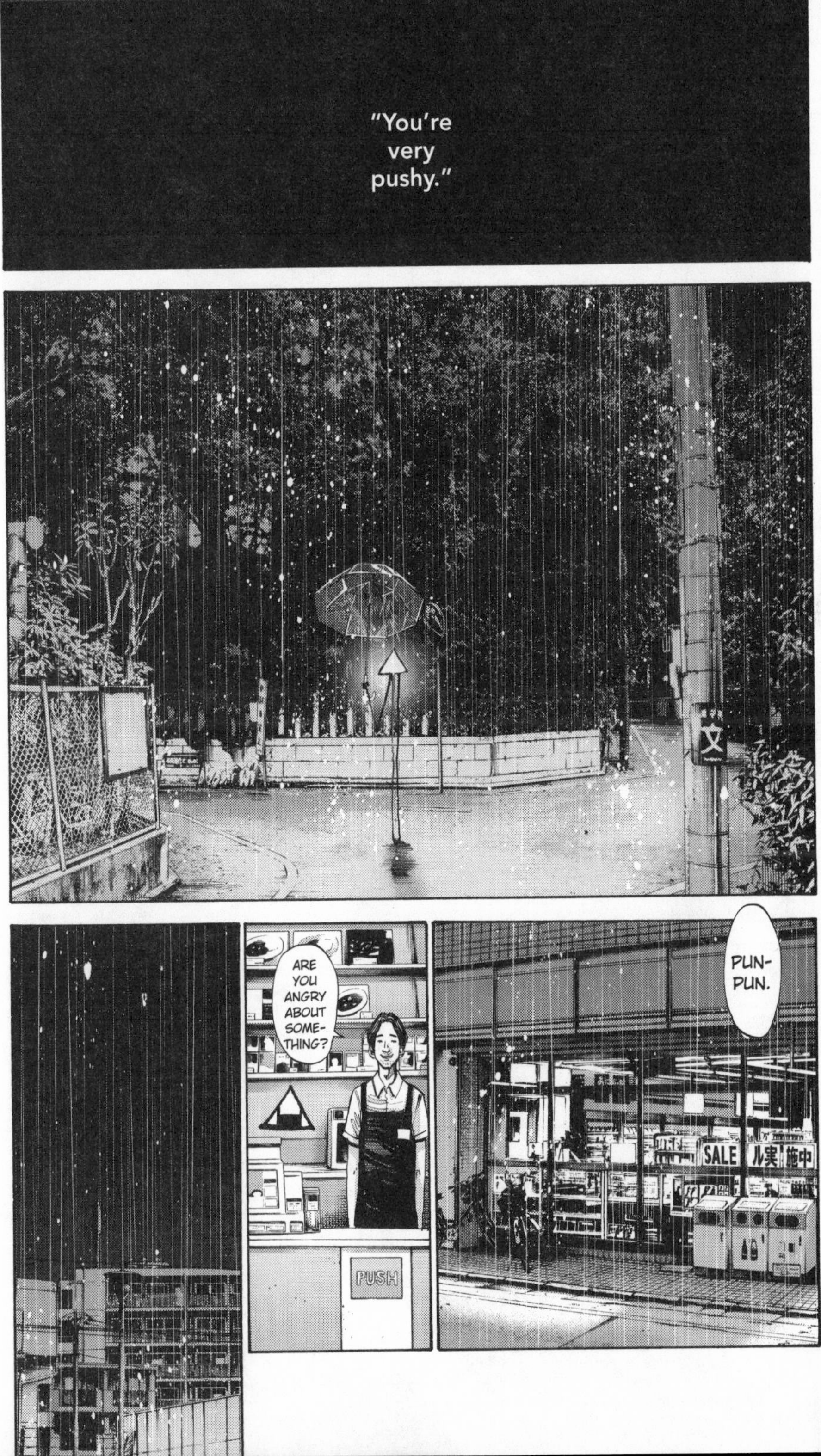
"You're very pushy."
PUN-PUN.
ARE YOU ANGRY ABOUT SOME-THING?
PUSH

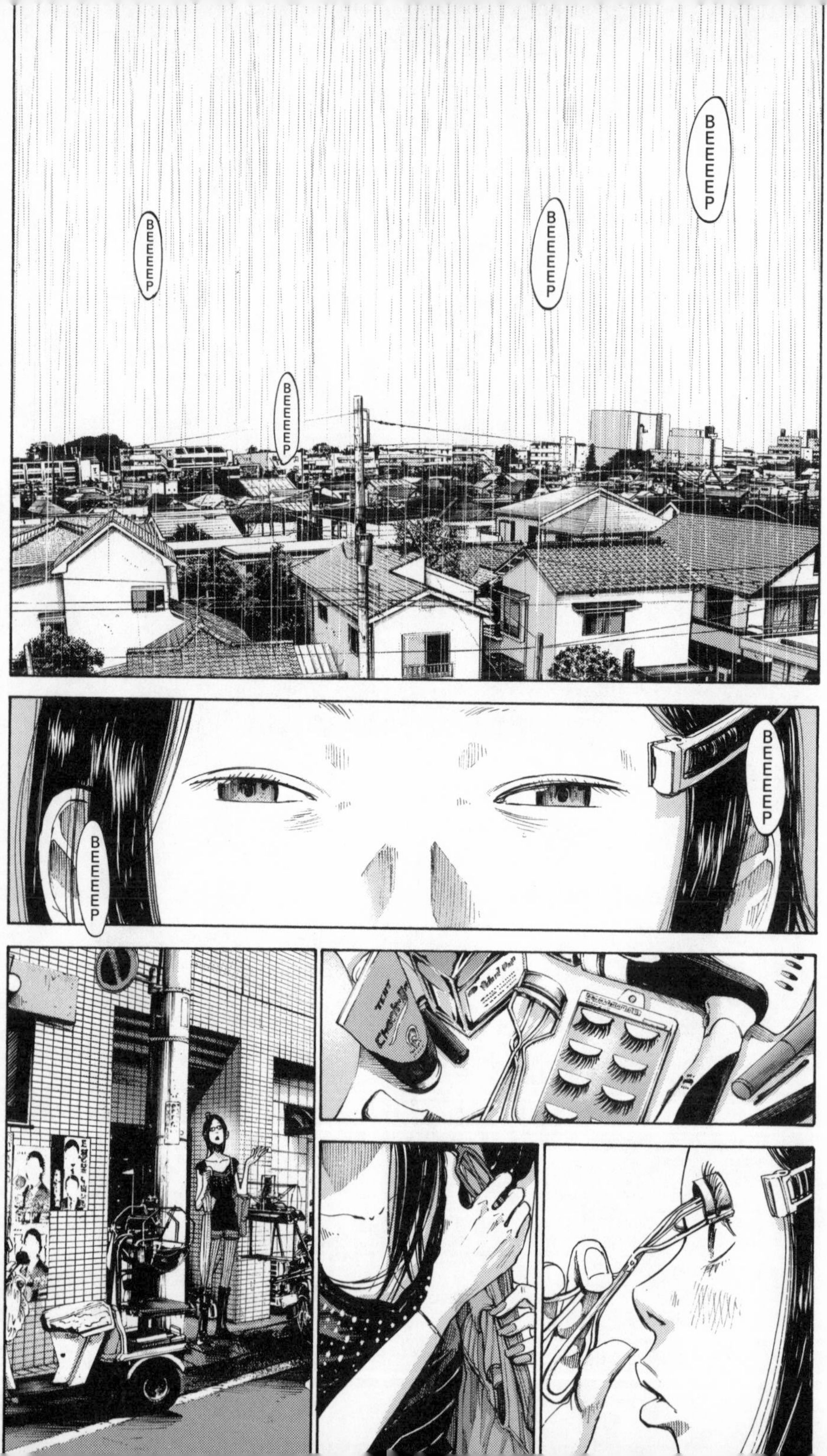
BEEEEP
BEEEEP
BEEEEP
BEEEEP
BEEEEP
BEEEEP

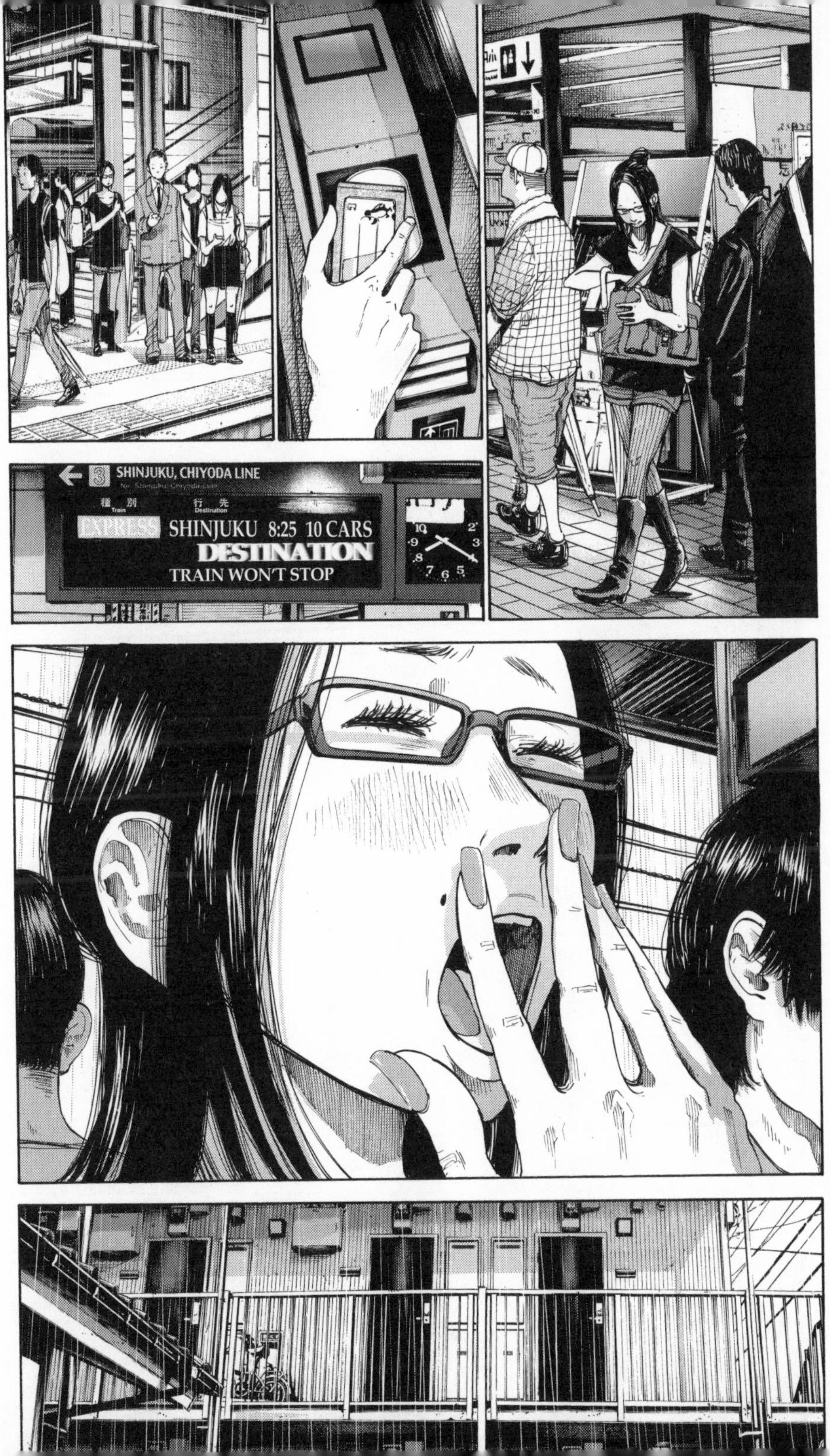

3 SHINJUKU, CHIYODA LINE
種別
Train
行先
Destination
EXPRESS
SHINJUKU 8:25 10 CARS
DESTINATION
TRAIN WON'T STOP

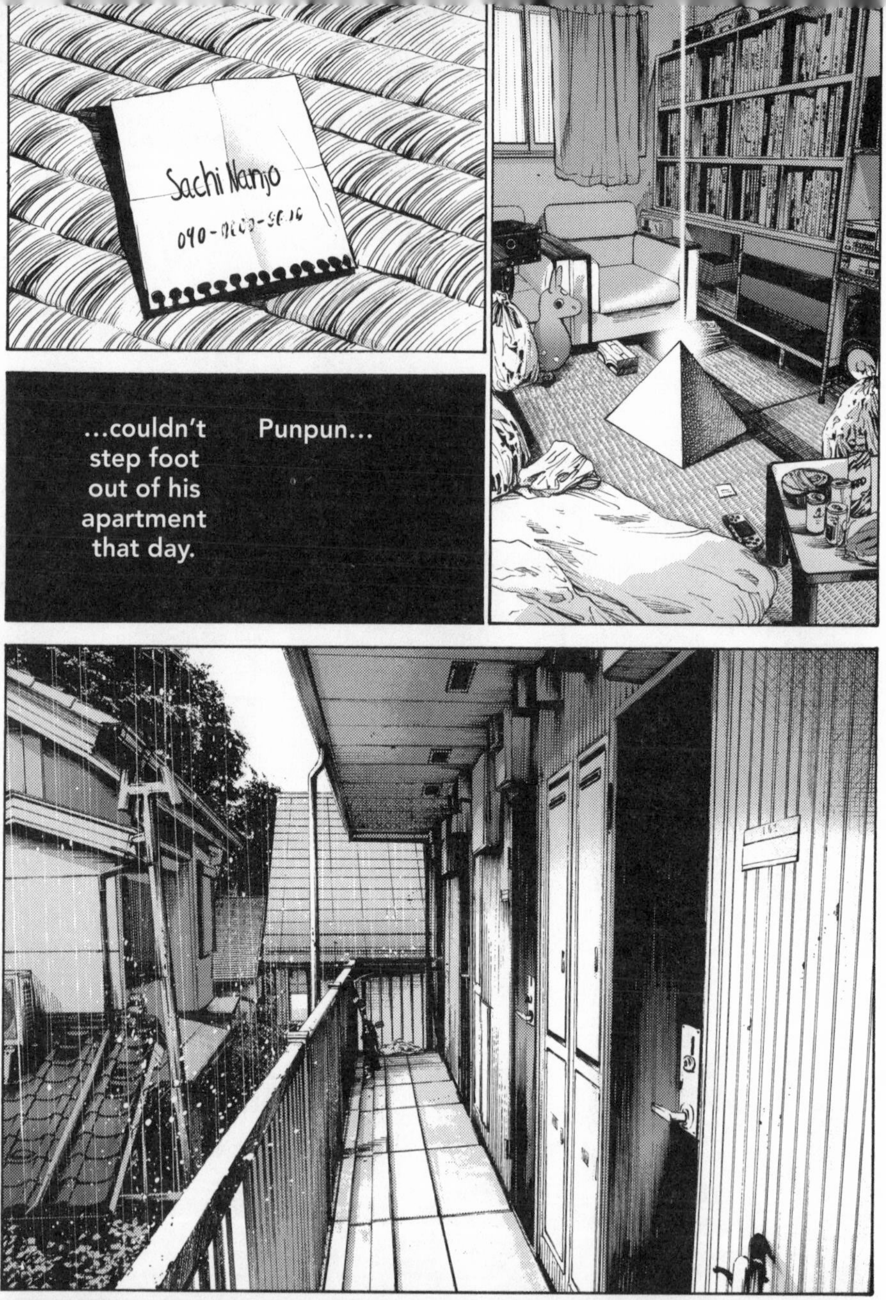
Sachi Nanjo
Punpun...
...couldn't step foot out of his apartment that day.

Chapter 82

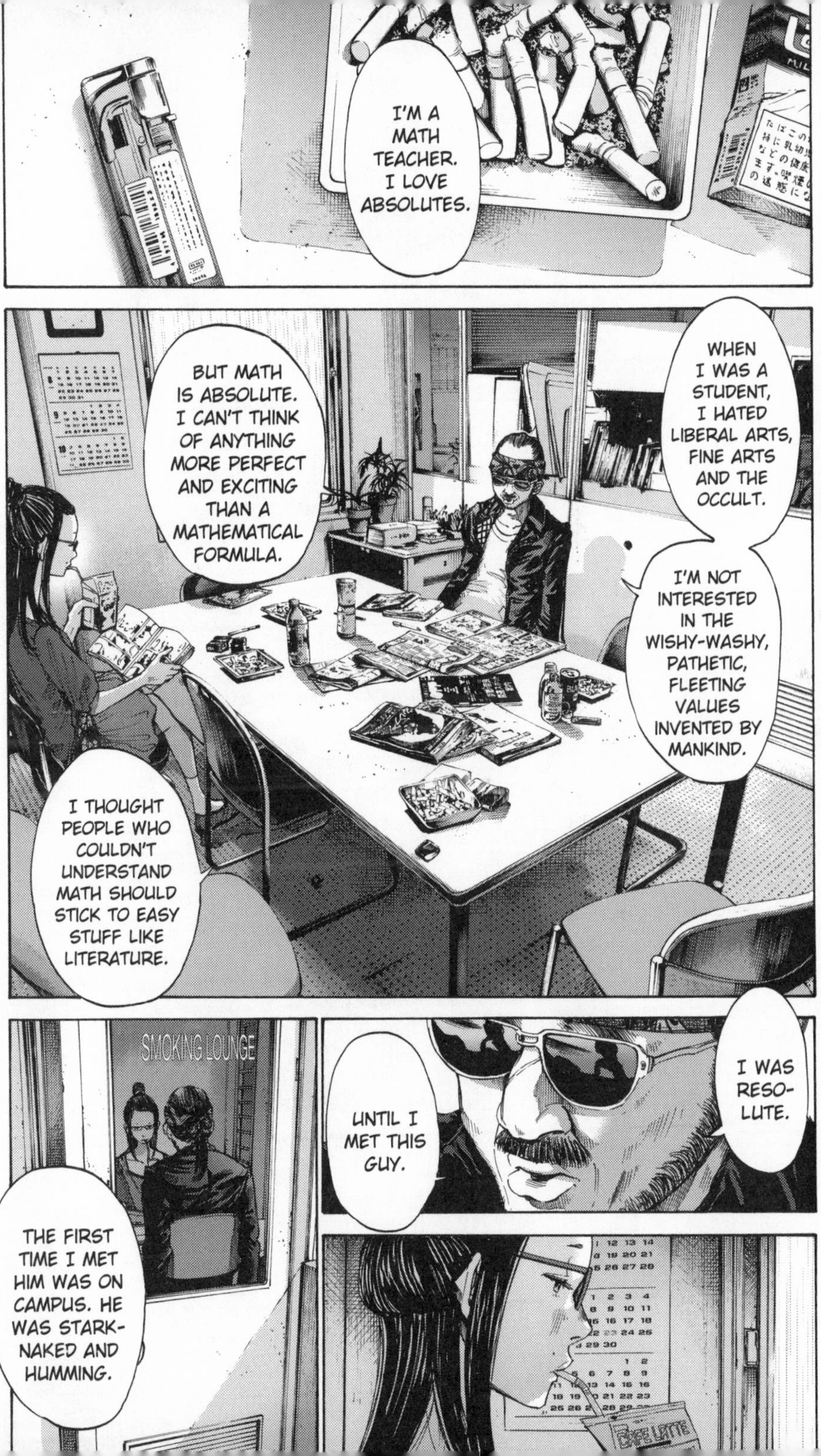
I'M A MATH TEACHER. I LOVE ABSOLUTES.
WHEN I WAS A STUDENT, I HATED LIBERAL ARTS, FINE ARTS AND THE OCCULT.
I'M NOT INTERESTED IN THE WISHY-WASHY, PATHETIC, FLEETING VALUES INVENTED BY MANKIND.
BUT MATH IS ABSOLUTE. I CAN'T THINK OF ANYTHING MORE PERFECT AND EXCITING THAN A MATHEMATICAL FORMULA.
I THOUGHT PEOPLE WHO COULDN'T UNDERSTAND MATH SHOULD STICK TO EASY STUFF LIKE LITERATURE.
I WAS RESO-LUTE.
UNTIL I MET THIS GUY.
SMOKING LOUNGE
THE FIRST TIME I MET HIM WAS ON CAMPUS. HE WAS STARK-NAKED AND HUMMING.

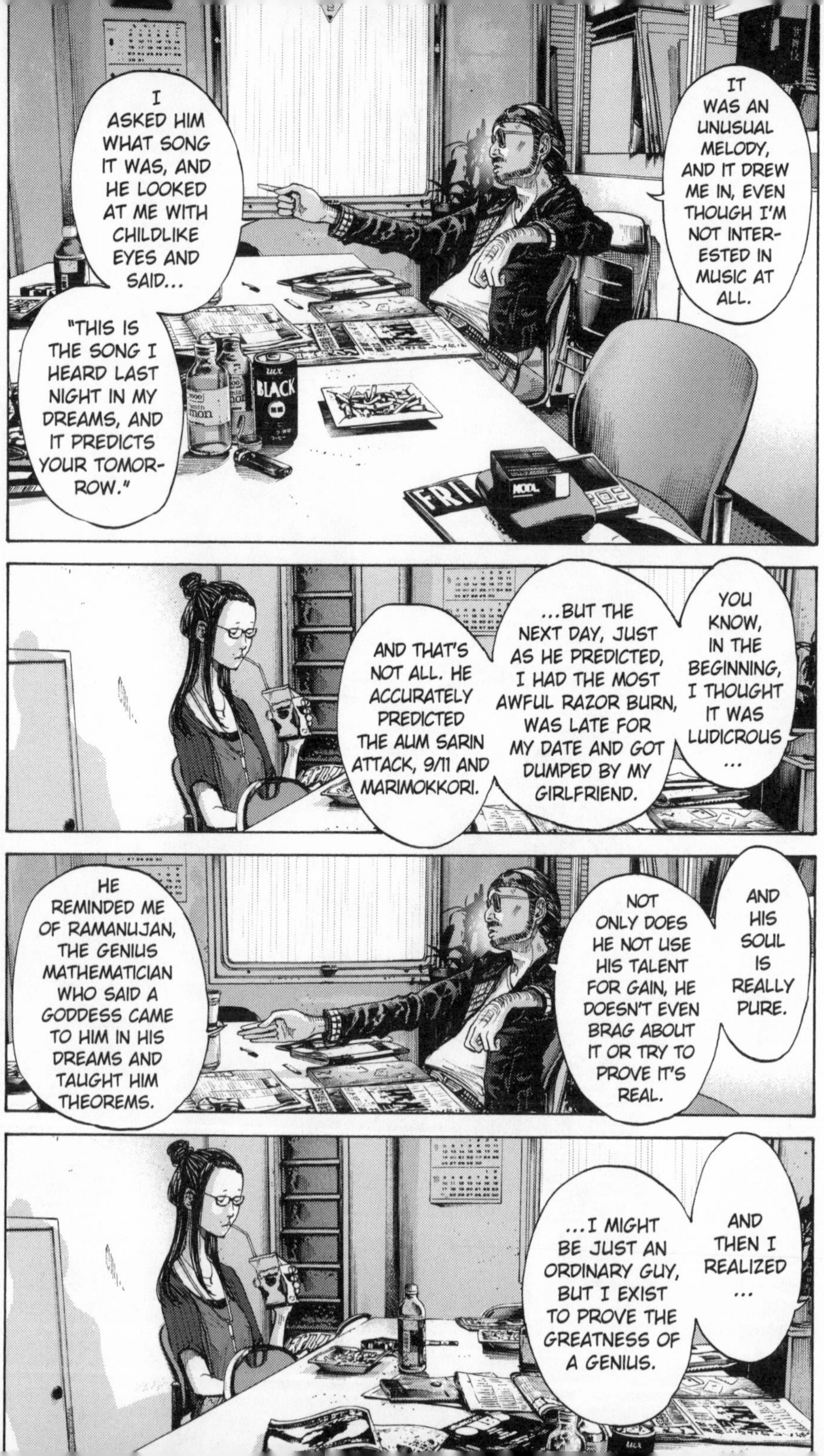
IT WAS AN UNUSUAL MELODY, AND IT DREW ME IN, EVEN THOUGH I'M NOT INTERESTED IN MUSIC AT ALL.
I ASKED HIM WHAT SONG IT WAS, AND HE LOOKED AT ME WITH CHILDLIKE EYES AND SAID...
"THIS IS THE SONG I HEARD LAST NIGHT IN MY DREAMS, AND IT PREDICTS YOUR TOMORROW."
YOU KNOW, IN THE BEGINNING, I THOUGHT IT WAS LUDICROUS...
...BUT THE NEXT DAY, JUST AS HE PREDICTED, I HAD THE MOST AWFUL RAZOR BURN, WAS LATE FOR MY DATE AND GOT DUMPED BY MY GIRLFRIEND.
AND THAT'S NOT ALL. HE ACCURATELY PREDICTED THE AUM SARIN ATTACK, 9/11 AND MARIMOKKORI.
AND HIS SOUL IS REALLY PURE.
NOT ONLY DOES HE NOT USE HIS TALENT FOR GAIN, HE DOESN'T EVEN BRAG ABOUT IT OR TRY TO PROVE IT'S REAL.
HE REMINDED ME OF RAMANUJAN, THE GENIUS MATHEMATICIAN WHO SAID A GODDESS CAME TO HIM IN HIS DREAMS AND TAUGHT HIM THEOREMS.
AND THEN I REALIZED...
...I MIGHT BE JUST AN ORDINARY GUY, BUT I EXIST TO PROVE THE GREATNESS OF A GENIUS.

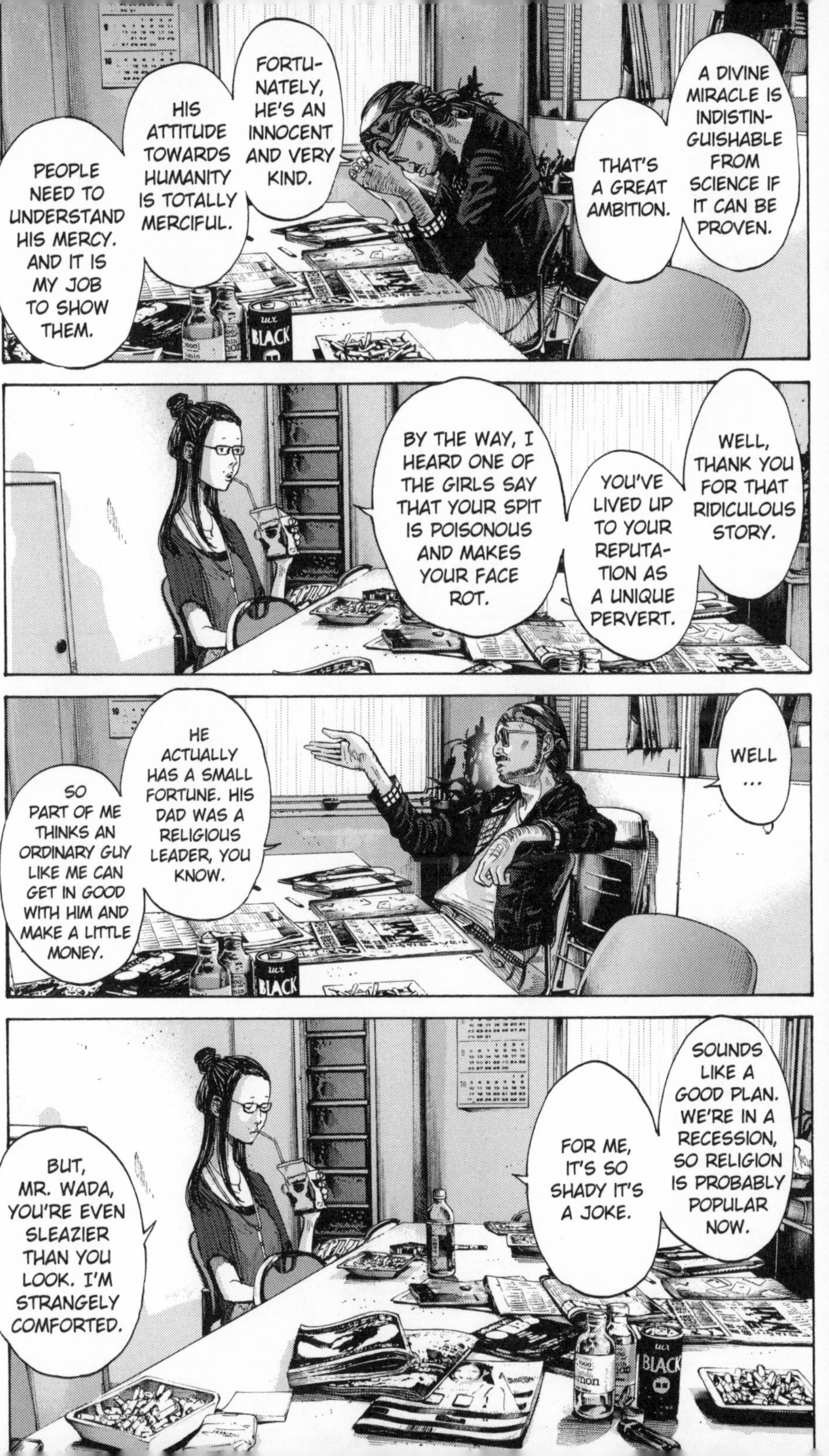
A DIVINE MIRACLE IS INDISTINGUISHABLE FROM SCIENCE IF IT CAN BE PROVEN.
THAT'S A GREAT AMBITION.
FORTUNATELY, HE'S AN INNOCENT AND VERY KIND.
HIS ATTITUDE TOWARDS HUMANITY IS TOTALLY MERCIFUL.
PEOPLE NEED TO UNDERSTAND HIS MERCY. AND IT IS MY JOB TO SHOW THEM.
WELL, THANK YOU FOR THAT RIDICULOUS STORY.
YOU'VE LIVED UP TO YOUR REPUTATION AS A UNIQUE PERVERT.
BY THE WAY, I HEARD ONE OF THE GIRLS SAY THAT YOUR SPIT IS POISONOUS AND MAKES YOUR FACE ROT.
WELL ...
HE ACTUALLY HAS A SMALL FORTUNE. HIS DAD WAS A RELIGIOUS LEADER, YOU KNOW.
SO PART OF ME THINKS AN ORDINARY GUY LIKE ME CAN GET IN GOOD WITH HIM AND MAKE A LITTLE MONEY.
SOUNDS LIKE A GOOD PLAN. WE'RE IN A RECESSION, SO RELIGION IS PROBABLY POPULAR NOW.
FOR ME, IT'S SO SHADY IT'S A JOKE.
BUT, MR. WADA, YOU'RE EVEN SLEAZIER THAN YOU LOOK. I'M STRANGELY COMFORTED.

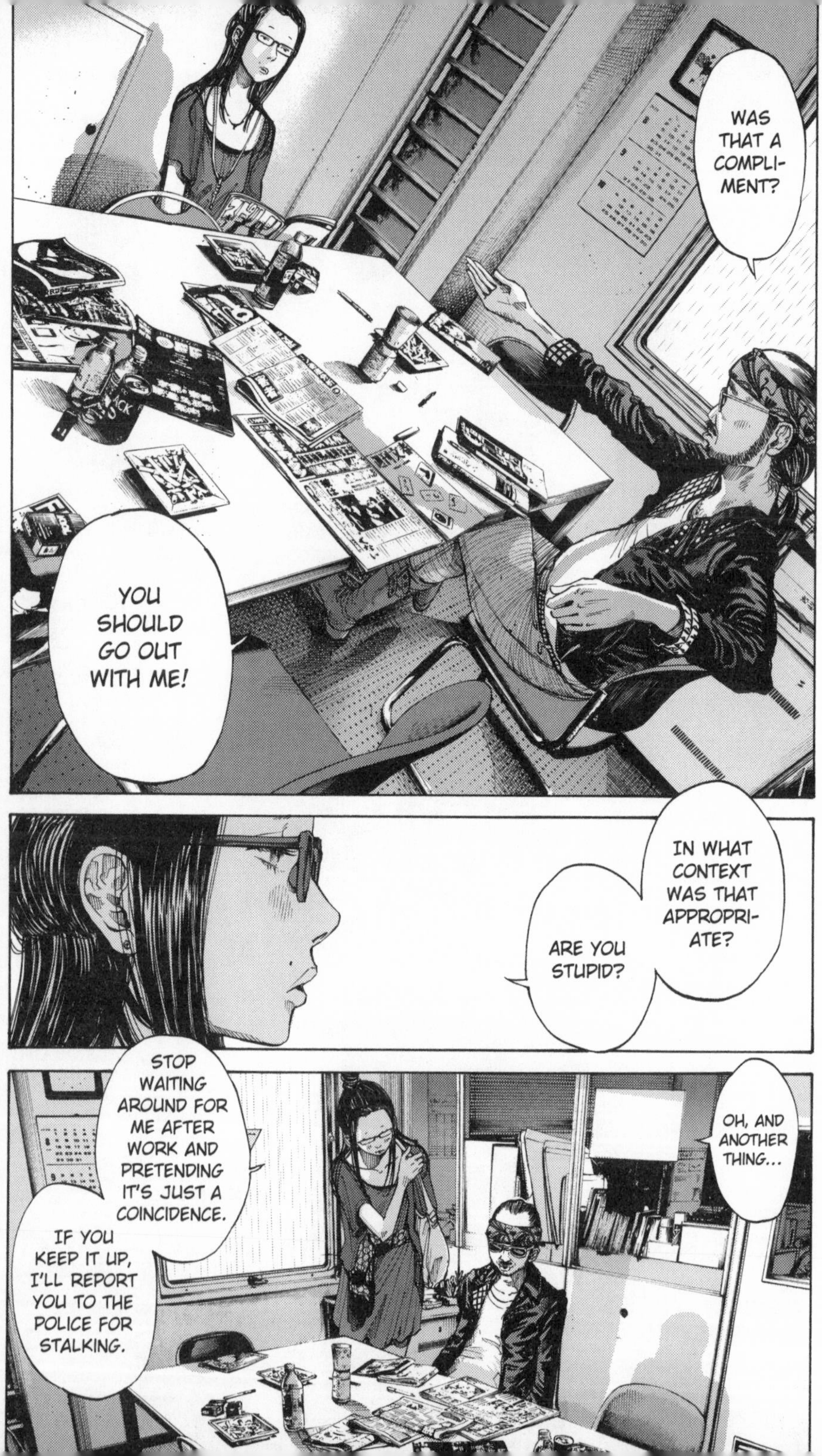
WAS THAT A COMPLIMENT?
YOU SHOULD GO OUT WITH ME!
IN WHAT CONTEXT WAS THAT APPROPRIATE?
ARE YOU STUPID?
OH, AND ANOTHER THING...
STOP WAITING AROUND FOR ME AFTER WORK AND PRETENDING IT'S JUST A COINCIDENCE.
IF YOU KEEP IT UP, I'LL REPORT YOU TO THE POLICE FOR STALKING.

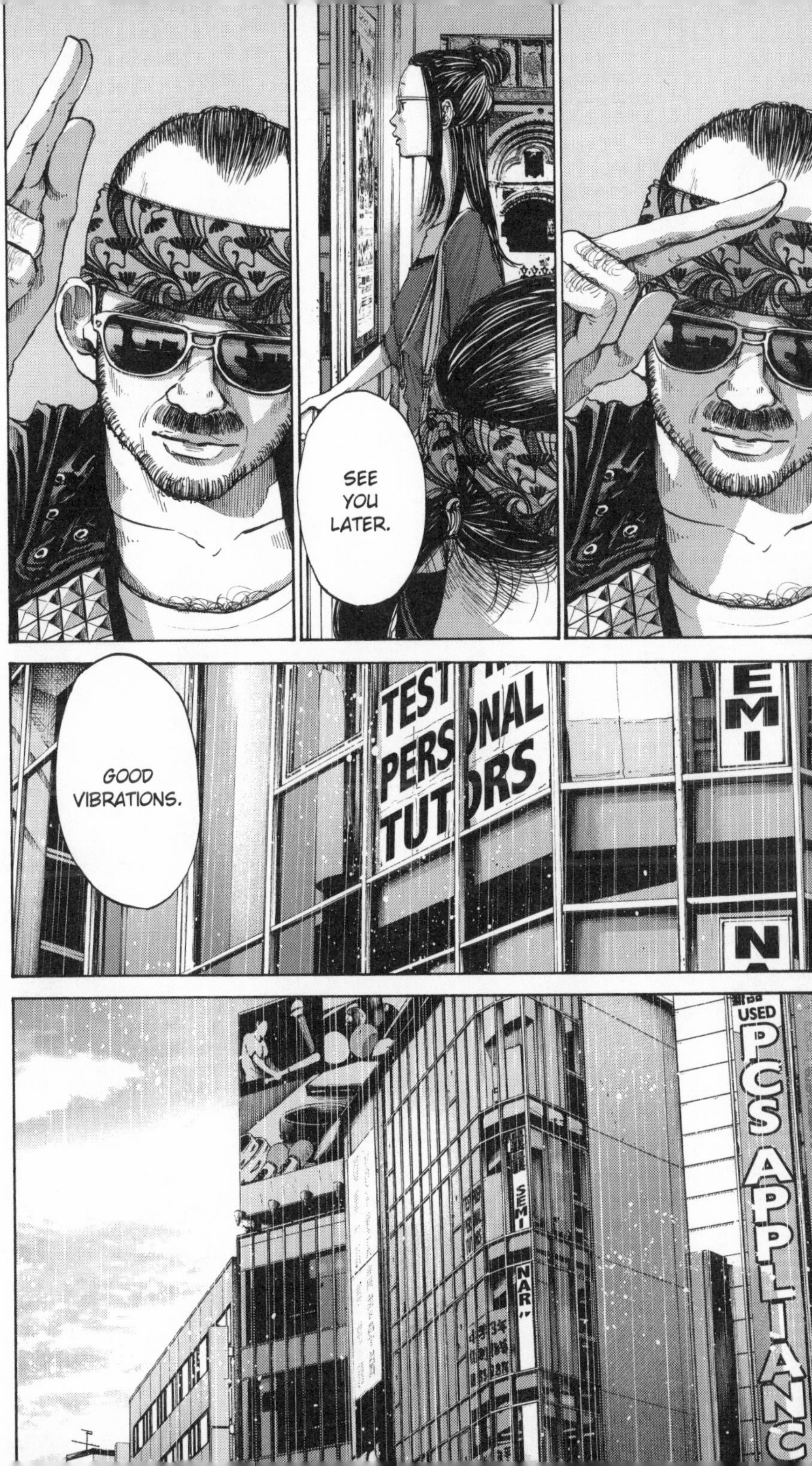
SEE YOU LATER.
GOOD VIBRATIONS.
USED
PCS
SEMI

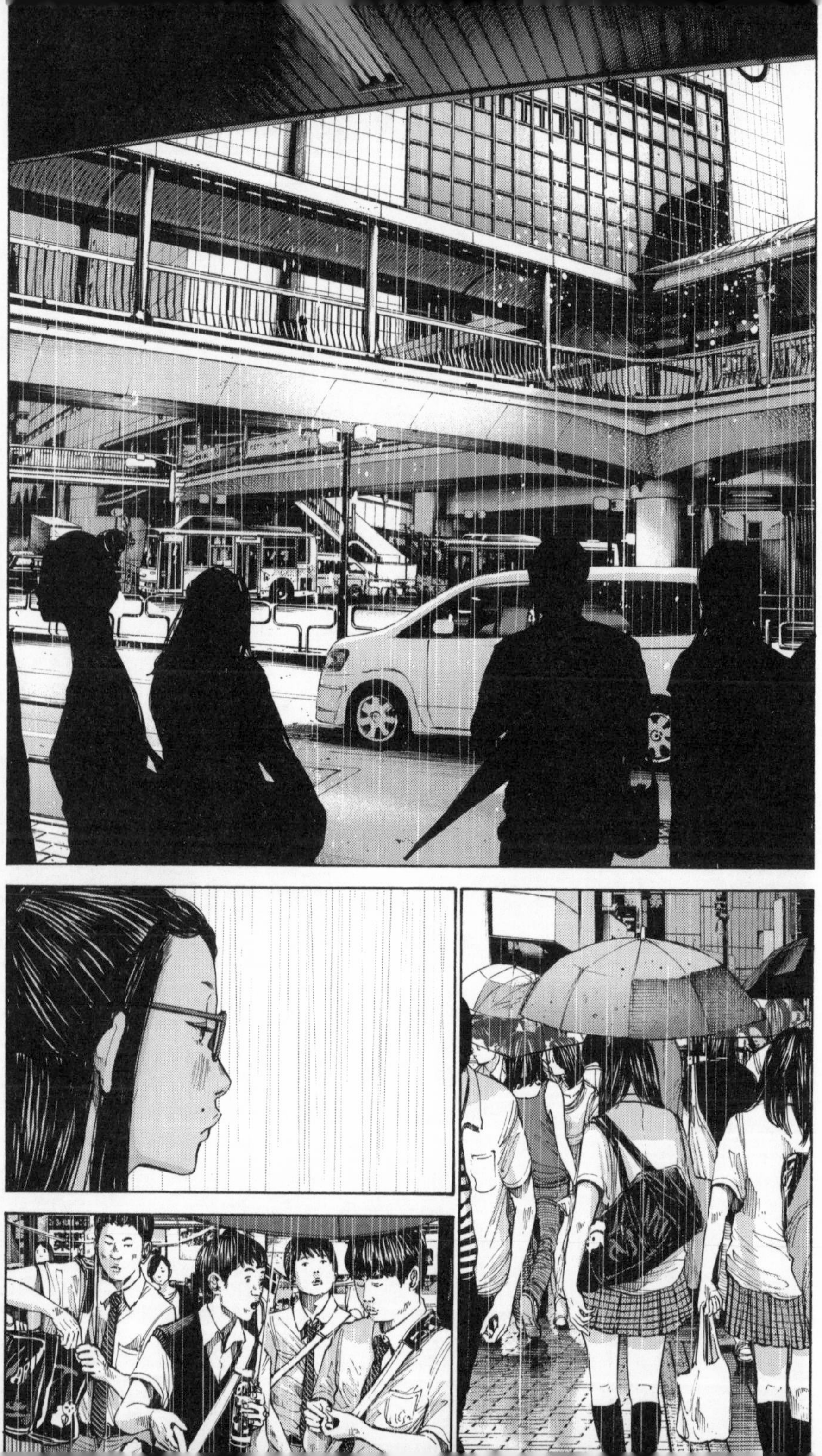

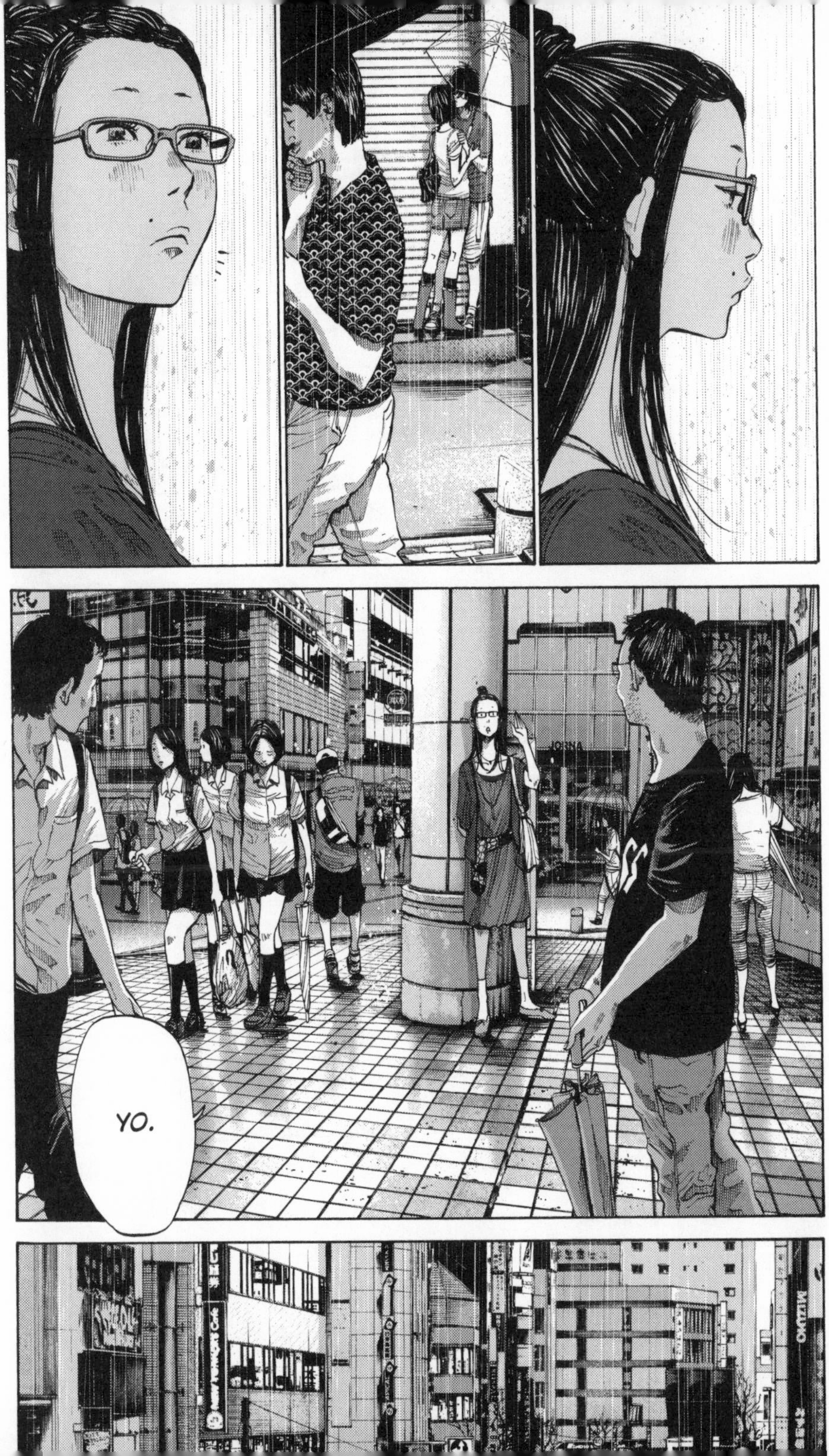
YO.

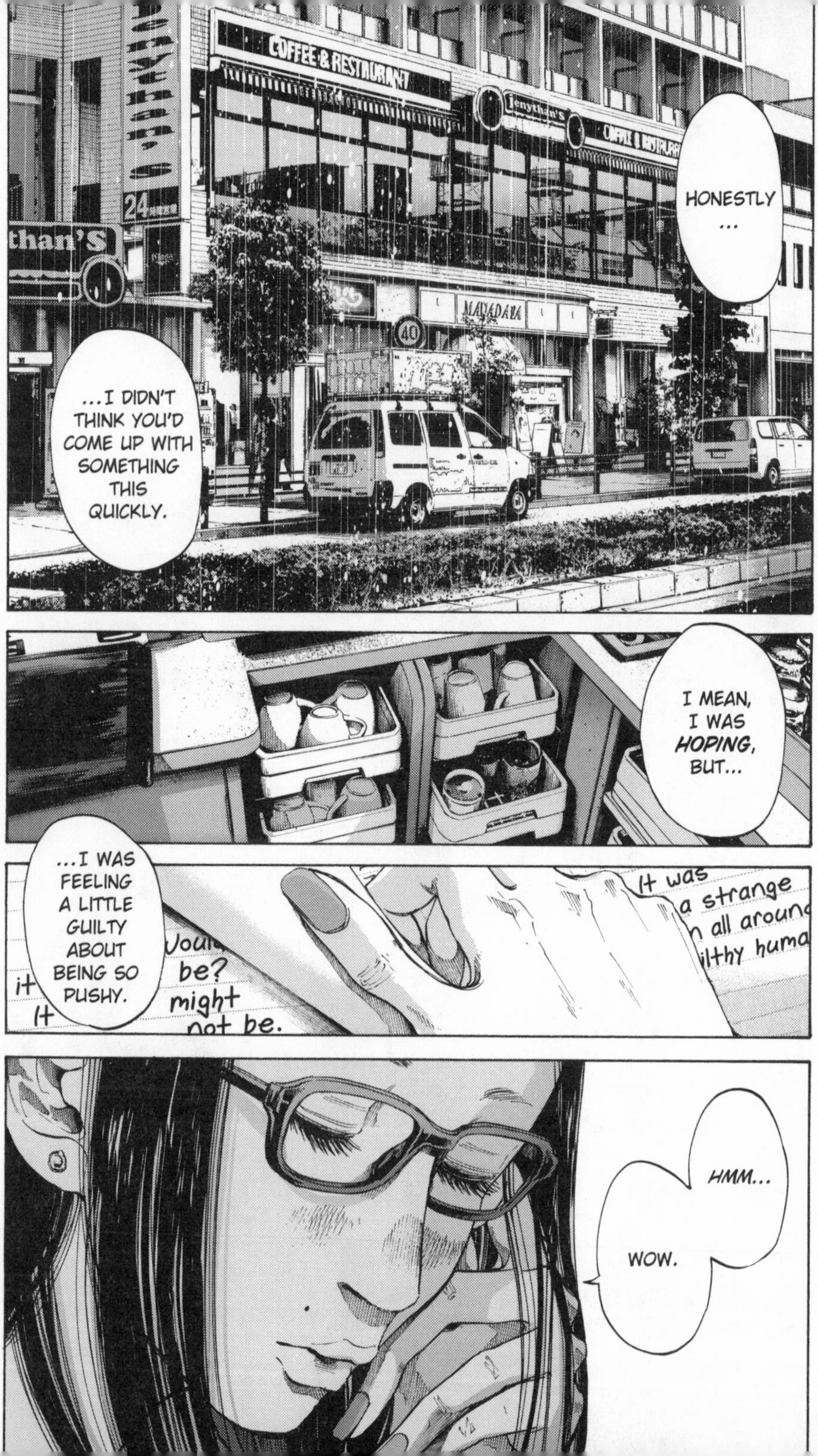
HONESTLY ...
...I DIDN'T THINK YOU'D COME UP WITH SOMETHING THIS QUICKLY.
I MEAN, I WAS *HOPING*, BUT...
...I WAS FEELING A LITTLE GUILTY ABOUT BEING SO PUSHY.
HMM...
WOW.

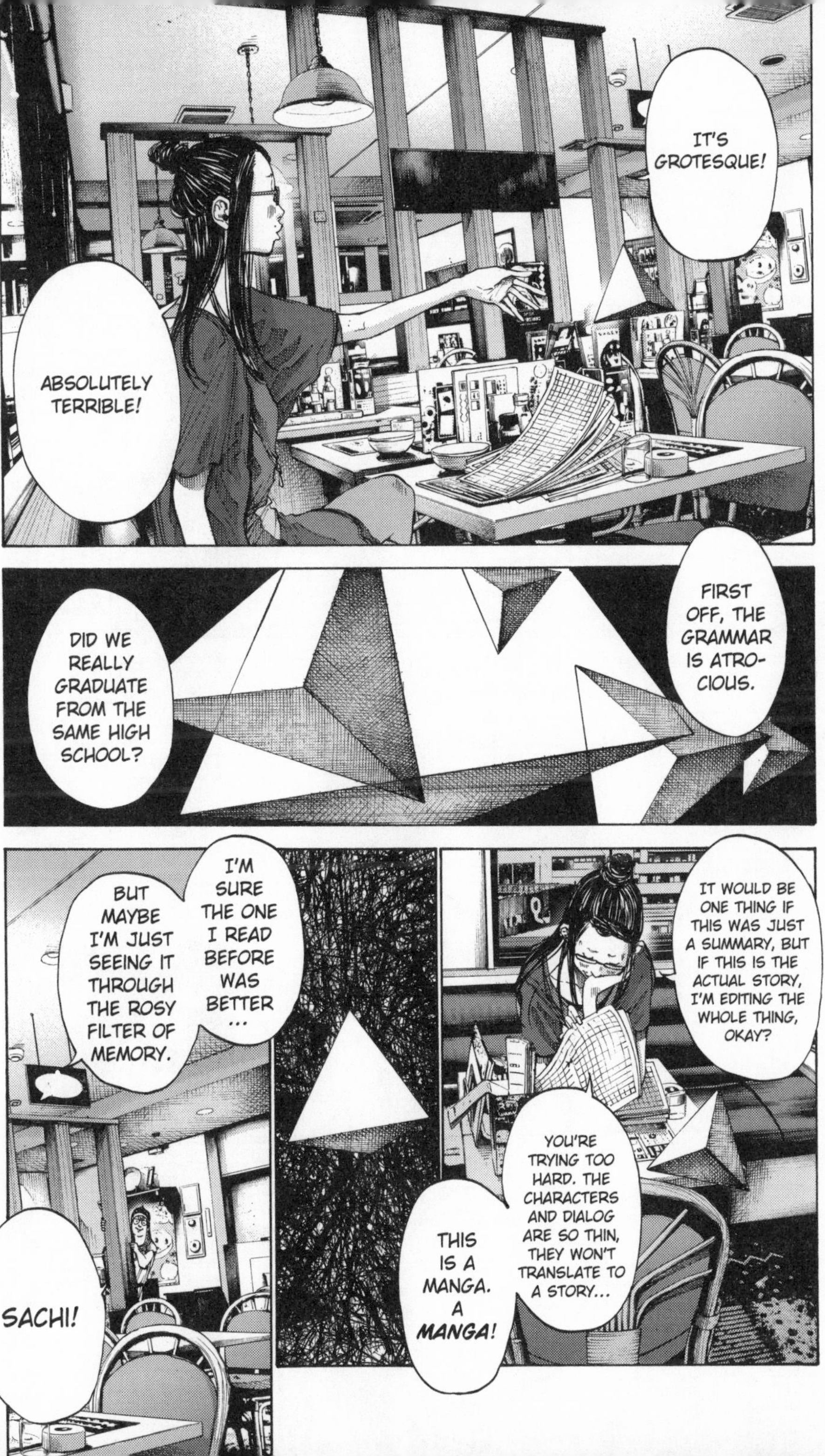
IT'S GROTESQUE!
ABSOLUTELY TERRIBLE!
FIRST OFF, THE GRAMMAR IS ATRO-CIOUS.
DID WE REALLY GRADUATE FROM THE SAME HIGH SCHOOL?
IT WOULD BE ONE THING IF THIS WAS JUST A SUMMARY, BUT IF THIS IS THE ACTUAL STORY, I'M EDITING THE WHOLE THING, OKAY?
YOU'RE TRYING TOO HARD. THE CHARACTERS AND DIALOG ARE SO THIN, THEY WON'T TRANSLATE TO A STORY...
THIS IS A MANGA. A *MANGA*!
I'M SURE THE ONE I READ BEFORE WAS BETTER...
BUT MAYBE I'M JUST SEEING IT THROUGH THE ROSY FILTER OF MEMORY.
SACHI!

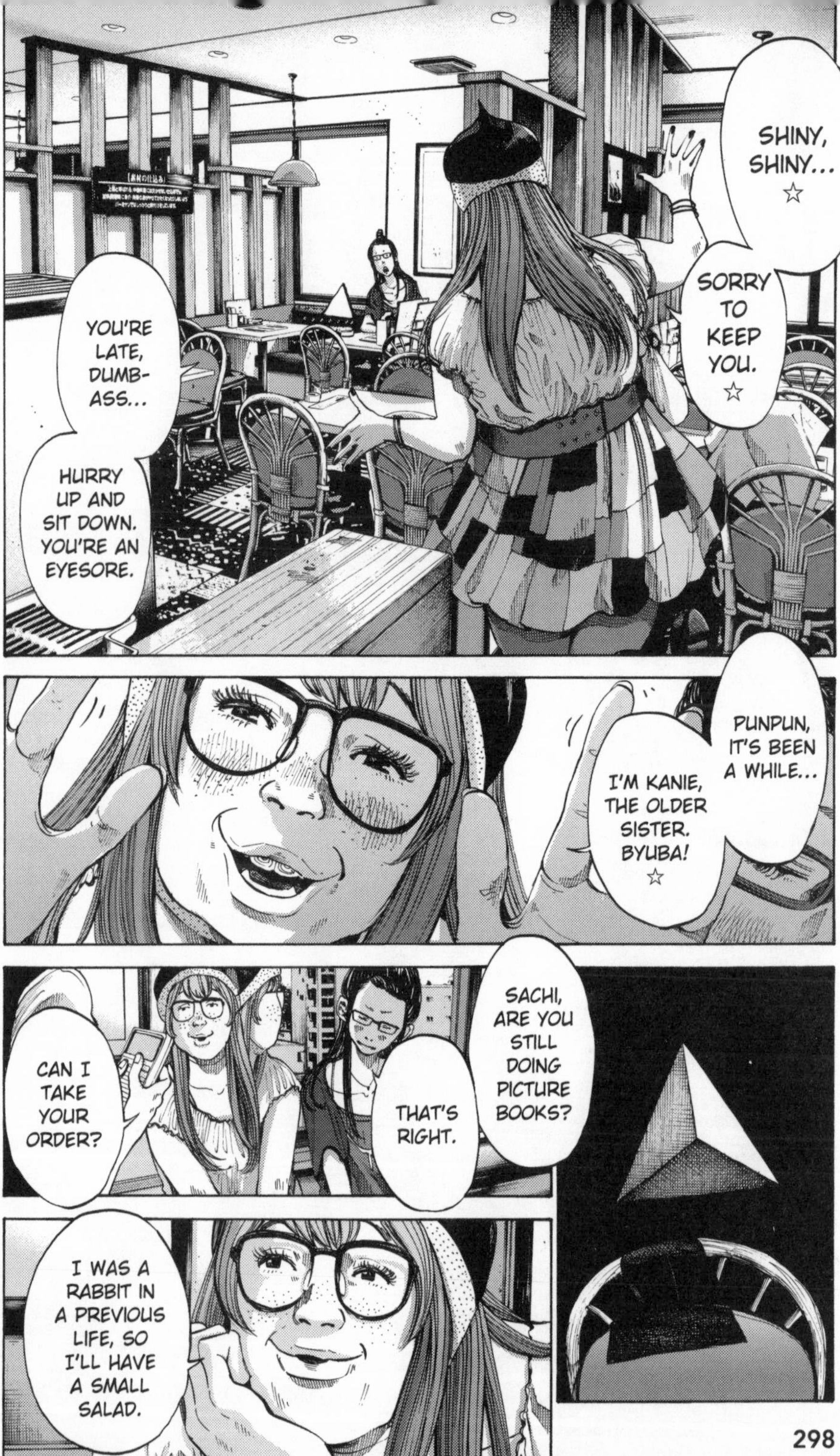
SHINY, SHINY... ☆
SORRY TO KEEP YOU. ☆
YOU'RE LATE, DUMB-ASS...
HURRY UP AND SIT DOWN. YOU'RE AN EYESORE.
PUNPUN, IT'S BEEN A WHILE...
I'M KANIE, THE OLDER SISTER. BYUBA! ☆
SACHI, ARE YOU STILL DOING PICTURE BOOKS?
THAT'S RIGHT.
CAN I TAKE YOUR ORDER?
I WAS A RABBIT IN A PREVIOUS LIFE, SO I'LL HAVE A SMALL SALAD.

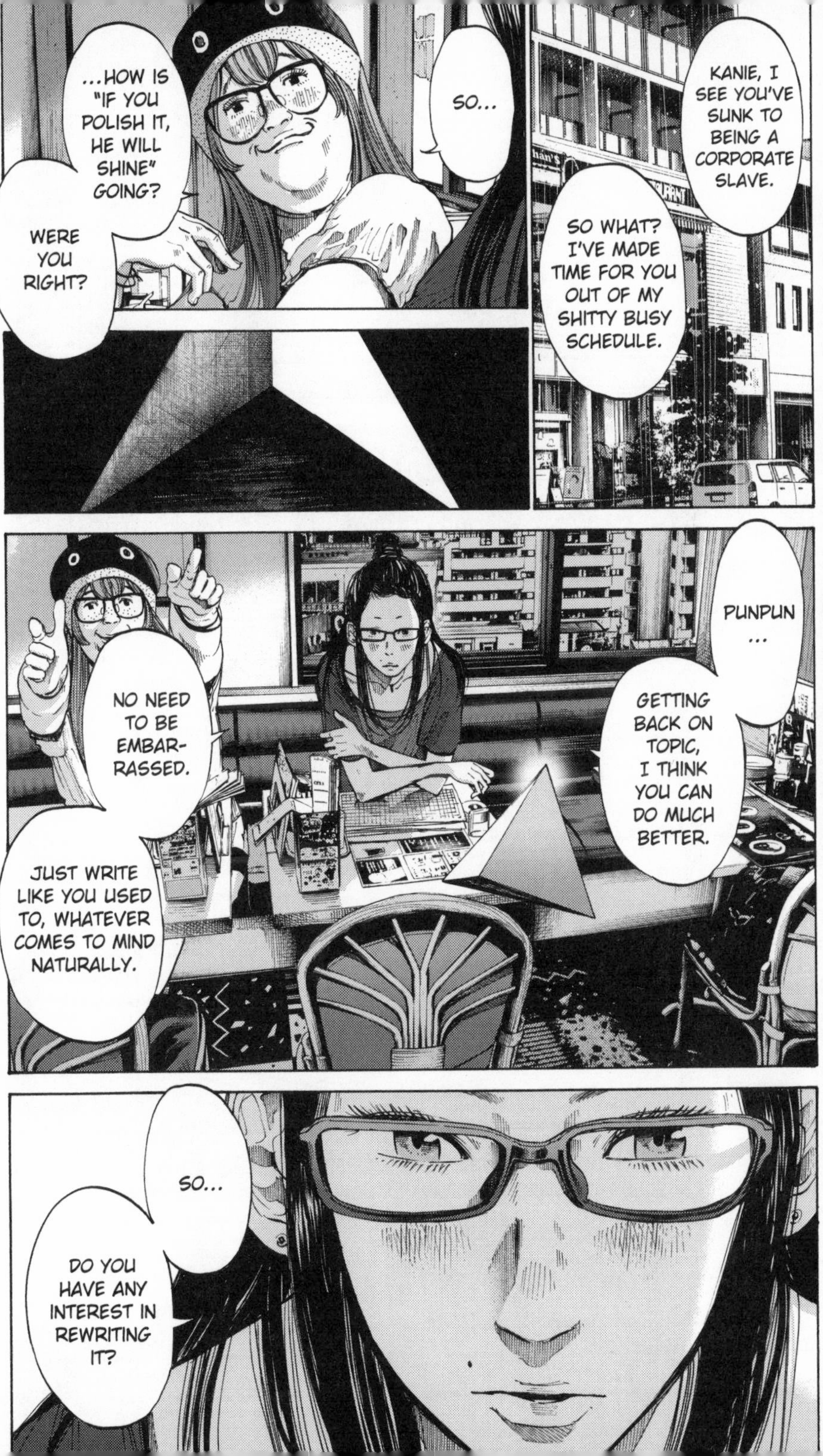
KANIE, I SEE YOU'VE SUNK TO BEING A CORPORATE SLAVE.
SO WHAT? I'VE MADE TIME FOR YOU OUT OF MY SHITTY BUSY SCHEDULE.
SO...
...HOW IS "IF YOU POLISH IT, HE WILL SHINE" GOING?
WERE YOU RIGHT?
PUNPUN ...
GETTING BACK ON TOPIC, I THINK YOU CAN DO MUCH BETTER.
NO NEED TO BE EMBAR-RASSED.
JUST WRITE LIKE YOU USED TO, WHATEVER COMES TO MIND NATURALLY.
SO...
DO YOU HAVE ANY INTEREST IN REWRITING IT?

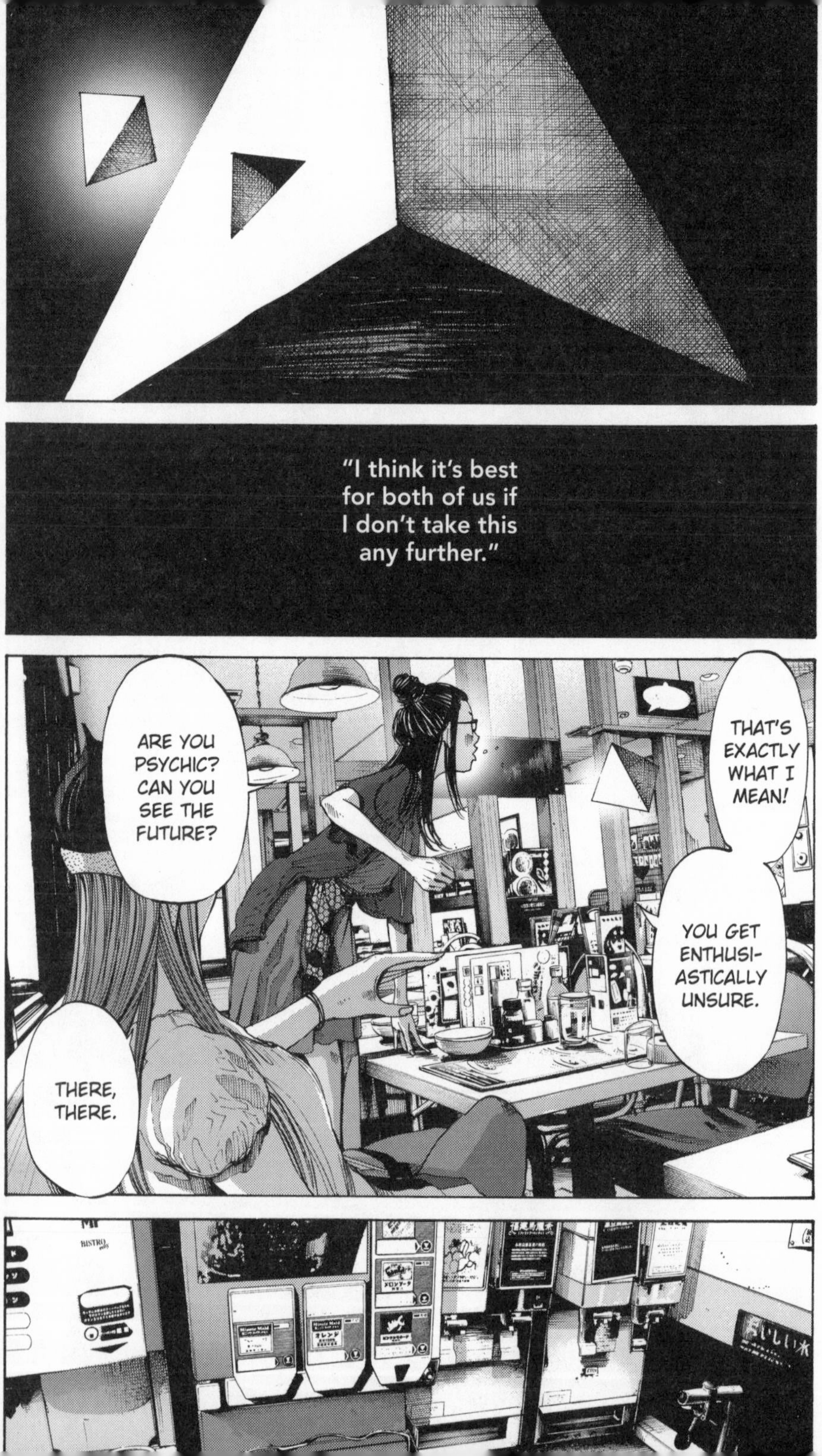
"I think it's best for both of us if I don't take this any further."
THAT'S EXACTLY WHAT I MEAN!
ARE YOU PSYCHIC? CAN YOU SEE THE FUTURE?
YOU GET ENTHUSI-ASTICALLY UNSURE.
THERE, THERE.

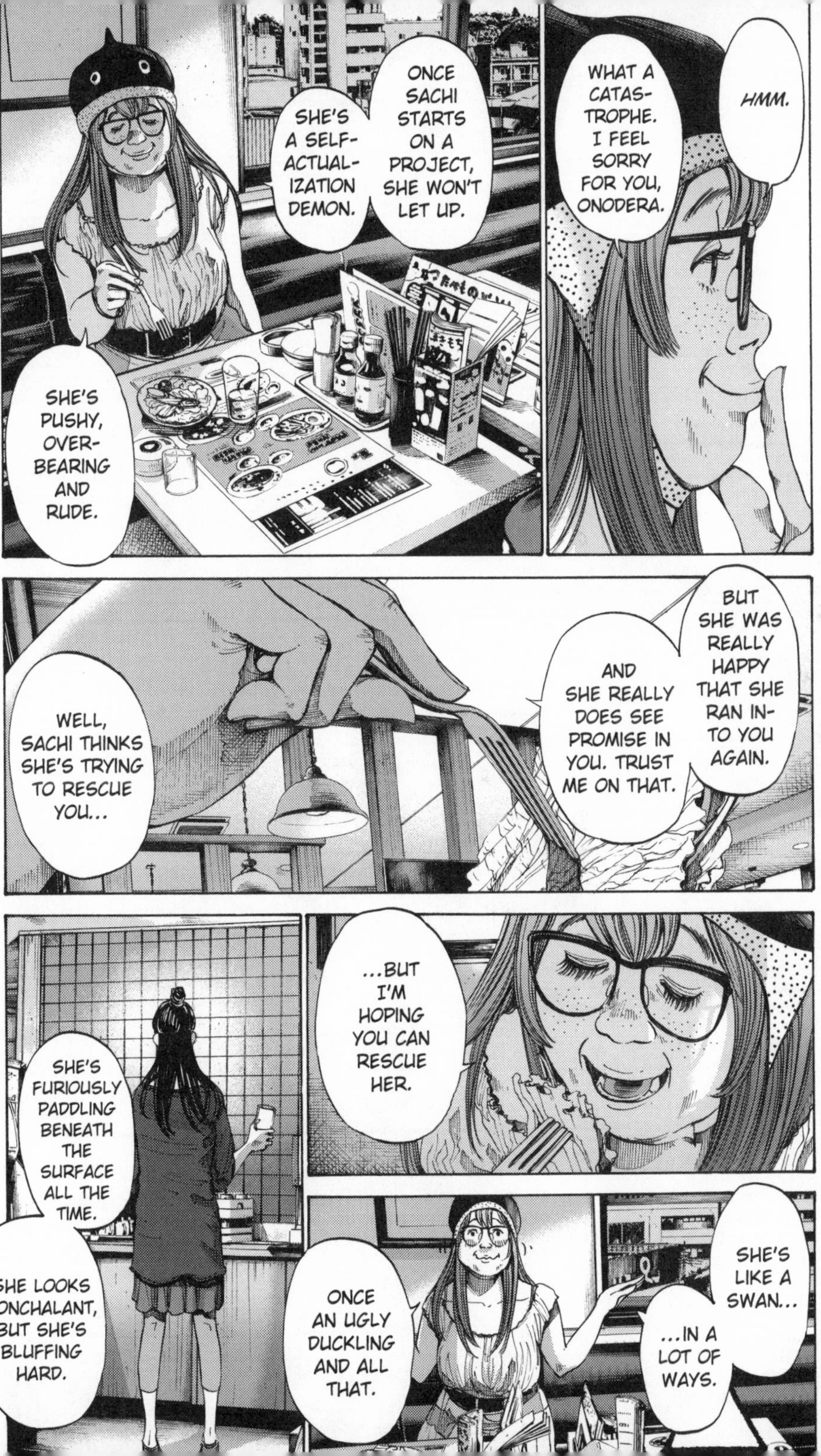
HMM.
WHAT A CATASTROPHE. I FEEL SORRY FOR YOU, ONODERA.
ONCE SACHI STARTS ON A PROJECT, SHE WON'T LET UP.
SHE'S A SELF-ACTUALIZATION DEMON.
SHE'S PUSHY, OVERBEARING AND RUDE.
BUT SHE WAS REALLY HAPPY THAT SHE RAN INTO YOU AGAIN.
AND SHE REALLY DOES SEE PROMISE IN YOU. TRUST ME ON THAT.
WELL, SACHI THINKS SHE'S TRYING TO RESCUE YOU...
...BUT I'M HOPING YOU CAN RESCUE HER.
SHE'S LIKE A SWAN...
...IN A LOT OF WAYS.
ONCE AN UGLY DUCKLING AND ALL THAT.
SHE'S FURIOUSLY PADDLING BENEATH THE SURFACE ALL THE TIME.
SHE LOOKS NONCHALANT, BUT SHE'S BLUFFING HARD.

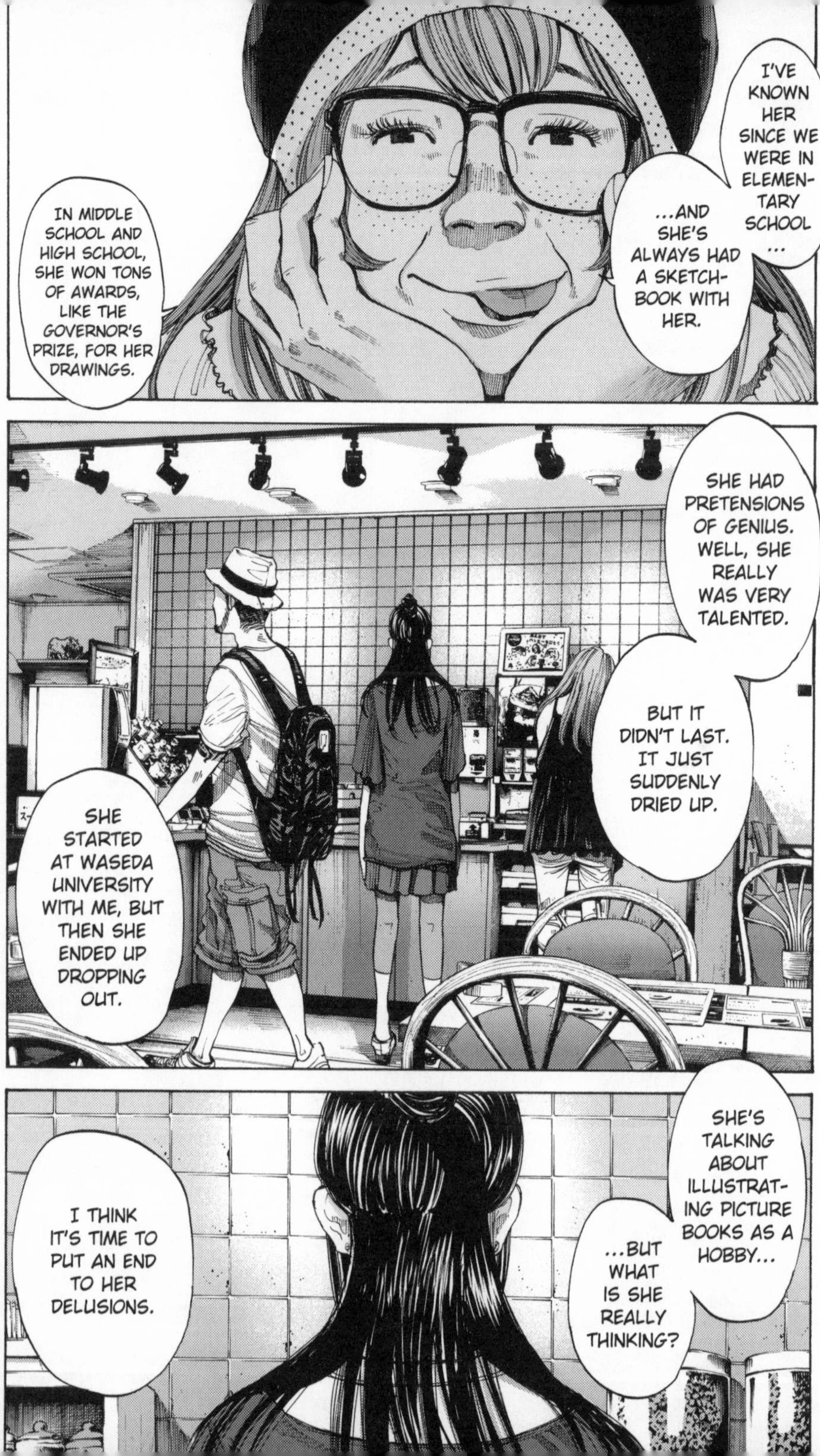

I'VE KNOWN HER SINCE WE WERE IN ELEMENTARY SCHOOL...
...AND SHE'S ALWAYS HAD A SKETCHBOOK WITH HER.
IN MIDDLE SCHOOL AND HIGH SCHOOL, SHE WON TONS OF AWARDS, LIKE THE GOVERNOR'S PRIZE, FOR HER DRAWINGS.
SHE HAD PRETENSIONS OF GENIUS. WELL, SHE REALLY WAS VERY TALENTED.
BUT IT DIDN'T LAST. IT JUST SUDDENLY DRIED UP.
SHE STARTED AT WASEDA UNIVERSITY WITH ME, BUT THEN SHE ENDED UP DROPPING OUT.
SHE'S TALKING ABOUT ILLUSTRATING PICTURE BOOKS AS A HOBBY...
...BUT WHAT IS SHE REALLY THINKING?
I THINK IT'S TIME TO PUT AN END TO HER DELUSIONS.

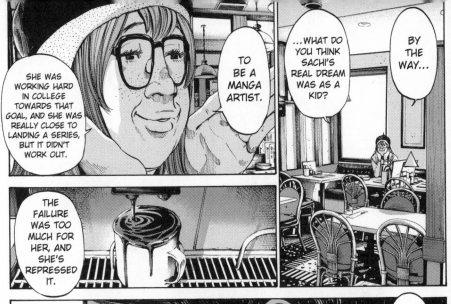

BY THE WAY...
...WHAT DO YOU THINK SACHI'S REAL DREAM WAS AS A KID?
TO BE A MANGA ARTIST.
SHE WAS WORKING HARD IN COLLEGE TOWARDS THAT GOAL, AND SHE WAS REALLY CLOSE TO LANDING A SERIES, BUT IT DIDN'T WORK OUT.
THE FAILURE WAS TOO MUCH FOR HER, AND SHE'S REPRESSED IT.
SHE CAN'T WRITE STORIES.
SHE USED TO GET ALL WORKED UP...
...ABOUT HOW SHE WAS GOING TO DESTROY THE WORLD WITH HER MANGA.

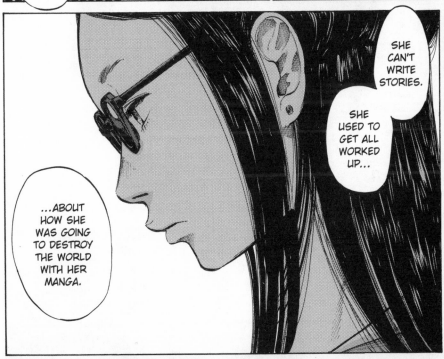

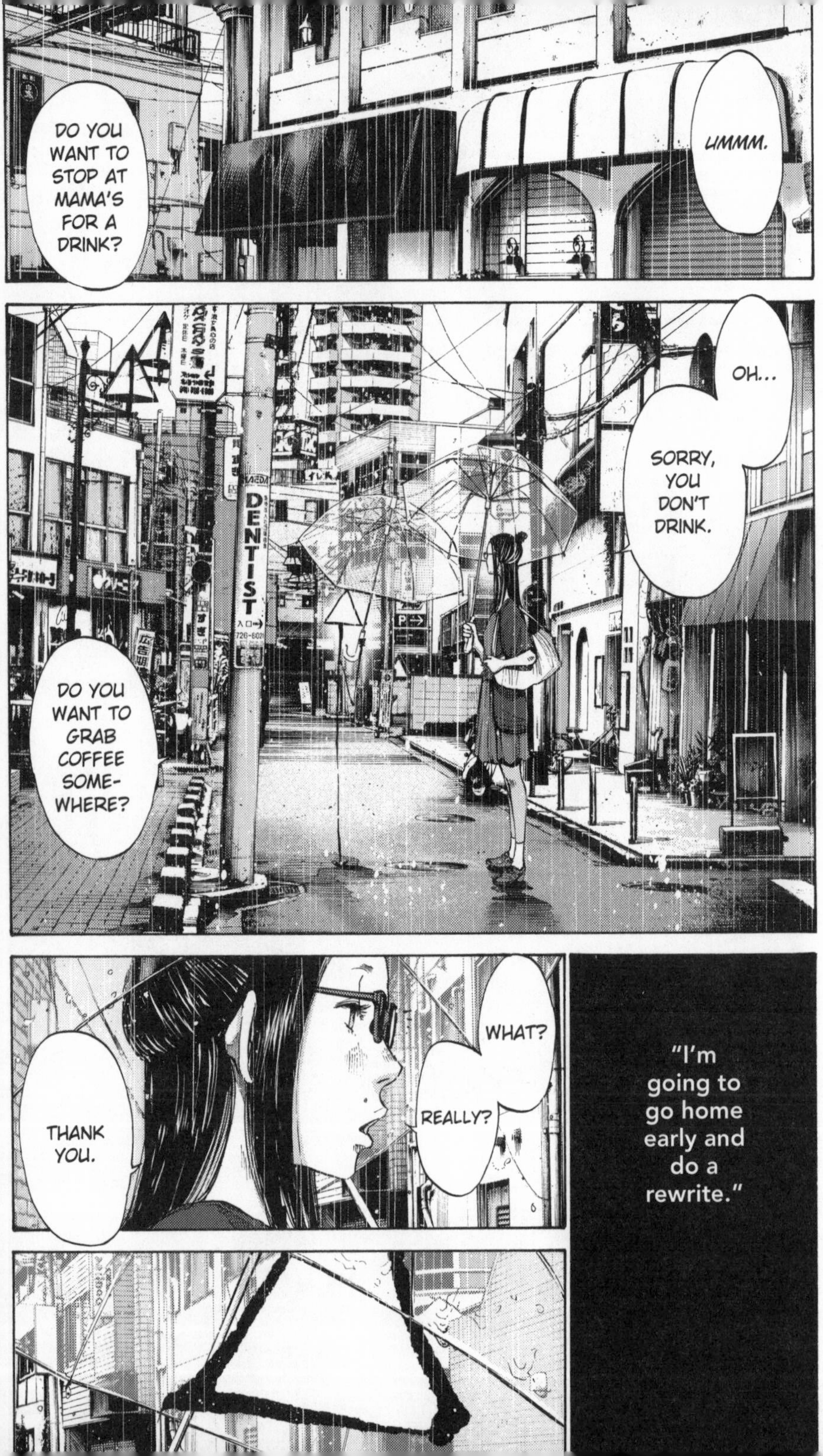
UMMM.
DO YOU WANT TO STOP AT MAMA'S FOR A DRINK?
OH...
SORRY, YOU DON'T DRINK.
DENTIST
DO YOU WANT TO GRAB COFFEE SOME-WHERE?
"I'm going to go home early and do a rewrite."
WHAT?
REALLY?
THANK YOU.

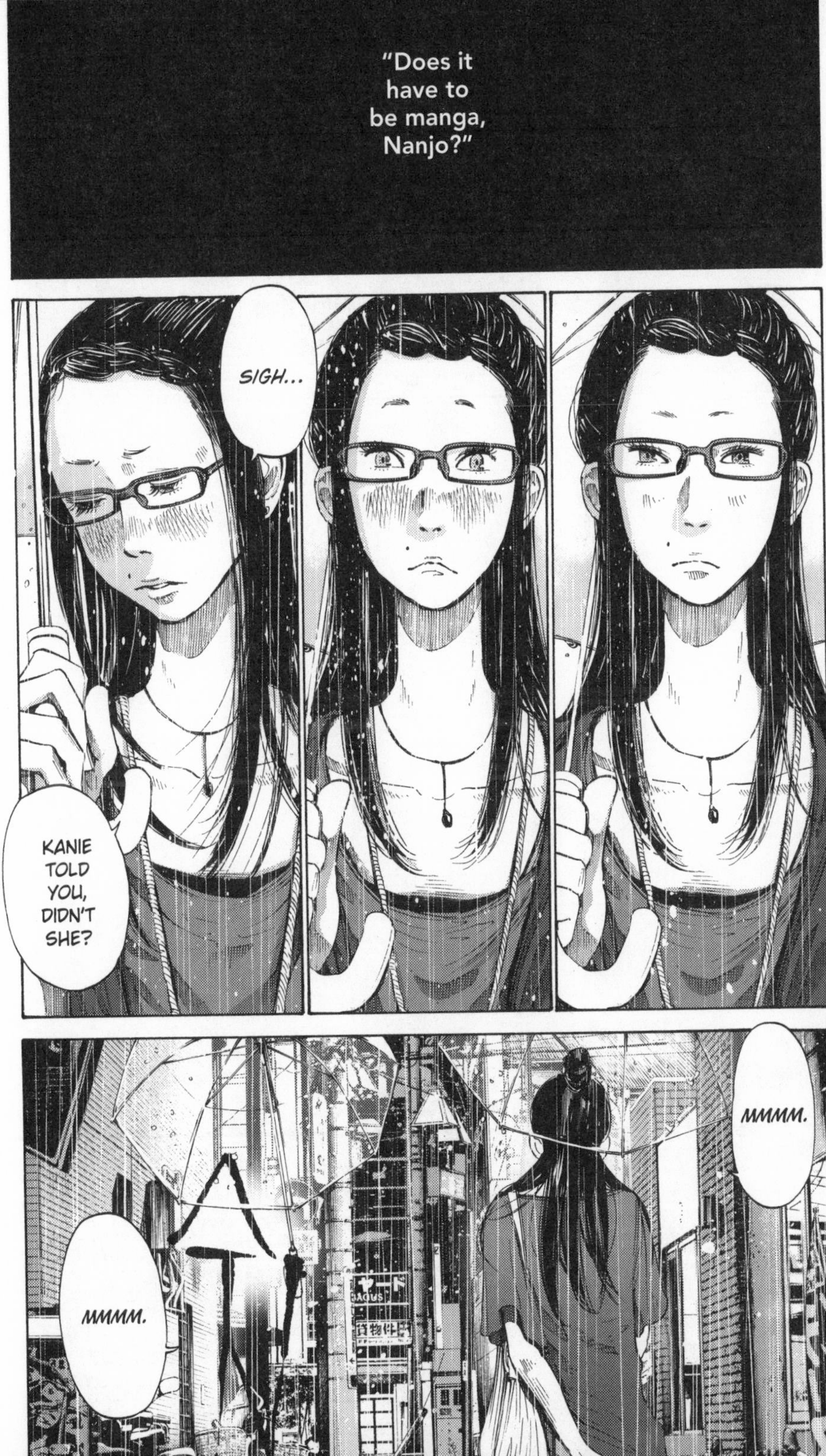
"Does it have to be manga, Nanjo?"
SIGH...
KANIE TOLD YOU, DIDN'T SHE?
MMMM.
MMMM.

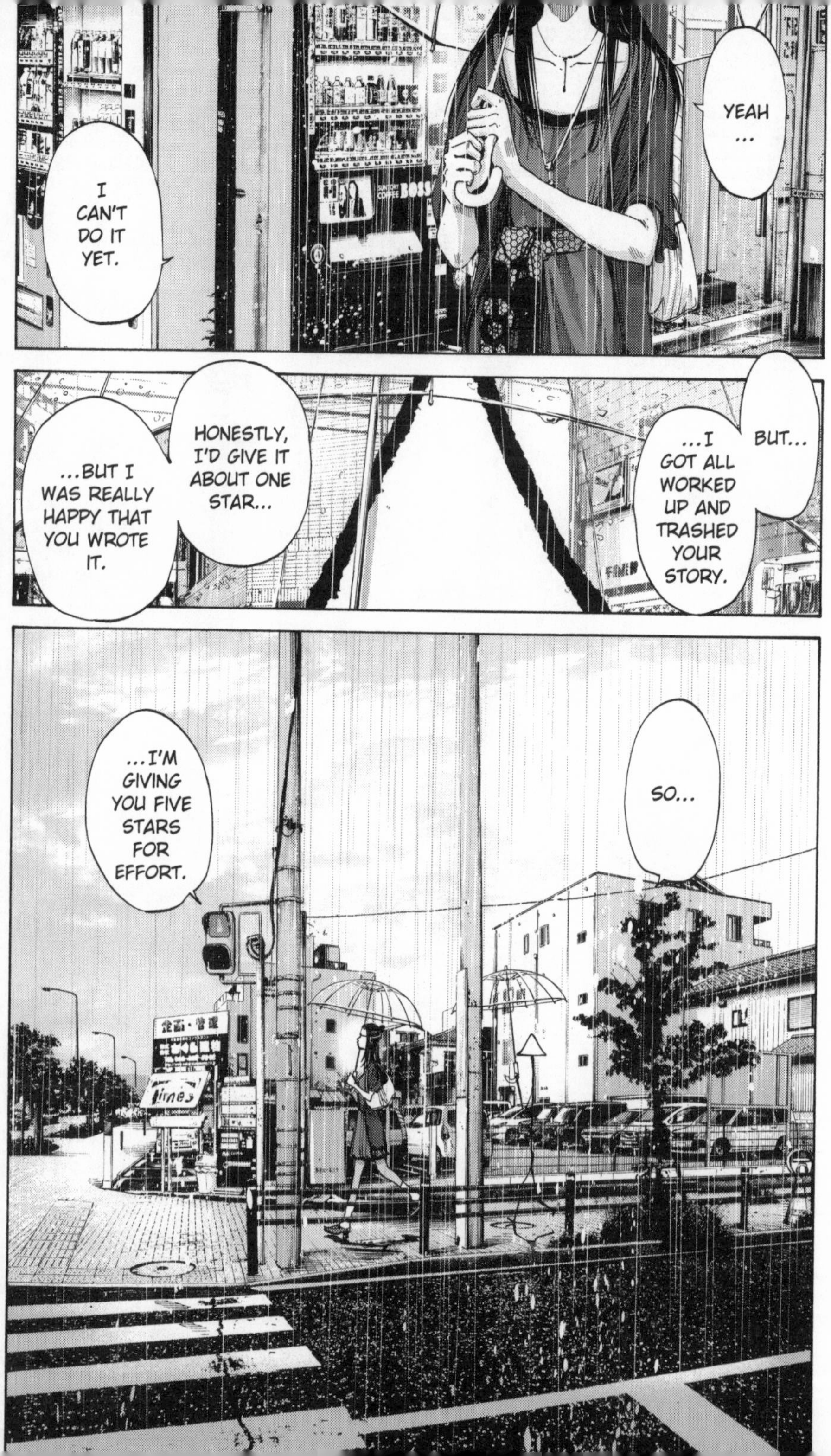
YEAH ...
I CAN'T DO IT YET.
BUT...
...I GOT ALL WORKED UP AND TRASHED YOUR STORY.
HONESTLY, I'D GIVE IT ABOUT ONE STAR...
...BUT I WAS REALLY HAPPY THAT YOU WROTE IT.
SO...
...I'M GIVING YOU FIVE STARS FOR EFFORT.

Chapter 83

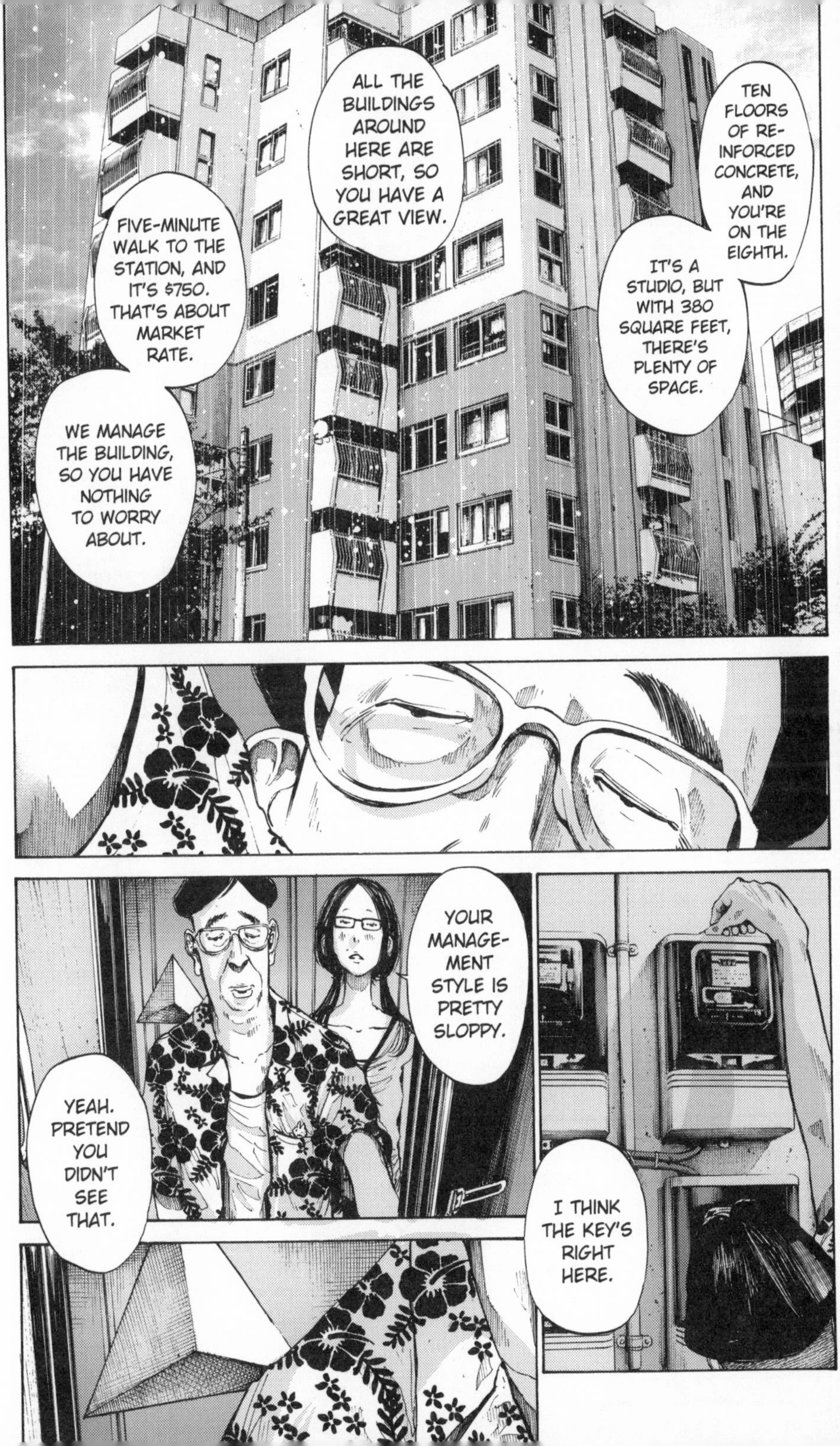

TEN FLOORS OF REINFORCED CONCRETE, AND YOU'RE ON THE EIGHTH.
IT'S A STUDIO, BUT WITH 380 SQUARE FEET, THERE'S PLENTY OF SPACE.
ALL THE BUILDINGS AROUND HERE ARE SHORT, SO YOU HAVE A GREAT VIEW.
FIVE-MINUTE WALK TO THE STATION, AND IT'S $750. THAT'S ABOUT MARKET RATE.
WE MANAGE THE BUILDING, SO YOU HAVE NOTHING TO WORRY ABOUT.
I THINK THE KEY'S RIGHT HERE.
YOUR MANAGEMENT STYLE IS PRETTY SLOPPY.
YEAH. PRETEND YOU DIDN'T SEE THAT.

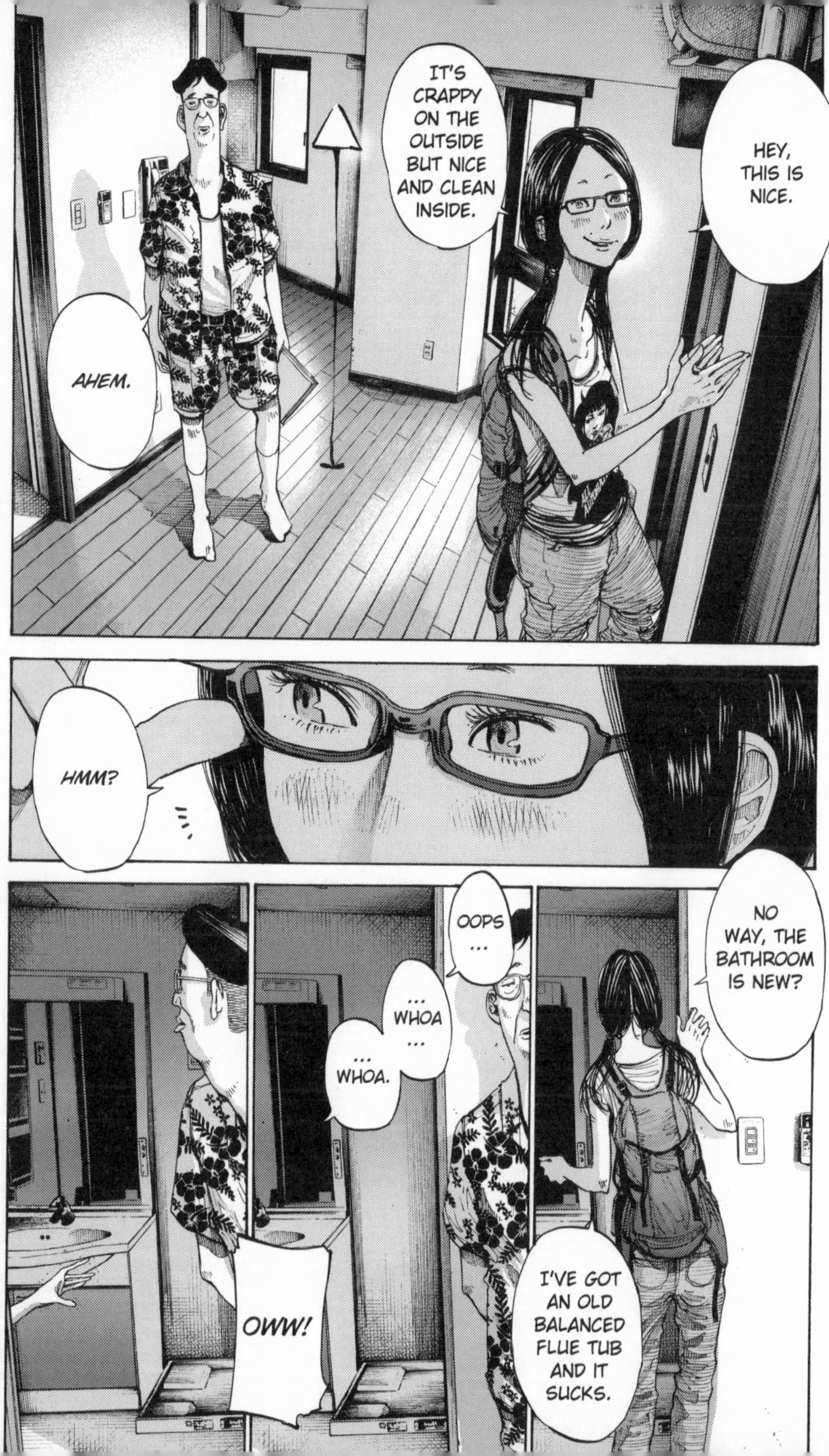
HEY, THIS IS NICE.
IT'S CRAPPY ON THE OUTSIDE BUT NICE AND CLEAN INSIDE.
AHEM.
HMM?
NO WAY, THE BATHROOM IS NEW?
I'VE GOT AN OLD BALANCED FLUE TUB AND IT SUCKS.
OOPS ...
... WHOA ...
... WHOA.
OWW!

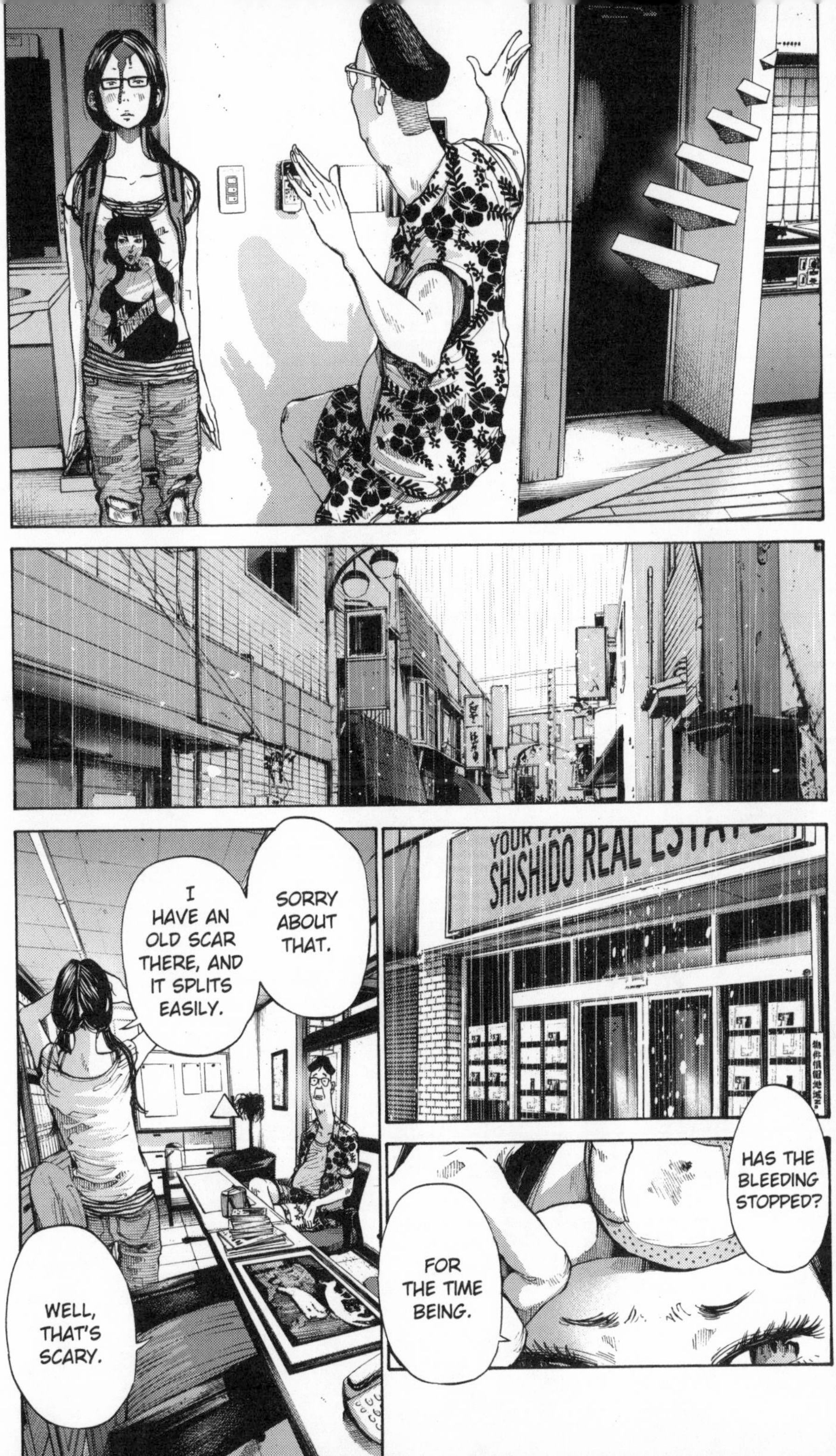
YOUR
SHISHIDO REAL ESTAT
HAS THE BLEEDING STOPPED?
FOR THE TIME BEING.
SORRY ABOUT THAT.
I HAVE AN OLD SCAR THERE, AND IT SPLITS EASILY.
WELL, THAT'S SCARY.

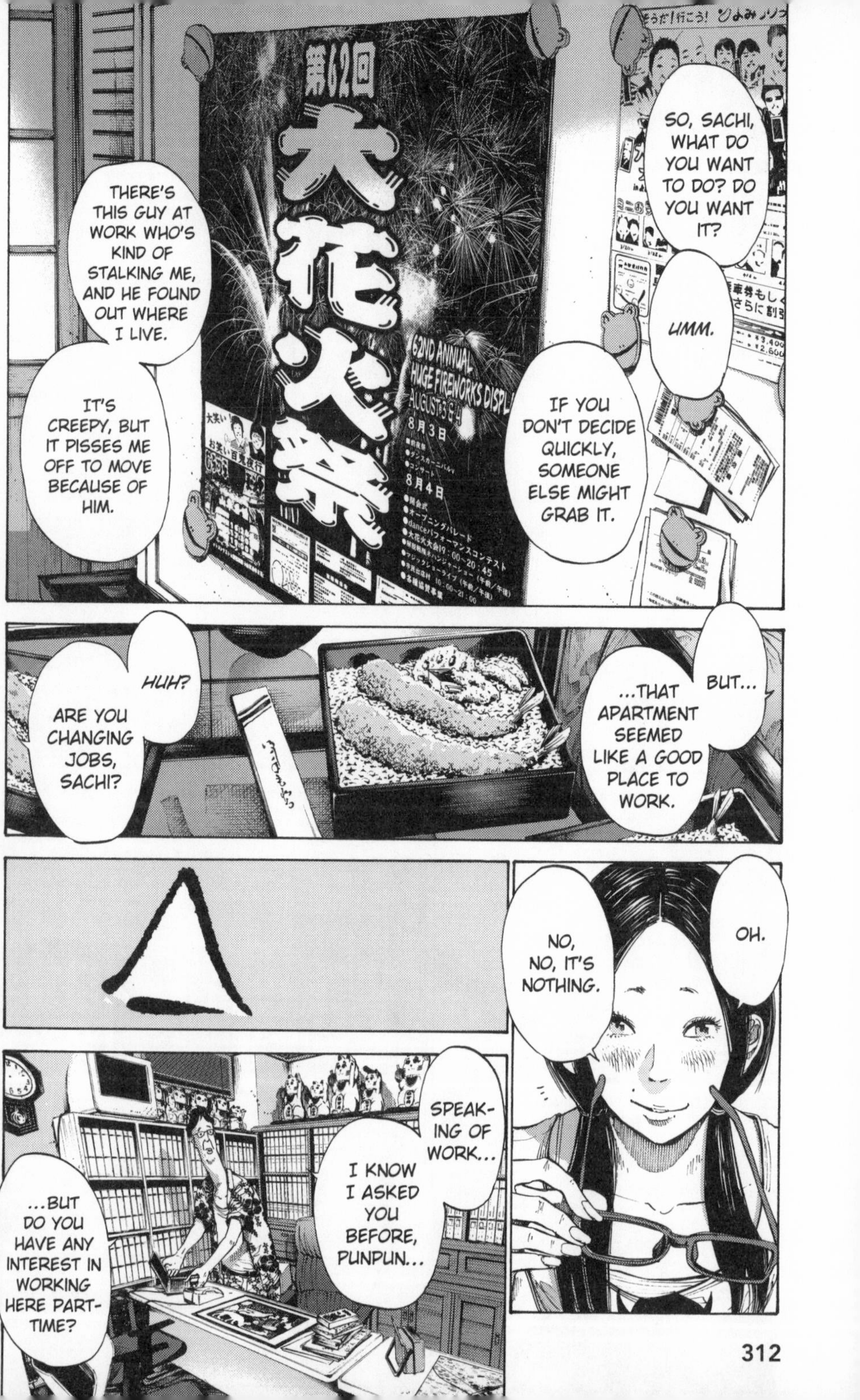

SO, SACHI, WHAT DO YOU WANT TO DO? DO YOU WANT IT?
UMM.
IF YOU DON'T DECIDE QUICKLY, SOMEONE ELSE MIGHT GRAB IT.
第62回
大花火祭
62ND ANNUAL HUGE FIREWORKS DISPL
AUGUST 3 & 4
8月3日
8月4日
THERE'S THIS GUY AT WORK WHO'S KIND OF STALKING ME, AND HE FOUND OUT WHERE I LIVE.
IT'S CREEPY, BUT IT PISSES ME OFF TO MOVE BECAUSE OF HIM.
BUT...
...THAT APARTMENT SEEMED LIKE A GOOD PLACE TO WORK.
HUH?
ARE YOU CHANGING JOBS, SACHI?
OH.
NO, NO, IT'S NOTHING.
SPEAKING OF WORK...
I KNOW I ASKED YOU BEFORE, PUNPUN...
...BUT DO YOU HAVE ANY INTEREST IN WORKING HERE PART-TIME?

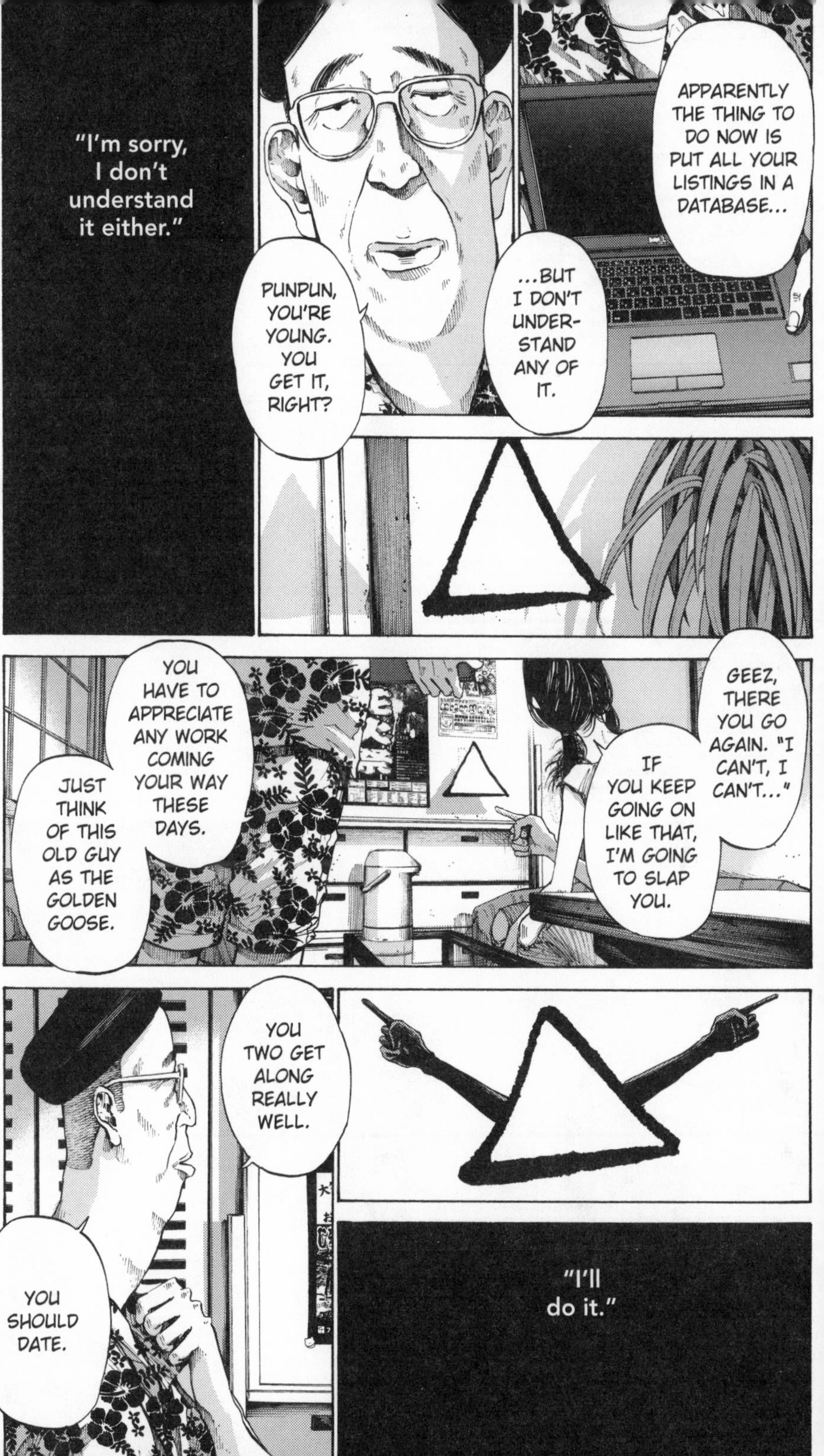
APPARENTLY THE THING TO DO NOW IS PUT ALL YOUR LISTINGS IN A DATABASE...
...BUT I DON'T UNDERSTAND ANY OF IT.
PUNPUN, YOU'RE YOUNG. YOU GET IT, RIGHT?
"I'm sorry, I don't understand it either."
GEEZ, THERE YOU GO AGAIN. "I CAN'T, I CAN'T..."
IF YOU KEEP GOING ON LIKE THAT, I'M GOING TO SLAP YOU.
YOU HAVE TO APPRECIATE ANY WORK COMING YOUR WAY THESE DAYS.
JUST THINK OF THIS OLD GUY AS THE GOLDEN GOOSE.
"I'll do it."
YOU TWO GET ALONG REALLY WELL.
YOU SHOULD DATE.

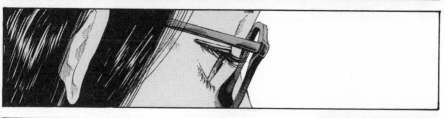

NO
WAY.

HEY!

OH.

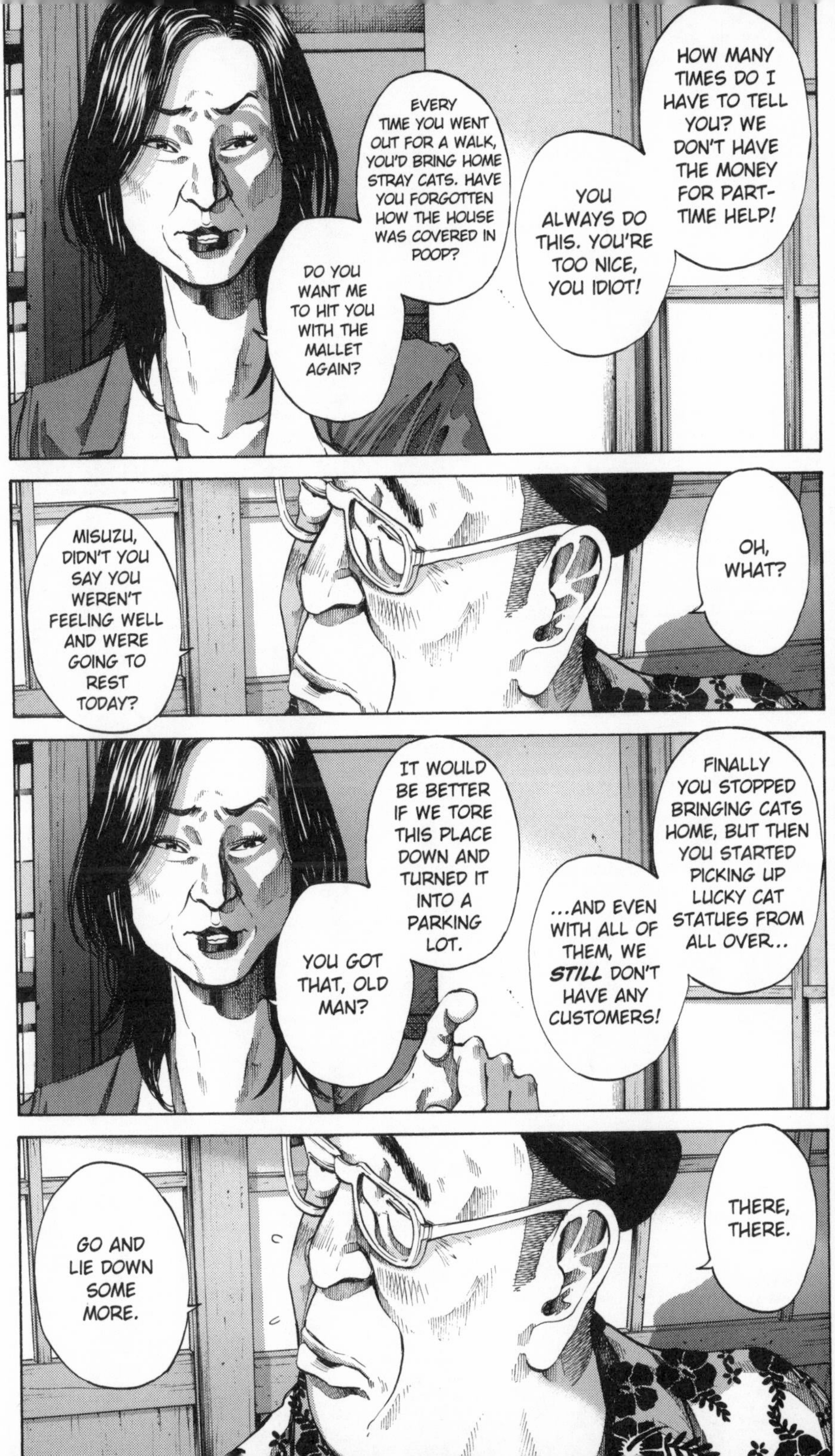
HOW MANY TIMES DO I HAVE TO TELL YOU? WE DON'T HAVE THE MONEY FOR PART-TIME HELP!
YOU ALWAYS DO THIS. YOU'RE TOO NICE, YOU IDIOT!
EVERY TIME YOU WENT OUT FOR A WALK, YOU'D BRING HOME STRAY CATS. HAVE YOU FORGOTTEN HOW THE HOUSE WAS COVERED IN POOP?
DO YOU WANT ME TO HIT YOU WITH THE MALLET AGAIN?
OH, WHAT?
MISUZU, DIDN'T YOU SAY YOU WEREN'T FEELING WELL AND WERE GOING TO REST TODAY?
FINALLY YOU STOPPED BRINGING CATS HOME, BUT THEN YOU STARTED PICKING UP LUCKY CAT STATUES FROM ALL OVER...
...AND EVEN WITH ALL OF THEM, WE *STILL* DON'T HAVE ANY CUSTOMERS!
IT WOULD BE BETTER IF WE TORE THIS PLACE DOWN AND TURNED IT INTO A PARKING LOT.
YOU GOT THAT, OLD MAN?
THERE, THERE.
GO AND LIE DOWN SOME MORE.

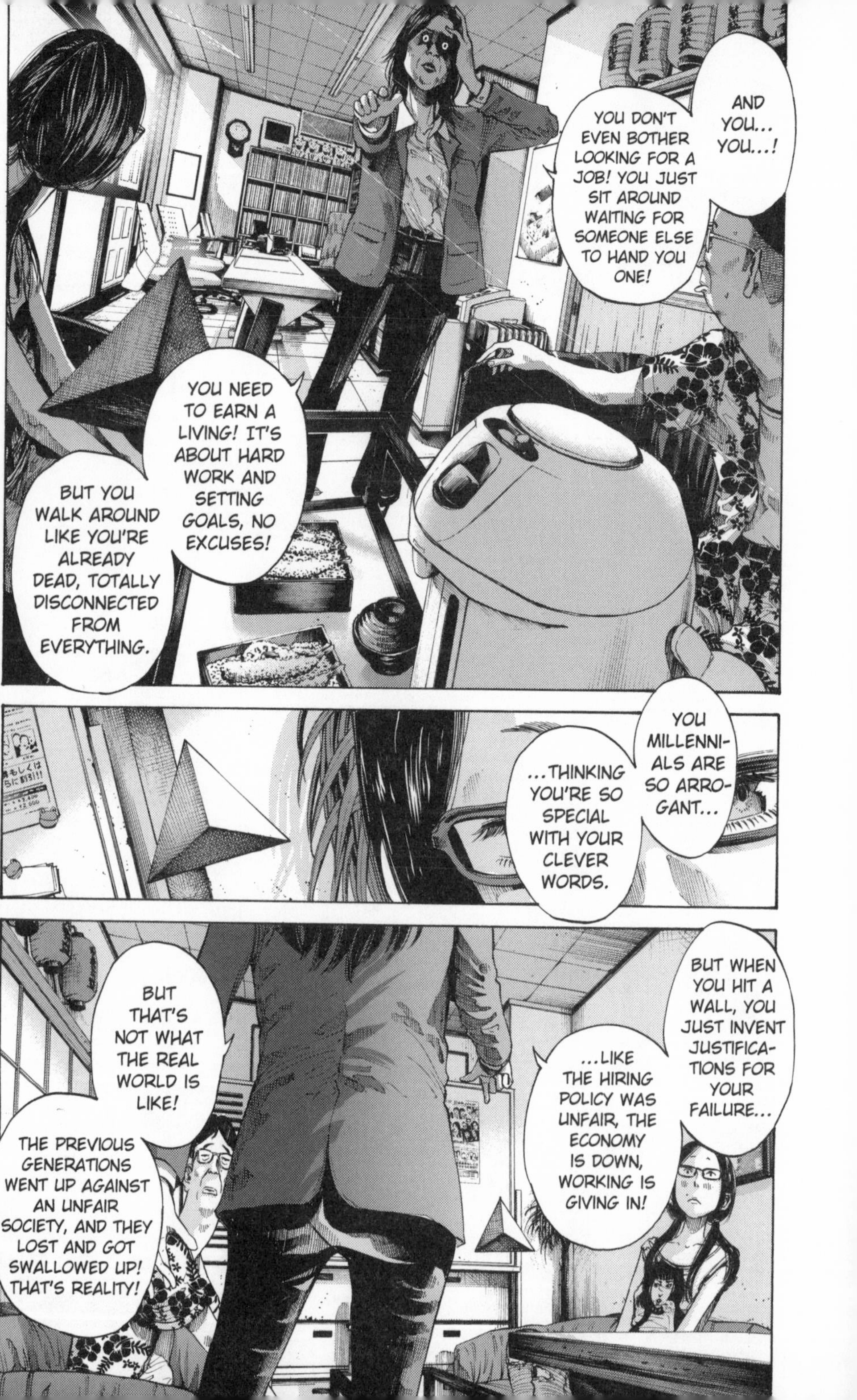
AND YOU... YOU...!
YOU DON'T EVEN BOTHER LOOKING FOR A JOB! YOU JUST SIT AROUND WAITING FOR SOMEONE ELSE TO HAND YOU ONE!
YOU NEED TO EARN A LIVING! IT'S ABOUT HARD WORK AND SETTING GOALS, NO EXCUSES!
BUT YOU WALK AROUND LIKE YOU'RE ALREADY DEAD, TOTALLY DISCONNECTED FROM EVERYTHING.
YOU MILLENNI-ALS ARE SO ARRO-GANT...
...THINKING YOU'RE SO SPECIAL WITH YOUR CLEVER WORDS.
BUT WHEN YOU HIT A WALL, YOU JUST INVENT JUSTIFICA-TIONS FOR YOUR FAILURE...
...LIKE THE HIRING POLICY WAS UNFAIR, THE ECONOMY IS DOWN, WORKING IS GIVING IN!
BUT THAT'S NOT WHAT THE REAL WORLD IS LIKE!
THE PREVIOUS GENERATIONS WENT UP AGAINST AN UNFAIR SOCIETY, AND THEY LOST AND GOT SWALLOWED UP! THAT'S REALITY!

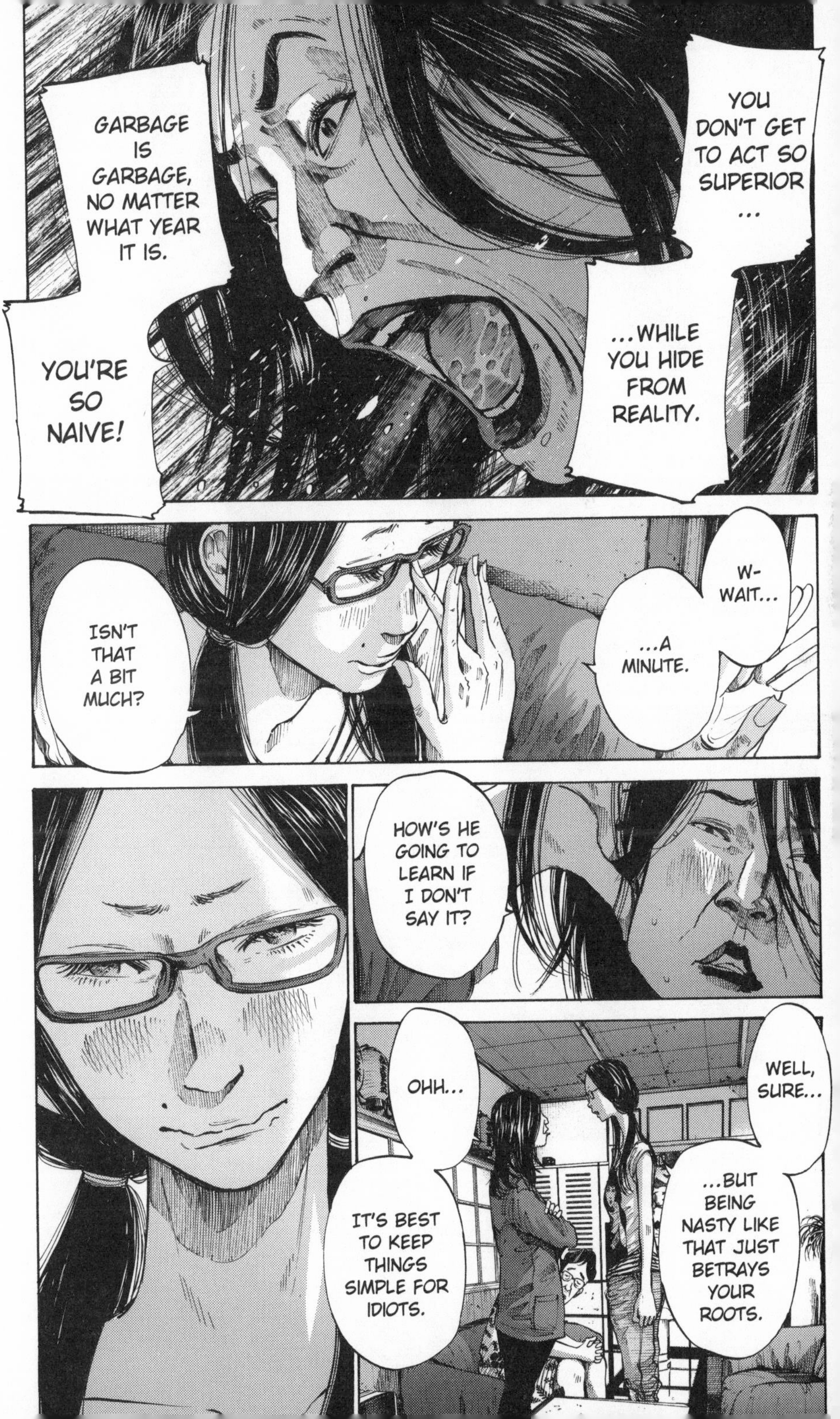
YOU DON'T GET TO ACT SO SUPERIOR ...
...WHILE YOU HIDE FROM REALITY.
GARBAGE IS GARBAGE, NO MATTER WHAT YEAR IT IS.
YOU'RE SO NAIVE!
W- WAIT...
...A MINUTE.
ISN'T THAT A BIT MUCH?
HOW'S HE GOING TO LEARN IF I DON'T SAY IT?
WELL, SURE...
...BUT BEING NASTY LIKE THAT JUST BETRAYS YOUR ROOTS.
OHH...
IT'S BEST TO KEEP THINGS SIMPLE FOR IDIOTS.

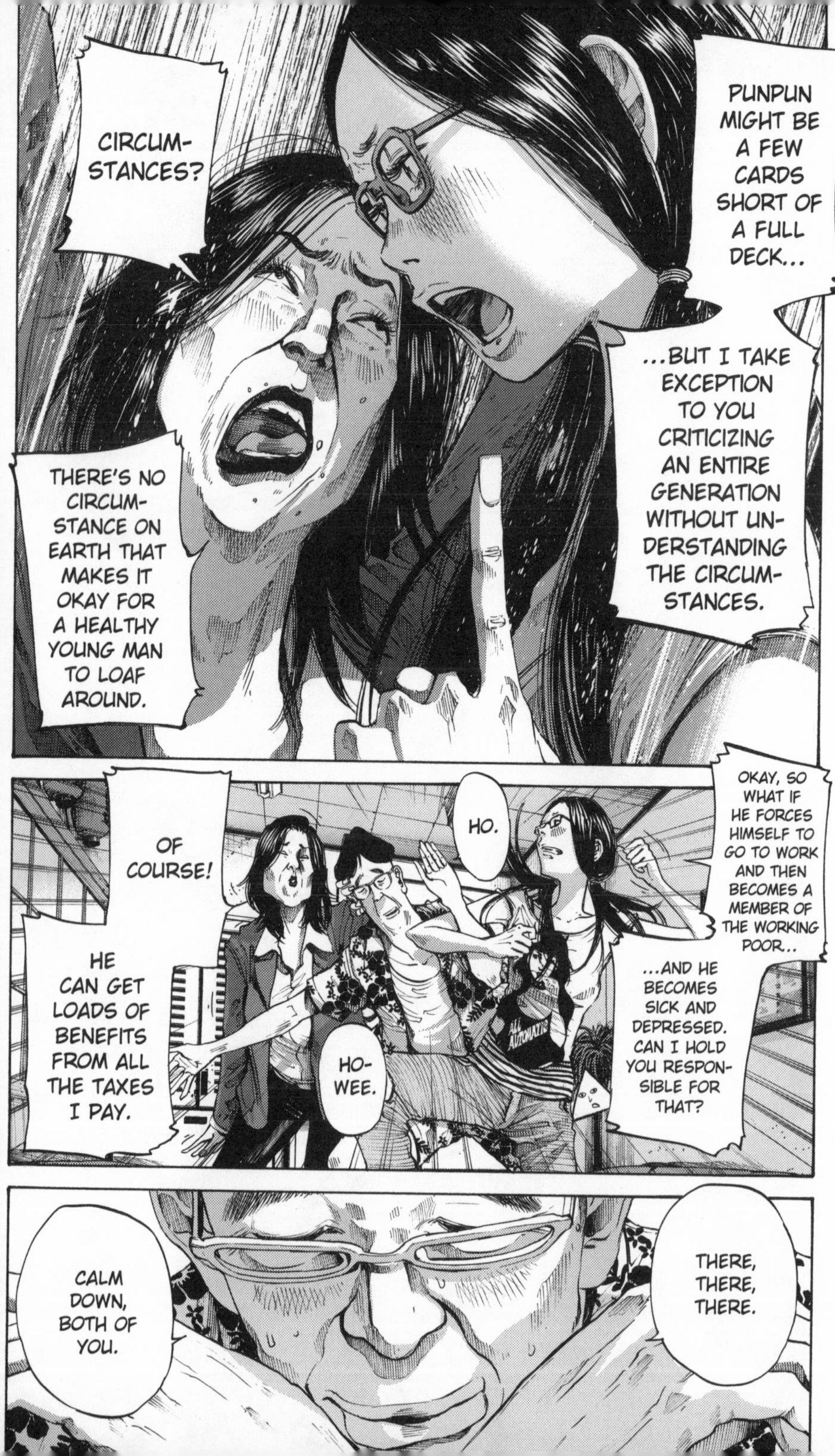
PUNPUN MIGHT BE A FEW CARDS SHORT OF A FULL DECK...
CIRCUM-STANCES?
...BUT I TAKE EXCEPTION TO YOU CRITICIZING AN ENTIRE GENERATION WITHOUT UN-DERSTANDING THE CIRCUM-STANCES.
THERE'S NO CIRCUM-STANCE ON EARTH THAT MAKES IT OKAY FOR A HEALTHY YOUNG MAN TO LOAF AROUND.
OKAY, SO WHAT IF HE FORCES HIMSELF TO GO TO WORK AND THEN BECOMES A MEMBER OF THE WORKING POOR...
HO.
OF COURSE!
...AND HE BECOMES SICK AND DEPRESSED. CAN I HOLD YOU RESPON-SIBLE FOR THAT?
HO-WEE.
HE CAN GET LOADS OF BENEFITS FROM ALL THE TAXES I PAY.
ALL AUTOMATIC
THERE, THERE, THERE.
CALM DOWN, BOTH OF YOU.

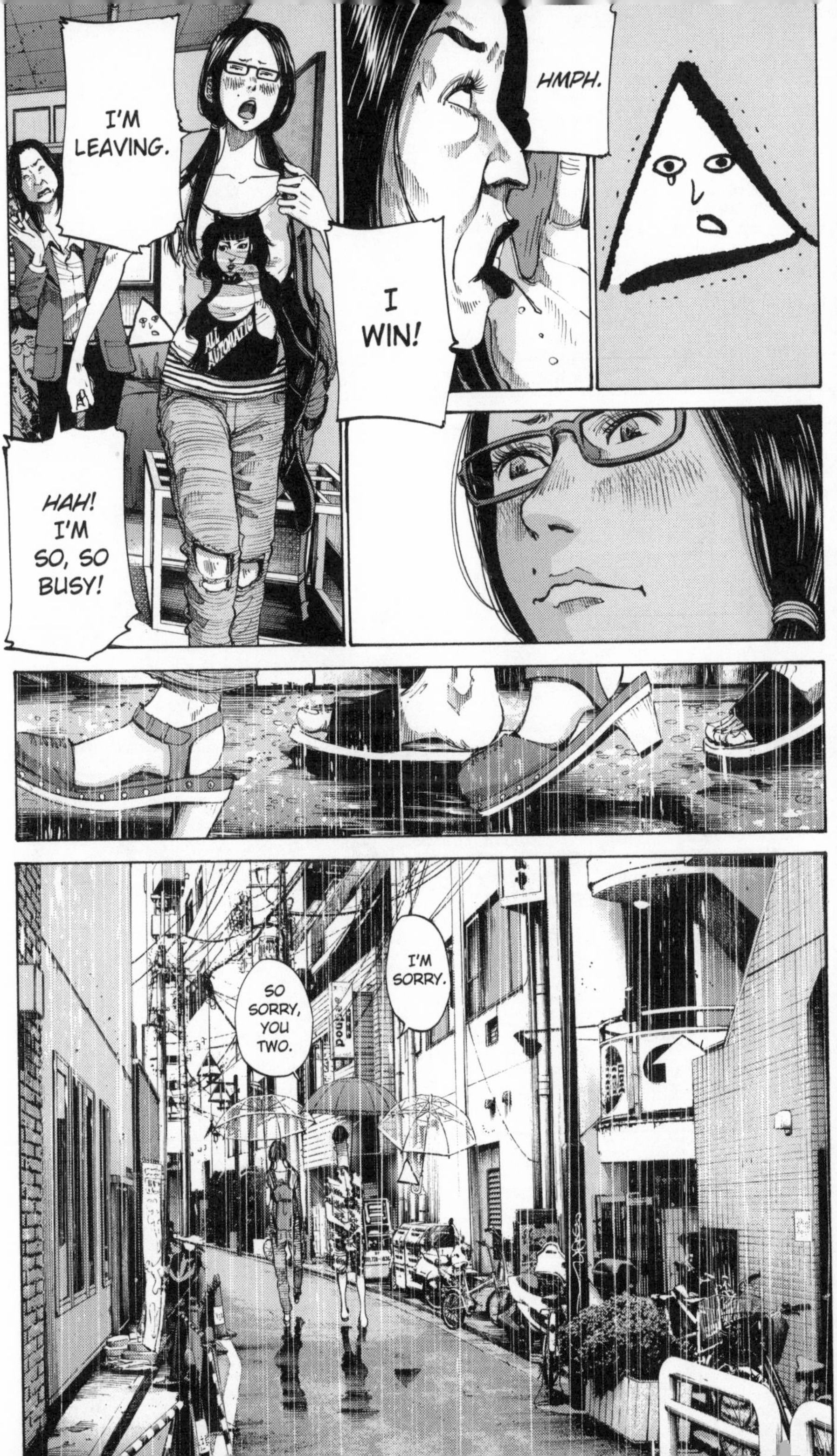
HMPH.
I WIN!
I'M LEAVING.
HAH! I'M SO, SO BUSY!
I'M SORRY.
SO SORRY, YOU TWO.

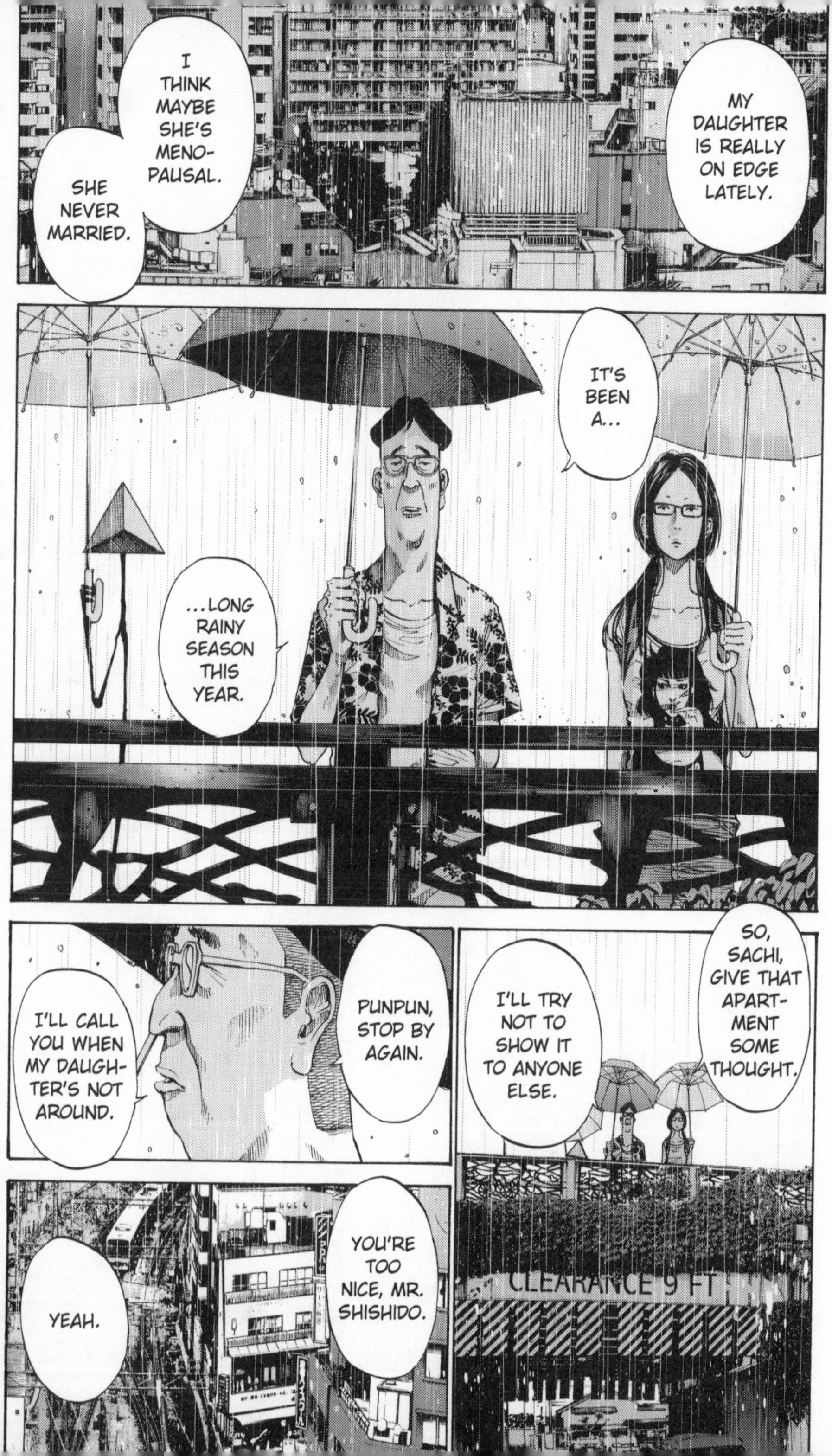
MY DAUGHTER IS REALLY ON EDGE LATELY.
I THINK MAYBE SHE'S MENO-PAUSAL.
SHE NEVER MARRIED.
IT'S BEEN A...
...LONG RAINY SEASON THIS YEAR.
SO, SACHI, GIVE THAT APART-MENT SOME THOUGHT.
I'LL TRY NOT TO SHOW IT TO ANYONE ELSE.
CLEARANCE 9 FT
PUNPUN, STOP BY AGAIN.
I'LL CALL YOU WHEN MY DAUGH-TER'S NOT AROUND.
YOU'RE TOO NICE, MR. SHISHIDO.
YEAH.

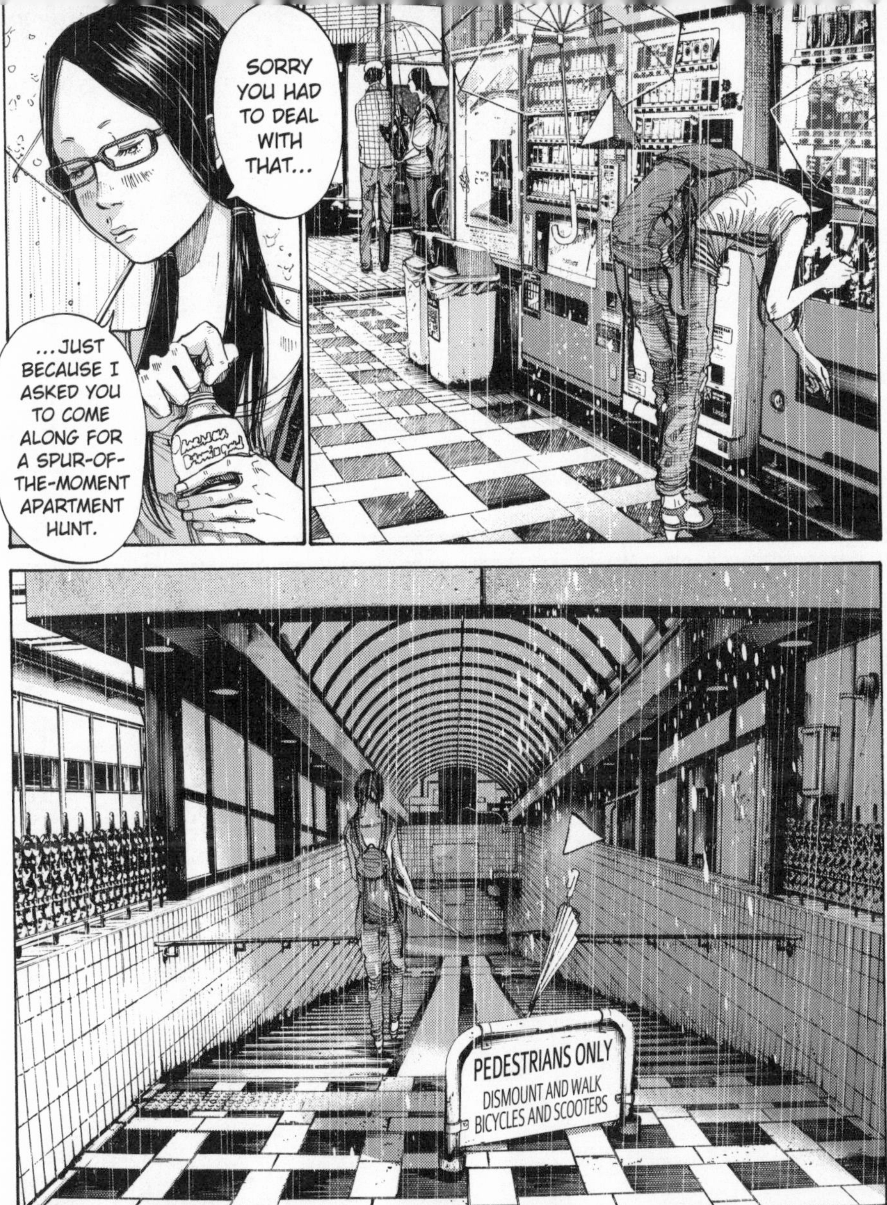
SORRY YOU HAD TO DEAL WITH THAT...
...JUST BECAUSE I ASKED YOU TO COME ALONG FOR A SPUR-OF-THE-MOMENT APARTMENT HUNT.
PEDESTRIANS ONLY
DISMOUNT AND WALK BICYCLES AND SCOOTERS

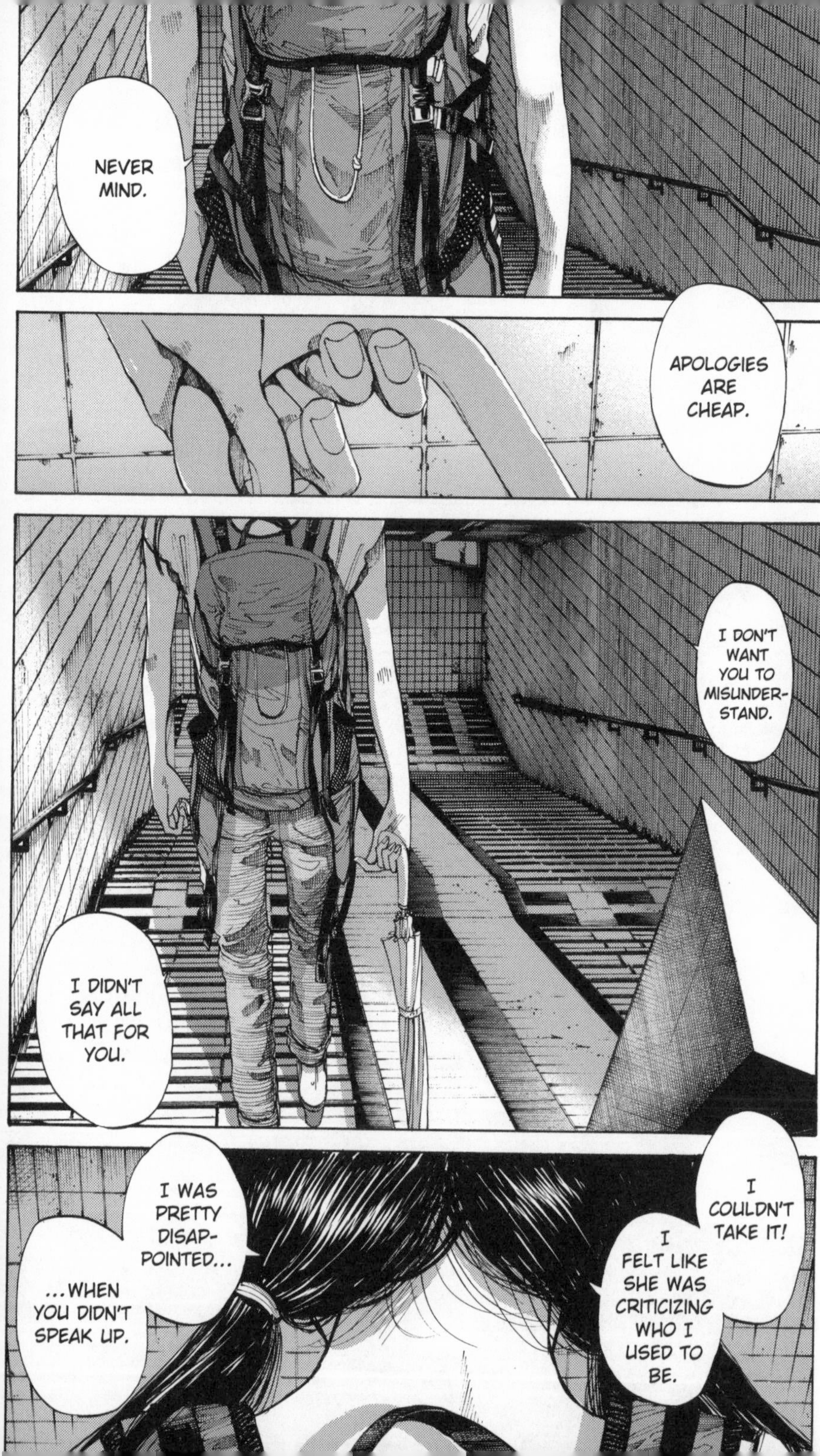
NEVER MIND.
APOLOGIES ARE CHEAP.
I DON'T WANT YOU TO MISUNDER-STAND.
I DIDN'T SAY ALL THAT FOR YOU.
I COULDN'T TAKE IT!
I FELT LIKE SHE WAS CRITICIZING WHO I USED TO BE.
I WAS PRETTY DISAP-POINTED...
...WHEN YOU DIDN'T SPEAK UP.

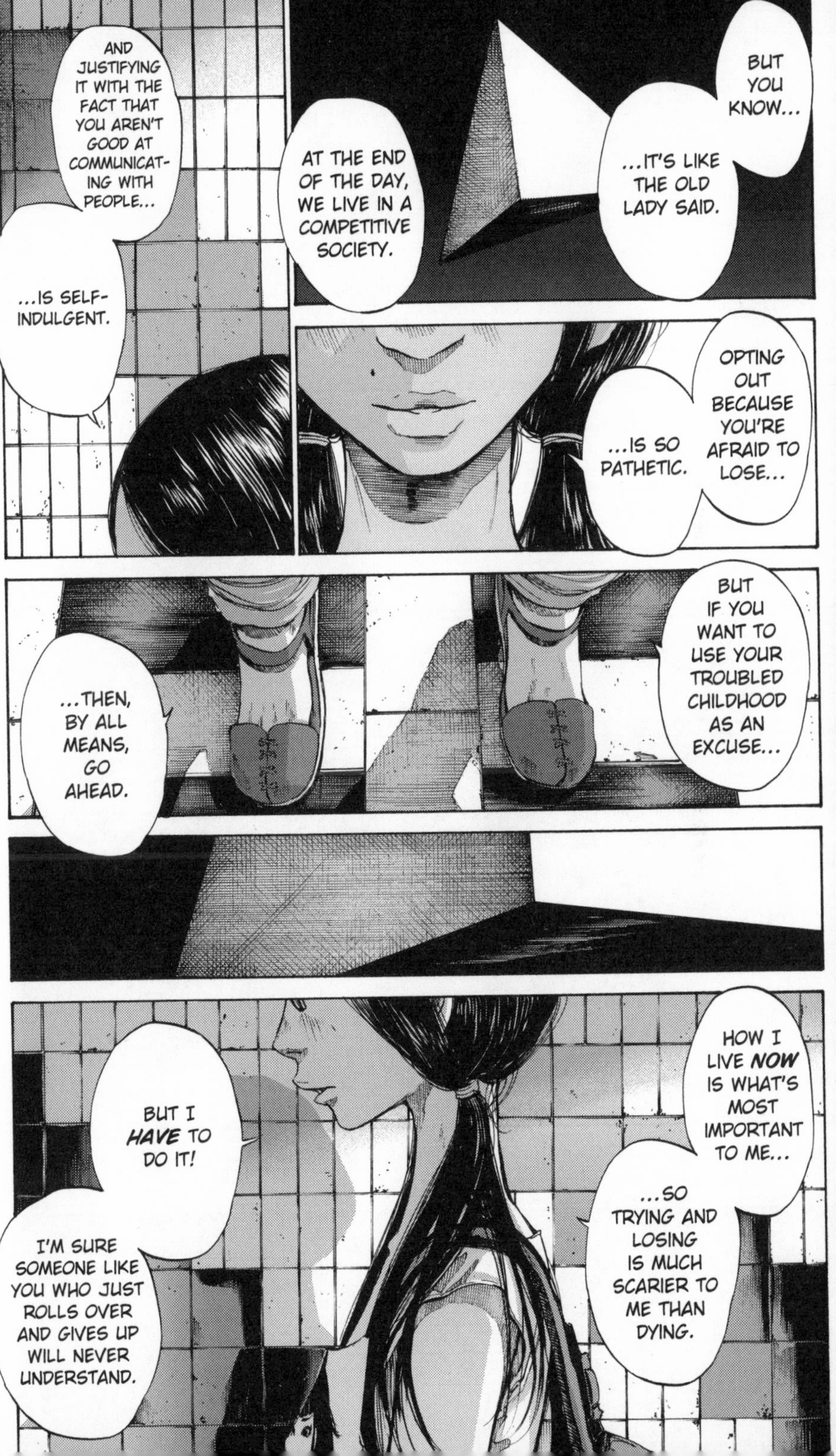
BUT YOU KNOW...
...IT'S LIKE THE OLD LADY SAID.
AT THE END OF THE DAY, WE LIVE IN A COMPETITIVE SOCIETY.
OPTING OUT BECAUSE YOU'RE AFRAID TO LOSE...
...IS SO PATHETIC.
AND JUSTIFYING IT WITH THE FACT THAT YOU AREN'T GOOD AT COMMUNICATING WITH PEOPLE...
...IS SELF-INDULGENT.
BUT IF YOU WANT TO USE YOUR TROUBLED CHILDHOOD AS AN EXCUSE...
...THEN, BY ALL MEANS, GO AHEAD.
HOW I LIVE *NOW* IS WHAT'S MOST IMPORTANT TO ME...
...SO TRYING AND LOSING IS MUCH SCARIER TO ME THAN DYING.
BUT I *HAVE* TO DO IT!
I'M SURE SOMEONE LIKE YOU WHO JUST ROLLS OVER AND GIVES UP WILL NEVER UNDERSTAND.

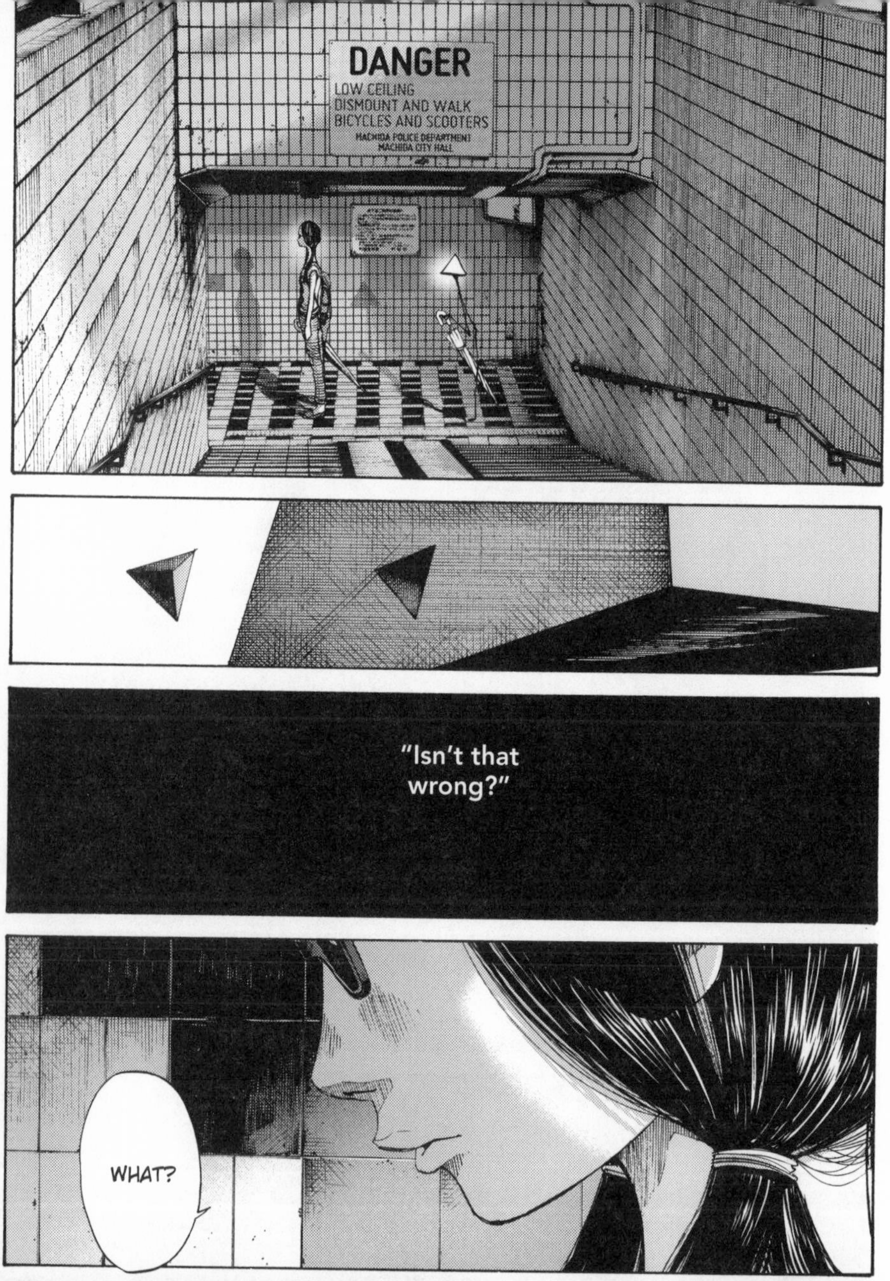
DANGER
LOW CEILING
DISMOUNT AND WALK
BICYCLES AND SCOOTERS
MACHIDA POLICE DEPARTMENT
MACHIDA CITY HALL
"Isn't that wrong?"
WHAT?

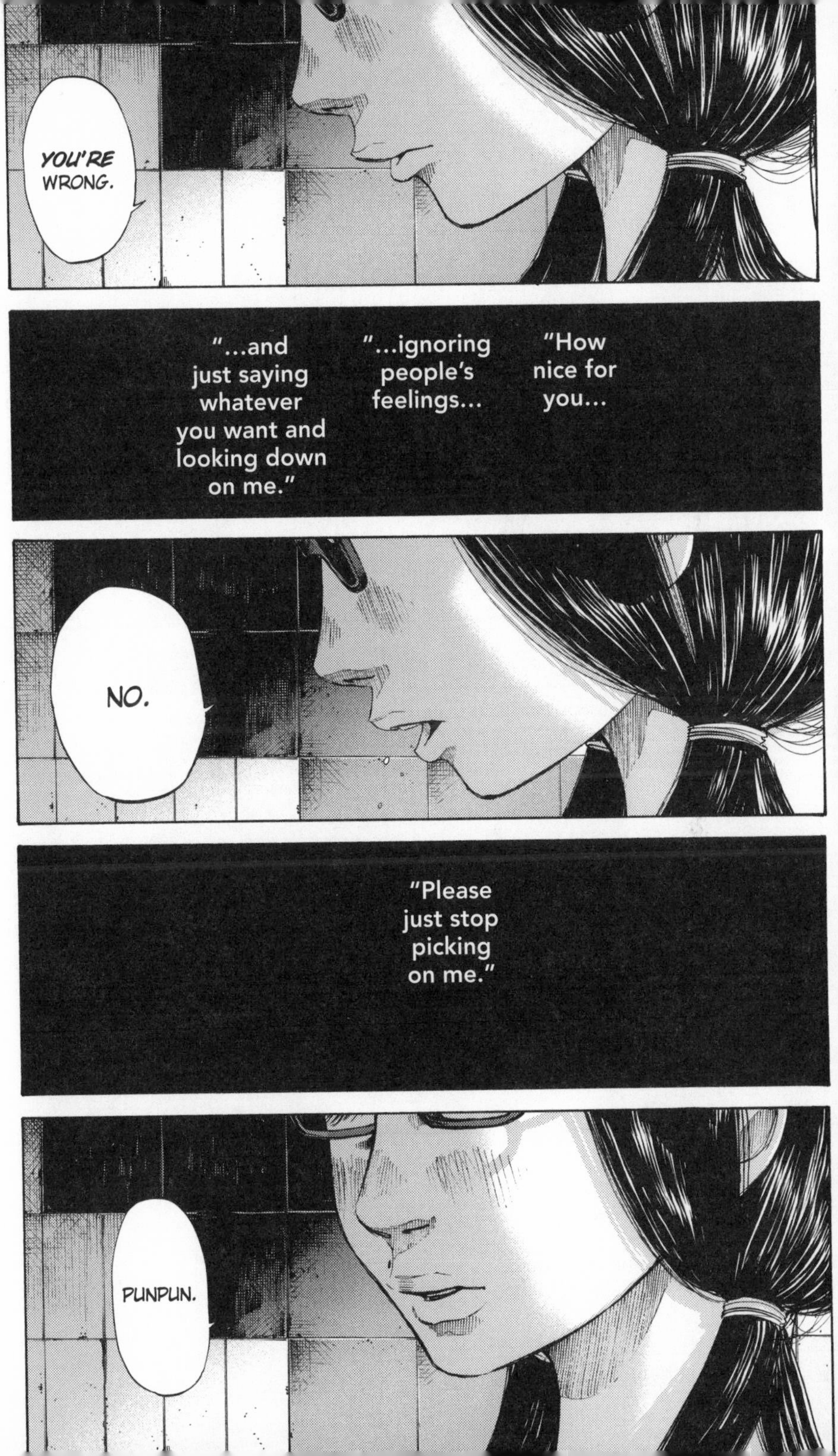
YOU'RE WRONG.
"How nice for you...
"...ignoring people's feelings...
"...and just saying whatever you want and looking down on me."
NO.
"Please just stop picking on me."
PUNPUN.

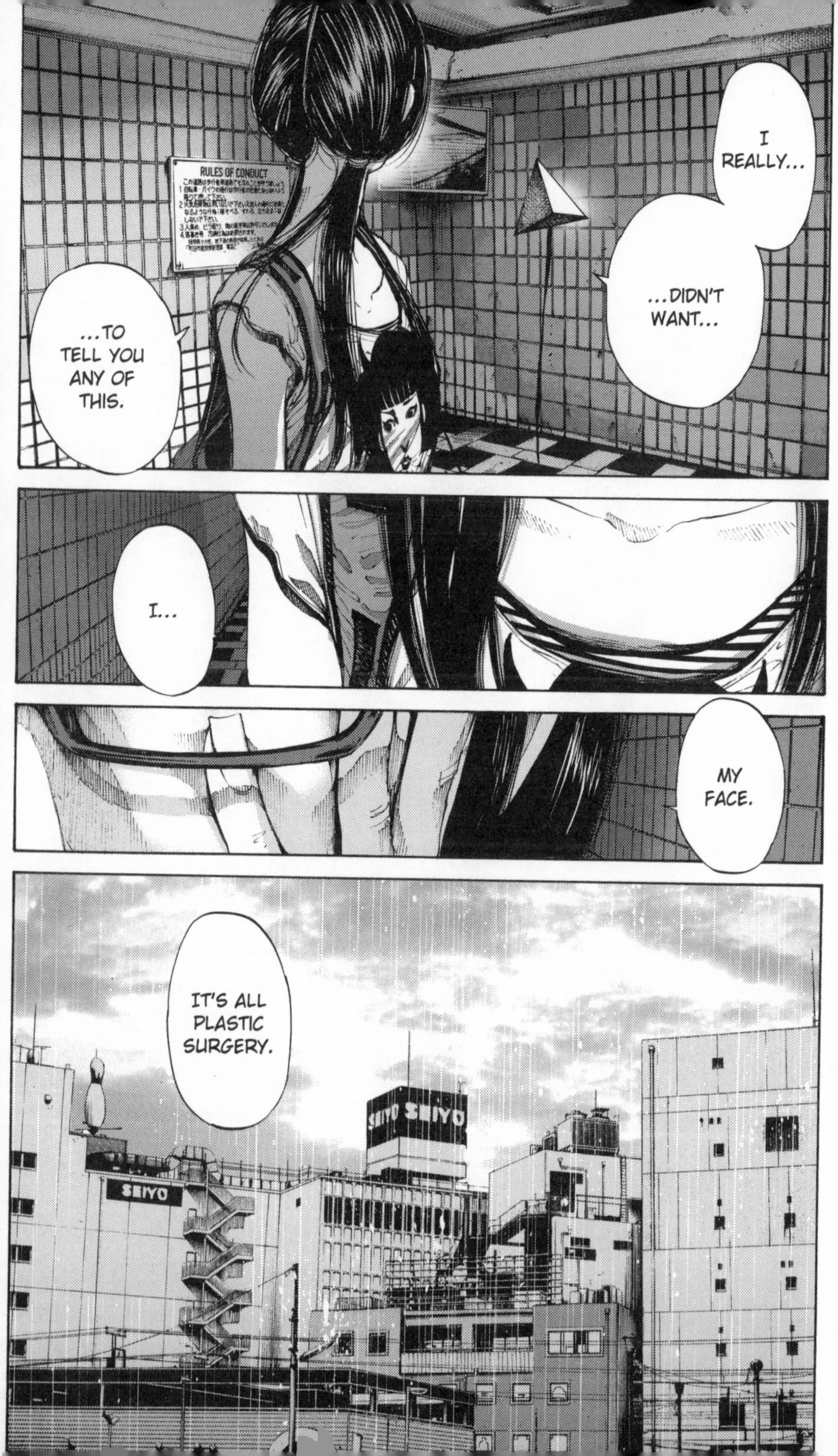
I REALLY...
...DIDN'T WANT...
RULES OF CONDUCT
...TO TELL YOU ANY OF THIS.
I...
MY FACE.
IT'S ALL PLASTIC SURGERY.
SEIYO SEIYO
SEIYO

Chapter 84

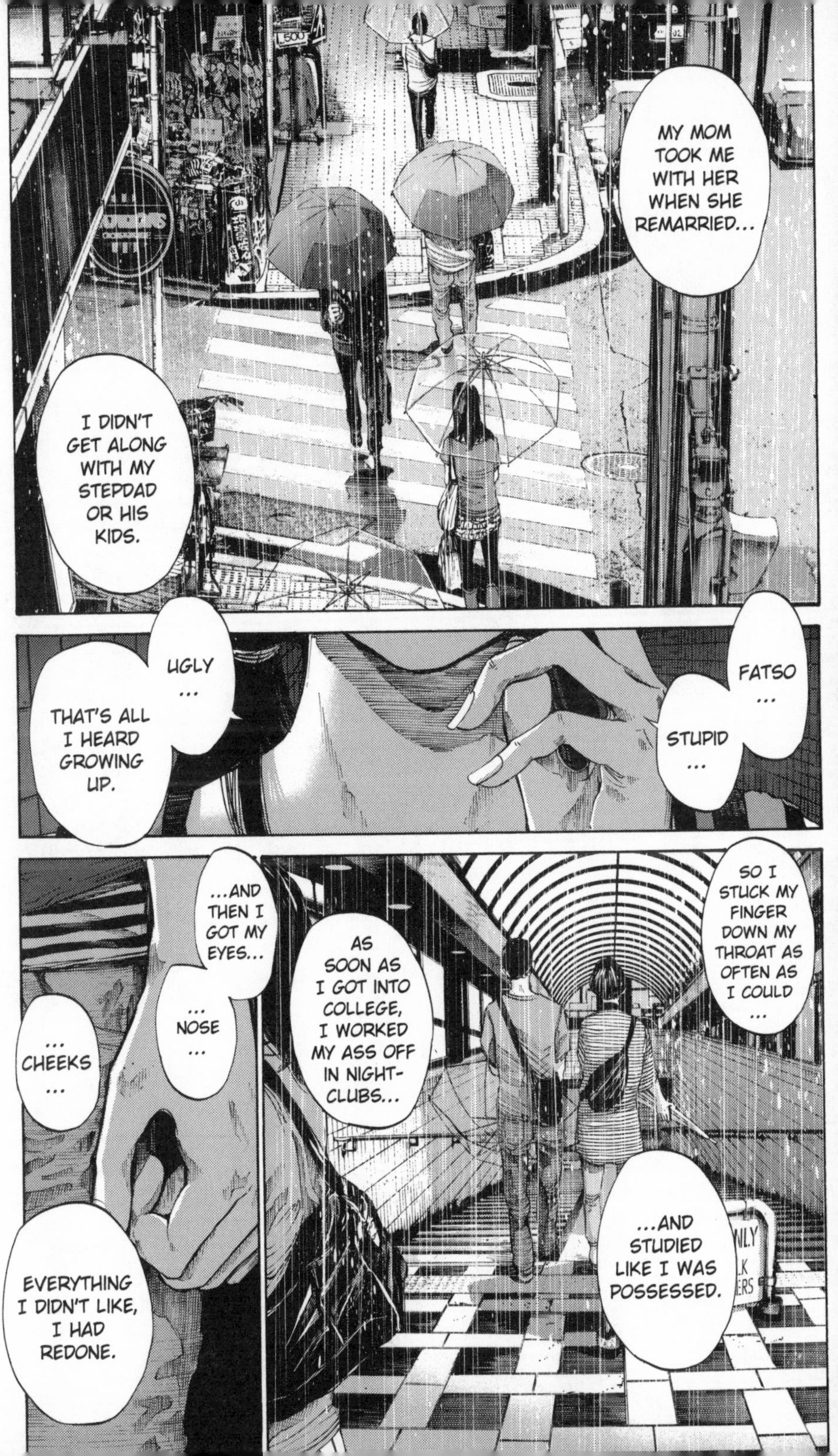
MY MOM TOOK ME WITH HER WHEN SHE REMARRIED...
I DIDN'T GET ALONG WITH MY STEPDAD OR HIS KIDS.
FATSO ...
STUPID ...
UGLY ...
THAT'S ALL I HEARD GROWING UP.
SO I STUCK MY FINGER DOWN MY THROAT AS OFTEN AS I COULD ...
AS SOON AS I GOT INTO COLLEGE, I WORKED MY ASS OFF IN NIGHT-CLUBS...
...AND STUDIED LIKE I WAS POSSESSED.
...AND THEN I GOT MY EYES...
... NOSE ...
... CHEEKS ...
EVERYTHING I DIDN'T LIKE, I HAD REDONE.

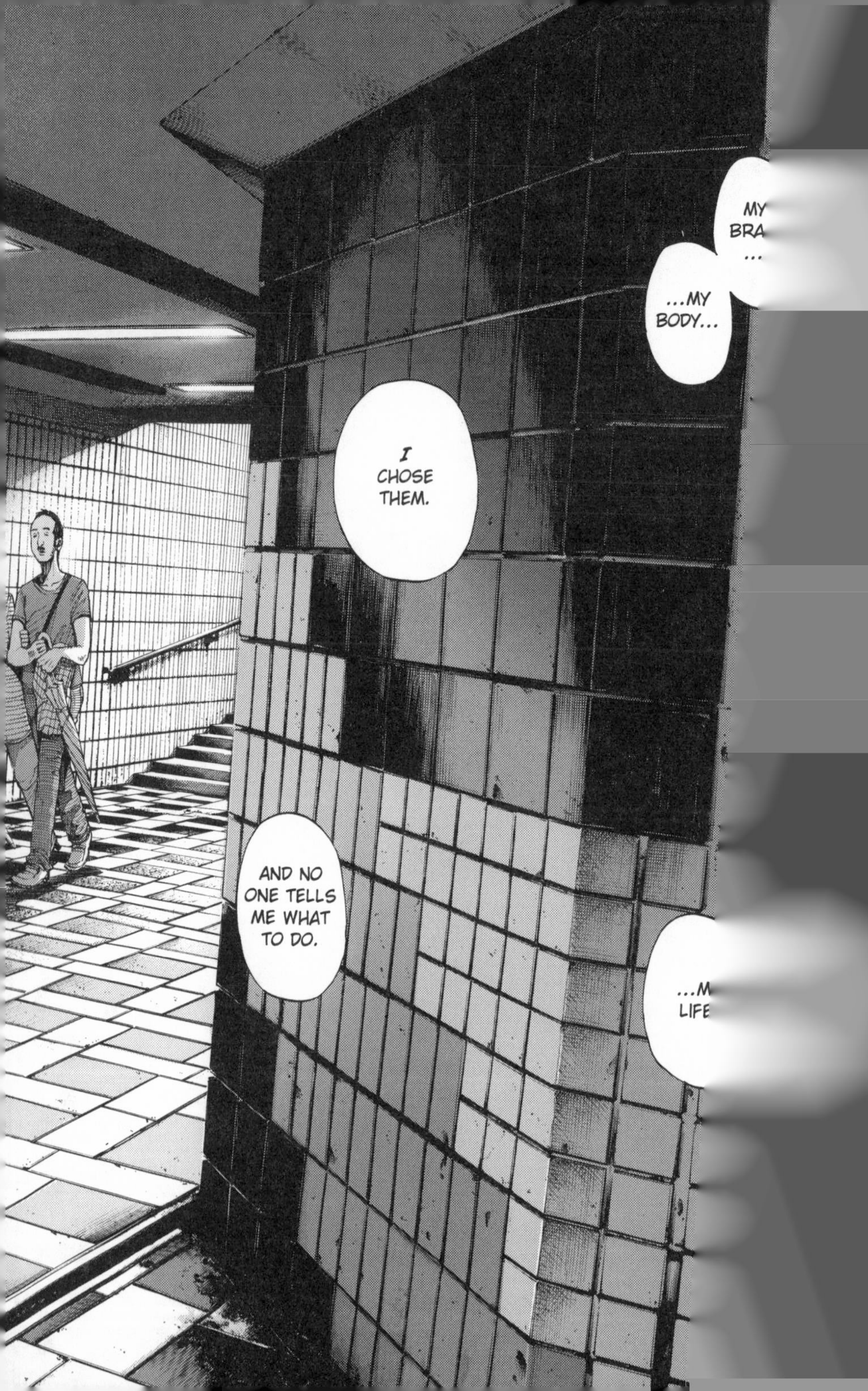
MY BRA...
...MY BODY...
I CHOSE THEM.
...M LIFE
AND NO ONE TELLS ME WHAT TO DO.

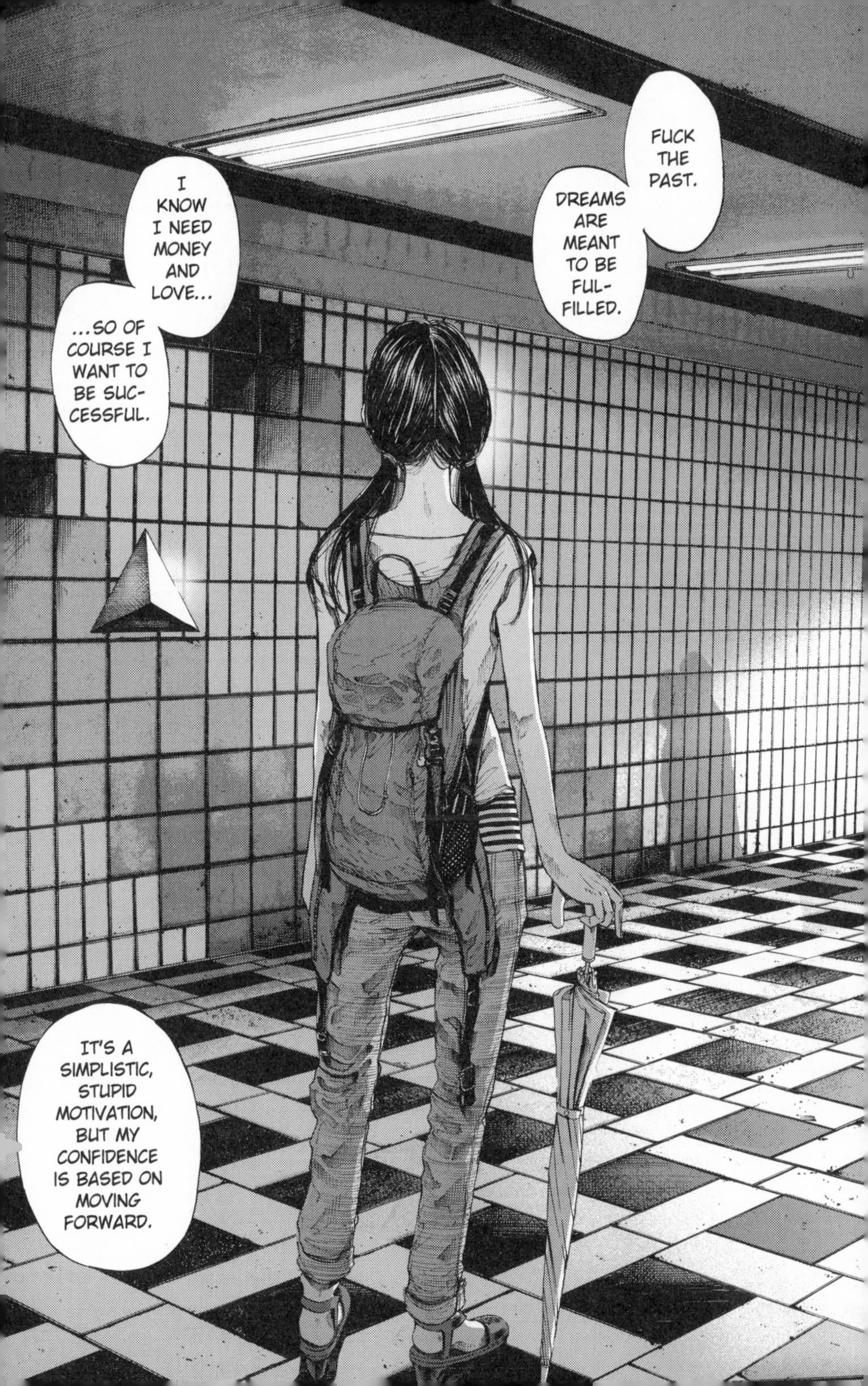
FUCK THE PAST.
DREAMS ARE MEANT TO BE FULFILLED.
I KNOW I NEED MONEY AND LOVE...
...SO OF COURSE I WANT TO BE SUCCESSFUL.
IT'S A SIMPLISTIC, STUPID MOTIVATION, BUT MY CONFIDENCE IS BASED ON MOVING FORWARD.

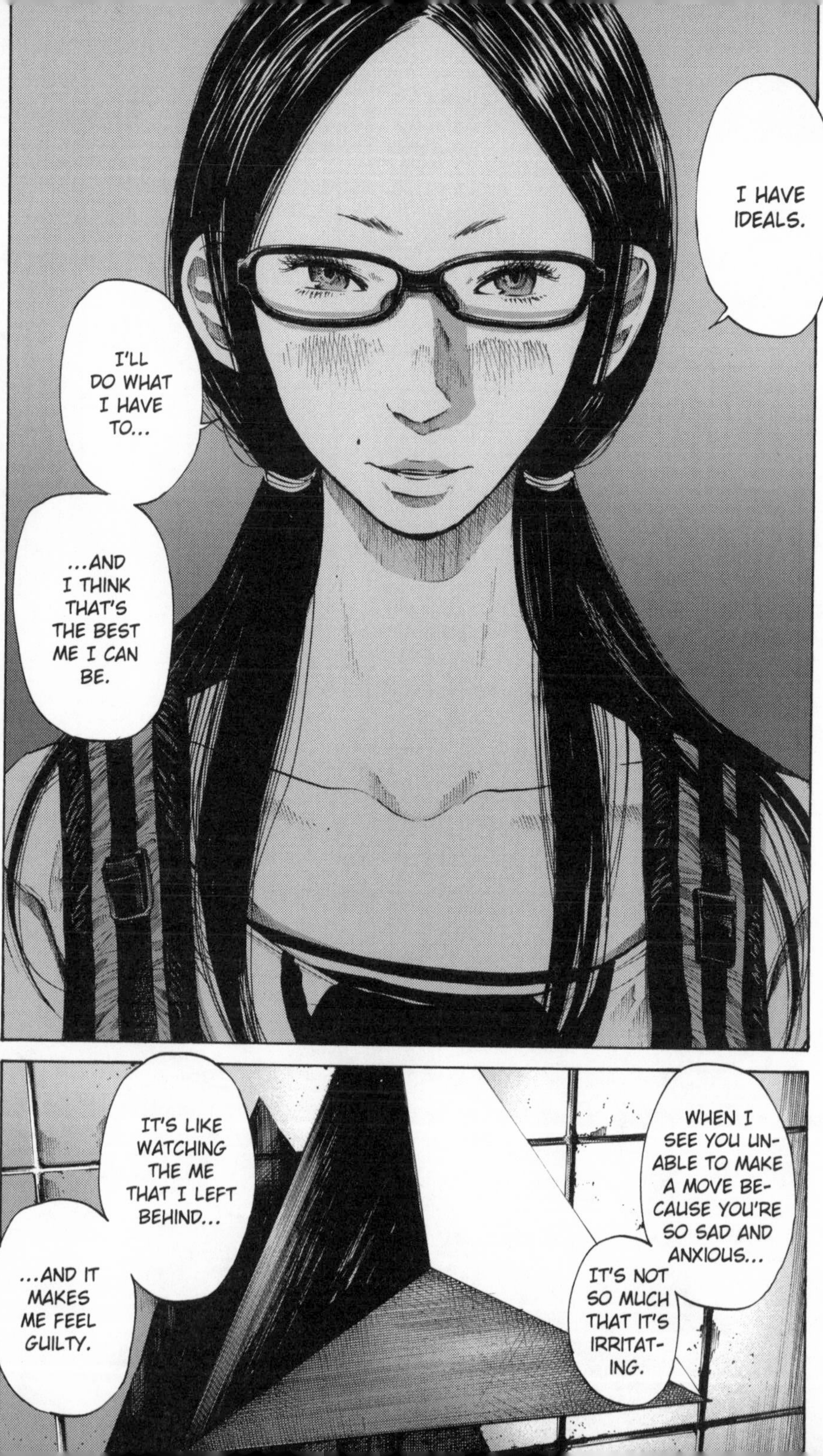
I HAVE IDEALS.
I'LL DO WHAT I HAVE TO...
...AND I THINK THAT'S THE BEST ME I CAN BE.
WHEN I SEE YOU UN-ABLE TO MAKE A MOVE BE-CAUSE YOU'RE SO SAD AND ANXIOUS...
IT'S NOT SO MUCH THAT IT'S IRRITAT-ING.
IT'S LIKE WATCHING THE ME THAT I LEFT BEHIND...
...AND IT MAKES ME FEEL GUILTY.

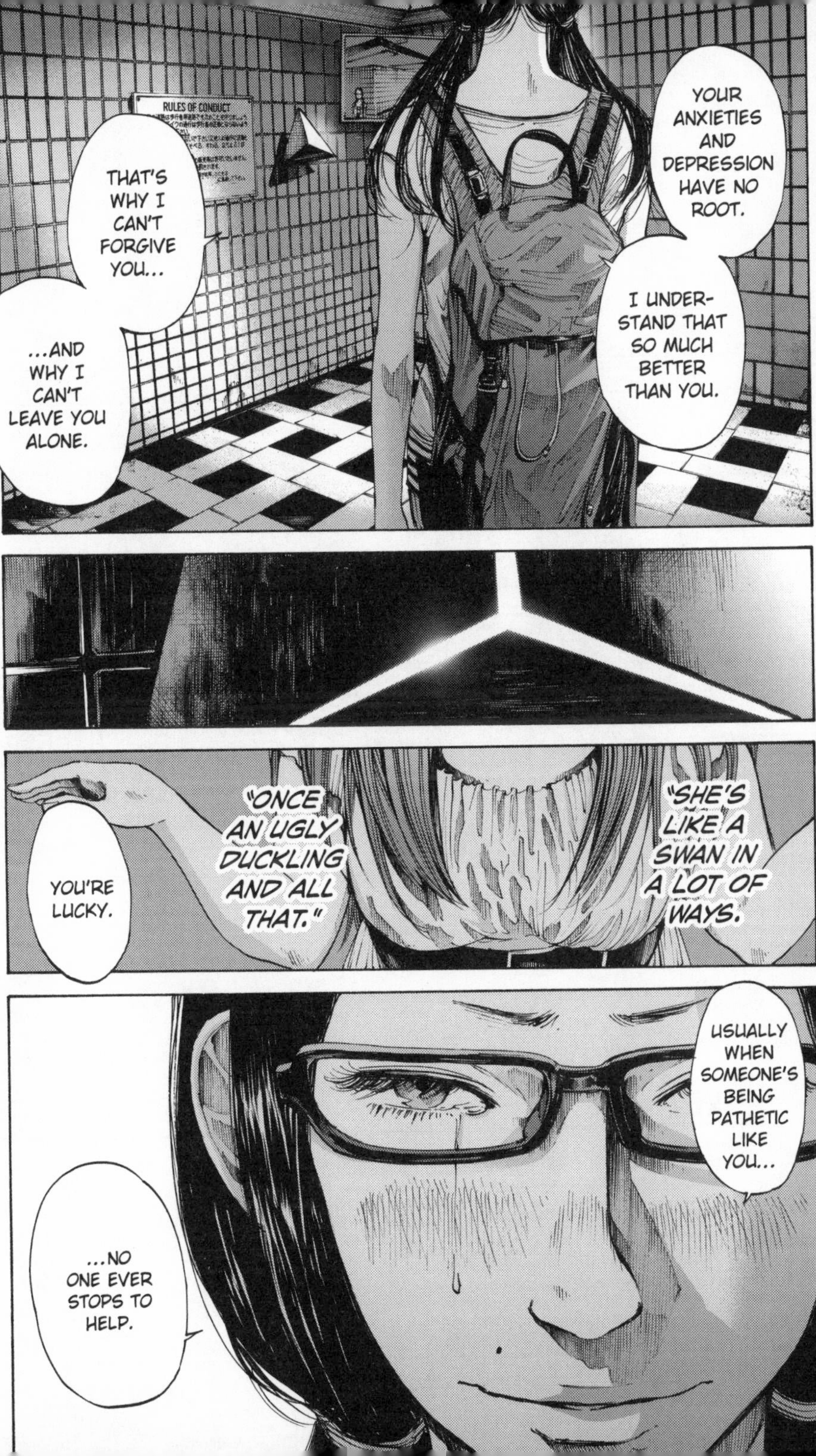

YOUR ANXIETIES AND DEPRESSION HAVE NO ROOT.
I UNDER-STAND THAT SO MUCH BETTER THAN YOU.
RULES OF CONDUCT
THAT'S WHY I CAN'T FORGIVE YOU...
...AND WHY I CAN'T LEAVE YOU ALONE.
"SHE'S LIKE A SWAN IN A LOT OF WAYS.
"ONCE AN UGLY DUCKLING AND ALL THAT."
YOU'RE LUCKY.
USUALLY WHEN SOMEONE'S BEING PATHETIC LIKE YOU...
...NO ONE EVER STOPS TO HELP.

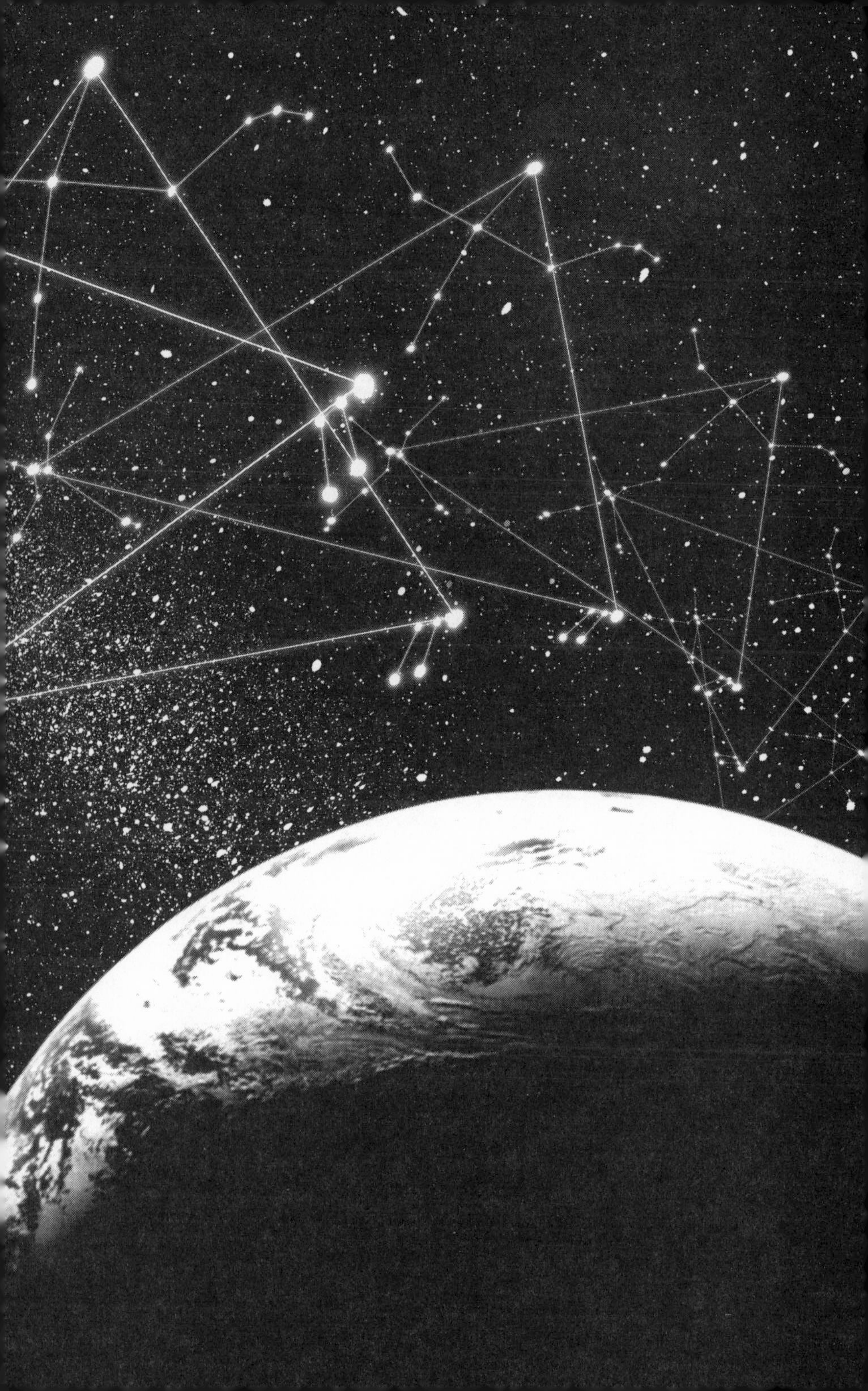

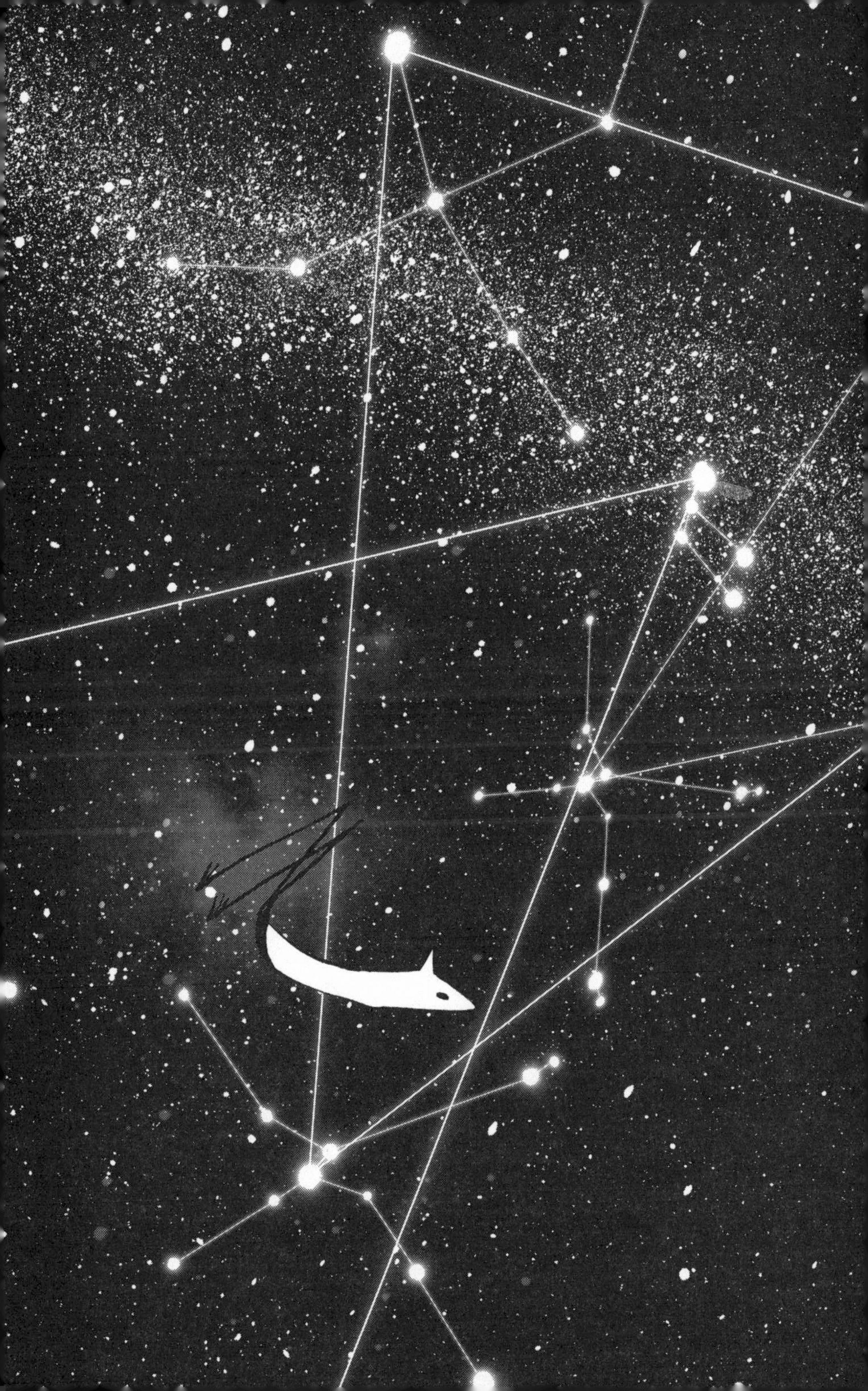

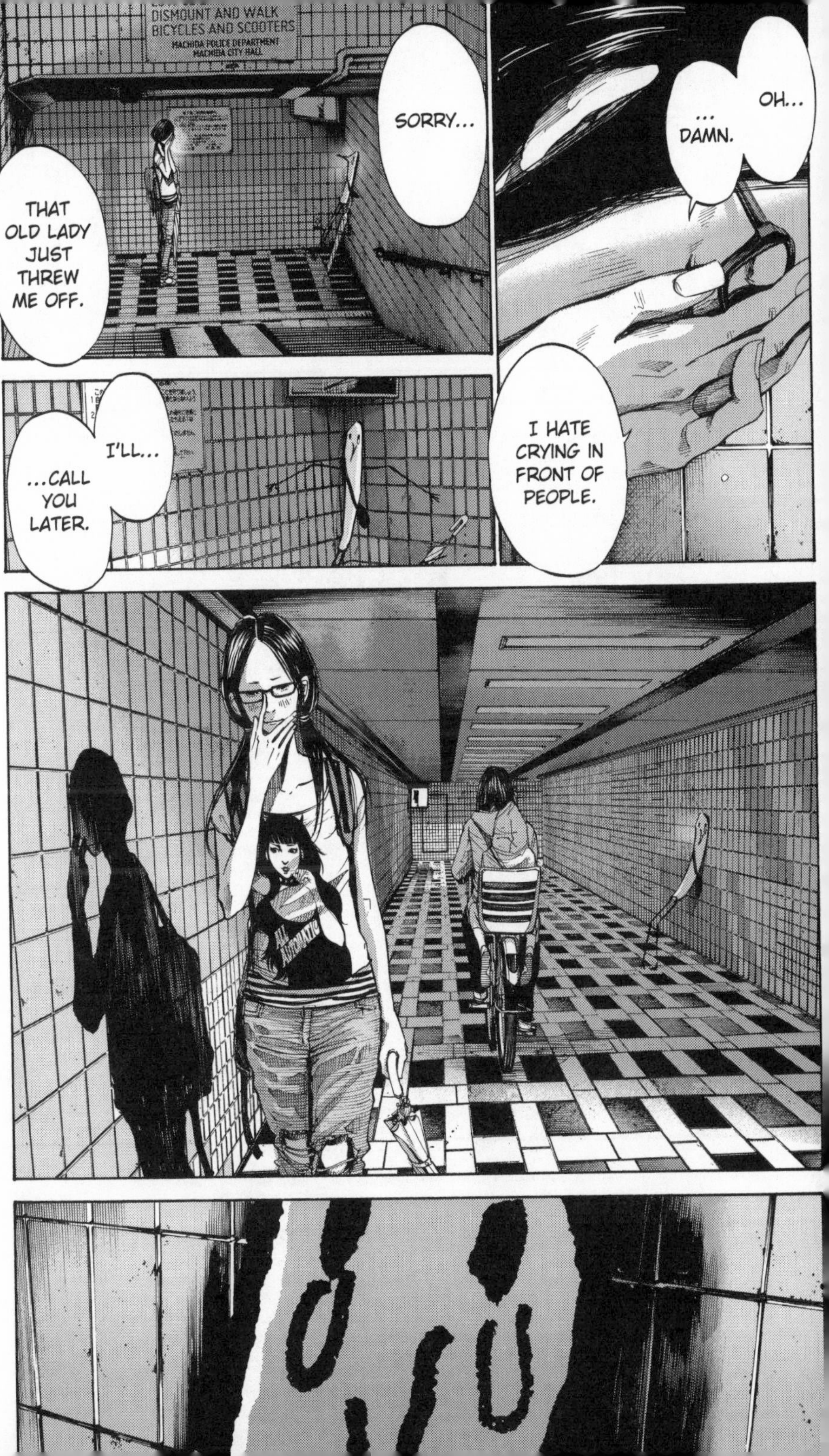
OH...
...DAMN.
I HATE CRYING IN FRONT OF PEOPLE.
DISMOUNT AND WALK BICYCLES AND SCOOTERS
MACHIDA POLICE DEPARTMENT
MACHIDA CITY HALL
SORRY...
THAT OLD LADY JUST THREW ME OFF.
I'LL...
...CALL YOU LATER.
ALL AUTOMATIC

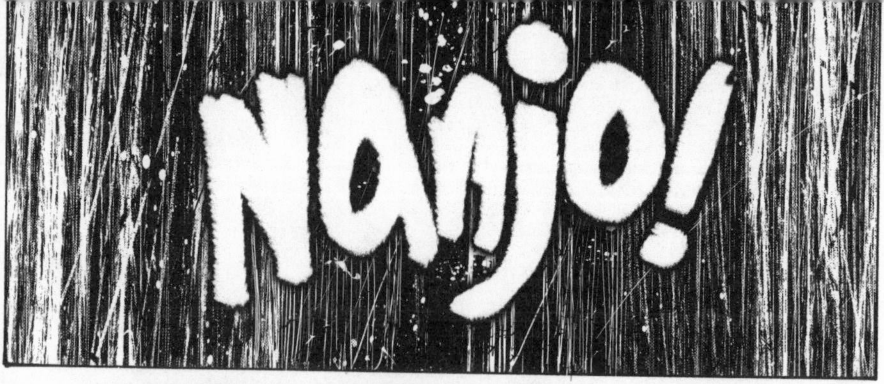
NANJO!
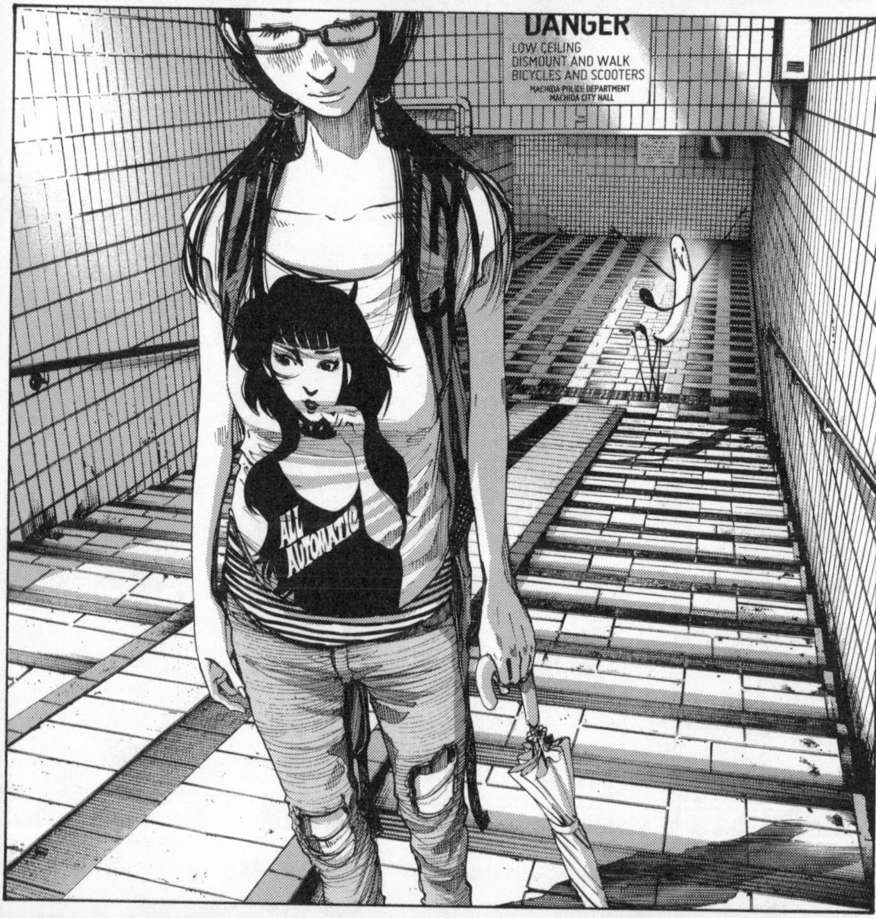
DANGER
LOW CEILING
DISMOUNT AND WALK
BICYCLES AND SCOOTERS
MACHIDA POLICE DEPARTMENT
MACHIDA CITY HALL
ALL AUTOMATIC

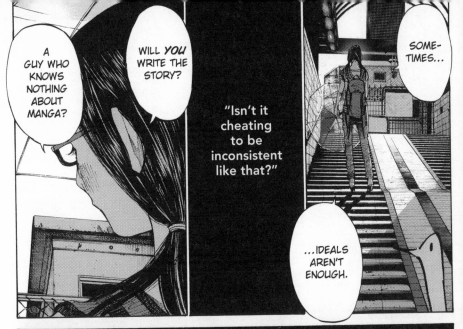

SOME-TIMES...
...IDEALS AREN'T ENOUGH.
"Isn't it cheating to be inconsistent like that?"
WILL *YOU* WRITE THE STORY?
A GUY WHO KNOWS NOTHING ABOUT MANGA?
"Will I...?
"Of course I will.
"I'll rewrite it until you approve."
HA HA!
WEIRD.
WHY ARE YOU SO GUNG HO ALL OF A SUDDEN?

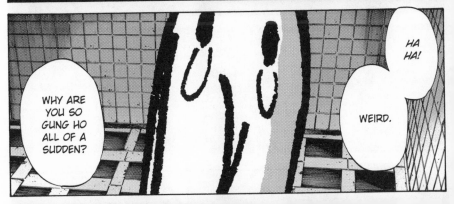

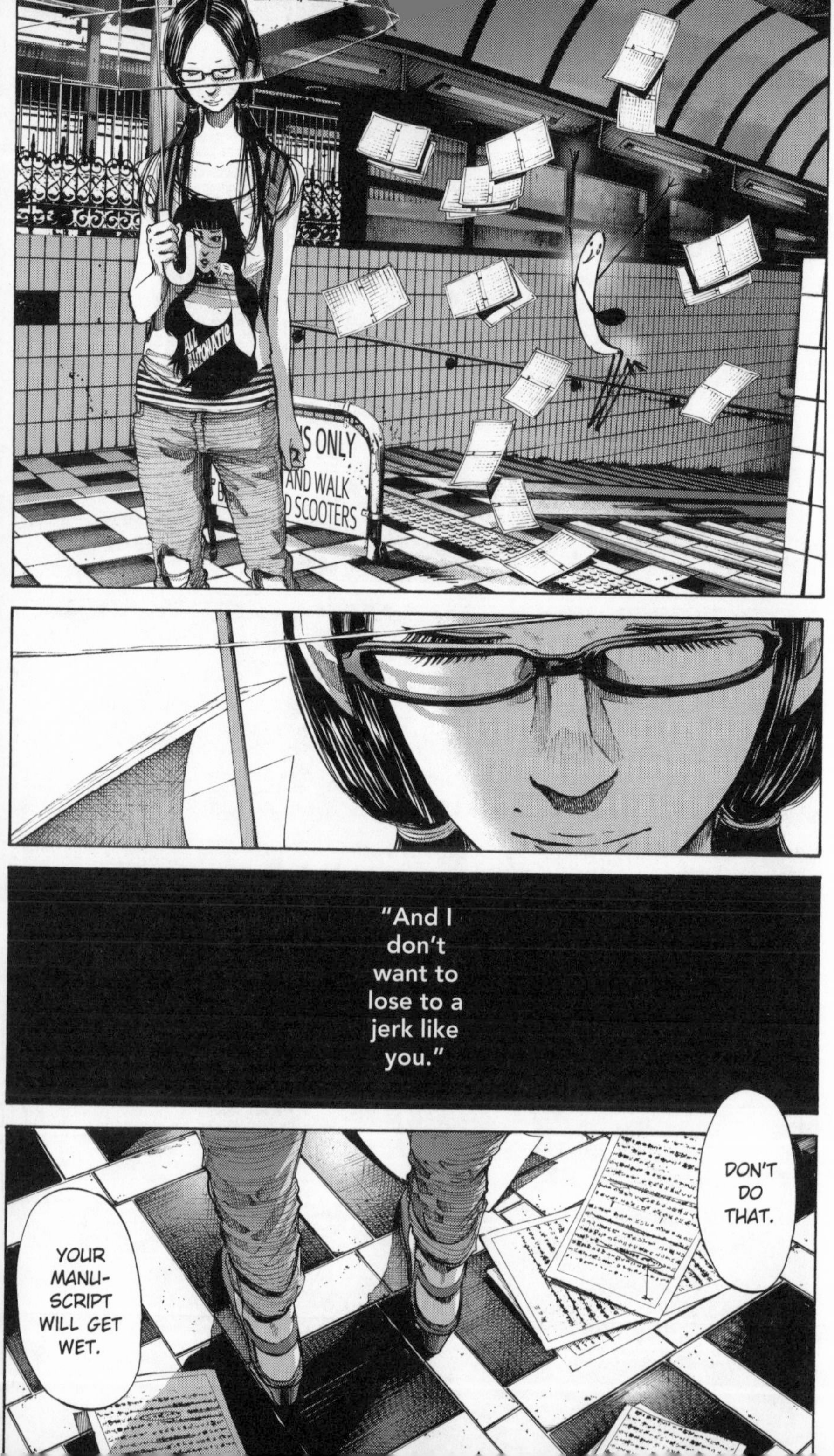
ALL AUTOMATIC
AND WALK
"And I don't want to lose to a jerk like you."
DON'T DO THAT.
YOUR MANUSCRIPT WILL GET WET.

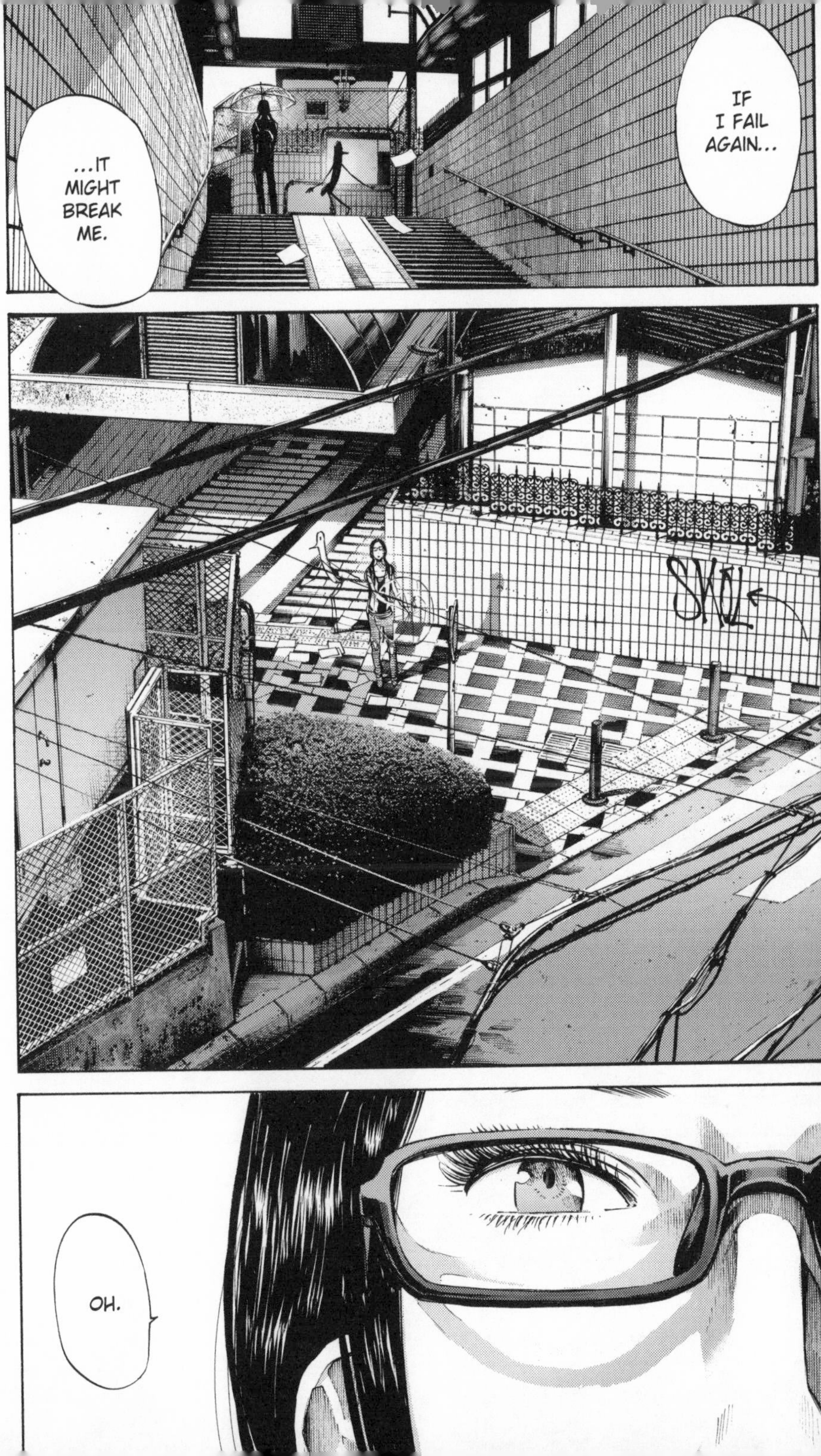
IF I FAIL AGAIN...
...IT MIGHT BREAK ME.
OH.

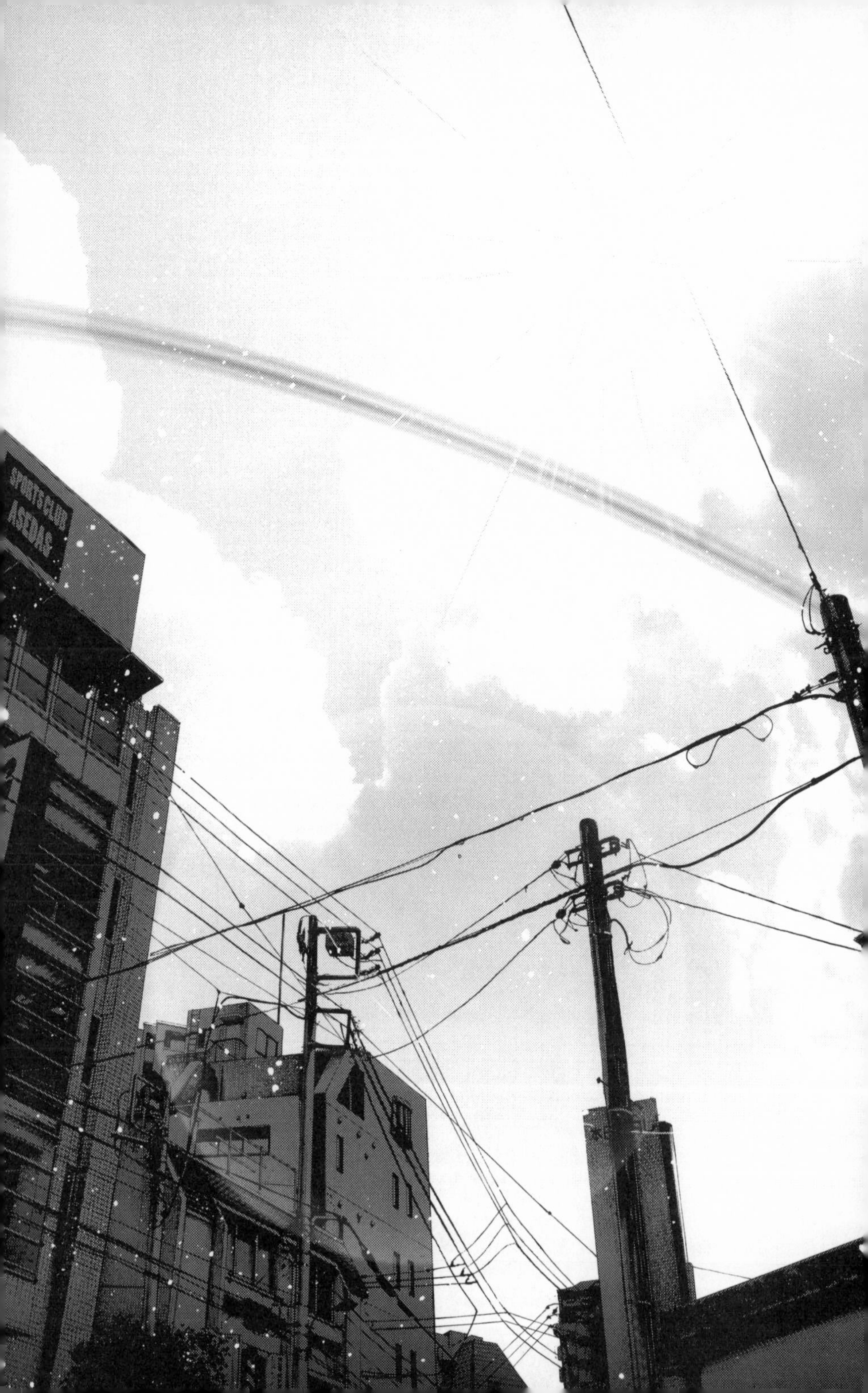
SPORTS CLUB
ASEDAS

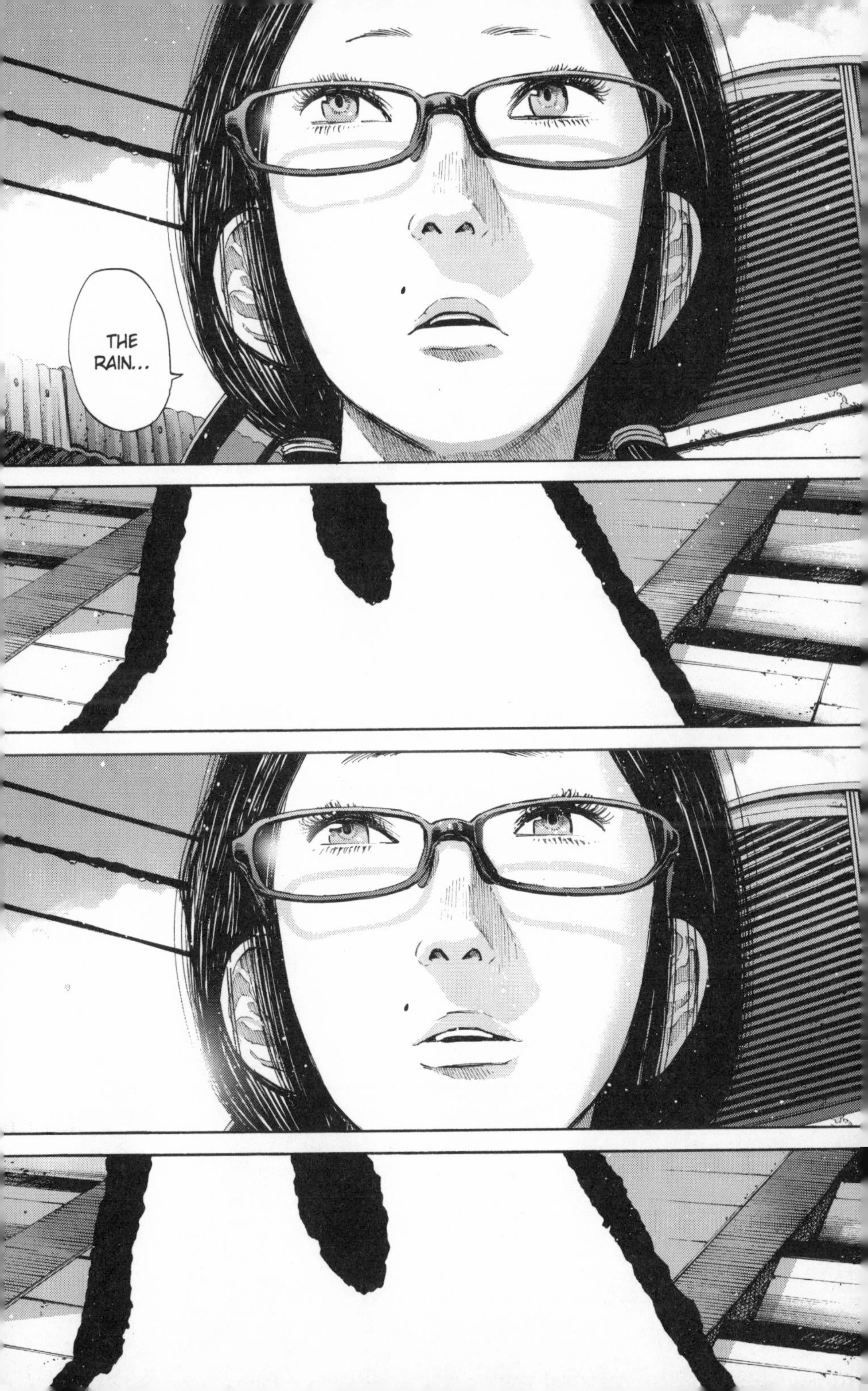
THE RAIN...

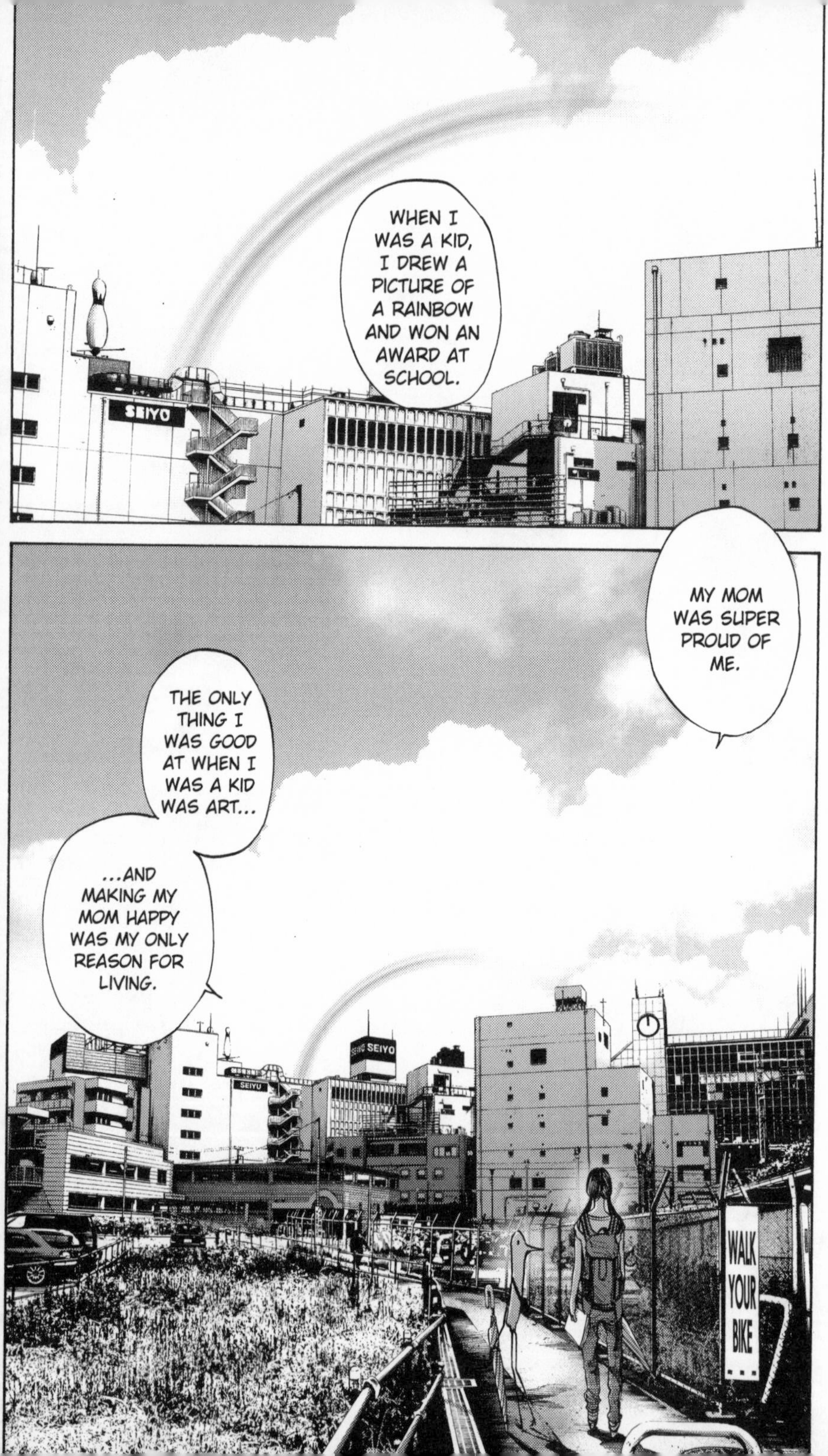
WHEN I WAS A KID, I DREW A PICTURE OF A RAINBOW AND WON AN AWARD AT SCHOOL.
SEIYO
MY MOM WAS SUPER PROUD OF ME.
THE ONLY THING I WAS GOOD AT WHEN I WAS A KID WAS ART...
...AND MAKING MY MOM HAPPY WAS MY ONLY REASON FOR LIVING.
SEIYO
SEIYO
WALK YOUR BIKE

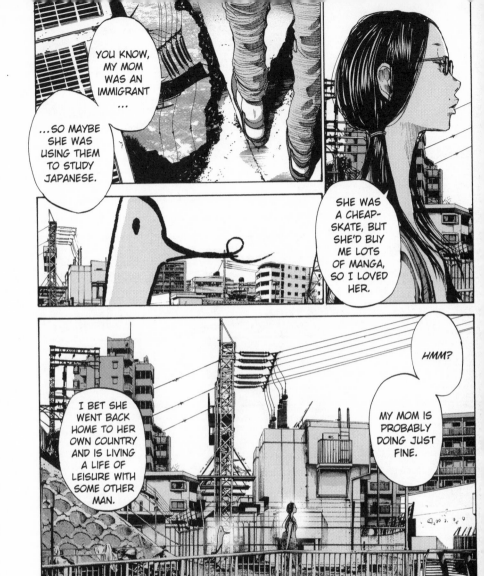

YOU KNOW, MY MOM WAS AN IMMIGRANT...

...SO MAYBE SHE WAS USING THEM TO STUDY JAPANESE.

SHE WAS A CHEAPSKATE, BUT SHE'D BUY ME LOTS OF MANGA, SO I LOVED HER.

HMM?

MY MOM IS PROBABLY DOING JUST FINE.

I BET SHE WENT BACK HOME TO HER OWN COUNTRY AND IS LIVING A LIFE OF LEISURE WITH SOME OTHER MAN.

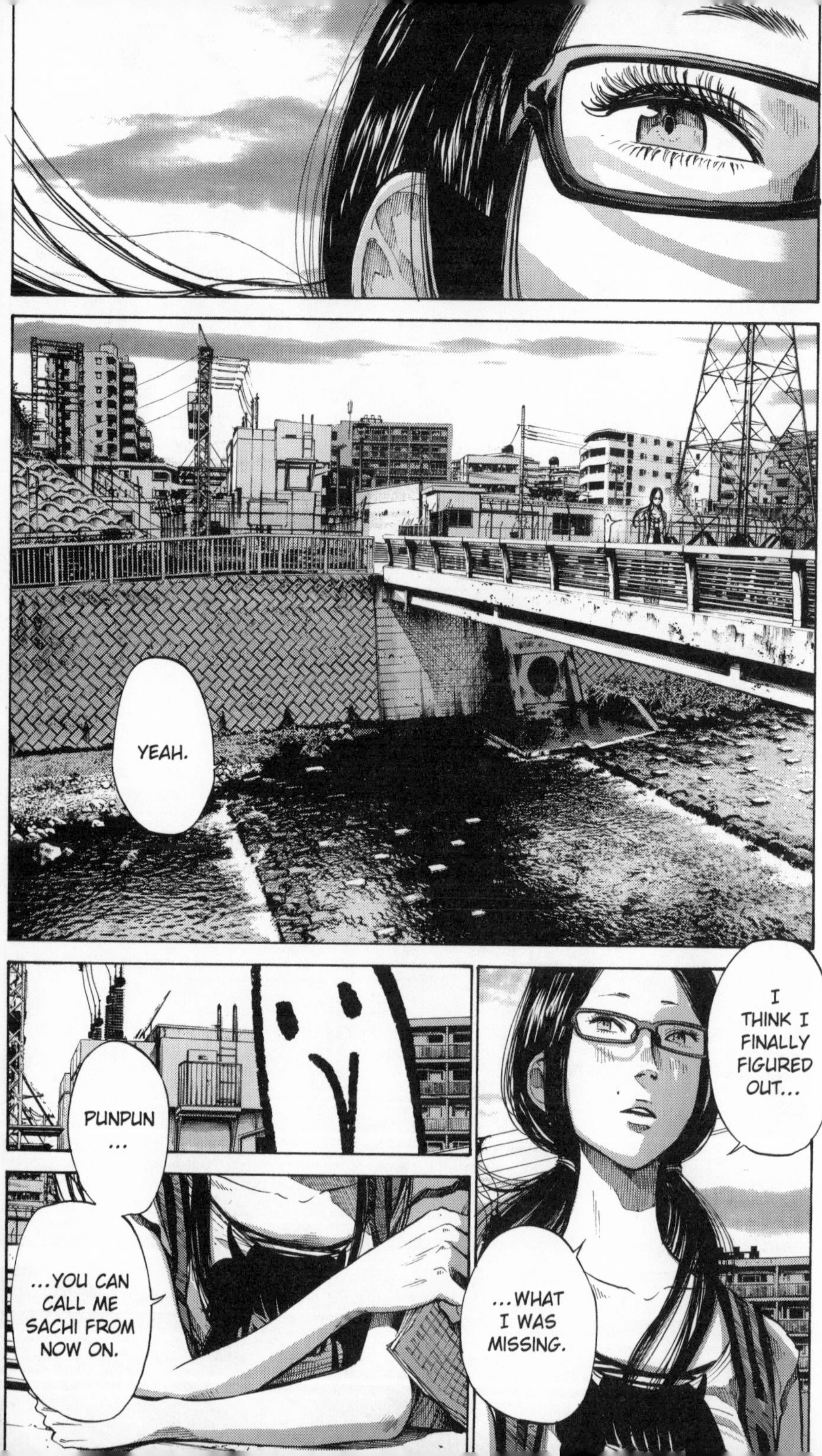
YEAH.
I THINK I FINALLY FIGURED OUT...
...WHAT I WAS MISSING.
PUNPUN ...
...YOU CAN CALL ME SACHI FROM NOW ON.

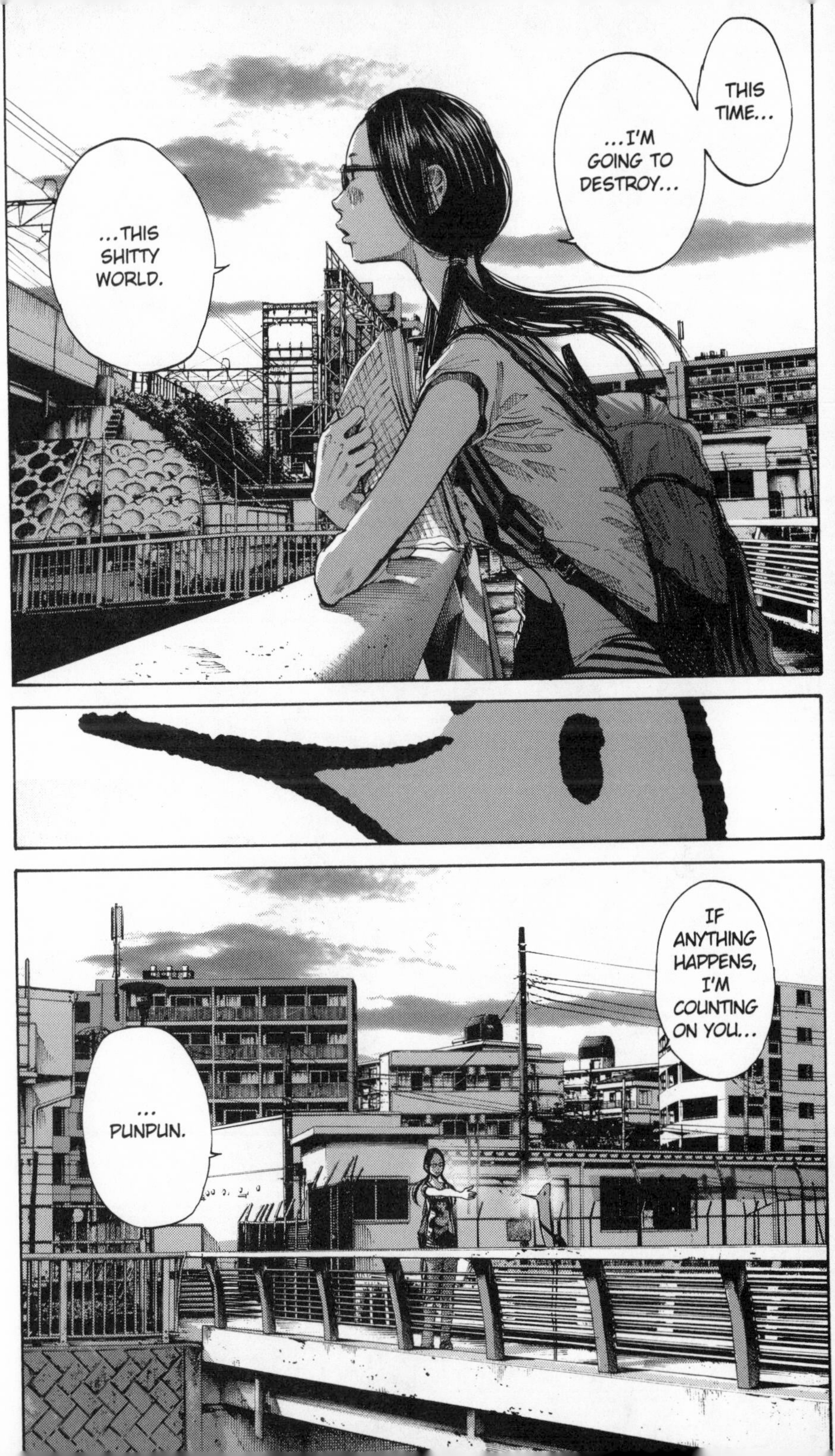
THIS TIME...
...I'M GOING TO DESTROY...
...THIS SHITTY WORLD.
IF ANYTHING HAPPENS, I'M COUNTING ON YOU...
... PUNPUN.

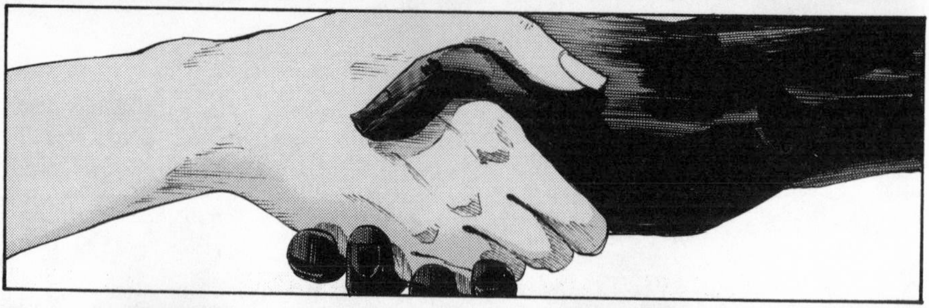

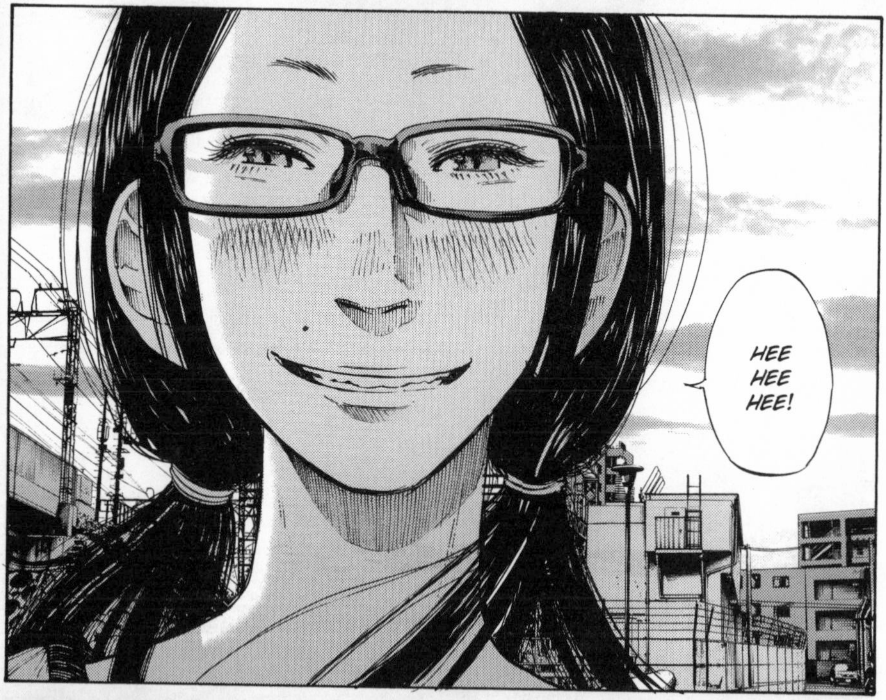
HEE HEE HEE!

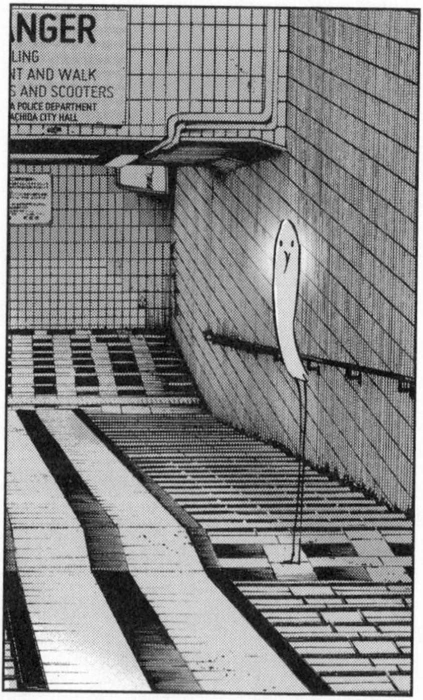
ANGER
LING
NT AND WALK
S AND SCOOTERS
A POLICE DEPARTMENT
ACHIDA CITY HALL

Chapter 85

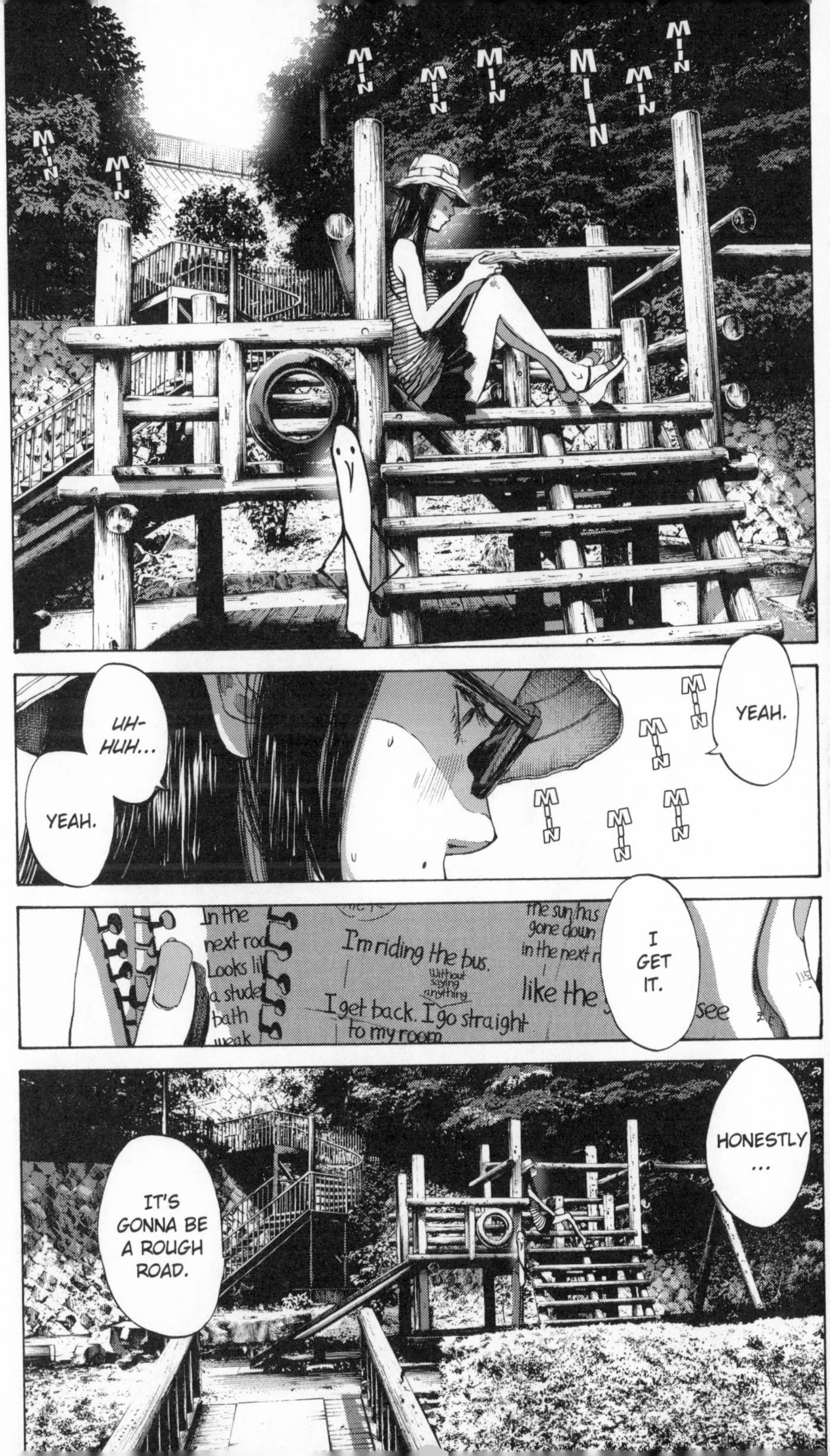
MIN
MIN
MIN
MIN
MIN
MIN
MIN
MIN
YEAH.
MIN
MIN
MIN
MIN
MIN
UH-HUH...
YEAH.
I GET IT.
I'm riding the bus.
Without saying anything
I get back. I go straight to my room
HONESTLY...
IT'S GONNA BE A ROUGH ROAD.

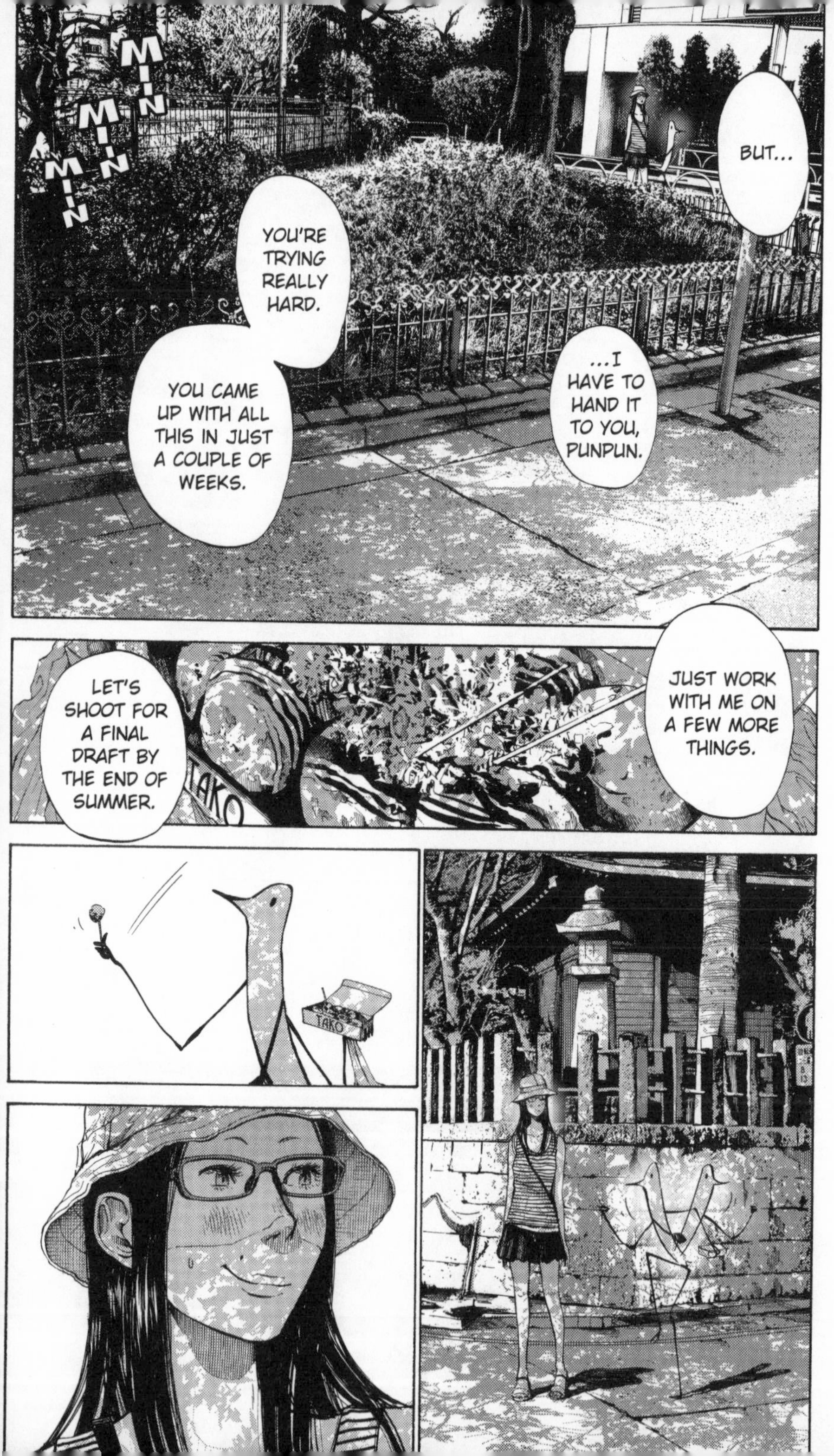
BUT...
...I HAVE TO HAND IT TO YOU, PUNPUN.
YOU'RE TRYING REALLY HARD.
YOU CAME UP WITH ALL THIS IN JUST A COUPLE OF WEEKS.
MIN MIN MIN
JUST WORK WITH ME ON A FEW MORE THINGS.
TAKO
LET'S SHOOT FOR A FINAL DRAFT BY THE END OF SUMMER.
TAKO

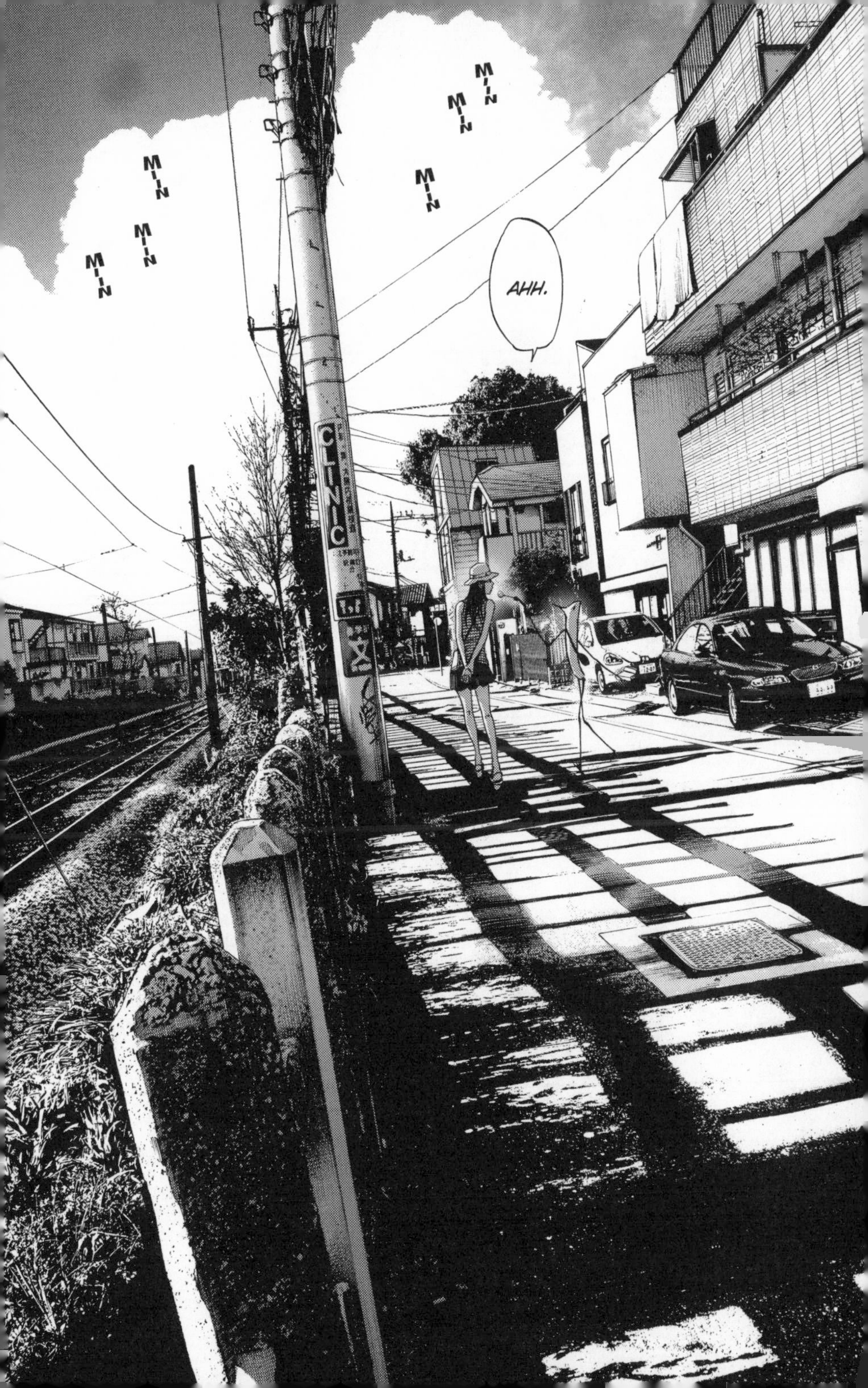
MIN MIN
MIN
AHH.
MIN
MIN
MIN MIN
CLINIC

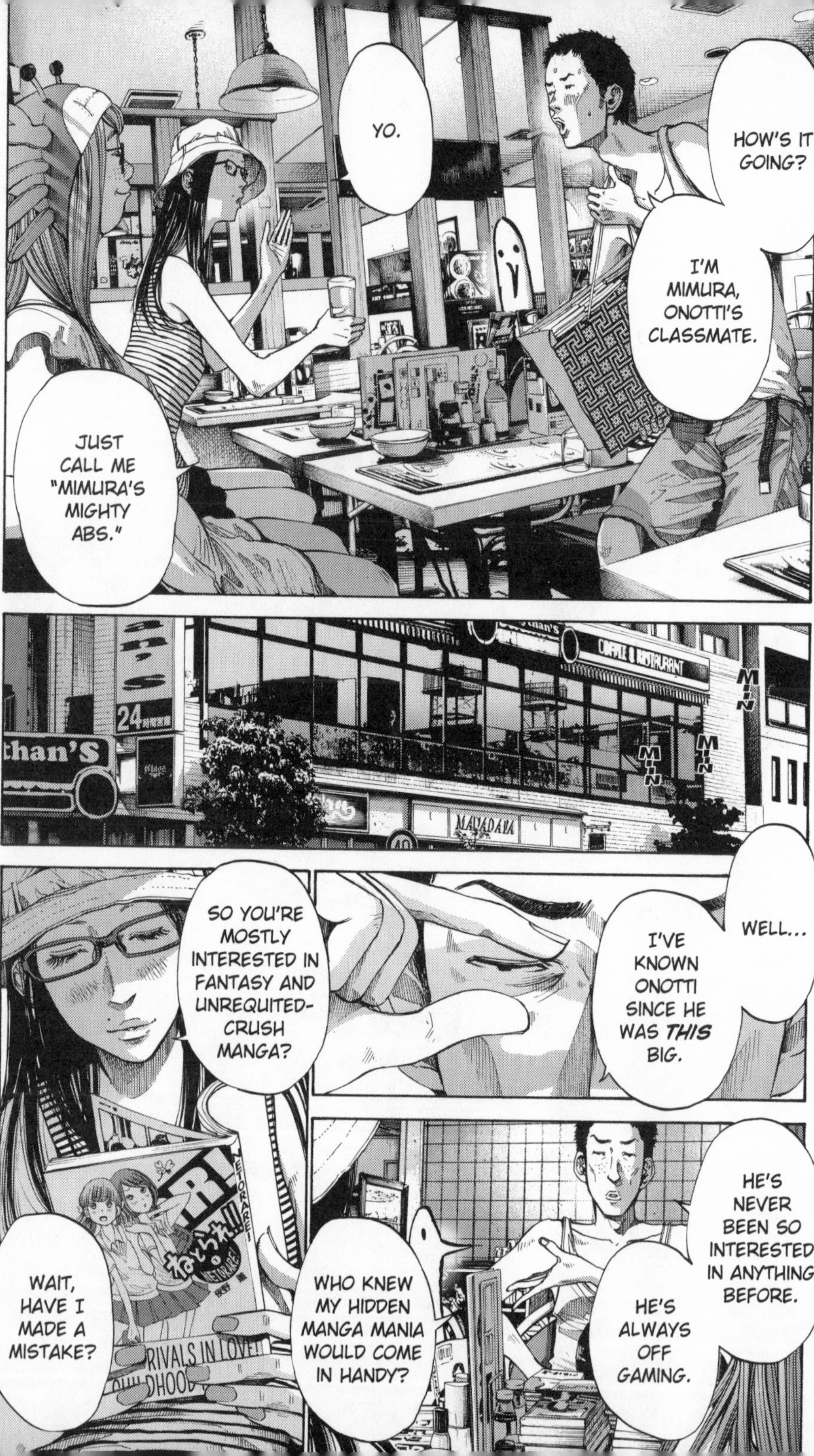
HOW'S IT GOING?
YO.
I'M MIMURA, ONOTTI'S CLASSMATE.
JUST CALL ME "MIMURA'S MIGHTY ABS."
MIN
MIN
MIN
than'S
WELL...
I'VE KNOWN ONOTTI SINCE HE WAS *THIS* BIG.
HE'S NEVER BEEN SO INTERESTED IN ANYTHING BEFORE.
HE'S ALWAYS OFF GAMING.
SO YOU'RE MOSTLY INTERESTED IN FANTASY AND UNREQUITED-CRUSH MANGA?
WHO KNEW MY HIDDEN MANGA MANIA WOULD COME IN HANDY?
WAIT, HAVE I MADE A MISTAKE?

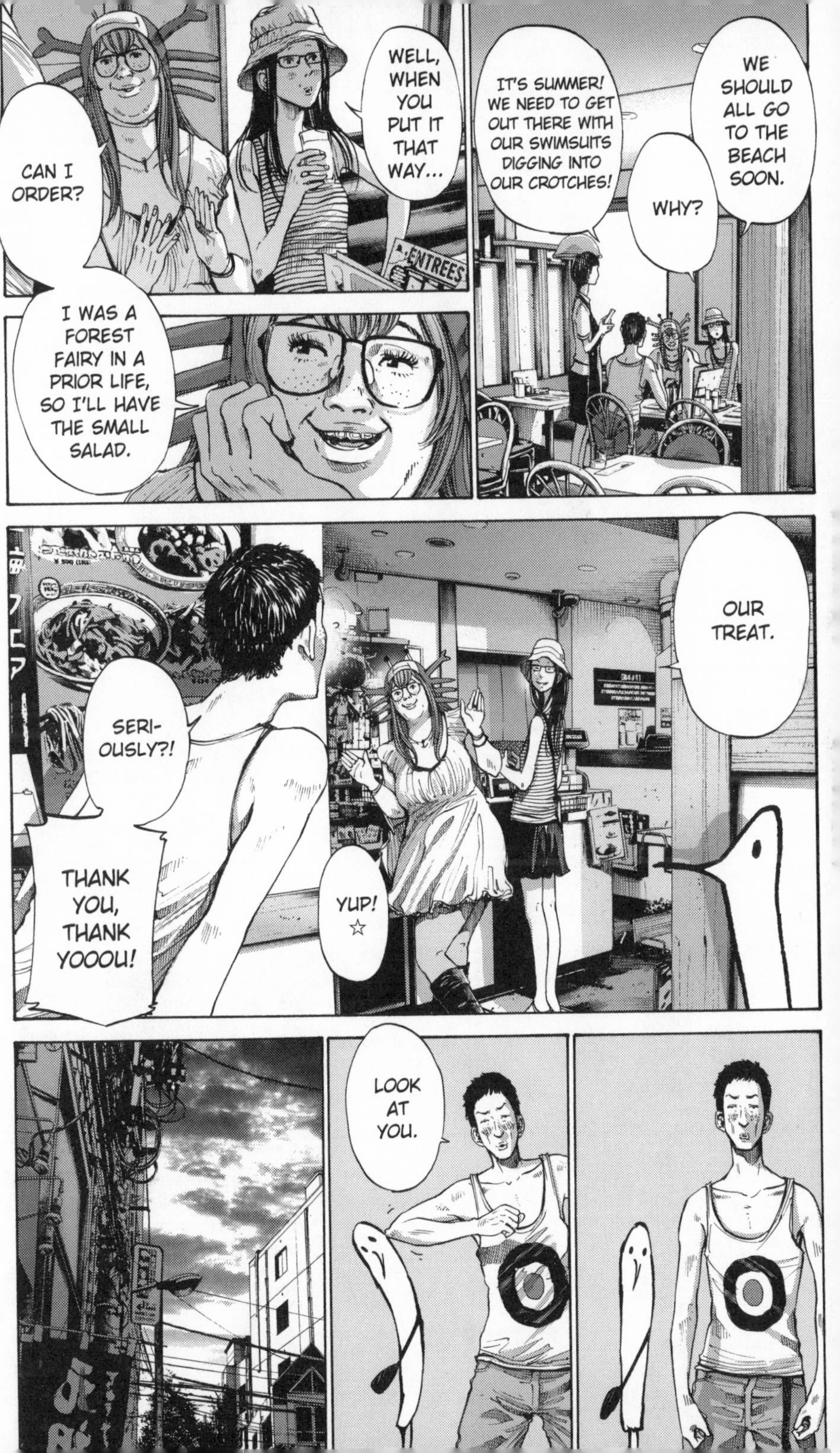

WE SHOULD ALL GO TO THE BEACH SOON.
WHY?
IT'S SUMMER! WE NEED TO GET OUT THERE WITH OUR SWIMSUITS DIGGING INTO OUR CROTCHES!
WELL, WHEN YOU PUT IT THAT WAY...
CAN I ORDER?
ENTREES
I WAS A FOREST FAIRY IN A PRIOR LIFE, SO I'LL HAVE THE SMALL SALAD.
OUR TREAT.
YUP! ☆
SERI-OUSLY?!
THANK YOU, THANK YOOOU!
LOOK AT YOU.

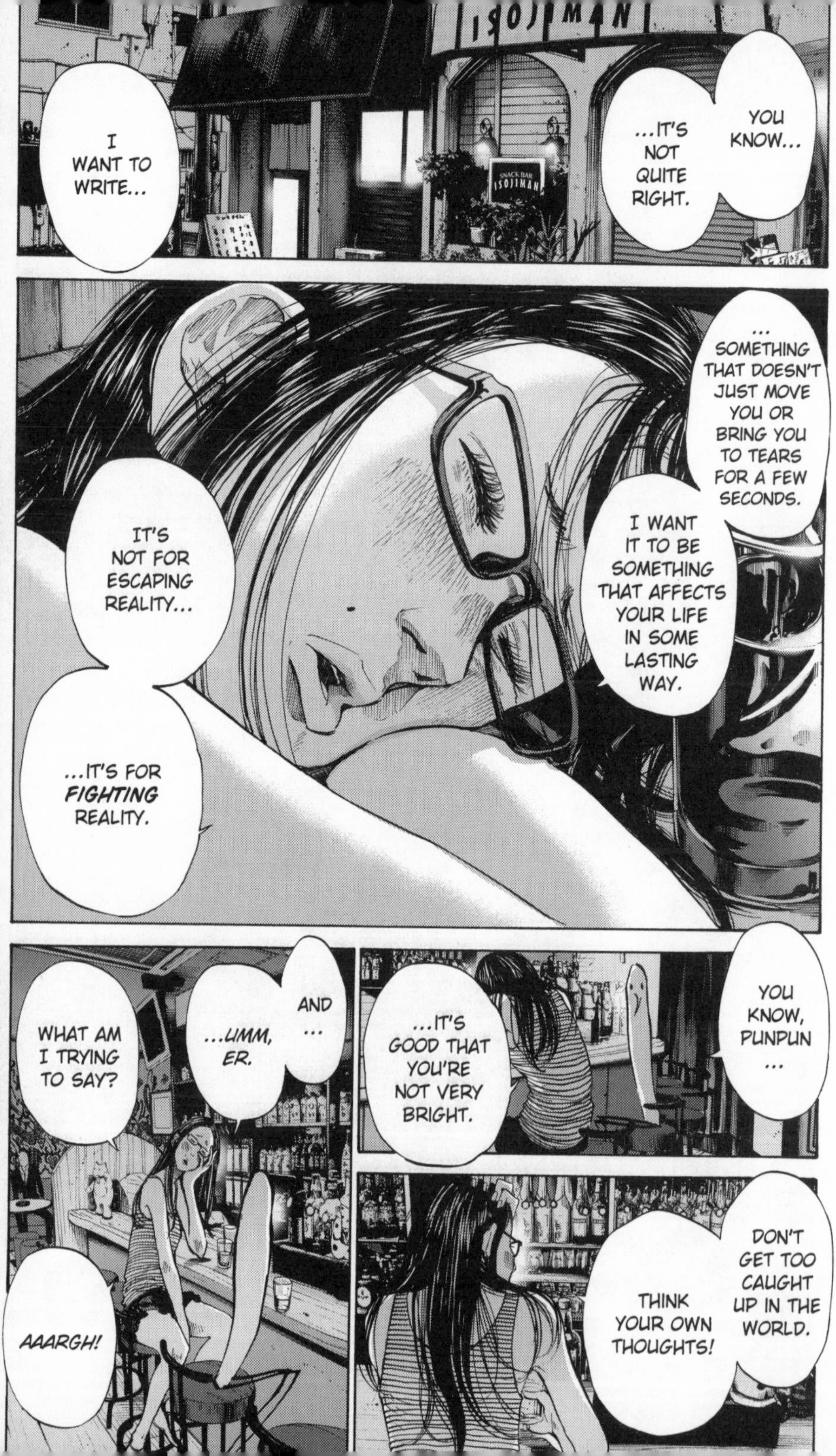
ISOJIMAN
SNACK BAR ISOJIMAN
YOU KNOW...
...IT'S NOT QUITE RIGHT.
I WANT TO WRITE...
...SOMETHING THAT DOESN'T JUST MOVE YOU OR BRING YOU TO TEARS FOR A FEW SECONDS.
I WANT IT TO BE SOMETHING THAT AFFECTS YOUR LIFE IN SOME LASTING WAY.
IT'S NOT FOR ESCAPING REALITY...
...IT'S FOR *FIGHTING* REALITY.
YOU KNOW, PUNPUN ...
...IT'S GOOD THAT YOU'RE NOT VERY BRIGHT.
DON'T GET TOO CAUGHT UP IN THE WORLD.
THINK YOUR OWN THOUGHTS!
AND ...
...UMM, ER.
WHAT AM I TRYING TO SAY?
AAARGH!

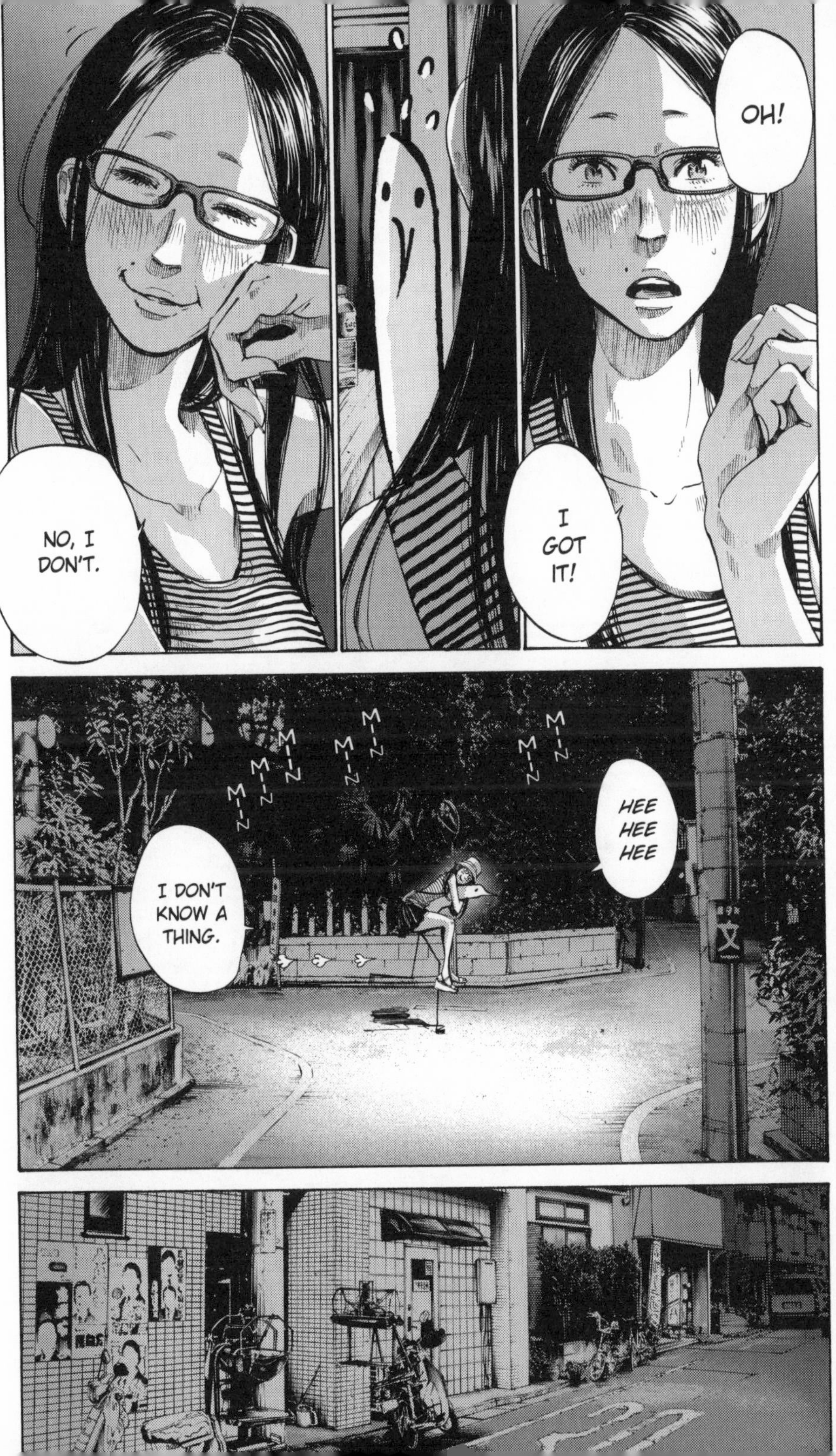
OH!
I GOT IT!
NO, I DON'T.
HEE HEE HEE
MIN MIN
MIN MIN
MIN MIN
MIN MIN
I DON'T KNOW A THING.

BEEP BEEP!

SO HOT.

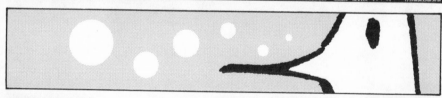

EL NIÑO.

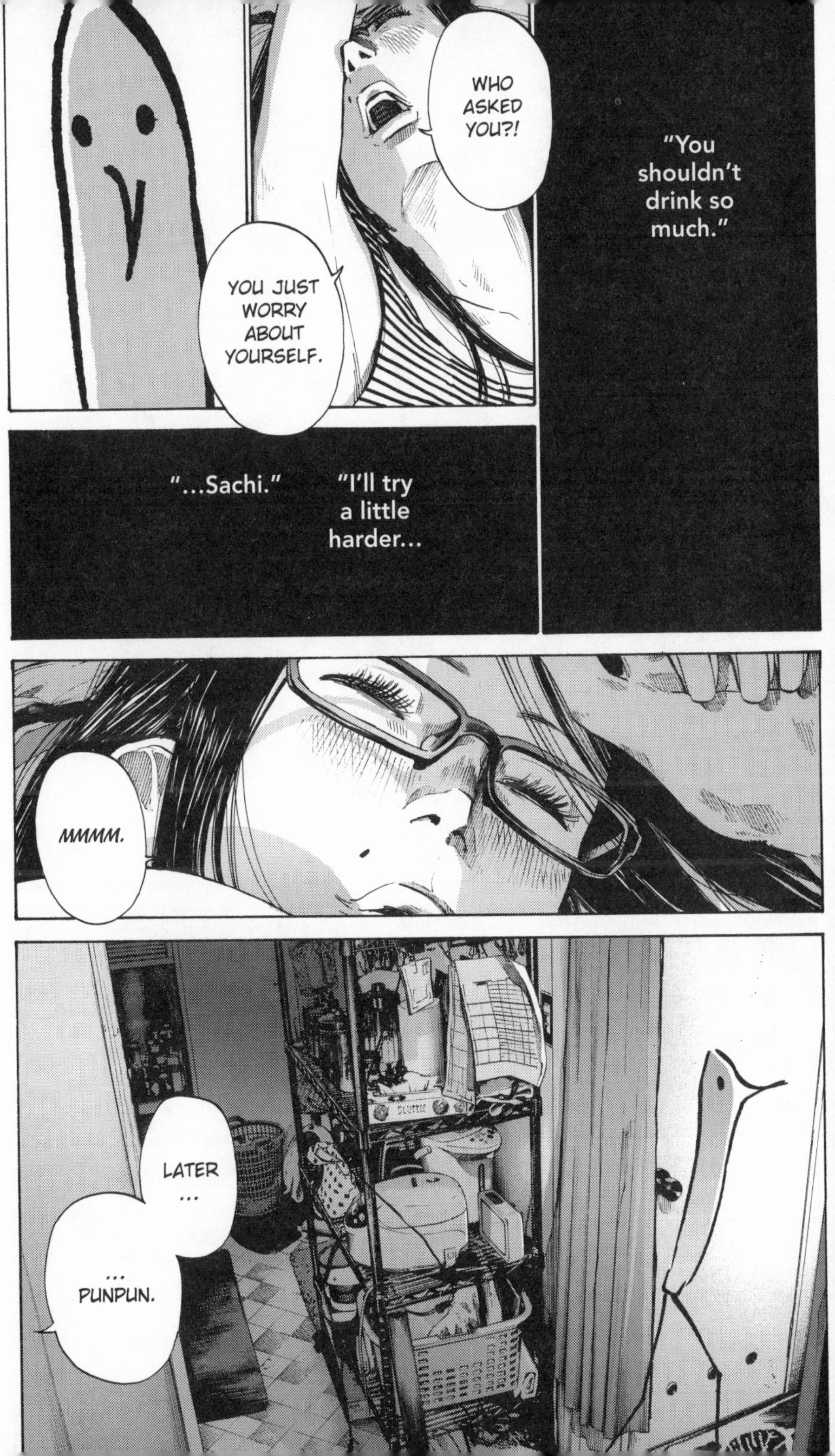
"You shouldn't drink so much."
WHO ASKED YOU?!
YOU JUST WORRY ABOUT YOURSELF.
"I'll try a little harder...
"...Sachi."
MMMM.
LATER ...
... PUNPUN.

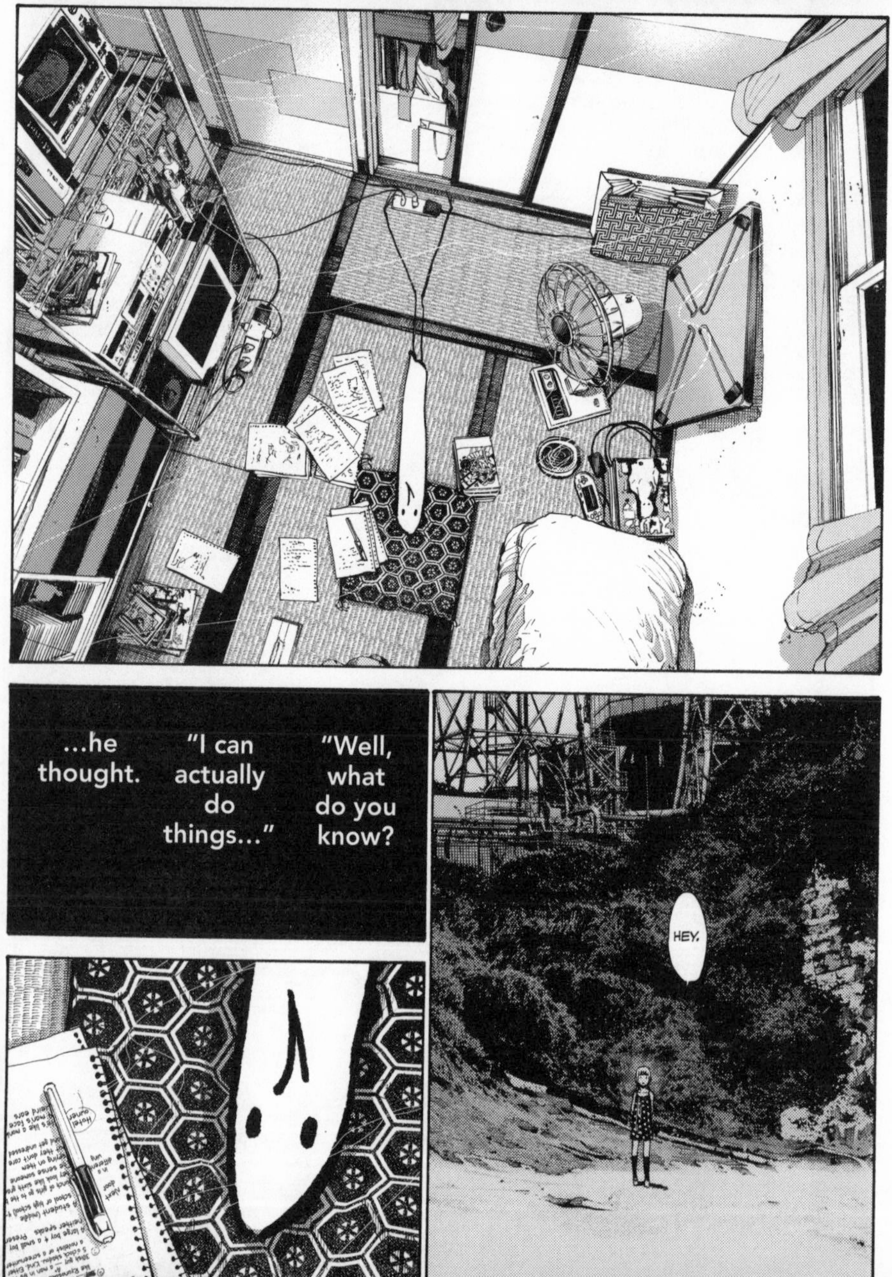
HEY.
"Well, what do you know?
"I can actually do things..."
...he thought.

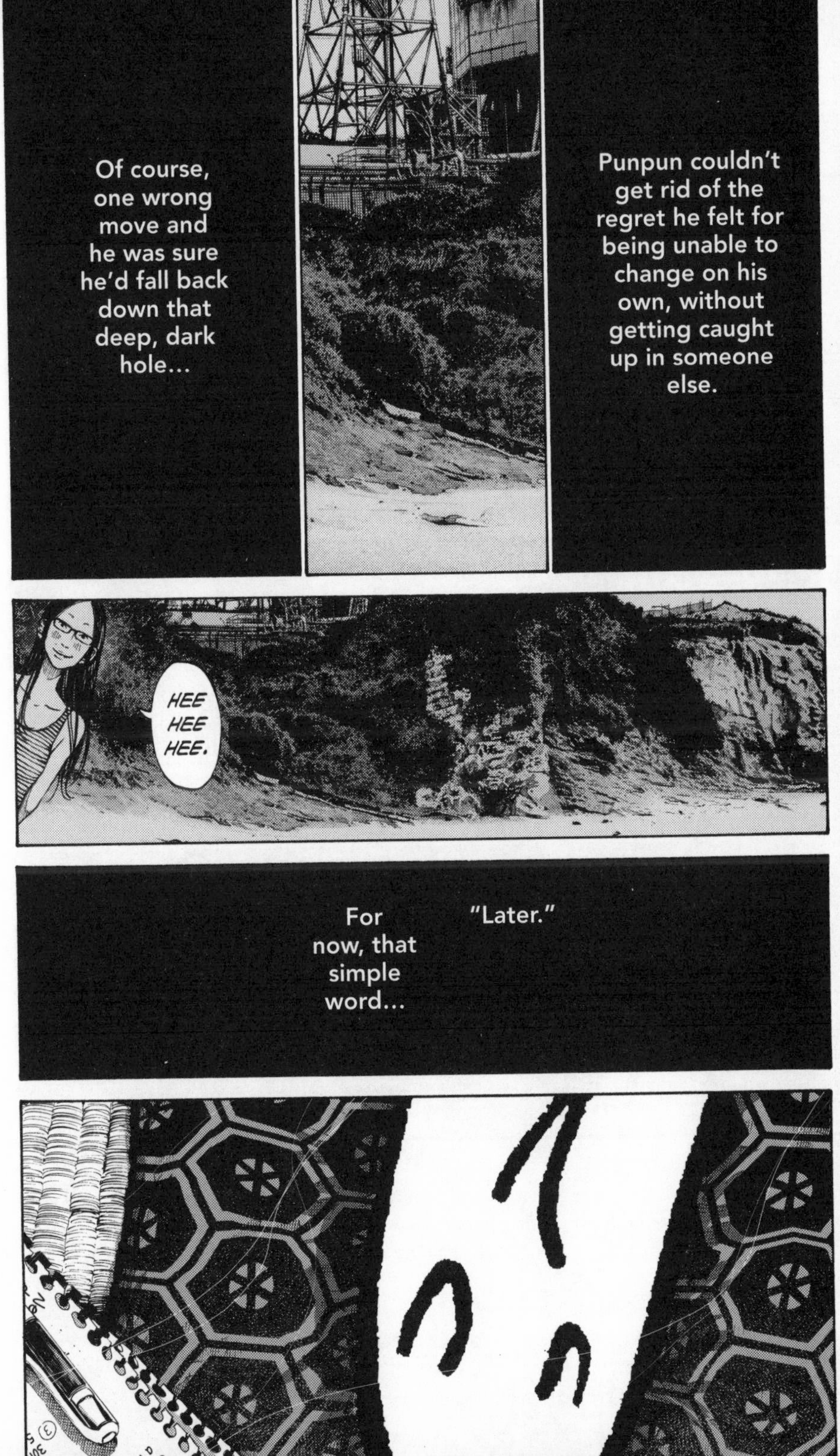
Punpun couldn't get rid of the regret he felt for being unable to change on his own, without getting caught up in someone else.
Of course, one wrong move and he was sure he'd fall back down that deep, dark hole...
HEE HEE HEE.
"Later."
For now, that simple word...

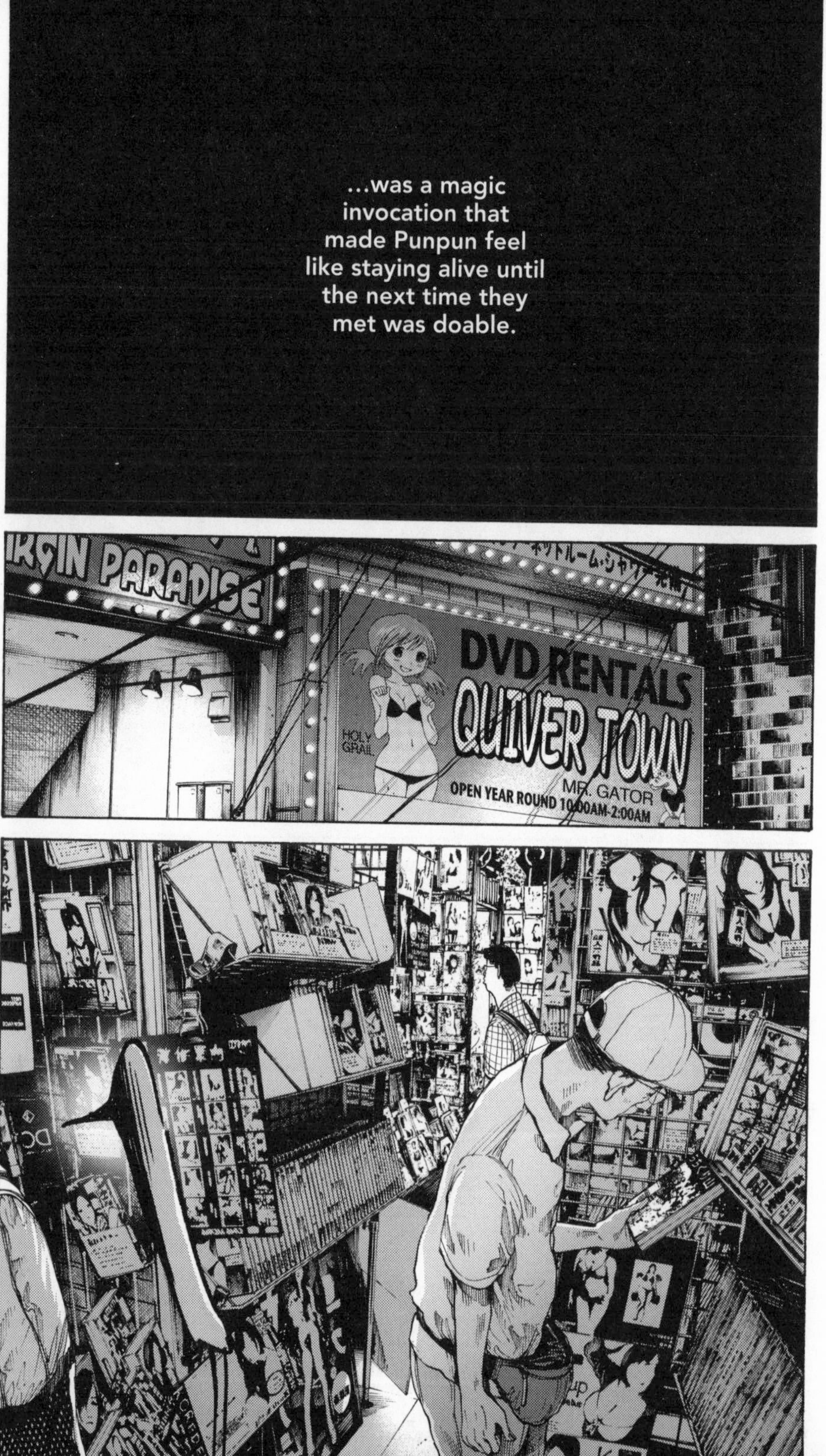
...was a magic invocation that made Punpun feel like staying alive until the next time they met was doable.
PARADISE
DVD RENTALS
QUIVER TOWN
HOLY GRAIL
MR. GATOR
OPEN YEAR ROUND 10:00AM-2:00AM

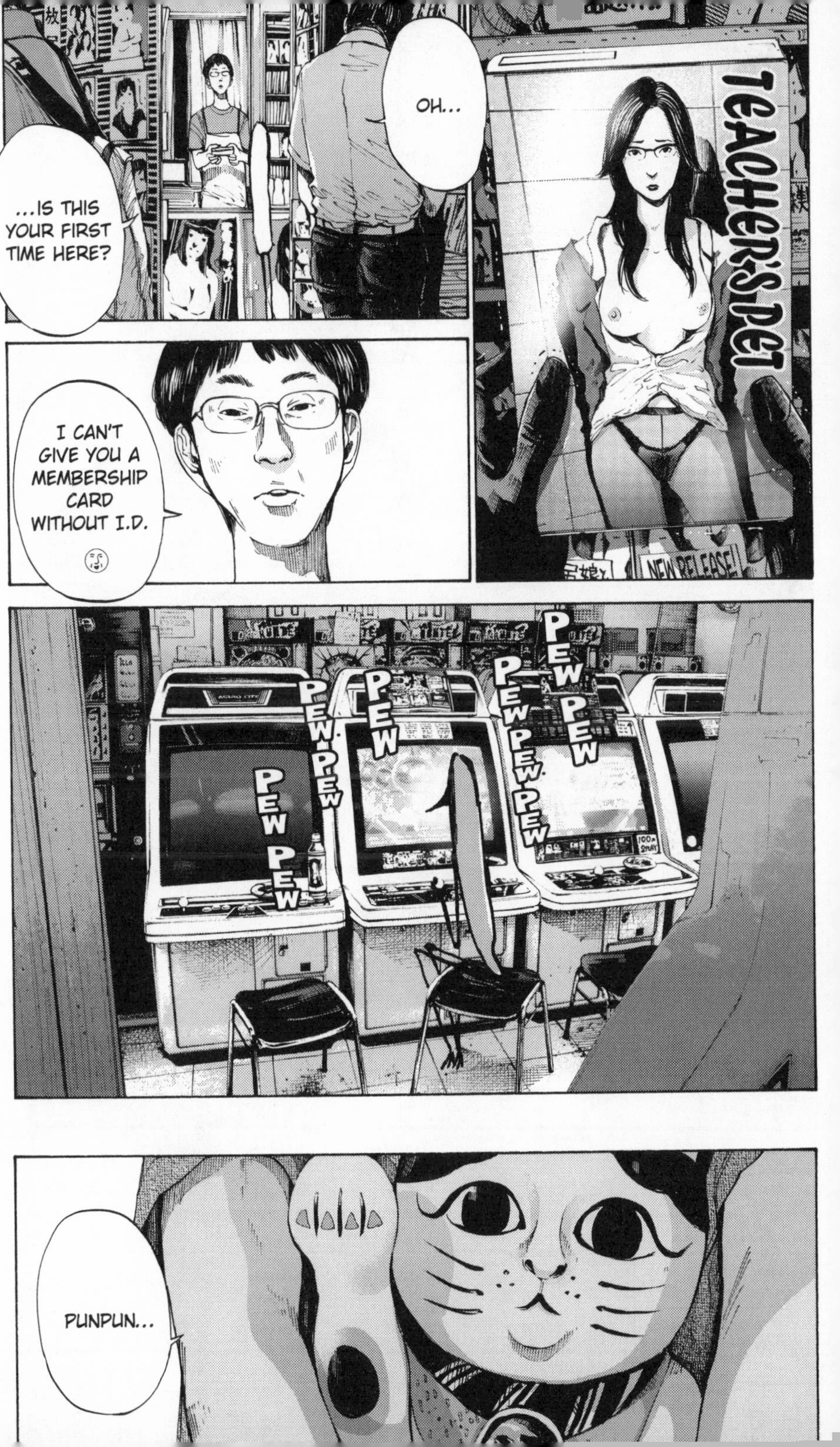
TEACHER'S PET
NEW RELEASE!
OH...
...IS THIS YOUR FIRST TIME HERE?
I CAN'T GIVE YOU A MEMBERSHIP CARD WITHOUT I.D.
PEW PEW
PEW PEW PEW PEW
PEW
PEW PEW
PEW PEW
PUNPUN...

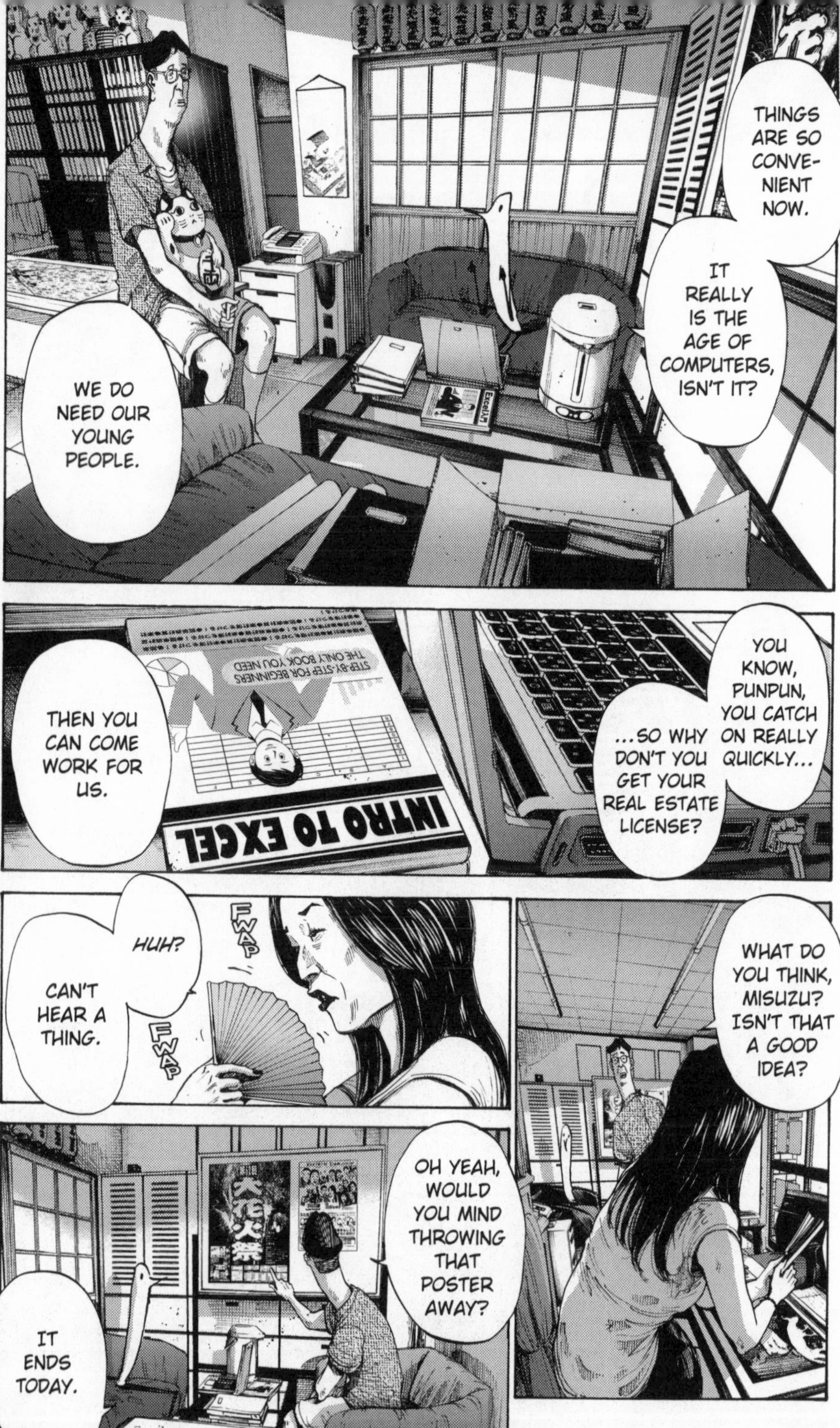
THINGS ARE SO CONVENIENT NOW.
IT REALLY IS THE AGE OF COMPUTERS, ISN'T IT?
WE DO NEED OUR YOUNG PEOPLE.
YOU KNOW, PUNPUN, YOU CATCH ON REALLY QUICKLY...
...SO WHY DON'T YOU GET YOUR REAL ESTATE LICENSE?
STEP-BY-STEP FOR BEGINNERS
THE ONLY BOOK YOU NEED
INTRO TO EXCEL
THEN YOU CAN COME WORK FOR US.
WHAT DO YOU THINK, MISUZU? ISN'T THAT A GOOD IDEA?
HUH?
FWAP
CAN'T HEAR A THING.
FWAP
OH YEAH, WOULD YOU MIND THROWING THAT POSTER AWAY?
IT ENDS TODAY.

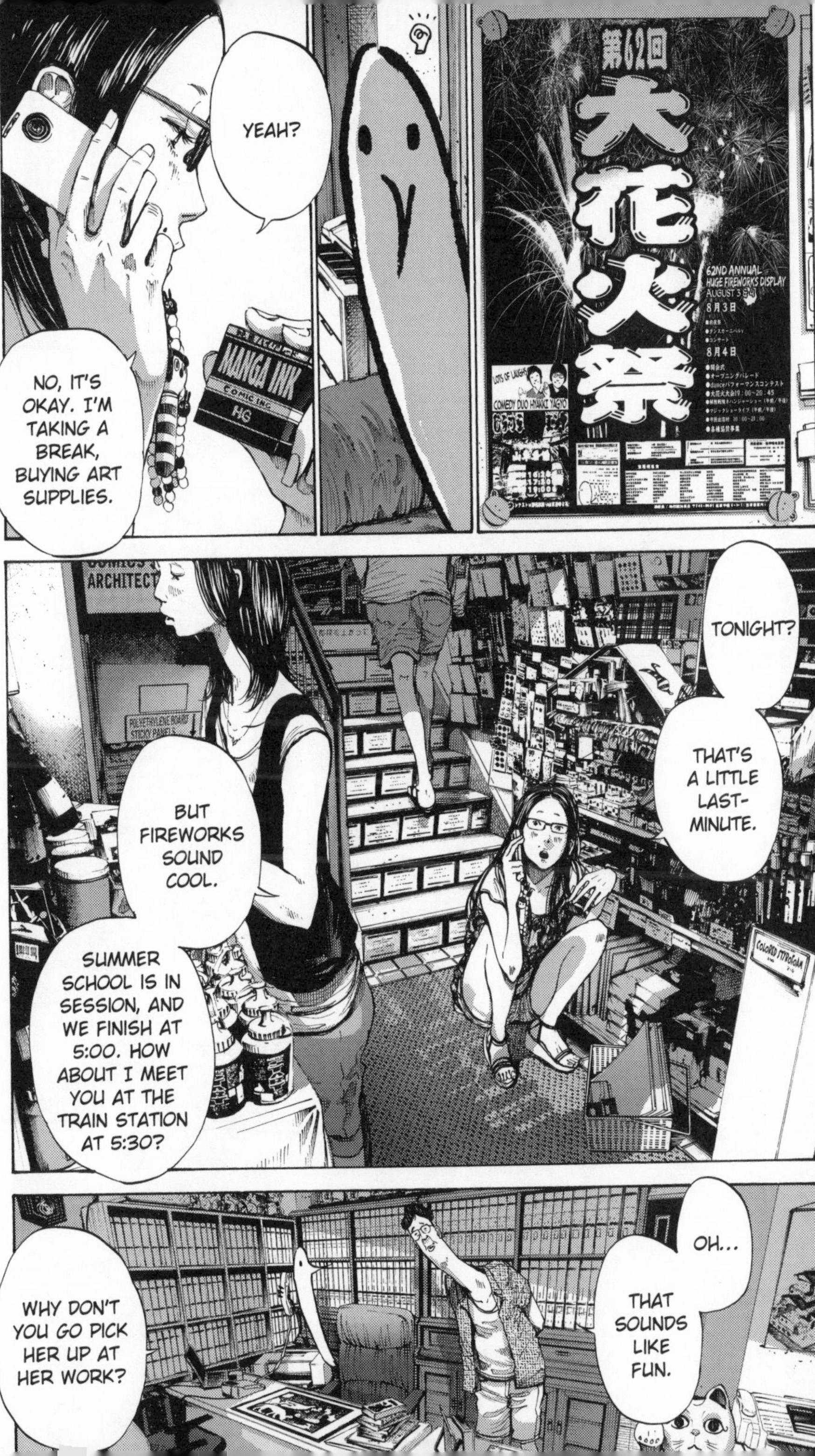
第62回
大花火大祭
62ND ANNUAL
HUGE FIREWORKS DISPLAY
AUGUST 3 & 4
8月3日
8月4日
LOTS OF LAUGHS
COMEDY DUO HYAKKI YAGYO
YEAH?
NO, IT'S OKAY. I'M TAKING A BREAK, BUYING ART SUPPLIES.
MANGA INK
COMICING
HG
TONIGHT?
THAT'S A LITTLE LAST-MINUTE.
BUT FIREWORKS SOUND COOL.
SUMMER SCHOOL IS IN SESSION, AND WE FINISH AT 5:00. HOW ABOUT I MEET YOU AT THE TRAIN STATION AT 5:30?
ARCHITECT
POLYETHYLENE BOARD
STICKY PANELS
COLORED STYROFOAM
OH...
THAT SOUNDS LIKE FUN.
WHY DON'T YOU GO PICK HER UP AT HER WORK?

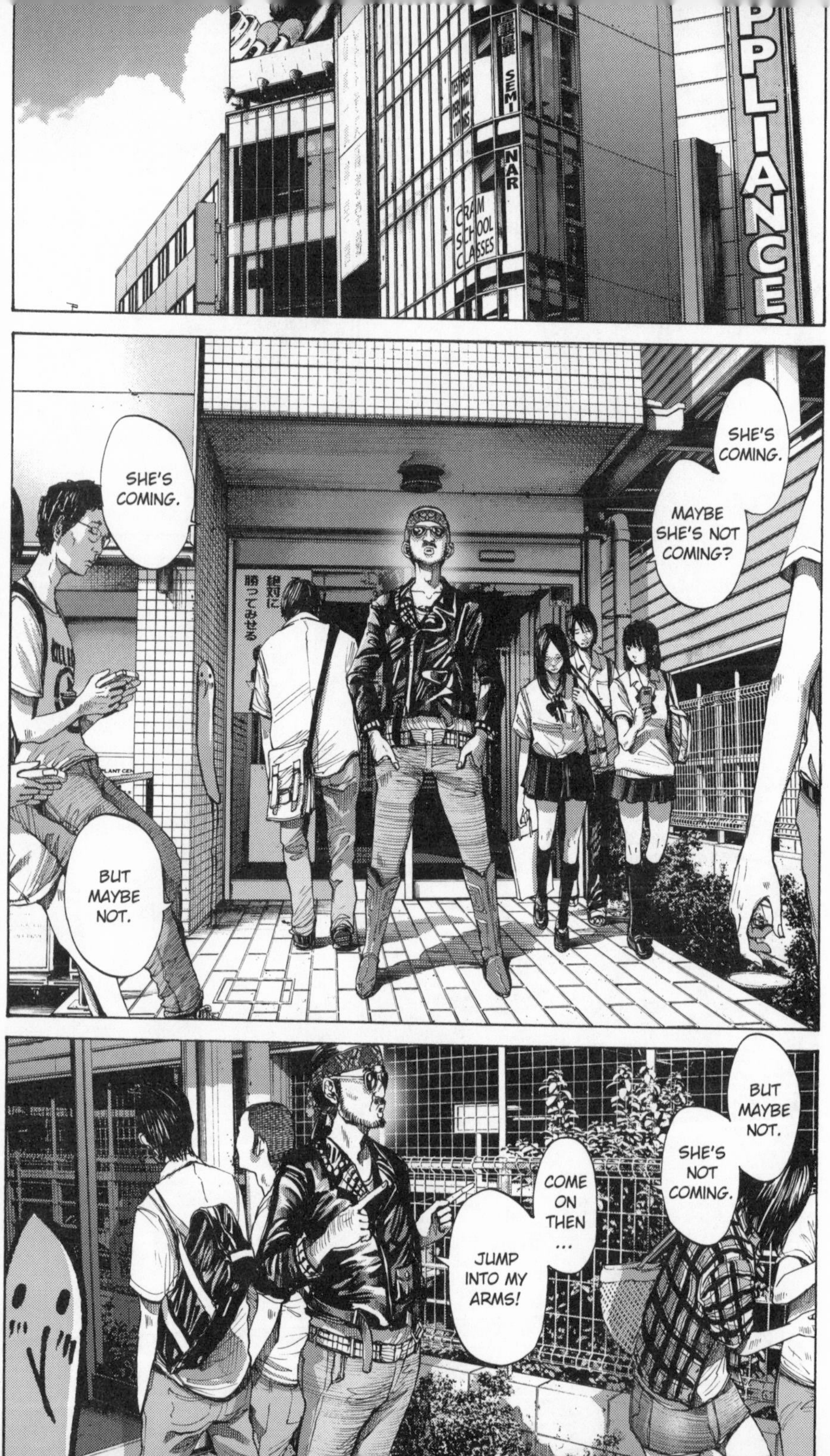
PPLIANCE
SEMI
NAR
CRAM SCHOOL CLASSES
SHE'S COMING.
MAYBE SHE'S NOT COMING?
絶対に勝ってみせる
SHE'S COMING.
BUT MAYBE NOT.
BUT MAYBE NOT.
SHE'S NOT COMING.
COME ON THEN...
JUMP INTO MY ARMS!

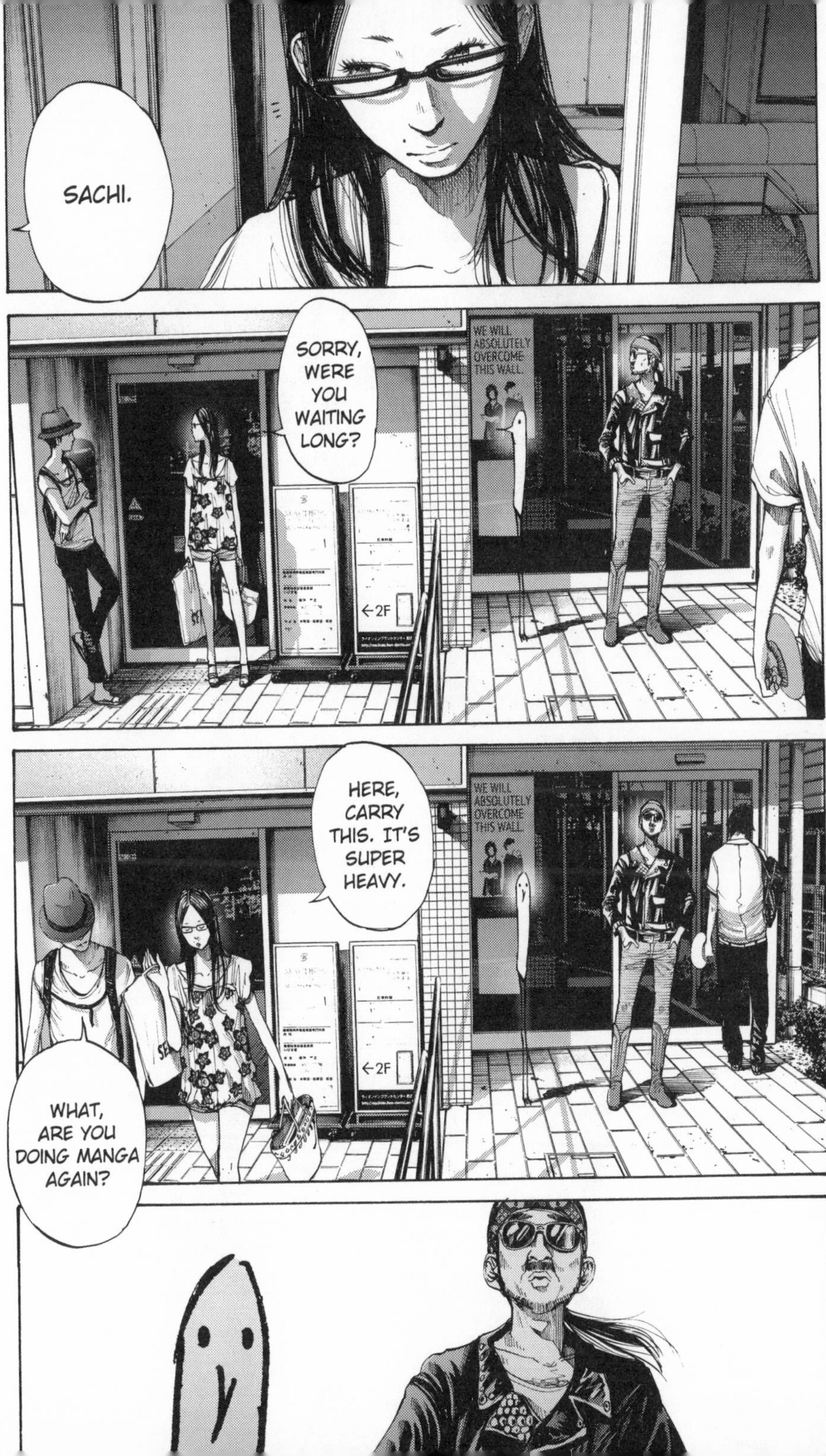
SACHI.
WE WILL ABSOLUTELY OVERCOME THIS WALL.
SORRY, WERE YOU WAITING LONG?
←2F
WE WILL ABSOLUTELY OVERCOME THIS WALL.
HERE, CARRY THIS. IT'S SUPER HEAVY.
←2F
WHAT, ARE YOU DOING MANGA AGAIN?

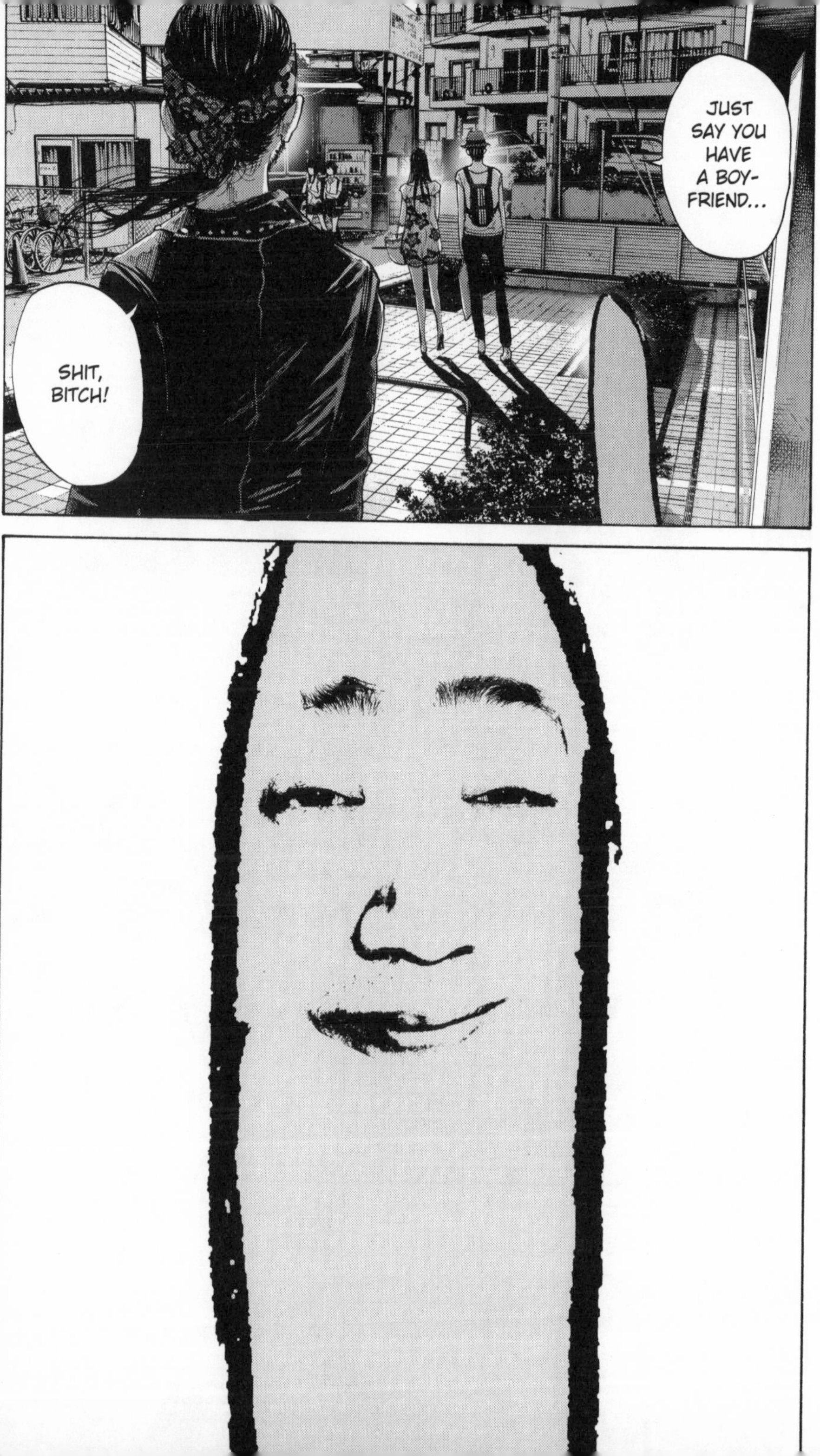
JUST SAY YOU HAVE A BOY-FRIEND...
SHIT, BITCH!

Chapter 86

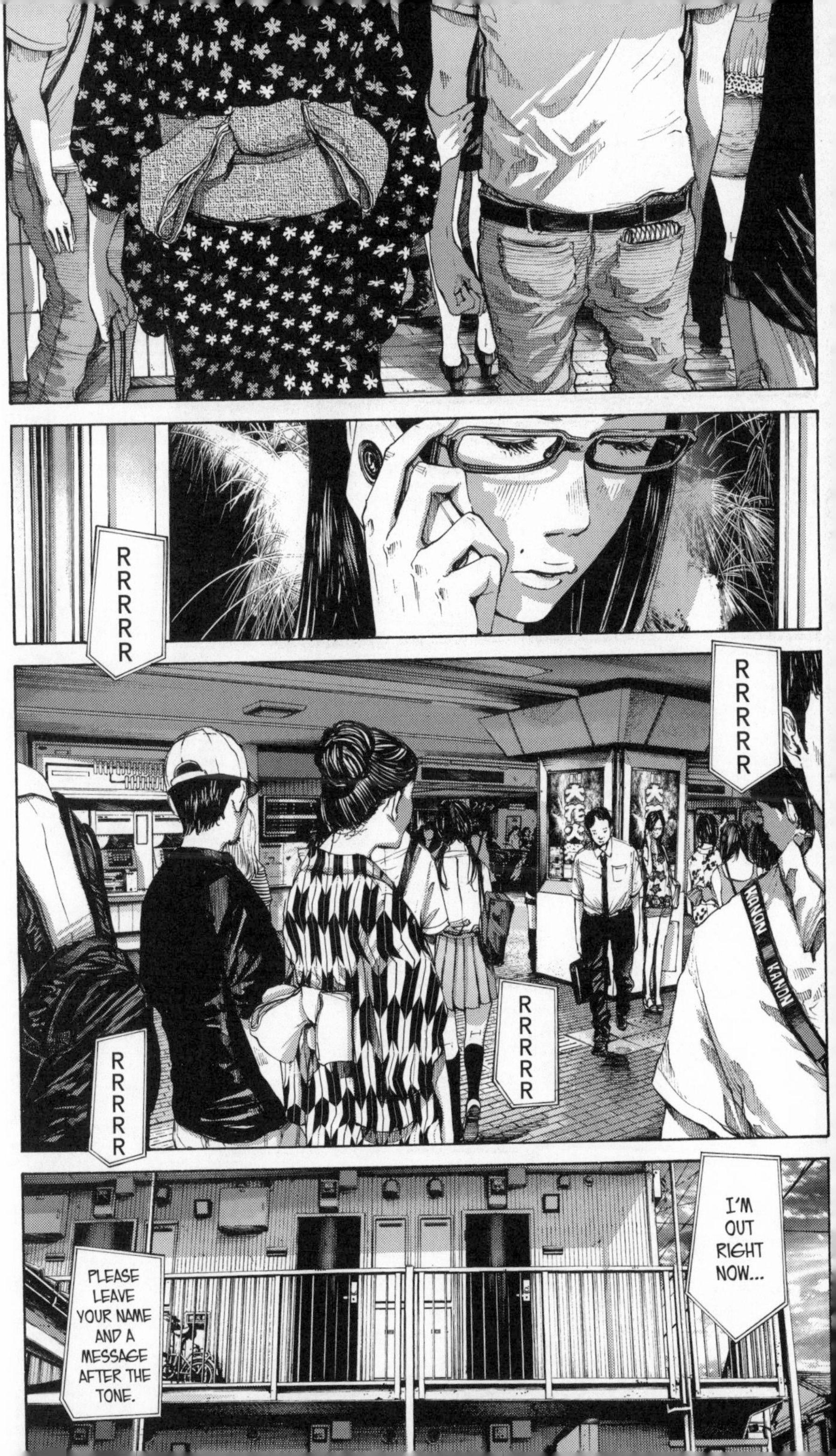

RRRRR
RRRRR
RRRRR
KANON
RRRRR
I'M OUT RIGHT NOW...
PLEASE LEAVE YOUR NAME AND A MESSAGE AFTER THE TONE.

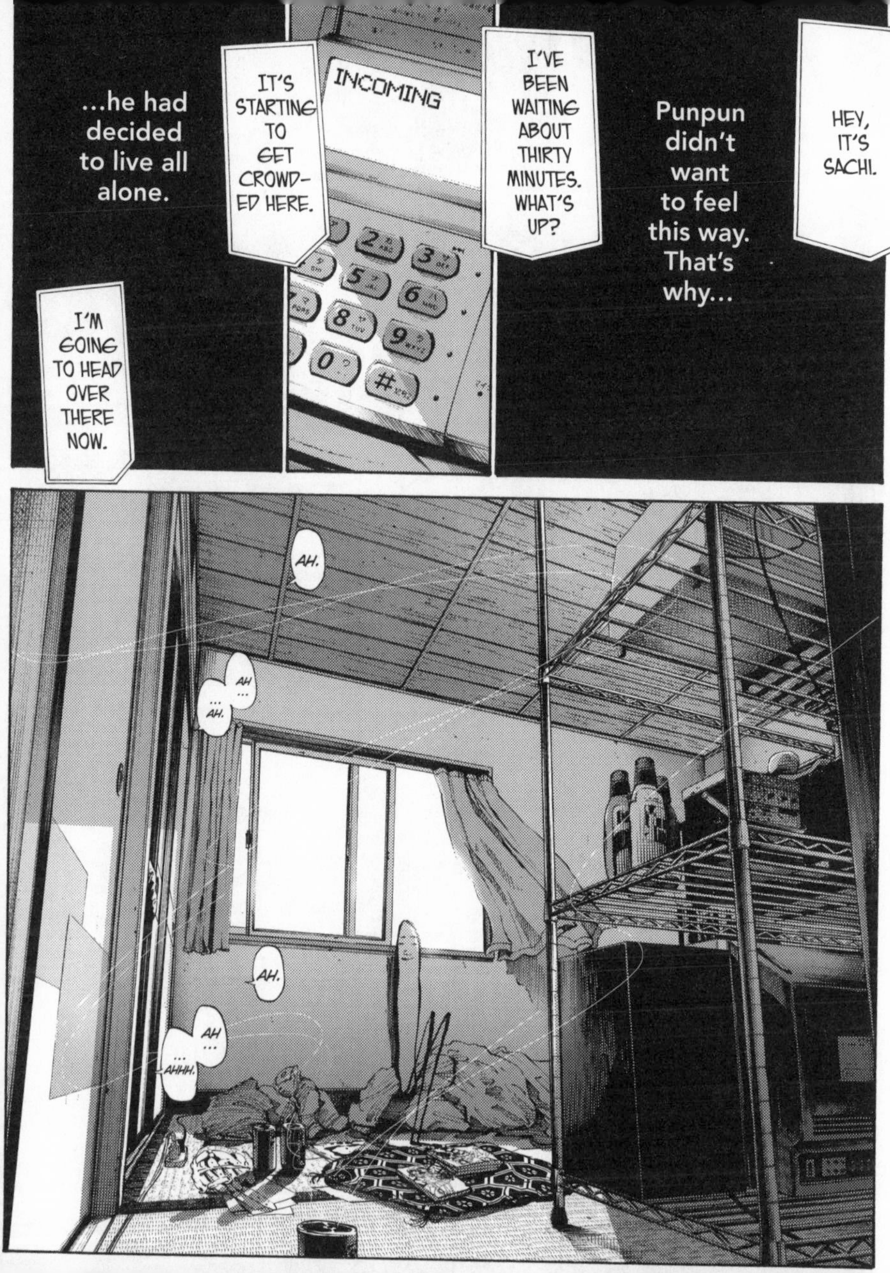
HEY, IT'S SACHI.
Punpun didn't want to feel this way. That's why...
I'VE BEEN WAITING ABOUT THIRTY MINUTES. WHAT'S UP?
INCOMING
IT'S STARTING TO GET CROWDED HERE.
...he had decided to live all alone.
I'M GOING TO HEAD OVER THERE NOW.
AH.
AH... ...AH.
AH.
AH... ...AHHH.

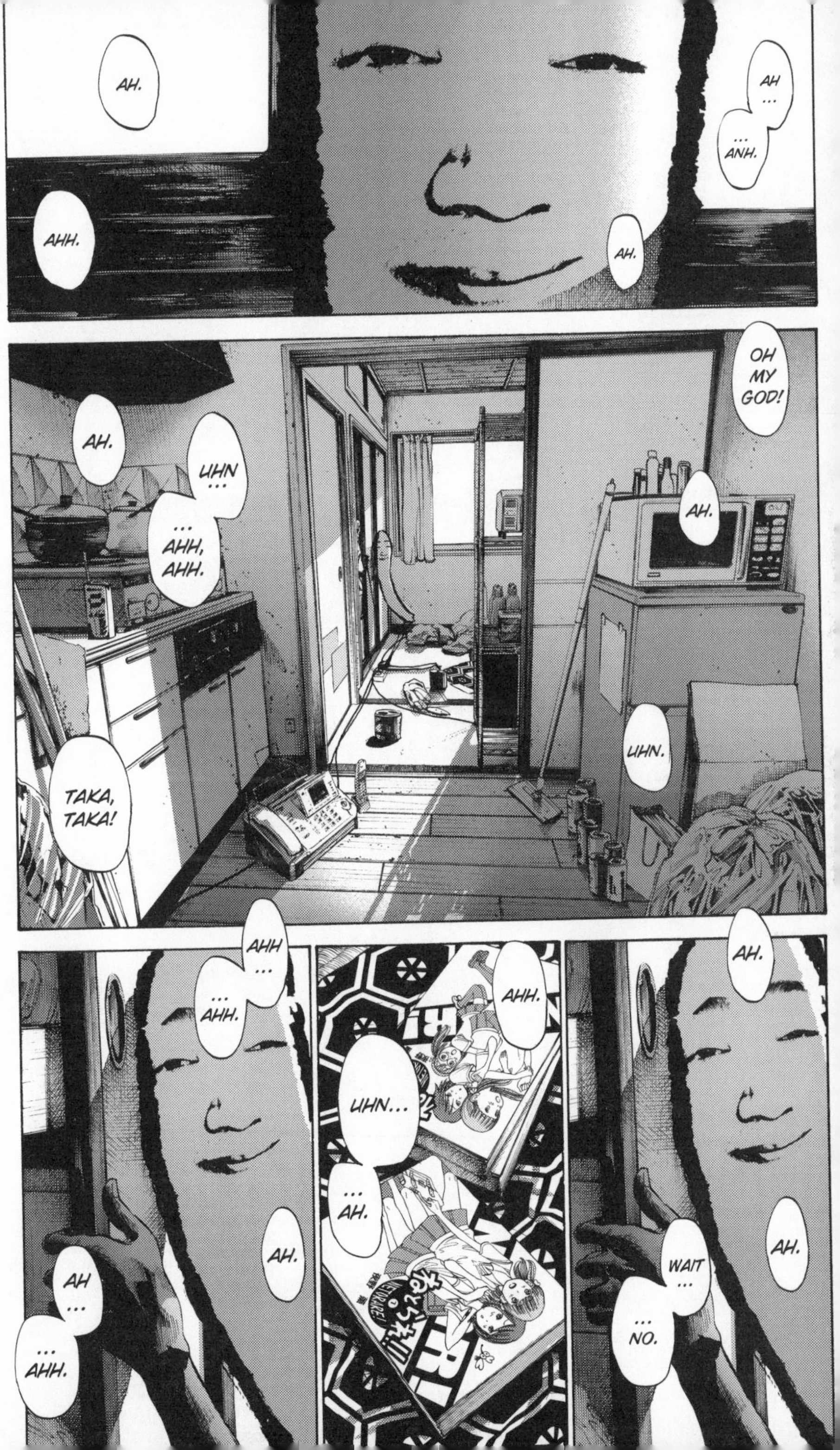
AH ...
... ANH.
AH.
AH.
AHH.
OH MY GOD!
AH.
UHN.
AH.
UHN ...
... AHH, AHH.
TAKA, TAKA!
AH.
AH.
WAIT ...
... NO.
AHH.
UHN...
... AH.
AHH ...
... AHH.
AH.
AH ...
... AHH.

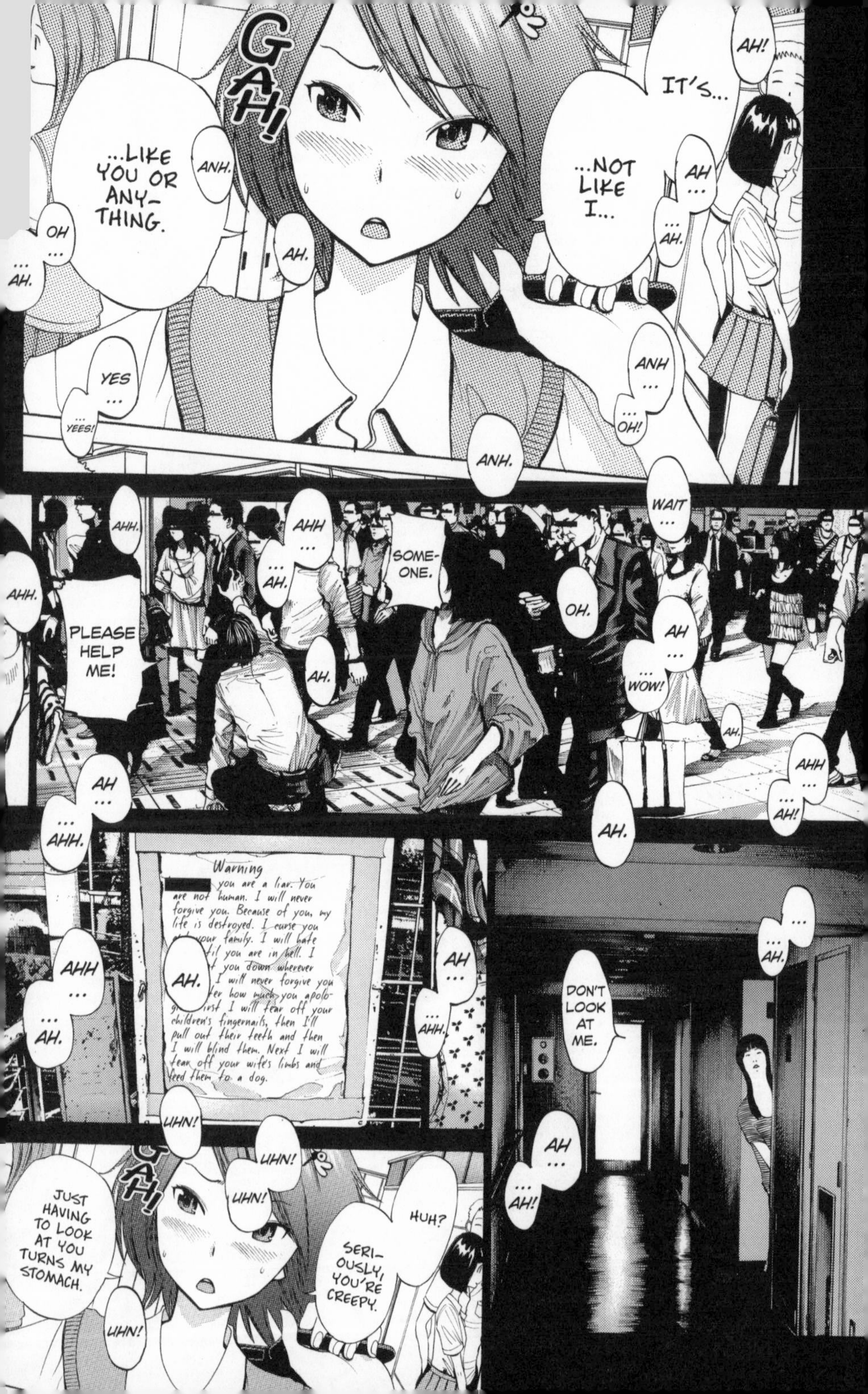
AH!
IT'S...
AH...
...AH.
...NOT LIKE I...
ANH...
...OH!
ANH.
GAH!
ANH.
...LIKE YOU OR ANY-THING.
AH.
OH...
...AH.
YES...
...YEES!
WAIT...
AHH...
...AH!
AH.
AH...
...WOW!
OH.
SOME-ONE.
AHH...
...AH.
AH.
AHH.
PLEASE HELP ME!
AHH.
AH...
...AHH.
...
...AH.
DON'T LOOK AT ME.
AH...
...AH!
AH...
...AHH.
Warning
[redacted] you are a liar. You are not human. I will never forgive you. Because of you, my life is destroyed. I curse you your family. I will hate til you are in hell. I you down wherever I will never forgive you how much you apolo- First I will tear off your children's fingernails, then I'll pull out their teeth and then I will blind them. Next I will tear off your wife's limbs and feed them to a dog.
AH.
AHH...
...AH.
UHN!
UHN!
UHN!
HUH?
SERI-OUSLY, YOU'RE CREEPY.
GAH!
JUST HAVING TO LOOK AT YOU TURNS MY STOMACH.
UHN!

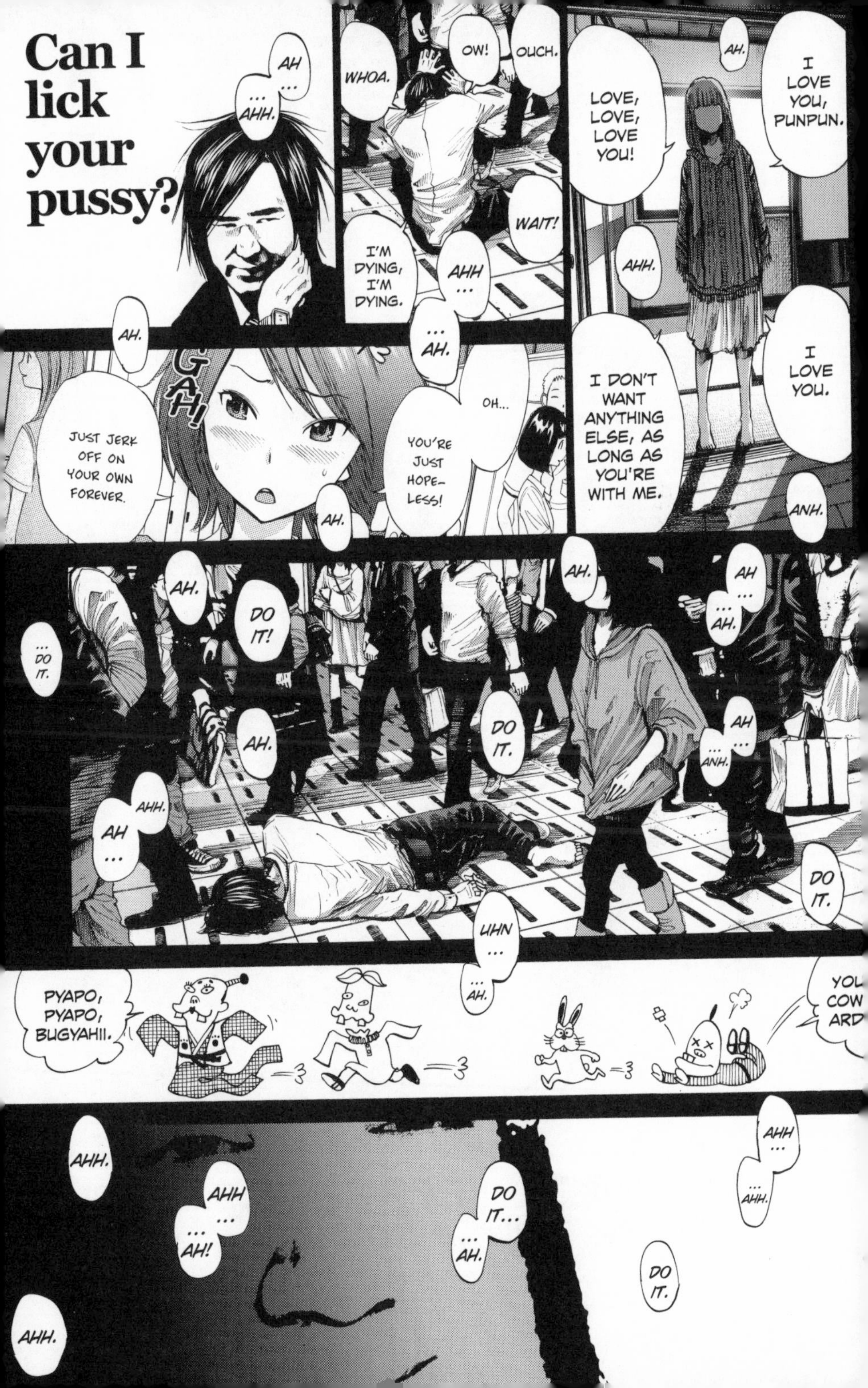
AH.
I LOVE YOU, PUNPUN.
LOVE, LOVE, LOVE YOU!
AHH.
I LOVE YOU.
I DON'T WANT ANYTHING ELSE, AS LONG AS YOU'RE WITH ME.
ANH.
OUCH.
OW!
WHOA.
WAIT!
AHH ...
I'M DYING, I'M DYING.
AH ... AHH.
Can I lick your pussy?
AH.
... AH.
OH...
YOU'RE JUST HOPELESS!
GAH!
JUST JERK OFF ON YOUR OWN FOREVER.
AH.
AH ... AH.
AH.
AH ... ANH.
DO IT.
DO IT.
AH.
DO IT!
AH.
... DO IT.
AHH.
AH ...
UHN ... ... AH.
YOU COWARD
PYAPO, PYAPO, BUGYAHII.
AHH ... ... AHH.
DO IT.
DO IT... ... AH.
AHH ... ... AH!
AHH.
AHH.

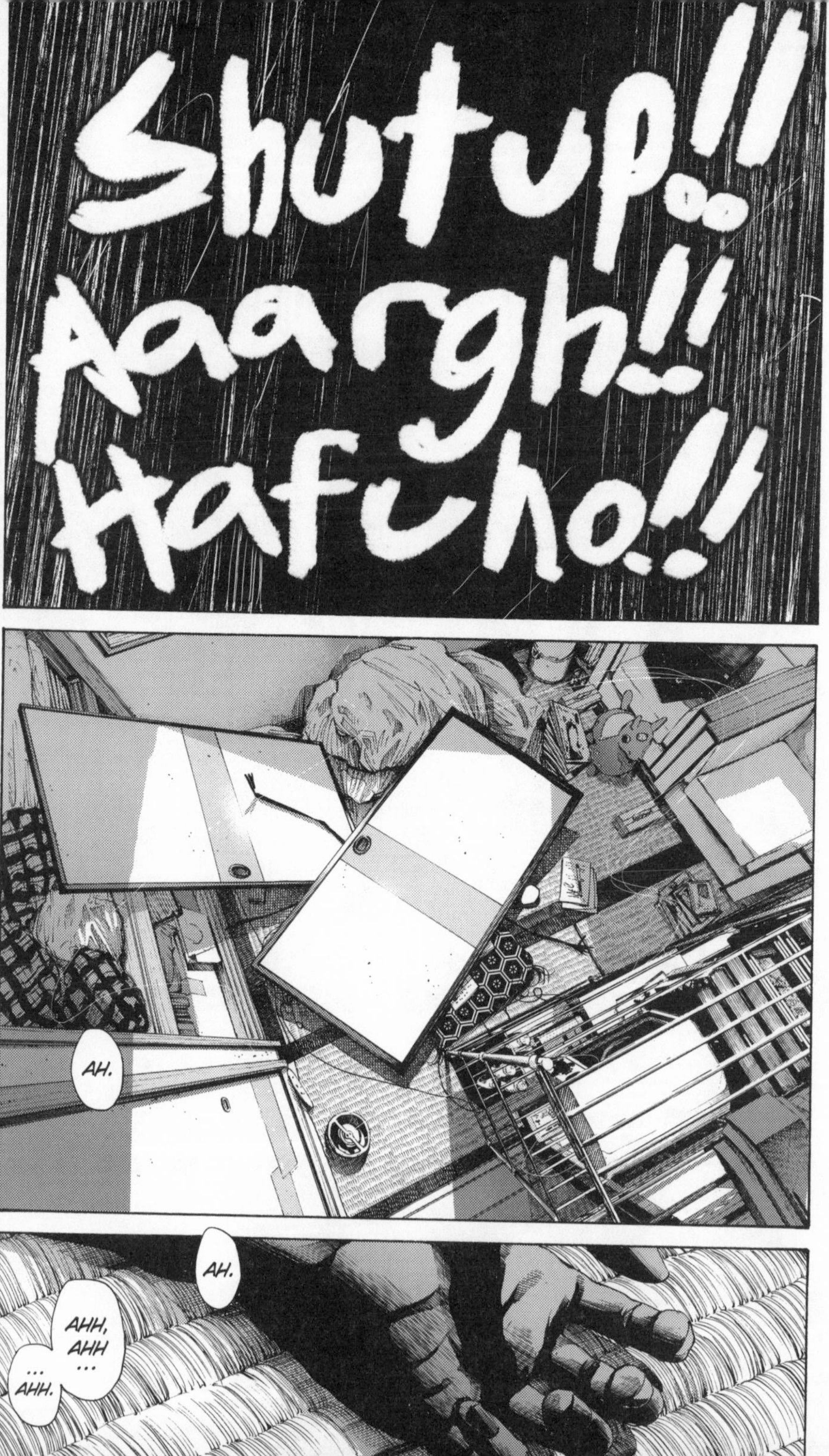
Shut up!! Aaargh!! Hafuho!!
AH.
AH.
AHH, AHH ...
... AHH.

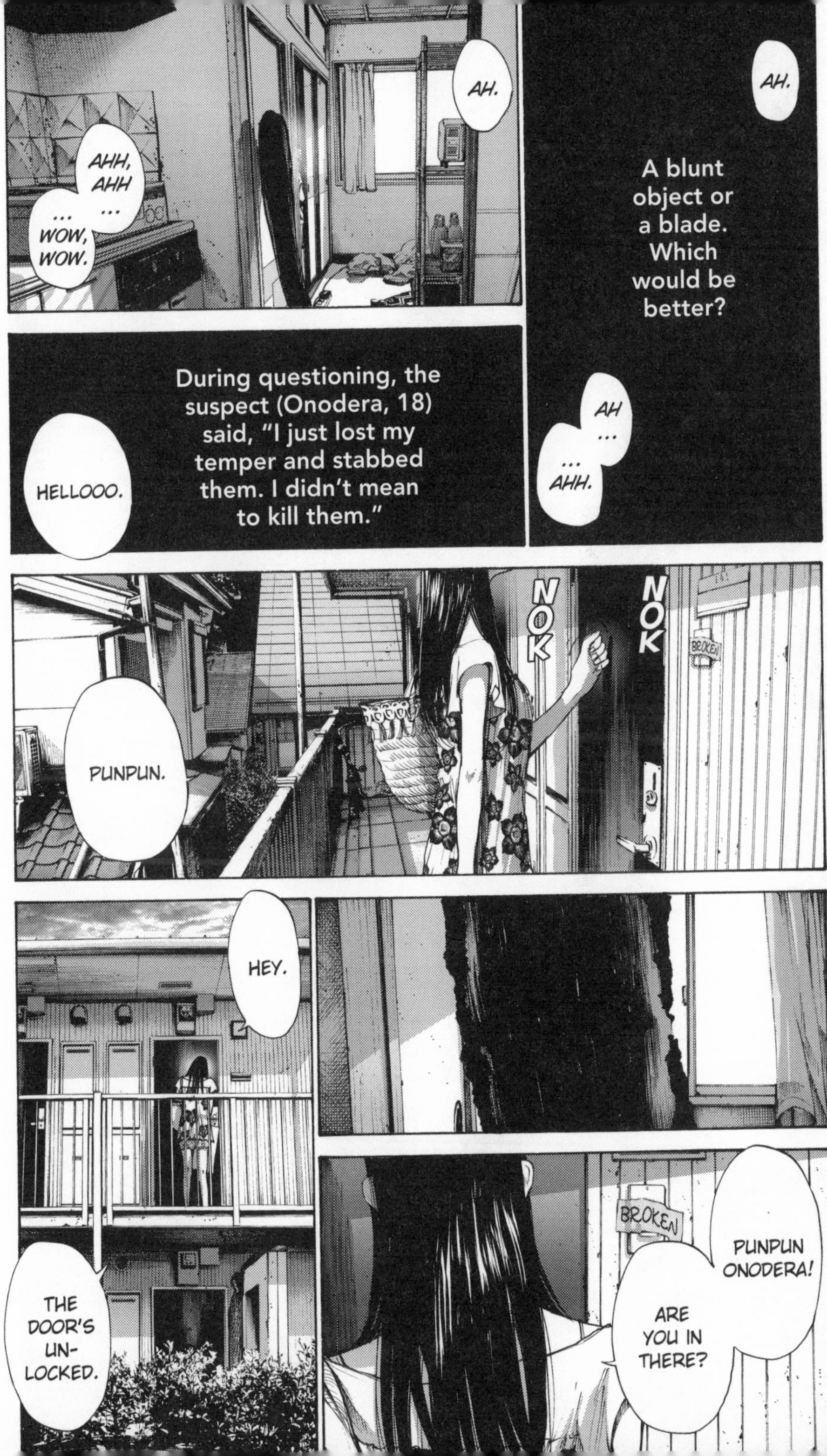
AH.
A blunt object or a blade. Which would be better?
AH ... ... AHH.
AH.
AHH, AHH ...
... WOW, WOW.
During questioning, the suspect (Onodera, 18) said, "I just lost my temper and stabbed them. I didn't mean to kill them."
HELLOOO.
NOK NOK
BROKEN
PUNPUN.
BROKEN
PUNPUN ONODERA!
ARE YOU IN THERE?
HEY.
THE DOOR'S UN-LOCKED.

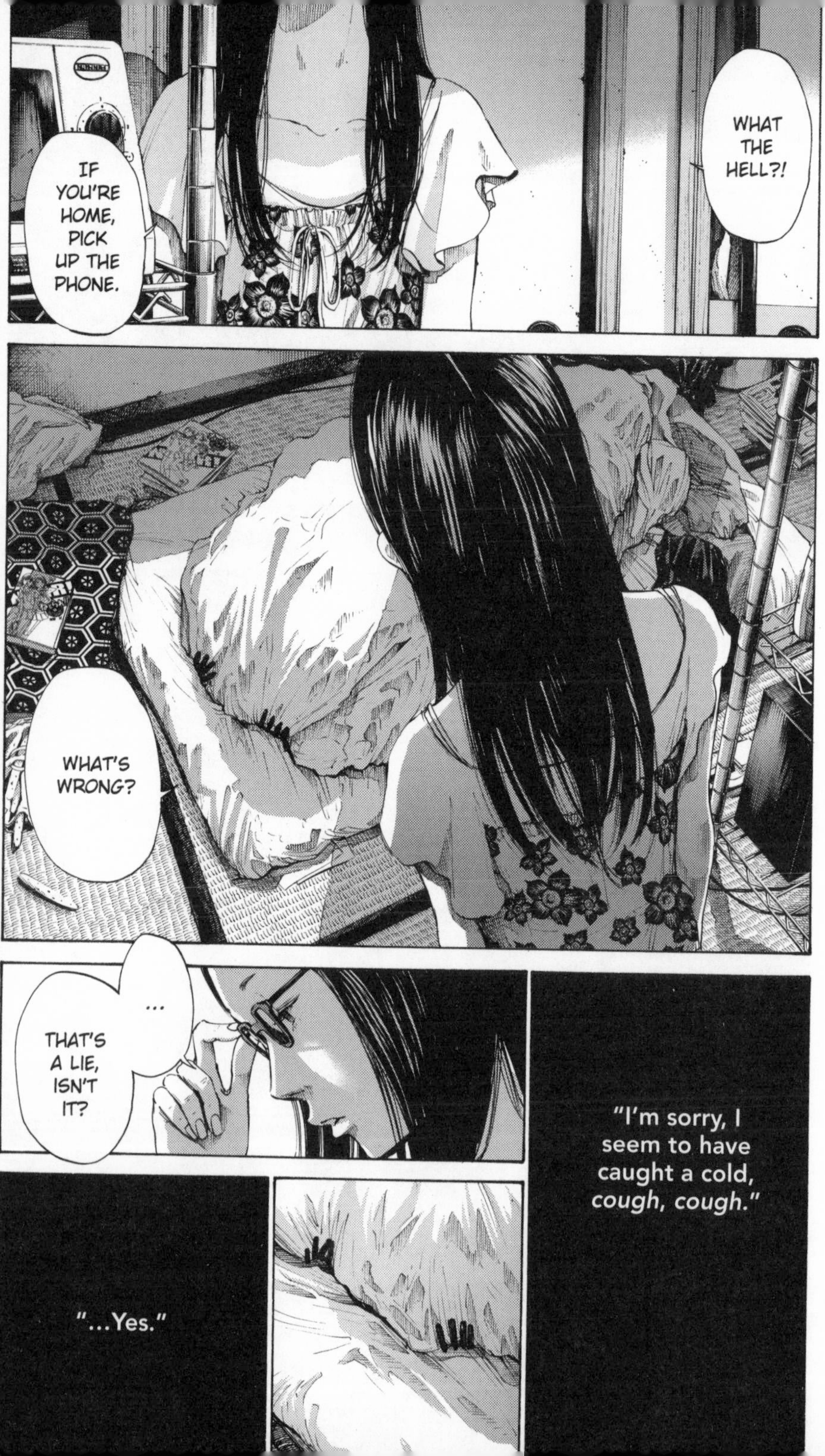
WHAT THE HELL?!
IF YOU'RE HOME, PICK UP THE PHONE.
WHAT'S WRONG?
"I'm sorry, I seem to have caught a cold, *cough, cough.*"
... THAT'S A LIE, ISN'T IT?
"...Yes."

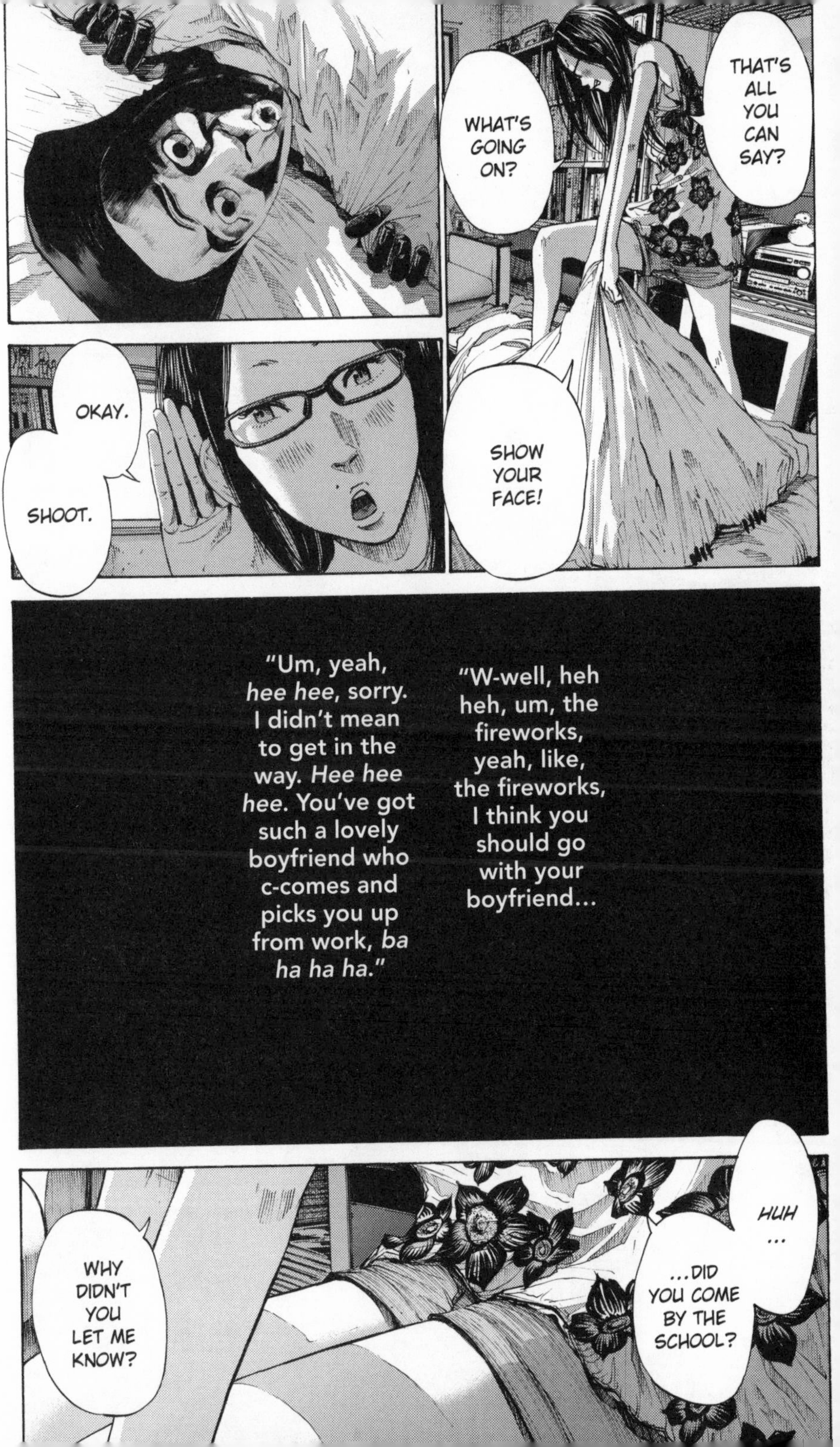
THAT'S ALL YOU CAN SAY?
WHAT'S GOING ON?
SHOW YOUR FACE!
OKAY.
SHOOT.
"W-well, heh heh, um, the fireworks, yeah, like, the fireworks, I think you should go with your boyfriend...
"Um, yeah, *hee hee*, sorry. I didn't mean to get in the way. *Hee hee hee*. You've got such a lovely boyfriend who c-comes and picks you up from work, *ba ha ha ha*."
HUH ...
...DID YOU COME BY THE SCHOOL?
WHY DIDN'T YOU LET ME KNOW?

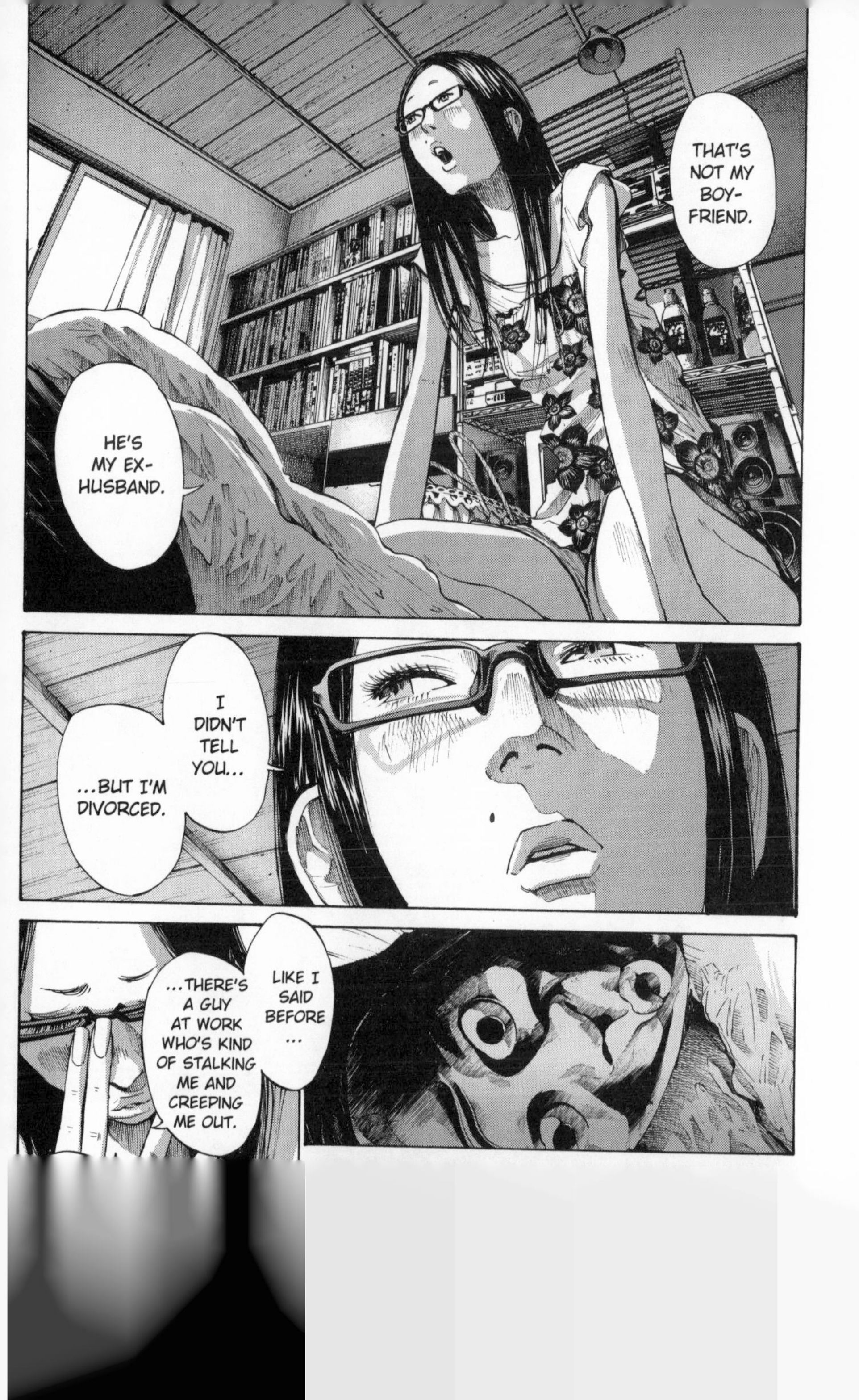
THAT'S NOT MY BOY-FRIEND.
HE'S MY EX-HUSBAND.
I DIDN'T TELL YOU...
...BUT I'M DIVORCED.
LIKE I SAID BEFORE...
...THERE'S A GUY AT WORK WHO'S KIND OF STALKING ME AND CREEPING ME OUT.

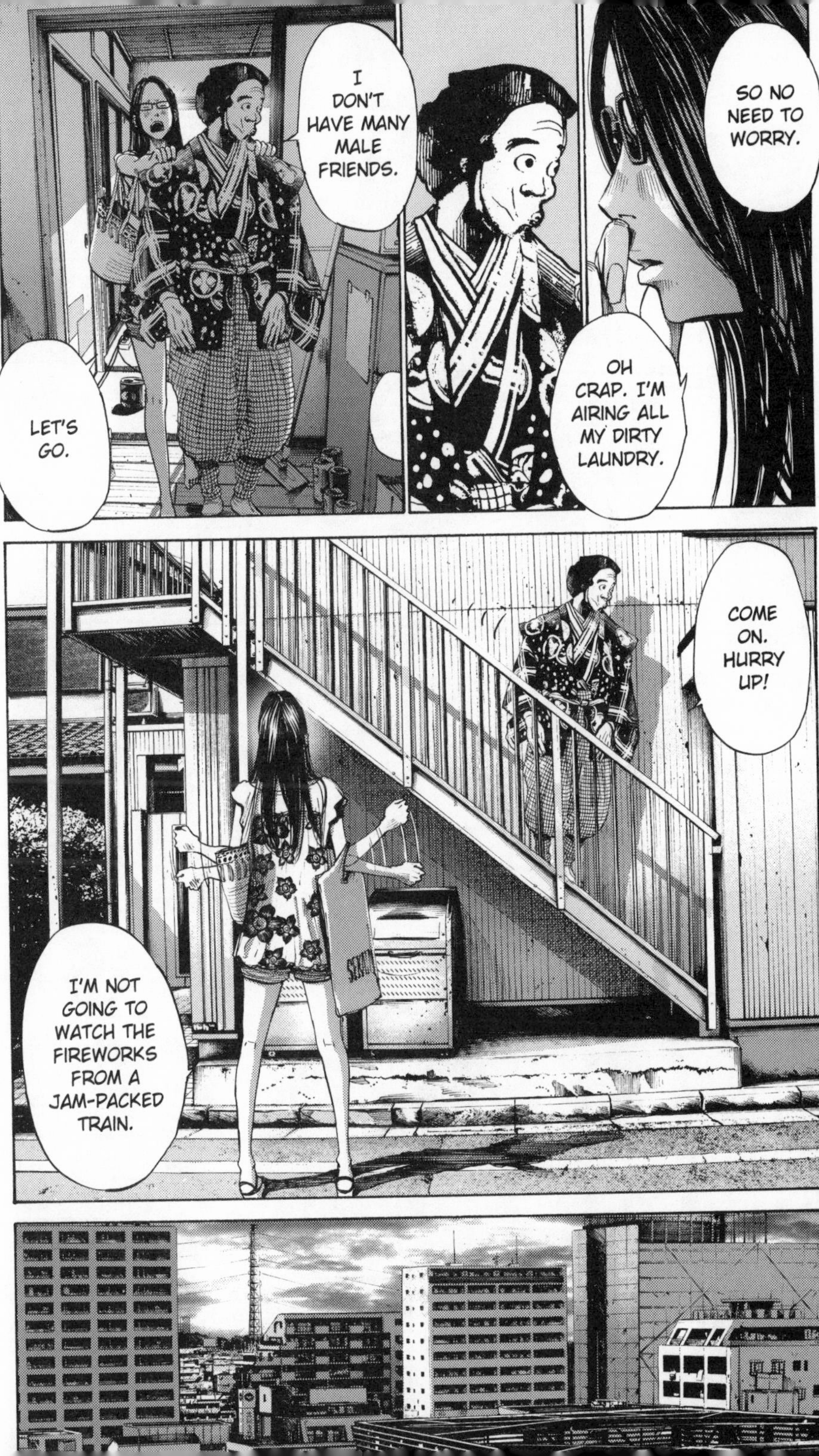
SO NO NEED TO WORRY.
OH CRAP. I'M AIRING ALL MY DIRTY LAUNDRY.
I DON'T HAVE MANY MALE FRIENDS.
LET'S GO.
COME ON. HURRY UP!
I'M NOT GOING TO WATCH THE FIREWORKS FROM A JAM-PACKED TRAIN.

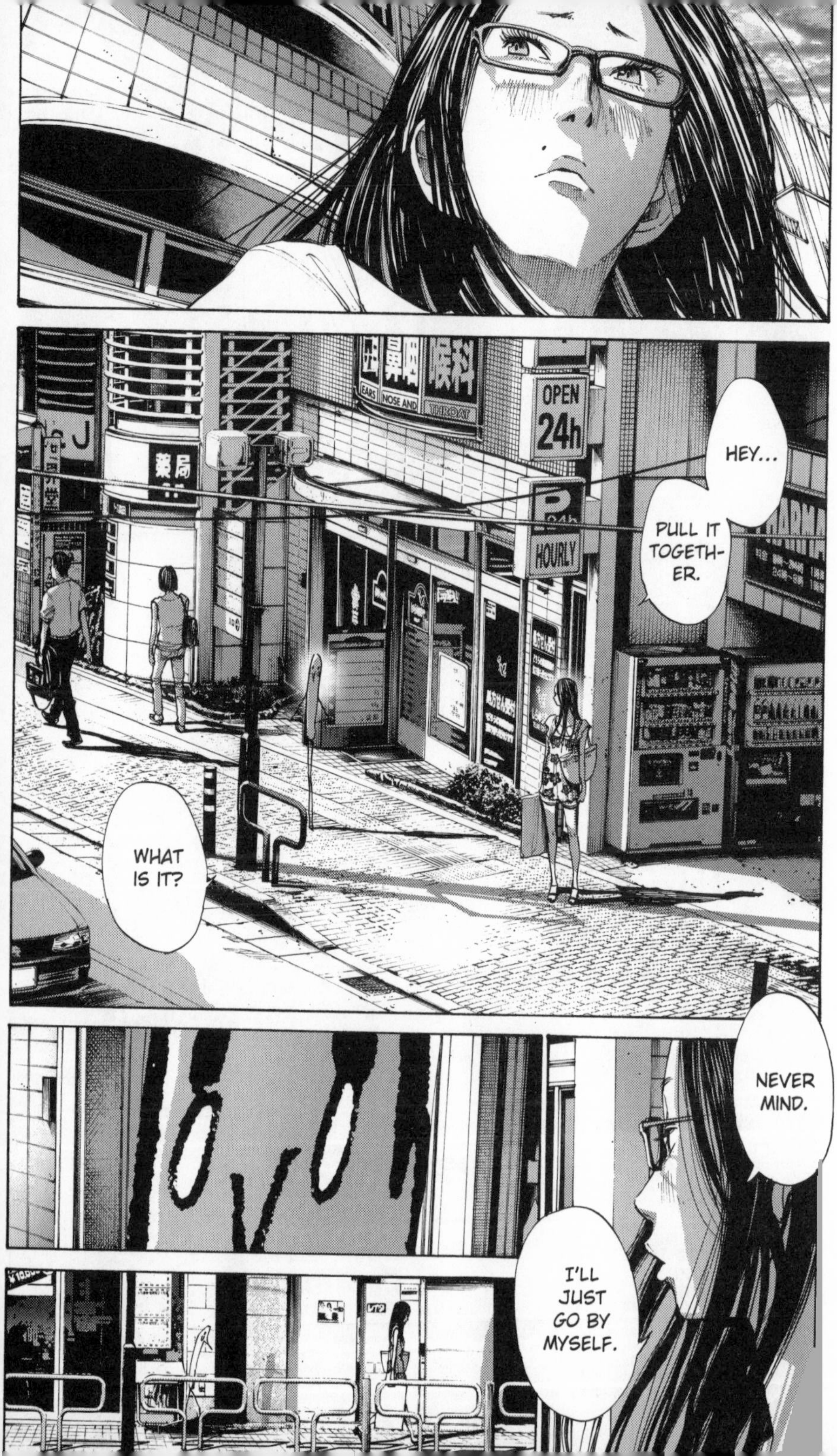
耳鼻咽喉科
EARS NOSE AND THROAT
OPEN 24h
HOURLY
薬局
HEY...
PULL IT TOGETHER.
WHAT IS IT?
NEVER MIND.
I'LL JUST GO BY MYSELF.

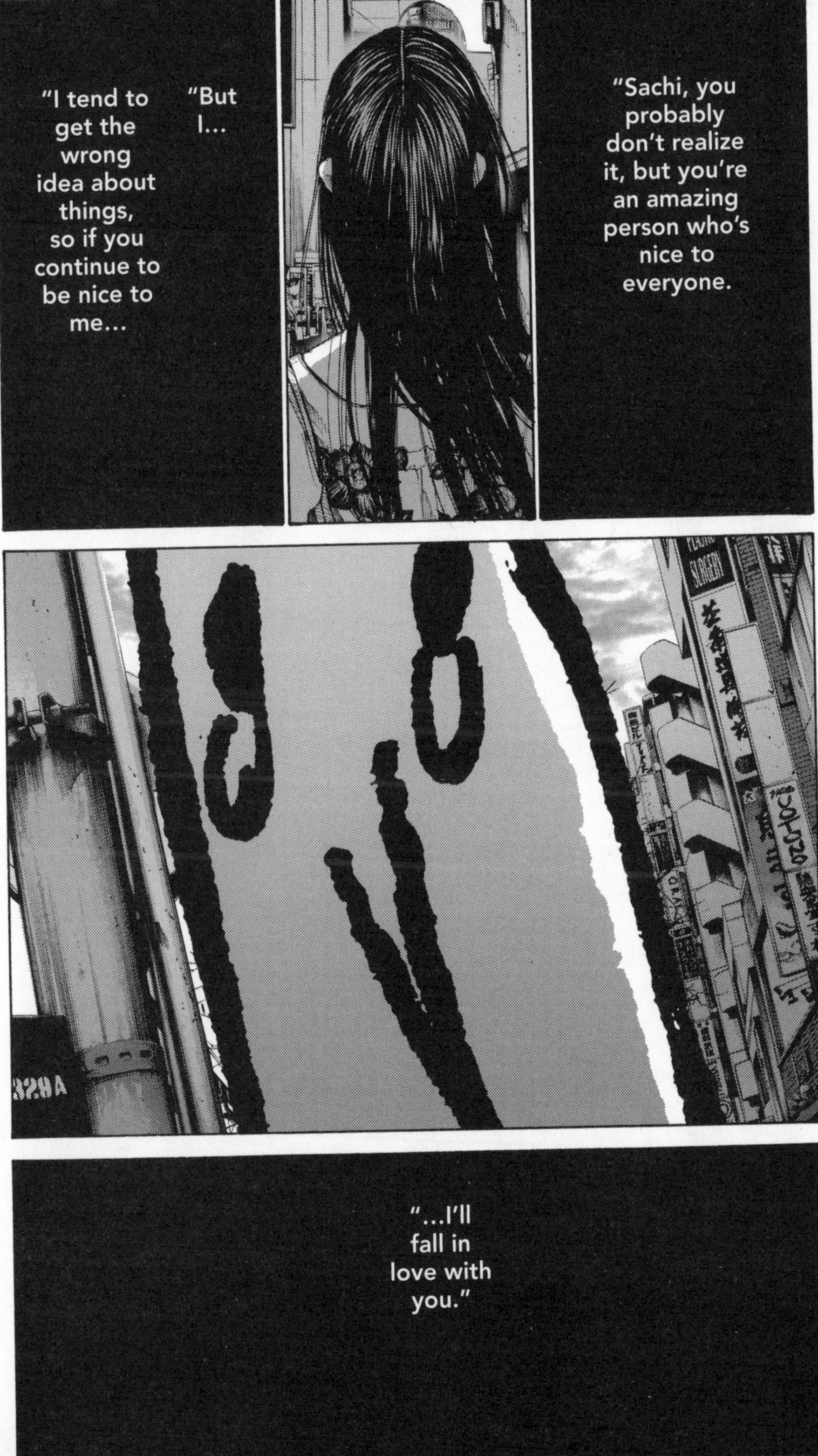
"Sachi, you probably don't realize it, but you're an amazing person who's nice to everyone.
"But I...
"I tend to get the wrong idea about things, so if you continue to be nice to me...
"...I'll fall in love with you."

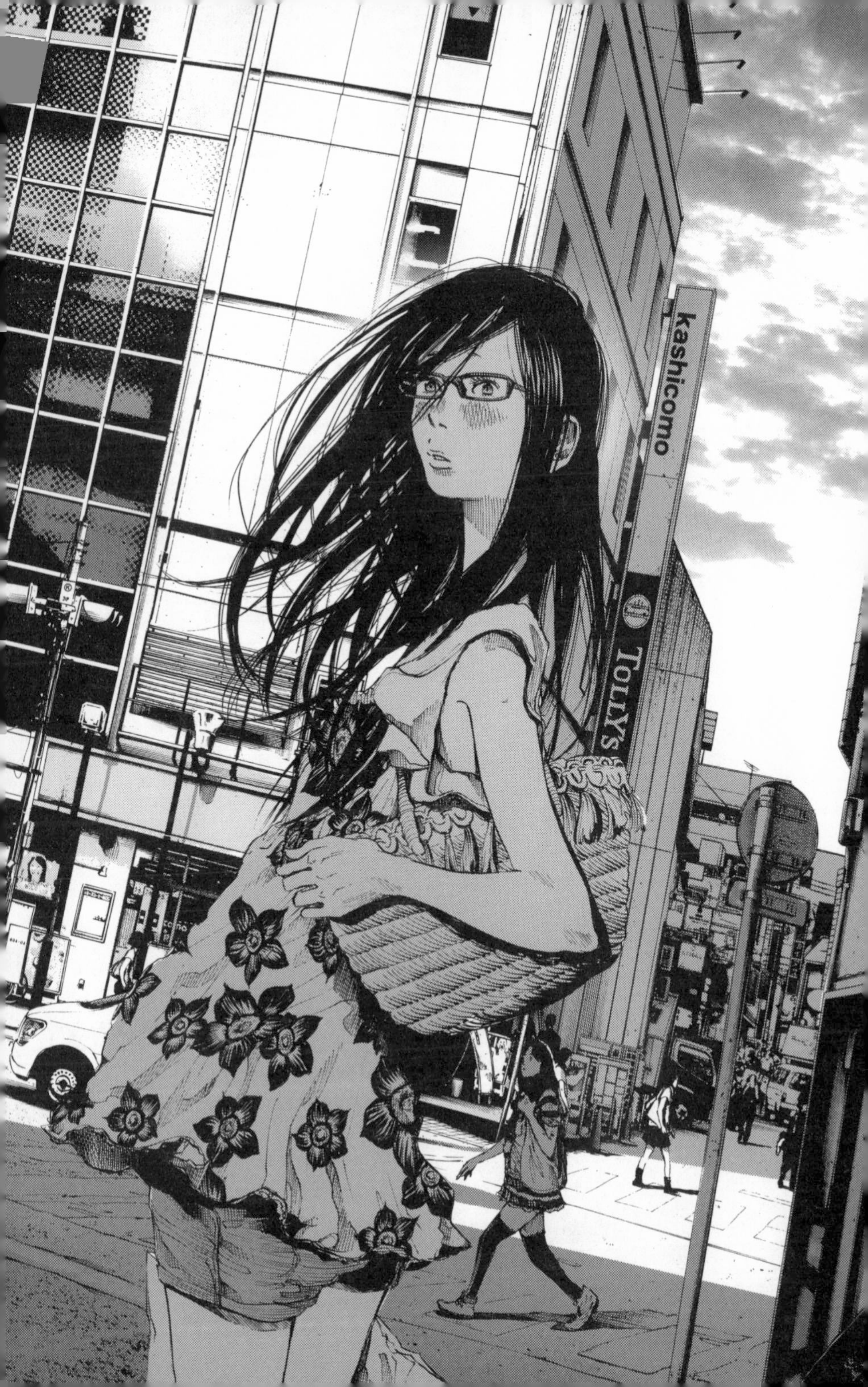
kashicomo
TOLLYS

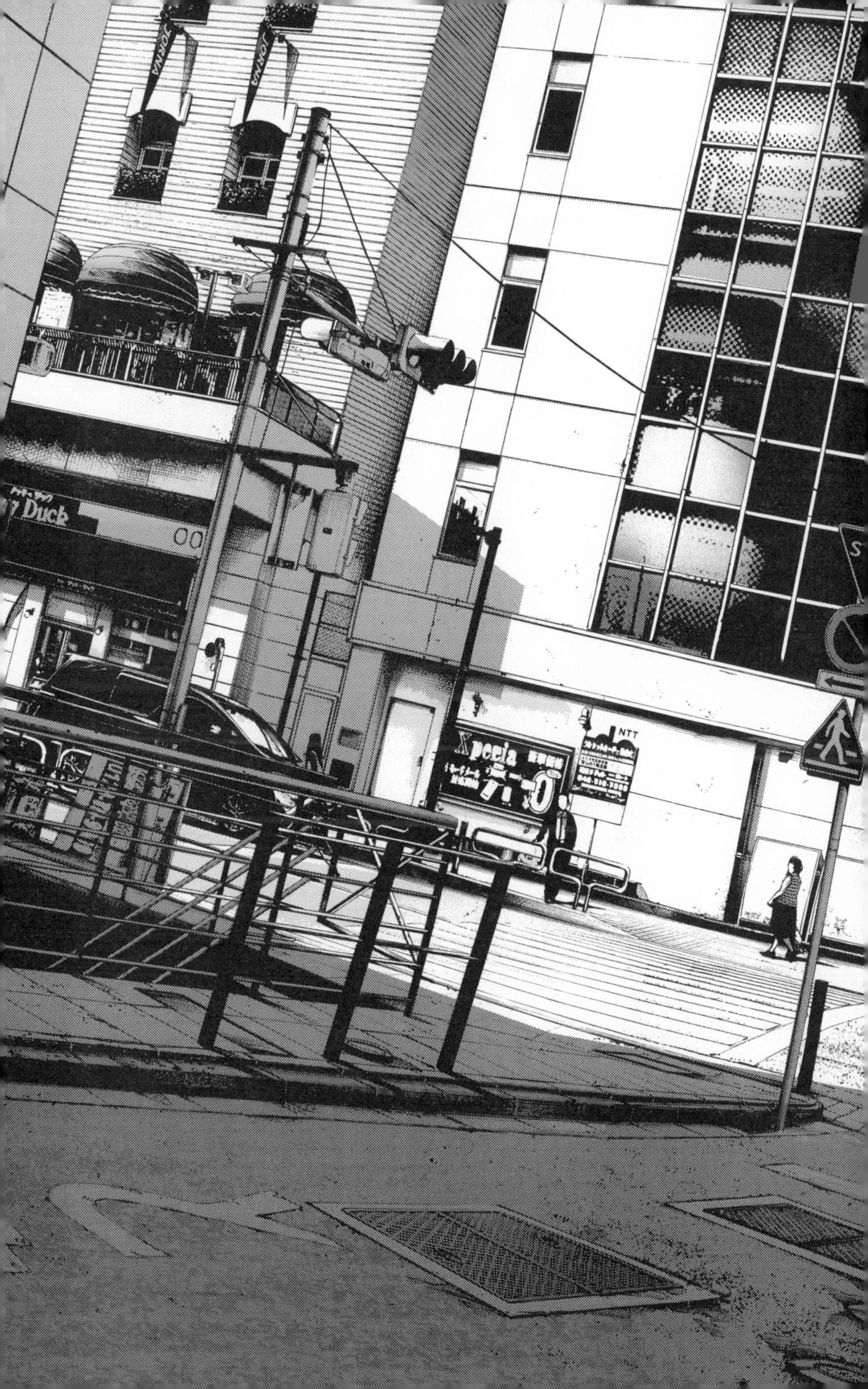
Xperia
NTT

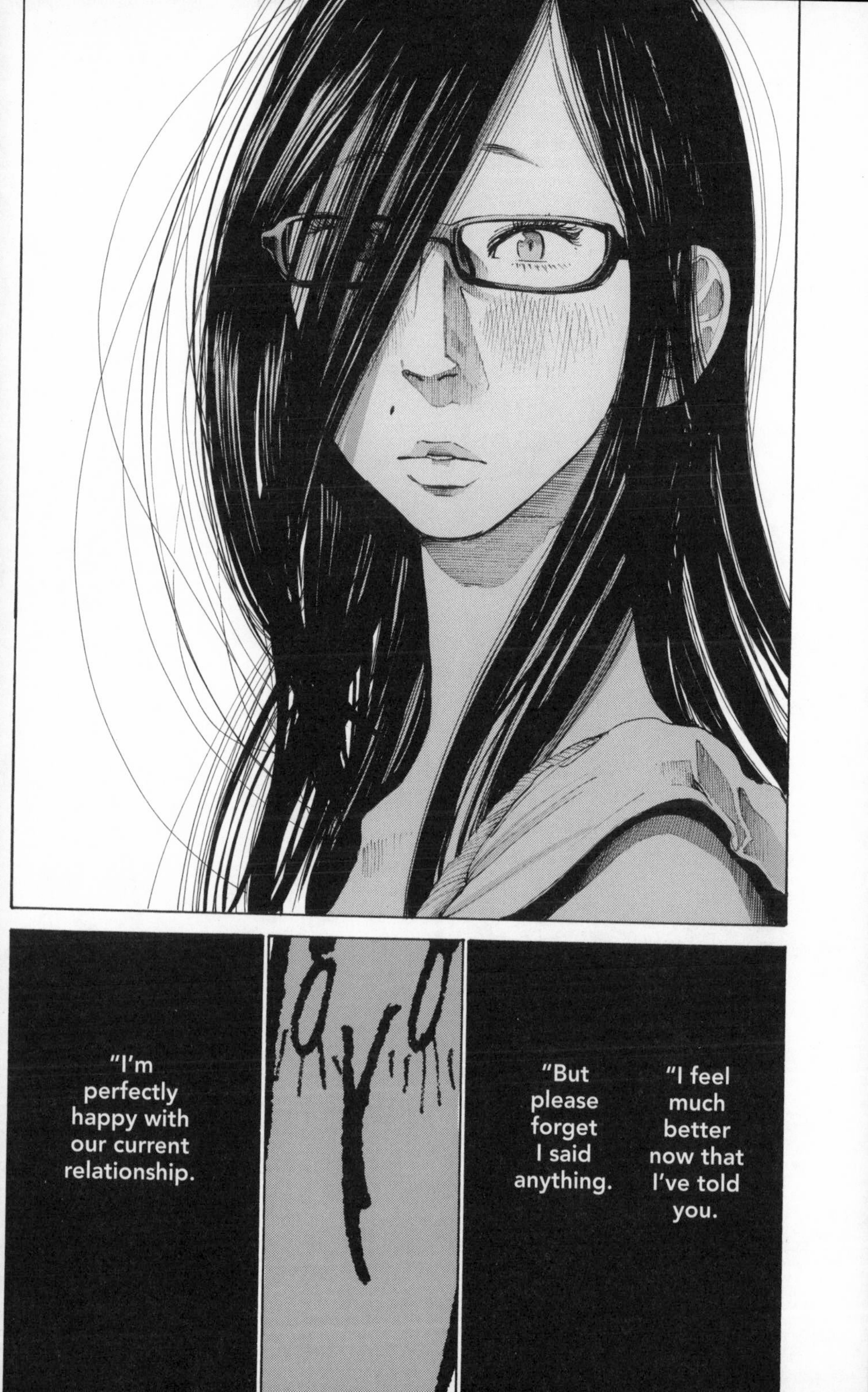
"I feel much better now that I've told you.
"But please forget I said anything.
"I'm perfectly happy with our current relationship.

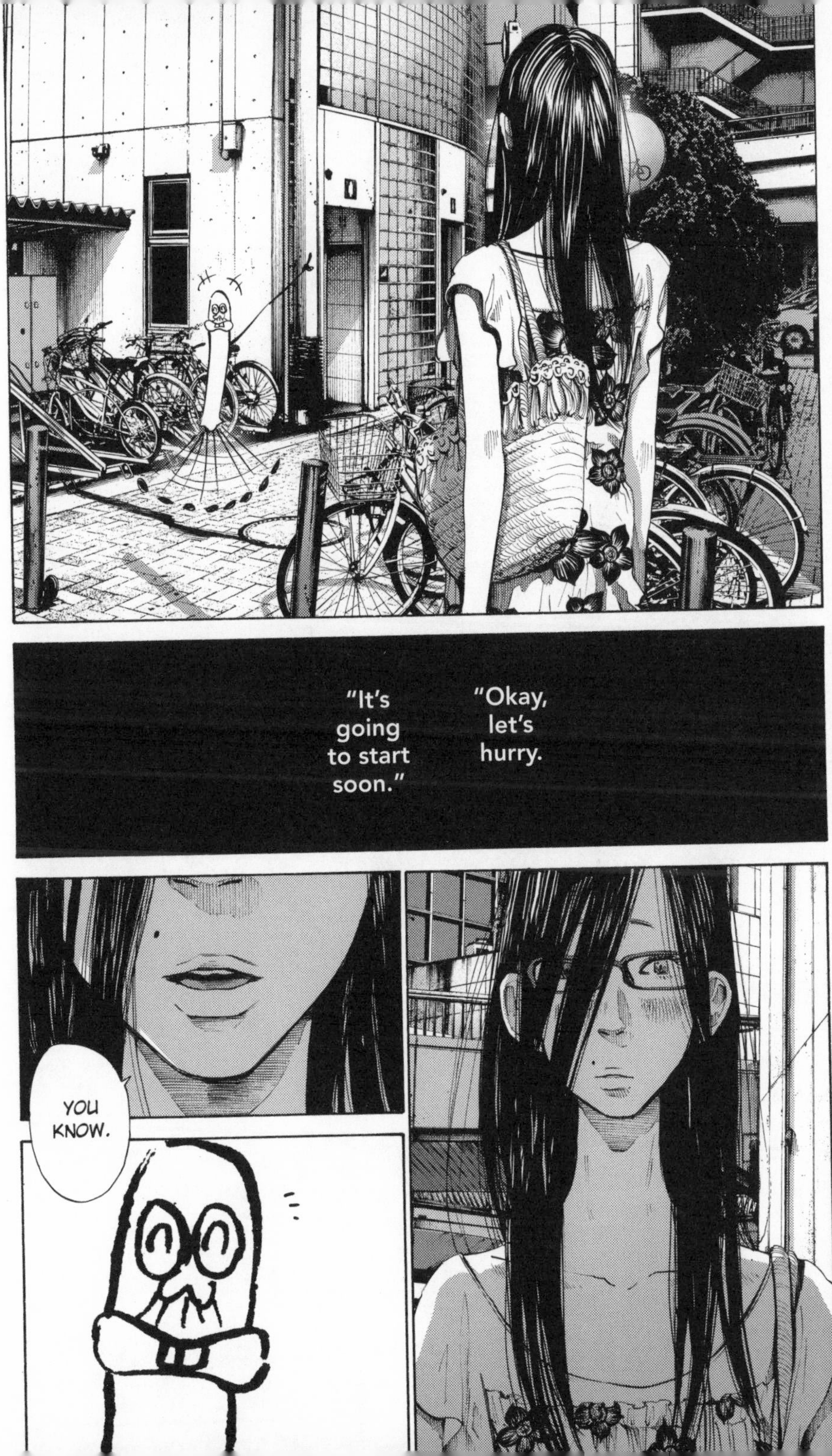
"Okay, let's hurry.
"It's going to start soon."
YOU KNOW.

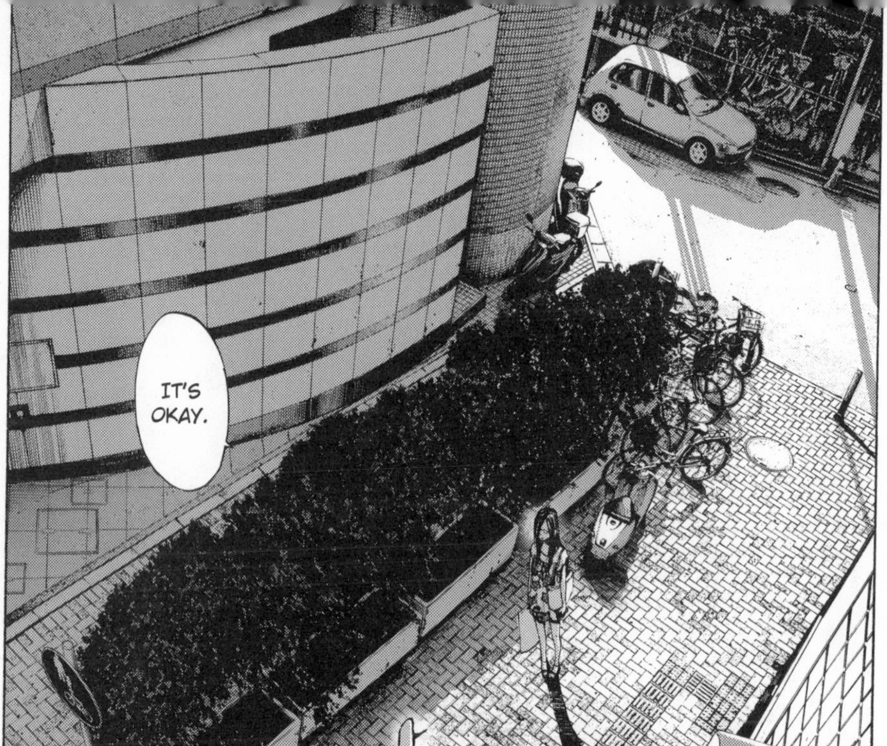
IT'S OKAY.

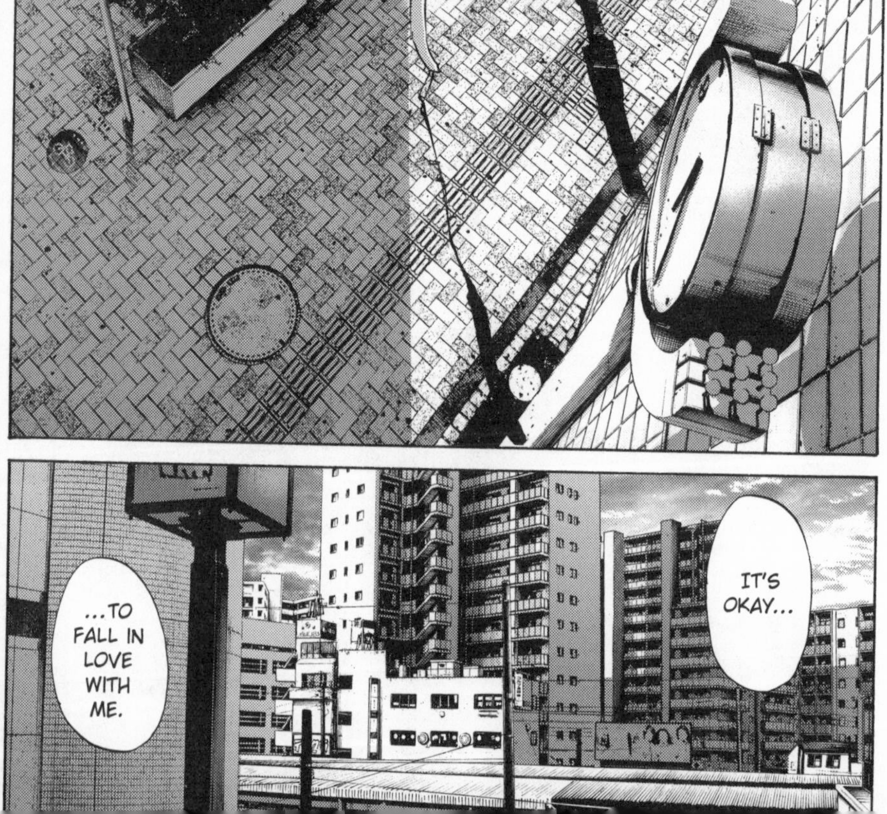
IT'S OKAY...
...TO FALL IN LOVE WITH ME.

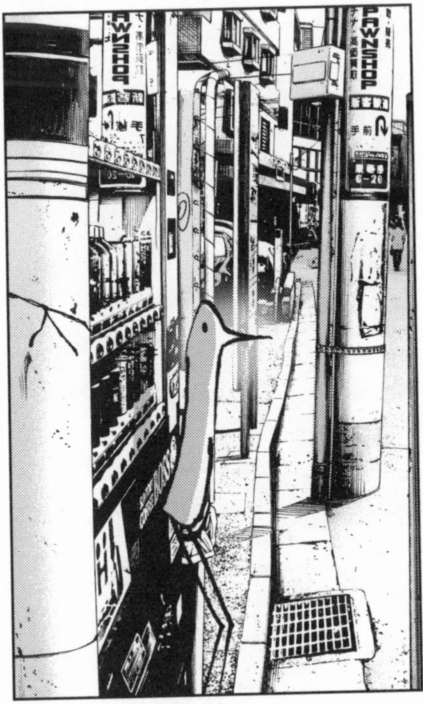
PAWNSHOP
手前
G-20
PAWNSHOP

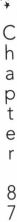

Chapter 87

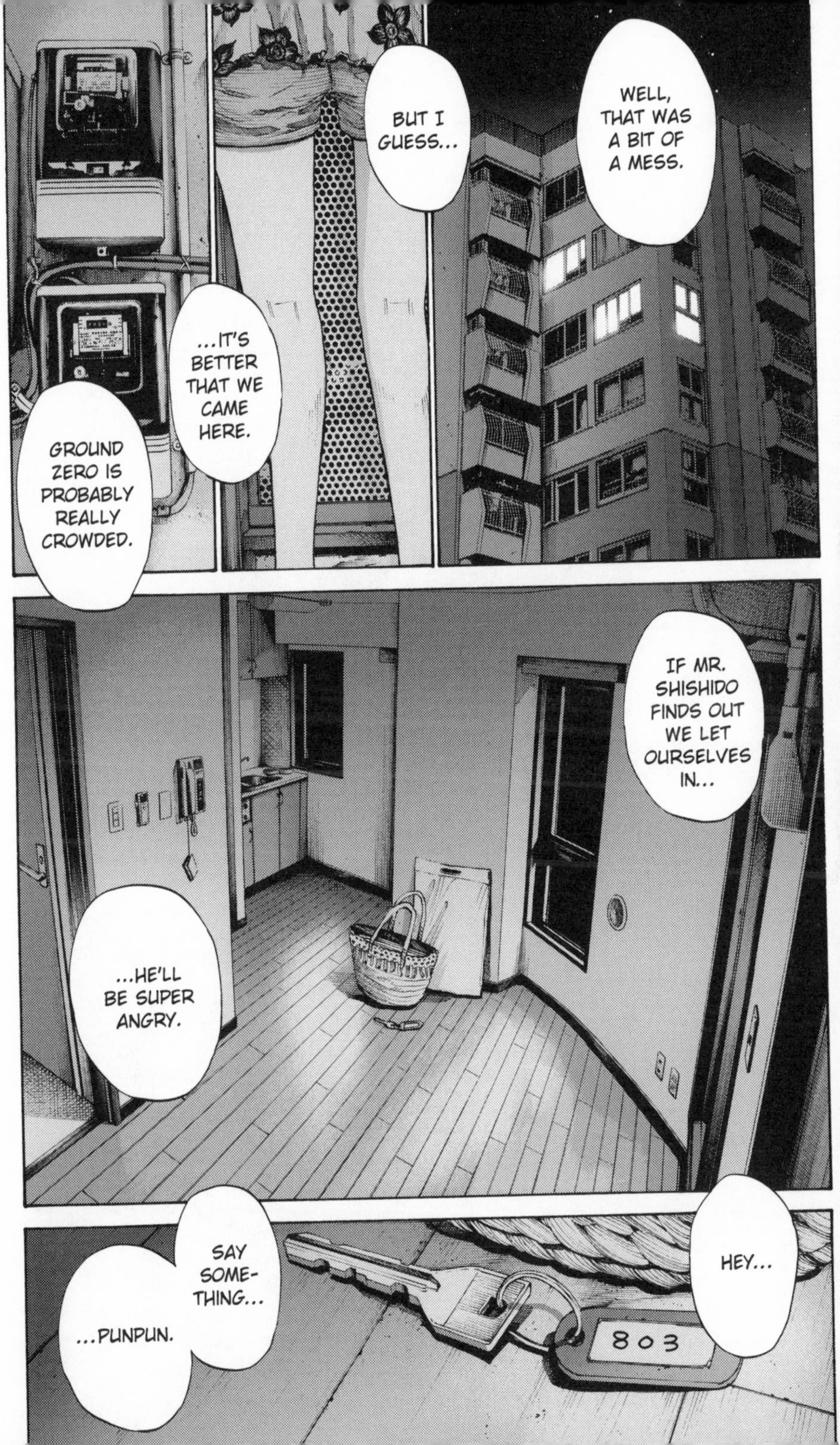
WELL, THAT WAS A BIT OF A MESS.
BUT I GUESS...
...IT'S BETTER THAT WE CAME HERE.
GROUND ZERO IS PROBABLY REALLY CROWDED.
IF MR. SHISHIDO FINDS OUT WE LET OURSELVES IN...
...HE'LL BE SUPER ANGRY.
HEY...
SAY SOME-THING...
...PUNPUN.
803

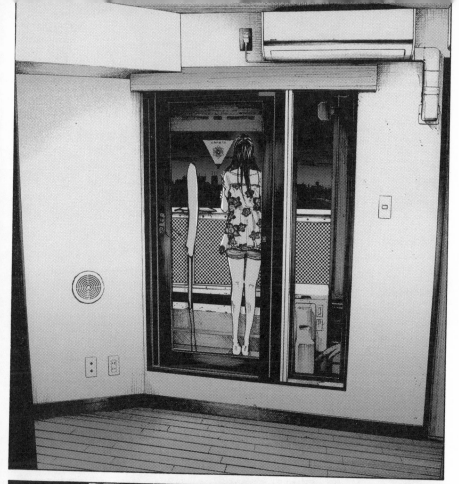

YEAH?

"Lately,
I've been
thinking
about
who you
remind
me of."

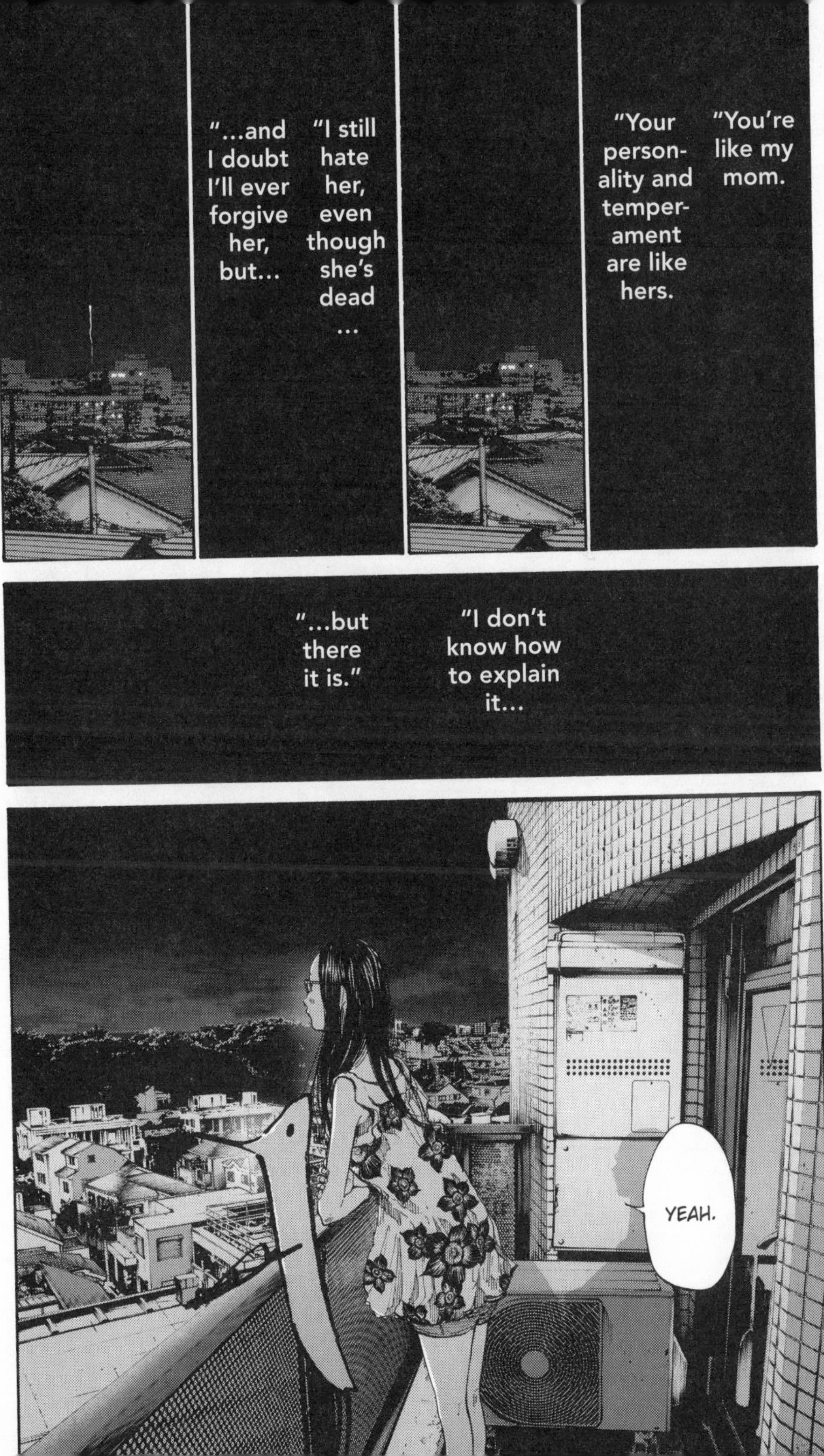
"You're like my mom.
"Your person-ality and temper-ament are like hers.
"I still hate her, even though she's dead...
"...and I doubt I'll ever forgive her, but...
"I don't know how to explain it...
"...but there it is."
YEAH.

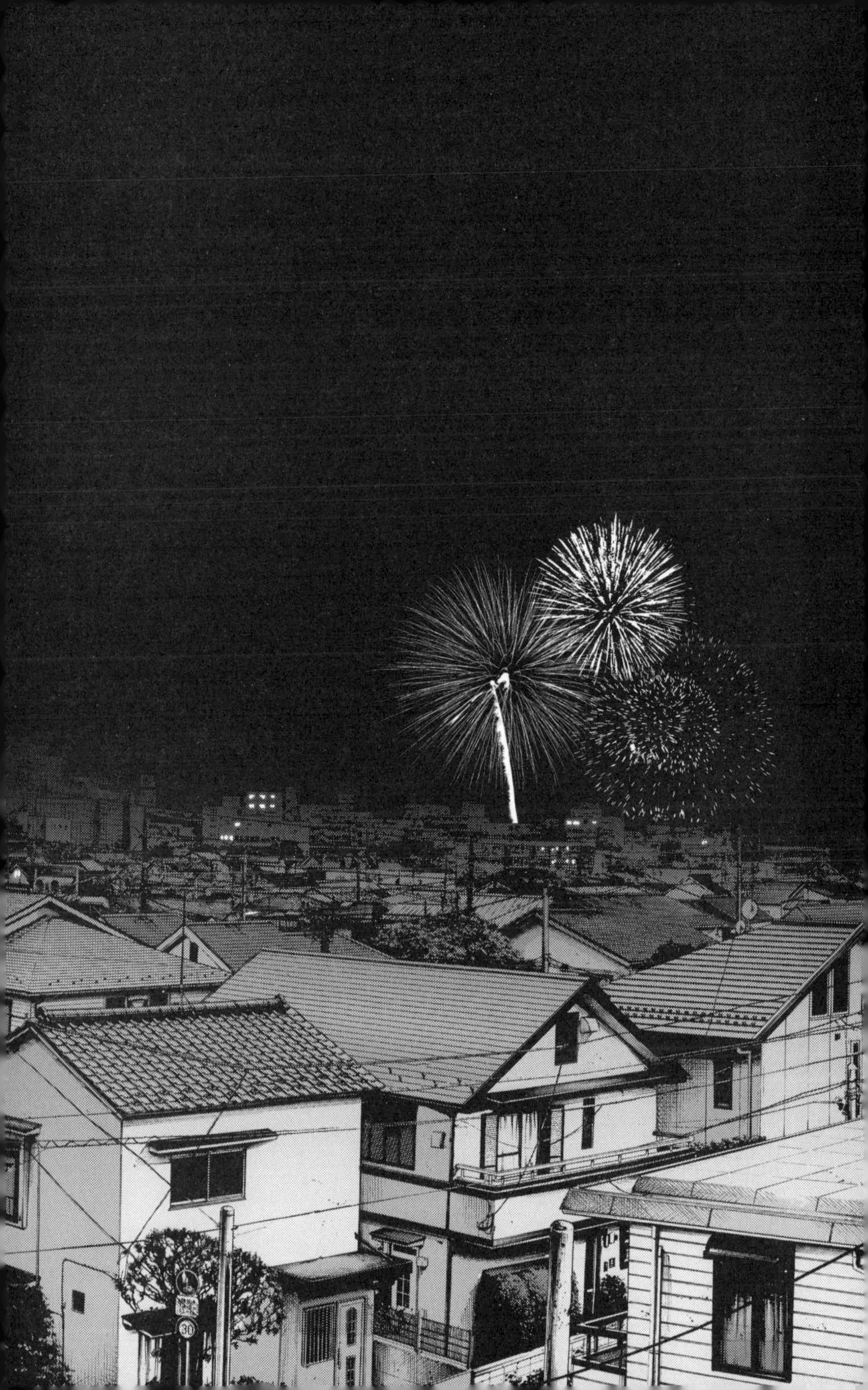

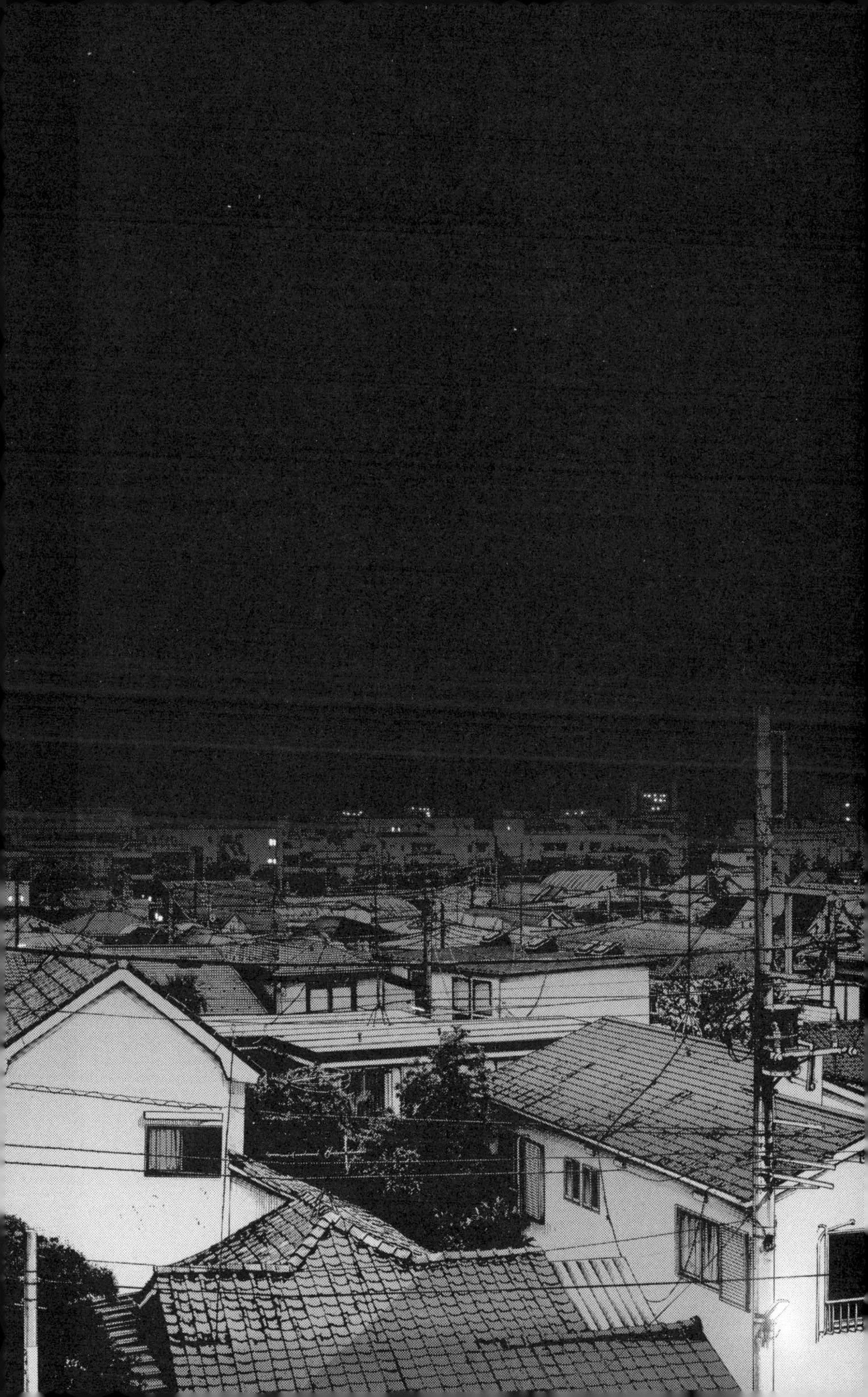

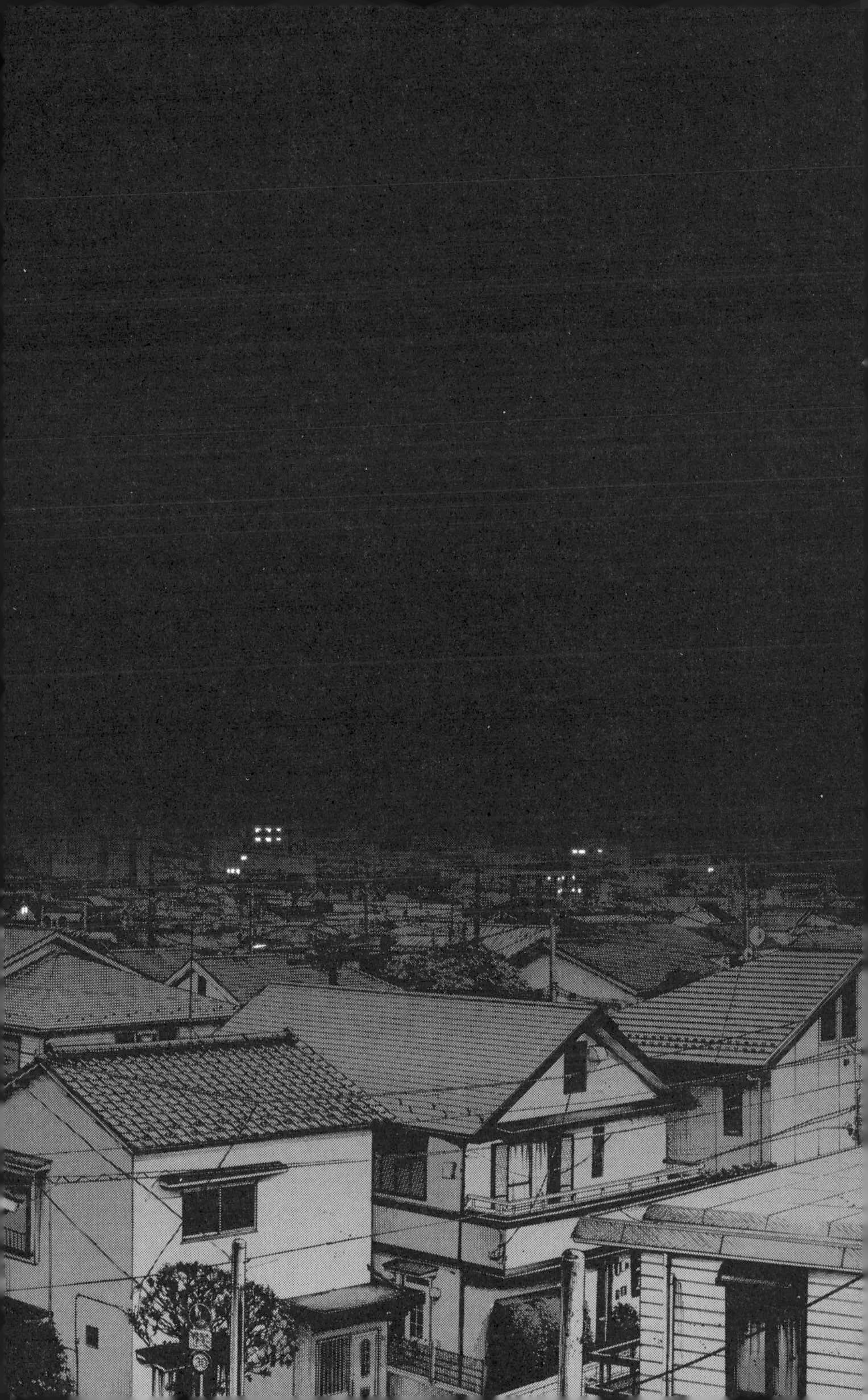

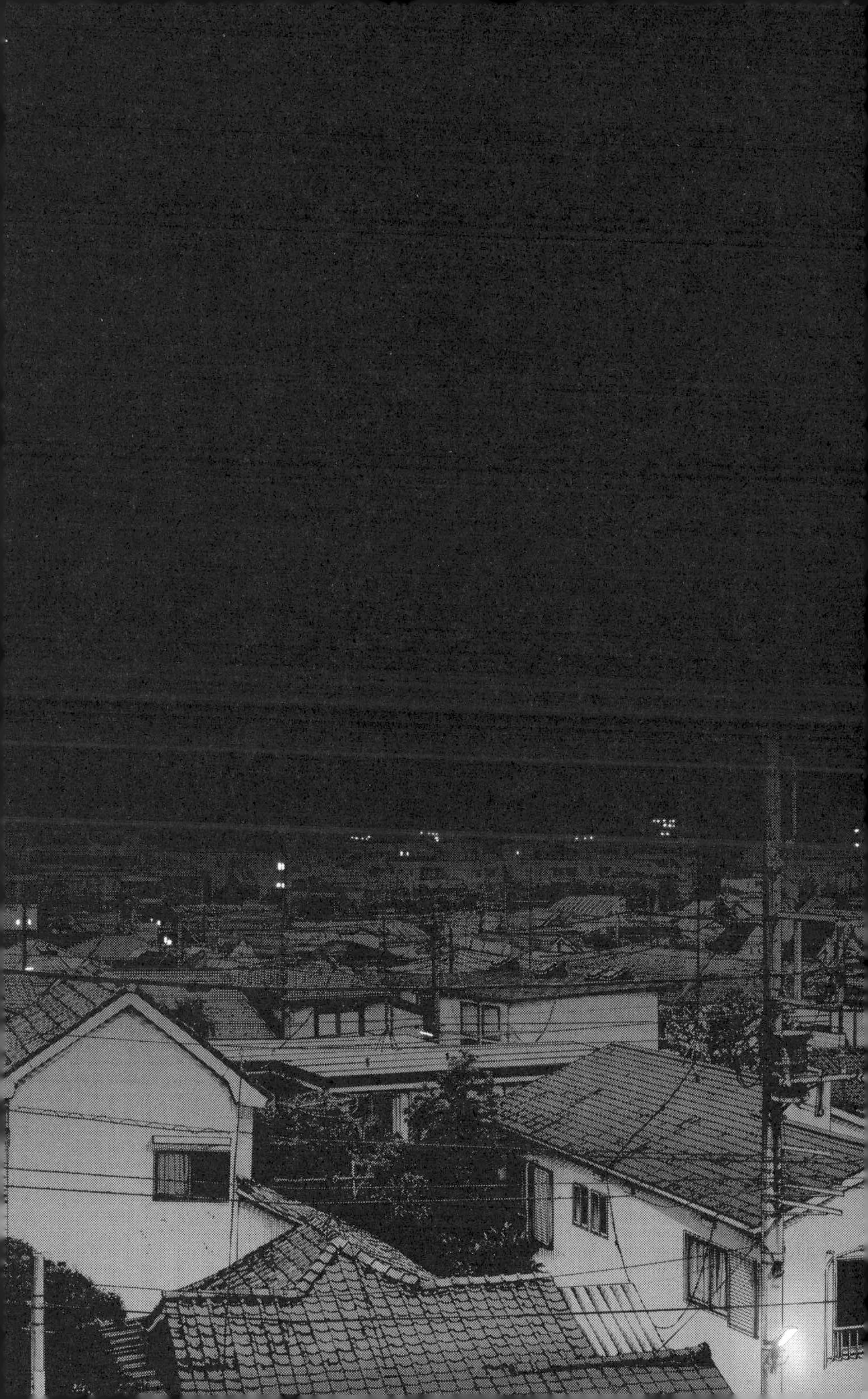

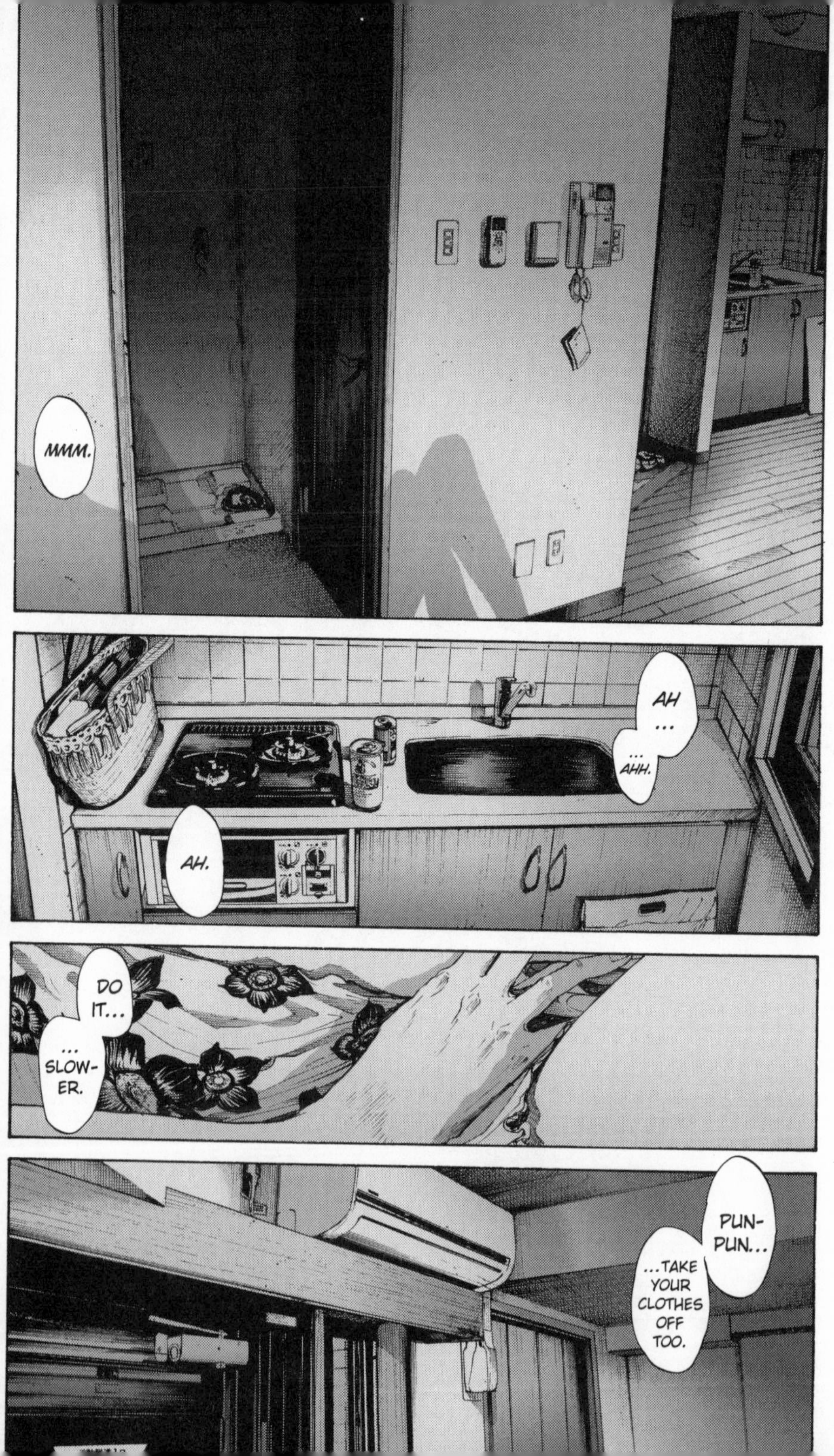
MMM.
AH ...
... AHH.
AH.
DO IT...
... SLOW-ER.
PUN-PUN...
...TAKE YOUR CLOTHES OFF TOO.

Goodbye,
Kanie.

Goodbye,
Midori.

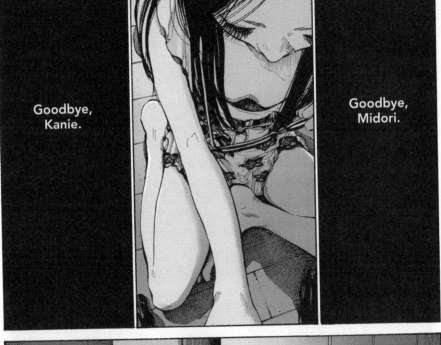

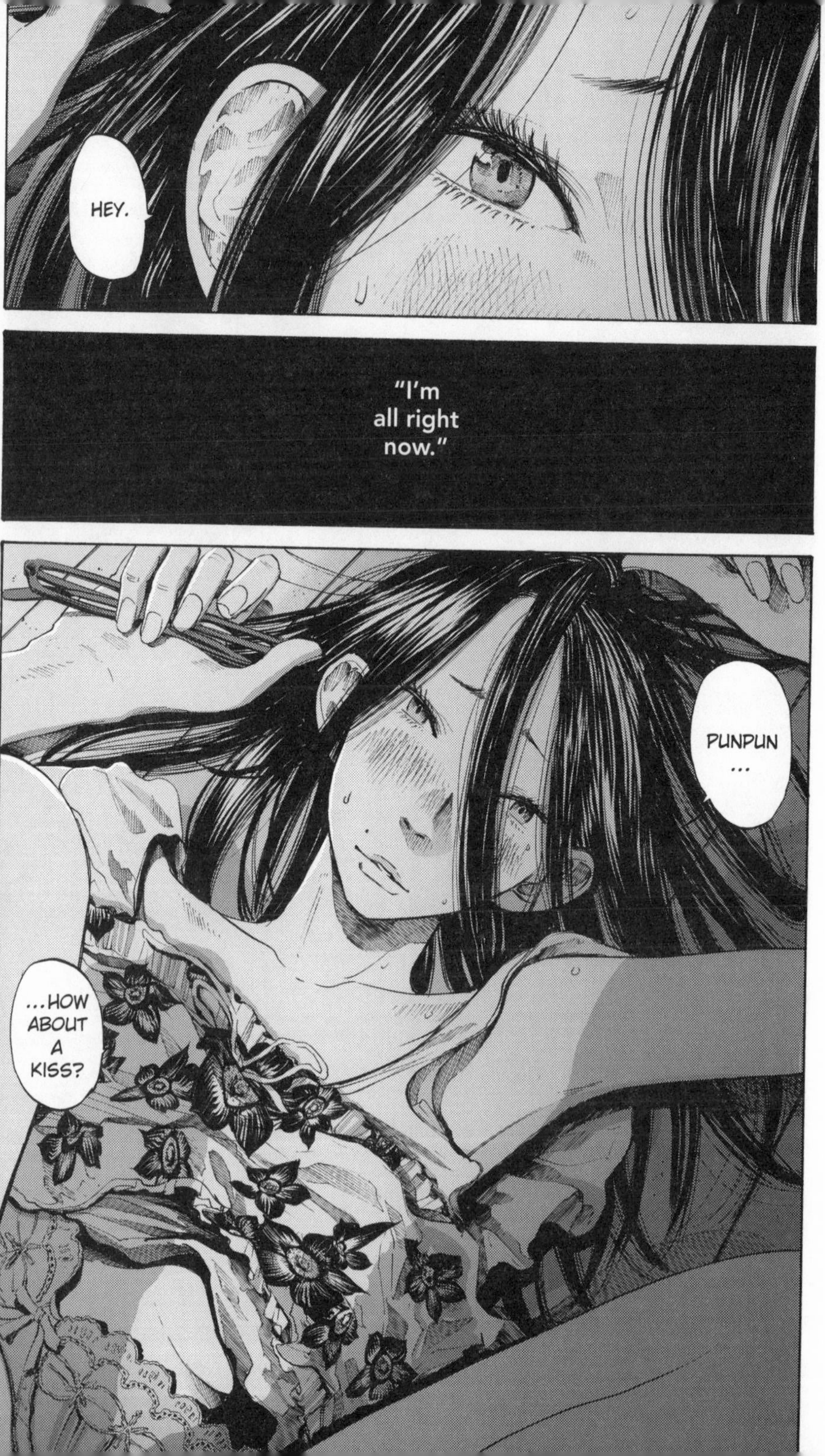
HEY.
"I'm all right now."
PUNPUN ...
...HOW ABOUT A KISS?

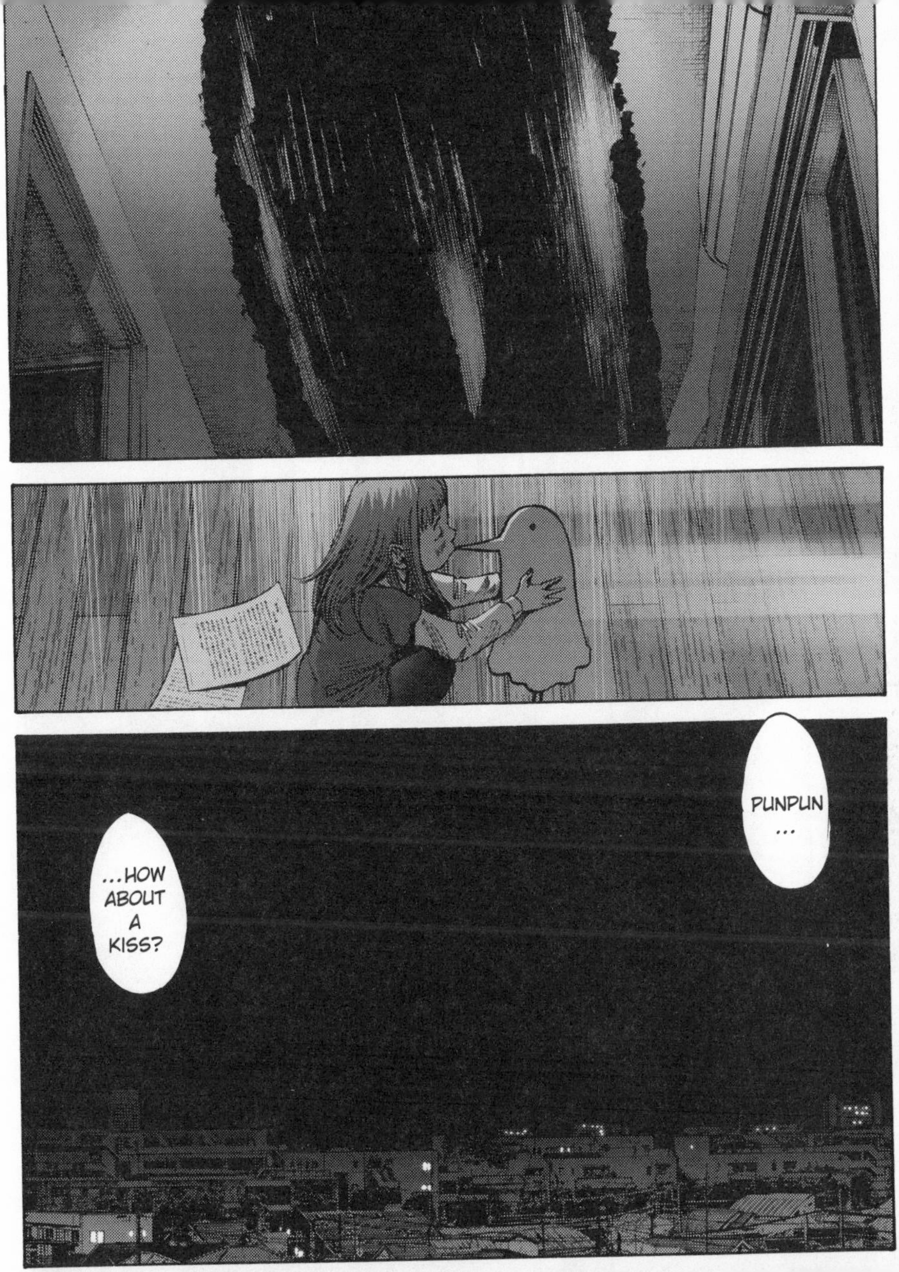
PUNPUN...
...HOW ABOUT A KISS?

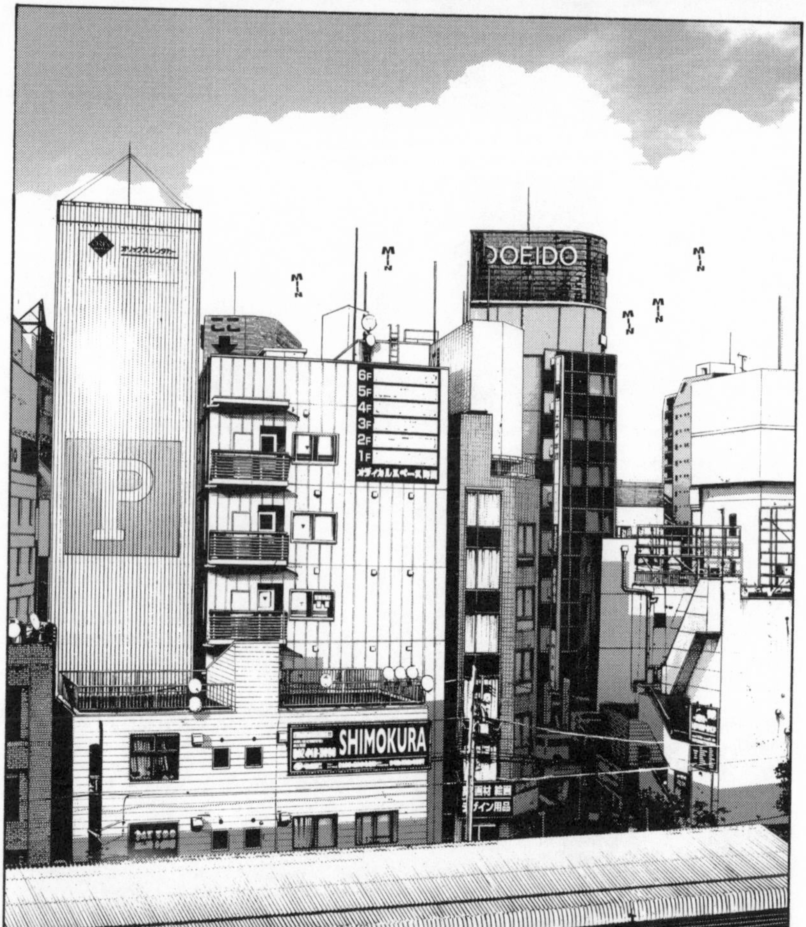
MIN
MIN
DOEIDO
MIN
MIN
MIN
6F
5F
4F
3F
2F
1F
SHIMOKURA
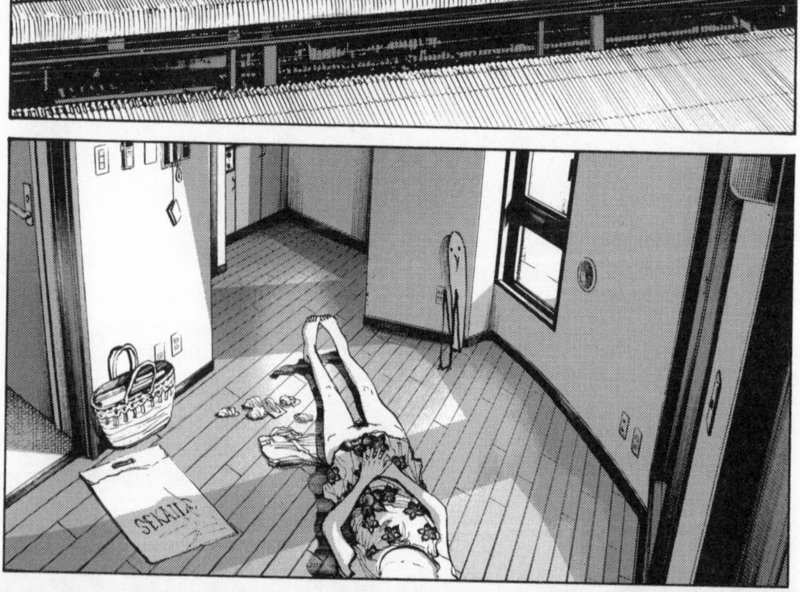
SEKAIDO

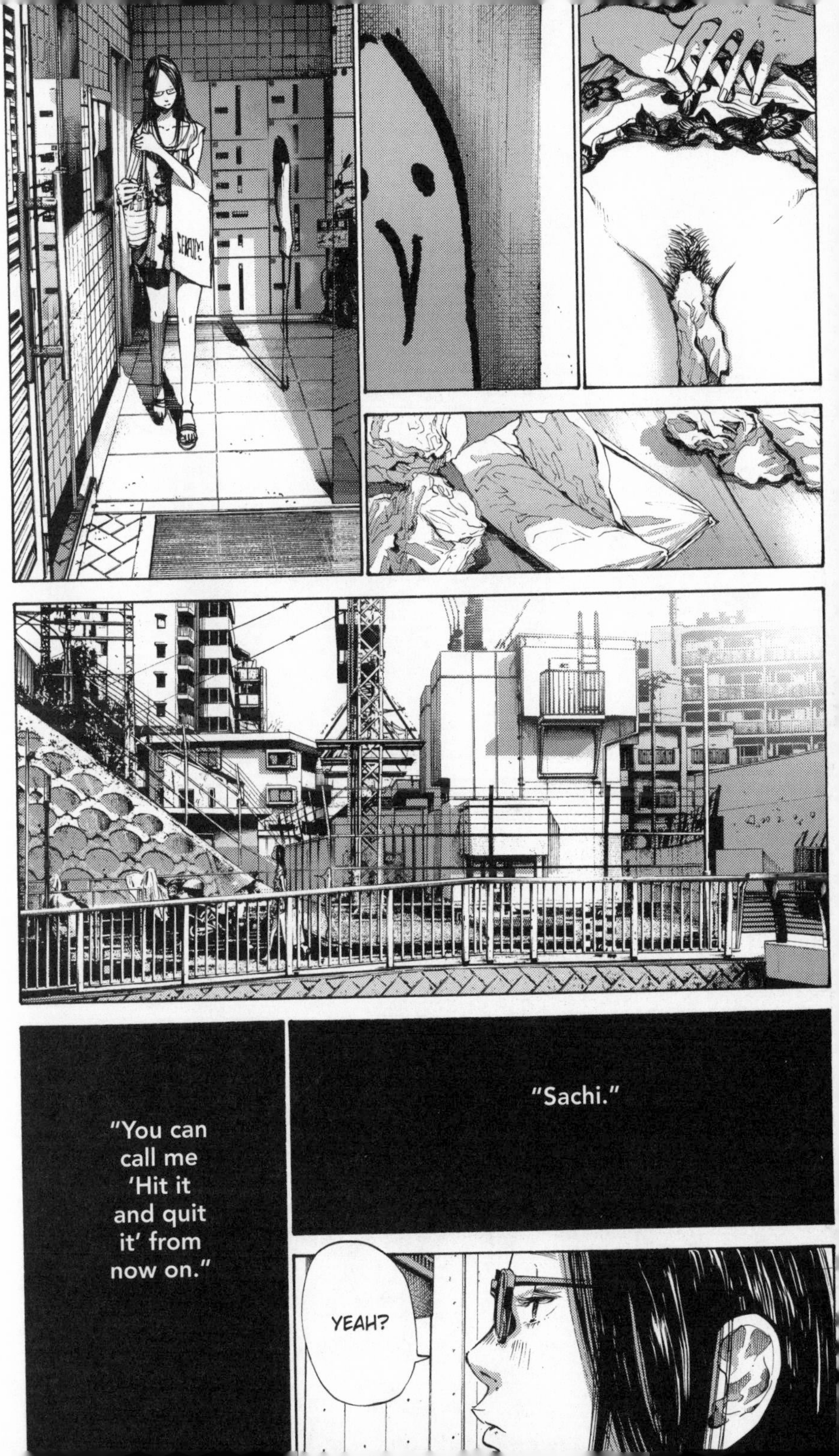
"Sachi."
YEAH?
"You can call me 'Hit it and quit it' from now on."

GET
UP.

...NOT
OVER
THAT GIRL,
ARE
YOU?

YOU'RE
STILL...

"In all my 18 years..."

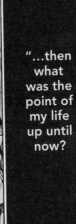

"...then what was the point of my life up until now?

YOU REALLY ARE...

...SUCH A PAIN.

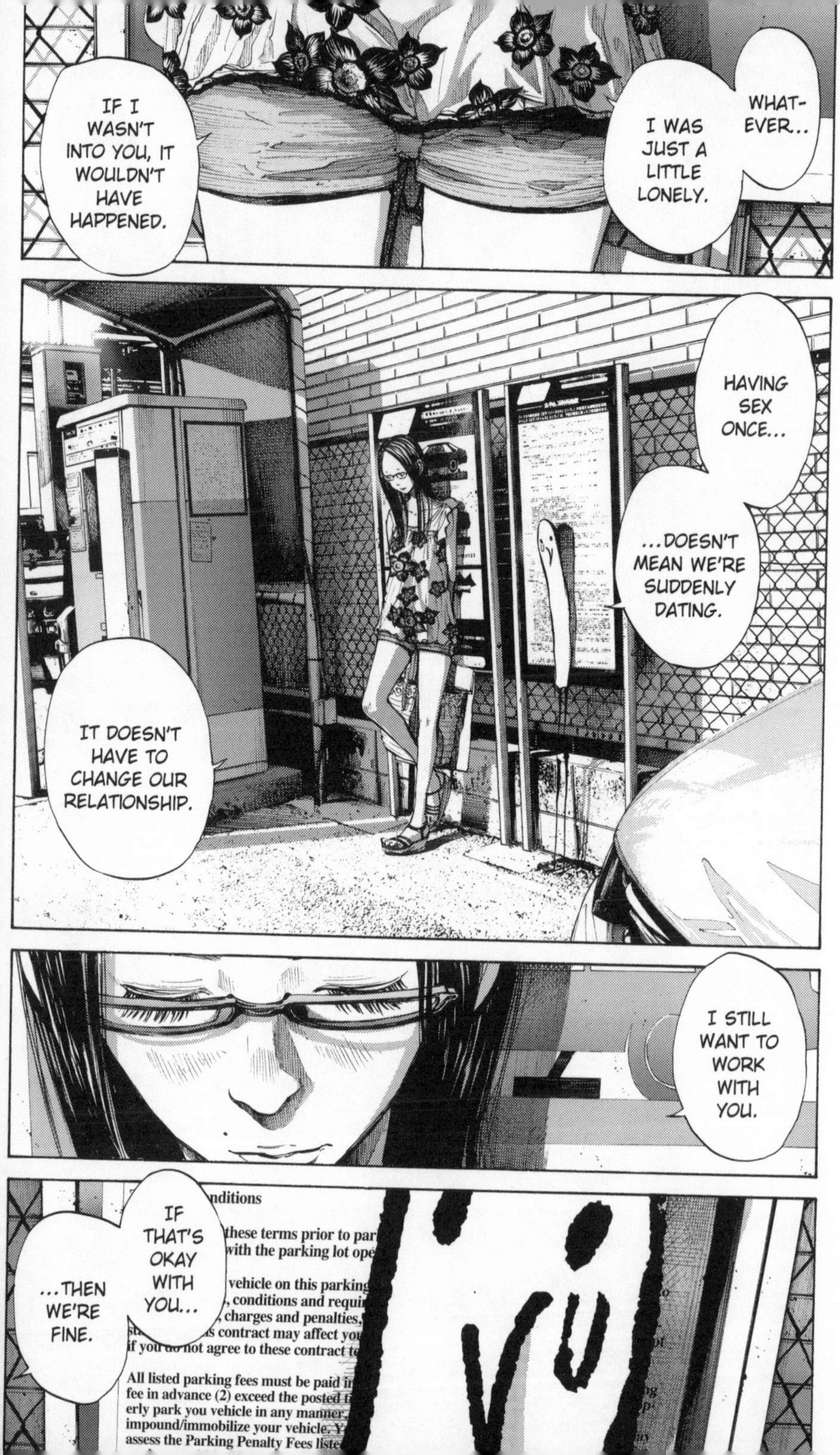

WHAT-EVER...
I WAS JUST A LITTLE LONELY.
IF I WASN'T INTO YOU, IT WOULDN'T HAVE HAPPENED.
HAVING SEX ONCE...
...DOESN'T MEAN WE'RE SUDDENLY DATING.
IT DOESN'T HAVE TO CHANGE OUR RELATIONSHIP.
I STILL WANT TO WORK WITH YOU.
IF THAT'S OKAY WITH YOU...
...THEN WE'RE FINE.

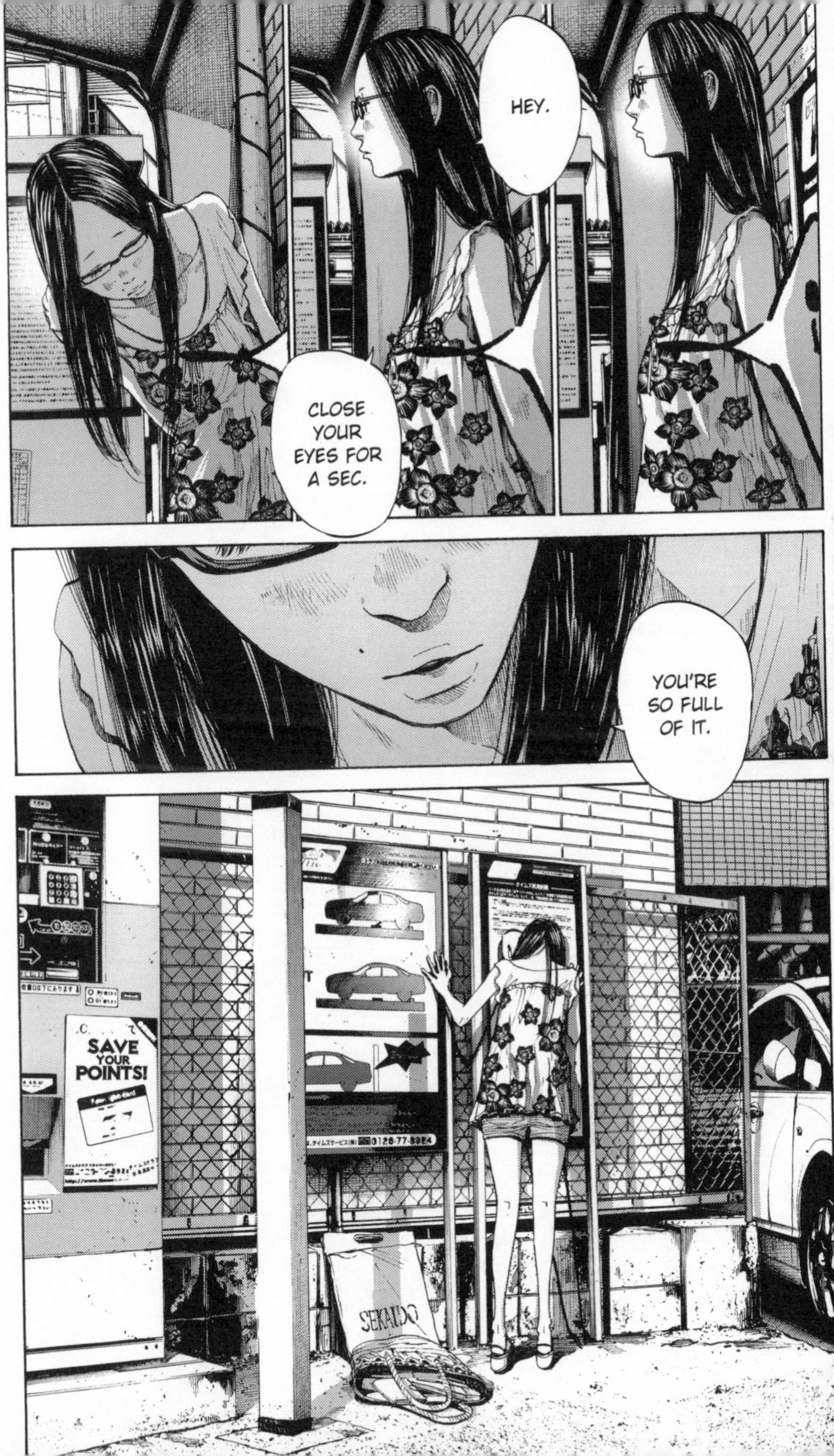
HEY.
CLOSE YOUR EYES FOR A SEC.
YOU'RE SO FULL OF IT.
SAVE YOUR POINTS!
SEKAIDO

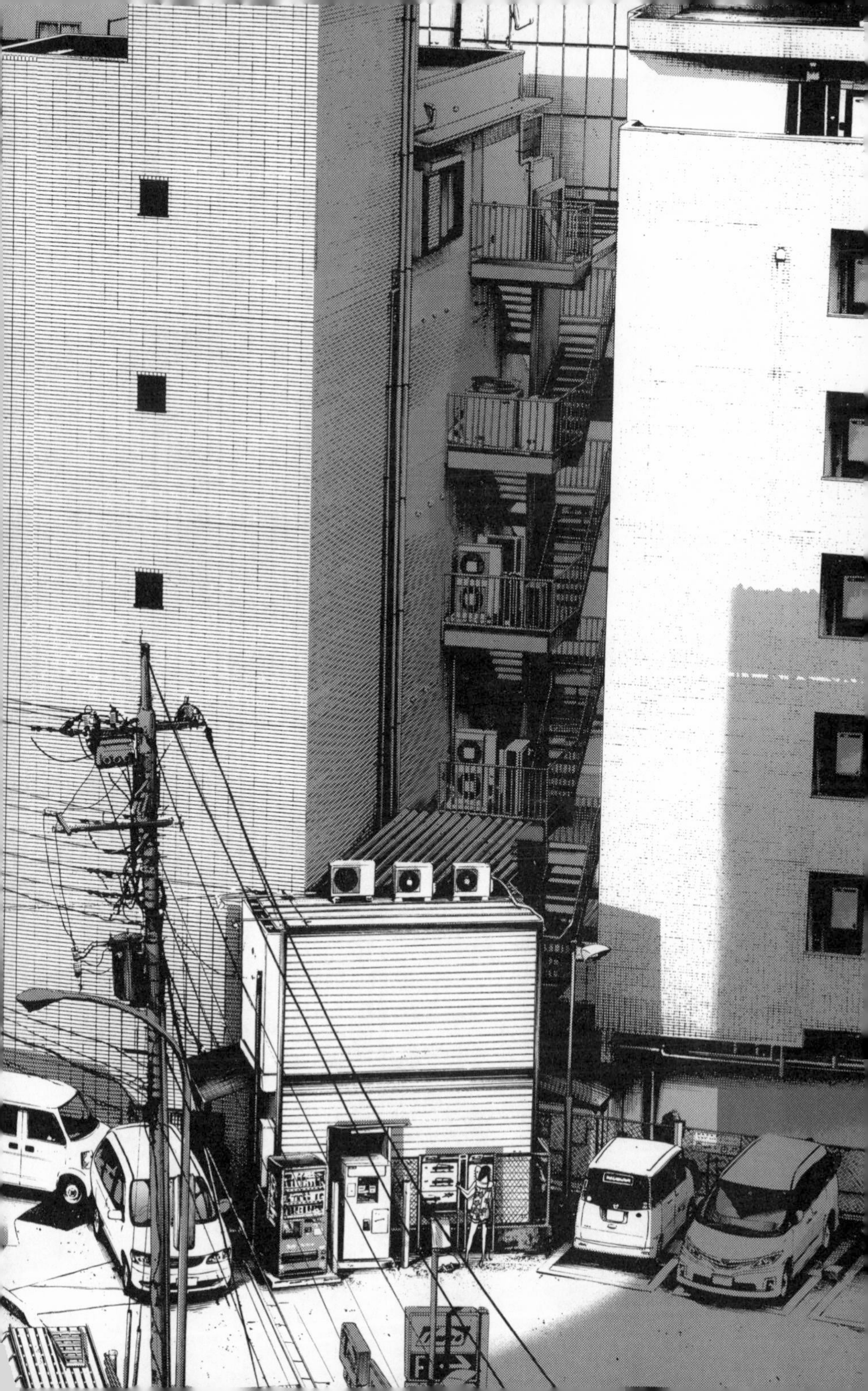

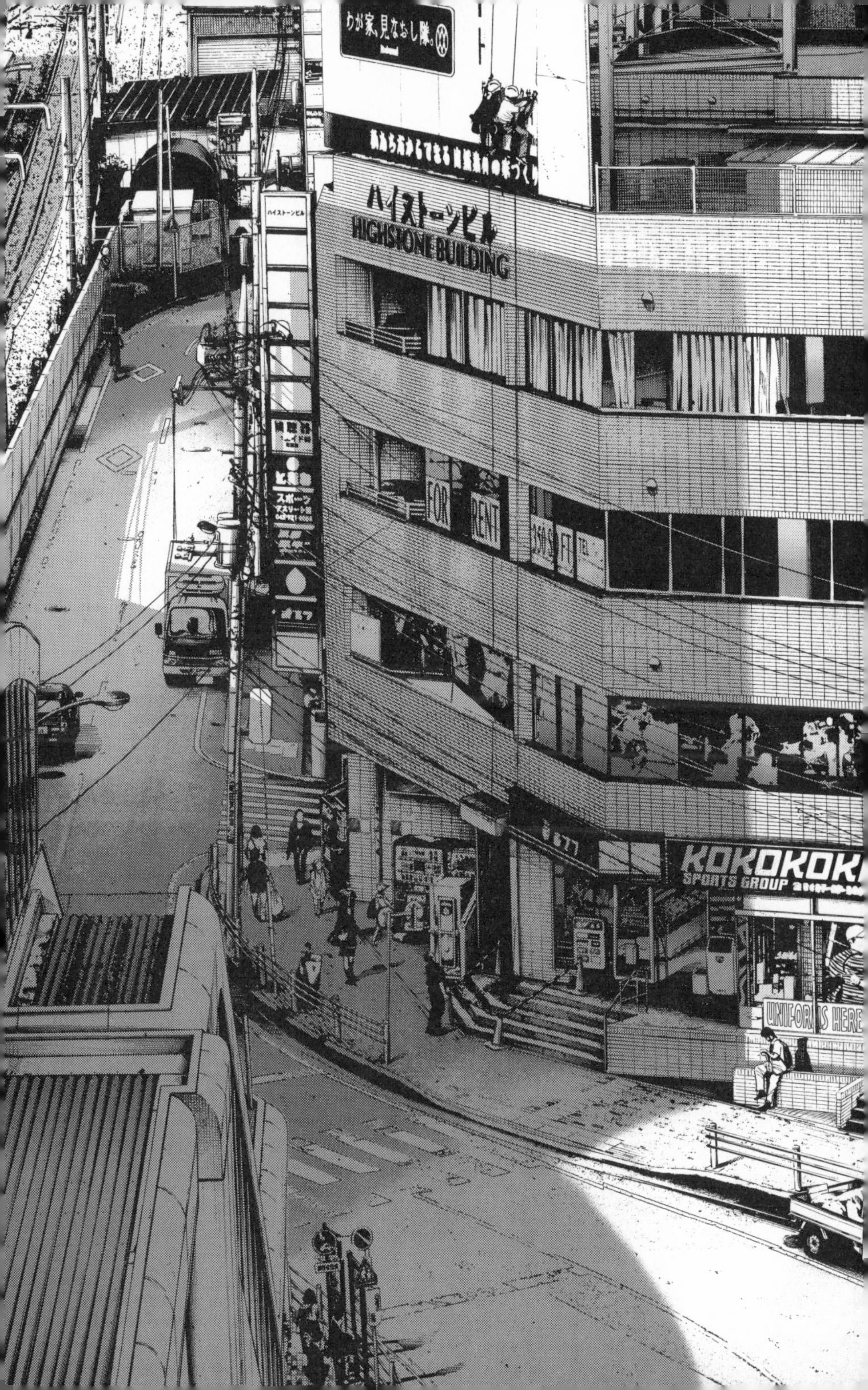
わが家、見なおし隊。
ハイストーンビル
ハイストーンビル
HIGHSTONE BUILDING
スポーツ
FOR RENT
SPORTS GROUP

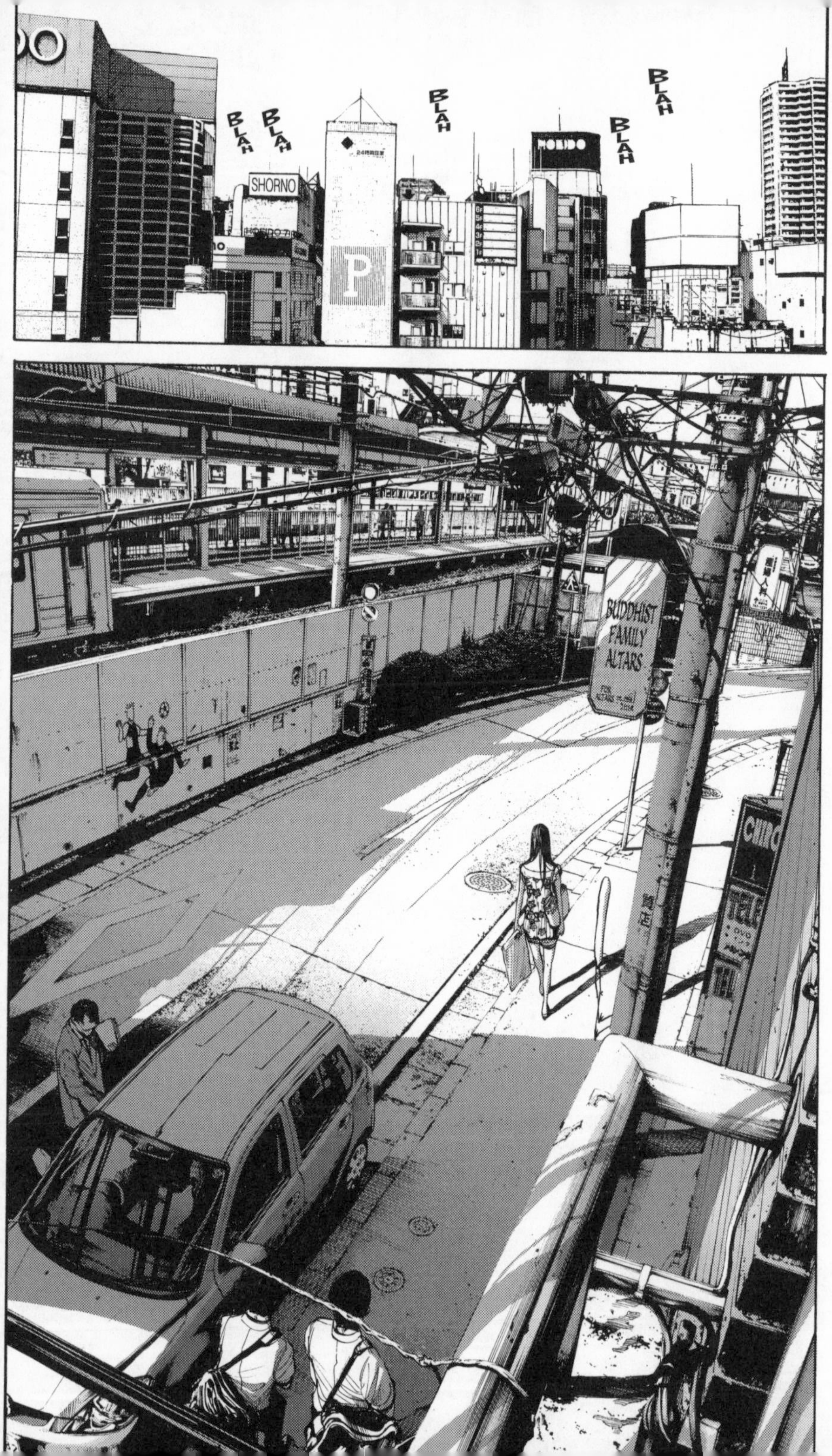
BLAH
BLAH
BLAH
BLAH
BLAH
SHORNO
BUDDHIST FAMILY ALTARS

Chapter 88

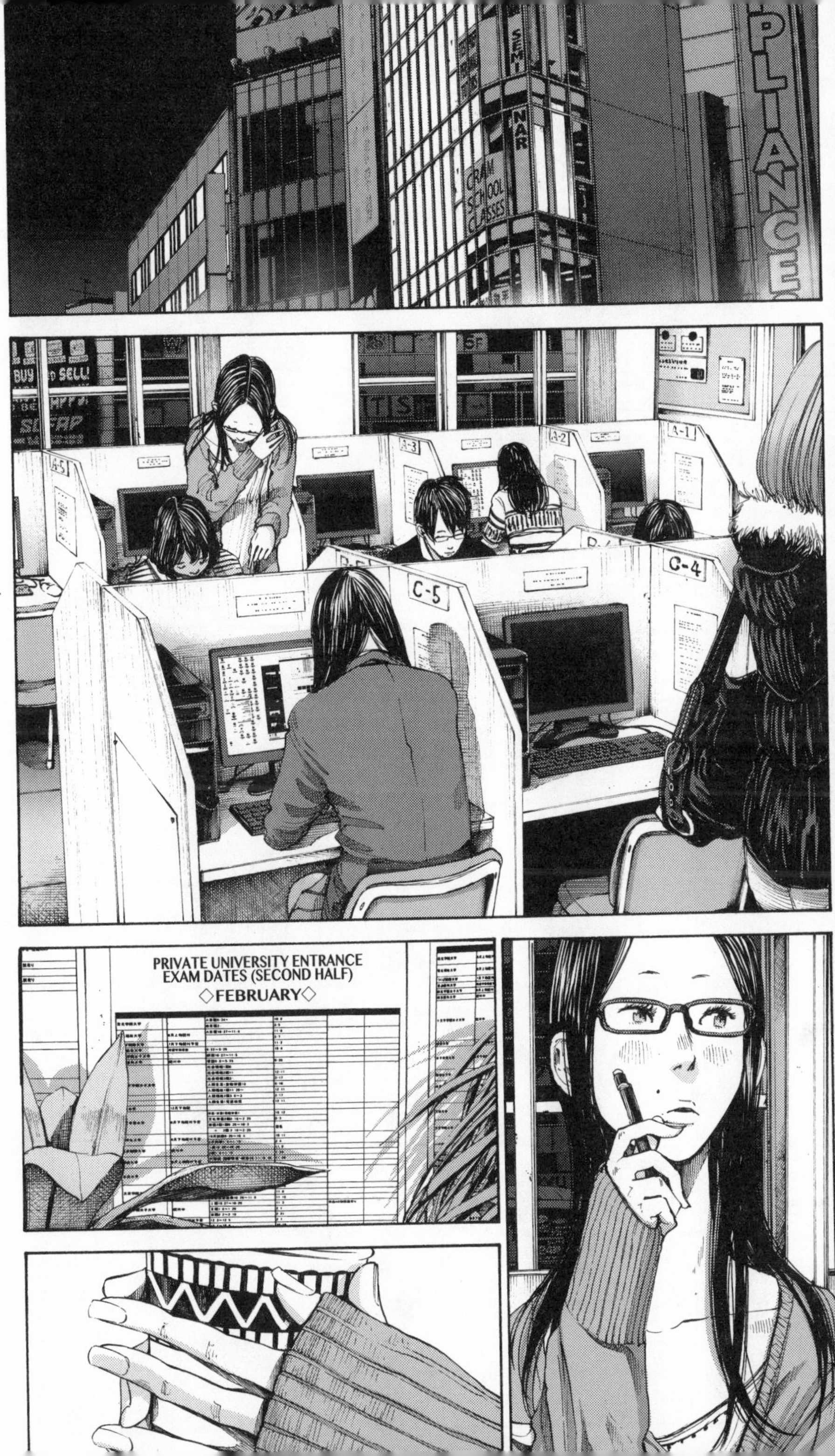
PLIANCE
CRAM SCHOOL CLASSES
NAR
SEMI
A-1
A-2
A-3
A-5
BUY SELL
C-4
C-5
PRIVATE UNIVERSITY ENTRANCE EXAM DATES (SECOND HALF)
◇FEBRUARY◇

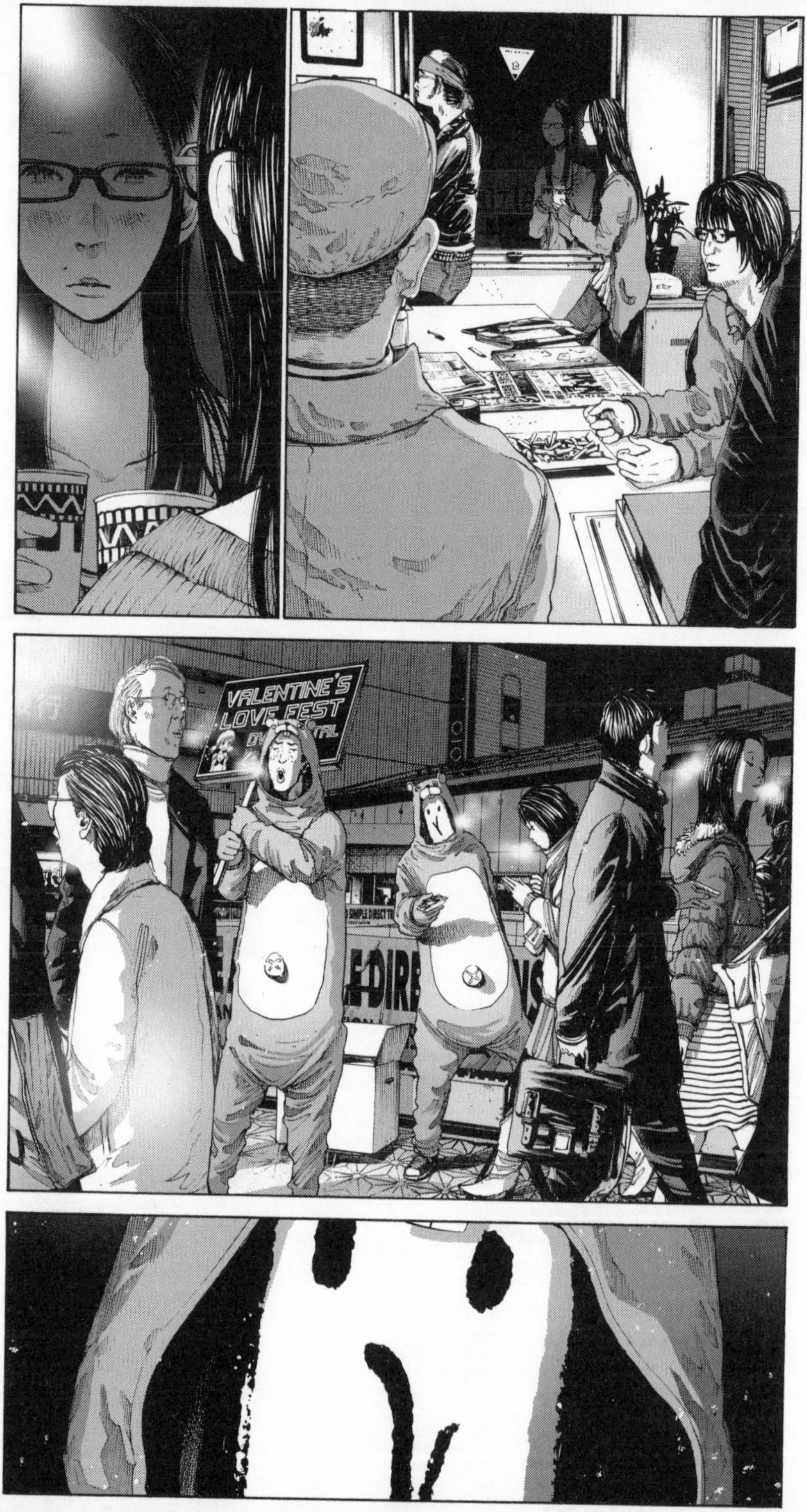
VALENTINE'S
LOVE FEST

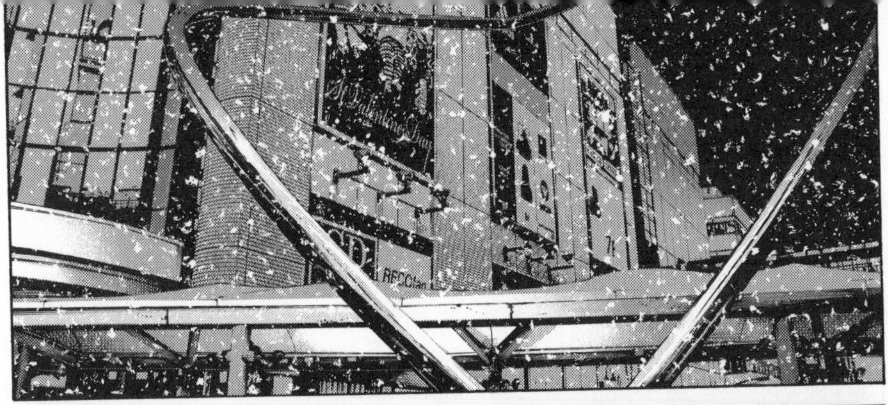
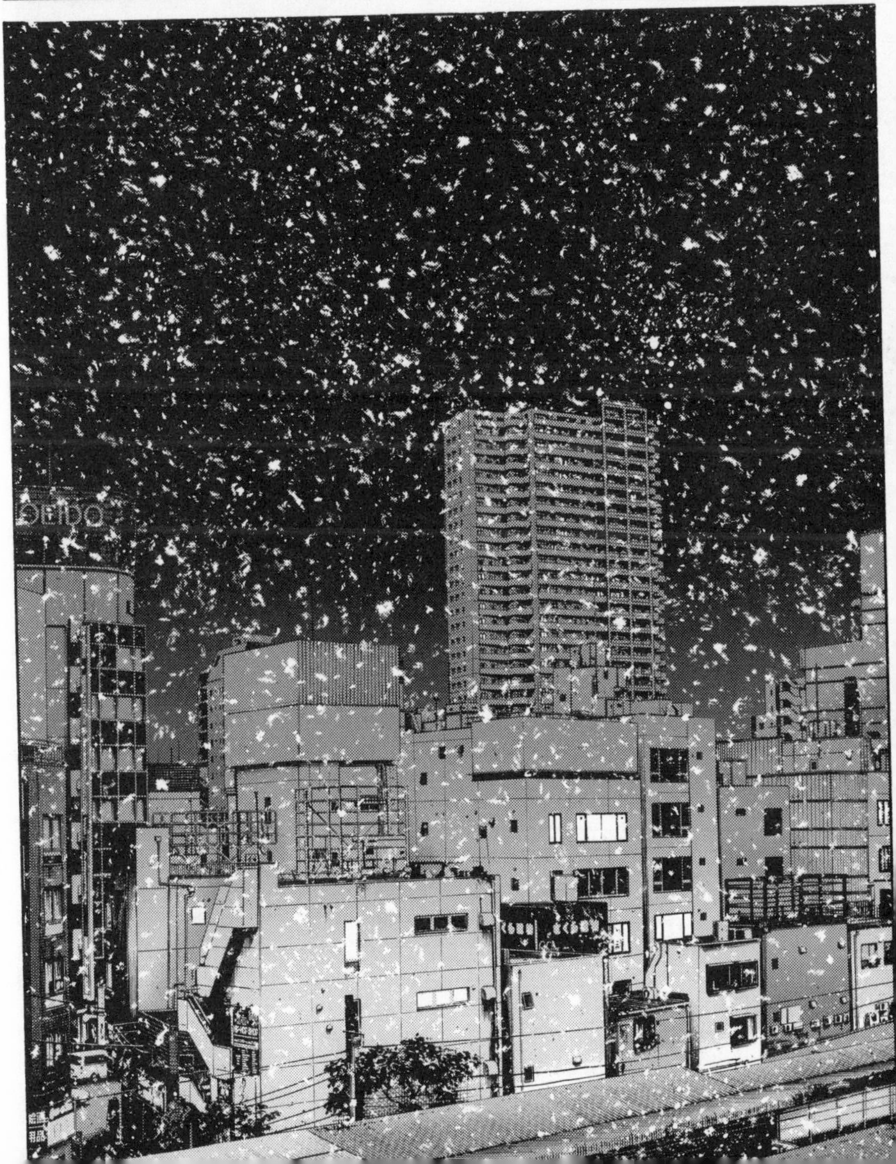

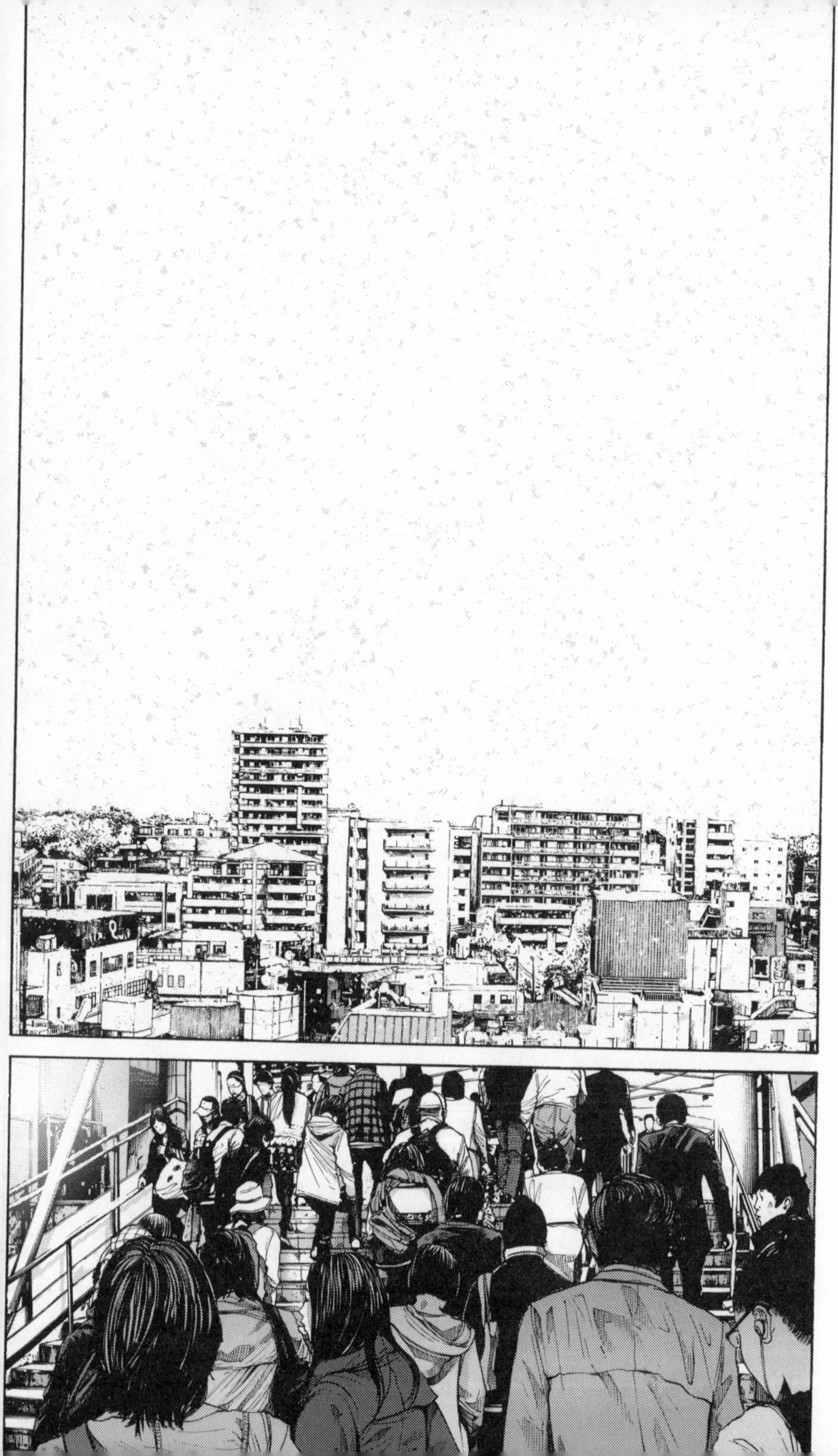

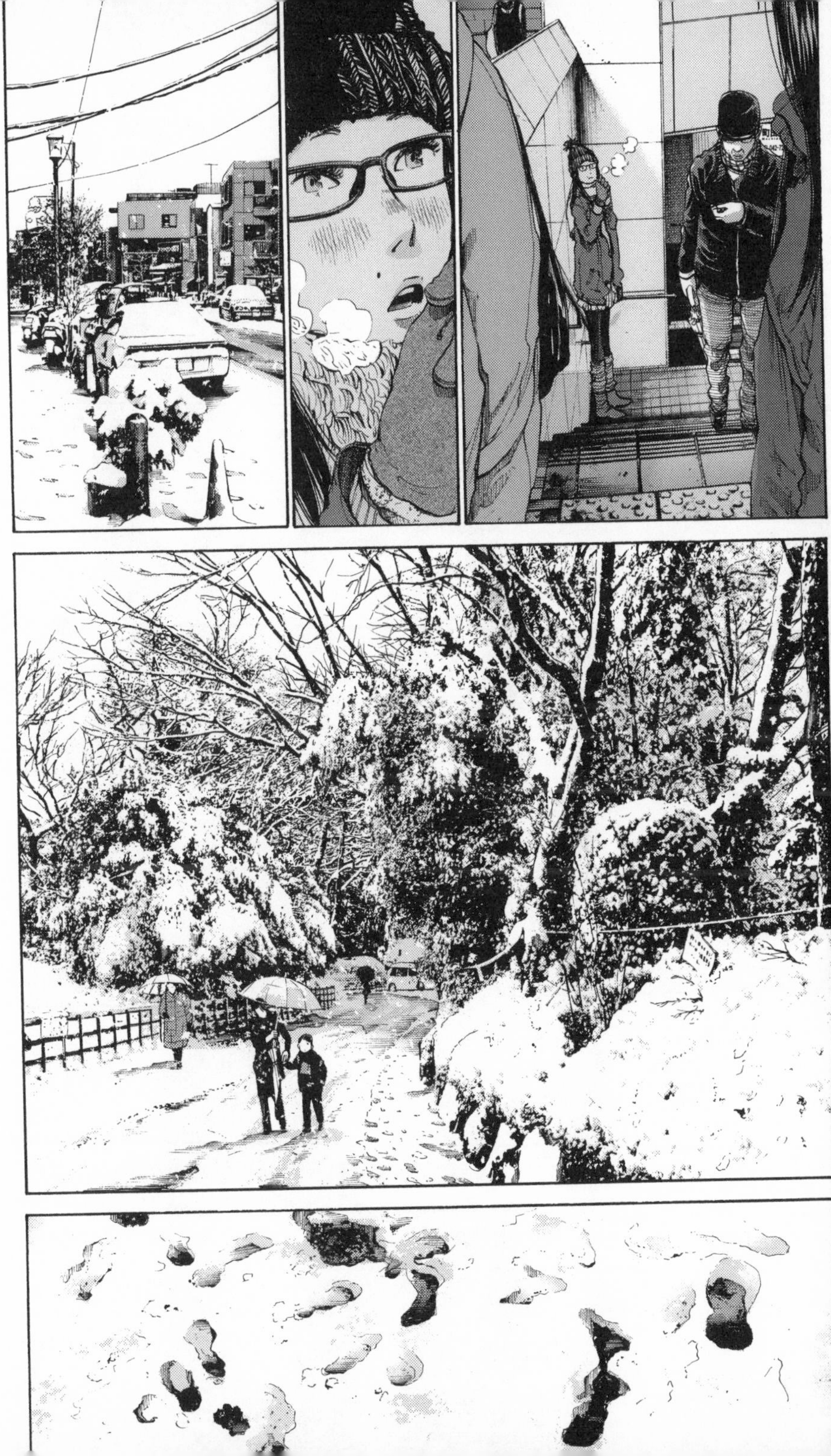

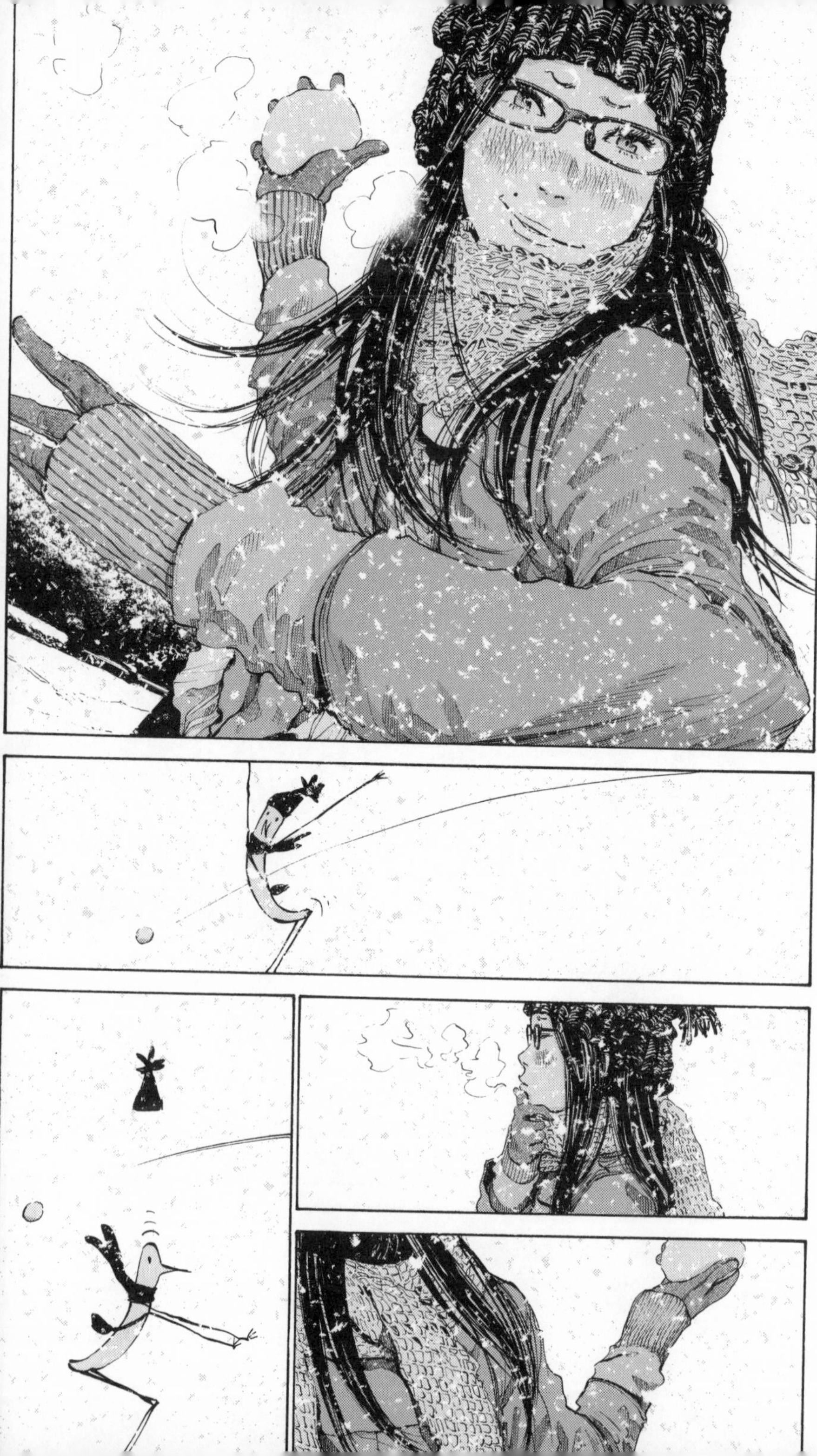

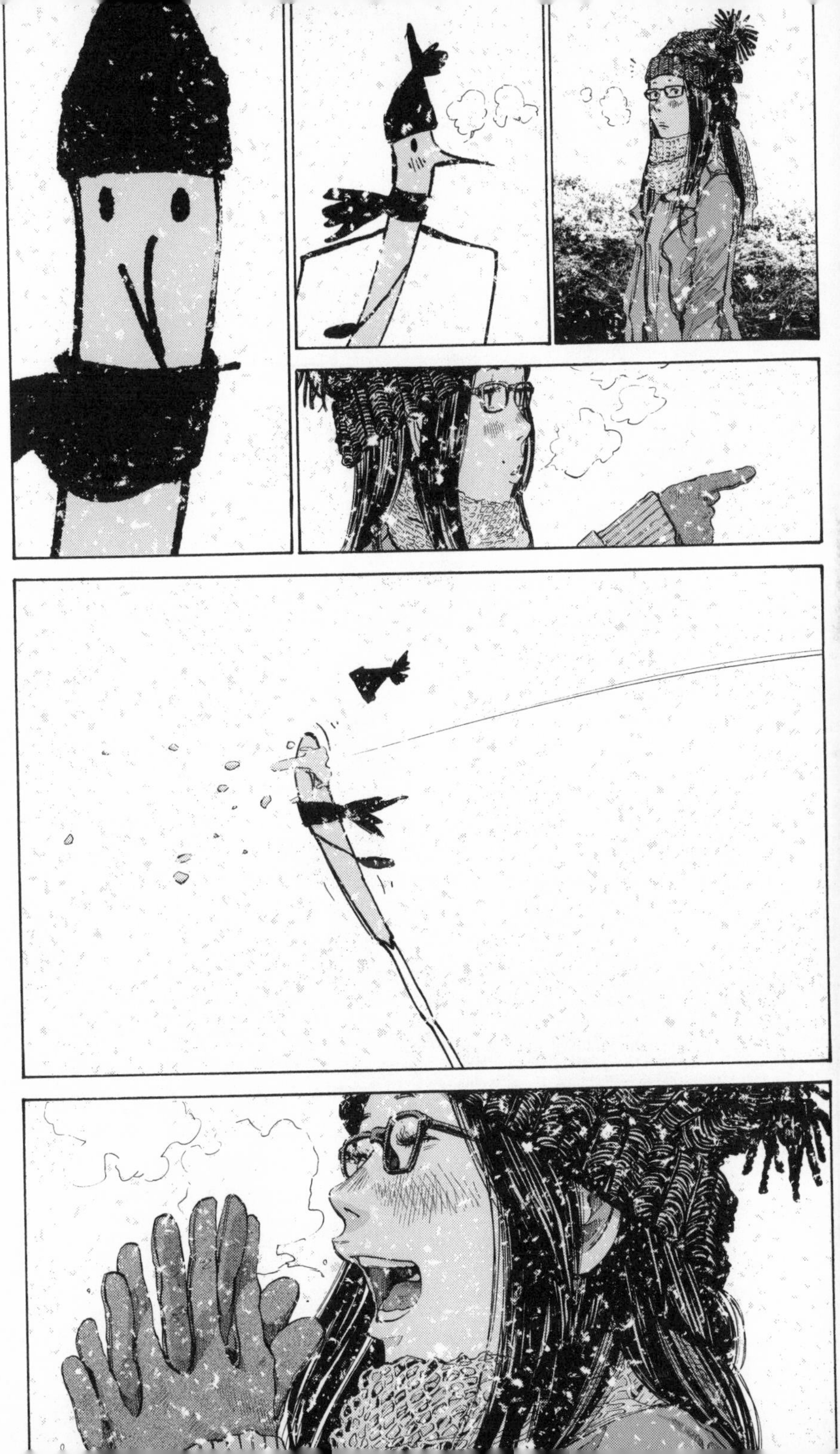

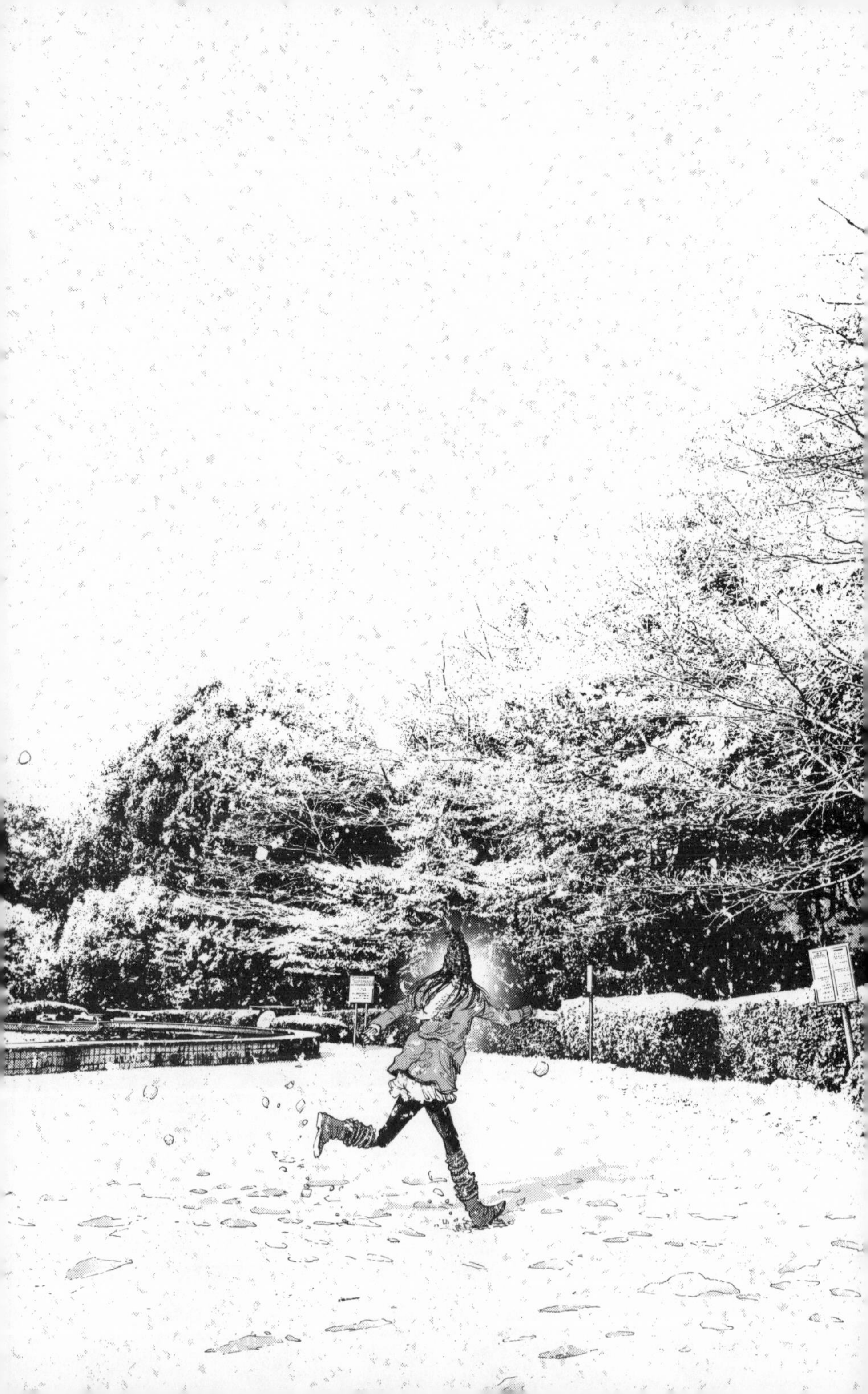

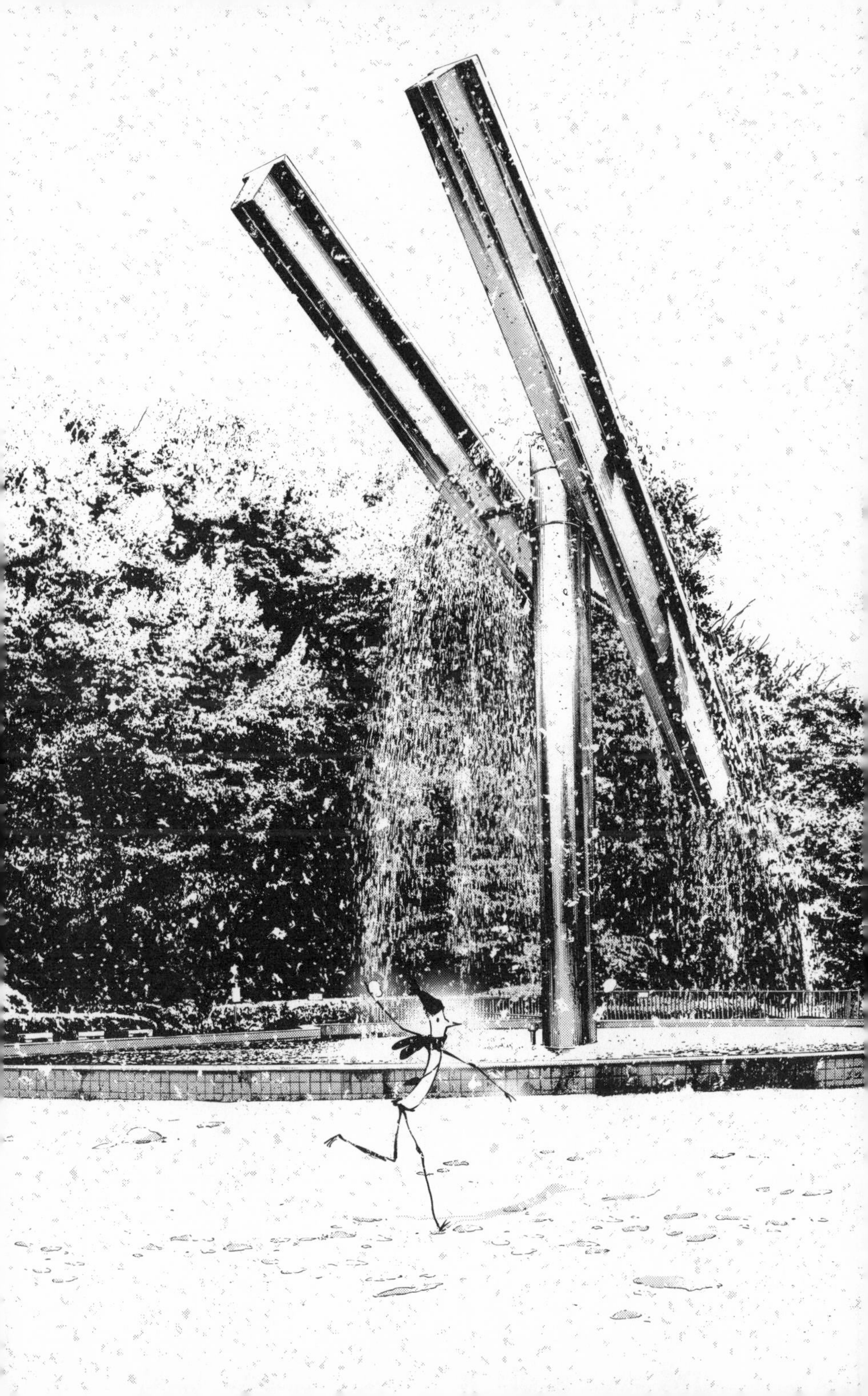

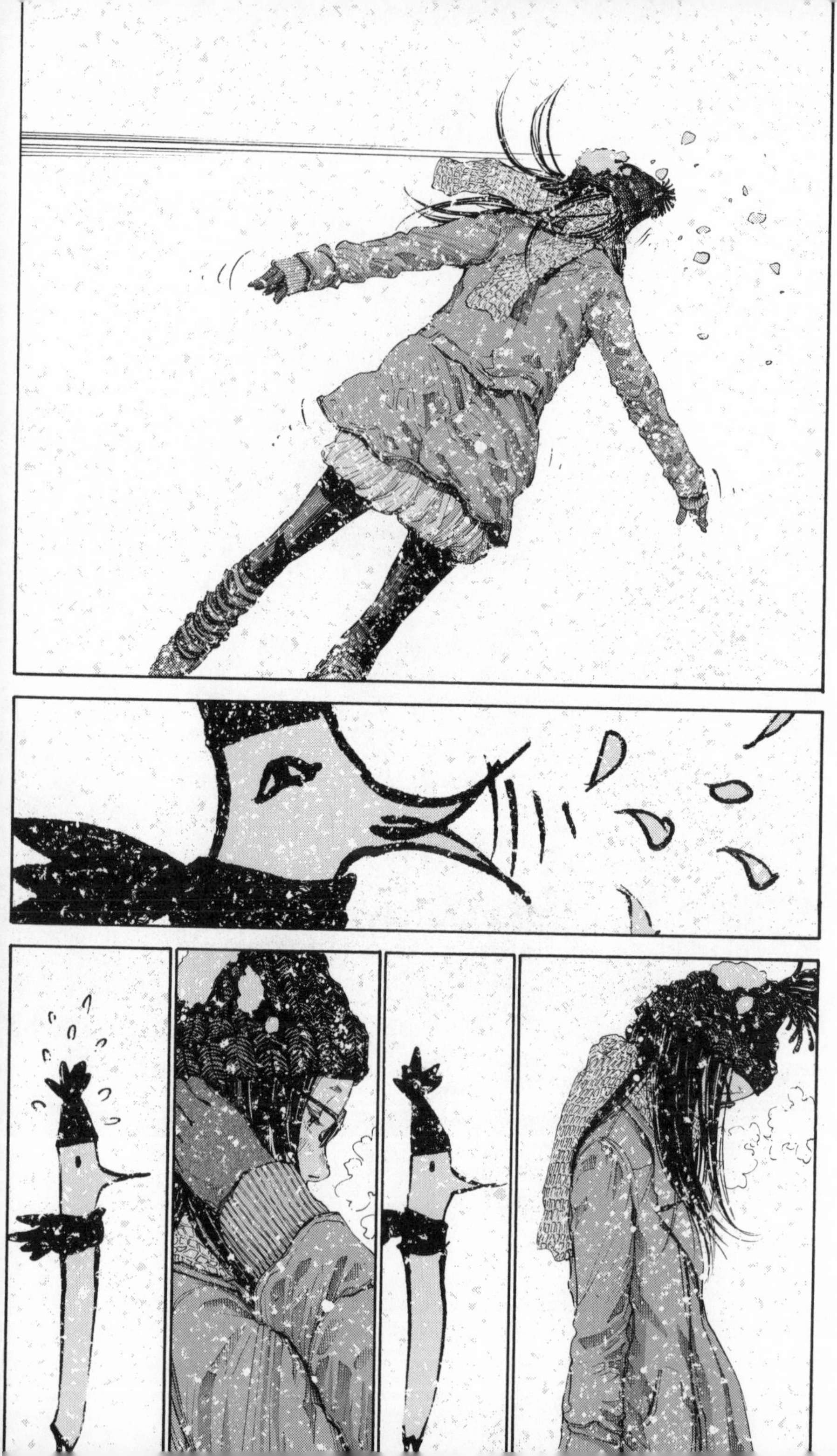

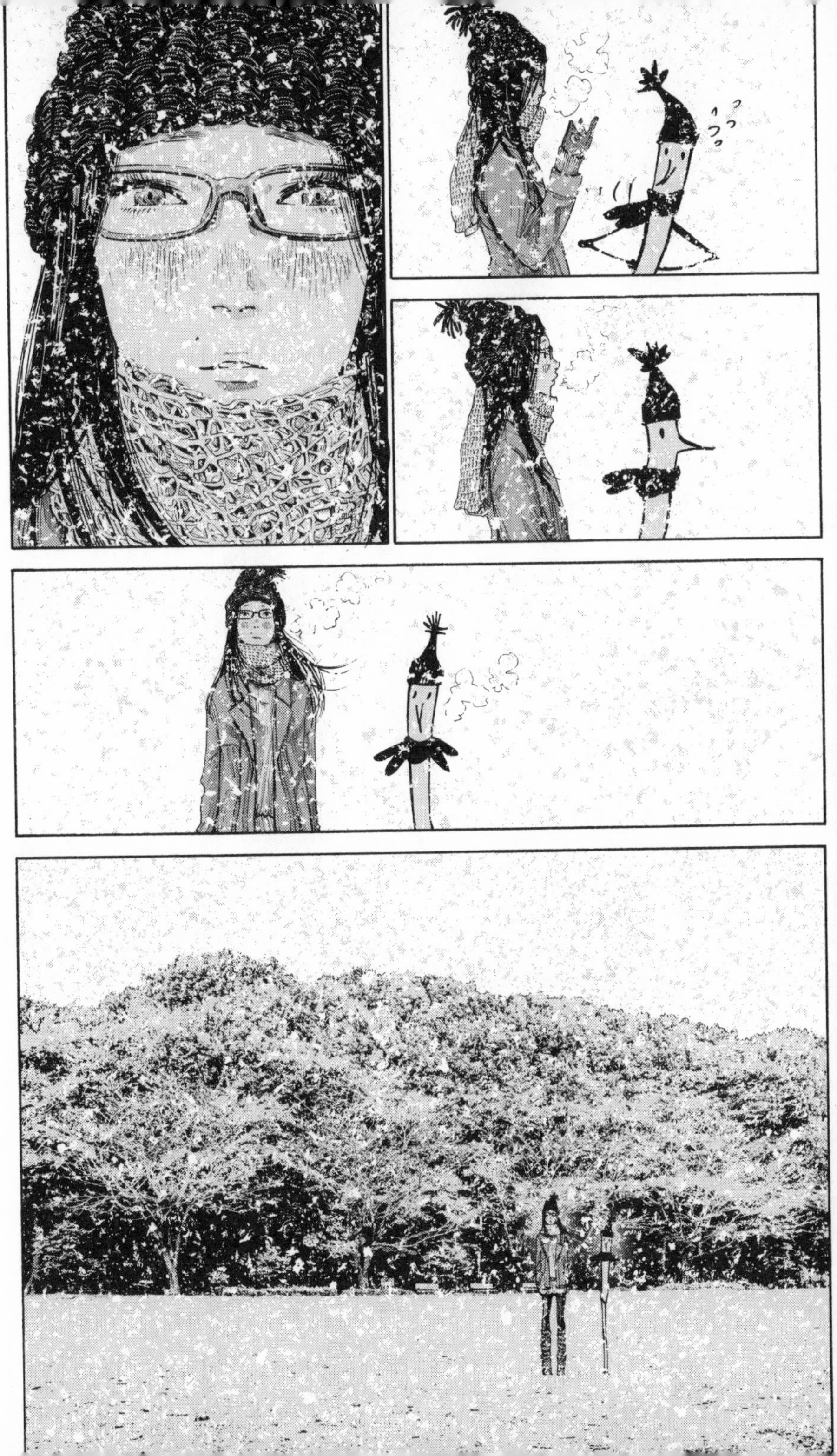

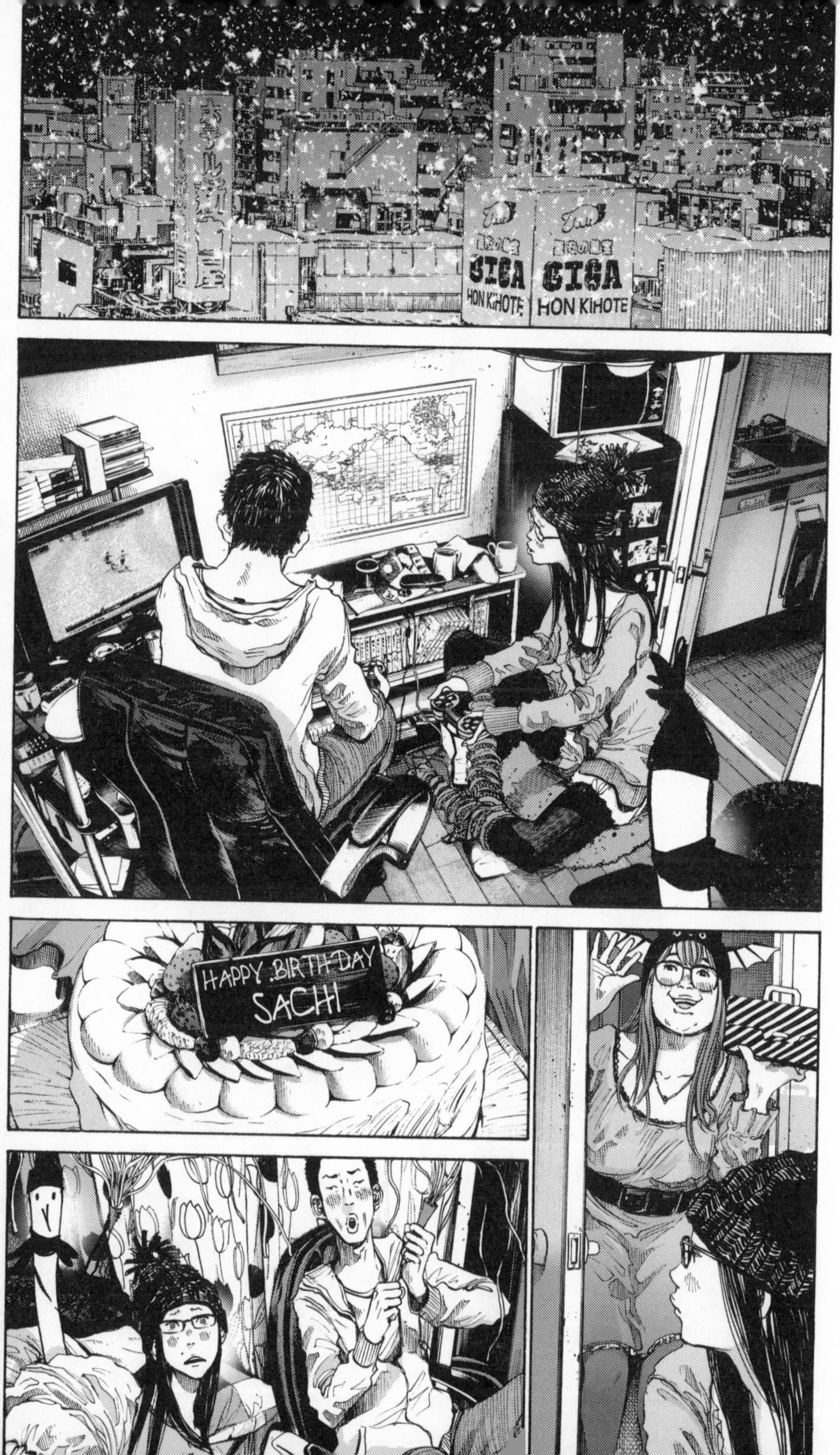
GIGA
HON KIHOTE
GIGA
HON KIHOTE
HAPPY BIRTH DAY
SACHI

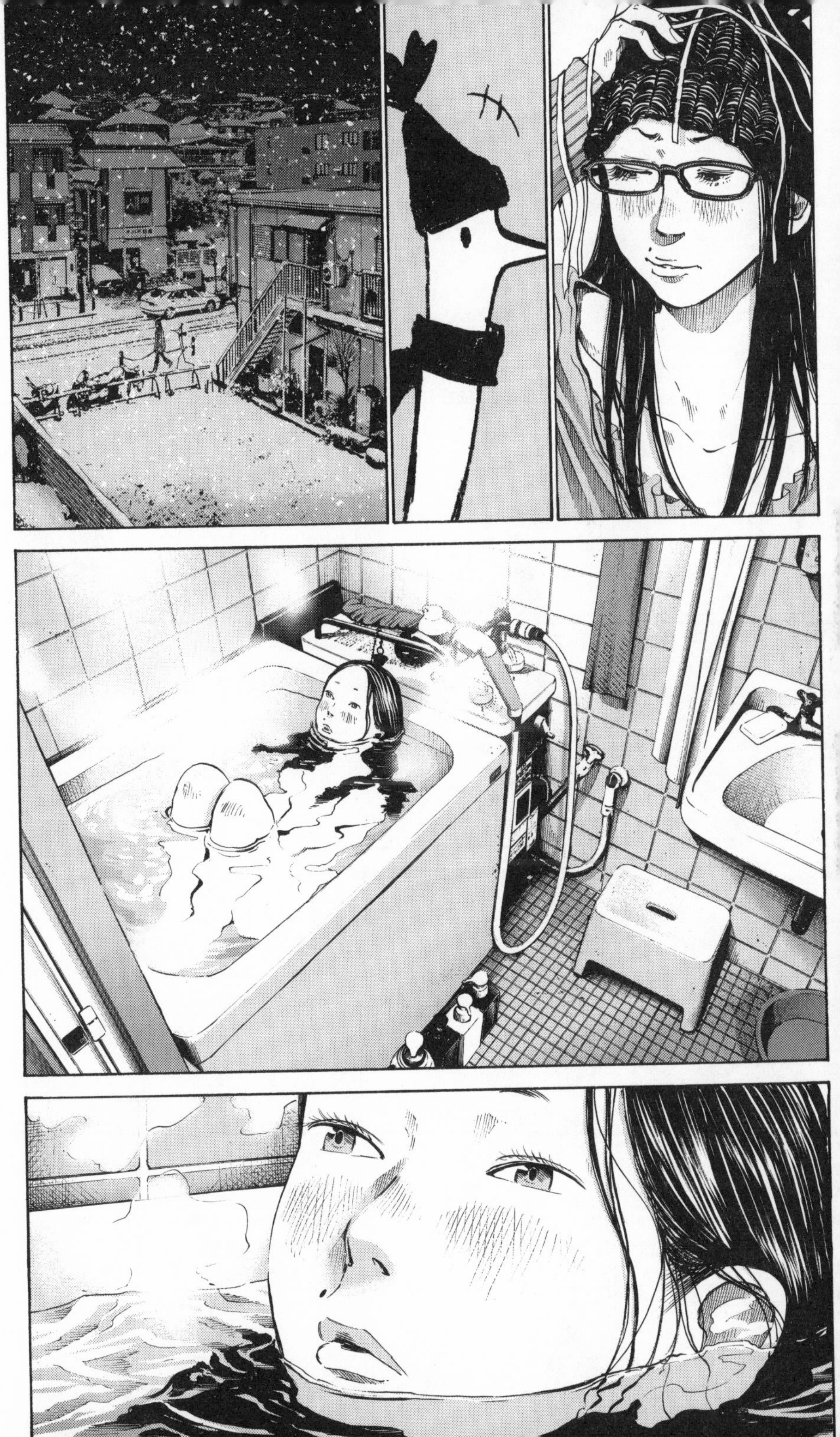

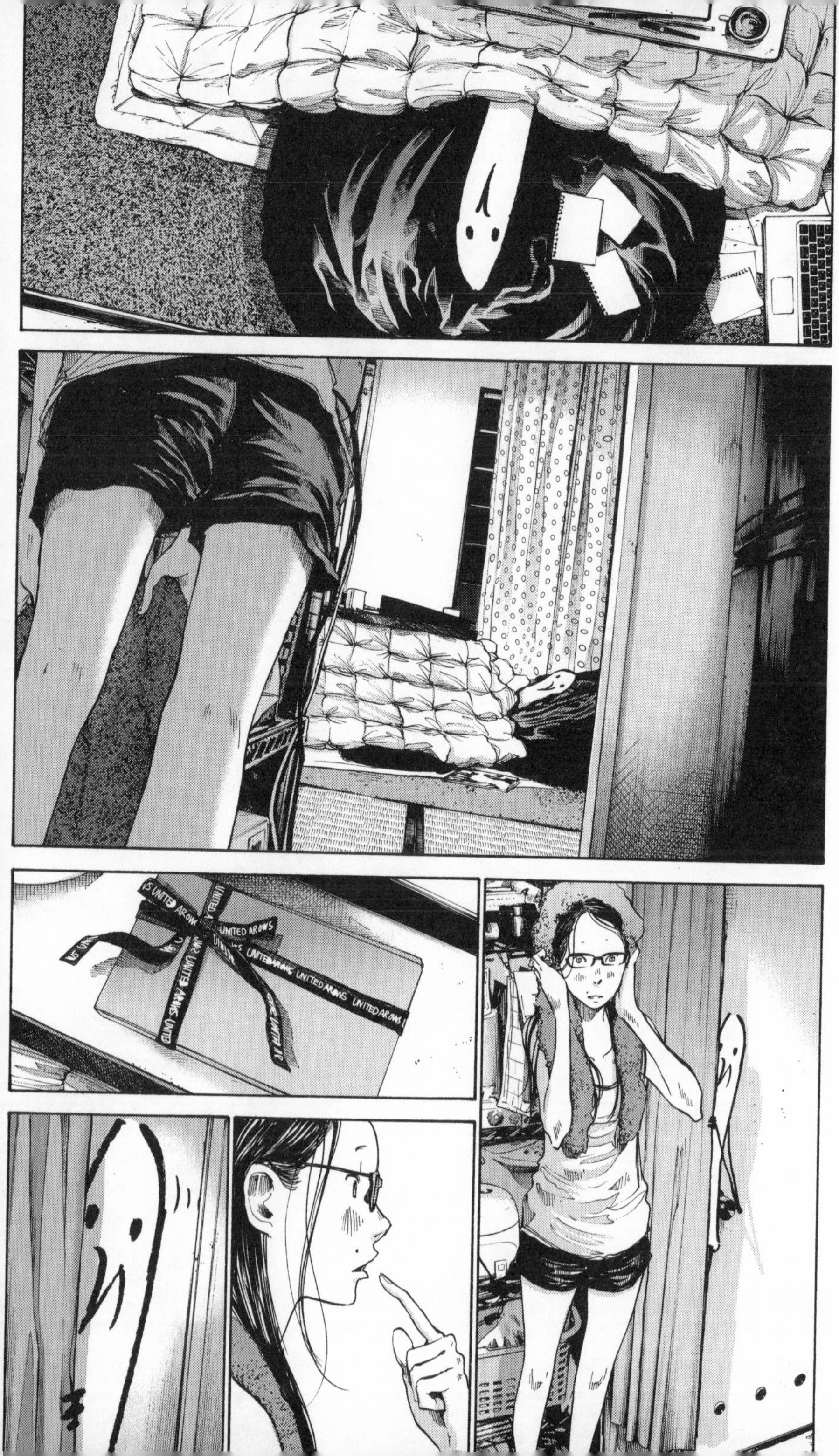
UNITED ARROWS

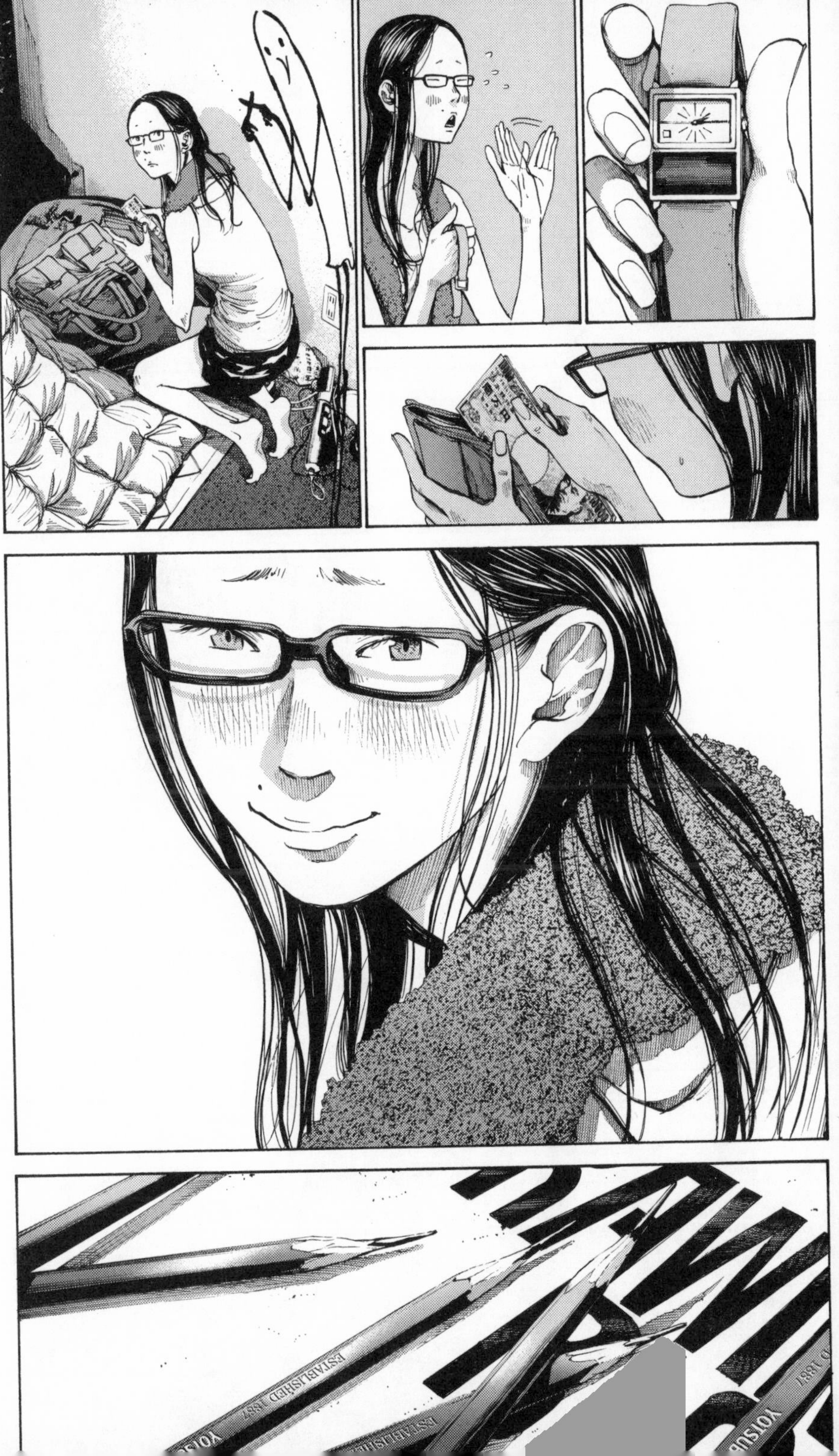

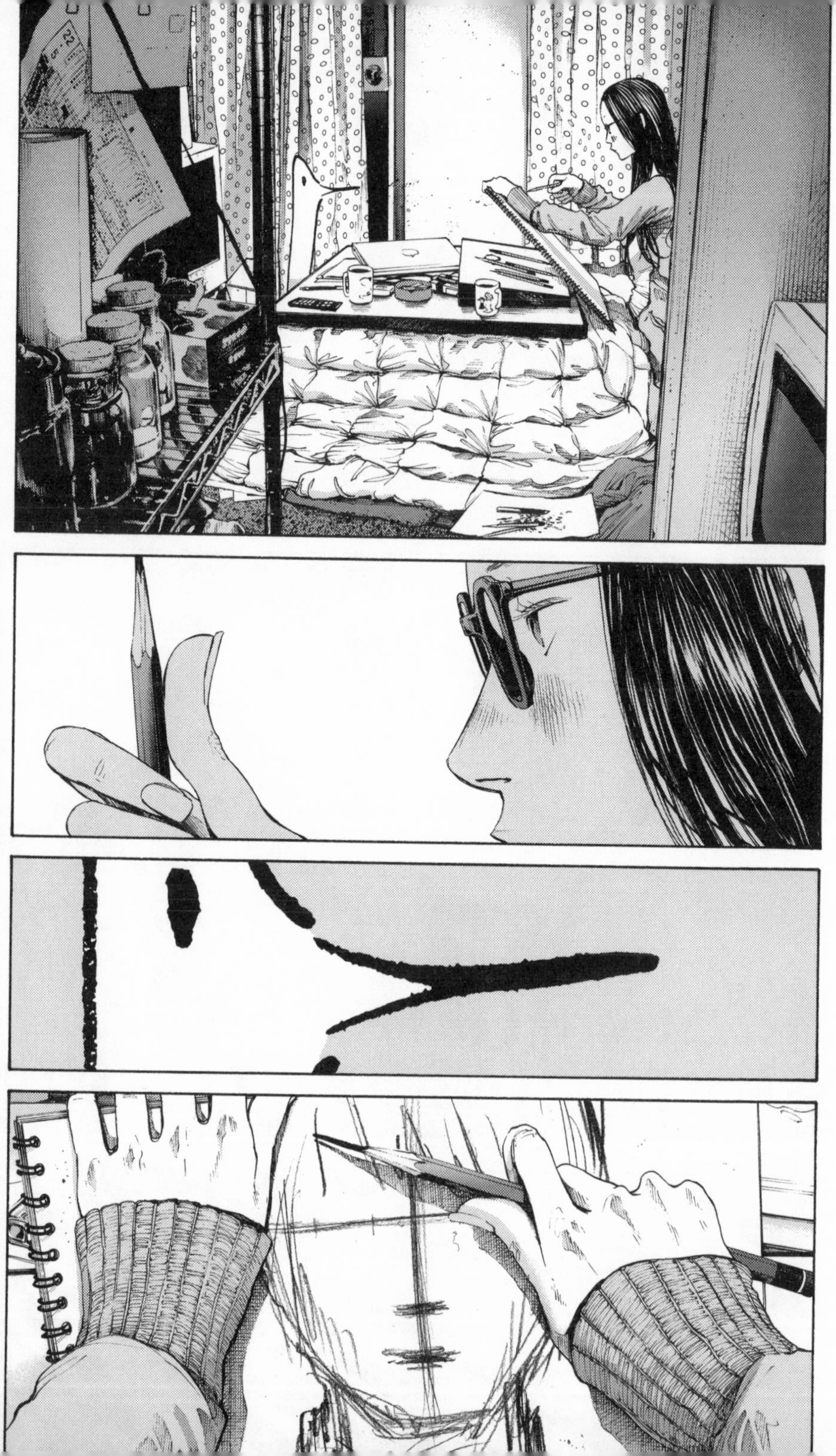

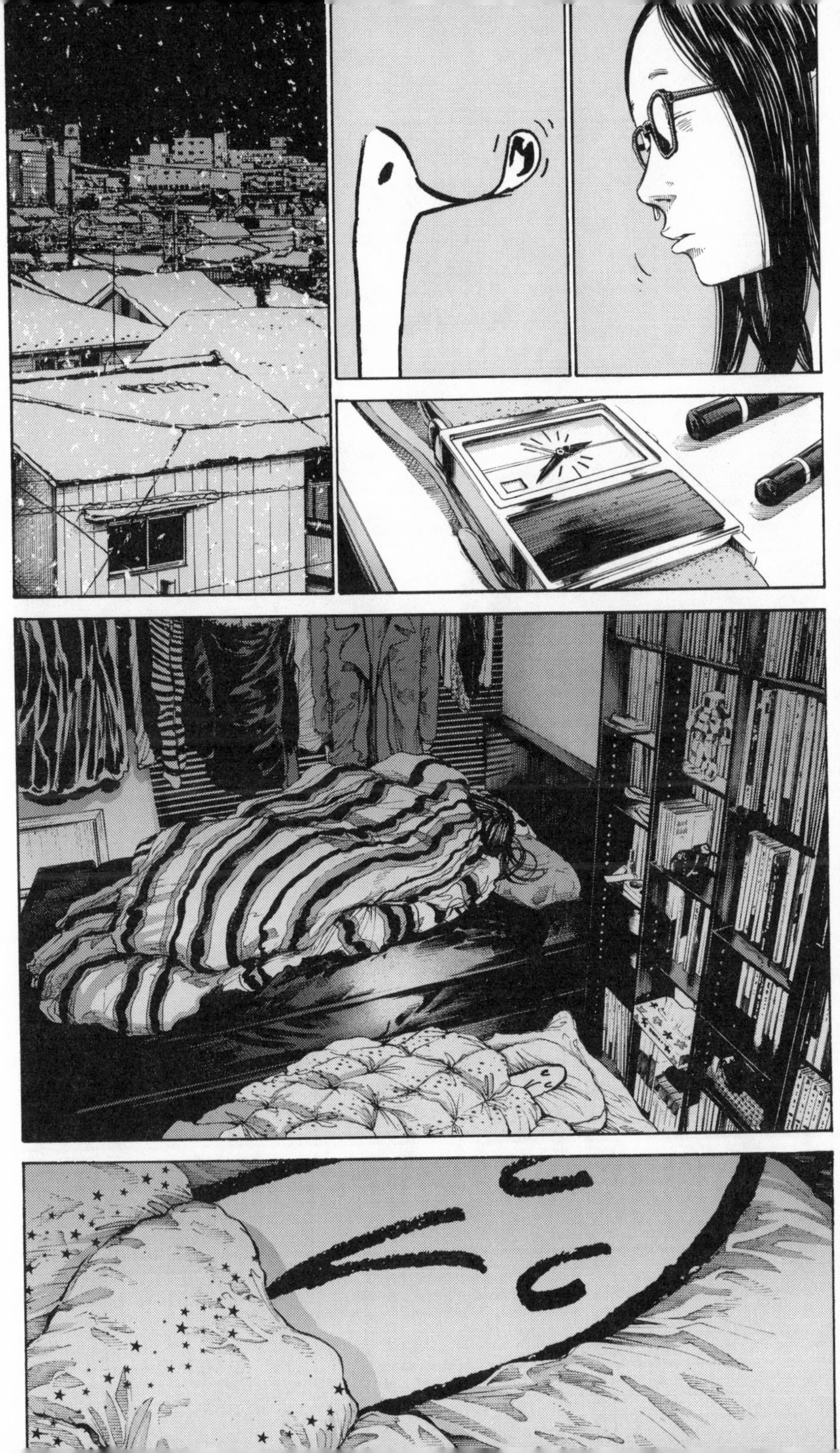

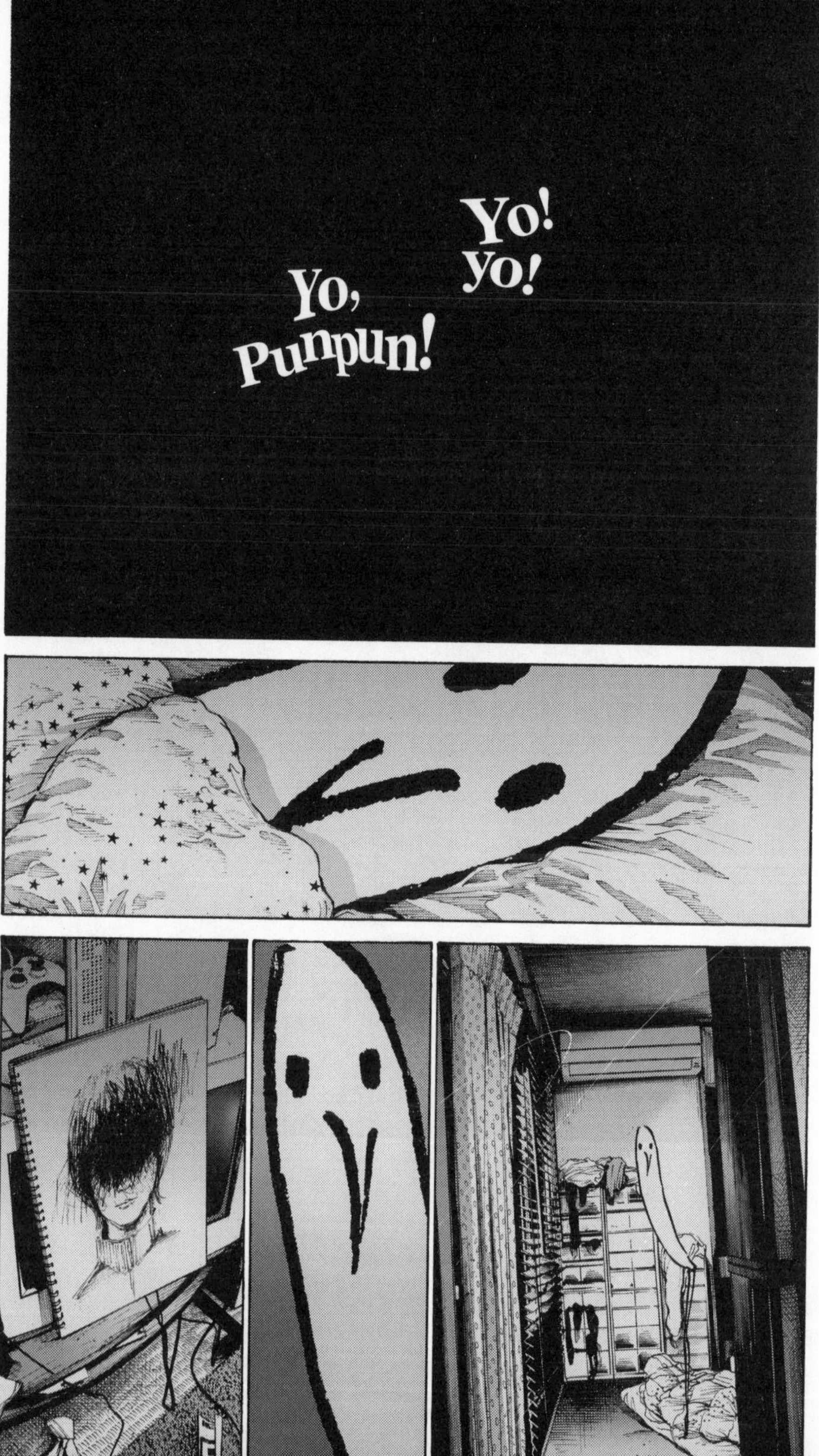
Yo! yo!
Yo, Punpun!

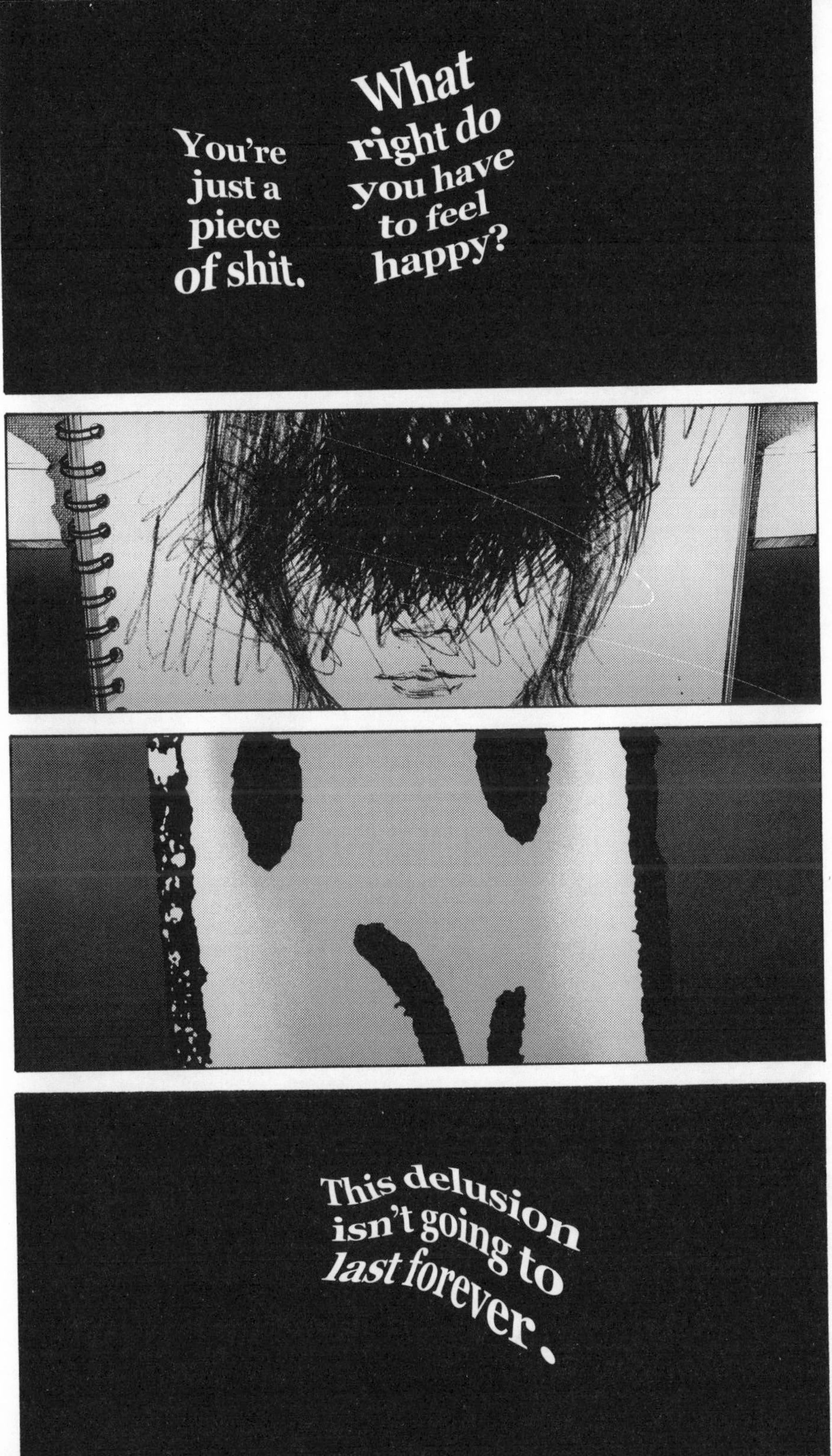

What right do you have to feel happy?
You're just a piece of shit.
This delusion isn't going to last forever.

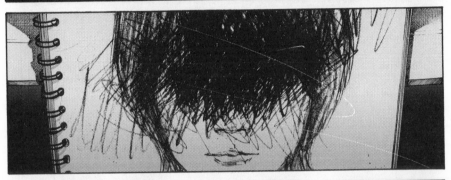

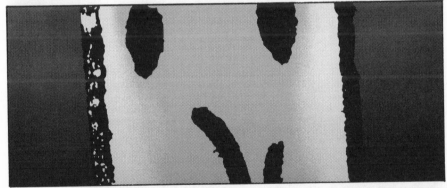

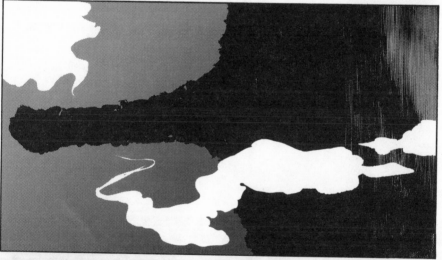

One
year
later.

Chapter 89

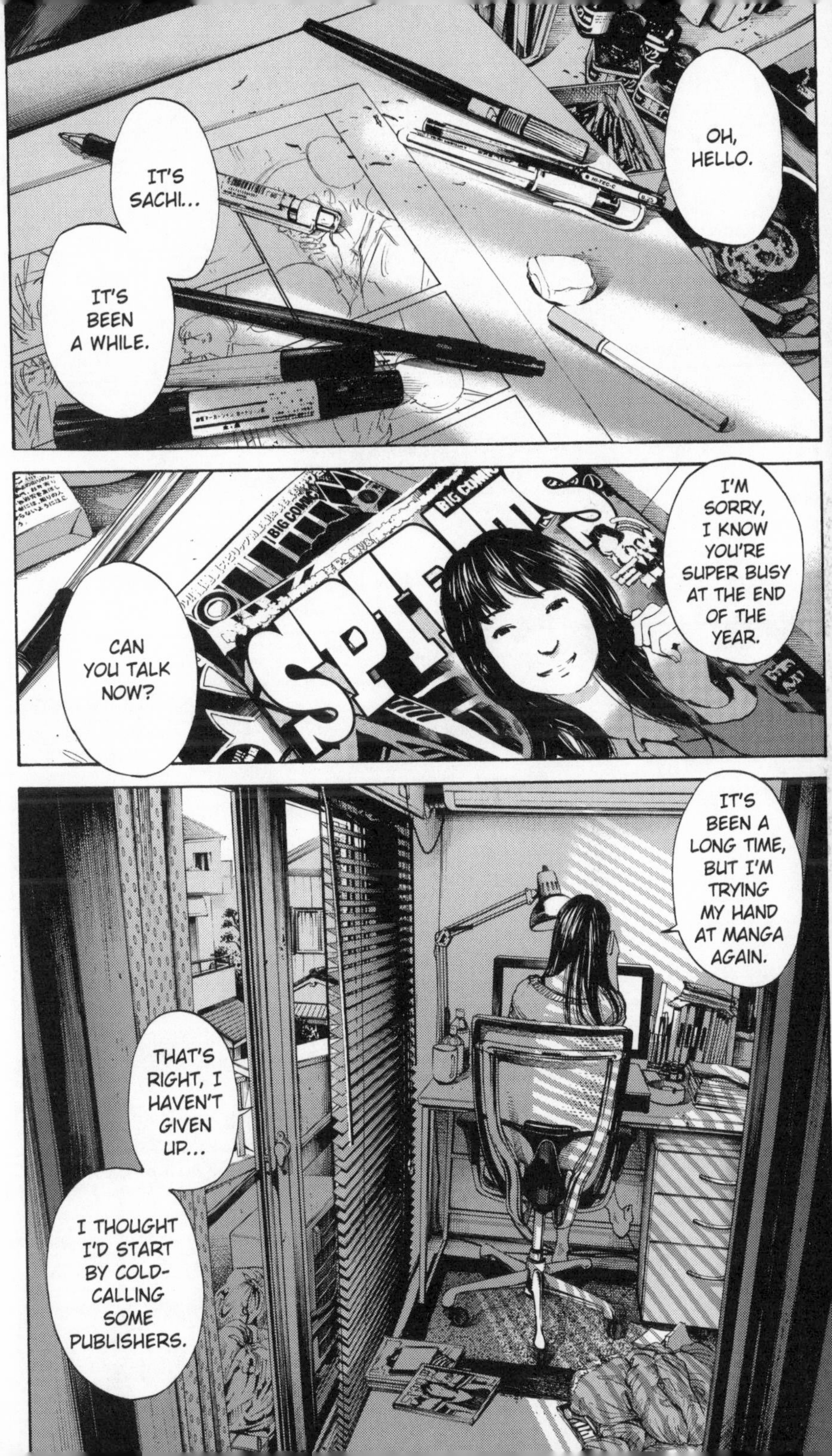
OH, HELLO.
IT'S SACHI...
IT'S BEEN A WHILE.
I'M SORRY, I KNOW YOU'RE SUPER BUSY AT THE END OF THE YEAR.
CAN YOU TALK NOW?
IT'S BEEN A LONG TIME, BUT I'M TRYING MY HAND AT MANGA AGAIN.
THAT'S RIGHT, I HAVEN'T GIVEN UP...
I THOUGHT I'D START BY COLD-CALLING SOME PUBLISHERS.

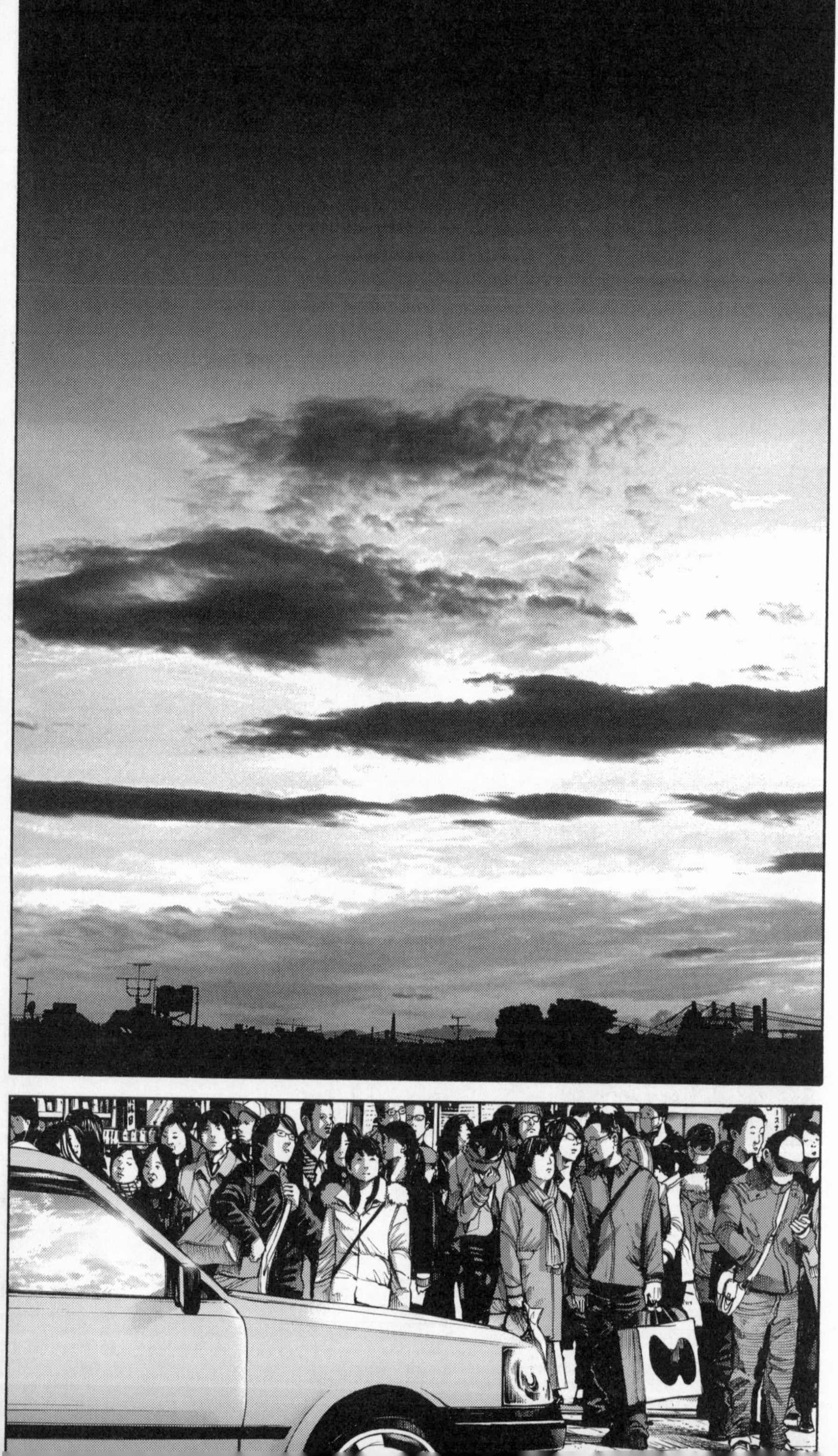

Once again...

...December in the city was full of hurried people bustling through the crowds...

...as if to make up for the laziness of the last 11 months.

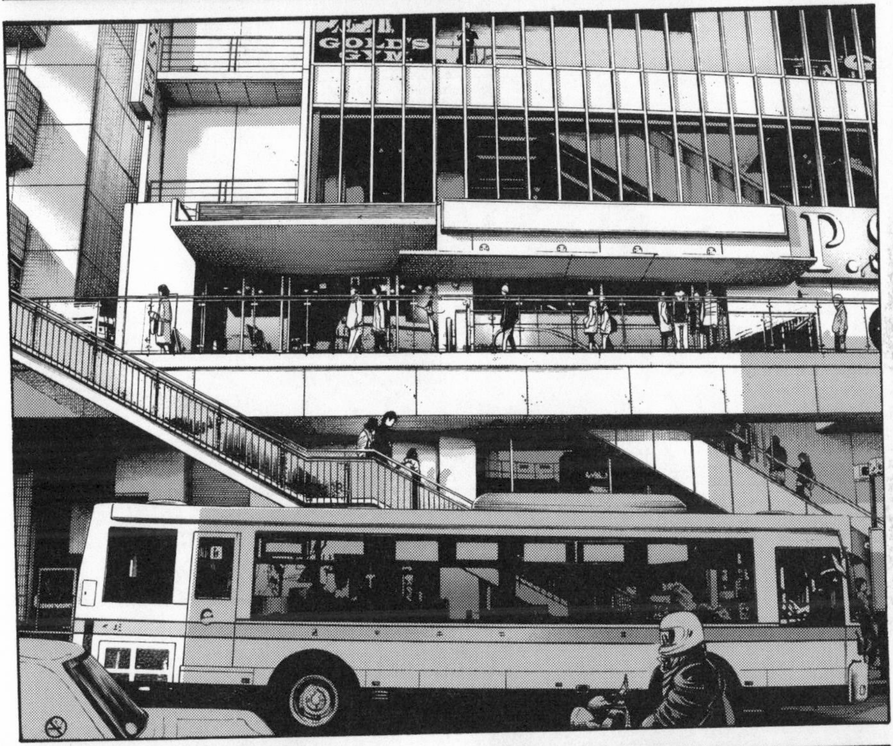
GOLD'S GYM

Unlike years past...

...Punpun had mastered the art of keeping step and blending with the crowd.

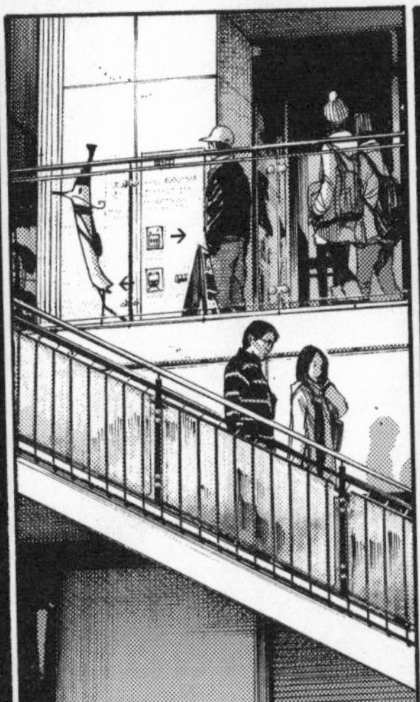

In the 18 months since he'd started living on his own...

...Punpun had changed.

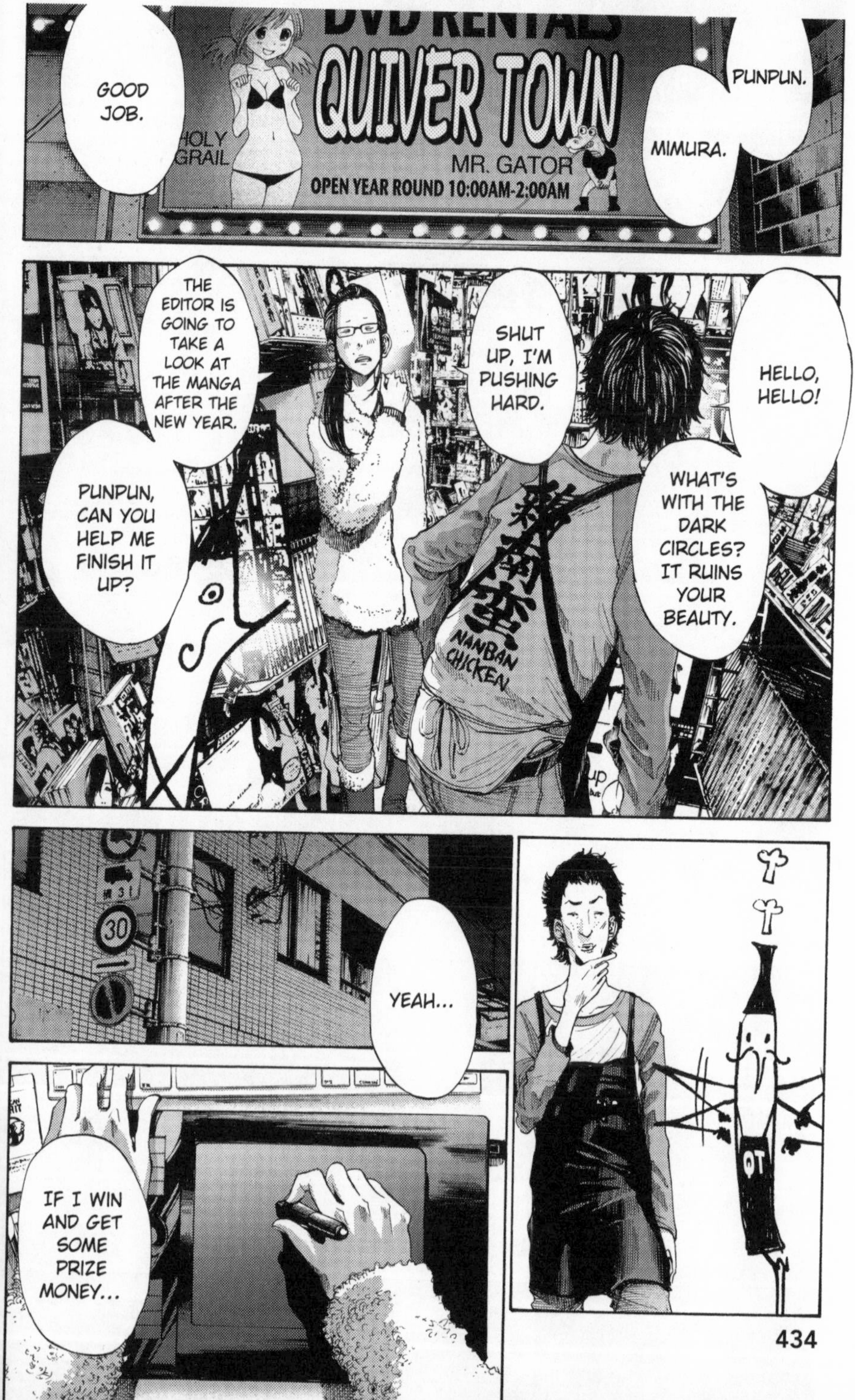
PUNPUN.
MIMURA.
DVD RENTALS
QUIVER TOWN
HOLY GRAIL
MR. GATOR
OPEN YEAR ROUND 10:00AM-2:00AM
GOOD JOB.
HELLO, HELLO!
WHAT'S WITH THE DARK CIRCLES? IT RUINS YOUR BEAUTY.
NANBAN CHICKEN
SHUT UP, I'M PUSHING HARD.
THE EDITOR IS GOING TO TAKE A LOOK AT THE MANGA AFTER THE NEW YEAR.
PUNPUN, CAN YOU HELP ME FINISH IT UP?
30
YEAH...
IF I WIN AND GET SOME PRIZE MONEY...

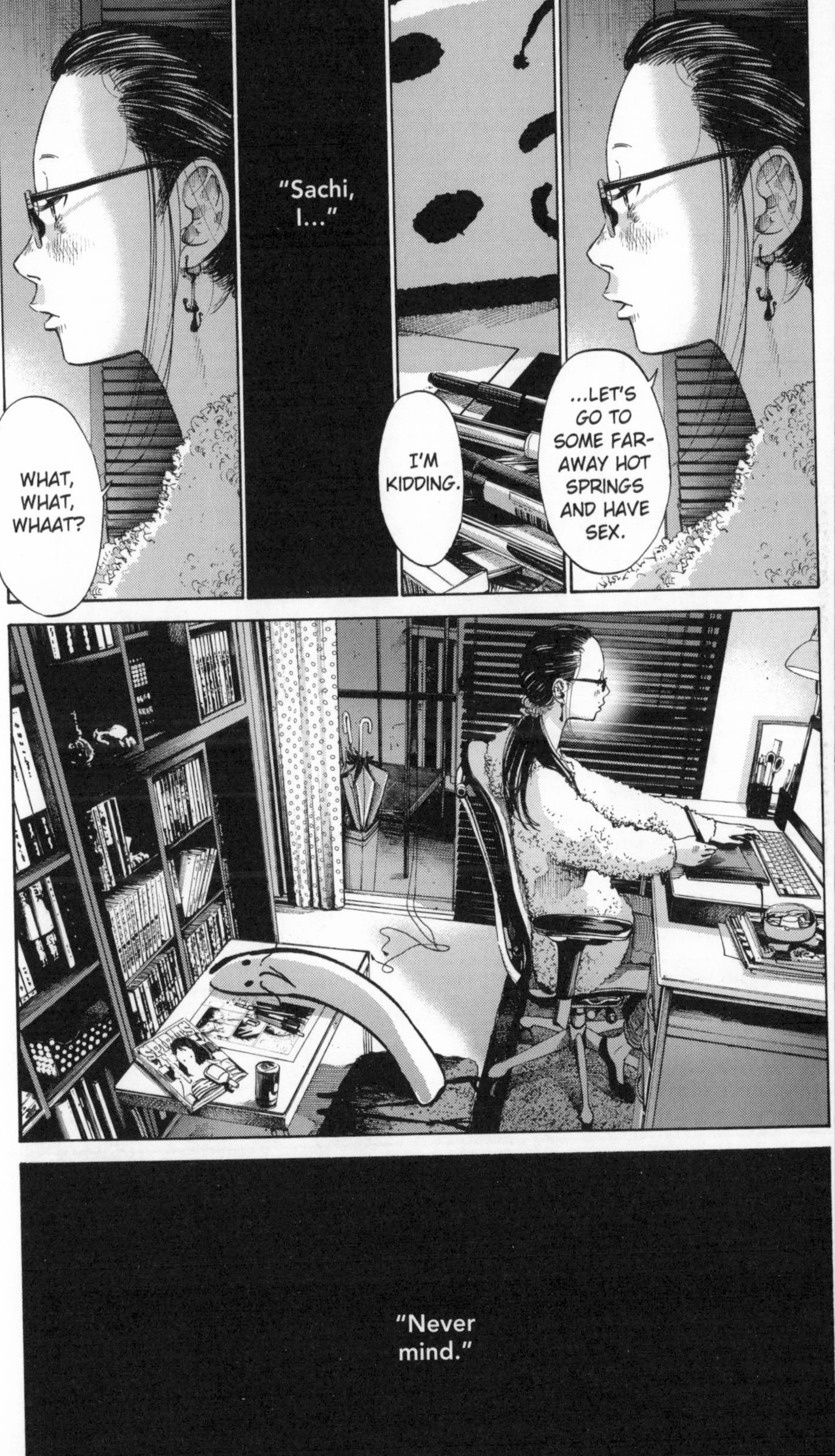
...LET'S GO TO SOME FAR-AWAY HOT SPRINGS AND HAVE SEX.
I'M KIDDING.
"Sachi, I..."
WHAT, WHAT, WHAAT?
"Never mind."

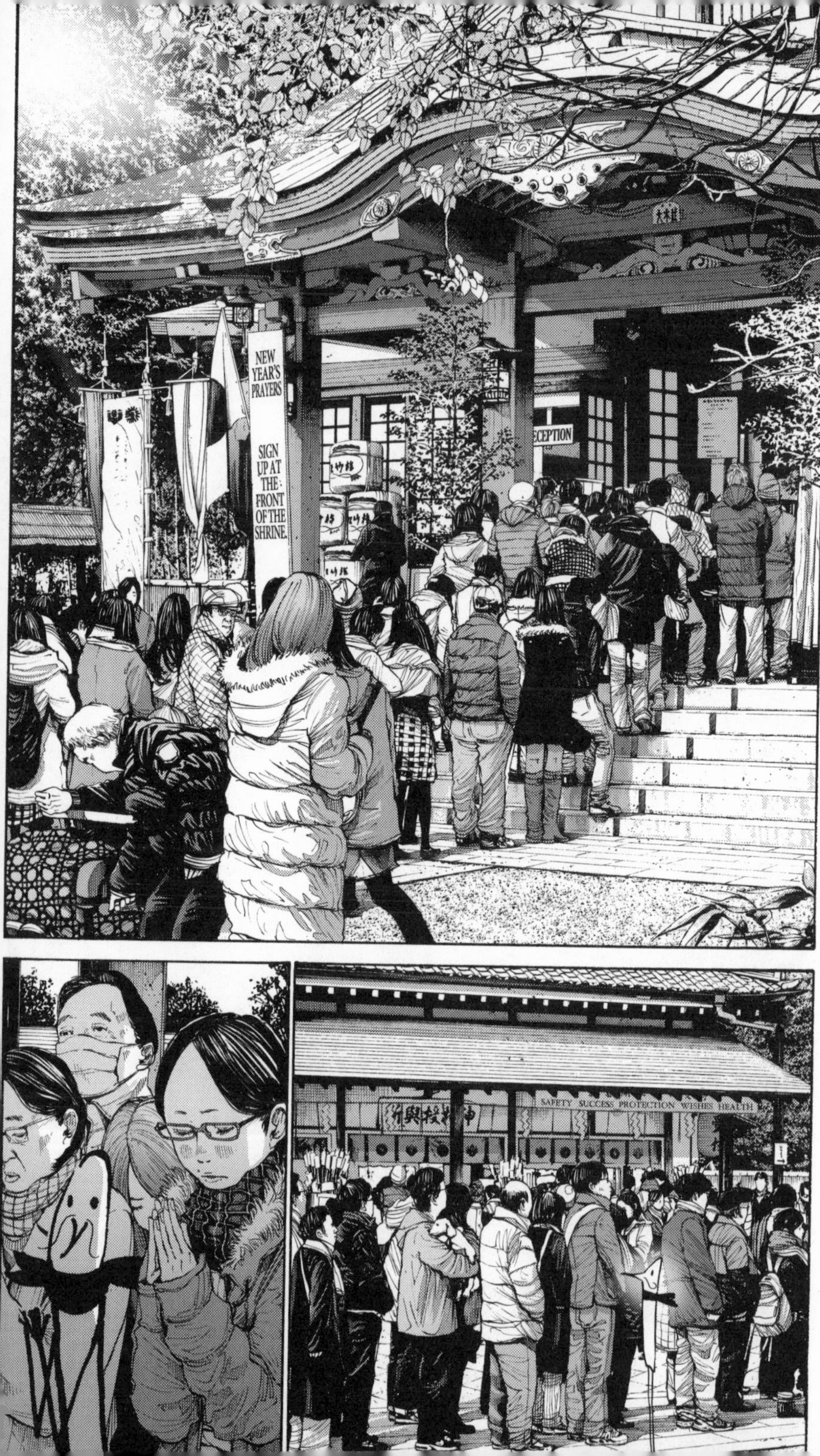
NEW YEAR'S PRAYERS
SIGN UP AT THE FRONT OF THE SHRINE.
ECEPTION
SAFETY SUCCESS PROTECTION WISHES HEALTH

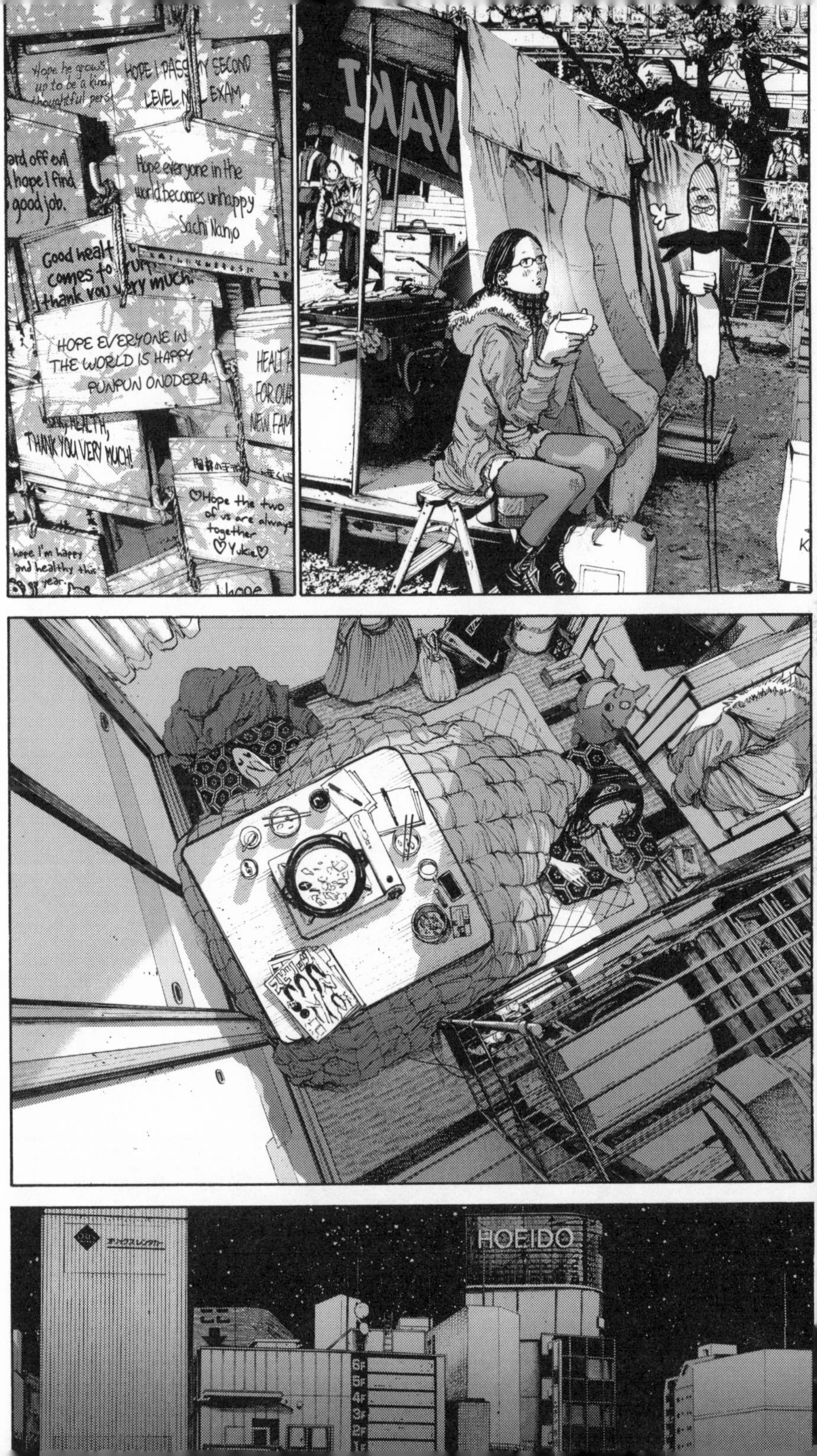
Hope he grows up to be a kind, thoughtful pers
HOPE I PASS MY SECOND LEVEL N L EXAM.
ard off evil hope I find good job.
Hope everyone in the world becomes unhappy Sachi Nanjo
Good healt comes to thank you very much.
HOPE EVERYONE IN THE WORLD IS HAPPY PUNPUN ONODERA.
HEALT FOR OUR NEW FAM
THANK YOU VERY MUCH!
♡Hope the two of us are always together ♡Yukie♡
hope I'm happy and healthy this year.
Hope
HOEIDO
6F
5F
4F
3F
2F

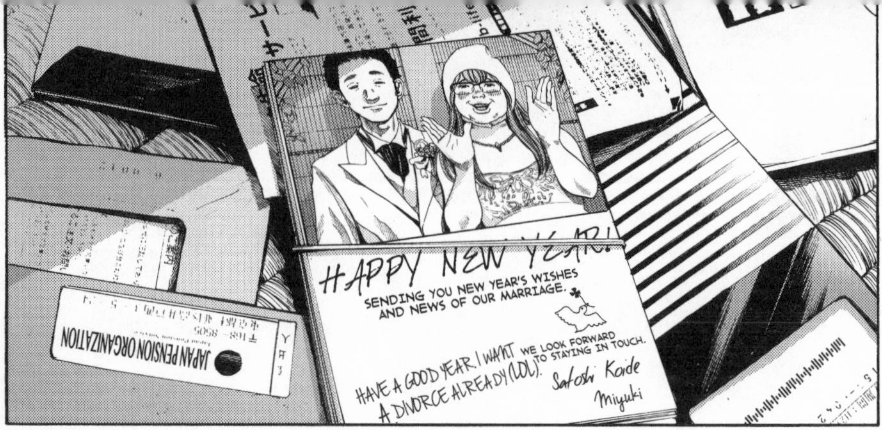
HAPPY NEW YEAR!
SENDING YOU NEW YEAR'S WISHES AND NEWS OF OUR MARRIAGE.
HAVE A GOOD YEAR. I WANT A DIVORCE ALREADY (LOL).
WE LOOK FORWARD TO STAYING IN TOUCH.
Satoshi Koide
Miyuki
JAPAN PENSION ORGANIZATION
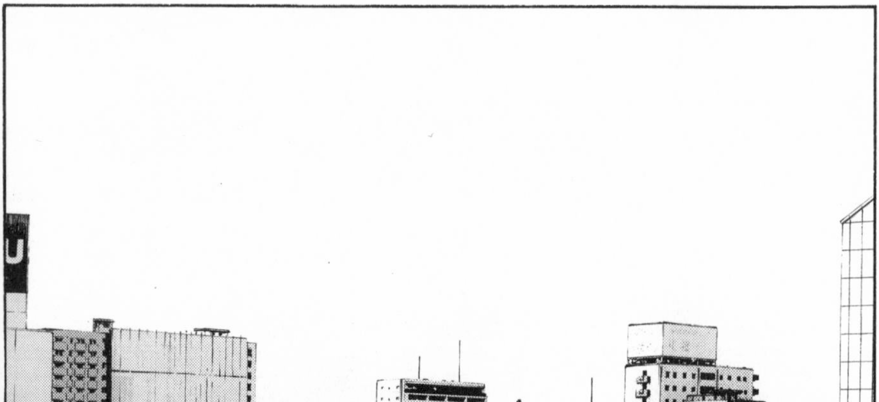
MIZUHO みずほ銀行
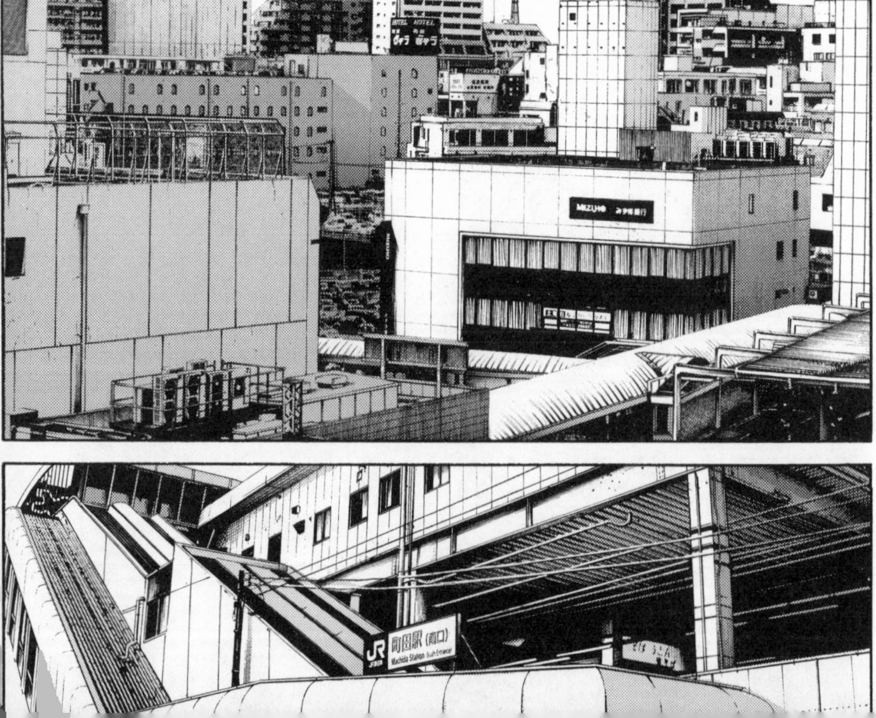
JR
町田駅 (南口)
Machida Station South Entrance

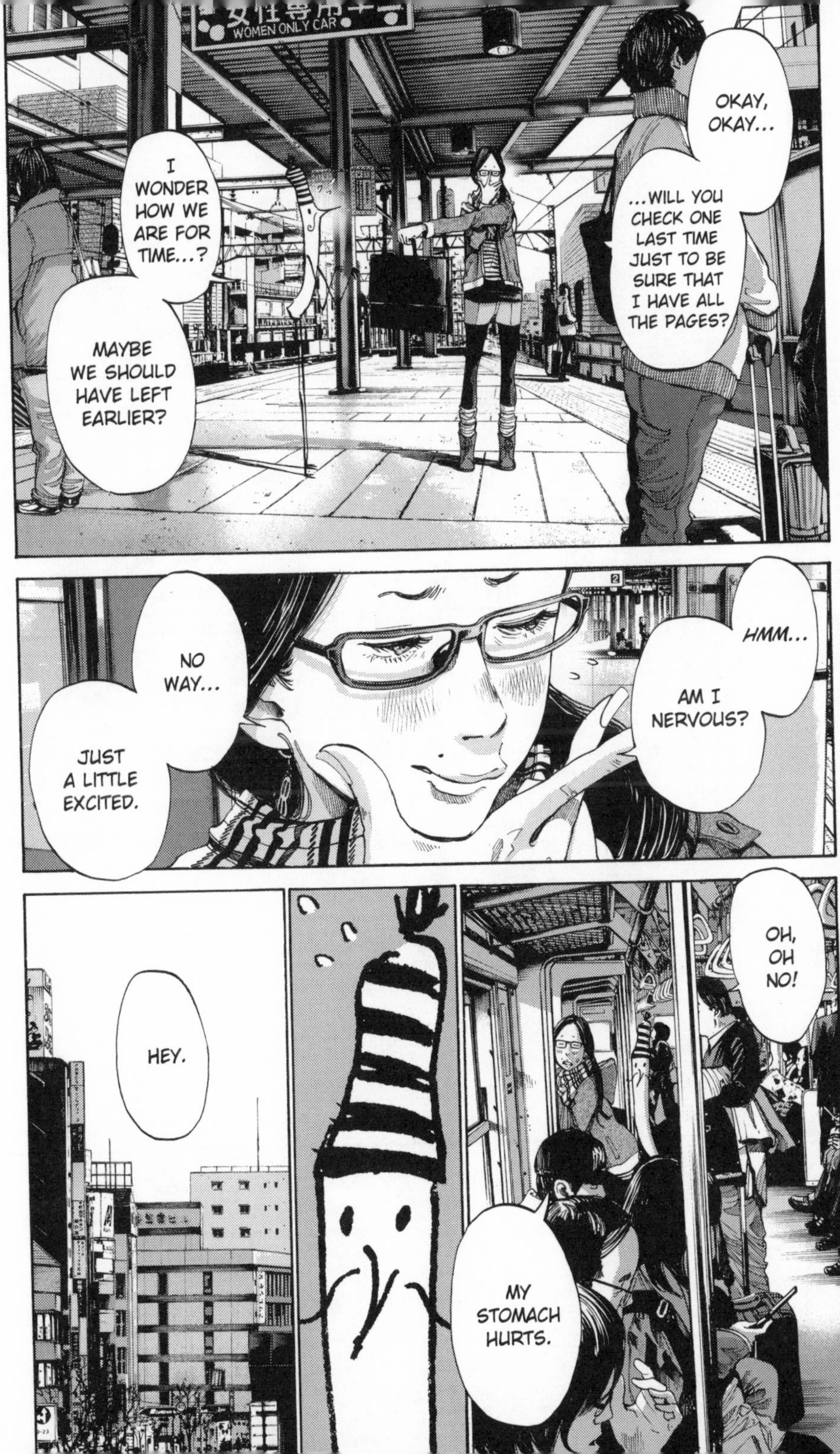
WOMEN ONLY CAR
OKAY, OKAY...
...WILL YOU CHECK ONE LAST TIME JUST TO BE SURE THAT I HAVE ALL THE PAGES?
I WONDER HOW WE ARE FOR TIME...?
MAYBE WE SHOULD HAVE LEFT EARLIER?
HMM...
AM I NERVOUS?
NO WAY...
JUST A LITTLE EXCITED.
OH, OH NO!
MY STOMACH HURTS.
HEY.

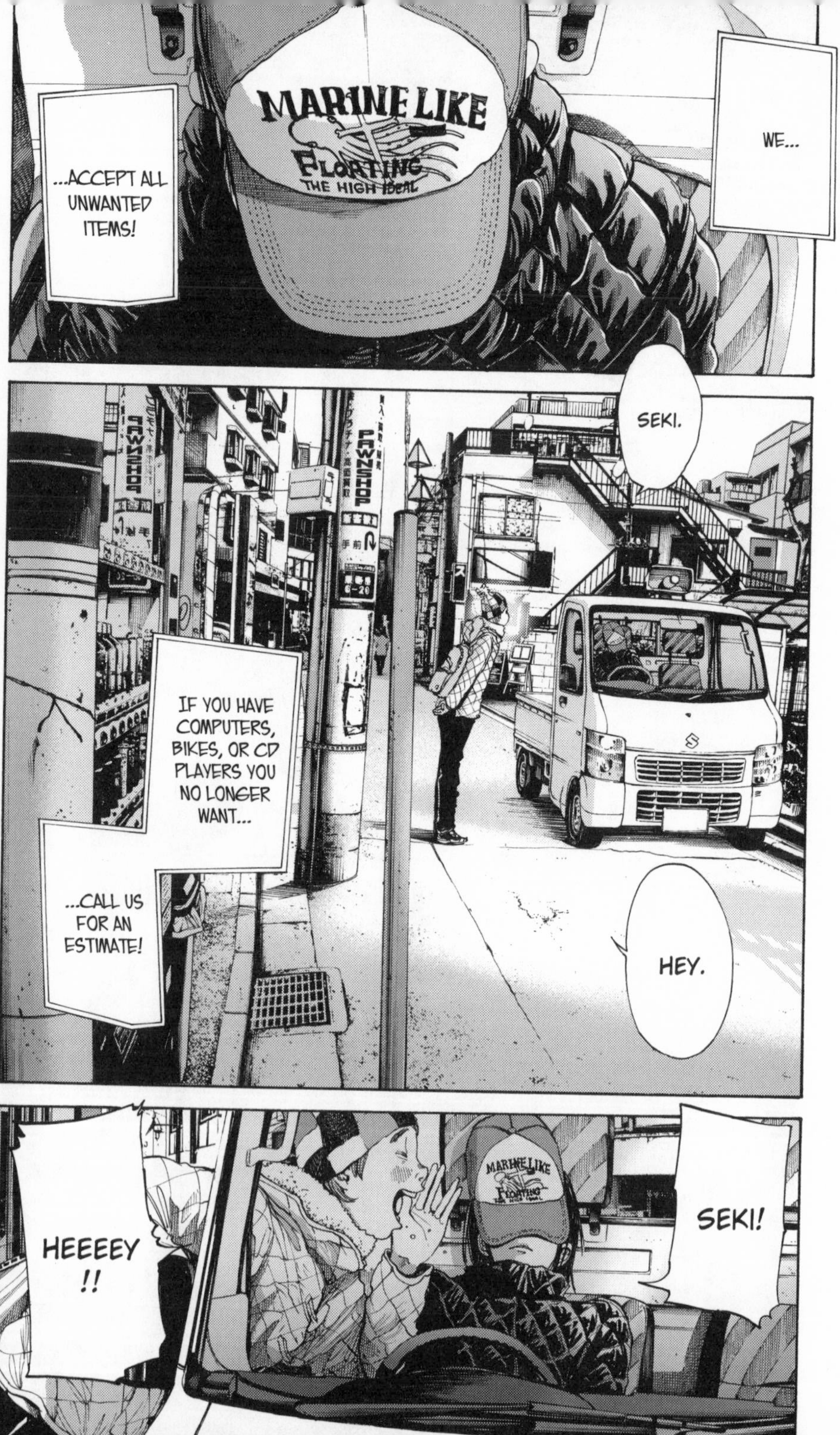
WE...
...ACCEPT ALL UNWANTED ITEMS!
MARINE LIKE
THE HIGH IDEAL
SEKI.
PAWNSHOP
IF YOU HAVE COMPUTERS, BIKES, OR CD PLAYERS YOU NO LONGER WANT...
HEY.
...CALL US FOR AN ESTIMATE!
SEKI!
HEEEEY !!

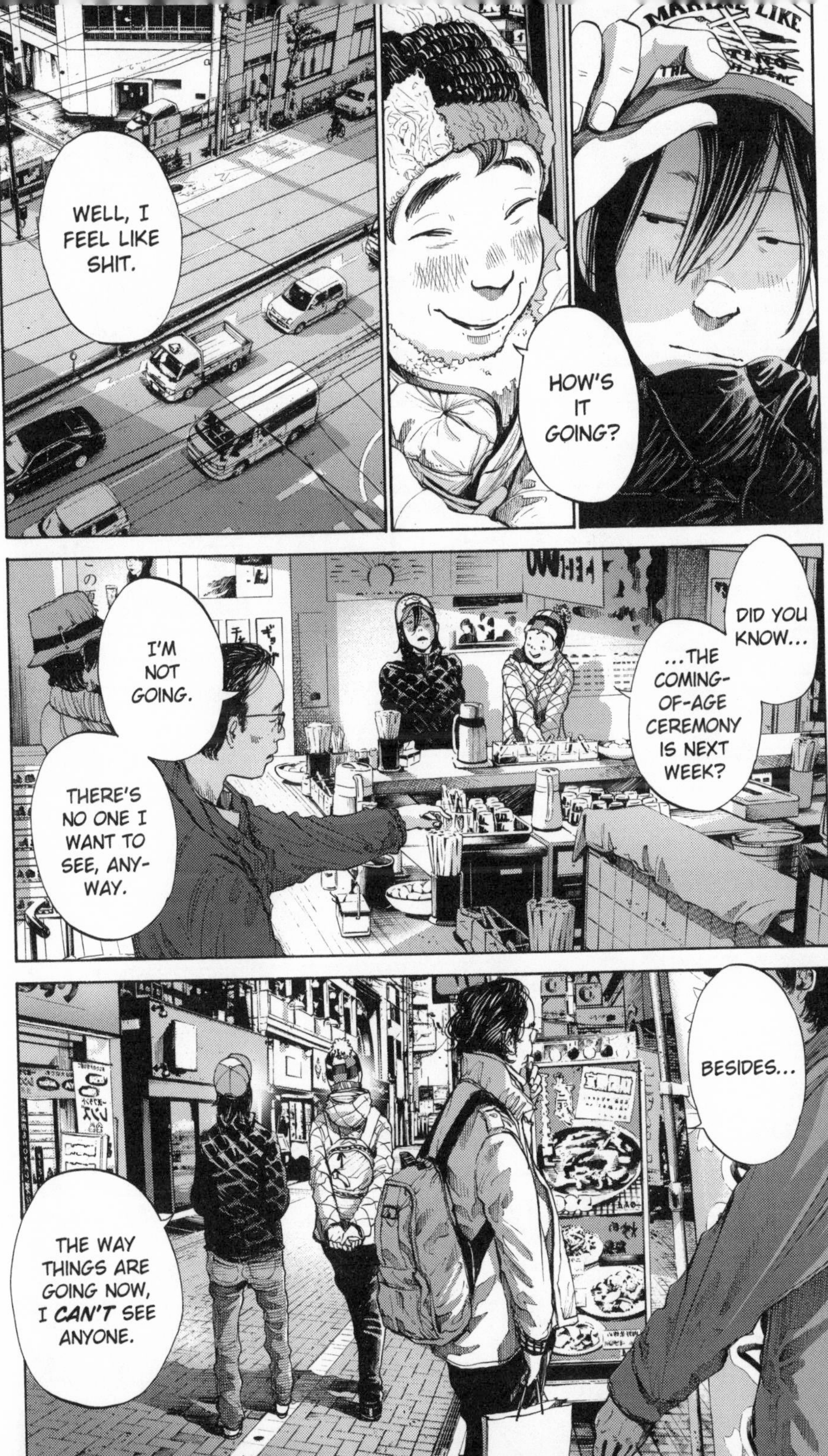
HOW'S IT GOING?
WELL, I FEEL LIKE SHIT.
DID YOU KNOW...
...THE COMING-OF-AGE CEREMONY IS NEXT WEEK?
I'M NOT GOING.
THERE'S NO ONE I WANT TO SEE, ANYWAY.
BESIDES...
THE WAY THINGS ARE GOING NOW, I *CAN'T* SEE ANYONE.

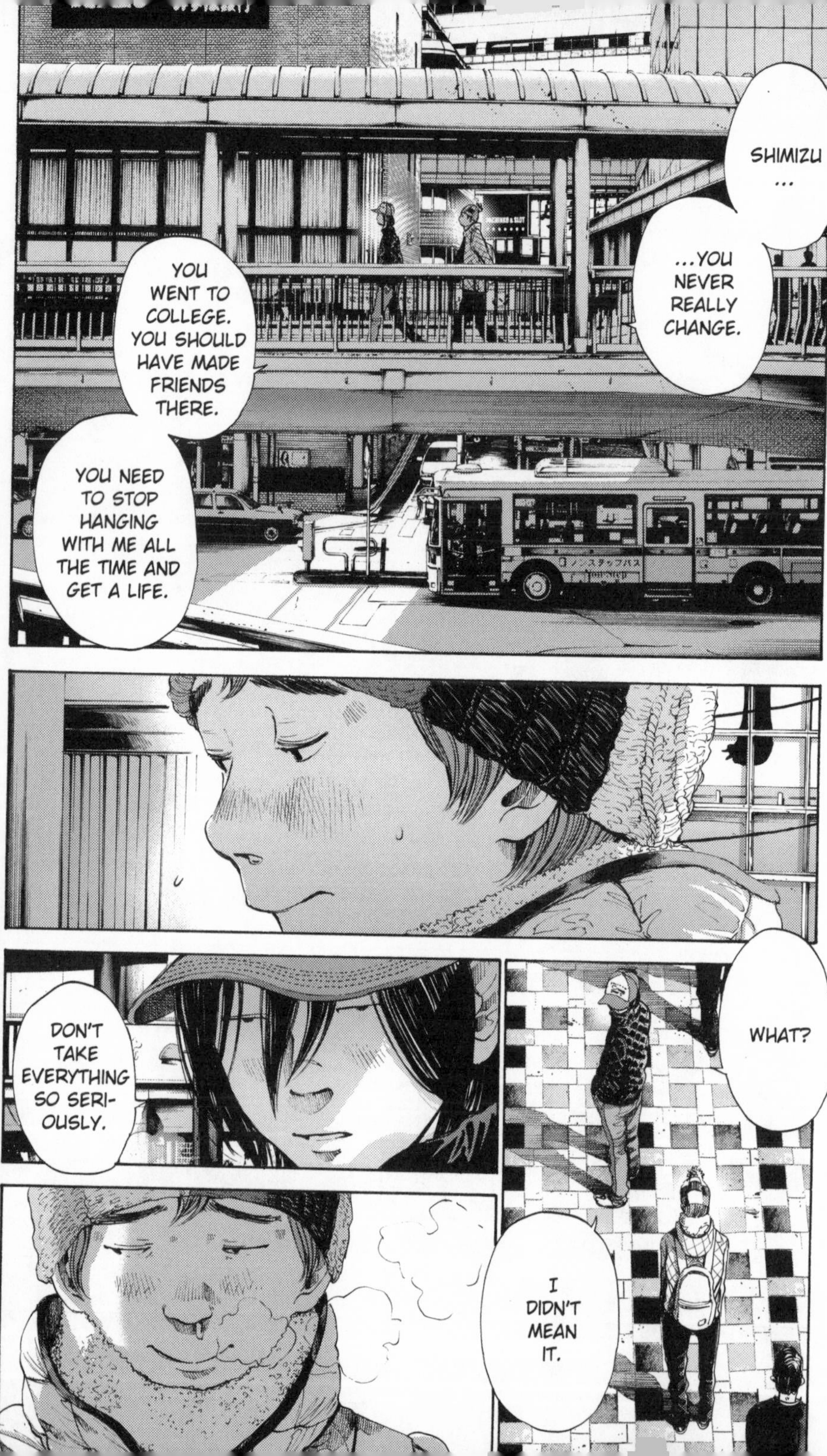
SHIMIZU ...
...YOU NEVER REALLY CHANGE.
YOU WENT TO COLLEGE. YOU SHOULD HAVE MADE FRIENDS THERE.
YOU NEED TO STOP HANGING WITH ME ALL THE TIME AND GET A LIFE.
WHAT?
I DIDN'T MEAN IT.
DON'T TAKE EVERYTHING SO SERI-OUSLY.

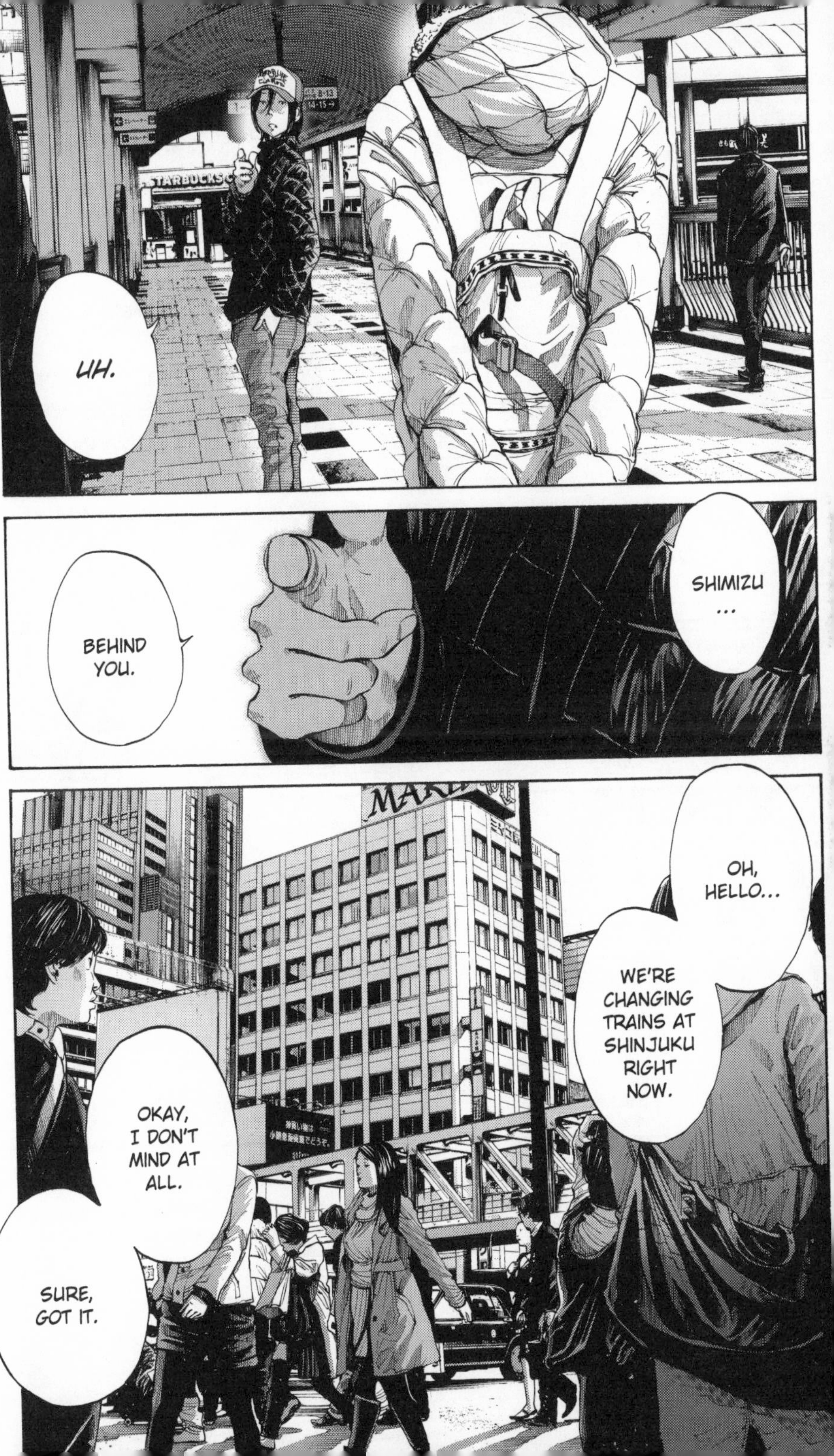
UH.
SHIMIZU ...
BEHIND YOU.
OH, HELLO...
WE'RE CHANGING TRAINS AT SHINJUKU RIGHT NOW.
OKAY, I DON'T MIND AT ALL.
SURE, GOT IT.

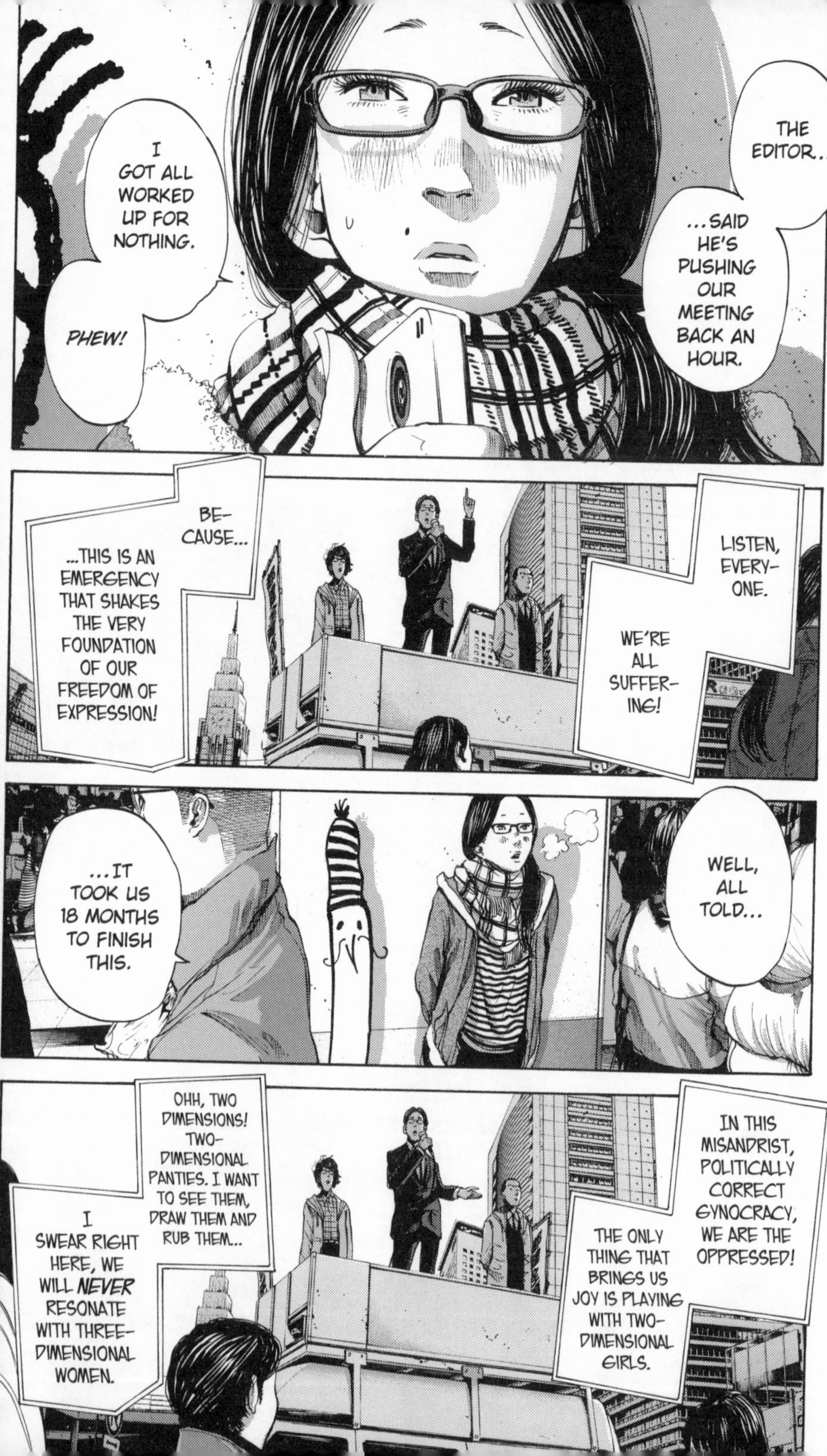
THE EDITOR...
...SAID HE'S PUSHING OUR MEETING BACK AN HOUR.
I GOT ALL WORKED UP FOR NOTHING.
PHEW!
LISTEN, EVERY-ONE.
WE'RE ALL SUFFER-ING!
BE-CAUSE...
...THIS IS AN EMERGENCY THAT SHAKES THE VERY FOUNDATION OF OUR FREEDOM OF EXPRESSION!
WELL, ALL TOLD...
...IT TOOK US 18 MONTHS TO FINISH THIS.
IN THIS MISANDRIST, POLITICALLY CORRECT GYNOCRACY, WE ARE THE OPPRESSED!
THE ONLY THING THAT BRINGS US JOY IS PLAYING WITH TWO-DIMENSIONAL GIRLS.
OHH, TWO DIMENSIONS! TWO-DIMENSIONAL PANTIES. I WANT TO SEE THEM, DRAW THEM AND RUB THEM...
I SWEAR RIGHT HERE, WE WILL *NEVER* RESONATE WITH THREE-DIMENSIONAL WOMEN.

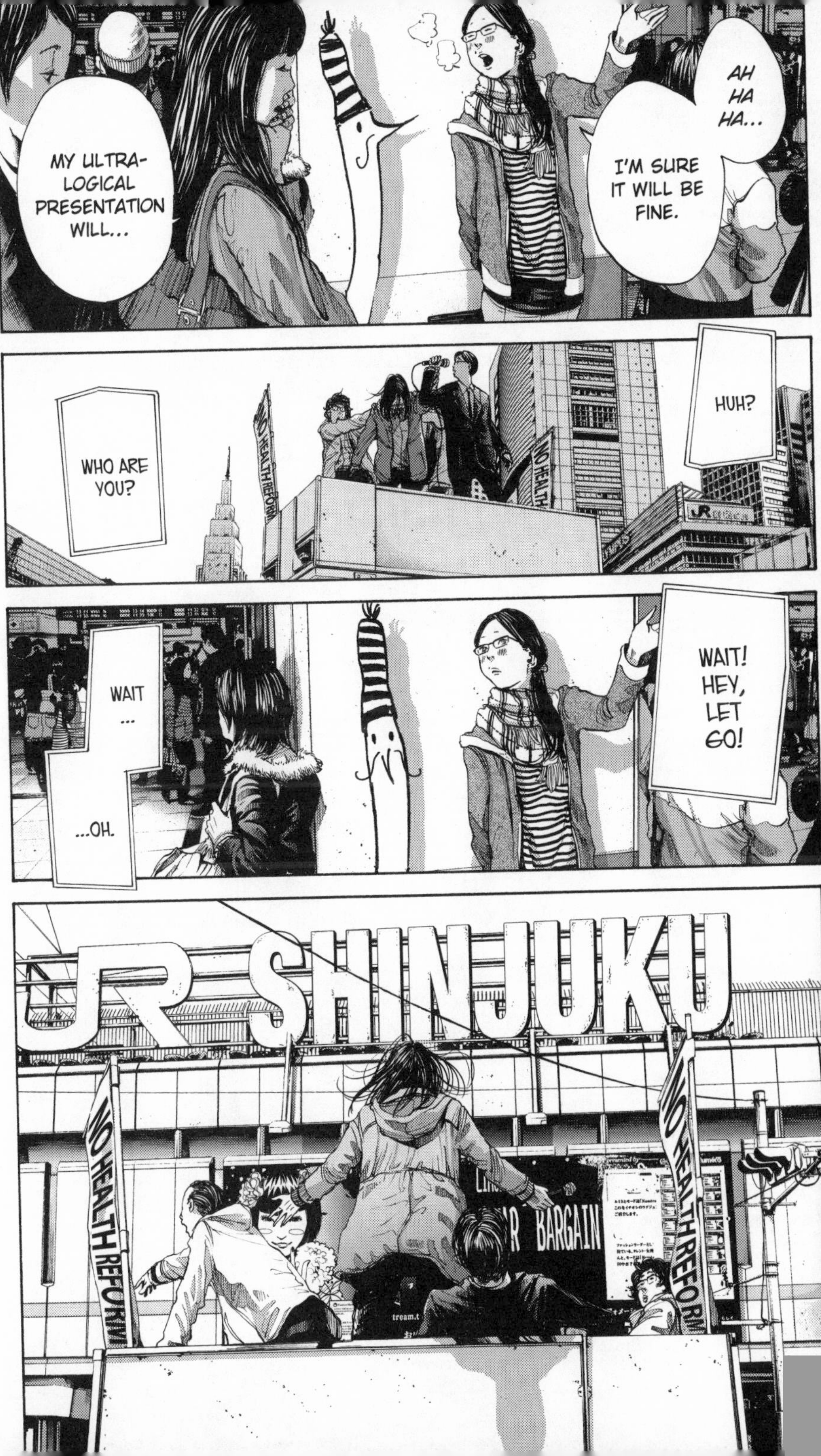
AH HA HA...
I'M SURE IT WILL BE FINE.
MY ULTRA-LOGICAL PRESENTATION WILL...
HUH?
NO HEALTH REFORM
NO HEALTH REFORM
WHO ARE YOU?
WAIT! HEY, LET GO!
WAIT ...
...OH.
JR SHINJUKU
NO HEALTH REFORM
BARGAIN
NO HEALTH REFORM

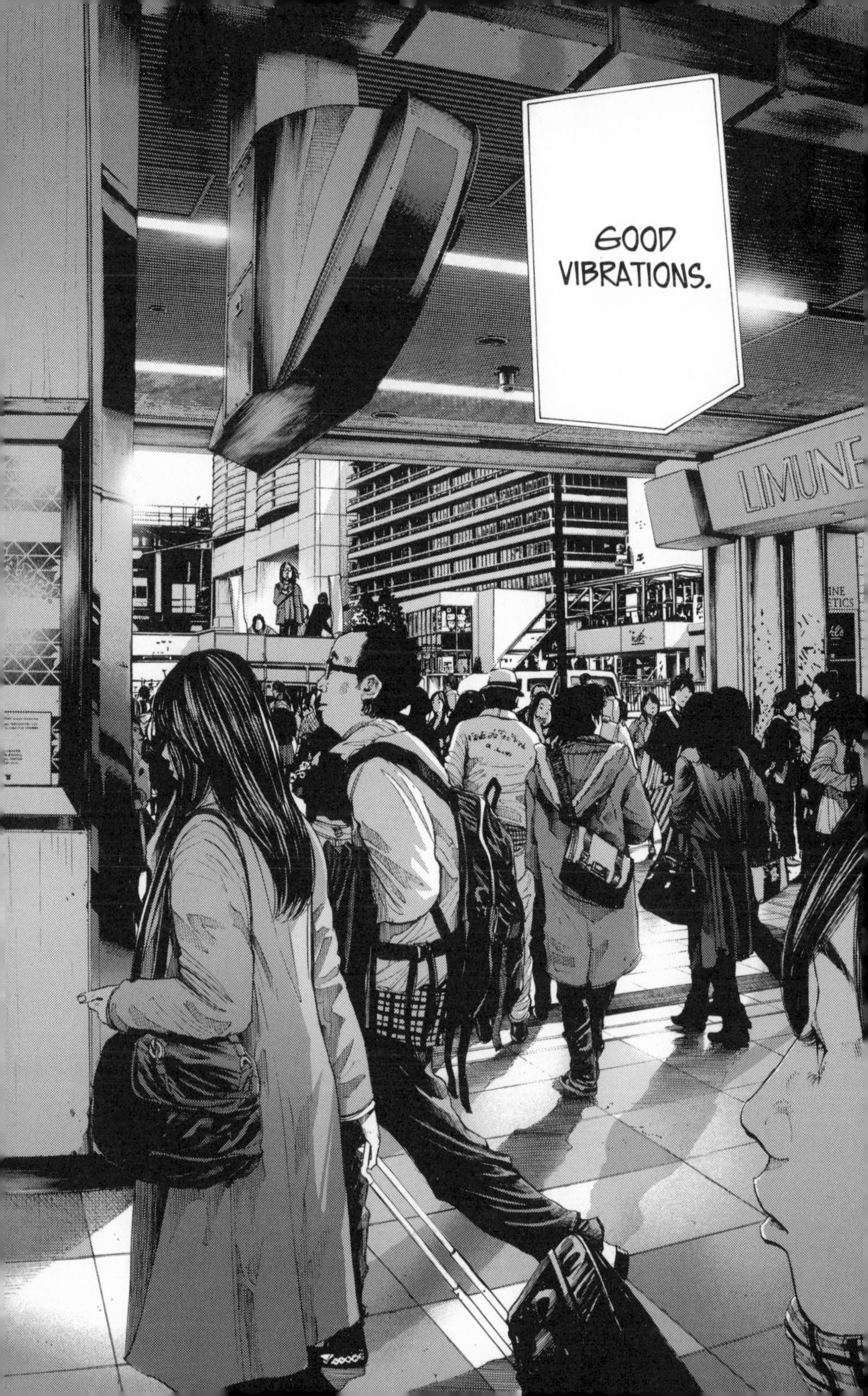
GOOD VIBRATIONS.
LIMUNE

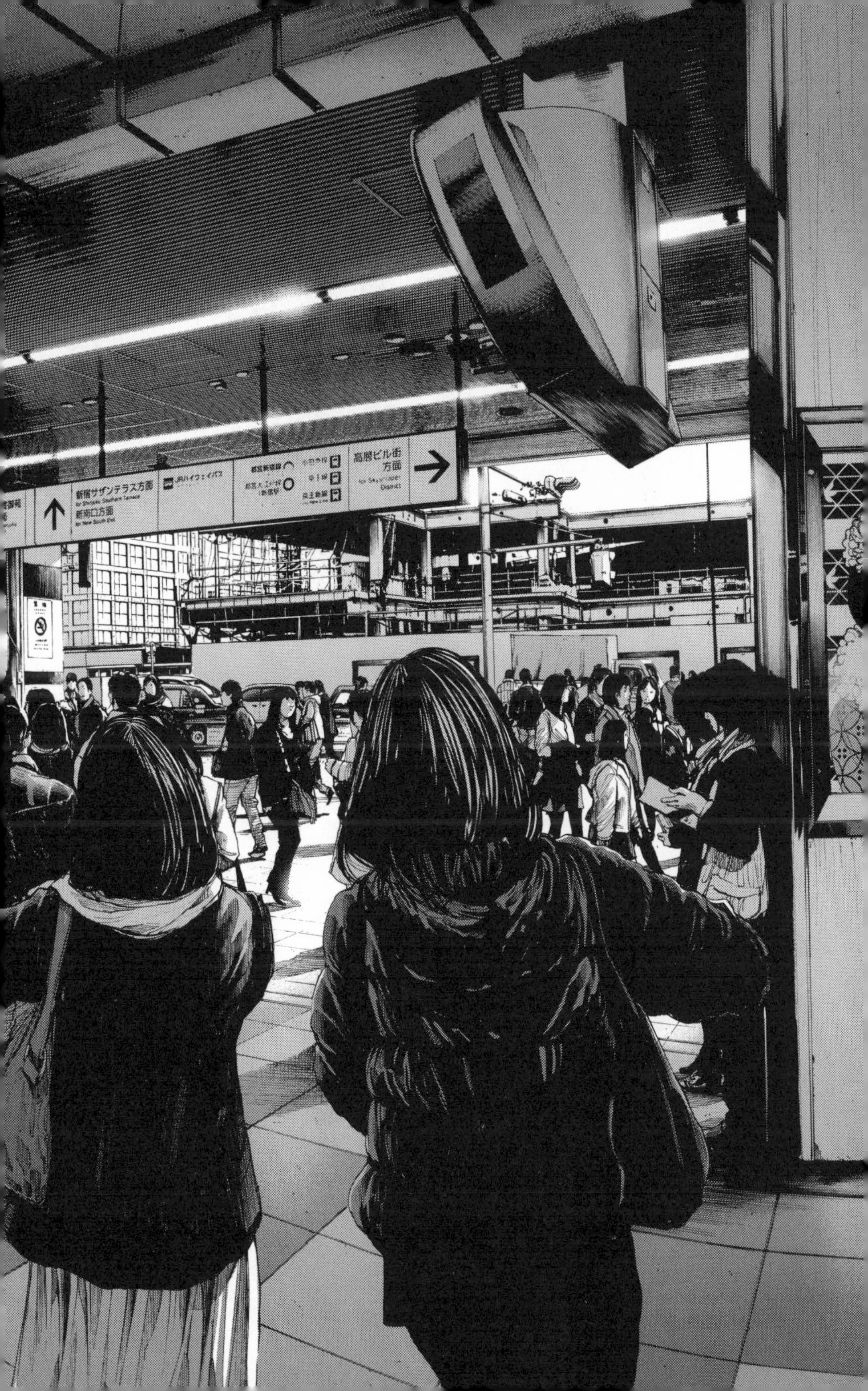

高層ビル街
方面
for Skyscraper District
都営新宿線
JRハイウェイバス
新宿サザンテラス方面
新南口方面

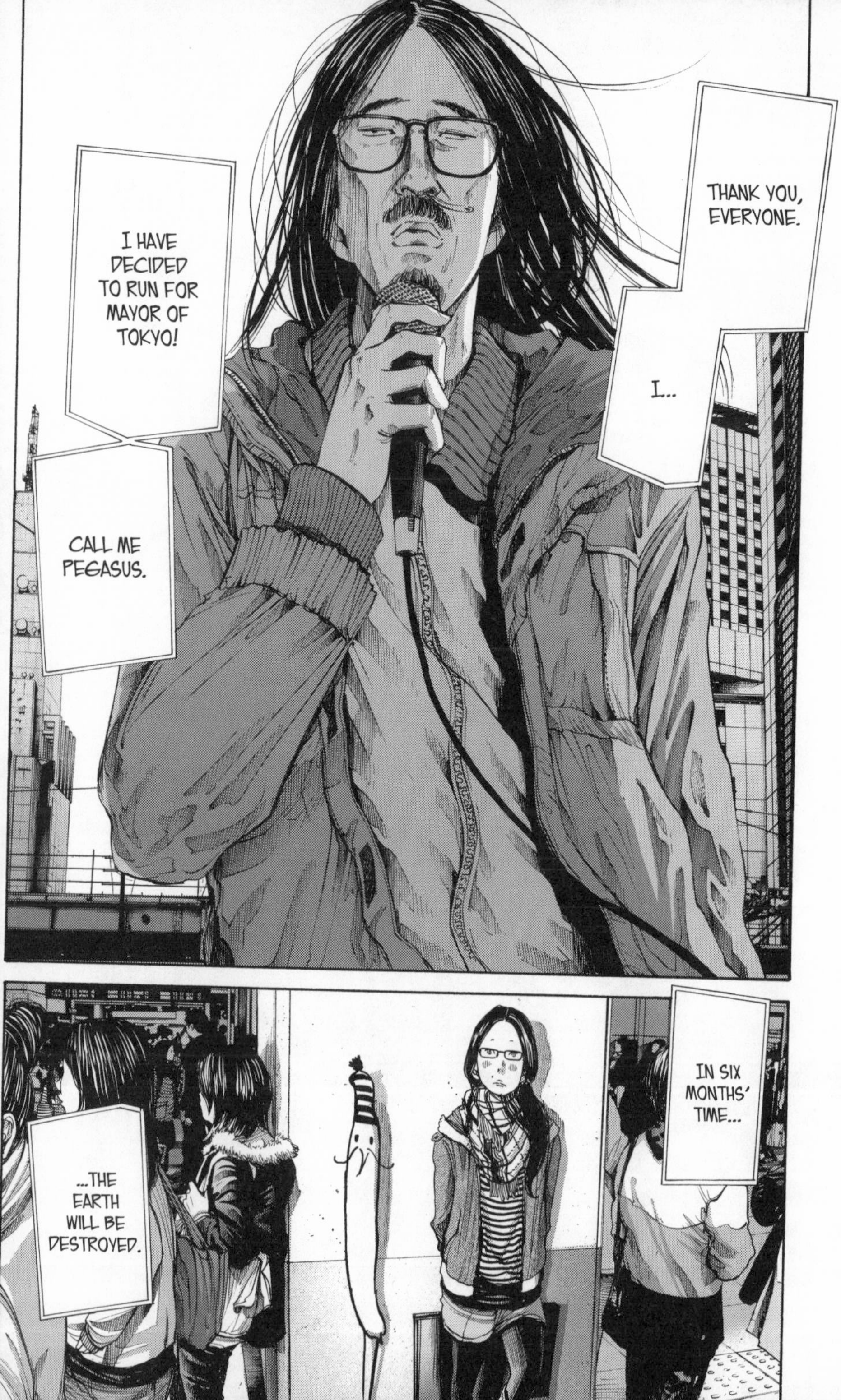
THANK YOU, EVERYONE.
I...
I HAVE DECIDED TO RUN FOR MAYOR OF TOKYO!
CALL ME PEGASUS.
IN SIX MONTHS' TIME...
...THE EARTH WILL BE DESTROYED.

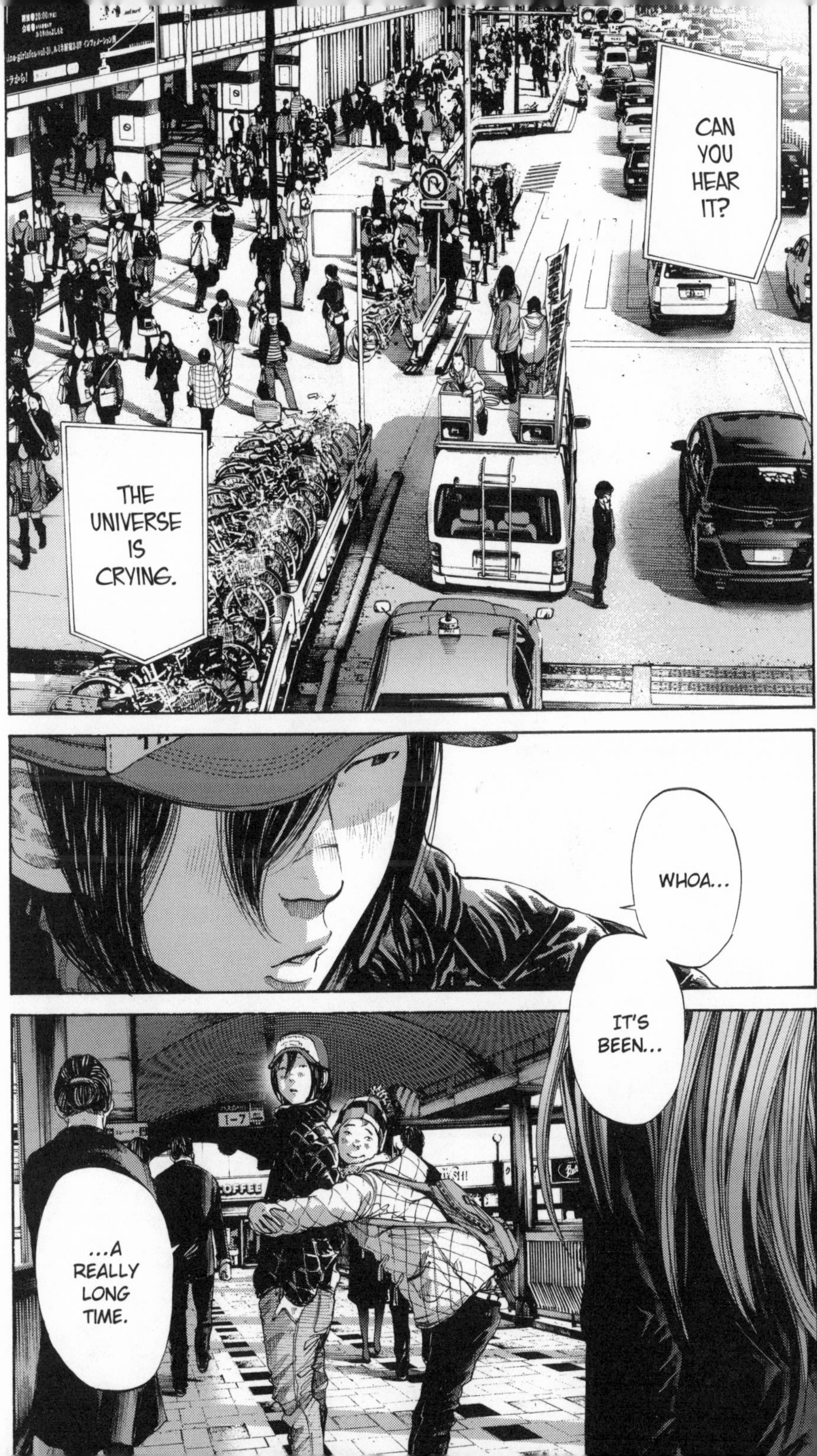
CAN YOU HEAR IT?
THE UNIVERSE IS CRYING.
WHOA...
IT'S BEEN...
...A REALLY LONG TIME.

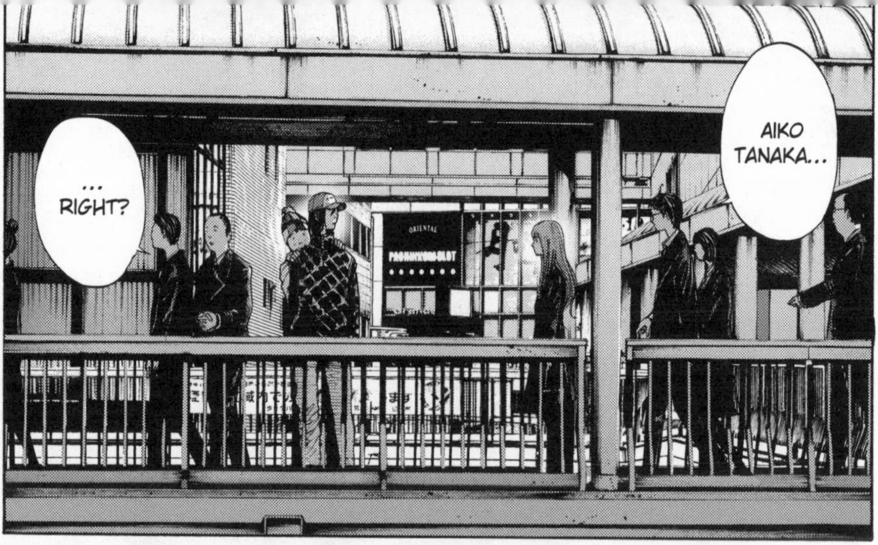
AIKO TANAKA...
... RIGHT?

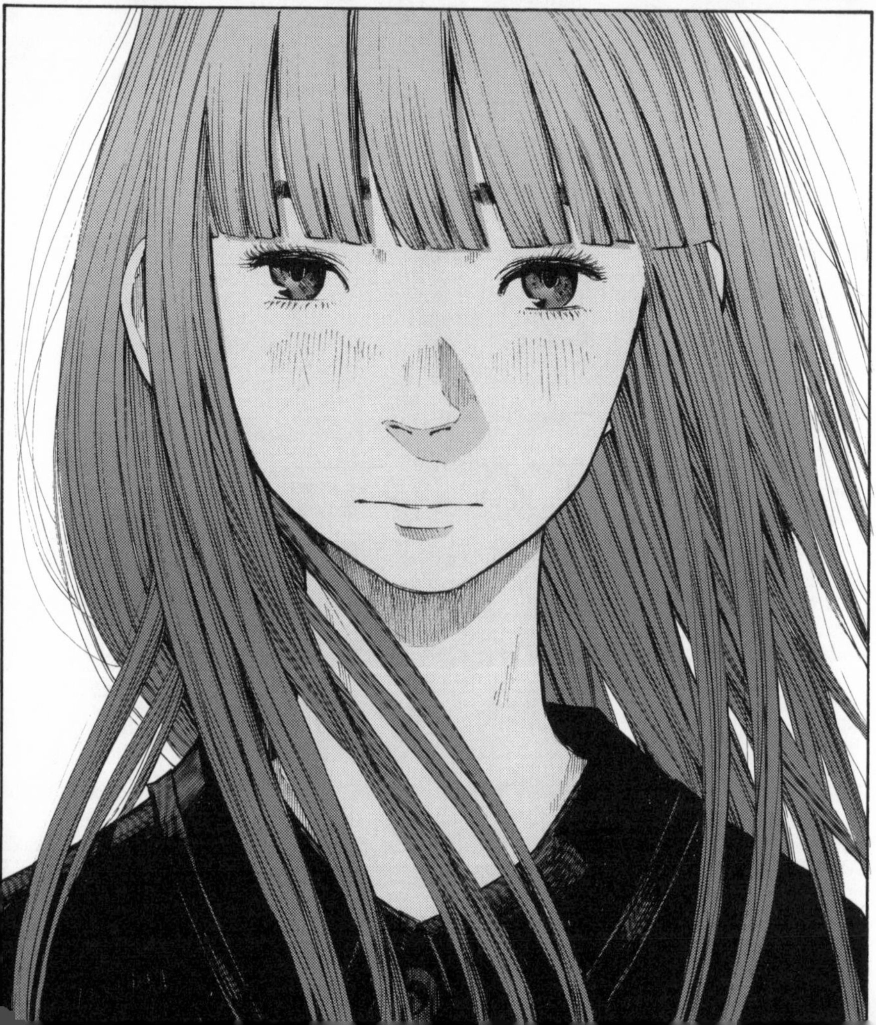

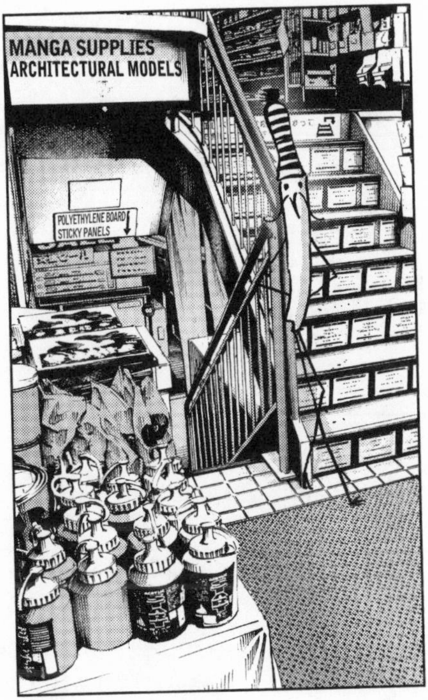
MANGA SUPPLIES
ARCHITECTURAL MODELS
POLYETHYLENE BOARD
STICKY PANELS

GOODNIGHT PUNPUN INIO ASANO

Part Eight

BACKGROUND ASSISTANTS: Yuki Toribuchi
Satsuki Sato
CG ASSISTANT: Hisashi Saito
COOPERATION: Kumatsuto
Yu Uehara

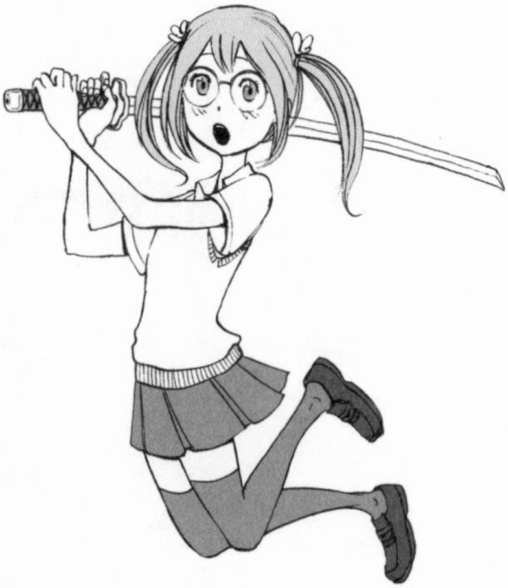

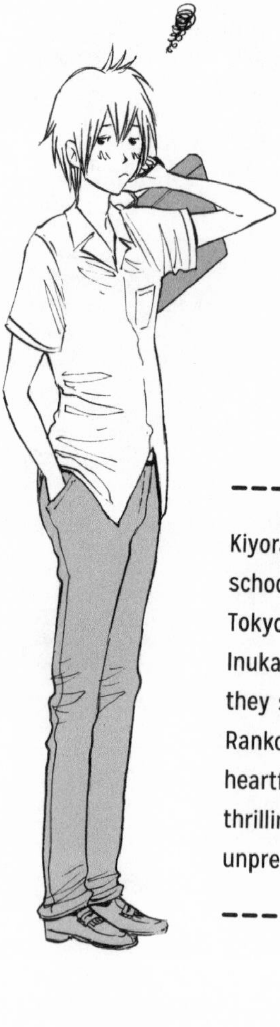

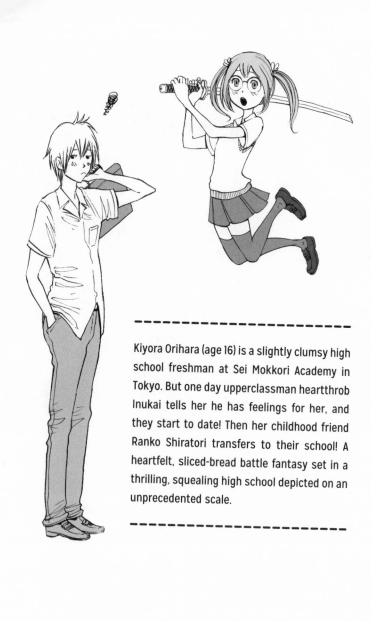

Kiyora Orihara (age 16) is a slightly clumsy high school freshman at Sei Mokkori Academy in Tokyo. But one day upperclassman heartthrob Inukai tells her he has feelings for her, and they start to date! Then her childhood friend Ranko Shiratori transfers to their school! A heartfelt, sliced-bread battle fantasy set in a thrilling, squealing high school depicted on an unprecedented scale.

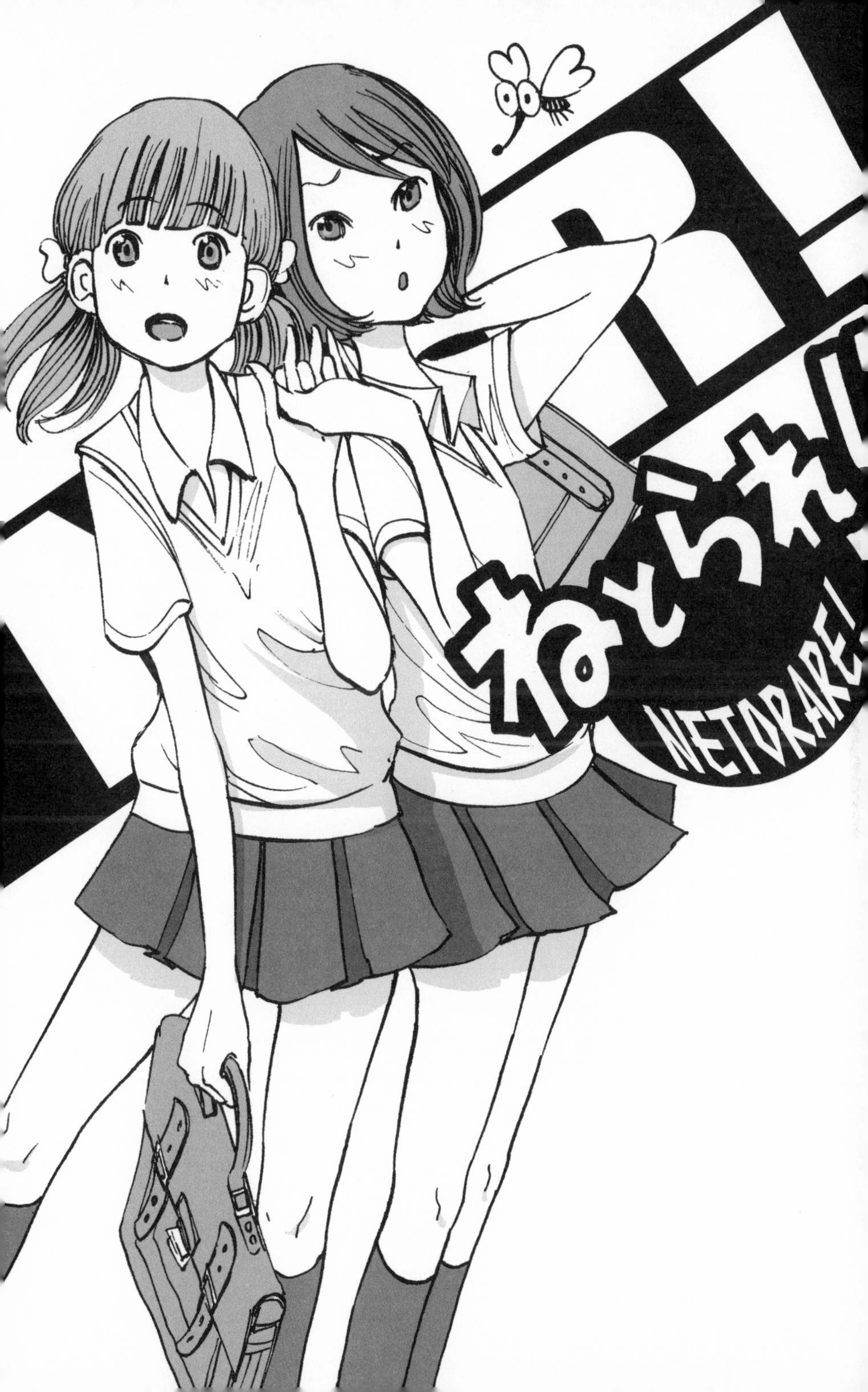
ねとられ
NETORARE

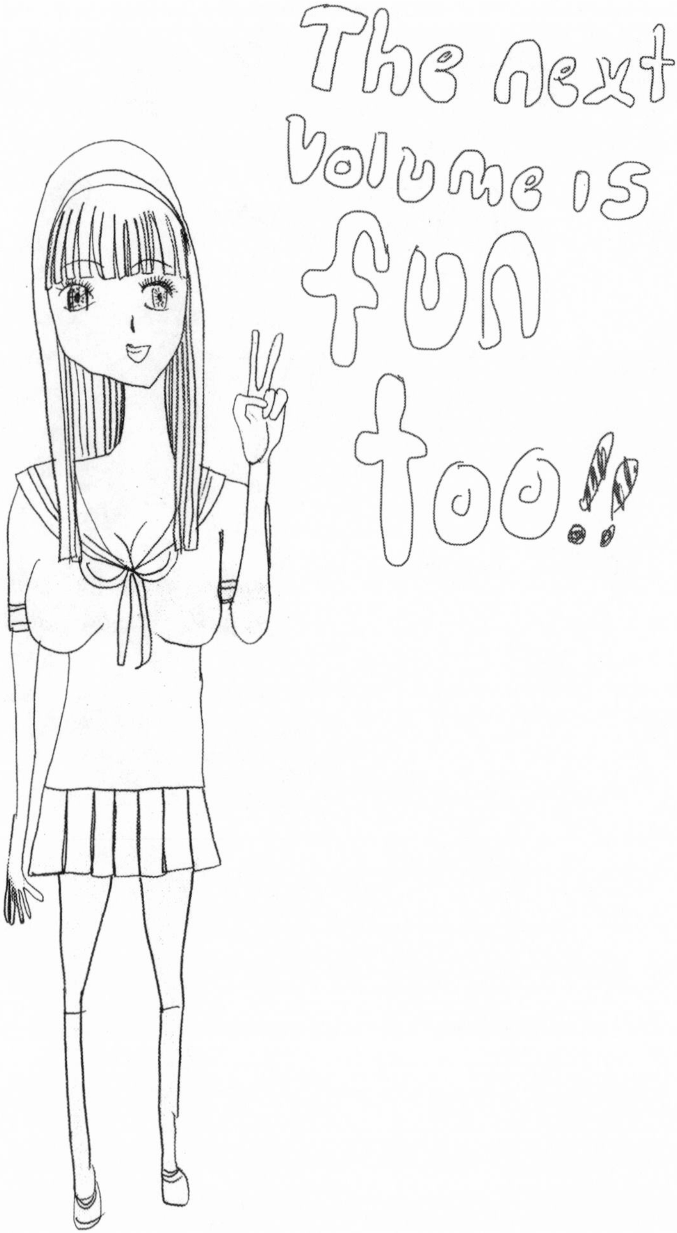
The next volume is fun too!!

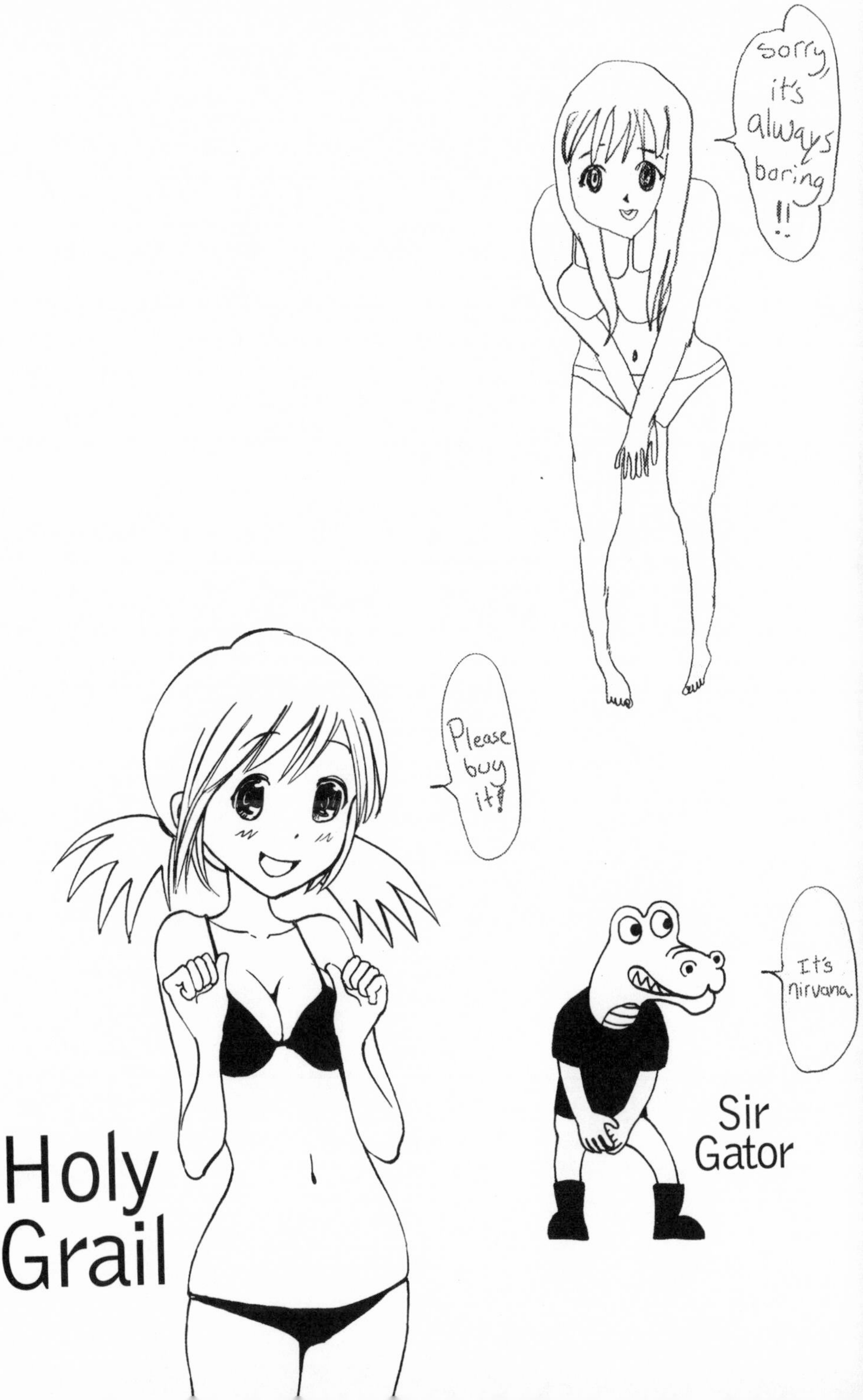
sorry it's always boring!!
Please buy it!
It's nirvana.
Sir Gator
Holy Grail

INIO ASANO, a bona fide earthling, was born in Ibaraki, Japan, in 1980. In 2001, his short story "Uchu kara Konnichiwa" (Hello from Outer Space) won the first Sunday GX Rookie Prize. Later, GX published his series *Subarashi Sekai*, available in English from VIZ Media as *What a Wonderful World!* His other works include *Hikari no Machi* (City of Light), *Nijigahara Holograph* and *Umibe no Onna no Ko* (A Girl on the Shore), as well as *solanin*, also available from VIZ Media.

GOODNIGHT PUNPUN
Volume 4
VIZ Signature Edition

Story and Art by INIO ASANO

OYASUMI PUNPUN Vol. 7, 8
by Inio ASANO
© 2007 Inio ASANO
All rights reserved.
Original Japanese edition published by SHOGAKUKAN.
English translation rights in the United States of America,
Canada, the United Kingdom and Ireland arranged with
SHOGAKUKAN.

Translation JN PRODUCTIONS
Touch-Up Art & Lettering ✦ ANNALIESE CHRISTMAN
Design ✦ FAWN LAU
Editor ✦ PANCHA DIAZ

Published by VIZ Media, LLC
P.O. Box 77010
San Francisco, CA 94107

10 9 8 7 6 5 4 3 2 1
First printing, December 2016

media
www.viz.com   **VIZ SIGNATURE**

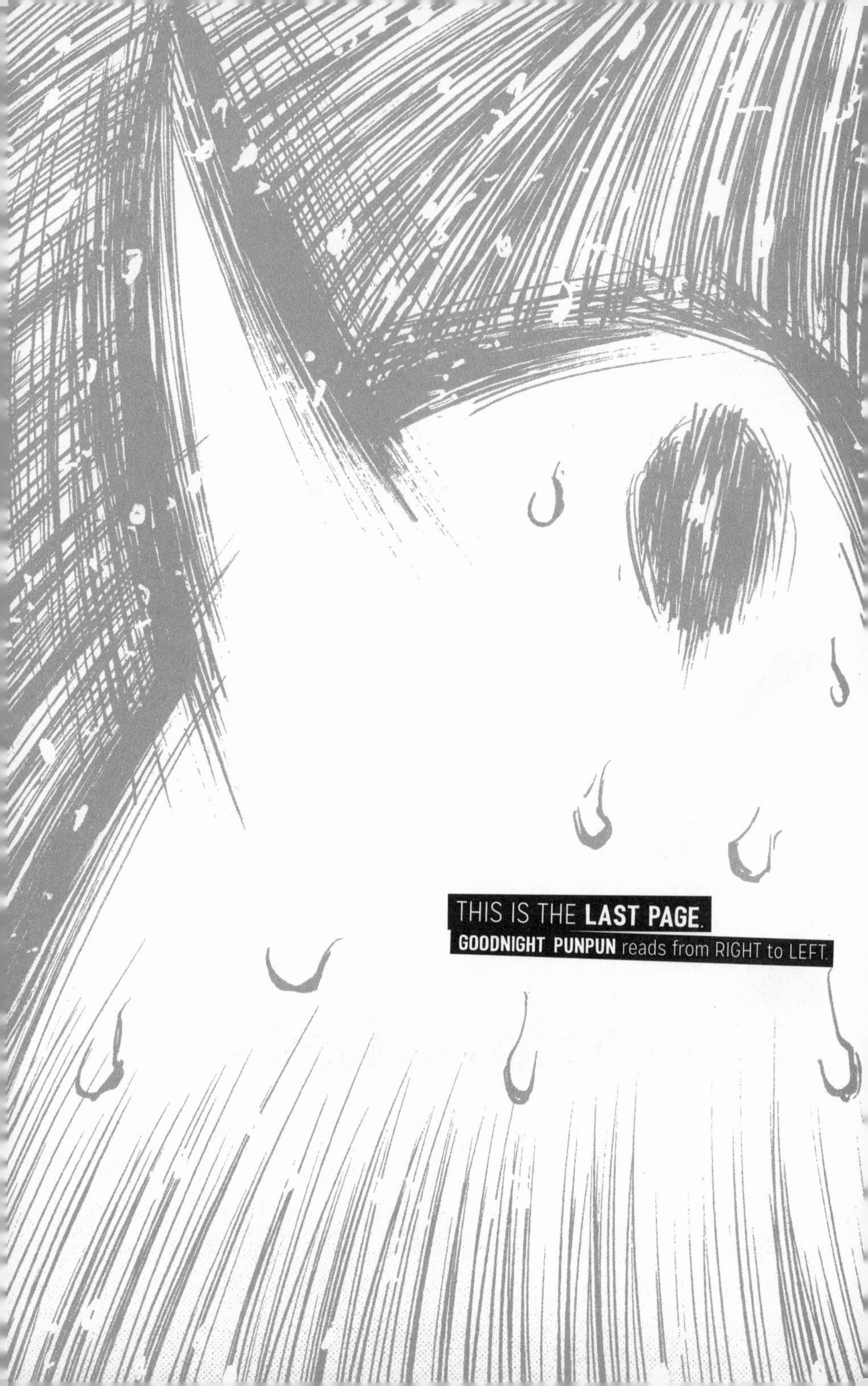

THIS IS THE **LAST PAGE**.

GOODNIGHT PUNPUN reads from RIGHT to LEFT.